THE COMPLETE ENCYCLOPEDIA OF
SOCCER

First published in 2004 by Carlton Books Limited

This edition published in 2010 by Carlton Books Limited
20 Mortimer Street
London W1T 3JW

Copyright © Carlton Books Limited 2004, 2006, 2007, 2010

A CIP catalogue record for this book is available from the British Library

ISBN 978 1 84732 657 7

Printed in Dubai

OPPOSITE: Spain celebrate winning the
2010 FIFA World Cup in South Africa.

THE COMPLETE ENCYCLOPEDIA OF
SOCCER

KEIR RADNEDGE

CARLTON
BOOKS

CONTENTS

PART 4: THE GREAT PLAYERS

FROM ABEGGLEN TO ZUBIZARRETA

PART 5: THE FAMOUS CLUBS

INTRODUCTION
BY KEIR RADNEDGE

Association football, also known since the late nineteenth century as soccer, has variously been labelled the "simplest game" and the "beautiful game" and the "people's game." But, above and beyond all that, it is the world's most popular game.

Politicians in newly-independent nations ponder over which organization to join first: the United Nations or FIFA and successive FIFA presidents Joao Havelange and Sepp Blatter have compared world soccer in global wealth and strength with the greatest multinational corporations.

But soccer is far more than a cold mess of financial statistics. The game appeals to peoples of all ages and social status from Afghanistan to Zimbabwe because of the passion it arouses: passion both for the player, whether in back street or Bernabeu, as much as for the spectator, whether on the sand of Copacabana or in the best seats in Berlin.

The basic concept is childishly easy to understand: for one team to score more goals than the other. A natural spirit of loyalty, along the way, picks up player adulation, club adherence and national team ambition.

This book seeks both to weave those threads together while also examining the single strands. That is just as it should be. Soccer is, after all, a team game played by individuals.

Italy and Brazil line up for the national anthems before kick-off at the 1970 World Cup Final in the Estadio Azteca in Mexico City.

PART 1:

THE HISTORY OF THE GAME

Association football is the formal title awarded by the 19th-century school teachers who turned an unruly physical pursuit into the codified game which, in due course, swept the world.

The likes of Lord Kinnaird and Charles Alcock had no idea how their part-time pastime would develop. The notion of billions of people around the world sitting down in front of a square screen to watch a match would have been beyond their comprehension.

Yet soccer has already conquered the world once. Ancient China, Japan, the Roman empire... all left fragments of their civilization etched or carved or embroidered with images of men kicking some sort of a ball around. Soccer may thus be described as a game almost as old as civilization itself.

Soccer is the world's most popular game and its competitions have broken down political barriers. Its laws surmount frontiers and borders and its world authority, FIFA, is probably more effective in its governance than any other global body. Its decisions on administration and the laws of the game command remarkable obedience.

In the 21st century there is no sign of a relaxation of soccer's grip on the public's imagination. That the world should have virtually stopped to watch Brazilians play the Dutch in a southern African city in the early years of the 21st century surely underlines the point. The soccer revolution is here to stay.

THE EARLY HISTORY OF SOCCER

The precise origins soccer are unknown. The modern format of 11 versus 11 can be attributed to the British in the nineteenth century, but there is evidence of a form of soccer played in China long before Caesar brought the game of harpastum to Britain.

China provides history's first soccer report, in the writings of the Han Dynasty 2000 years ago. They made it a proud boast in support of their hosting of the Beijing Olympic Games in 2008. The rules may have changed down the centuries but the pursuit of what we term a soccer or football has remained one of man's most consistent entertainments.

It was just so for the Greeks and the Romans. Pollux describes the pastime of harpastum in the following terms: "The players divided themselves into two bands. The ball was thrown upon the line in the middle. At the two ends behind the places where the players were stationed there were two other lines (which would seem to be equivalent to modern goal-lines), beyond which they tried to carry it, a feat that could not be done without pushing one another backward and forward." This suggests that harpastum was the origin of both rugby football and association football.

Ball games in Britain seem to have started as annual events staged over Shrovetide. As a rule these contests began in the market-place and involved two teams of unlimited numbers trying to propel a ball into the opposite side's goal, which was usually some convenient spot not too remote from the centre of town.

It was very hostile, violent and extremely dangerous. Householders had to barricade their lower windows as the mobs did battle along the streets. The hero was the lucky player who eventually grounded the ball in goal. Not that it was always a ball. The followers of the rebel leader Jack Cade kicked a pig's bladder in the streets of London. In Chester the object of the boot was a little more distasteful. There the game originated as a celebration of victory over the marauding Danes, and the head of one of the vanquished army was used as a football. Later generations were content to boot a leather ball at their Shrove Tuesday festivals.

There is a record of London schoolboys playing organized soccer before Lent in 1175, and so popular had the game become in the streets of London in the reign of Edward II that the merchants, fearing this most robust and violent activity was affecting their trade, petitioned the king to prohibit the game.

On April 13, 1314, Edward II issued the following proclamation forbidding the practice as leading to a breach of the peace: "Forasmuch as there is great noise in the city caused by hustling over large balls, from which many evils may arise, which God forbid; we command and forbid on behalf of the King, on pain of imprisonment, such game

One of the myriad early variations on the soccer theme survives to this day, in the Eton Wall Game.

to be used in the city in future."

This was just one of many attempts to stamp out this popular activity. In 1349 Edward III tried to put an end to soccer because he felt the young men of the day were spending more time playing soccer than practising archery or javelin throwing. He commanded his sheriffs to suppress "such idle practices." Similar orders were issued by Richard II, Henry IV and James III, without any lasting effect. One such royal proclamation in 1491 forbade the people to participate in soccer and golf: it was to be an offence if "in a place of the realme ther be used futeball, golfe, or other sik unprofitable sports."

Despite these spoilsport measures the game flourished in the Tudor and Stuart epochs. It took Cromwell to effectively suppress the activity, after which the game did not come back into vogue until the Restoration. Samuel Pepys, writing a hundred years after the event, describes how, in the great freeze of January 1565, "the streets were full of footballs."

There were still no rules, the game basically being an excuse for an uninhibited ruck. Sir Thomas Elyot, in a well-known book entitled *The Governour*, published in 1564, waxes wroth against soccer, which he dismisses as "beastlike furie and extreme violence deserving only to be put in perpetual silence." But the lusty men of England were not to be denied their vigorous activity. During the reign of Elizabeth I soccer was played widely, and, in the absence of rules and referees, there were frequent and sometimes fatal accidents.

In the seventeenth century, soccer

appears to have had various titles. In Cornwall it was termed "hurling", a name subsequently applied to hockey; while in Norfolk and Suffolk it was known as "campynge" or "camping".

Carew, in his Survey of Cornwall, suggests that the Cornish were the first to adopt regular rules. He records that no one was permitted to "but or handfast under the girdle", which presumably meant that tripping, charging, or grabbing below the waist was prohibited. He goes on to state that it was also not allowed "to deal a foreball", which suggests that it was forbidden to pass forward, another similarity with rugby football.

Such rules were obviously not in general use. Strutt, in his Sports and Pastimes, describes soccer thus: "When a match at soccer is made, two parties, each containing an equal number of competitors, take the field and stand between two goals, placed at the distance of eighty or one hundred yards the one from the other. The goal is usually made with two sticks driven into the ground about two or three feet apart. The ball, which is commonly made of blown bladder and cased with leather, is delivered in the midst of the ground, and the object of each party is to drive it through the goal of their antagonists, which being achieved, the game is won.

"The abilities of the performers are best displayed in attacking and defending the goals, and hence the pastime was more frequently called a goal at soccer than a game at soccer. When the exercise becomes exceeding violent, the players kick each other's shins without the least ceremony, and some of them are over-thrown at the hazard of their limbs."

It seems that "hacking" was as keenly relished in those days as it was when the game's modern renaissance began in the mid-19th century. By the start of the 21st century, of course, the very idea of "hacking" for its own sake would be considered with horror.

1848
- First code of rules compiled at Cambridge University

1855
- Sheffield FC, world's oldest club, formed

1862
- Notts County, world's oldest league club, formed

1863
- The Football Association is formed in England, October 26

1871
- FA Cup inaugurated in England

1872
- Size of ball fixed
- Scotland draw 0-0 with England in first official international at West of Scotland cricket ground

1874
- Shinguards introduced by Sam Weller Widdowson of Nottingham Forest and England

1875
- Crossbar replaces tape

1878
- Referee's whistle used for first time at Nottingham Forest's ground
- Almost 20,000 people watch first floodlit match, between two Sheffield teams, with lighting provided by four lamps on 30ft wooden towers

THE NINETEENTH CENTURY

Soccer's sometime image as the "working man's game" is complicated by one salient piece of history: it was the public schools, and Oxford and Cambridge Universities in particular, which brought shape and order out of the almost aimless fury of violence.

Nearly all the schools and numerous clubs which had mushroomed in the wake of the Industrial Revolution had their own sets of rules. Some catered for the ball to be handled, some did not; some limited the number of participants on each side, some did not. The overall situation was chaotic so, in 1846, the first serious attempts to unify a code of rules was instigated at Cambridge University by messrs H de Winton and JC Thring. They met representatives from the major public schools with a view to formulating a standard set of rules.

Their deliberations took seven hours 55 minutes and were published as the Cambridge Rules. These were well accepted and years afterwards, with very few alterations, became the Association Rules. Unfortunately there is no copy of the original regulations, and the earliest set of rules to which those of the Football Association may be traced are those issued by Thring in 1862 when he was the assistant master at Uppingham. These were the rules for what he termed "The Simplest Game," and as they are so important to the development of association football

as we know it today they are worthy of reproduction (see below).

The Football Association came into being in October 26, 1863, following a meeting at the Freemasons' Tavern, Great Queen Street, London, "for the purpose of forming an association with the object of establishing a definite code of rules for the regulation of the game".

Representatives of all the major clubs were present and they appointed Arthur Pember as president and Ebeneezer Morley as honorary secretary. Morley was asked to write to the captains of the leading schools inviting them to co-operate in the movement but at a second meeting, held a few days later, it was revealed that replies from Harrow, Charterhouse and Westminster indicated they preferred their own rules.

At a third meeting a letter of acceptance was read from Mr Thring of Uppingham School and considerable progress was made with the laws, which were published on December 1, 1863. At the sixth meeting held that month the first committee of the Association was appointed.

It was at this meeting that the "split" between the rugby unionists (as they were now termed) and the associationists occurred. Blackheath withdrew their membership, though Campbell agreed to stay in office.

Although there were no further major upsets it seems there was still unease about the way the game should be played. At the Association's annual meeting in February, 1866, a representative of the No Names (from Kilburn, north London) complained that only Barnes and Crystal Palace were playing strictly to Association rules. All present, apart from the Lincoln club who withdrew, agreed that no member clubs should ever play under any other rules.

The Association and the game grew steadily in public favour following the introduction of the FA Cup (in 1871-72) and international fixtures (in 1872), but the comparatively peaceful progress enjoyed until 1880 was followed by a decade of drastic reforms, including the launch of the Football League in 1888-89.

The number of the rules of the Association had by now increased from 10 to 15. Scotland still refused to adopt the English throw-in, or the English understanding of the offside rule; apart from that the two

HOW IT BEGAN

The Simplest Game

1. **A goal is scored whenever the ball is forced through the goal and under the bar, except it be thrown by hand.**
2. **Hands may be used only to stop a ball and place it on the ground before the feet.**
3. **Kicks must be aimed only at the ball.**
4. **A player may not kick the ball whilst in the air.**
5. **No tripping up or heel kicking allowed.**
6. **Whenever a ball is kicked beyond the side flags, it must be returned by the player who kicked it, from the spot it passed the flag line, in a straight line towards the middle of the ground.**
7. **When a ball is kicked behind the line of goal, it shall be kicked off from that line by one of the side whose goal it is.**
8. **No player may stand within six paces of the kicker when he is kicking off.**
9. **A player is "out of play" immediately he is in front of the ball, and must return behind the ball as soon as possible. If the ball is kicked by his own side past a player, he may not touch or kick it, or advance, until one of the other side has first kicked it, or one of his own side has been able to kick it on a level with, or in front of, him.**
10. **No charging allowed when a player is out of play; that is, immediately the ball is behind him.**

Royal Engineers were runners-up to Wanderers in the first FA Cup Final in 1872.

Associations were on friendly terms with each other. But there loomed another crisis which was to become as significant as that which separated the associationists from the rugby followers. It was the advent of the paid player – the first professionals.

Amid persistent rumours that many of the northern contingent were paying men to play for them the following new rule (No. 16) was added in 1882: "That any member of a club receiving remuneration or consideration of any sort above his actual expenses and any wages actually lost by any such player taking part in any match, shall be debarred from taking part in either cup, inter Association, or International contests, and any club employing such player shall be excluded from this Association."

The liberty to pay "wages lost" was extensively abused and this falling away from amateurism was seen by those in the south as a reflection of an unsportsmanlike spirit spreading through northern and Midlands clubs.

Soccer had flourished with far greater rapidity in Scotland than in the rest of the UK and English clubs looked north of the border to strengthen their teams. The FA at first turned a blind eye, but its hand was forced by the Sheffield, Lancashire, and Birmingham Associations, each of which held inquiries into charges of professionalism. In January 1883 an FA commission was appointed to look into the allegations. They proved nothing. Yet the disquiet among the best amateur clubs continued and there was a veiled threat by some to boycott the FA Cup at the start of the 1883-84 season.

The row came to a head early in 1884 when the Upton Park Club lodged a complaint against Preston North End on the grounds of professionalism. The case attracted wide publicity and William Sudell, the president of the Preston club and in effect the manager, admitted that they did pay their players and that he could prove that nearly every other important club in Lancashire and the Midlands did likewise.

Preston were disqualified from that season's FA Cup but the frankness of Sudell's confession brought home to the FA councillors the need to face reality. At their next committee meeting the progressive Charles Alcock proposed "that the time has come for the legalization of professionalism". This was seconded by Dr Morley but a concerted battle to repress the move raged until July 1885 when the soccer professional was at last legalized.

The British were the original missionaries of modern, organized soccer. As communications and travel developed, so sailors, soldiers, merchants, engineers, teachers, students and other professional classes took their sports – cricket and soccer – around the world.

Local people joined in and soccer, consequently, gained universal popularity. Towards the end of the nineteenth century the game invaded Austria. There was a sizeable British colony in Vienna and their influence is manifest in the names of the two oldest clubs, the First Vienna FC and the Vienna Cricket and Football Club, from which FK Austria descended.

THE PERFECT SEASON
The Invincibles

Preston North End, founded in 1881, won the first-ever Football League championship in 1888-89. They also completed the first League and FA Cup double that season. They defeated Wolverhampton Wanderers 3-0 in the final to complete their cup without conceding a goal. Preston also set an English goalscoring record when they thrashed Hyde 26-0 in the FA Cup; inside-forward James Ross set a First Division record by scoring seven goals in one match. Preston, who finished 11 points clear of Aston Villa, won the league again the following season. The inaugural season recorded 586 goals in 132 matches, an average of more than four goals per game.

The rest of the Hapsburg empire followed suit. Young students returning from England imported the first soccer into Hungary in the 1890s and two Englishmen, Arthur Yolland and Ashton, were included in the first representative team.

In Italy too the English - albeit along with the Swiss - played a key role in developing the game, as the names of some of the clubs reflect: Genoa Football and Cricket Club (founded by Englishmen in 1892) and Milan (not Milano). The game was introduced to Italy by a Turin businessman, Edoardo Bosio, in 1887, but Genoa were the first great club.

But Europe was not alone. Soccer, by the end of the 19th century, was being exported to all four corners of the world.

1901
- Maximum wage rule formalized
- Southern League Tottenham Hotspur become first professional club to take FA Cup south
- First 100,000 attendance (110,802) at FA Cup Final, venue Crystal Palace
- Argentina beat Uruguay 3-2 in first international between South American countries

1902
- Ibrox Park disaster: 25 killed when part of new wooden stand collapses at Scotland v England match
- Real Madrid formed
- Austria beat Hungary 5-0 in Vienna, the first international between teams outside the home countries
- The Mexican League Championship, the first in Central and North America, is founded

1904
- FIFA formed in Paris with seven members: Belgium, Denmark, France, Holland, Spain, Sweden and Switzerland
- Galt FC from Canada beat Christian Brothers College from the USA 2-0 in an Olympic medal game

1905
- England join FIFA
- First £1,000 transfer sees Alf Common (below) move from Sunderland to Middlesbrough
- Argentina and Uruguay meet in Buenos Aires in the first official international in South America

1906
- The laws of the game are substantially rewritten for the first time

1907
- FIFA admits Bohemia to membership - then excludes it because it is only a region within the Austro-Hungarian empire

1900-1919: Global organization

Soccer had planted significant roots in South America by the start of the 20th century. In Argentina, although the game had been imported earlier by British residents of Buenos Aires, it had proved slow to catch on until after the migrant influx from Italy and Spain. The British influence in South America remains clear to this day through the adopted names of clubs such as River Plate, Newell's Old Boys and Rosario Central in Uruguay, Liverpool and Wanderers in Uruguay, Everton and Rangers in Chile as well as the likes of Corinthians – after the great English amateur club – in Brazil, by achievement the world's greatest soccer nation.

The first club comprising mainly Brazilians was the Associaciäo Athletica Mackenzie College in São Paulo while other organizations such as the Flamengo sailing club in Rio de Janeiro added soccer sections in the early years of the century. In due course Flamengo and their perpetual derby rivals Fluminense, would become synonymous with futebol.

In Africa and Asia not only the English but the French and, to a lesser extent, German and Portuguese colonial movements played predominant roles in introducing the game.

The worldwide momentum was reflected in the launch of the world federation FIFA (Federation Internationale de Football Association)

in Paris on May 21, 1904. In fact, it could have been launched two years earlier but for the ponderous ways of the Football Association. In the spring of that year the initial proposal for an international governing body was sent to Sir Frederick Wall, the FA secretary in London.

The letter, posted on May 8, had been drafted by the secretary of the Dutch federation, CAW Hirschmann, and a French journalist, Robert Guerin of Le Matin, who was also treasurer of the Union des Societes Francaises de Sports Athletiques.

They believed that the fast-growing popularity of soccer throughout Europe deserved international co-

ordination some ten years after another Frenchman, Baron Pierre de Coubertin, had presided from Paris over the revival of the Olympic Games. Unusually in this case, the French did not want to take the initiative. Guerin and Hirschmann believed, respectfully, that the Football Association should lead the way forward, summon the inaugural meeting, lay down the statutes and welcome all soccer-playing countries into the fold.

Wall did not see it that way. In fact, he did not see it at all. He replied on June 4, saying his council would review the issue "though my council will not meet again until August." It is fascinating to speculate what might have happened if Charles Alcock had still been running the FA. Alcock was renowned, with good reason, as the "father of modern sport" a visionary who would probably have appreciated the opportunity. But illness had taken its toll and he died four years later. Wall ignored Guerin and Hirschmann's specific invitation and countered that the FA had decided to invite foreign associations to a "conference to be held in England." It never happened.

In November 1903 the 'pupils' tried another tack. Guerin, on behalf of the USFSA, wrote to the FA proposing a federation of specifically European soccer associations. Wall did reply more quickly this time but in no more encouraging terms. The French would wait no longer. On May 1, 1904, as

Coaching visionary Jimmy Hogan was more appreciated in central Europe than in England.

France and Belgium played their first international so Guerin and Belgian federation secretary Louis Muhlinghaus agreed to go ahead regardless. Just under three weeks later, on May 21, 1904, delegates representing Belgium (Louis Muhlinghaus and Max Kahn), Denmark (Ludvig Sylow), France (Guerin and his assistant Andre Espir), Holland (Carl Anton Wilhelm Hirschmann), Spain, Sweden and Switzerland (Victor E Schneider) met at the USFSA offices at 229 rue Sainte-Honoré in Paris and created FIFA. The meeting voted to itself the right to organize a world championship.

France did not have a specific soccer federation so the USFSA took the lead. Spain, though soccer had

1908
- Transfer limit of £350 introduced in January, withdrawn in April
- Great Britain beat Denmark to win the first official Olympic soccer title at Shepherds Bush
- England travel to Vienna to beat Austria 6-1 in their first international on foreign soil

1910
- Argentina win the first unofficial South American Championship
- A national championship is launched in the Philippines, the first in Asia

1913
- China and the Philippines meet in the first international in Asia

1914
- Brazil make their international debut, against Argentina

1915
- In what becomes known as the "Khaki Cup Final", Sheffield United beat Chelsea in front of a crowd mostly dressed in army uniform (right, injured soldiers in the crowd)

1916
- CONMEBOL, in South America, is created as the first regional confederation

1919
- The Football League is extended to 44 clubs as league soccer in England is resumed after the war

been introduced in the 1860s, did not have a federation either. Thus one of their club presidents took it upon himself to represent Spain: his name was Carlos Padros from Madrid FC (now, of course, Real Madrid). This was one of the reasons why FIFA president Sepp Blatter went out of his way to take a FIFA executive meeting to Madrid in December 2003. He believed FIFA was duty bound to honour the centenary of the club which helped give FIFA life a century earlier.

The stranger truth is that Padros did not, as many subsequent accounts claimed, attend FIFA's founding meeting. He sent his apologies and Frenchman Andre Espir voted as Spanish proxy. Similarly, no Swede was present and Sylow spoke and voted for Sweden. Thus FIFA's foundation was attended by seven men representing seven countries but by men of only five nationalities.

Guerin was the first, reluctant, president. But a year later, on April 14, 1905, Baron Edouard de Laveleye, president of the Belgian federation, persuaded the Football Association to come on board. However, irritated that not one of FIFA's members had entered the proposed world championship, Guerin quit as president. Schneider took over briefly before the election to the presidency in 1906 of England's Daniel (DB) Woolfall, who led for 12 years until his death in 1918.

It was under Woolfall's leadership that the suspicious, superior, insular British magnanimously agreed to admit foreign representation on the law-making International Board. It was also under Woolfall's leadership that FIFA became a truly world federation rather than a European one: in 1910 South Africa was admitted to membership and, in 1912, Argentina.

The notion of competitive international soccer took shape once FIFA had formalized the notion of the nation state as a soccer entity. The British home championship was the forerunner followed by the Olympics. The sport entered the Games in a one-match exhibition form in Athens in 1896 and further unofficial competitions followed in 1900 and 1904.

Great Britain then had the honour of being first Olympic champions when they scored a fortunate 2-0 win over Denmark in the final in 1908. Britain won again in 1912. Meanwhile the South Americans, cut off from the Eurocentric Olympic movement by travel restrictions, responded by organizing their own regional championship, (the future Copa America). The first, unofficial, tournament was staged in 1910 to celebrate the centenary of Argentine independence, with the first formal championship in 1916.

Almost all domestic and international soccer in Europe had, by this time, been halted by war.

Elsewhere repercussions of the grim hostilities brought both national and even personal implications for the likes of English coaching missionaries such as Jimmy Hogan and Steve Bloomer – the former an England and Derby County inside-right – who were both interned in Germany where they had been working.

INFAMOUS HISTORY

Across the lines

During the First World War, on Christmas Day, 1915 a truce was observed between German and British forces. At Laventie in northern France soldiers of both sides ventured out of their trenches to exchange seasonal greetings. The last survivor of those Royal Welsh Fusiliers, Bertie Felstead, recalled: "When we met them, someone suggested soccer. It wasn't a game as such, more of a kick around and a free-for-all. There could have been 50 on each side for all I know. I played because I really liked soccer. I don't know how long it lasted, probably half an hour. No-one was keeping score." The soccer truce ended with the order: "to kill the Hun, not make friends with him." Felstead died in July 2001, aged 106.

1920
- The four home FAs withdraw from FIFA when other members reject their demand not to play matches against First World War enemies
- Third Division South formed, containing a further 22 clubs

1921
- Third Division North formed
- Jules Rimet becomes president of FIFA
- Goalkeepers ordered to wear yellow jerseys at future Olympic tournaments to distinguish them from other players

1922
1923
- Football pools introduced
- First Wembley FA Cup Final sees Bolton beat West Ham 2-0 in the "White Horse Cup Final"

1924
- First Wembley international: England 1, Scotland 1 (Scotland take to the field, left)
- Goal can be scored direct from corner kick
- The four home FAs rejoin FIFA
- Uruguay become the first non-European nation to win the Olympic tournament

1920s: Mixed emotions

The First World War proved disastrous for Europe and FIFA suffered from the fall-out. Federations from the First World War allies, meeting in Brussels, decided to boycott international contact with wartime antagonists Austria, Hungary and Germany and demanded their withdrawal or expulsion.

Other nations, notably the Scandinavians and Italy, insisted on their rights to play soccer against whoever they chose. They were then blacklisted by the allies. Compromise was shunned. On April 23, 1920, the British quartet resigned from FIFA and banned FIFA's representatives from the International Board.

Britain's absence lasted four years and the home FAs quit again in 1928 in a row over broken-time payments. There were other issues. For instance, FIFA (in acquiring IOC approval for broken-time payments) had told the Olympic committee that it was now the "highest authority in all matters pertaining to soccer," phraseology which put the FA's nose out of joint.

The battle between traditionalist amateurs and progressive professionals caused chaos in many countries. Two championships ran simultaneously in Argentina, for example, for three years at the end of the 1920s – one amateur, one professional. Nowadays countries who quit, are expelled or suspended from FIFA are barred from all match contact with FIFA members. Not so in

the 1920s. The home countries continued to play friendly matches against their former partners in FIFA. The only arena in which the Brits would later miss out was, however, the most important – the World Cup.

The histories of FIFA and the World Cup are bound inextricably and the competition took 26 years to get off the ground. In the meantime Austrian official Hugo Meisl had forced through the launch of two other international competitions at national team and club level. The Dr Gero Cup was the first for European national teams outside the United Kingdom while the Mitropa Cup – a contraction of the German Mittel Europa (Central Europe) – proved a successful and dramatic forerunner of today's European club events. The Gero Cup – also known variously as the International Cup, Nations Cup and Europe Cup – was in part a response to the allied nations attempt to freeze out their wartime opponents.

The Gero Cup has been largely forgotten in the mists of time, during which the World Cup, European Championship and Copa America have established an all-stifling supremacy where national team competitions are concerned. Meisl would have been surprised to know that it was the club-based Mitropa Cup whose aura has lingered far stronger, far longer.

Founding nations included three of

the Gero Cup participants in Austria, Hungary and Czechoslovakia plus Yugoslavia. Swiss clubs did not fancy the travelling involved at that stage though later the success of the

competition attracted clubs from further and wider afield, including the rising giants of northern Italy.

The progress made by the game within Czechoslovakia was underlined

THE GREAT GAMES
"The White Horse Cup Final"
BOLTON WANDERERS 2–0 WEST HAM UNITED
FA Cup Final, Wembley Stadium London, April 28, 1923

King George V was there, and somehow a match was laid on for him which, through good fortune and the crowd's good sense, was not the tragedy it might have been. Thanks to the self-discipline of the fans in a less impatient age, and to the police – led by Constable George Scorey on his legendary white horse, Billy – the Cup Final took place, starting almost an hour late. Capacity was officially 125,000, but the combination of a fine spring day, the new arena and the appearance of a London club in the final led to an estimated 250,000 trying to gain admittance – with most succeeding. The first goal came as an opponent was trying to climb back out of the crowd. The second was a rebound, either off a post... or spectators standing alongside the goal.

1925
- Offside rule change: a player needs two, not three, players between him and goal to stay onside
- German becomes, after French and English, the third official FIFA language

1926
- Huddersfield complete first hat-trick of championships

1927
- Hughie Ferguson's goal against Arsenal makes Cardiff first club to take FA Cup out of England
- The Mitropa Cup, predecessor of the European club cups, is launched in central Europe
- English fans hear a first radio commentary (Arsenal v Sheffield United)

1928
- The four home countries withdraw from FIFA again, in a row over broken-time payments for amateurs
- Bill "Dixie" Dean scores 60 First Division goals, still a record
- Arsenal pay Bolton a world record £10,000 for inside-forward David Jack
- Uruguay win the Olympic title a second time to prompt FIFA into formulating a World Cup

1929
- FIFA's Barcelona congress awards hosting rights of the first World Cup to Uruguay in 1930
- Goalkeepers ordered to stay on goal-line until penalty is kicked
- England lose to foreign opposition for the first time, by 4-3 to Spain in Madrid
- Unified Italian league championship set up

---

by the fact that Sparta from Prague were the first Mitropa winners in 1927 and old rivals Slavia were runners-up in 1929. The momentum and interest in the competition also stemmed from its staging on an annual basis. Sparta and Slavia, Hungary's Ujpest and Ferencvaros and Austria Rapid and FK Austria were among the clubs whose status was established via Meisl's brainchild.

The free-scoring which helped popularize the Mitropa and Gero cups among European fans had been encouraged by probably the most significant change ever in the laws of the game. Over the years the features of modern soccer – referee's whistle, penalty spot, crossbar, etc – had been welcomed and accepted. But the change in the offside law of 1925 was a revolutionary step towards increasing (briefly) scoring rates and forcing a tactical balance which gave the game greater shape and linear attraction.

The original style of play in the mid-19th century had been "dribbling" until Queens Park developed the "passing" game after realizing that the ball could always travel forward faster than the man. In 1873 the specificity of offside was recognized in the Laws; corners were exempted (on the grounds of sheer logic) in 1881; offside was limited to the opponents' half of the pitch in 1907; and throw-ins were excluded from the rigour in 1921. Otherwise, when the ball was played forward the law demanded that three opponents should be between attacker and goal.

Irish international Billy McCracken forced a change in the offside law.

Anti-hero of the subsequent offside revolution was the Irish fullback Billy McCracken of Newcastle United. Born in Belfast, McCracken played for local Distillery before moving to the northeast of England with Newcastle in 1904. He played more than 400 games for them, winning two championship medals and appearing in three FA Cup Finals, once as a winner, twice as a loser. In his latter years as a player, in the early 1920s, he perfected the ruse of stepping forward just in time to catch countless forwards offside.

His success prompted an increasing number of imitators and the furore ultimately prompted the Scottish FA to propose to the International Board the decisive change in wording and numbers: instead of "three" it would now be "two."

The immediate effect of the change, in British soccer at least, was for goal-scoring rates to rocket upwards. In the season before the law change the 462 matches of the English first division produced 1,192 goals at an average of 2.58 goals per game. The next season, 1925-26, the 462 games generated 1,703 goals at a match average of 3.68. Two seasons later, benefiting to a record extent, the Everton centre-forward Bill "Dixie" Dean fired 60 goals. The law change contributed to Dean ultimately ending his career in 1939 boasting a prolific 379 goals in 437 league matches.

League champions both sides of the law change were Huddersfield Town, guided by one of the greatest and most innovative managers in the game's history: Herbert Chapman. Chapman was subsequently lured south to London where his initial 18 months at Highbury coincided with the last days at the club of one of their greatest players – Charlie Buchan. Both were great thinkers and strategists and between them they came up with the answer to the goal glut of the new era: the stopper centre-half.

At that point, soccer all over the world played largely to a simple tactic of one goalkeeper, two full-backs (who took it in turns to cover the centre of defence), two wide wing-halves, a

Telling the world
January 22, 1927, marked the date of the first radio broadcast of an English First Division match, a 1-1 draw between Arsenal and Sheffield United, at Highbury in North London. In 1930 a commentary on an international against Italy in Turin was broadcast back to Germany. The first television transmission was highlights of the 1937 FA Cup Final in which Sunderland beat Preston North End 3-1 at Wembley.

centre-half between them who was – in modern parlance – the playmaker, and five forwards – two wingers who stuck to their touchlines like railway tracks, two versatile inside-forwards in channels on right and left of the opponents' half and the traditional centre-forward.

Buchan and Chapman recognized that the change in the offside law left the two full-backs and the goalkeeper exposed. Their answer was to pull the centre-half back between the fullbacks and pull the wing-halves in towards the centre of midfield where they could form a new playmaking base with the inside-forwards.

The new WM formation caught on quickly enough in British soccer, partly thanks to slavish copying of a method which brought Chapman's Arsenal so much success. The scheme would spread far and wide over the next 25 years, though it was not until the late 1940s that it became standard across the whole of Europe. The nations of South America found a different tactical route altogether.

1930
- Hosts Uruguay win the first World Cup
- Austria's "Wunderteam" beat Scotland 5-0, beat Germany 6-0 and lose only 4-3 to England at Stamford Bridge

1931
- Argentina becomes the first South American country to accept professionalism
- Athletic Bilbao win the Spanish league and Cup double for the second successive season

1932
- Stanley Matthews starts his first senior season
- Substitutions are permitted for the first time in non-competitive matches when mutually agreed

1933
- Numbered shirts worn in the FA Cup Final for first time, winners Everton wearing 1-11, Manchester City 12-22
- Uruguay decide to ignore the second World Cup because so many European nations stayed at home in 1930

1934
- Sudden death of Arsenal manager Herbert Chapman (below) on Jan 6
- Hosts Italy win the first World Cup to be staged in Europe
- Bologna of Italy win the Mitropa Cup for the second time in three years

1930s: Internationals

The 1930s proved a watershed in international soccer with the launch of the World Cup. Its success would lead to the concept and the very name itself being copied down the years by every other major sport.

At club level the Mitropa Cup expanded with increasing success in central Europe while Arsenal established their legend in England by winning the League five times in eight seasons and the FA Cup twice, as George Allison took over the reins after Chapman's premature death.

England, outside FIFA, continued to play friendly matches against FIFA members but they were barred from entering the first three World Cups in 1930, 1934 and 1938.

FIFA had voted in 1929 to hand organization of the first World Cup to Uruguay. Celebrating a centenary of independence, the country had offered to foot the travel bill for European entries and had promised to build a giant new stadium (naturally, the Centenario) to host many of the matches. In early 1930, however, FIFA president Jules Rimet was staring failure in the face. The Europeans who had supported the Uruguayan theory turned their backs. None entered. It was too far and demanded too much time of players and officials in the days before full-time professionalism was a worldwide standard.

Rimet eventually persuaded his French Federation to send a team. A few others followed suit, and the Belgian, Romanian and French parties (including Rimet and his daughter) all sailed together on the Conte Verde.

Uruguay were the winners, as they beat neighbours Argentina 4-2 in the final in Montevideo.

The "Celeste" – the nickname of the Uruguayans because of their sky blue shirts – were the outstanding national team of their age. Indeed, a significant factor in their gaining World Cup hosting rights was their success in having won both the 1924 and 1928 Olympic titles. Their World Cup triumph, however, raised a conundrum which bothers FIFA to this day: intercontinental transfers. Immediately after the 1930 finals Italian clubs raided Uruguay and Argentina and used men from both countries to win the World Cups of 1934 in Italy itself and 1938 in neighbouring France.

This was not the only negative issue to emerge as the World Cup took a grip on the passions of the international game. The 1930s also saw the rise of the sports event as political propaganda. The Uruguayans had, innocently, set the trend by winning World Cup host rights to celebrate their centenary in 1930. But their wish to use a soccer event to enhance the national party was a far cry from the sinister developments afoot in Europe.

Dictator Benito Mussolini saw the 1934 World Cup as an ideal vehicle to promote the fascist "wonders" of Italy while Adolf Hitler's will to use the 1936 Berlin Olympics as a showcase for "Aryan supremacy" has been recorded in numerous books and films and has remained a grim focus for sports politics historians down the years.

In Germany the Schalke club from Gelsenkirchen, in the industrial Ruhr,

THE GREAT GAMES

The first world champions

URUGUAY 4-2 ARGENTINA

World Cup Final, Centenary Stadium, Montevideo, July 30, 1930

Few papers outside South America and Central Europe bothered to report the match. Yet the game went into history simply because it could not be repeated. The first World Cup was over and international soccer now had a standard to emulate. Hosts Uruguay just managed to get a stadium built in time and fittingly reached the Final against neighbours Argentina. The Uruguayans took the lead, fell behind, then went ahead again at 3-2 before Stabile, top scorer in the competition with eight goals, hit their bar. Castro, who had lost part of an arm in childhood, then headed the goal which clinched Uruguay's victory, to be greeted by a national holiday in his country... and bricks through the windows of the Uruguayan Embassy in Buenos Aires. (above) Jules Rimet hands the World Cup to the Uruguayan national team.

1935
- Nurnberg beat Schalke 2-0 in Dusseldorf in the first German Cup Final
- Juventus win a fifth successive Italian league title
- Sparta Prague win the Mitropa Cup for the second time

1936
- Joe Payne scores an English record 10 goals in one game in Luton's 12-0 win over Bristol Rovers
- Italy add Olympic gold to their World Cup success
- Civil war brings Spanish league soccer to a halt for three years

1937
- A world attendance record of 149,547 watch Scotland v England at Hampden Park, Glasgow
- The official weight of the ball is increased from 13/15 oz to 14/16 oz
- Germany's legendary "Breslau-Elf" thrash Denmark 8-0

1938
- First live television transmission of Cup Final (Preston 1-0 Huddersfield)
- FA secretary Stanley Rous (left) rewrites the laws of the game
- Arsenal set a world transfer record by paying £14,000 for Wolves' forward Bryn Jones

1939
- England turn down invitation to play in the World Cup after the withdrawal of Austria following the Anschluss with Germany
- Italy become the first double winners of the World Cup, in France
- All normal English competitions suspended because of war
- Mysterious death in Vienna of Austria's superstar centre-forward Matthias Sindelar

INFAMOUS HISTORY

Shamed England hit six

GERMANY 3-6 ENGLAND

Olympic Stadium, Berlin, May 14, 1938

One of England's most effective displays followed a shameful incident brought about by the political pressures of the era. In an effort to placate Hitler, still furious at the way the majority of his athletes had been humbled in the same stadium at the 1936 Olympics, the England team were ordered to join the Germans in giving the Nazi salute as the German national anthem was played. The instruction came after talks between the British Ambassador, Sir Neville Henderson, and Stanley Rous, then FA secretary. The players reluctantly got on with it, then showed their feelings by beating a very good German team out of sight. Don Welsh, one of two men making their England debut, was to say later: "You couldn't have asked for a greater team performance than this. Only when the heat got to us in the second half did we have to slow down a bit. I honestly thought we could have scored ten." Jackie Robinson, only 20, was a perfect partner for Stan Matthews, and little Len Goulden hit a tremendous 30-yard goal.

long struggled to escape the shadow of Nazi-allied suspicions. Schalke commanded pivotal analysis because the club won the old German title in 1934, 1935, 1937, 1939 (and then again in 1940 and 1942). Not only did they win the title six times in nine seasons, they were also runners-up in 1933 and 1938 and third in 1936.

Modern historians have suggested that Schalke benefited indirectly and then only from prominent Nazis' wish to bask in their glory. "There were no special privileges for us," recalled Herbert Burdenski, Schalke's goalkeeper and later coach. "Once we were refused admittance to a youth tournament in Breslau [now Wroclaw in Poland] because we weren't wearing Hitler Youth uniforms. It didn't matter that we were Schalke."

The link with Breslau/Wroclaw remains significant. The German national team in the late 1930s was built on a Schalke nucleus. On May 16, 1937, Germany thrashed Denmark 8-0. It was the birth of the so-called "Breslau-Elf" which remains a legend to this day. They might even have threatened the Italian team at the 1938 World Cup finals. But the Anschluss prompted political pressure to mix the Schalke-Kreisel 'spinning top' with the "Vienna School."

It did not work for both stylistic and personal reasons. The warning signs were not heeded after Greater Germany lost 6-3 to England in Berlin on May 14, 1938, and Germany then took their mixed-up, defeated team to the World Cup in France where they lost to Switzerland in the first round, with the Germans questioning Austrian allegiance.

England, despite being outside FIFA, could have played at those finals. The field had been cut from 16 to 15 when Hitler's armies had marched into Austria that spring and the German federation had swallowed up its Austrian counterpart. FIFA offered England the spare place... and were turned down. Italy, jeered by the French crowds for their crude switch from traditional blue to sinisterly significant black shirts, won the cup for a second successive time.

In 1934 Italy, managed by Vittorio Pozzo, had beaten Czechoslovakia 2-1 in the final in Rome. Four years later eastern Europe took a another beating as Hungary lost 4-2. Pozzo and Italy, in tactical terms, had moved with the times. In 1934 they had won by using an "old-fashioned" attacking centre-half in the Argentine Luisito Monti; victory in 1938 was accomplished by the effective use of a new-style "stopper" central defender in the Uruguayan, Michele Andreolo. Only two players survived from the 1934 winners to 1938: inside-forwards Gianni Ferrari and skipper Giuseppe Meazza – who gave the fascist salute just before hoisting the World Cup trophy high in the Stade Colombes.

It was some 15 months later that resistance to Nazism took a different form in a very different field of conflict. Yet while soccer in Britain halted immediately war was declared on Sunday, September 3, 1939, it continued in Germany and Italy for several more years.

1940
- Central American championship launched
- Representative soccer is revived in England (Captains Eddie Hapgood for an FA XI and Stan Cullis of The Army shake hands before a match at Selhurst Park, London, left)1941
- Rapid Vienna defeat favourites Schalke 4-3 in controversial German league championship play-off final

1942
- Italy beat Croatia and Spain both 4-0 in April in their last matches before war halts the Azzurri's international activity

1943
- Santiago Bernabeu, new president of Real Madrid, launches an investment scheme to build the stadium which would later bear his name

1944
- Dresdner SC defeat LSV Hamburg 4-0 in the last wartime championship play-off in Germany
- Malmo win the Swedish championship for the first time in one of the few European leagues uninterrupted by war

1945
- Retirement of John Langenus, Belgian referee of the first World Cup Final back in 1930
- Moscow Dynamo make a sensational tour of Britain

1940s: Global halt

The 1940s were confused years for soccer. Official competition had been suspended in the United Kingdom on the outbreak of the Second World War but was maintained through the early years of fighting in both Italy and Germany. Meanwhile soccer continued in South America and, in a vacuum for the duration, in both Portugal and Spain. Their respective dictators, Antonio Salazar and Francisco Franco, had tried to maintain a relationship with the Axis powers best described as "sympathetically neutral."

Spain, in any case, had barely emerged from its own civil war of 1936 to 1939, which saw the Soviet-supported Republic overcome by the fascist-backed armies of the rebellious General Franco. Further confusion was generated by the various anarchist and regional independence movements. Decades later the stigma of political enmity scarred matches between Barcelona (supposedly representing regional independence), Real Madrid (Franco-directed centralism) and Athletic Bilbao (separatism).

In Germany, political pressure began seriously to compromise all-conquering Schalke in 1941. Nazi leaders were growing concerned about fading enthusiasm for the Greater German cause in Austria. Coincidentally, Schalke's rivals in the German Championship Final that year were Rapid Vienna. Schalke cruised to a 3-0 lead in 52 minutes. Yet Rapid recovered to win 4-3. Austrian pride was, apparently, vindicated.

Gradually even Germany's soccer

Wreckage of Torino's flight home from Lisbon at the foot of the Superga basilica in 1949.

players were called up for military service though the national coach, Sepp Herberger, used his restricted influence to protect his favoured players as best he could. Not even Herberger could help his most talented player, however, in the closing years of the war. Fritz Walter, who had played 24 times for Germany before the war closure, was sent to the Russian front. Remarkably, he later returned from a prisoner of war camp to pick up the threads of a World Cup-winning career. The German domestic championship had continued, amid increasing chaos, until 1944.

Greater Germany also went on playing national team soccer until 1944. Opposition was drawn exclusively from a close circle such as Finland and Switzerland, sympathetic or occupied nations of eastern Europe such as Bulgaria, Hungary, Romania and Yugoslavia, newly "Nazi-independent" Croatia and Slovakia and their Axis partners from Italy.

The Italians continued national team soccer until 1942 when they beat Croatia and Spain. They remained World Cup holders, of course, although early plans to decide on hosts for 1942 were scrapped. FIFA itself, now with a membership of 50, moved from Paris to Zurich in neutral Switzerland but Ottorino Barassi, secretary of the Italian federation, had no way of getting the World Cup trophy to safety. Instead he hid it under his bed and then in a chicken

THE GREAT STADIUMS
Pride of Madrid
ESTADIO SANTIAGO BERNABEU Madrid, Spain

It is thanks to the visionary foresight of long-time president Santiago Bernabeu in the early 1940s that Real Madrid boast their imposing edifice on Madrid's most prestigious street, the Castellana. The ground, which began life in 1944 on five hectares of prime land, was Bernabeu's brainchild. He decided that a super new stadium was needed to help raise the funds to build a new team. Madrid, who include the King and Queen of Spain among their members, raised an astonishing 41 million pesetas and the stadium was opened, with a 75,000 capacity, in December 1947. In the 1950s the finance raised by Real's dominance of the European Cup enabled capacity to be extended to 125,000. The name Estadio Santiago Bernabeu was adopted in 1955 and the floodlights were switched on in 1957 for the European Cup Final.

1946
- British Associations rejoin FIFA
- Norman Adcock, at Padova, becomes the first modern English professional to play in Italy
- 33 killed and 500 injured as wall and crowd barriers collapse at Bolton v Stoke FA Cup tie
- FIFA expels Germany from membership at its Luxembourg congress

1947
- First £20,000 transfer: Tommy Lawton (right), from Chelsea to Notts County
- A Great Britain XI beats the Rest of Europe 6-1 at Hampden Park, Glasgow, in a match to mark the return of the British home nations to FIFA membership

1948
- England win first European youth championship
- A separate federation is set up in East Germany
- Sweden, managed by Englishman George Raynor, surprisingly win the London Olympic Games title

1949
- Barcelona beat Sporting Lisbon 2-1 to win the Latin Cup, another precursor to the European club cups
- England's first home defeat by a non-home nation (0-2 vs. Republic of Ireland at Goodison Park)
- Entire Torino team wiped out when aircraft taking Italian champions home from Lisbon crashes near Turin
- Argentine league players undertake the first soccer players' strike for better pay and terms
- First post-war World Cup is postponed for one year to give hosts Brazil more time to prepare
- Colombian clubs, outside FIFA, poach some of the world's best players (Pedernera, Di Stefano, Nestor Rossi) without paying transfer fees

coop on a farm to keep it out of the hands of the Nazis. (The trophy was finally lost because of the lack of Brazilian security 30 years later. It was on display in the offices of the CBF in Rio de Janeiro when it was stolen by a group of thieves who had it melted down for its gold content: a sorry day for the Brazilian confederation).

When FIFA recovened in 1946 it had 57 members and no money. Congress decided optimistically, even so, to stage the first post-war World Cup in Brazil in 1949 (later postponed until 1950) and also decided to name the trophy after Jules Rimet himself.

Thus was formalized the legend of Rimet as father of the World Cup. In fact, a school of thought suggests that the trophy, if it were to be named after anyone, should have been named after Carl Hirschmann, FIFA's general secretary from 1906 to 1931. Rimet had been a comparative late arrival at the World Cup party, but Hirschmann had

stood aside in Rimet's favour when it had come to picking a new president in 1921, and it was on Rimet's "watch" that the World Cup was launched.

Simultaneously the secretary of the Football Association, Stanley Rous, negotiated the re-entry of the four "home countries" into FIFA. Rous swung the deal by offering FIFA the gate receipts from a Hampden Park friendly between the four home countries on the one hand and the Rest of the World on the other.

As part of the deal Rous also shrewdly negotiated a formal undertaking from FIFA guaranteeing the individual status of the four home nations in terms of both playing international soccer and of four individual votes within FIFA. It would say much about the surviving status of Britain, and more specifically England, that the status quo was retained when the FIFA statutes were revised in 2004. Suggestions that the British exception

be scrapped met with resounding opposition within the FIFA executive.

The final piece of the jigsaw would be the admission of the British home countries to the World Cup. Results from two seasons of the British Home Championship were to be used as the qualifying competition with the top two teams going to the finals. In fact, only group winners England went: the Scottish FA decided, for reasons which remain a mystery, that they would attend only if they won the group.

International club competitions were revived in the late 1940s. The Mitropa Cup had lost its status. But in western Europe the club baton was picked up by the federations of France, Italy, Portugal and Spain. The Latin Cup featured a four-team end-of-season tournament between the champion clubs of the four countries; points would be awarded which would be tallied up after four years to provide a winner. The first "edition" took place in 1949. Barcelona won by defeating Reims in the semi-finals and Sporting Clube of Portugal 2-1 in the final. In the other semi-final Sporting had won 3-1 against Torino who then beat Reims 5-3 in the third-place play-off.

But this was not the Torino team who had just won the Italian league title for a record-equaling fifth successive year. The senior first-team had been wiped out in its entirety a month earlier. Eighteen players died, along with management and coaching staff and crew, as the

plane, returning from a testimonial match against Benfica in Lisbon, crashed through the rain clouds into the perimeter wall of the Superga basilica above Turin. The dead included 10 Italian internationals, among them Valentino Mazzola as well as the Czecho-Hungarian inside-forward Gyula Schubert.

This was not the only soccer disaster of the immediate post-war era: 33 died in 1946 when a wall collapsed at Bolton before an FA Cup tie against Stanley Matthews' Stoke City.

BACK FROM THE USSR
Snow on their boots

In October and November 1945 Moscow Dynamo embarked upon one of the strangest yet memorable soccer goodwill missions in a four-match tour of Britain. Playing superb skilled, passing soccer, the Russians drew 3-3 with Chelsea, thrashed third division Cardiff City 10-1, scored a 4-3 win over a reinforced Arsenal (including Stanley Matthews) in the White Hart Lane fog then drew 2-2 with Rangers in Glasgow. On the journey home they beat Norrkoping 5-0 in Sweden. The players who made the greatest impression included the legendary goalkeeper Alexei "Tiger" Khomich, captain and playmaker Mikhail Semichastny, the forwards Konstantin Beskov (a future national manager) and Sergei Solovyov. They also brought their own referee, future FIFA official Nikolai Latyshev. He refereed the match against Arsenal in which Dynamo had 12 men on the pitch for 20 minutes after confusion over a substitution...

Wilf Mannion (centre) is denied by Rest of the World goalkeeper Julien Darui in 1947.

1950
- The English Football League is extended from 88 to 92 clubs
- England humbled 1-0 by US in World Cup group match, and world record crowd (203,500) see Uruguay beat Brazil 2-1 in the Final in Rio
- Scotland first beaten at home by foreign team (Austria, 1-0)
- West Germany is readmitted to FIFA

1951
- White ball comes into use
- First official match under floodlights played at Highbury: between Arsenal and Hapoel Tel Aviv
- Milan win Italy's Serie A for the first time
- Argentina play England for the first time, losing 2-1 at Wembley

1952
- Newcastle become first club to win successive FA Cup finals at Wembley
- Ferenc Puskas's Hungary win Olympic gold in Helsinki

1953
- Stanley Matthews (below) inspires Blackpool to beat Bolton 4-3 in the FA Cup Final
- Hungary beat England 6-3 at Wembley and then 7-1 the next year in Budapest

1954
- Favourites Hungary are surprisingly beaten 3-2 by West Germany in the World Cup Final
- European federation UEFA is founded
- Colombia is reintegrated into FIFA, ending the pirate league era
- Real Madrid, inspired by Alfredo Di Stefano, win their first Spanish league title since 1933

1950s: Great clubs

THE GREAT MATCHES

Brazil fail at the finish

BRAZIL 1-2 URUGUAY

World Cup final pool, Maracana, Rio de Janeiro, July 16, 1950

Figures for attendance vary, but this was certainly the highest at any match since Wembley 1923. The first post-war World Cup, played without a knockout final stage, provided what was in effect a final and established the tournament as the leading worldwide competition. Brazil, huge favourites, won their first two games, scoring 13 goals to 2. Uruguay trailed both Spain and Sweden 2-1, but drew the first game and won the second. So they had to beat Brazil at the newly-built Maracana, while Brazil needed only to draw. Coach Flavio Costa's warnings about previous encounters in which Uruguay had disturbed Brazil went unheeded. Even after Friaca hit their 22nd goal in 6 games, Brazil kept pressing forward: Costa later protested that he had ordered men back, but his words had gone either unheard or unheeded. Uruguay, calm amid the crescendo, equalized through Juan Schiaffino. Then Alcides Ghiggia slipped through on the right and shot between Barbosa and his near, left-hand post. All Brazil went into mourning.

Soccer took its first modern steps towards becoming the planet's dominant sport in the 1950s. The game provided showcase tournaments for the greatest players, in the World Cup and the new European Champions Club Cup, which were transmitted into the homes of millions by television.

The first post-war World Cup was staged in Brazil in 1950. Building and administrative problems had forced the tournament's delay by one year from the originally-scheduled 1949. Even then the massive new Maracana stadium, the biggest in the world with its 200,000 capacity, was barely ready to welcome the event.

Brazil and England, competing for the first time, started out as joint favourites. Holders Italy, robbed of their playing nucleus by the 1949 Torino air crash, failed in the first round – just like England who lost humiliatingly by 1-0 to the United States. Brazil went all the way to the effective final before they were upset, losing 2-1 to tiny old enemy Uruguay in front of around 200,000 home fans in Maracana. At least Brazil tried their best – unlike Argentina who stayed away for political and sporting reasons.

By this time a new force was rising in Europe in the shape of Hungary. The Magical Magyars underlined their status by winning the Olympic title in 1952 in Helsinki and then, the following year, by thrashing England 6-3 at Wembley. It was the first time England

had lost at home to continental opposition and the first time managers, players and fans had been forced to confront the realization that the rest of the world had left the game's founders behind.

An even bigger shock than Brazil's 1950 defeat was awaiting at the 1954 finals in Switzerland, however. Hungary, an amalgam of players dragooned into their two top clubs by the communist regime and unbeaten in four years, lost the one match which mattered most: the World Cup Final. West Germany, remarkably, hit back from 2-0 down and against all the odds to win 3-2. What made victory such a shock was the fact that skipper Ferenc Puskas and his Hungarians had beaten West Germany 8-3 in the first round in front of 30,000 furious German fans in the St Jakob stadium in Basel. Three weeks later manager Sepp Herberger, skipper Fritz Walter, two-goal Helmut Rahn and their team were heroes. But controversy erupted in the autumn after half the team went down with jaundice linked to revelations of vitamin injections.

Walter had received the World Cup from the hands of the increasingly frail Jules Rimet, who then stepped down as president of FIFA. Belgium's Rodolphe Seeldrayers succeeded him, too late; he died the following year. Englishman Arthur Drewry was next in line but the apparent curse of the FIFA

1955
- First floodlit FA Cup tie (replay): Kidderminster vs. Brierley Hill Alliance
- The European Champions Club Cup is launched on the initiative of the French sports newspaper, L'Equipe

1956
- First floodlit league match: Portsmouth vs. Newcastle
- Real Madrid, from an entry of 16 teams, win first European Cup
- South Korea defeat Israel to win first Asian Cup

1957
- First African Nations Cup Final: Egypt 4-1 Ethiopia
- Juventus pay a world record £91,000 for Omar Sivori (left) from River Plate

1958
- Munich air disaster kills 19, including eight Manchester United players
- English League restructured into four divisions
- Barcelona beat a London Select team 8-2 over two games to win first Inter City Fairs Cup
- Pele, at 17, becomes youngest World Cup-winner with Brazil

1959
- Billy Wright of Wolves, first man to reach 100 caps for England, retires on 105
- Real Madrid win their fourth European Champions Cup by defeating Reims - their opponents in the first final
- Alfredo Di Stefano become the first player to win the European Footballer of the Year for a second time

presidency saw him die in office as well, in 1961. Drewry was followed by another Englishman in Stanley Rous.

It was an era of expansion which also brought a significant development in the administration of the game worldwide. Later FIFA presidents such as Joao Havelange and Sepp Blatter would talk about the "FIFA pyramid" as if this were the original blueprint for world soccer administration. FIFA is at the apex, with the six regional confederations next, then the national associations who comprise the confederations' memberships. In fact, the structure was not a planned, peaceful creation - it erupted out of dissatisfaction with this remote tiny body in Switzerland.

South America had created the first regional confederation in 1916. But that was an early exception for geographical and communications reasons. It was the gathering of nations at the 1954 World Cup which prompted the birth of the Asian and European federations (AFC and UEFA). Three years later Africa would create CAF with CONCACAF following in 1961 and Oceania in 1966. Thus the famous pyramid came into being through an accident of frustration and may indeed need to be redesigned in due course to recognize the changing balance in power between leagues and associations, clubs and countries.

To be fair, Rous welcomed all these initiatives. He had also been one of the moving forces in the early 1950s behind the launch of the Inter-City Industrial Fairs Cup, whose conception narrowly preceded L'Equipe's creation of the European Champions Club Cup, which gave UEFA an immediate administrative purpose.

The European Cup quickly took on a life and power of its own and UEFA, taking the hint, created the European Championship for national teams (initially called the Nations Cup) in its wake. The initial Nations Cup, an expanded version of the Gero Cup set up by Hugo Meisl back in the late 1920s, attracted only 17 entries in 1958. But within less than two decades it was established in national team status as second only to the World Cup.

European fans, meanwhile, were thrilled by the European Champions Cup. Officials turned blind eyes to political conventions as when Partizan of Yugoslavia flew to Spain to face pioneering power Real Madrid in the winter of 1955. The two countries had no political relations but the Yugoslav players were allowed to slip into the airport through a side door with no passport checks.

But the thrills were accompanied by disaster. In February 1958 eight Manchester United players died after their plane crashed at Munich after a refuelling stop following a match against Red Star in Belgrade. Just as Italy's 1950 World Cup bid was wrecked by the Superga air crash, so England's hopes for Sweden in 1958 were undermined by the deaths of Roger Byrne, Duncan Edwards and Tommy Taylor.

England did manage a goalless first round draw with ultimate winners Brazil, but failed to reach the quarter-finals after losing a play-off to the Soviet Union. Brazil reacted to the England draw by producing the explosive genius of Pele and Garrincha. Brazil also opened up a new tactical front. Not for them the old WM. Instead Brazil strung four players across defence, pulled one inside-forward back into midfield to partner an attacking wing-half, and attacked with four men instead of five. Suddenly everyone woke up to 4-2-4.

THE GREAT MATCHES

The match that changed the game
ENGLAND 3-6 HUNGARY
Friendly international, Wembley Stadium, London, November 25, 1953

Why were England so confident? Did they not know that Hungary had won 25 and drawn 6 of their previous 32 games, scoring in every match they had played for six seasons? Yet England still looked on the match as a training spin, fooled by a xenophobic Press with little or no knowledge of Puskas and his colleagues. "This will be easy," said one England player, "they've all got carpet slippers on." Hungary's footwear did look like slippers compared with England's boots, but they could smack the ball pretty hard. As Hidegkuti did in the opening seconds, from 20 yards, arrow-straight past Merrick. The Hungarians played in tight triangles, then suddenly opened up with a raking pass of 30, 40, 50 yards or more to a sprinting colleague. The defeat was England's first by a continental invader and the manner and margin forced a furious tactical rethink in succeeding seasons.

1960
- FA recognizes Sunday soccer
- European champions Real Madrid win first World Club Championship, beating South American champions Penarol over two legs
- Soviet Union win the first European Championship
- Penarol of Uruguay win first Copa Libertadores

1961
- Tottenham complete first League and Cup double of 20th century
- Maximum wage (£20) abolished
- First British £100-a-week wage paid to Johnny Haynes by Fulham
- First £100,000 British transfer: Denis Law (right) from Manchester City to Torino
- Fiorentina beat Rangers 4-2 over two games to win first European Cup-winners' Cup

1962
- Brazil win second successive World Cup
- Pele's club, Santos, win the Copa Libertadores for the first time

1963
- Tottenham beat Atletico Madrid 5-1 in Cup-winners' Cup Final to become first British club to win European trophy
- First pools panel is organised in England to assess the likely results of weather-hit Saturday match schedules

1964
- First televised Match of the Day (BBC 2, Liverpool 3-2 Arsenal, August 22)
- 318 die and 500 injured in riot over disallowed goal during Peru v Argentina Olympic tie in Lima
- Oryx Douala of Cameroon defeat Stade Malien of Mali 2-1 to win first African Champions Club Cup

1960s: Refining the game

The 1960s saw soccer's last romantic era washed away by a wave of pragmatism at both club and country and tactical level.

Brazil and England won the decade's two World Cups, Iberian adventure gave way to Italian cynicism in the European Champions Cup, the greed for European money prompted the launch of the Cup-Winners' Cup and revamp of the Fairs Cup while South America sought its own chunk of the action. Amid the explosion of international club competitions so the concept of "prestige friendlies" at national team level faded into history.

If anything, this was the decade in which the balance of financial power began to turn in favour of the clubs and away, perceptibly, from the amateur officials who had run the game for a century but whose time was fast running out.

The tactics of success underlined the nature of the change. Brazil introduced 4-2-4 to the world in 1958 but an ageing team demanded a more cautious approach in Chile in 1962. Thus left-winger Mario Zagallo was pulled back on the left side of midfield and the conversion made to 4-3-3.

Brazil won with a final victory over Czechoslovakia. Consolation for the Czechs was to have scored first and to see Josef Masopust crowned later as European Footballer of the Year.

Masopust and the Soviet goalkeeper Lev Yashin were the two greatest individuals to rise above the stereotyping which was reducing the potential of the eastern Europe nations at international level. Communist sport doctrine forbade professionalism but the edifice was a sham. Dukla Prague (Czechoslovakia), CCA later known as Steaua Bucharest (Romania), Vorwarts Berlin (East Germany), Legia Warsaw (Poland), Honved (Hungary), CDNA later CSKA Sofia (Bulgaria) and CSKA Moscow (Soviet Union) were the army clubs who dominated their countries' league championships and returned, time and again, to the Champions Cup. Masopust was the commander at Dukla, Ivan Kolev – the so-called "Pocket Puskas" – at CDNA and Kaziu Deyna at Legia.

But they rarely progressed beyond the quarter-finals. Every season the eastern Europeans were caught out by the traditional mid-winter shutdowns forced by icy weather. The Soviet Union won the inaugural European Championship in 1960 but the best they could acheive at the World Cup was fourth in 1966 in England.

Tactics were changing. By the time England reached the final for the first time, against West Germany, manager Alf Ramsey had decided to scrap wingers in favour of a four-man midfield in which the effort and energy of Nobby Stiles and Alan Ball were balanced by the perception of

Sir Stanley Matthews is shouldered into retirement by Lev Yashin and Ferenc Puskas.

Martin Peters and brilliance of Bobby Charlton. Ramsey's tactical pragmatism had already been pre-empted in the European club competitions by Milan and neighbours Internazionale.

In 1960 Real Madrid had reached a glorious pinnacle of Champions Cup perfection with the manner of their 7-3 victory over Germany's Eintracht Frankfurt in the Hampden Park Final. Not content with their fifth European crown they then collected the first World Club Cup. This was launched under the formal title of Inter-continental Club Cup at the instigation of the South American confederation and with the acquiescence, if not full-hearted approval, of UEFA.

THE GREAT MATCHES

Glasgow sees the greatest

REAL MADRID 7-3 EINTRACHT FRANKFURT

European Cup Final, Hampden Park, Glasgow, May 18, 1960

Real Madrid's fifth successive European Cup was achieved by their greatest performance in front of yet another great crowd. In their seven matches they scored 31 goals and were watched by 524,097 people – an average of nearly 75,000 per game. In the semi-final Real beat Barcelona 3-1 home and away, after Barça had crushed Wolves, the English champions, 9-2 on aggregate. In the other semi-final, Eintracht performed the barely credible feat of twice scoring six goals against Rangers, but in the Final they conceded hat-tricks to both Di Stefano and Puskas in a wonderful performance watched by a crowd so big that only one larger attendance has been recorded in Britain since. Hardly any left early, even though the Germans were a beaten team well before the end. The fans stayed to bay a seemingly never-ending roar of tribute to one of the finest displays ever put on by any team, anywhere. The Scots were quick to appreciate their good fortune.

1965
- Ten Football League players jailed and banned for life for match-fixing
- Stanley Matthews knighted
- Substitutes allowed for injured players in English league matches

1966
- Hosts England win World Cup, beating West Germany 4-2 after extra time at Wembley; manager Alf Ramsey is knighted
- Real Madrid win a record-extending sixth European Champions Cup

1967
- Jock Stein's (right) Celtic beat Internazionale 2-1 to become first British winners of European Cup

1968
- 74 die at Nunez, Buenos Aires, when panic breaks out during River Plate v Boca Juniors match
- Alan Mullery becomes first England player sent off, vs. Yugoslavia in European Championship
- Manchester United become first English winners of European Cup beating Benfica 4-1 after extra time

1969
- Ajax Amsterdam become the first Dutch club to reach the Champions Cup Final, albeit losing 4-1 to Milan in Madrid
- 200 die in the so-called "football war" between El Salvador and Honduras after a contentious World Cup qualifier

Nobby Stiles, Bobby Moore, Geoff Hurst and Martin Peters celebrate England's World Cup triumph in 1966.

South America's big clubs had seen the success of the European Champions Cup and demanded that CONMEBOL sanction an equivalent. Thus was born, in 1960, the Copa Libertadores. At first this was competed between the champions of the South American countries. Later, and before UEFA got around to the idea, the Copa Libertadores was expanded to include the runners-up from each country. First champions of South America were the Uruguay giants, Penarol of Montevideo. They beat a Bolivian team in the first Libertadores final to qualify to face Madrid over two legs. Madrid forced a goalless draw in Montevideo then handed out a 5-1 hiding back in Spain.

Every club has its era and that was the pinnacle for Madrid. They were almost instantly eliminated from the next European Cup by Barcelona – of all teams – and the Catalans then lost the 1961 final to Benfica.

They were deposed in turn by Milan who were duly succeeded by neighbours Internazionale. Coached by the Moroccan-born Argentine-educated Spaniard Helenio Herrera, Inter took Italian caution to new lengths. Herrera brought a cynical new rigour to the catenaccio defensive system by which a "free" defender lingers behind the rest of a man-marking defence to sweep away any danger.

Twice in a row Inter ground out Champions Cup victory and, each time, went on to grind down Independiente of Argentina for the world title. But that approach demanded the highest levels of fitness and when Inter began to fray at the physical edges they were prey to the sort of one-off, marauding masterpiece which Celtic produced in 1967 to become the first British club to win the Champions Cup. One year later and Manchester United had followed in their footsteps: skipper Bobby Charlton, a Munich survivor, scored in the 4-1 defeat of Benfica at Wembley under manager Matt Busby.

Simultaneously, however, and as if negative tactics were not enough, lax and corrupt refereeing around the world threatened to bring the game to its knees. Santos kicked their way to victory over Milan in the 1963 World Club Final while controversial Argentine referee Juan Brozzi turned a blind eye. Celtic gave way to immense provocation and had six players sent off against Racing of Argentina in 1967; and Manchester United had Nobby Stiles and George Best sent off in the two legs of their defeat by Estudiantes de La Plata. The message of the 1960s was that negativity paid, both in terms of defensive tactics and physical assault.

To say the professional game was dying on its feet was trite, however, because a very real death toll was mounting. More than 600 fans died in stadia accidents in the 1960s, the

THE GREAT MATCHES

Lisbon's Lions
CELTIC 2-1 INTERNAZIONALE
European Cup Final, National Stadium, Lisbon, May 25, 1967

Celtic, one of Scotland's big two clubs, were minnows in the mainstream of Europe. They were led by Jock Stein, a manager wondrously adept at making the whole much greater than the sum of the parts. Inter, European champions in 1965, returned to the Final with the help of a "deal" that would not now be allowed: after two draws with CSKA, Inter won the right to stage a vital play-off at home by promising the other team 75 per cent of the takings. Inter won and many neutrals turned against them: Celtic had incredible support in a comparatively small crowd at Lisbon. Celtic's faith in hard work and un-complicated, attacking soccer paid off with two late goals.

majority – 318 – in Lima, Peru, after a late penalty claim was rejected in an Olympic qualifier against Argentina. Players died too with the increase in air travel: Green Cross of Chile in 1961 and The Strongest of Bolivia in 1969 both lost entire first-team squads.

Worst of all, soccer even prompted a border war after El Salvador beat Honduras in 1969 in a World Cup qualifying play-off. The future looked bleak indeed.

1970
- Brazil beat Italy 4-1 to capture World Cup for third time and win the Jules Rímet trophy outright
- Feyenoord become the first Dutch club to win the European Champions Cup

1971
- 66 fans trampled to death and 100 injured in second Ibrox disaster, as they tumbled down a stairway just before the end of Rangers vs. Celtic New Year's Day game
- Arsenal set British transfer record by paying £220,000 for Alan Ball from Everton
- Ajax Amsterdam win the first of three successive Champions Cups

1972
- Fairs Cup becomes UEFA Cup and is won by Tottenham, who defeat Wolves 3-2 over two games
- West Germany beat the Soviet Union 3-0 to win European Championship

1973
- Barcelona pay world record £922,000 to buy Johan Cruyff (below) from Ajax
- Russia expelled from the World Cup after refusing to play Chile in the "concentration camp" Estadio Nacional of Santiago

1974
- English league soccer played on Sunday for first time
- Magdeburg become first and last East German winners in Europe, beating Milan in Cup-Winners' Cup final
- Last FA Amateur Cup Final
- Hosts West Germany beat Holland 2-1 to win the World Cup after conceding first Final penalty in the event's history

1970s: Popularity

On and off the pitch, the 1970s belonged to Brazil. The national team became the first three-times World Cup winners, and four years later Joao Havelange seized administrative power at the head of FIFA.

In fact, 1970 began inauspiciously for Brazil. The journalist/coach Joao Saldanha who had been put in charge of the World Cup bid was no friend of the superstar culture. The Brazilian confederation accepted his strategy up to a point but when that strategy threatened the omission of Pele, Saldanha had to go.

In the World Cup Brazil had more and better skilled individuals than anyone else. They beat holders England 1-0 in the first round and crushed Italy 4-1 in the Final in Mexico City. Four years later Brazil were winning again but this time off the pitch as Havelange, president of the Brazilian confederation, ousted England's Sir Stanley Rous as FIFA leader. Rous had reigned for 13 years, in which time FIFA expanded from 90 countries to more than 130 and launched its first development schemes in Africa and Asia. The fact that African votes ultimately cost Rous his presidency was not the only irony: seeds for that rebellion had been sown by Rous and FIFA's own organization of the 1966 World Cup, back "home" in England.

Rous was one of the towering sports administrators of the 20th century. He was first an international

THE GREAT MATCHES

Losers at the last gasp
ITALY 4-3 WEST GERMANY
World Cup semi-final, Azteca Stadium, Mexico City, June 17, 1970
Six goals in 21 minutes made this one of the most exciting matches in the history of the World Cup. Sadly, such are the demands of modern tournament structures, both teams ended up as losers; four days later, an unchanged Italian side crashed 4-1 in the Final. Players, no matter how fit, need ample time to recuperate from two tense, testing hours in the Mexican sun. Italy led for nearly all normal time, after Boninsegna's early snap shot, but Schnellinger, playing in his fourth World Cup, equalized for West Germany in injury time – only seconds from defeat. That began a remarkable scoring burst, with Germany leading 2-1, Italy levelling then leading 3-2, Germany getting level again – Muller's tenth goal of the tournament – and Rivera carefully rolling in what proved to be the decider, straight from the restart.

referee then secretary of the Football Association and he wrote the "modern" version of the laws of the game.

North Korea's participation at the 1966 World Cup finals is one of the legends of the game. Yet the Koreans probably would not have been there had it not been for Rous's intransigence. The African nations wanted one guaranteed place at the finals. Rous refused so the Africans boycotted the entire event.

On its own that would not have proved fatal to the Rous presidency. But, in 1973, he alienated a significant chunk of European votes through his handling of the Santiago stadium affair which followed the overthrow of the elected Marxist government of Salvador Allende in Chile. The Estadio Nacional in Santiago, which had staged the 1962 World Cup Final, had been put to use as concentration camp and interrogation (i.e. torture) facility. So it was hardly surprising later that year that the Soviet Union, when due to meet Chile in a qualifying play-off to reach the World Cup finals, refused point-blank to play there.

Rous flew to and fro trying to find a compromise. In the end FIFA insisted the match be fulfilled, the Soviets refused to go and Chile were awarded a walk-over. The Soviets turned on Rous and put eastern bloc support behind the politically far more astute Havelange at the Frankfurt congress on the eve of the 1974 World Cup finals.

1975
- FIFA appoints Swiss Sepp Blatter as development director
- English hooliganism makes its first mark on the Champions Cup Final after Leeds United lose to Bayern Munich at the Parc des Princes in Paris

1976
- Czechoslovakia become the first European champions courtesy of a penalty shootout – against holders West Germany
- East Germany win Olympic gold in Montreal
- Bayern Munich win their third European Champions Cup in a row

1977
- Liverpool win League Championship and European Cup
- Allan Simonsen becomes the first Dane voted as European Footballer of the Year

1978
- Freedom of contract accepted for English league players
- Ban on foreign players in English soccer lifted. Tottenham take advantage of rule change to sign Argentine World Cup stars Osvaldo Ardiles and Ricardo Villa (right)
- Argentina, as hosts, win the World Cup; Holland are again runners-up
- Paolo Rossi, at Perugia, becomes world's most expensive player at £3.5million

1979
- First £1m British transfer: Trevor Francis, from Birmingham City to Nottingham Forest
- Forest win the European Cup Final – with Francis' goal beating Malmo

Liverpool's Phil Neal, Emlyn Hughes and Jimmy Case share European Cup-winning delight.

No incumbent president had ever faced an election challenge before. Rous was outmanoeuvred, utterly. Havelange came to power on a promise to expand the World Cup to accommodate third world ambitions and supported by the political power of the German sportswear company Adidas. This was being wielded with increasing effect by Horst Dassler, son of the (literal) founding father, Adi (hence the company name).

Horst Dassler, shy but hugely effective behind the scenes as he pulled the political strings, teamed up with British super-salesman Patrick Nally. They brought in Coca-Cola to finance FIFA's repurchase of rights to its own images. They also created the concept of central event sponsorship sold at premium rates with the guarantee of worldwide television exclusivity.

Between them, the triumvirate of Havelange, Dassler and Nally revolutionized the finances of the World Cup and FIFA.

But if a Brazilian had grasped the levers of power in 1974, on the pitch, at least, command reverted to Europe. These were the days of so-called "total football." The soccer players of Holland and, to a lesser extent West Germany, did not possess the natural technique of the 1970 Brazilians but they countered with a more scientific appreciation of the qualities demanded to win World and European cups.

Three years in a row Dutch club Ajax won the European Champions Cup and then the baton of so-called 'total football' was picked up by their relentless pursuers, Bayern Munich. Bayern's three-year reign was launched in 1974 – the same year

Germany beat Holland in the World Cup Final in Munich. The Germans were managed by Helmut Schön, the former Dresdner inside-forward and later No. 2 to the legendary Sepp Herberger. His achievement was not only in winning the second World Cup for the Germans but in turning them into the first team to hold both world and European titles: two years earlier they had defeated the Soviet Union 3-0 to win the European Championship. Gerd Müller scored two of the goals just as he then scored the winner in the 1974 World Cup Final. Holland completed a double four years later when they were again runners-up, this time in Argentina.

The club game was changing. UEFA had scrapped the old Fairs Cup, taken full control of a ragged competition and rebranded it as the UEFA Cup. At domestic level across Europe and South America the big clubs began establishing a new level of command. In England six clubs won the league title in the 1950s and seven in the 1960s. In the 1970s, however, Liverpool launched themselves on a takeover bid of the Football League which brought them eight championships in 12 years under inspirational Bill Shankly, then erstwhile assistant Bob Paisley.

Simultaneously Liverpool achieved a hitherto unattainable dominance of the European Champions Cup – by English standards at least – despite competition from Leeds United and Nottingham Forest.

But while clubs remained happy to spend ever larger sums on players, they refused to spend similar sums on the safety and security of fans – with catastrophic consequences. In 1971 some 66 fans died and 150 were injured as they tumbled down a steep stairway while leaving a few minutes before the end of an Old Firm derby at Ibrox Park, Glasgow, between Rangers and Celtic. That, tragically, was just the start.

THE GREAT STADIUMS
Fair shares in Milan
STADIO GIUSEPPE MEAZZA Milan, Italy
Impressive and intimidating are the most appropriate words to describe the home of two of Europe's leading clubs in the city which claims to be the continent's premier soccer centre. The cylindrical towers which allowed builders to construct a third tier and roof in advance of the 1990 World Cup have become just as much a trademark as the ramp system which gave access to the original two tiers of what used to be known as the San Siro. The stadium reopened for the two clubs in 1955 with an increased capacity of 82,000 and was renamed Stadio Giuseppe Meazza in 1979 to honour the memory of one of the only two players to appear in both Italy's 1934 and 1938 World Cup-winning sides. The inside-forward had played for both Milan clubs in the 1930s.

1980
- West Germany win European title for second time in Italy
- All four semi-finalists in the UEFA Cup are West German clubs: Eintracht Frankfurt then beat Borussia Monchengladbach in the final

1981
- Tottenham win 100th FA Cup Final
- Liverpool win European Cup, becoming first British side to hold it three times
- Three points for a win introduced in Football League
- Record British transfer: Bryan Robson, from West Bromwich Albion to Manchester United for £1.5m
- Queens Park Rangers lay the first artificial pitch in English soccer

1982
- 340 fans crushed to death during Spartak Moscow v Haarlem UEFA Cup tie at Lenin Stadium
- Aston Villa become sixth consecutive English winners of European Cup (right)
- Tottenham retain FA Cup, for the first time since 1961-62
- Italy defeat West Germany 3-1 in Madrid to complete third World Cup triumph

1983
- England's Football League sponsored by Canon for three years
- Hamburg break the six-year English monopoly of the European Champions Cup

1984
- Aberdeen win Scottish Cup for third straight season and win championship
- Northern Ireland win last British Home Championship
- France win their first honour – the European Championship
- Britain's biggest score of 20th century: Stirling Albion beat Selkirk 20-0 in Scottish Cup

1980s: Tragedy

Diego Maradona and Michel Platini were the dominant players of the 1980s; Liverpool, Juventus, Milan plus Penarol and America Cali the leading clubs; Italy and Argentina the decade's two World Cup-winners. But the 1980s will be remembered, most of all, for an almost criminal negligence by many associations, officials and clubs which led to unnecessary death and destruction on the terraces.

This was the decade in which soccer had to fight for its soul against the threat of the hooligan menace. Almost every year brought a terrace disaster somewhere in the world, starting in Colombia in 1981 when 18 fans died after a wall collapsed in Ibague. One year later, again in Colombia, 22 died in a supporter stampede in Cali.

That same year more than 300 Soviet fans died on the icy terracing and staircases of the Lenin Stadium in Moscow at a UEFA Cup tie between Spartak and Haarlem of Holland.

By now the curse of hooliganism had eaten its way deep into the heart of the game and the English game in particular. In 1985 English soccer drew the horrible consequences of inadequate stadia and inadequate security. First, 56 fans were burned to death and more than 200 injured when fire swept through Bradford City's 77-year-old wooden stand before half-time in the last match of the season. It was one of the club's biggest crowds of the season.

From Bradford to Brussels: just 17 days later the world's television viewers watched more tragedy. The scene was the Champions Cup Final between holders Liverpool and Juventus in the

THE GREAT MATCHES

Rossi's timely return

ITALY 3-2 BRAZIL

World Cup Group C, Sarria Stadium, Barcelona, July 5, 1982

On the morning of April 29, 1982, Paolo Rossi returned from suspension, having been banned for three years – later reduced to two – for allegedly accepting a bribe and helping "fix" a match in the Italian league. 11 weeks later Rossi was the hero of all Italy. He scored three goals in this vital group qualifying match and one in the Final, when Italy beat West Germany 3-1. His six goals made him the tournament's leading marksman and completed a remarkable comeback for one of the most effective strikers of his generation. He had always protested his innocence – and his demonic efforts to regain match fitness, plus his finishing, took Italy to a merited success. Brazil needed a draw to reach the semi-finals, but their two brilliant goals encouraged them to keep on attacking and their over-stretched defence made too many errors against a forward in such inspired mood as Rossi.

ageing Heysel stadium in Brussels, capital of Belgium. An hour before the match, missiles began to be exchanged between fans who were separated only by a frail net fence.

Provoked perhaps by one more missile, the Liverpool-supporting horde suddenly swept across the terracing, bulldozed the fence and threw themselves headlong upon the Juventus fans. They retreated against a maintence shaft wall... which collapsed under the pressure. Some 39 Juve fans died, crushed. As ambulances and aid workers dashed to the scene, so it was decided to play the match. One hour 25 minutes after the scheduled kick-off, the game got under way. Juventus duly won 1-0 with a penalty.

The European federation in general and its secretary Hans Bangerter in particular were later excoriated and summoned to answer in the Belgian courts for going on with the match when fans lay dead and dying only yards from the pitch. The official answer was that a postponement or cancellation would have risked further angry violence from fans and would also have let out people across the stadium concourses which were being used as emergency field hospitals.

In the immediate aftermath the president of the Football Association, Sir Bert Millichip, withdrew English clubs from European competitions. Later UEFA formalized the separation with a wholesale ban. The absence lasted five years and a further five were taken in making up the educational time lost from a lack of competition against top foreign opposition.

1985
- Bradford City fire disaster kills 56
- Kevin Moran (Manchester United) is first player sent off in Cup Final
- Heysel disaster: 39 die as a result of rioting at Liverpool v Juventus European Cup Final in Brussels. UEFA bans English clubs indefinitely from European competition

1986
- Sir Stanley Rous dies, aged 91
- Wales FA move HQ from Wrexham to Cardiff after 110 years
- Diego Maradona's Argentina win the World Cup for the second time on its second hosting in Mexico

1987
- Play-offs introduced for last promotion place; re-election abolished; automatic promotion for winners of Conference
- The 18-strong squad plus youth players and officials of Alianza Lima die in plane crash

1988
- Wimbledon (below) beat Liverpool in FA Cup Final
- Holland win the European Championship, beating the Soviet Union 2-0 in Munich

1989
- Hillsborough disaster: 95 crushed to death at Liverpool v Nottingham Forest FA Cup semi-final
- Milan win their first European Champions Cup of the Berlusconi era, beating Steaua Bucharest 4-0 in the final in Barcelona

This was indeed soccer's killing fields decade. In 1988 more than 30 fans died in Libya and another 100 in Katmandu, Nepal. But worse was to come in April 1989 when 95 Liverpool supporters were crushed to death before an FA Cup semi-final against Nottingham Forest at Sheffield Wednesday's Hillsborough.

Subsequent inquiries and investigations laid bare a string of basic security and crowd control errors. The first problem was a flood of Liverpool fans arriving close to kick-off time. Police, fearing crush injuries outside the ground, opened the gates... and the fans rushed for the tunnel leading to the Leppings Lane terracing behind one goal. They pushed their way out on the terracing unaware that fans at the front of the terraces were being crushed against the fencing and that police failed to understand what was happening and refused to open the security gates for fear of the mob. When realization did strike home, it proved too late to save many.

English soccer could, apparently, sink no lower. Prime Minister Margaret Thatcher demanded radical action. That prompted the Taylor Report which forced the introduction of all-seater stadia at top league level and new security systems.

FIFA and UEFA duly picked up the all-seater concept and a host of new grounds began to arise throughout not only English soccer but Europe-wide. European Union grants in some countries and lottery support in others helped finance the structural redevelopment of the game.

Wreaths of flowers turn the Kop into a memorial to the Hillsborough victims in 1989.

Clubs were also attacked for using the seats provision too readily as an excuse for raising prices and thus switching the game's appeal to a middle-class sector and away from its traditional working-class roots.

Amid the gloom Maradona and Platini played some of the best soccer for years. Their shadows had first touched at the 1978 World Cup. Maradona was in hosts' Argentina's initial squad of 25 but was then among one of the three players omitted because manager Cesar Luis Menotti doubted he could withstand the pressure. Menotti had a point: four years later Maradona was sent off at the 1982 World Cup for sticking a boot into a Brazilian's groin.

Platini, five years older, had played for France at the 1978 finals, then took a starring role when they reached the semi-finals in Spain in 1982 and in Mexico in 1986. In between he scored a tournament record nine goals as hosts France won the European Championship for the first time in 1984. That was also the year in which Barcelona sold Maradona to Napoli for a world record £3 million. Two years later he led Napoli to the Serie A crown and Argentina to World Cup glory. Now captain of his country, Maradona led by example, scoring wondrous solo goals in the quarter-finals against England and in the semis against Belgium. He also laid on the winner for Jorge Burruchaga against West Germany in the final.

Argentina's manager Carlos Bilardo had been a member of the Estudiantes team who roughed up the best clubs in South America and Europe in the late 1960s. But, as a coach, he proved a pragmatic thinker and inventive tactician. At the 1986 World Cup Bilardo quickly realized that most opponents played with only two strikers and he was wasting his "fourth" defender. Midway through the tournament Bilardo thus replaced fullback Oscar Garre with midfielder Julio Olarticoechea. He pushed up into what was now a five-man midfield, leaving a three-man defence.

Several countries had played with a similar 3-5-2 formation at the 1984 European Championship but Bilardo was the first coach to set out his stall that way. The catch of the system, as he explained later, was that it demanded players of a particular footballing intelligence. "That's why I am not so

The best man
WEST GERMANY 3-3 FRANCE
World Cup semi-final, Sanchez Pizjuan Stadium, Seville, July 8, 1982

The first World Cup finals match to be decided on penalties was resolved because indomitable German spirit proved just too much for French skill. West Germany were lucky to go through after an appalling foul by 'keeper Harald Schumacher on French substitute Patrick Battiston. France recovered so well after a poor opening that they might well have won inside 90 minutes. Then two quick goals in extra time seemed to have made them safe, and delighted all neutrals. Yet the Germans pulled the game round. Rummenigge went on as a sub and scored and an overhead hook from Fischer levelled the scores. Even then France should have won but at 4-4 in the shootout Schumacher saved and Germany went through with the next kick.

sure about 3-5-2 at club level," he said. "With all due respect, the quality of the players is just not the same. It could then be a pretty risky tactic.

"On the other hand, with Maradona in your side the tactical shape does not matter quite so much: what matters is picking the players who know how to give him the ball."

1990
- International Board amends offside law (player level no longer offside); FIFA makes professional foul a sending-off offence
- English clubs (Manchester United and Aston Villa) restored to European competition
- Giuseppe Lorenzo of Bologna sets a world record by being sent off after 10 seconds for striking Parma opponent
- West Germany avenge their 1986 defeat by beating Argentina 1-0 in the World Cup Final

1991
- Manchester United climax first season back in Europe by winning Cup-Winners' Cup
- End of artificial pitches in Division One (Oldham and Luton)

1992
- Premier League of 22 clubs launched; Football League reduced to 71 clubs
- Yugoslavia expelled from European Championship finals on security grounds
- 15 killed and 1,300 injured when temporary stand collapses at Bastia, Corsica, during Bastia v Marseille in French Cup semi-final
- Late entrants Denmark, replacing Yugoslavia, score shock victory in European finals in Sweden

1993
- Marseille are the first French team to win European Cup, but cannot defend their trophy following bribery scandal

1994
- Manchester United win "double"
- Colombia defender Escobar shot dead after returning home following World Cup own goal in game against hosts United States
- Brazil become first country to win the World Cup on penalties

1990s: Evolution

The 1990s proved one of the most energizing decades in soccer history both on and off the pitch. Yet they were launched to an inauspicious start by a World Cup in Italy in which the quality of soccer and standards of refereeing fell far below expectations.

The Italian public made some amends by providing a great carnival atmosphere but their semi-final defeat by Argentina left the tournament to end in anti-climax. Argentina produced angry soccer which raised unpleasant memories of the 1960s. It all reached a nadir in the Final in Rome when they had two players sent off, the first World Cup Final dismissals in history. Germany won.

Off the pitch European club soccer was entering a new, enriched phase of development. In 1992 in England the top division clubs broke away from the Football League and created the Premier League under the auspices of the Football Association. The Premier League, or Premiership as the competition would be labelled, was in truth a very effective rebranding – underpinned by the hitherto undreamed-of monies generated by satellite television in general and Rupert Murdoch's Sky in particular.

Internationally, the club elite took command as well, when UEFA was carried down the Champions League road. The origins of the concept were to be found in the commercial foundations laid for FIFA by Horst

Dassler and Patrick Nally back in the mid-1970s. In 1982 Dassler had forced Nally out of the picture and created the ISL company which became FIFA's long-term marketing and commercial partner. However Dassler's premature death in 1987 sparked a battle for control of the company which drove joint bosses Klaus Hempel and Jurgen Lenz off to set up a rival, TEAM, which went to UEFA with the Champions League concept and the rest is history. Selling the TV rights to an exclusive group of broadcasters and signing up a band of multinational sponsors revolutionized UEFA's finances.

Suddenly the European federation could afford prize money of up £12 million for the competition winners. This not only headed off talk of pirate superleagues; the remaining largesse could be spread around the rest of European soccer to head off complaints that the minnows were denied their share of the glamour.

Not satisfied, the likes of Milan, Real Madrid and Juventus pushed UEFA even further, into opening up the competition to the second and even third and fourth-placed teams in the domestic leagues. This further enhanced the status of the Champions League while utterly undermining the other two club competitions. The UEFA Cup struggled to maintain its status while the Cup-Winners' Cup was scrapped altogether in 1999. Controversy raged over the shadow

THE GREAT MATCHES

Unfortunate end to a classic

WEST GERMANY 1-1 ENGLAND

World Cup semi-final, Stadio delle Alpi, Turin, July 4, 1990

Two of soccer's oldest rivals served up a magnificent match, sadly decided by FIFA's only solution to draws after 120 minutes: the penalty shoot-out. England went so very, very close to reaching the Final for only the second time but their post-1966 record of failing to win a competitive match against Germany continued. Despite the trials and tribulations besetting their manager, Bobby Robson, and despite the lack of class players – in the English game at large, let alone the squad – there was only the merest fraction between the teams. The splendid spirit in which the match was contested was another bonus. So, on a more personal level, was the flood of tears released by the enigma, Paul Gascoigne, which made him a media and public darling overnight and earned him a wallet of gold to go with his later-revealed feet of clay. Germany ground their way through 4-2 on penalties.

1995

- Jean-Marc Bosman wins landmark European Court judgement against European Union player transfer restrictions
- Manchester United's Eric Cantona is suspended for six months by the FA for a kung-fu assault on a Crystal Palace supporter

1996

- Manchester United become first club to win English "double" twice
- Germany beat the Czech Republic to win the first European Championships hosted in England

1997

- Ronaldo becomes the first Brazilian to be voted European Footballer of the Year after a change in the rules
- Eric Cantona announces his sudden retirement from soccer

1998

- Arsenal remain unbeaten in the league for last five months of season to win the "double-double"
- Real Madrid beat Juventus to win first European Champions Cup in 32 years
- Former general secretary Sepp Blatter elected new president of FIFA
- France defeat Brazil 3-0 to win the World Cup for the first time

1999

- Manchester United, managed by Alex Ferguson, win historic treble of Premiership, FA Cup, and European Cup
- Lazio win the last ever European Cup-Winners' Cup at Villa Park, England

cast by this money mountain. The mini-league section gave clubs a minumum of three home matches and the income unbalanced domestic competition.

The pursuit of Champions League riches raised an even more sinister issue: match fixing. Not in the continental competition but, rather, in domestic competition. Worst case scenario was provided by Marseille who won the old European Cup in 1993. President of Marseille was the millionaire businessman and MP, Bernard Tapie. He sought to fix the result of the French league match the weekend before their Champions Cup final duel with Milan. A draw with Valenciennes ensured Marseille another league title and their players could play knowing they had nothing to lose. They went on to beat Milan 1-0. But within days it emerged that senior aides of Tapie and various agents had set up a string of front companies abroad. Money was used for a multiplicity of corrupt purposes... bribes to players and referees, under-the-counter bonuses, etc. Marseille were kicked out of the Champions League and relegated; Tapie went to jail.

Milan bounced back and regained the Champions League Cup in 1994. Milan had been on the brink of bankruptcy when media magnate Silvio Berlusconi took over in the mid-1980s. He paid off debts and Milan won three European Champions Cups in the years which saw European soccer plunder media millions.

Soccer's progress now knew no

Jean-Marc Bosman, more effective off the pitch than he ever was on it.

bounds. In 1994 even the United States was conquered with the staging there of the World Cup finals.

But confidence within soccer's governing bodies about the status quo off the pitch was about to be shattered for ever. In December 1995 the European Court of Justice threw the game's administration into confusion by ruling in favour of a restraint of trade claim from a minor Belgian footballer named Jean-Marc Bosman.

His contract with second divison Liege had expired and he wanted to transfer to Dunkerque in France. Liege demanded a minimal fee which was still beyond Dunkerque's means. Bosman took legal action in Belgium from where the case was directed to the European courts. The Belgian FA refused to settle; when it went to the European court UEFA also failed

to agree a settlement. It was a failure of revolutionary proportions.

Bosman won his case. Not only that but the court declared illegal the attempt to hold a player for a fee beyond the end of his contract; it also declared illegal any and all restrictions on the number of European Union players clubs could both employ and select to play.

At first FIFA and UEFA huffed and puffed and pretended it would all go away. It did not. Within months leagues in all the EU countries had unilaterally scrapped restrictions on the cross-border movement of EU citizen players and accepted the right of a player to move fee-free within the EU on the expiry of his contract. Domesday warnings were issued on behalf of smaller clubs about a collapse in transfer fees though such fears ultimately proved unfounded – even after FIFA and the European Commission had rebuilt the entire international transfer system to fall in line with European law.

Clubs across western Europe – and not only the giants – threw a tidal wave of Champions League income into the international transfer market. Soon the big Italian clubs had more foreign players on their books than home-grown talent. Juventus, Real Madrid and Manchester United firmed up the club establishment's command of the Champions League Cup. Meanwhile FIFA president Joao Havelange and his general secretary, Sepp Blatter, railed in powerless impotence against the impending threat to the old national team/nation

state concept on which FIFA had been founded. But by the mid-1990s Havelange was attracting increasingly brazen criticism from UEFA for the way in which he went about achieving his ends. He took the hint and stood down. Blatter then nimbly outmanoeuvred UEFA president Lennart Johansson to win election to the FIFA high command on the eve of France's 1998 World Cup victory.

THE GREAT STADIUMS

Sunrise on Yokohama

YOKOHAMA INTERNATIONAL
Yokohama, Japan

In 1993, amid a fanfare of pop music and fireworks, Japan welcomed professional soccer with the launch of the J. League. This was a significant step in convincing FIFA to bring the World Cup to the Far East in 2002. In 1996 the world governing body decided that Japan would be co-hosts with South Korea, but that the Final would be staged in the new International Stadium in Yokohama. The stadium, with an all-seater capacity of 72,327, was opened in March 1998 as home for Yokohama Marinos. It staged the Final of the 2002 World Cup and later finals of the Club World Championship.

2000
- First all-Spanish European Champions' final ends in 3-0 win for Real Madrid against Valencia
- FIFA executive awards 2006 World Cup to Germany after controversial one-vote win over South Africa

2001
- FIFA is convulsed by the financial collapse of the marketing group ISL, the television rights agency Kirch and the cancellation of its World Cup insurance by Axa
- Some 176 fans die in three African stadia disasters in South Africa, DR Congo and Ghana

2002
- Real Madrid mark their centenary by winning a record ninth UEFA Champions League, beating Bayer Leverkusen 2-1 in Glasgow
- Sepp Blatter re-elected as FIFA president
- First World Cup in Asia is the first to be co-hosted – by South Korea and Japan
- Brazil win a record fifth World Cup; fit-again Ronaldo wins Golden Boot

2003
- Milan wins sixth UEFA Champions League, beating Juventus on penalties in the Final
- Boca Juniors win their fifth Copa Libertadores
- Cameroon's Marc-Vivien Foe collapses and dies in Lyon during a Confederations Cup semi-final against Colombia
- Russian billionaire Roman Abramovich sensationally invests more than £200million in Chelsea, wiping out the club's debt and buying a comspolitan new squad of superstars

2004
- Greece score a shock success in the European Championship
- FIFA decides that the first World Cup to be staged in Africa will be held in South Africa in 2010
- New champions Arsenal become the first English club since Preston's "Invincibles" in 1888-89 to complete a season unbeaten
- The International Board scraps golden and silver goal solutions to drawn matches

2000s: The future of the game

FIFA president Sepp Blatter said, at the start of the new millennium, that "in the 21st century the face of soccer will be feminine." What he meant, presumably, was that men's soccer had taken over planet sport in the previous century and now the changing nature of society would bring the women's game on in its wake.

In fact, the early signs of the 21st century were anything but encouraging for his vision. The 2003 Women's World Cup had to be switched from China to the United States because of the SARS epidemic in the Far East; then, on the eve of the finals the women's soccer league in the US collapsed for lack of sponsors.

The men's game was still the game which dominated. Indeed, apart from the United States where progress remained steady if not spectacular, association soccer worldwide had achieved a position of virtual sports dictatorship. That status was enhanced and underlined by FIFA's decision to take the World Cup out beyond its traditional homes of Europe and the Americas. In 2002 South Korea and Japan brought first-time co-hosting to the first World Cup in Asia. On a world level co-hosting was an excessively expensive indulgence born of political compromise. Japan had been lobbying unofficially for years to host the World Cup but then, in the formal process, Korea rushed in with a late campaign to share the spoils. Co-hosting for the

Japanese was a defeat, for the Koreans a victory. In the event – and after initial problems stemming from a legacy of historical enmity – the finals were organized extremely well. Brazil made up for their final failure in 1998 to regain the trophy with a Final win over Germany.

THE GREAT MATCHES

Liverpool back from the brink
LIVERPOOL 3-3 MILAN (3-2 ON PENALTIES AFTER EXTRA TIME)
UEFA Champions League Final, Ataturk Stadium, Istanbul, May 25, 2005

Liverpool won their fifth European club crown in the most dramatic of circumstances. They were 3-0 down at half-time, then recovered with three goals in seven second half minutes, and after extra time finally triumphed in a penalty shootout. The first half was an Italian walkover. Milan went ahead in the opening minutes through skipper Paolo Maldini and added two further goals through Argentinian striker Hernan Crespo before the interval. The Milan players denied later that they had begun noisy celebrations at half-time but they relaxed fatally and Liverpool hit back with rapid-fire goals from the inspirational midfielder Steven Gerrard, Vladimir Smicer and Xabi Alonso. The comeback effort left Liverpool dangerously wearied in extra time but they held out for a shootout in which Polish keeper Jerzy Dudek starred with saves from Andrea Pirlo and, finally, Andriy Shevchenko.

Buck-toothed centre-forward Ronaldo scored both goals then returned to European controversy as he transferred from Italy's Internazionale to join Real Madrid's so-called Galacticos. Zinedine Zidane, Luis Figo, Spain's own Raul and later England's David Beckham would be his partners in glamour. However, Madrid, if anything, had too much ego and not enough energy. Playing and promotional pressures on the game's stars in the initial years of the 21st century appeared to rule out any club matching the long-term dominance over five or even three years as had once been achieved by the likes of Madrid, Ajax Amsterdam and Bayern Munich.

The year 2002 saw not only repeat – if temporary – success for Brazil and Madrid but turmoil within FIFA. President Sepp Blatter faced opposition at the presidential election from Cameroon's Issa Hayatou, president of the African confederation. Blatter was vulnerable after the corporate suicide of ISL, the collapse of the Kirch media empire and the cancellation – in the wake of the 9/11 terror attack on New York's World Trade Center – of Axa's World Cup insurance.

At the Seoul Congress, in one of the most adroit public displays of political manoeuvring, Blatter rode out some ferocious punches before delivering a knock-out blow of world heavyweight title proportions. He

2005
- Liverpool comeback from being 3-0 down at half-time against AC Milan to win the Champions League Final.

2006
- Drawing 1-1 after extra time Italy defeat France 5-3 on penalties to win the World Cup for the fourth time

2007
- International investors take over ownership of three English Premiership clubs, Aston Villa, Liverpool and West Ham United.
- Juventus, the only Serie A club to be relegated in the match-fixing scandal, win the Serie B championship.
- MLS changes its salary-cap rules to allow high-priced superstars to play in America. David Beckham is first, joining LA Galaxy.
- Milan avenge their 2005 Champions League Final loss by beating Liverpool 2-1 in Athens

2008
- Spain end a 44-year title drought by defeating Germany 1-0 to win the European Championship
- Manchester United win the Club World Cup, European Champions League and English Premier League
- LDU of Quito become the first Ecuadorian club crowned champions of South America
- Manchester City sign Robinho for a British record £32m

2009
- Rookie coach Pep Guardiola guides Barcelona to a treble of Champions League plus Spanish league and cup
- Jose Mourinho wins, with Inter in Italy, a third league in a different country (after Portugal and England)
- Shakhtar Donetsk become, in the UEFA Cup, the first club from an independent Ukraine to win a European trophy

2010
- Portuguese coach Jose Mourinho leads Inter Milan to Champions League triumph before departing for Real Madrid.
- The first World Cup to be held on African takes place. Spain win their first World Cup defeating Holland 1-0 in extra time thanks to an Andrés Iniesta goal.

then purged FIFA of any elements who were not demonstrably in his corner and set the world federation on a new course.

Danny Jordaan, leader of South Africa's bids to host the World Cup in 2006 and then 2010, summed it up by saying: "Everything that has happened over the last few years has changed FIFA's emphasis. It's had to take all the commercial stuff and business management in-house to prevent another ISL or Kirch fiasco. It is not so much a sports association now as a business empire."

The South African bid for 2006 had fallen short by one vote after the Oceania president, Charles Dempsey, quit the FIFA executive meeting ahead of the decisive vote, muttering darkly about death threats. Germany, their bid spearheaded by the midas touch of Franz Beckenbauer, won the day instead. But the South African debacle prompted FIFA to introduce a rotation system and, in 2004, Jordaan and Co duly secured the 2010 finals.

A fortnight later the FIFA bandwagon rolled on from Zurich to Paris for a centenary celebration congress in a conference centre beneath the Louvre not far from the Rue St-Honoré where the world soccer authority had been founded back in May 1904. The change in emphasis was spelled out in the presentations. Players barely received a look-in as awards were handed out to the Adidas and Coca-Cola corporations, the IOC and Blatter's presidential mentor Joao Havelange. At least a posthumous award did go to Jules Rimet, the World Cup's founding FIFA president. FIFA's second century will bear little resemblance to its first. National team soccer will continue but under increasing pressure from the richest clubs. The creation of the G-14 group of Europe's most powerful clubs – including three each from Italy, Spain and England – was a manifestation of growing unrest over the terms of the game's governance.

One of G-14's major complaints was the absence of compensation payments from national associations for players summoned for international duty. A non-G-14 club, Charleroi of Belgium, sued FIFA in the Belgian and then European courts over a serious injury to Moroccan midfielder Abdelmajid Oulmers while on national team duty.

FIFA and Blatter refused to give way. He insisted: "If we are not careful, soon we won't have any more national team soccer or any national associations." However in 2006 FIFA created an insurance and compensation system for clubs whose players went to the major championship finals. As part of the deal, G-14 folded itself into a new European Club Association.

The clubs have survival concerns of their own. UEFA introduced a licensing system in 2004 which compels clubs to produce stable accounts if they wish to compete in European competitions. As if to underline the need for greater control and transparency, some of Europe's greatest clubs tottered to the brink of financial collapse.

In England Leeds United spent extravagantly to try to secure Champions League permanence then crashed to relegation after the gamble failed to pay off.

In Italy Fiorentina, one-time winners of the Cup-Winners' Cup, did indeed go bankrupt. The club born out of the financial ashes had to start all over again in the fourth division. Roma, Lazio, Parma and Napoli all teetered over the abyss but somehow survived; in France Monaco were threatened by the French league with relegation over accounting problems – yet revived effectively enough to reach the Champions League Final 15 months later; Kaiserslautern – home club of 1954 World Cup-winning hero Fritz Walter – sold a share of centre-forward Miroslav Klose to the local authority to buy financial time; in Spain Real Madrid pulled every available political string so their sports city land could be reclassified for development to purge a £100m-plus debt.

The battle for control of the club game intensified after the multi-million investment in Chelsea launched in 2003 by the Russian oligarch Roman Abramovich. Not that money was everything. Chelsea won three Premier League titles in six seasons but could not match Arsenal's achievement in becoming the first club to complete a league season unbeaten since Preston's "Invincibles" in 1889.

In Europe Liverpool and Barcelona each briefly regained the Champions' crown before Italy carried off the World Cup for a European record fourth time and Milan laid their hands on their seventh European Cup. The chill wind of the world global recession had comparatively little initial impact on the game. However, while Barcelona and Manchester United dominated the European soccer headlines in 2008-09, a sub-plot was developing concerning the professional's game debt mountain. Ongoing TV contracts cushioned the game against instant meltdown but the outlook was not altogether rosy.

The Bottom Line

The near-collapse of English Premier League club Portsmouth in the spring of 2010 focused concern on the level of the debt being built up by many of Europe's leading clubs. Michel Platini, former France captain turned UEFA president, decided that the European federation should take action. He promoted the introduction of "financial fairplay" rules designed to bar access to the lucrative Champions League and Europa League to clubs which cannot balance their books. This system was considered a threat to the way in which the likes of Roman Abramovich and Sheikh Mansour bin Zayed Al Nahyan provided personal multi-million backing to Chelsea and Manchester City respectively.

PART 2:

THE MAJOR COMPETITIONS

Soccer has always been competitive. The very simple core of the game is one team's effort to score more goals than their rivals. That competitive spirit developed first into a direct elimination competitions, such as the FA Cup and then into more complex formats such as league championships.

Such structures have been adopted by almost every sport though some have preferred one to the other. The knock-out format has retained greatest domestic popularity in the United Kingdom and Europe while the league format has ruled South America.

At international level a mixture of the two has entranced fans from Chile to China, Moscow to Montevideo.

The first international club competition to try to balance the demands of knock-out and fair opportunity was the Mitropa Cup and almost 30 years later the same system was used for the fledgling European Champions Club Cup.

Managers and directors down the years have boasted of the greater authority of a league competition for presenting a worthy champion team. But for fans the world over it is the one-off drama of a great cup competition which throws up the greatest memories – whether through the exploits of a Johan Cruyff at club level or Pele at a World Cup...

THE WORLD CUP

The World Cup was conceived by FIFA's founders, but the driving force behind its launch was Frenchman Jules Rimet, the president of both FIFA and the French federation in the 1920s. The British had shunned FIFA's first meeting in Paris in 1904, and by the time the inaugural World Cup tournament was introduced in 1930 they had both joined and then withdrawn from the world governing body over the question of broken time payments for amateurs.

Italy, Holland, Spain, Sweden and Uruguay had all applied to stage the tournament, but the Europeans withdrew after an impassioned plea from the Latin Americans, who in 1930 would be celebrating one hundred years of independence. Uruguay were to build a new stadium in Montevideo and would pay all travelling and hotel expenses for the competing nations. However, faced by a three-week boat trip each way, the Europeans were reluctant to participate, and two months before the competition not one European entry had been received. Meanwhile, Argentina, Brazil, Paraguay, Peru, Chile, Mexico and Bolivia had all accepted, as had the United States of America.

The Latin American federations were bitter and threatened to withdraw from FIFA. Eventually France, Belgium, Yugoslavia and, under the influence of King Carol, Romania, all relented and travelled to Uruguay.

Because of the limited response the 13 teams were split into four groups. Uruguay, Argentina, Brazil and the USA were the seeded nations.

On the afternoon of Sunday, July 13, France opened the tournament against Mexico, and in the 10th minute lost goalkeeper Alex Thepot, who was kicked on the jaw. Left-half Chantrel took over between the posts (there would be no substitutes for another 40 years), but even with 10 men the French proved too good. Goals by Laurent, Langiller and Maschinot gave them a 3–0 advantage before Carreno replied for Mexico. Maschinot then grabbed a second to complete a 4–1 victory for France.

Two days later France lost to Argentina through a goal scored by Monti, nine minutes from time. The game had ended in chaos when Brazilian referee Almeida Rego blew for time six minutes early as Langiller raced through for a possible equalizer. In their next match, against Mexico, Argentina brought in young Guillermo Stabile, known as "El Infiltrador". He scored three goals in Argentina's 6–3 victory – in a game of five penalties – and finished as the top scorer of the tournament.

Argentina topped Group 1, while from Group 2 Yugoslavia qualified with victories over Brazil and Bolivia. The USA were most impressive in Group 4, reaching the semi-final without conceding a goal. However, their hit-on-the-break tactics were no match for Argentina, who cruised into the Final with a 6–1 win. In the other semi-final Uruguay dispatched Yugoslavia by the same margin to set up what was to be a repeat of the 1928 Olympic Final.

On this occasion Pablo Dorado shot Uruguay into a 12th-minute lead but Peucelle equalized and Argentina forged ahead in the 35th minute with a disputed goal by Stabile – who the Urugayans claimed was offside! Excitement grew when Pedro Cea made it 2–2 just after the break. In the 65th minute outside-left Santos Iriarte made it 3–2 for Uruguay, who underlined their victory with a fourth goal, smashed into the net by Castro in the closing seconds.

Uruguayan goalkeeper Enrique Ballestrero is beaten by Carlos Peucelle's equalizer for Argentina.

Hector Castro, Enrique Ballestrero and Hector Scarone celebrate Uruguay's triumph in 1930.

1934

Uruguay are the only winners of the World Cup who did not defend their title. Still upset by the European reluctance to participate in 1930 and plagued by players' strikes, they opted to stay at home.

No fewer than 32 countries – 22 from Europe, eight from the Americas and one each from Asia and Africa – contested a qualifying series in which even hosts Italy had to take part, and before the competition proper got under way the USA beat Mexico in Rome, but then crashed 7-1 to Italy in Turin.

Of the 16 finalists, Italy and Hugo Meisl's Austrian "Wunderteam" were the clear favourites, though the Austrians – who were just past their peak – were taken to extra time by a spirited French side in the first knockout round. Belgium led Germany 2-1 at half-time, then crumbled as Conen, Germany's centre-forward, completed a hat-trick in a 5-2 win.

Brazil, beaten 3-1 by Spain, and Argentina, defeated 3-2 by Sweden, had travelled 8,000 miles to play one solitary game.

Spain forced Italy to a replay in the second round after a physical 1-1 draw was not resolved by extra time. In the replay, the following day, Meazza's 12th-minute header put Italy into the semi-finals. Austria, who led Hungary 2-0 after 51 minutes through Horwarth and Zischek, then found themselves in what Meisl described as "a brawl,

not an exhibition of soccer". Sarosi replied for Hungary from the penalty spot, but the Magyars' expected comeback was spoiled when Markos foolishly got himself sent off.

Italy and Austria now faced each other in the semi-finals. A muddy pitch was not conducive to good soccer and Italy won when right-winger Guaita capitalized on a brilliant set-play routine following a corner, to score in the 18th minute. Czechoslovakia, the conquerers of Romania and Switzerland, joined Italy in the Final after a 3-1 victory over Germany, with two goals by Nejedly.

In the Final, Puc shot the Czechs into a deserved 70th-minute lead, Italian keeper Combi reacting late to the shot from 20 yards. Sobotka then

squandered a fine opportunity and Svoboda rattled a post as the Czechs impressed with their short-passing precision. With eight minutes left the Slavs were still 1-0 ahead. Then Italy's left-winger Raimondo Orsi left defenders in his wake as he dribbled through on goal. He shaped to shoot with his left but hit the ball with his right boot. The ball spun crazily goalwards, and though Planicka got his fingers to it, he could not prevent a goal. Schiavio grabbed the Italian winner seven minutes into extra time. Italy were world champions.

1938

Europe was in turmoil, Argentina and Uruguay were absent but the tournament welcomed for the first time Cuba, Poland and Dutch East Indies.

In the first round it was only Hungary, who eclipsed the Dutch East Indies 6-0, and France – 3-1 winners over Belgium – who came through in 90 minutes; all the other ties went to extra time or replays. Defending champions Italy were saved by their goalkeeper Olivieri, who made a blinding save from Norwegian centre-forward Brunyldsen in the last minute of the game to earn extra time, and Piola struck to see them through.

Brazil emerged from the mud of Strasbourg after an 11-goal thriller. A Leonidas hat-trick gave the South Americans a 3-1 half-time lead, but the Poles ran riot after the break to force extra time. Willimowski netted four times but by then Leonidas had grabbed his fourth to help Brazil to a 6-5 win! The second round provided no shocks, though Brazil needed two games to eliminate Czechoslovakia and earn a semi-final joust with Italy, whose captain, Meazza, converted the winning penalty. In the other semi-final, Hungary beat Sweden, 5-1.

When Italy met Hungary in the Final, Colaussi drilled Italy ahead in the sixth minute after a scintillating run almost the length of the field

from Biavati, but Titkos equalized from close range within a minute. Then, with inside-forwards Meazza and Ferrari in dazzling form, Italy asserted themselves. Piola scored in the 15th minute, and Colaussi made it 3-1 in the 35th. In the 65th minute Sarosi forced the ball over the Italian line, but a magnificent back-heeled pass from Biavati set up Piola to smash in the decisive goal.

Italy's Giuseppe Meazza greets Hungary's Gyorgy Sarosi before the 1938 Final.

1950

Brazil hosted the first tournament after the war – for what was now known as the Jules Rimet Trophy – and it proved to be a thriller. Argentina refused to play in Brazil, and the Czechs and Scots declined to take their places, but England were there for the first time.

The competition was arranged, as in 1930, on a pool basis. Brazil won Pool 1 despite a 2-2 draw with Switzerland, and Uruguay topped two-team Pool 4, where they thrashed Bolivia 8-0. The shocks came in Pools 2 and 3, starting with holders Italy's 3-2 defeat by Sweden. The greatest shock of all time, however, was to beset England. After a 2-0 victory over Chile, the game against the USA in Belo Horizonte seemed to be a mere formality. Instead it turned into a fiasco. England hit the bar and found the goalkeeper unbeatable. In the 37th minute the impossible happened. Bahr shot from the left and Gaetjens got a touch with his head to divert the ball into the net: 1-0 to the USA!

There was to be no final in this competition, Brazil, Uruguay, Sweden and Spain qualifying for the Final Pool. The hosts were favourites as they

Pele breaks down in tears on the shoulders of goalkeeper Gilmar after Brazil's 1958 triumph in Stockholm.

faced Uruguay in the last game (final by any other name), a point ahead. A draw would make Brazil champions.

It proved to be a real thriller. Brazil's much-acclaimed inside-forward trio of Zizinho, Ademir and Jair, weaving gloriously through the Uruguayan defence, found goalkeeper Maspoli playing the game of his life. The giant Varela proved another stumbling block, as did Andrade. They cracked in the 47th minute, Friaca shooting past Maspoli. Uruguay's response was positive, and in the 65th minute Ghiggia's cross found Schiaffino unmarked – his thunderous shot gave Barbosa no hope. Brazil were shaken, the fizz went out of their game, and when Ghiggia ran in to shoot home in the 79th minute they were beaten. After 20 years the World Cup made its way back to Uruguay.

1954

Hungary arrived in Switzerland as the hottest ever World Cup favourites. The magic of Puskas, Hidegkuti and Kocsis had added a new dimension to the beautiful game and, what is more, had proved an unbeatable combination in the 1952 Olympic tournament.

No one was really surprised when the Magyars rattled in 17 goals in their opening pool matches against Korea and Germany. Kocsis scored four against the Germans but Hungary were left a significant legacy by their opponents, centre-half Werner Liebrich delivering a fateful kick on Puskas that forced him out of the match in the 30th minute. Even so Hungary cruised their way to the quarter-finals, where they dispatched Brazil 4-2, while Germany beat Turkey in a play-off for the right to face Yugoslavia. England began with a 4-4 draw with Belgium then secured a quarter-final place with a 2-0 win over Switzerland. The Scots were not so successful. They failed to score and were beaten by Austria and Uruguay.

In the quarter-finals Stanley Matthews and Schiaffino took the individual honours as Uruguay beat England 4-2 but the competition was sullied by a notorious clash between Brazil and Hungary, labelled "The Battle of Berne". Three players were sent off and a fight followed in the dressing-rooms afterwards. If that was infamous, then the Austria v Switzerland tie was incredible. The Swiss scored 3 in 20 minutes, and Austria replied with 3 in 3

minutes. Eventually Austria came out 7-5 winners.

Puskas returned for the Final, but it was a mistake. Although he scored the opening goal in a devastating start which saw Hungary score twice in eight minutes, his ankle was not fully healed. Morlock replied for Germany in the 11th minute and Rahn struck two fine goals – the last seven minutes from time – to win it for Germany.

1958

Brazil enthralled the world in Sweden in a competition notable for the emergence of 4-2-4 and the outstanding individual talents of Didi, Garrincha, Vava and the teenage Pele. France were to perform with style too, with Just Fontaine and Raymond Kopa providing the magic, while hosts Sweden also provided their share of surprises.

West Germany headed Pool 1, where Northern Ireland, who had eliminated Italy in the qualifying rounds, caused an upset by beating Czechoslovakia in a play-off to earn a quarter-final tie with France, who headed Pool 2 with Yugoslavia. Wales also made the quarter-finals after a play-off with Hungary and did themselves proud by limiting Brazil to one goal, inevitably scored by Pele. Brazil had comfortably emerged from Pool 4 without conceding a goal, but England were knocked out 1-0 by Russia in another play-off.

The semi-finals pitted Sweden against West Germany and Brazil against France. Schäfer volleyed West Germany into the lead only for Sweden to equalize fortunately through Skoglund even though Liedholm handled blatantly in the build-up. Juskowiak was sent off in the 57th minute and Sweden took full advantage to clinch their Final place with goals from Gren and Hamrin. Brazil took a second-minute lead against France through Vava, Fontaine equalized within nine minutes but Didi restored Brazil's lead and, in the second half, Pele ran riot with three more goals.

The final got off to a sensational start when Liedholm shot Sweden into a fourth-minute lead. It was the first time in the tournament that Brazil had been behind, but that lasted only six minutes. Garrincha exploded down the right, and cut the ball back for Vava to shoot home. A fascinating spectacle saw Pele hit a post at one end and Zagallo head out from beneath the bar at the other. In the 32nd minute the Garrincha–Vava combination struck again, and when Pele made it 3-1 in the 55th minute with a touch of magic, the game was won. Bringing a dropping ball down on a thigh in a crowded penalty area, he hooked it over his head, spun and volleyed thunderously into the net. Zagallo and Pele added further goals, either side of a second from Agne Simonsson. There was no doubt that Brazil were the best in the world.

THE FINAL

1958 (Sweden)
BRAZIL   **5 (2)**
Vava (2), Pele (2), Zagallo
SWEDEN   **2 (1)**
Liedholm, Simonsson
         Rasunda, Stockholm, 49,737
BRAZIL
Gilmar, Santos D., Santos N., Zito, Bellini (capt.), Orlando, Garrincha, Didi, Vava, Pele, Zagallo.
SWEDEN
Svensson, Bergmark, Axbom, Boerjesson, Gustavsson, Parling, Hamrin, Gren, Simonsson, Liedholm (capt.), Skoglund.

TOP SCORER
13 FONTAINE (France)

1962

Brazil retained their world crown as Garrincha took centre stage and 4-3-3 became the subtle change. But this was a World Cup marred by violence.

The Soviet Union and Yugoslavia comfortably overcame the Uruguayan and Colombian challenge in Group 1, while in Group 3 Brazil's only hiccup was their goalless draw with Czechoslovakia, the surprise package of the event.

England made a bad start. Unable to break down the massed Hungarian defence after Springett was beaten by a thunderous long-range effort from Tichy, they equalized from a Ron Flowers penalty, but the impressive Albert clinched it for Hungary 18 minutes from time with a well-worked individual goal. England did find some form to beat Argentina 3-1. Another Flowers penalty, a Bobby Charlton special and Jimmy Greaves clinched their first World Cup finals victory since 1954.

The Chile-Italy tie turned into a very violent confrontation, with spitting, fighting, and a plethora of two-footed tackles. That referee Ken Aston sent only two players off was remarkable.

Brazil, meanwhile, continued to thrill, even without Pele, who was injured in a group match against Mexico. Garrincha mesmerized England to defeat, then took Chile apart in the semi-final, only to be sent off.

In Vina del Mar a tiny crowd of 5,000 watched Czechoslovakia earn their Final place at the expense of Yugoslavia, and the Czechs threatened to upset all the odds when Masopust cleverly gave them the lead over Brazil in the 16th minute. Amarildo – Pele's replacement – quickly equalized but it was not until the 69th minute that Zito headed them into the lead. Vava made it 3-1 when Czech goalkeeper Schroiff fumbled a lob.

THE FINAL

1962 (Chile)
BRAZIL   **3 (1)**
Amarildo, Zito, Vava
CZECHOSLOVAKIA   **2 (1)**
Masopust
         Nacional, Santiago, 68,679
BRAZIL
Gilmar, Santos D., Mauro (capt.), Zozimo, Santos N., Zito, Didi, Garrincha, Vava, Amarildo, Zagallo.
CZECHOSLOVAKIA
Schroiff, Tichy, Novak (capt.), Pluskal, Popluhar, Masopust, Pospichal, Scherer, Kvasniak, Kadraba, Jelinek.

TOP SCORERS
4 GARRINCHA, VAVA (Brazil), **SANCHEZ L.** (Chile), **JERKOVIC** (Yugoslavia), **ALBERT** (Hungary), **IVANOV V.** (USSR)

Referee Ken Ashton tries to cool tempers in the 1962 'Battle of Santiago'.

England's glory: skipper Bobby Moore is hoisted high by his team-mates at Wembley after the 4-2 defeat of West Germany.

1966

For the first time in 32 years the host nation - England - won the title. This was a finals series that had everything - passion, controversy, fine soccer, and one of the greatest upsets of all time when North Korea knocked out Italy in Middlesbrough.

The tournament got off to a slow start, with England held 0-0 by Uruguay, but in Group 2 West Germany quickly showed their potential with a 5-0 win over Switzerland. Brazil disappointed. Having beaten Bulgaria 2-0, they lost an encounter with Hungary, for whom Albert was the dominating factor, then lost to Portugal, whose striker Eusebio was to be one of the stars of the competition. The Soviet Union, efficient and technically

sound, cruised through to the quarter-finals without alarm. For the Italian team, however, there was to be a rude awakening. They lost 1-0 to the Soviets, and had to beat North Korea to stay in the competition. What seemed a formality turned to a nightmare. In the 42nd minute Pak Doo Ik dispossessed Rivera, advanced and crashed a searing shot past Albertosi. It was the only goal. Italy were out.

At Goodison Park there was a sensational opening to Korea's quarter-final with Portugal. There was a goal in the opening minute, followed by a second and a third - and all for Korea. It was then that Eusebio showed his genius and, thanks to him and the towering Torres, the Portuguese team

clawed back the deficit to win what was a sensational game 5-3.

The England-Portugal semi-final produced an emotional classic, Bobby Charlton upstaging the mercurial Eusebio with what many felt was his greatest game for England. This display was a wonderful advertisement for the game, and miles away from the bad-tempered quarter-final shambles with Argentina, when Rattin was sent off and Geoff Hurst arrived on the scene as a new shooting star.

West Germany had edged out the Soviet Union, in a disappointing tie, to secure their place in the Final, and there they struck the first blow through Haller. Hurst equalized and his West Ham colleague Martin Peters

gave England the lead. But a scrambled goal from Weber just before time forced the game into extra time. In the 100th minute controversy raged. Alan Ball crossed and Hurst, coming in on the near post, hammered his shot goalwards. It thumped against the underside of the bar and dropped - but which side of the line? The Swiss referee Dienst was not sure, but the Soviet linesman Bakhramov was. 3-2 England! Any feeling of injustice felt by the Germans was quickly irrelevant. Bobby Moore swept a long ball upfield for Hurst to chase, and the big striker slammed his shot into the roof of Tilkowski's net to become the first player to score a hat-trick in a World Cup Final.

1970

Soccer triumphed again in Mexico where the colourful free-flowing Brazilians delighted. They overcame the heat, the altitude and – in a Final full of drama – Italy, the acknowledged masters of defensive caution.

There were no surprises in groups one and two where Russia, Mexico, Italy and Uruguay all qualified comfortably. The fixture between Brazil and England in group three provided the outstanding tie of the series.

In the 10th minute Jairzinho, a wonderful player of power and pace, sent over the perfect cross from the line. Pele timed it to perfection, his header hard and true angled to bounce before entering just inside the left post. The shout of "Goal!" was already in the air when Gordon Banks, who anticipated the shot going the other way, twisted athletically to pounce and incredibly push the ball over off the bounce! It was one of the greatest saves ever.

Jairzinho scored the only goal in the second-half and was to score in all three of their subsequent matches. England faltered in the quarter-final. Without Banks (out with an upset stomach), they wasted a two-goal lead to lose to West Germany in extra-time.

The semi-final between Italy and West Germany was dramatic. Having taken the lead through Boninsegna Italy withdrew in the second-half to protect their advantage. Given midfield Germany took the initiative but did not equalize until the third minute of injury-time through Schnellinger. The goals came thick and fast in extra-time. Muller for Germany 1–2; Burgnich then Riva for Italy 3–2! Muller again, 3–3 before Rivera clinched it for Italy.

The Final proved to be a marvellous affirmation for attacking soccer. Pele, opened the scoring and made two more after Boninsegna had made it 1–1, capitalizing on a dreadful error by Clodoaldo.

Gerson drove in a powerful cross-shot in the 66th minute and the match was sewn up with goals from Jairzinho and Carlos Alberto.

THE FINAL

1970 (Mexico)
BRAZIL 4 (1)
Pele, Gerson, Jairzinho, Carlos Alberto
ITALY 1 (1)
Boninsegna

Azteca, Mexico City, 107,000

BRAZIL
Felix, Carlos Alberto (capt.), Brito, Piazza, Everaldo, Clodoaldo, Gerson, Jairzinho, Tostao, Pele, Rivelino.

ITALY
Albertosi, Cera, Burgnich, Bertini (Juliano 75), Rosato, Facchetti (capt), Domenghini, Mazzola, De Sisti, Boninsegna (Rivera 84), Riva.

TOP SCORER
9 **MULLER** (West Germany)

THE FINAL

1966 (England)
ENGLAND 4 (1)
Hurst (3), Peters
WEST GERMANY 2 (1)*
Haller, Weber

Wembley, London, 96,924
* After extra time

ENGLAND
Banks, Cohen, Wilson, Stiles, Charlton J., Moore (capt.), Ball, Hurst, Hunt, Charlton R., Peters.

WEST GERMANY
Tilkowski, Höttges, Schulz, Weber, Schnellinger, Haller, Beckenbauer, Overath, Seeler (capt.), Held, Emmerich.

TOP SCORER
9 **EUSEBIO** (Portugal)

Pele leaps for joy after heading Brazil in front in the 1970 Final.

1974

European teams dominated the 1974 series in which a strong West Germany regained the World Cup after 20 years. It was another triumph for positive tactics, as Holland and Poland - who had eliminated England - demonstrated to the maximum the attributes of skill and technique. The term "Total Football" crept into the soccer vocabulary, with Cruyff, Neeskens and Rep leading the Dutch masters who abandoned the rigidity of 4-2-4 and 4-3-3 to introduce the concept of "rotation" play.

Half of the 16 competing nations had been eliminated after the first series of group matches. The two Germanys qualified for the second phase comfortably, as did Holland and Sweden, and Poland from Group 4, where Argentina just pipped Italy on goal difference thanks to a 4-1 victory over Haiti, whom Italy had beaten 3-1.

Group 2 proved to be the most competitive. Brazil, now sadly without the retired Pele, could only draw 0-0 with Yugoslavia and Scotland. Zaire were to be the key factor. Scotland defeated them 2-0, but Yugoslavia overwhelmed them 9-0 to clinch pole position on goal difference. As they went into the final round Scotland needed victory over Yugoslavia to win the group. They only managed to draw 1-1, and Brazil squeezed through, by virtue of one goal, thanks to a 3-0 win over Zaire.

Holland looked impressive. They topped Group A to qualify for the Final without conceding a goal. Brazil, a shadow of their former selves, bowed out leaving us with one significant memory, their winning goal against East Germany. Jairzinho, standing on the end of the German wall facing a free-kick, ducked as Rivelino crashed his shot towards him, the ball swerving past the bewildered goalkeeper Croy.

West Germany's passage was a bit more uncertain. It hinged on their clash with the impressive Poles in the final game of Group B. On a

Johan Neeskens fires Holland ahead from the first-ever World Cup Final penalty.

waterlogged pitch they made their physical strength pay. Tomaszewski saved a Hoeness penalty, but the German atoned for his miss when his shot was deflected to "The Bomber", Gerd Muller, who booked the date with Holland for his team.

The Dutch produced probably the most dramatic opening to a Final in the history of the competition. Right from the kick-off the ball was fluently played into the German area, where Cruyff was brought down by Hoeness. Neeskens calmly converted the first penalty awarded in a World Cup Final to record the fastest Final goal ever. And the Germans had yet to play the ball. After being outplayed for the first quarter of the game, West Germany managed to get themselves

off the hook. On a rare break from Dutch indulgence, Bernd Hölzenbein was homing in on goal when he was tripped by Wim Jansen, and Paul Breitner duly rammed in the resultant penalty to make it 1-1. A 43rd-minute goal from Gerd Muller - his 68th, last and most important for his country - won the World Cup.

It was hard for Holland to blame anyone but themselves. Having taken an immediate advantage, they had failed to make their domination count with a second goal, and for all their luxurious touches, the killer instinct was beyond them. Even the much-hyped duel between Beckenbauer and Cruyff - battling it out to replace Pele as the greatest player in the world - had gone the Germans' way.

1978

Ecstasy and euphoria greeted Argentina's eventual triumph on home soil, yet for neutrals the failure of Holland, as in 1974, to claim their rightful crown as the best team in the world left a void.

The home nation, backed by fanatical support and animated tickertape adoration in the River Plate Stadium, staged a colourful and dramatic tournament. Yet their passage to the Final was not without controversy, both on and off the pitch. After repeated frustrations in their attempts to stage the finals, Argentina were finally granted their wish in 1966, but by the time 1978 came around many people were concerned about the internal political situation of the country. Argentina's military government gave unnerving signals to the rest of the world, while organizations such as Amnesty International stepped up campaigns highlighting the flagrant human rights abuses, so that at one stage a relocation of the event to Holland and Belgium emerged as a possible option. The Argentine players, though, faced the responsibility of exploiting their home advantage and emulating neighbours Uruguay and Brazil by winning the greatest prize. Their opening game proved a torrid affair, despite the impassioned River Plate crowd roaring them on. Hungary took the lead in 12 minutes through Zombori only for Leopoldo Luque to equalize three minutes later. The Hungarians were to have two players sent off before Bertoni fired in the winning goal. Italy and Argentina had already qualified for the second stage when they met to decide the final Group 1 places. The Italians played it tight and snatched the win through Bettega in the 67th minute.

In Group 2 Poland carried on where they left off in Germany, with slick and precise play. The shock result featured Tunisia, who held West Germany to a goalless draw and could have won. Brazil once again failed to inspire, and

only a fortunate 1-0 victory over Austria, who topped their group, squeezed them into the second phase. Scotland, the United Kingdom's only representatives, suffered humiliation. Rocked by a 3-1 defeat by Peru, they received a further blow to morale when Willie Johnston failed a drugs test and was ordered home. A 1-1 draw with Iran added to the troubles, but they went out in style against Holland.

While Italy and West Germany played not to lose, Holland thrilled with their adventurous attitude. The "reprise" of the 1974 Final between them and Germany provided one of the best games. The final score was 2-2 and Holland were back in the Final. Meanwhile, the fact that Brazil had defeated Poland 3-1 left Argentina needing to beat Peru by at least four goals. They beat them by six in a shambolic exercise that tarnished the image of the whole competition.

The Final, more dramatic than distinguished, saw the European-based Mario Kempes score twice as once more Holland fell at the final hurdle.

THE FINAL	
1978 (Argentina)	
ARGENTINA	**3 (1)**
Kempes (2), Bertoni	
HOLLAND	**1 (0)***
Nanninga	
Monumental, Buenos Aires, 77,260	
* After extra time	

ARGENTINA
Fillol, Olguin, Galvan, Passarella (capt.), Tarantini, Ardiles (Larrosa), Gallego, Kempes, Bertoni, Luque, Ortiz (Houseman).

HOLLAND
Jongbloed, Krol (capt.), Poortvliet, Brandts, Jansen (Suurbier), Van de Kerkhof W., Neeskens, Haan, Rep (Nanninga), Rensenbrink, Van de Kerkhof R.

TOP SCORER
6 **KEMPES** (Argentina)

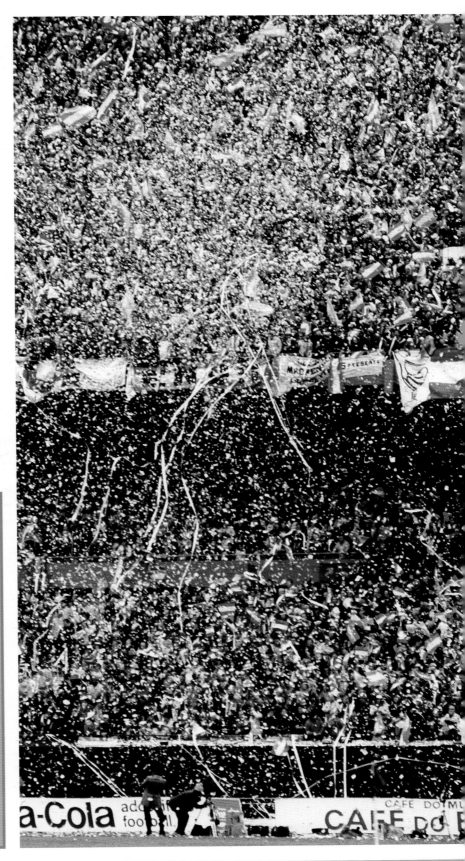

Marco Tardelli races off on his unstoppable celebratory dash after shooting Italy's second goal against West Germany in Madrid.

1982

Italy deservedly won in Spain after a slow start in which they drew all three games in Group 1 and qualified on the slenderest goal difference. West Germany, who were to finish runners-up, were on the wrong end of a shock 2-1 defeat in their opening tie against Algeria but, like Italy, got better as the tournament progressed.

England, in contrast, started with a bang then gradually eased up. Skipper Bryan Robson got them off to a dream start against France with a goal in 27 seconds, but although Ron Greenwood's team proved hard to beat, without the injured Kevin Keegan and Trevor Brooking they had little guile. The outstanding game was that between Italy and the favourites, Brazil. Three times Italy took the lead,

twice Brazil came back to level the score in a classic that would not be matched for quality. Paolo Rossi, back after a two-year suspension, was the hero with a brilliant hat-trick.

In the semi-finals Rossi scored twice more to beat the impressive Poland, while West Germany and France, who had both grown in stature and confidence following that initial setback against England, took part in a pulsating thriller. With Michel Platini, Jean Tigana and Alain Giresse at their teasing best, many fancied France as winners. In a tense 90 minutes they carved out the better chances but failed to make them count, then in extra-time fell victim on penalties after the German goalkeeper Toni Schumacher got away with a blatant,

appalling foul on Patrick Battiston.

The less glamorous sides also had their moments. Algeria, Honduras and Kuwait caught the eye, and Northern Ireland – whose Norman Whiteside was, at 17, the youngest ever to play in the finals – distinguished themselves in a win over Spain.

The Final, sadly, did not live up to its billing. There was not one shot on target in the opening 45 minutes, and that includes Cabrini's effort from a penalty. But in the second half the Germans paid, in fatigue, the price of their extra-time victory over France. Italy were inspired by the effort of Marco Tardelli and the counter-attacking pace of Bruno Conti, and were the deserving winners – thus sealing a World Cup hat-trick.

1986

Mexico staged its second World Cup amid a certain amount of controversy, but ultimately set records all round with 52 matches played before a total of 2,406,511 spectators.

Initially the finals had been awarded to Colombia. However, that was before the number of teams had been expanded from 16 to 24 ahead of the Spanish hosting. The uncertain security situation in Colombia was an issue already when the domestic federation brought an ultimatum to FIFA president Joao Havelange towards the end of 1982. Colombia insisted it would happily play host but only on condition that the scale of the finals was reverted back to 16 teams.

FIFA refused, Colombia withdrew and a race against time started to find a new host in the Americas at short notice. Mexico, the United States of America and Canada all applied. The Americans, bringing the political power of former Secretary of State Henry Kissinger on board, thought their case irresistible. Instead, FIFA opted for Mexico. It was a decision which later prompted a whole host of recriminations and accusations, largely based around the professional and sporting links between Havelange and the FIFA vice-president Guillermo Canedo – a senior figure in a broadcasting chain which indirectly underwrote much of the hosting costs in return for host TV rights.

The dust had barely settled on that furore when Mexico, in September of 1985, was struck by an earthquake which killed thousands of people. FIFA considered switching the finals yet again . . . then yielded to government appeals from Mexico who said that staging the finals had become more important than ever to the population.

Eventually, on 31 May, the Azteca Stadium in Mexico City saw the finals get under way with holders Italy making do with a tentative 1–1 draw against Bulgaria. Alessandro Altobelli, who had scored the Italians' third goal in the 1982 final, struck the opening blow in their title defence. Nasko Sirakov levelled five minutes from time, his goal a warning of greater things to come over the next eight years from the rapidly-improving Bulgarians.

But no one had a player to match the inspirational Diego Maradona. Argentina's captain proved a creator and scorer of crucial – not to mention controversial – goals as he benefited from the tactical creativity of Carlos Bilardo, his manager. Bilardo's development of the 3-5-2 system provided Maradona with the most solid of stages on which to work his magic.

Various moments stood out as the tournament progressed: Gary Lineker's hat-trick for England against Poland; Emilio Butragueno's four-goal tirade as Spain defused the Danish Dynamite; and a quarter-final in which France beat Brazil on penalties... after three of the world's greatest players, Zico, Socrates and Michel Platini – had all missed spot-kicks.

Argentina topped their first round group ahead of Italy then saw off old enemy Uruguay in the second round to set up a high-tension quarter-final with England. The legacy of the Falklands War hung over the match in the Azteca, which Argentina won 2–1 in the most notorious fashion. Their first goal was the infamous "hand of God" incident, when Maradona knocked the ball past goalkeeper Peter Shilton with a hand, unseen by Tunisian referee Ben Naceur. But there was nothing to argue about Argentina's second goal, a brilliant solo run by Maradona, taking him past the entire England defence before he popped the ball beyond Shilton for one of the greatest goals in World Cup history.

To prove it was no fluke Maradona scored a similar goal in the next game, a win over Belgium, which sent the Argentinians on into the Final against West Germany, who were now under the management of former Cup-winning captain Franz Beckenbauer. The Germans had again eliminated France in the semi-finals and appeared to sleepwalk into the final, however, as Argentina led 2–0 after 56 minutes through goals from Jorge Brown and Jorge Valdano.

Almost too late, West Germany awoke to launch a remarkable comeback and draw level through Karl-Heinz Rummenigge and Rudi Völler. It was all in vain. Five minutes remained when Maradona wriggled free in midfield and sent Jorge Burruchaga away to snatch Argentina's winner and their second World Cup win. Maradona, dropped because of his youth from the squad before the victorious 1978 campaign, had fulfilled his destiny. From here, it would all be downhill.

Diego Maradona's 'Hand of God' raises the World Cup in Mexico City.

THE FINAL

1986 (Mexico)

ARGENTINA   3 (1)
Brown, Valdano, Burruchaga
WEST GERMANY   2 (0)
Rummenigge, Völler

Azteca, Mexico, 114,590

ARGENTINA
Pumpido, Cuciuffo, Olarticoechea, Ruggeri, Brown, Giusti, Burruchaga (Trobbiani 89), Batista, Valdano, Maradona (capt.), Enrique

WEST GERMANY
Schumacher, Berthold, Briegel, Jakobs, Förster, Eder, Brehme, Matthäus, Allofs (Völler 46), Magath (Hoeness, D. 63), Rummenigge (capt)

TOP SCORER
6 **LINEKER** (England)

1990

The 14th World Cup finals did not live up to the passionate Italian setting. There was a miserly shortage of goals, but perhaps the saddest failure of all was on the part of the established stars who failed to enhance their reputations.

It started dramatically enough with Cameroon beating the champions Argentina – François Omam Biyik with the only goal in a rugged match that saw Cameroon finish with nine men after the expulsions of Andre Kana Biyik and Benjamin Massing.

The Africans went on to top Group B, with Argentina trailing in third place, and were later to frighten the life out of England when they took a 2-1 lead before losing to two late goals 3-2 in the quarter-finals.

"Toto" Schillaci's tense expressions were to reflect the Italian mood. The Juventus centre-forward had played only once for Italy before the finals. Yet he became an overnight national hero after scoring the winner against Austria and the first against Czechoslovakia as Italy comfortably topped Group A.

Scotland were humiliated 1-0 by Costa Rica in Group C, bounced back against Sweden, then slipped out 1-0 to Brazil after taking them all the way. The Scots' gloom contrasted with the Republic of Ireland's popular success. The managerial guile of Jack Charlton

had brought them to the finals for the first time and a shoot-out win over Romania earned them a tilt at the hosts in the quarter-finals. Italy edged it 1-0, Schillaci again the scorer.

West Germany started as they meant to go on with a 4-1 win over Yugoslavia in Group D while Spain topped Group E and England headed a graceless Group F which had been played out in administrative quarantine on Sardinia to contain the feared hooligan menace.

The second round brought England to the mainland to face Belgium in Bologna. A goalless stalemate looked destined for penalties when Paul Gascoigne arrowed a quick, artful free kick into the heart of the Belgian penalty box and David Platt volleyed the winner. The goal had enduring significance; it earned Platt admirers who would later bring him back to Italy to star with Juventus, among others; and for Gascoigne, his boyish impudence gained cult status after the semi-final against West Germany when he burst into tears on being booked, realizing he would miss the final if England got there. Shootout failures by Stuart Pearce and Chris Waddle meant none of his teammates managed it either.

The other semi-final pitted Argentina against their Italian hosts at Diego Maradona's adopted Serie

Andy Brehme shoots Germany's Final winner past Sergio Goycochea.

A home in Naples. Extra time in the game ran over by seven minutes until the French referee, Michel Vautrot, realized his watch had stopped. Italy failed to take advantage and Argentina went through on penalties thanks to Italian nerves and goalkeeper Sergio Goycochea.

Italy at least took the consolation prize of third place by defeating a deflated England 2-1 in the play-off in Bari. It was the last managerial duty for Bobby Robson: he had already accepted an offer to take over PSV Eindhoven in Holland after the Football Association dithered too long over his contract extension.

Rome's Stadio Olimpico saw a final duel between two tired teams. Both Germans and Argentinians had been taken to their physical and mental limits in semi-finals that had featured not only extra time, but penalties. What was worse, the Argentinians were weighed down by their own paranoid suspicions of high-level plotting against them – as evidenced, in their minds, by the semi-final yellow card that brought about the suspension of Claudio Caniggia, robbing them of his services.

Diego Maradona was still there, but knee injuries had reduced his pace and mobility which was why Caniggia – a high-speed fetcher and carrier – proved an invaluable attacking partner.

The Germans brought their own bad memories of 1986 and an ugly

mood pervaded the entire event. It was one of the worst finals in the history of the World Cup. West Germany were the deserved winners on their overall contribution though their goal was controversial. Argentina accused Rudi Völler of diving for the 81st-minute penalty. Skipper Lothar Matthäus, claiming injury, handed responsibility for taking it to Andy Brehme and Goycochea was, for once, beaten from the spot.

Argentina still managed to make history, even in defeat; Pedro Monzon and Gustavo Dezotti were the first players ever sent off in a World Cup final.

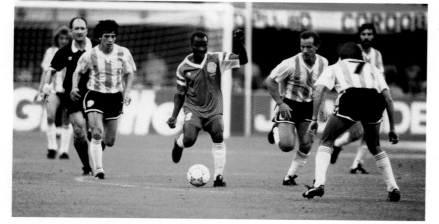

Roger Milla leads Cameroon to their shock opening win over Argentina.

1994

History was made twice over in the United States when Brazil secured a fourth title. To do so they needed to win the first-ever penalty shoot-out at the end of extra time in a goalless Final.

FIFA introduced radical measures in an attempt to improve the quality of the action: three points for a win in the first round group matches; a relaxation over the offside law by which play was to be stopped only if an attacking player was interfering with play; a crackdown on the tackle from behind and violent conduct in general; and finally, injured players would be taken off the field immediately.

In statistical terms these changes added up to 15 sendings-off and a record 235 bookings but on the positive side, they also computed to 141 goals in 52 matches, a match average of 2.71 and an improvement on Italia 90.

The team of Group A were undoubtedly Romania, inspired by their attacking general Gheorghe Hagi. The well-organized Swiss team qualified in second place, but Colombia – among the pre-tournament favourites – played without conviction or pattern and were eliminated.

Group B offered clear favourites in Brazil and they did not disappoint their colourful, noisy and musical supporters. Brazil's strength was the striking partnership of Romario and Bebeto. Romario either scored or had a creative hand in 10 of Brazil's 11 goals.

Group C included the formal opening match in which holders Germany beat Bolivia 1-0. The Germans appeared laboured, and Stefan Effenberg was expelled from the squad at the end of the first round for making a rude gesture towards jeering German fans in the narrow 3-2 win over South Korea. This was the other group which provided only two, rather than three, second round qualifiers. Germany finished top followed by Spain.

In Group D Argentina's Diego Maradona was his team's attacking inspiration in the opening 4-0 win over Greece and in the 2-1 follow-up defeat of Nigeria, but it was after this game that he failed a dope test. It was all over for Maradona and Argentina lost their next game 2-0 to Bulgaria.

In Group E, Ireland shocked Italy with a 1-0 victory in their opening match, and Norway appeared on the verge of inflicting a second defeat on the group favourites when goalkeeper Gianluca Pagliuca was sent off. Remarkably, however, Italy fought back to win, 1-0, when defeat would have resulted in almost certain elimination. Wasting that numerical superiority cost Norway dear. All four teams ended up on four points and zero goal difference, but Norway finished bottom of the group on goals scored and were thus eliminated.

Another favoured team who struggled in the first round were Holland. They escapted early elimination by defeating Morocco 2-1 in their final match, to qualify along with Belgium and World Cup newcomers Saudi Arabia – who beat Belgium 1-0 along the way.

The second round saw Germany defeat Belgium, the Republic of Ireland commit defensive suicide against Holland, Spain beat Switzerland and Sweden beat Saudi Arabia. Brazil spoiled Independence Day by defeating the USA. The other second-round games were even more dramatic: Bulgaria beat Mexico on penalties in the first shoot-out of the finals, Romania saw off Argentina, and Italy dramatically defeated Nigeria.

In the quarter-finals, Sweden defeated Romania on penalties. Baggio confirmed his star rating with Italy's late second goal in their 2-1 victory over Spain. Another tight game saw Brazil defeat Holland 3-2. Completing the semi-final line-up were rank outsiders Bulgaria, who beat holders Germany for the shock of the finals. The two-goal brilliance of Roberto Baggio lifted Italy into their fifth Final while, in the other semi, Brazil saw off a lacklustre and leg-weary Sweden.

Italy gambled twice over, in playing superstar striker Baggio despite a hamstring strain and in recalling veteran sweeper Franco Baresi for his first appearance after an operation.

Baresi was Italy's man of the match. The game saw Brazil employing their technical brilliance to try and outflank Italy's defensive discipline while the Italians waited for the right moment to unleash their rapid counter-attacks.

It was a game of few chances, most of which fell to Brazil, although Baggio went close with one effort in each half of extra time while Brazil should again have taken the lead in the 109th minute when the industrious Cafu crossed to the far post and Romario put the ball fractionally the wrong side of the post from four yards out.

In the penalty shoot-out, Taffarel benefited immediately when Baresi shot over. Baresi sank to his knees in despair. Pagliuca saved from Marcio Santos and Italy went briefly ahead as Albertini scored from kick two. Romario squared for Brazil, Evani netted for Italy and Branco for Brazil. This was the point at which it fell apart for Italy: Taffarel saved from Massaro and Dunga shot what proved the vital Brazilian kick. Baggio needed to score with Italy's last kick of the five to keep his country alive. He scooped the ball over the bar. Brazil were back on top.

Joy and disaster: Brazil celebrate Roberto Baggio's penalty miss.

THE FINAL

1994 (United States)
BRAZIL	**0(0)**
ITALY	**0(0)***

Brazil won 3-2 on pens

Rose Bowl, Pasadena, 94,000

* After extra time

BRAZIL
Taffarel, Jorginho (Cafu 20), Aldair, Marcio Santos, Branco, Mazinho (Viola 106), Dunga (capt.), Mauro Silva, Zinho, Romario, Bebeto.

ITALY
Pagliuca, Mussi (Apolloni 34), Maldini, Baresi (capt.), Benarrivo, Berti, Albertini, D. Baggio (Evani 94), Donadoni, R. Baggio, Massaro.

TOP SCORERS
6 SALENKO (Russia),
STOICHKOV (Bulgaria)

1998

France, the nation that invented the World Cup, finally won it in 1998 with a spectacular 3-0 victory over Brazil on home soil.

It was the Frenchman Jules Rimet who introduced the idea of a worldwide tournament of nations in 1930. He would have been delighted that 68 years on, France should host the finals and be crowned champions.

Even before it began, France 98 was billed as the biggest and most glamorous of World Cups, not least because it featured 32 teams instead of the previous 24. The ever-increasing popularity of soccer plus the ever-expanding sponsorship and media circus made it virtually impossible to escape the tournament anywhere.

The line-up included four nations – Jamaica, Japan, South Africa and Croatia – making their finals debuts, which both added to the anticipation and increased predictions of upsets ahead. In fact, although Croatia provided the fairy story, France 98 only confirmed the status quo, with European and South American countries dominating and the African and Asian nations failing to make an impact.

The opening game saw champions Brazil win 2-1 against the Tartan Army of Scotland thanks to an unfortunate own goal from Tommy Boyd. When the samba stars went on to crush Morocco 3-0 they became the first team to qualify for round two.

There was still plenty of drama to come, however. Scotland (having held Norway to a draw) faced Morocco in the final fixture with each team thinking that the winners would go through – provided Norway did not do the unthinkable and beat Brazil. The Moroccans were already partying after they went 3-0 up only to find that Norway had turned the tables by winning 2-1. The pictures of Moroccan celebrations turning to tears were highly memorable.

In Group B Italy came back to draw 2-2 with Chile when Roberto Baggio, who missed a penalty in the 1994 World Cup Final shootout, volunteered to take a spot kick when his side were 2-1 down – and duly converted. The Azzurri went on to crush Cameroon and Austria to reach the second round with striker Christian Vieri helping himself to four goals. Chile, led by three-goal striker Marcelo Salas,

finished the group as runners-up.

Hosts France defied fears that they would struggle for goals by beating South Africa 3-0, Saudi Arabia 4-0 (despite Zinedine Zidane being sent off) and runners-up Denmark 2-1.

Nigeria topped Group D by winning their opening two games and became the only African nation in the second round. The key to their progress was a stunning 3-2 victory over Spain in which they twice came from behind. But it was an awful mistake from the experienced Spanish keeper Andoni Zubizarreta, credited as an own goal, which turned the game.

There was far more misery to come for Spain who had to beat Bulgaria to go through in the final group game. They romped to a thrilling 6-1 victory only to find that Paraguay (without a goal up to that point) had done the unexpected and beaten a weakened Nigeria 3-1 to snatch second place.

In Group E Holland posted a 5-0 win against South Korea and drew 2-2 with Mexico in a thrilling game. The Mexicans won many fans with their never-say-die attitude, twice coming back from 2-0 down to secure draws. Striker Cuauhtemoc Blanco provided one of the light-hearted moments of the tournament with his 'bunny hop' trick that served to baffle defenders.

Group F saw German captain Jurgen Klinsmann, playing his farewell tournament, turn back the years by firing goals against the United States and Iran to send his side comfortably into round two. But perhaps the most memorable match of Group F, and the entire first round, was the politically sensitive clash between the United States and Iran. Both sets of players exchanged gifts before the kick-off and posed for a joint team picture, arms around each other as if to prove that politics has no place on the soccer field. Iran won 2-1.

Group G saw England, tipped as one of the big guns of France 98, open with a comfortable 2-0 win over

Tunisia. But then they slipped up 2-1 against Romania for whom Chelsea's Dan Petrescu rolled home the winner.

England's consolation was the prowess of teenage substitute Michael Owen who scored a goal and hit the post in the last minute. It came as no surprise that he started England's crucial third game against Colombia, and helped them to a comfortable 2-0 win, sealed by a stunning David Beckham free kick.

Group H was more clear-cut. Argentina dominated, winning all three of their games including a 5-0 thrashing of Jamaica in which Gabriel Batistuta hit a hat-trick. Croatia took second spot and Jamaica's Reggae Boyz scored their first finals victory – 2-1 over a dispirited Japan.

Tension increased in round two where Vieri handed Italy a narrow win over Norway and the Klinsmann-Oliver Bierhoff combination sent Germany through against Mexico. A Davor Suker penalty edged Croatia past Romania; Brazil cruised home against South American rivals Chile with Ronaldo and Cesar Sampaio scoring twice each in a 4-1 win; and Denmark easily disposed of Nigeria by the same score.

Holland, though, needed a dramatic 90th-minute strike from Edgar Davids to beat Yugoslavia, while France relied on a 'golden goal' from defender Laurent Blanc to see off a stoic challenge from Paraguay.

England vs. Argentina proved to be the tie of the round. A penalty for each side, both converted, made for an exciting opening and then Owen ran all the way from the centre circle to score the goal of the tournament. The Argentinians hit back with a cleverly-worked free kick and must have expected to win after Beckham was controversially sent off for petulantly kicking out at Diego Simeone. But the English showed their bulldog spirit by surviving with ten men all the way to the end of 90

David Beckham is sent off in England's second round defeat by Argentina.

Zinedine Zidane heads France into the lead against Brazil in the 1998 Final in the Stade de France.

minutes, then extra time before losing 4-3 on penalties.

In the quarter-finals Croatia confirmed their status as the surprise of the tournament by crushing Germany (who had defender Christian Worns sent off) 3-0 with goals from Jarni, Vlaovic and Suker yet again. Holland beat Argentina 2-1 with a glorious goal from Dennis Bergkamp in the last minute, while France needed a penalty shootout to beat Italy after a 0-0 draw. The match of this round was Brazil's exciting 3-2 win over Denmark, decided by the two-goal brilliance of Rivaldo.

In the semi-finals, Holland more than matched Brazil and Patrick Kluivert sent the game into extra-time by equalizing a Ronaldo strike in the 87th minute. The Dutch then lost on

penalties. In contrast, France, cannily coached by Aimé Jacquet, sent the home fans wild with a 2-1 victory over Croatia. As usual, the French team struggled up front but found an unlikely hero in the shape of right-back Lilian Thuram who scored twice. The only blot was a red card for Laurent Blanc (the 15th of the finals) after some appalling play-acting by Slaven Bilic. Suker, of course, scored for Croatia and he did so again in a 2-1 third place play-off win over Holland to clinch the golden boot with a total of six goals.

The final, between hosts France and champions Brazil, proved to be dramatic, controversial and yet disappointing all at the same time. The drama began when Brazil boss Mario Zagallo handed in his teamsheet, which did not include Ronaldo. Then,

15 minutes later, they sent in a correction with the striker back in the line-up. Later it transpired that Ronaldo had suffered a convulsive fit earlier in the day and had been passed fit to play only after a hospital check-up.

The affair clearly affected Brazil who looked out of spirits from the start. France, by contrast, were simply magnificent. Two headed goals from the inspirational Zidane, both from corners, put them in control and Emmanuel Petit rounded off the 3-0 win after dashing the full length of the pitch in the closing minutes. The scale of the victory equalled the largest winning margin in a final.

The celebrations around the Champs Elysees were remarkable, with millions packing the streets for days.

THE FINAL

1998 (France)

FRANCE   **3(2)**
Zidane (2), Petit
BRAZIL   **0(0)**

Stade de France, Paris, 75,000

FRANCE
Barthez, Thuram, Leboeuf, Desailly, Lizarazu, Petit, Deschamps (capt), Karembeu (Boghossian 58), Zidane, Guivarc'h (Dugarry 66), Djorkaeff (Viera 76)

BRAZIL
Taffarel, Cafu, Junior Baiano, Aldair, Roberto Carlos, Dunga (capt), Cesar Sempaio (Edmundo 75), Leonardo (Denilson 45), Rivaldo, Bebeto, Ronaldo

TOP SCORER
6 **SUKER** (Croatia)

2002

Brazil won the World Cup for a record fifth time as Ronaldo took revenge over the fates of 1998 to score the goals in Yokohama which beat Germany 2-0 at the climax of the first co-hosted finals.

The first World Cup in Asia had been full of surprises for fans far beyond South Korea and Japan. Co-hosting worked exceptionally well, despite the countries' uneasy history while hooligans were conspicuous by their absence from the 20 superb, mostly new, stadia. The only major snag concerned the perennially problematic issue of refereeing. Newcomers Senegal provided a sensational start by defeating holders France 1-0 in the opening match in Group A. Papa Bouba Diop stole the show on the half-hour by snatching the winner. France badly missed their injured playmaker Zinedine Zidane. For FIFA the result was a godsend, overshadowing controversies over a new ticketing system and the presidential re-election of Sepp Blatter.

France never recovered. Thierry Henry was sent off next time out in a frantic 0-0 draw with Uruguay which left France needing to beat group leaders Denmark in their last match. Half-fit Zidane was recalled but France lost 2-0. Senegal came through as runners-up, after Uruguay recovered from being 3-0 down at half-time to snatch a draw with the Lions of Turangi.

Spain topped Group B with one of only two 100 per cent records in the opening round (Brazil boasted the other). Runners-up Paraguay pipped South Africa on goal difference after beating Slovenia 3-1 on late goals from substitute Nelson Cuevas.

Group C was dominated by Brazil who scored 11 goals in their three victories although they struggled in their opening 2-1 beating of Turkey on strikes from Ronaldo and Rivaldo. But Rivaldo was fortunate to escape with only a fine after pretending he had

been hit in the face by a soccer kicked at him before a corner. Debutants China, under classic coach Bora Milutinovic, lost all three games.

South Korea escaped the first round for the first time as they took Group D by athletically irresistible storm. They beat a spiritless Poland 2-0, drew 1-1 with the United States and outran Portugal 1-0. Crowds of up to five million turned out to watch public-screen broadcasts and hailed Dutch coach Guus Hiddink and stars such as forward Ahn Jung Hwan as national heroes.

Germany opened in explosive style in Group E by crushing Saudi Arabia 8-0 thanks to a headed hat-trick from Miroslav Klose. It was the biggest finals victory in 16 years. Ireland took the runners-up spot despite the pre-finals loss of skipper Roy Keane after a bust-up with manager Mick McCarthy.

Group F was called the Group of Death though the label proved over-stated. Spiritless Nigeria were eliminated after losing their first two games while Argentina were a huge disappointment. The group turned on Argentina's 1-0 defeat by England in Sapporo. Michael Owen was tripped and skipper David Beckham, with a score to settle from 1998, converted the penalty. England duly finished runners-up behind Sweden.

Mexico topped Group G, using their neat possession soccer to maximum effect to beat Croatia 1-0 and finals debutants Ecuador 2-1. Italy edged through as runners-up despite struggling for a 1-1 draw with Mexico in their last game. The Italians would have gone out but Croatia, inexplicably, lost their last game 1-0 to Ecuador.

Japan followed the example of co-hosts South Korea by topping Group H. The hero of their similarly hard-running efforts was midfielder Junichi Inamoto who had emerged from Arsenal reserves to score goals which helped inspire an opening 2-2 draw with ultimate group runners-up

Korean fans exhort their fellow countrymen to 'Be the Reds.'

Belgium and subsequent 1-0 win over Russia. That was Japan's first victory in the finals and they followed up neatly with a 2-0 win over Tunisia.

Bizarre fixture scheduling denied the players any chance to catch their breath between the end of the groups and the switch into knock-out mode for the second round. It came as no surprise that it was the athletes who won through rather than the technicians. Germany ground down Paraguay 1-0 with a late goal from Oliver Neuville, while the USA ran over Mexico 2-0. Latin America was thus left with only Brazil who needed late goals from Rivaldo and Ronaldo to see off Belgium.

The Nordic challenge evaporated in contrasting ways. Sweden lost only 2-1 on Henri Camara's golden goal for Senegal while Denmark collapsed 3-0 against England. Sunderland goalkeeper Thomas Sorensen gifted England their first goal in only four minutes by knocking a header from Rio Ferdinand into his own net, Owen grabbed a close-range second while Emile Heskey fired a third courtesy of more poor defending. It was all over before half-time.

The co-hosts enjoyed mixed fortunes. Japan's unremitting effort went in vain after they allowed Turkey's Umit Davala a free header at a 12th-minute corner. South Korea, however, overcame an embittered Italy 2-1 on a golden goal from Ahn Jung Hwan. His celebratory comments after the match earned him instant dismissal from his club – Perugia of Italy.

The quarter-finals provided more glory for Korea who beat angry Spain on penalties after a goalless draw in which Ivan Helguera and Fernando Morientes (twice) both had goals disallowed. But Senegal lost on a golden goal to Turkey, while the USA succumbed 1-0 to Germany who owed victory to the brilliance of captain and goalkeeper Oliver Kahn.

Brazil beat England 2-1 more easily

Ronaldo punishes a slip by Oliver Kahn to put Brazil ahead against Germany in Yokohama.

than the scoreline suggested after goalkeeper David Seaman was caught out by a free kick from Ronaldinho which floated over his head and into the net for the winner. Michael Owen had given England a 23rd-minute lead after a mistake by Lucio but Brazil squared through Rivaldo before the interval.

A harsh red card cost Ronaldinho suspension from Brazil's semi-final against Turkey, the European team reaching this stage for the first time in their history. But a virtuoso display from Rivaldo, making up for his sins of the first meeting, inspired Brazil to a 1-0 win courtesy of a 48th-minute goal from Ronaldo.

Korea's magnificent adventure was ended by Germany in the semi-final. The only goal came 15 minutes from time, from the boot of German playmaker Michael Ballack. But Germany's delight at reaching the

Final – against all predictions – was tempered by the suspension of Ballack, who was shown his second yellow card in Seoul.

Turkey's consolation was to claim third place after beating Korea 3-2 in the losers' play-off with Hakan Sukur scoring the fastest goal in finals history after 10.8 seconds.

In the Final, physical endeavour, mental willpower and the reflexes of Kahn kept Germany on level terms for 66 minutes. Then the goalkeeper spilled a drive from Rivaldo and Ronaldo shot Brazil ahead. Germany had to open up, lacked the necessary attacking panache and the on-form Ronaldo punished them a second time. He finished as the tournament's eight-goal top scorer and equalled Pele's Brazilian record of 12 goals in 14 World Cup ties. Cafu marked his 111th international by becoming the first player to appear in three consecutive

finals. He was the worthy captain of ultimately very deserving champions.

2006

Italy carried off the World Cup for a European record fourth time but the Final in Berlin is more likely to be remembered as the night on which the great Zinedine Zidane's career ended in disaster. He was sent off in extra time as the Italians beat France in the second penalty shootout in the Final's history.

Zidane, who had put France ahead from a "normal" penalty in only the seventh minute of the game, was dismissed by Argentine referee Horacio Elizondo on his assistant's evidence. The French captain had head-butted Italian defender Marco Materazzi in the chest in an off the ball clash in the 19th minute of extra-time. Elizondo, who had earlier sent off England's Wayne Rooney in the quarter-finals, had no option.

France, who had already substituted Thierry Henry, thus lacked their two finest penalty exponents for the shootout which the Italians had earned with a 19th-minute equaliser from the same Materazzi.

All nine players in the shootout hit the target with the sole tragic exception of French striker David Trezeguet. His shot, France's second, flew up past his Juventus club colleague Gigi Buffon – and ricocheted back down off the crossbar. Minutes later Fabio Grosso rasped home Italy's fifth penalty and finally, after 12 years, they had claimed a fourth World Cup and righted the sad memory of their own shootout defeat by Brazil in Pasadena in 1994. Yet Italy's new heroes flew home uncertain of their own futures since victory had been achieved in the shadow of a major corruption investigation.

This was all a major contrast to the flair and panache with which hosts Germany had set the party under way in Munich just over a month earlier all the way back in Group A.

Few local fans had much faith in manager Jurgen Klinsmann or his players ahead of the party. Klinsmann

had been a surprise choice as boss in 2004 after the Germans' first-round flop at the European finals. He was not the DFB's first choice and insisted on commuting from his home on California's Pacific coast, to the fury of the media and bemusement of fans.

Yet his players made the best possible start with a superb early goal from leftback Philipp Lahm in the opening match win against Costa Rica. Torsten Frings struck another from long-range to round off a 4-2 win which saw Jens Lehmann controversially picked as No1 keeper ahead of 2002 skipper Oliver Kahn.

Next time out was serious business in the soccer bearpit of Dortmund. Poland needed at least a draw and came within minutes of achieving it. Much had been made before the game of the Polish origins of German strikers Lukas Podolski and Miroslav Klose but it was substitute Oliver Neuville who snatched the hosts' last-ditch winner.

Klose (two) and Podolski fired the goals as Germany beat Ecuador 3-0 to finish top of the group but the South Americans also celebrated after securing progress beyond the groups for the first time.

England topped Group B but with none of Germany's flair or sense of fun. Preparation had been overshadowed by a metatarsal fracture which had threatened to sideline Wayne Rooney. A late scan finally cleared him to join the squad but England stumbled forward after narrow wins over Paraguay and Trinidad & Tobago and 2-2 draw with runners-up Sweden.

Manager Sven-Goran Eriksson's attacking options were reduced further by a serious knee ligament injury to Michael Owen in the second minute against the Swedes. Thus only Trinidad went home happy after claiming an opening goalless draw with Sweden in which keeper Shaka Hislop played the game of his life.

Trinidad coach Leo Beenhakker's

Argentinian midfielder Esteban Cambiasso finishes a memerising multi-pass move with a superb strike.

Dutch fellow countrymen had been drawn in the so-called "Group of death" along with Argentina, newcomers Ivory Coast plus Serbia and Montenegro.

Marco Van Basten, in his first managerial post, had dropped most of the old guard in an attempt to build a unified young team. Holland duly qualified in second place behind Argentina whose 6-0 dismantling of Serbia was the outstanding performance of the groups.

Esteban Cambiasso's strike, Argentina's second, was the goal of the finals – superbly struck after a move between nine players with 55 touches of the ball over 58 seconds.

Group D saw Portugal progress for, surprisingly, the first time since their third-place finish in 1966. Three victories over runners-up Mexico, outclassed Iran and newcomers Angola – the former Portuguese colony – earned coach Luiz Felipe Scolari a finals record of 10 successive victories. He had stored up the initial seven as boss of winners Brazil in 2002.

The one African nation out of five to progress were Ghana. An opening two-goal defeat by Group E winners Italy could have been fatal but the Ghanaians' extrovert Serb coach Ratomir Dujkovic maintained morale so successfully than they beat the Czech Republic 2-0 next time out.

The luckless Czechs missed injured strikers Jan Koller and Milan Baros but the Ghanaians' quality was underlined

when they beat a disappointing United States 2-1 in their last game.

Brazil virtually sleep-walked to three wins out of three, scoring seven goals and conceding only one in Group F. They relied lazily on the individual opportunism of Kaka against Croatia, Adriano and Fred against Australia and then Ronaldo to see off Japan.

Ronaldo, an eight-goal hero in 2002, had emerged from a wretched season at Real Madrid disrupted by injuries and criticism that he was overweight. Yet he would still overtake Gerd Muller's old record aggregate of 14 World Cup goals.

Australia, appearing for the first time since West Germany in 1974, came through as runners-up thanks in so small part to the managerial nous of PSV Eindhoven's Guus Hiddink, a semi-finalist manager of Holland in 1998 and co-hosts South Korea in 2002.

Croatia, Poland, Serbia and the Czechs made up a quartet out of the 14 European starters who failed to make the last 16. Stuttering France and Switzerland in Group G and Spain and newcomers Ukraine in Group H provided a European one-two to mirror the England-Sweden command of Group B.

The failures of Iran, Japan, South Korea and Saudi Arabia suggested that Asian soccer had made no progress since 2002. As for the almost equally disappointing Africans, Togo made headlines for all the wrong reasons. They sacked coach Stephen Keshi after a poor African Nations performance and replacement Otto Pfister walked out briefly in disgust after the federation refused to pay the players' qualifying bonuses.

In the end FIFA decided to pay the bonuses direct and deduct the sum from Togo's profit-share.

Sadly, the knockout stage saw the quality of both the soccer and the refereeing fall away alarmingly. The nadir was reached in Portugal's 1-0 win over Holland in which Valentin Ivanov showed a record haul of four red cards and 16 yellow. But the Russian was betrayed by the players of both sides who revived ill-feeling from the Euro 2004 semi-final which Portugal had also won.

Ivanov was not the only referee released early. So was Englishman Graham Poll who showed Croatia's Josip Simunic two yellow cards but mistakenly let him play on against Australia. Again Poll, while

badly at fault, was let down by not only his fellow officials but by the players themselves.

An equally awful game, for different reasons, was the goalless draw after which newcomers Ukraine beat Switzerland in the first penalty shootout of the finals. The Swiss missed all their three kicks, prompting a newspaper to ask: "If William Tell could hit an apple from 60metres why couldn't three of our players hit a net from 11?"

England and Italy scored narrow victories which were barely less gruesome. The Azzurri scrambled past Australia despite the expulsion of defender Materazzi and with the help of a controversial last-minute penalty from Francesco Totti; England needed a free kick from the unwell Beckham to see off Ecuador.

Thus only three of the eight matches provided soccer worth the memory. Germany struck twice in an explosive first 12 minutes to see off a Sweden side whose lack of belief was

reflected in Henrik Larsson's second-half penalty miss; Brazil benefited from two "offside" goals in a 3-0 win over Ghana; and Argentina were saved from the lottery of a penalty shootout against Mexico by Maxi Rodriguez.

But his superb late strike kept the Gauchos riding for only one more match. Lehmann's bravura performance in a quarter-finals shootout took Germany to victory after a 1-1 draw while Portugal also needed penalties to see off an over-hyped England who were doomed after Rooney's expulsion on the hour for treading on Ricardo Carvalho.

Brazil, like England, failed to match expectations and were fortunate to lose only 1-0 against the reviving French for whom Henry volleyed a superb winning goal.

Italy had it easy. They cruised to a 3-0 win over Ukraine and were thus fresher and fitter for the semi-final against Germany in which they dismissed their hosts with late extra-

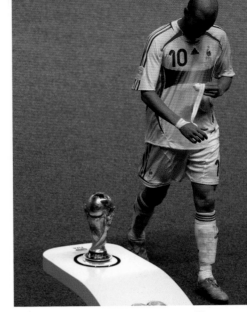

France's Zinedine Zidane walks past the World Cup trophy after being sent off in the Final.

time strikes from Fabio Grosso and Alessandro Del Piero.

Germany went on to win the third-place match 3-1 against a tired Portugal who had lost the other semi-final to France. Zidane had scored the winner from a first-half penalty. Little did he know, as he and Les Bleus celebrated, what fate had in store five days later in Berlin.

Captain Fabio Cannavaro lifts Italy's fourth World Cup after defeating France 5-3 on penalties in the Final following their 1-1 draw after extra time.

THE FINAL

2006 (Germany)

ITALY	**1(0)***
Materazzi	
FRANCE	**1(0)**
Zidane	
Italy won 5–3 on pens	
	Olympiastadion, 69,000
	* After extra time

ITALY
Buffon, Zambrotta, Cannavaro (capt.), Materazzi, Grosso, Camoranesi (Del Piero), Pirlo, Gattuso, Perrotta (Iaquinta), Totti (De Rossi), Toni
FRANCE
Barthez, Sagnol, Thuram, Gallas, Abidal, Ribery (Trezeguet), Vieira (Diarra 56), Makelele, Zidane (capt.), Malouda, Henry (Wiltord)

TOP SCORER
5 KLOSE (Germany)

2010

South Africa's hosting of the 2010 World Cup finals was hailed as a remarkable success and outstanding reward for FIFA's vision in taking its elite event to the African continent for the first time. But the soccer on view was of a modest quality and it was lucky that Spain, by far the best team on view, emerged as winners. Amazingly, considering Spain's power and achievements at club level this was their first World Cup triumph.

The 1-0 extra-time victory over Holland in Soccer City came courtesy of a 116th-minute goal from Andres Iniesta, one of the Barcelona core at the service of coach Vicente Del Bosque. The goal came after the over-aggressive Dutch had been reduced to 10 men by the expulsion of defender Johnny Heitinga by Howard Webb – the fourth Englishman to referee the Final, but first since Jack Taylor officiated over the first of Holland's three Finals defeats back in 1974.

Spain became only the eighth nation to be crowned as champions in the World Cup's 80 years and they were also the lowest-scoring winners, having mustered a meagre eight goals in their seven games. The outcome of the eighth all-European final edged Europe 10-9 ahead of South America in the inter-continental rivalry.

The fringe honours saw Germany claim a record fourth win in the third-place play-off while losers Uruguay had the consolation of seeing forward Diego Forlan hailed as best player. German pride in their young team was boosted by 20-year-old Thomas Muller from Bayern Munich carrying off the awards for young player and top scorer; his points total computed from five goals and three assists was better than that of Forlan, Holland's Wesley Sneijder and Spain's David Villa.

South Africa had campaigned initially to win host rights in 2006 but had been outmanoeuvred politically by Germany. FIFA, at president Sepp

South Africa's Siphiwe Tschabalala scores the first – and one of the best – of the finals' 145 goals.

Blatter's behest, then introduced a system of rotation which designated 2010 for Africa and made it inevitable that Nelson Mandela and his countrymen would win at second attempt. Only one hitch dampened local enthusiasm and that was the failure of the host team – Bafana Bafana, The Boys – to rise to the occasion. Carlos Alberto Parreira, World Cup-winning coach of Brazil in 1994, had been called in just before the tournament to build a worthy team. But a lack of time, experience and playing ability saw them register unwanted history as the first host not to advance past the first round.

At least they began and ended their Group A campaign in style. Siphiwe Tschabalala provided one of the goals of the tournament in an opening 1-1 draw with Mexico in the majestic Soccer City in Johannesburg; then The Boys saw off France 2-1 in their last game in Bloemfontein.

Firmly-focused Uruguay and entertainingly fragile Mexico progressed, with South Africa missing out only on goal difference and France finishing bottom and in disgrace. Striker Nicholas Anelka had raged at coach Raymond Domenech at half-time in their defeat by Mexico and his expulsion by federation bosses

prompted a training ground strike by the rest of the squad. Even President Nicolas Sarkozy became caught up in the 'national crisis' sentiment which the idiosyncratic Domenech and his players found on their return home.

By contrast Argentina were on a different plane entirely in Group B. Diego Maradona was an inexperienced, contentious choice as coach but he was carried along by the technical prowess of his team.

The double former world champions were one of only two teams – Holland were the other – to win all their three group games. Inspiration was provided by the eel-like pocket genius of World Player of the Year Leo Messi from Barcelona while most of the goals came from Gonzalo Higuain of Real Madrid. Nigeria's last-place finish in Group B was matched by Algeria in Group C, though the latter's plight was not unexpected, and most of the focus surrounded England's struggle to find their way into the second round.

The Football Association had hired Italian Fabio Capello as manager at world record expense, a reported £6m-a-year, after England had failed to qualify for Euro 2008. Capello's authoritarian style worked wonders in the qualifying round, but the wheels

began to come off with lack-lustred displays in the run-up to the finals and a run of injuries to key players. England looked in vain for Manchester United's Wayne Rooney to impose his brilliance on the finals. England drew 1-1 with the United States, 0-0 with Algeria and snatched a 1-0 win over Slovenia. One extra goal would have made them group winners; but the US beat Algeria in the dying seconds to take top spot on goals scored. England, fatally, were paired with Germany in the second round.

The Germans had come into the finals handicapped by a string of injuries and thus little expectation. That changed at once with the high-tempo nature of their opening 4-0 rout of Australia which led to a top-spot finish after a concluding single-goal win over Ghana, who finished runners-up, and were the only one of six African nations to capitalise on 'home continent' advantage.

Cameroon finished bottom of Group E, one of only two teams – North Korea were the others – not to gain a point. Holland topped the group, followed by lively Japan, for whom Keisuke Honda was a lively attacking spark. But the 2006 winners Italy, in Group F, were a disaster. They finished bottom after stuttering draws against not only section winners Paraguay but minnows New Zealand and then a defeat by 3-2 to Slovakia. Coach Marcello Lippi fought back tears afterwards as he accepted "full responsibility." In truth, he was undermined partly by the limitations of the players available to him.

The same could not be said for multi-talented Brazil. Coach Dunga duly saw his team through to top spot with wins over North Korea and Ivory Coast and a goalless draw with Portugal. This had been labelled the 'Group of Death' but Portugal, who gave North Korea a seven-goal thrashing, went through in second place. The Ivory Coast never overcame the upset of a pre-tournament injury to skipper Didier Drogba.

After 116 minutes of often fractious and spiteful soccer, Andres Iniesta (6) shoots past Holland goalkeeper Maarten Stekelenburg to give Spain the World Cup.

Spain made a bad start in Group H before topping the group. Their opening 1-0 defeat by Switzerland led to them becoming the only team to win the World Cup after losing their opening game. Chile claimed the second spot from the group.

The crowded tournament format meant that the group phase ran straight on into the knockout second round without even a day's break. It saw resurgent Uruguay, adopted 'home' team Ghana, Holland, Brazil, Paraguay (albeit only on penalties) and Spain emerge as predictable winners over South Korea, the US, Slovakia, Chile, Japan and Portugal. But the other two ties generated the major storm of the finals.

Germany were as deserving of their thumping 4-1 win over England as were Argentina of their 3-1 dismissal of Mexico. But the Germany-England game was marred by a mirror-image repeat of the contentious over-the-line goal from way back at the 1966 World Cup Final. Then, Geoff Hurst was awarded the goal which put England 3-2 ahead; now, Frank Lampard was denied a clear goal which would have pulled England level at 2-2 just before half-time. Uruguayan referee Jorge Larrionda and assistant Mauricio Espinoza were among the

few people in Bloemfontein's Free State Stadium who did not see that the ball had bounced back into play.

Hours later Argentina's Carlos Tevez was awarded an opening goal against Mexico despite clearly being in an offside position. Italian referee Roberto Rosetti let the goal stand and Mexico, concentration snapped, gifted a soft second shortly afterwards.

The explosion of fury at these two major refereeing blunders was so intense that it prompted FIFA president Blatter into apologising to both England and Mexico and also swept aside his resistance to the exploration of goal-line technology for use at future World Cups.

The morning of Friday, July 2, saw the quarter-finals field viewed as a judgment on Europe's obsession with club soccer; only Holland, Germany and Spain had made it this far compared with four South American nations. By midnight the next day all perceptions of European indifference to the World Cup had been shattered.

The empire struck back first when Holland overturned Brazil 2-1. The Brazilians had gone ahead in the opening minutes through Robinho but took their foot complacently off the pedal and conceded two rapid-fire second-half goals to outstanding

Dutch playmaker Wesley Sneijder. When Felipe Melo was dismissed for stamping on the pacy Arjen Robben it was all up for not only Brazil but for the derided Dunga.

Argentina and Paraguay joined the queue at the transatlantic flight desk the following day. Muller followed up his two goals against England with another against Argentina in the third minute. Maradona's men lost their poise and, with Messi shuffled into Cape Town cul-de-sacs, were shredded by three further goals in the second half. Miroslav Klose scored two of them to take his all-time total to 14 goals, one short of the overall World Cup record held by Brazil's Ronaldo.

Hours later, David Villa scored his fourth goal of the finals to edge Spain onward after a dramatic second-half in which both Paraguay's Oscar Cardozo and Spaniard Xabi Alonso missed penalties within two minutes of each other.

Europe's trio thus marched into the last four, together with South America's last surviving hope, Uruguay, who had appeared on the brink of elimination when, at 1-1 against Ghana, the Africans were awarded a last-minute penalty in extra-time after a punch off the goal-line by Ajax forward Luis Suarez. His tears of pain,

as he left the pitch, suddenly turned into tears of joy as Ghana's Asamoah Gyan banged his penalty against the top of the crossbar. Gyan, bravely, made no mistake in the subsequent shootout but Uruguay advanced 4-2.

Uruguay owed an enormous debt to the attacking inspiration of Forlan but, without the suspended Suarez, it was too much to expect that he alone could conjure up enough solo magic to overcome Holland. He did indeed manage one goal but was ultimately outgunned by Giovanni Van Bronckhorst, Sneijder yet again and Robben. Maxi Pereira pulled a goal back late on, but Holland, with six wins out of six, deserved a third final appearance.

The certainty of a first-ever European winner outside their own continent emerged after Spain defeated Germany 1-0 in Durban. Veteran centre-back Carles Puyol thundered home a late winning header to take them on to the ultimate Soccer City showdown.

THE FINAL	
SPAIN	**1 (0)***
Iniesta	
HOLLAND	**0 (0)**

Soccer City, Johannesburg, 84,490
*After extra-time: 0-0 at 90min

SPAIN
Casillas, Sergio Ramos, Pique, Puyol, Capdevila, Sergi Busquests, Xabi Alonso (Fabregas 87), Pedro (Navas 60), Xavi, Iniesta, Villa (Torres 106)
HOLLAND
Stekelenburg, Van der Wiel, Heitinga, Mathijsen, Van Bronckhorst (Braafheid 105), Van Bommel, De Jong (Van der Vaart 99), Robben, Sneijder, Kuyt (Elia 71), Van Persie

TOP SCORERS
5 **MULLER** (Germany), VILLA (Spain), SNEIJDER (Holland), FORLAN (Uruguay)

THE EUROPEAN CHAMPIONSHIP

The European Championship was the last of the continental tournaments to get under way and, like the World Cup and the European Champions Cup, was another French innovation. It was originally launched in 1958-60.

Four nations were involved, playing knock-out semi-finals, with a third place play-off and Final. France should have been in that final themselves. They led Yugoslavia 4-2 in their semi-final opener with 15 minutes to play. The Slavs, however, were spurred by a sense of injustice over the second of Francois Heutte's two goals which should have been disallowed for offside. They thus battled back with astonishing results – putting three goals past Georges Lamia in the France goal within three minutes. French fans excused the result on the grounds that playmaker Raymond Kopa and star striker Fontaine were out injured. Georges Lamia, his confidence shattered by the Slavs' great revival, never played for France again.

The Soviet Union, including legendary goalkeeper Lev Yashin, thrashed Czechoslovakia 3-0 in Marseille in the other semi-final. The Final was played in the old Parc des Princes – just like the first Champion Clubs Cup Final four years earlier. The first goal was almost an own goal, Soviet skipper Igor Netto deflecting a strike from Milan Galic though the latter was credited with the goal just two minutes before the interval. Soviet right-wing Slava Metrevelli equalized four minutes after half-time to send the final into extra time.

Yugoslavia had been the better team. Only the brilliance of Lev Yashin in the Soviet goal had denied them victory. But in extra time they lost heart and defensive discipline. Soviet centre-forward Viktor Ponedelnik snatched his one chance of the game... and the Soviet Union were first European champions.

The 1964 tournament saw England enter for the first time – only to crash out in the first round. Alf Ramsey's first competitive experience in charge ended in a defeat by France. The finals were staged in Spain who had put their faith in a new generation of home-grown youngsters. The final four were completed by the Soviet holders, Hungary and Denmark.

Yashin and Co beat Denmark easily 3-0 but Spain needed extra-time to defeat Hungary 2-1. Real Madrid's new hero Amancio scored the winner, five minutes from the end. Spain's most influential player was Luis Suarez from Internazionale Milan who pulled the midfield strings in the final. Spain took an early lead against the Soviets in the Estadio Bernabeu through Jesus Pereda. Galimzyan Khusainov struck back for the Soviet Union but a second-half strike from Zaragoza centre-forward Marcelino was the signal for Spanish celebrations. General Franco, watching from the VIP box, was reported to have greatly appreciated another victory over the forces of Communism.

For the 1968 event, the qualifying tournament was expanded to eight mini-league groups. The knock-out

Fans prepare to invade the Heysel pitch in the closing minutes of West Germany's 1972 defeat of the Soviet Union.

quarter-finals were staged on a two-leg basis and the winners went through to the finals in Italy. The hosts beat the Soviet Union in the first semi-final, but only by the rather dubious method of tossing a coin. World champions England also reached the semi-finals, but were beaten 1-0 by Yugoslavia. The final went to a replay, where goals by Luigi Riva and Pietro Anastasi were too much for the exhausted Yugoslavs, who again had to be content with runners-up medals.

The Soviets reached their third final out of four in 1972, but were no match for the West Germans. Gerd Müller was at his peak, and two goals by him in the Final set up a 3-0 victory, and confirmed the Germans as favourites for the World Cup to be held two years later on home soil.

The 1976 tournament threw up

Spain's Jesus Pereda (left) beats Lev Yashin to open the scoring in the 1964 Final.

surprises from start to finish. England, Italy and France were eliminated in the qualifying round, and the semi-final line-up comprised Czechoslovakia, 1974 World Cup winners West Germany, runners-up Holland and hosts Yugoslavia. Both semi-finals went to extra-time, the Czechs beating the Dutch 3-1 and the West Germans defeating the Yugoslavs 4-2, with a hat-trick from substitute Dieter Müller.

West Germany were clear favourites, but the Czechs had other ideas. Goals by Jan Svehlik and Karel Dobias gave them a 2-0 lead inside half an hour, but West Germany fought back, Bernd Holzenbein snatching an equalizer in the 89th minute. Extra time failed to separate the teams, and in the penalty shoot-out, Antonin Panenka chipped his penalty past Sepp Maier to win the trophy.

In 1980 the format for the final stages of the competition changed. The quarter-finals were abolished and the seven qualifying group winners proceeded straight to the finals along with the hosts, Italy, who received a bye direct to the final stage. The eight teams divided into two groups of four, with the winners meeting in the final.

The Soviets failed to qualify for their "favourite" tournament, and the Yugoslavs also missed out, but there was a first-ever finals appearance for Greece. Belgium proved the surprise package, reaching the final after conquering England, Spain and Italy in the group matches. West Germany won the other group and became the only nation to win the trophy twice when they beat the Belgians 2-1.

The 1984 tournament was the best to date, with the flamboyant French hosts in unstoppable form. They had Michel Platini to thank for it. His nine goals in five games was a superb achievement as the French swept aside Denmark, Belgium and Yugoslavia in the group matches. Unfancied Spain clinched the other group and then squeezed past the impressive Danes on

penalties after a 1-1 draw in the re-introduced semi-finals. The Final was more conclusive as the host country won for the third time in seven events.

The 1988 finals in West Germany saw the Soviet Union qualify with Holland to reach the semi-finals, where they met – and beat – Italy and West Germany respectively. With Rinus Michels in charge, the Dutch played irresistible soccer, beating the hosts 2-1 in the semi-final with a splendidly taken goal by Marco Van Basten two minutes from time. Van Basten did even better in the Final against the Soviet Union, crashing home a volley from an almost impossible angle to seal a 2-0 victory following Ruud Gullit's first-half opener.

Sweden hosted the 1992 finals. They and Scotland were making their finals debut and the former Soviet Union played under the banner of Commonwealth of Independent States, but the biggest surprises were Denmark, last-minute replacements for the suspended Yugoslavia. They arrived with little time to prepare and walked off with the trophy after beating Holland on penalties in the semi-finals and then a shocked Germany by 2-0 in the final in Gothenburg. Midfielders John Jensen and Kim Vilfort were their goal-scoring heroes.

Gullit and Van Basten celebrate in 1988.

THE FINALS 1960-1992

1960 (Paris)
SOVIET UNION 2
(Metreveli, Ponedelnik)
YUGOSLAVIA 1 (Galic)
Att: 18,000

1964 (Madrid)
SPAIN 2 (Pereda, Marcelino)
SOVIET UNION 1 (Khusainov)
Att: 105,000

1968 (Rome)
ITALY 1 (Domenghini)
YUGOSLAVIA 1 (Dzajic)
Att: 85,000.
Replay (Rome)
ITALY 2 (Riva, Anastasi)
YUGOSLAVIA 0
Att: 85,000

1972 (Brussels)
WEST GERMANY 3 (Müller G. 2, Wimmer)
SOVIET UNION 0
Att: 65,000

1976 (Belgrade)
CZECHOSLOVAKIA 2 (Svehlik, Dobias)
WEST GERMANY 2 (Müller D., Holzenbein) (aet).
Czech. won 5-4 pens. Att: 45,000

1980 (Rome)
W. GERMANY 2 (Hrubesch 2)
BELGIUM 1 (Vandereycken)
Att: 48,000

1984 (Paris)
FRANCE 2 (Platini, Bellone)
SPAIN 0
Att: 47,000

1988 (Munich)
HOLLAND 2 (Gullit, Van Basten)
SOVIET UNION 0
Att: 72,000

1992 (Stockholm)
DENMARK 2 (Jensen, Vilfort)
GERMANY 0
Att: 37,000

EURO 96

The 1996 event was the most exciting soccer extravaganza in England since the 1966 World Cup.

Czech players claim offside in vain after Oliver Bierhoff's golden goal winner for Germany.

The enlargement of the tournament from eight to 16 teams was one of the decisive factors in England winning host rights in the first place. However, part of the political process later came back to haunt the Football Association. Part of the political trade-off was that England called a halt to their campaign to win host rights to the 1998 World Cup in favour of France. But when Euro 96's success persuaded the FA to revive the World Cup bid for 2006 chairman Bert Millichip and co found themselves outflanked by German opportunism – just as they had been pipped by the Germans on the pitch in the European Championship itself.

England drew 1-1 against Switzerland in the opening match before pulling themselves together with a dramatic 2-0 victory over old enemy Scotland and a high-class 4-1 defeat of Holland.

France topped Group B ahead of Spain and Italy were notable failures in Group C from which both the Germans and Czechs qualified.

The quality of soccer faded in the knock-out stages in which spot-kicks proved decisive for both England (against Spain) and France (against Holland). The Czechs beat Portugal 1-0 while Germany triumphed 2-1 in a bad-tempered duel with Croatia.

Penalties were needed to resolve both the semi-finals with the Czechs pipping France and England vs. Germany provided a night of exciting intensity which a 76,000 crowd at Wembley and 26 million domestic television viewers will never forget.

England secured a magnificent start with Shearer heading home in the third minute, but the Germans soon levelled through their only fit striker, Stefan Kuntz. The drama rolled on into golden goal extra time when Darren Anderton struck the post and Kuntz had a headed effort disallowed.

Both sides converted their five spotkicks but Gareth Southgate sent the ball straight into the arms of keeper Andy Kopke, and Germany won the Final place.

Domestic euphoria might have been punctured like a toy balloon. Yet it said everything for the manner in which Euro 96 had gripped the public imagination that 73,611 turned out for the Final. The vast majority – English fans converted into honorary Czechs for the night – were celebrating when Patrick Berger fired home a 59th-minute penalty. Germany had lost to the underdogs in the Final – against Denmark – four years earlier and history appeared to be repeating itself. But then German coach Berti Vogts played his hidden ace, bringing on substitute centre-forward Oliver Bierhoff. Within minutes Bierhoff had headed the Germans level then, in the fourth minute of extra time, he fired home the Golden Goal. The Czechs protested that Kuntz had been in an offside position but referee Pierluigi Pairetto waved away their protests.

Paul Gascoigne explodes England's first goal beyond Scotland keeper Andy Goram at Wembley.

THE FINAL	
1996 (England)	
GERMANY	**2 (0)**
Bierhoff 73, 94	
CZECH REPUBLIC	**1 (0)***
Berger 58 pen	

Germany win on golden goal in extra time
Wembley, London, 76,000

GERMANY
Köpke, Babbel, Sammer, Helmer, Strunz, Hässler, Eilt (Bode 46), Scholl (Bierhoff 69), Ziege, Klinsmann, Kuntz
CZECH REPUBLIC
Kouba, Hornak, Rada, Kadlec, Suchoparek, Poborsky (Smicer 88), Nedved, Bejbl, Berger, Nemec, Kuka

EURO 2000

France regained the European title they had won in 1984 with a thrilling 2-1 golden goal victory over Italy.

The first major European international event of the 21st century made history as the first to be co-hosted, by Belgium and Holland. The result was magnificent, with thrill-a-minute soccer and a catalogue of matches which will live in the nemory.

The Final was no exception. Italy, in defiance of their defensive traditions, traded lightning raids blow for blow with the World Cup holders in a goalless first half and went ahead through Marco Delvecchio 11 minutes into the second half. Even man of the tournament Zinedine Zidane appeared unable to work his usual magic as the match ran over the 90 with Italy on the brink of glory.

Then the Italian defence failed to clear one last, despairing up-and-under from France and substitute Sylvain Wiltord equalized seconds from the whistle. Italy, physically and psychologically the worse for wear

after a tougher semi-final, ultimately subsided 13 minutes into extra time when Monaco's Juventus-bound striker David Trezeguet jabbed home the winner. It was the second successive victory for France by a golden goal and the second consecutive European Championship to have been decided that way.

Such a spectacular conclusion was exactly what the tournament deserved. The event was full of exciting, skilful soccer with plenty of goals and remarkable matches.

It was a miserable tournament for England who went out in the same group as fellow under-achievers Germany. Against expectations, their opening group was lifted by the impressively disciplined Romania and an inspired Portugal. The Portuguese made their mark right from the start. They went 2-0 down to England in 17 minutes in Eindhoven yet hit back to

win 3-2. On the same day only awful finishing by Viorel Moldovan let Germany escape their clash with Romania with a 1-1 draw. That placed extra weight on the long-awaited meeting of Germany and England in Charleroi. Police had long dreaded this day, ever since the draw had placed two old rivals together in a small provincial town on a weekend when every hooligan within hundreds of miles would have time to travel. England won 1-0 with a 53rd-minute header by skipper Alan Shearer. They then lost 3-2 to a Romanian side weakened by the absence through suspension of Gheorghe Hagi.

All four quarter-finals were decided in 90 minutes without recourse to extra-time or shoot-outs. Portugal beat Turkey 2-0 while Italy defeated Romania by the same margin. Holland thrashed Yugoslavia 6-1 with a hat-trick from Patrick Kluivert.

Zidane fired France ahead against Spain from a free kick after 32 minutes only for Gaizka Mendieta to equalize from a penalty four minutes later. The French regained the lead through Youri Djorkaeff right on half-time yet squeezed through only because Raul lofted a last-minute penalty over the bar.

The drama factor increased in the semi-finals which were both decided from the penalty spot. France maintained the thrill-a-minute standard by defeating Portugal 2-1 on Zidane's golden goal penalty in Brussels.

The second semi-final was decided by the only penalty shootout of the event, Holland falling 3-1 to Italy after a 0-0 extra-time draw. The cliché about a team 'paying the penalty' was never more apt. Holland's Frank De Boer and Kluivert not only both missed penalties in normal time but De Boer, Jaap Stam and Paul Bosvelt also failed in the shootout. Italy got through despite playing all but the first half hour with only ten men after the expulsion of Gianluca Zambrotta.

Didier Deschamps adds the European Championship to his trophy collection.

EURO 2004

Greece generated the wildest shock in European Championship history when they beat hosts Portugal 1-0 in the Final.

A second-half goal from striker Angelos Charisteas in the Estadio da Luz in Lisbon punctured the hosts' euphoria and handed the Greeks their first major title. They thus became the first nation to beat both hosts and holders – France – in the same competition. Greece's triumph was one of fitness, organization and discipline, thanks to the pragmatic management of veteran German Otto Rehhagel.

Back at the start of the finals the Greeks had not figured among the nine nations with title hopes alongside their Portuguese hosts: England, holders France, Germany, Italy and Spain plus the Czech Republic, Denmark, Holland and Sweden.

The Big Five were the biggest embarrassment. Germany, Italy and Spain all crashed in the first round and England and France fell in the quarter-finals along with Denmark and Sweden. A pedestrian Dutch side reached the semi-finals almost by default before falling to Portugal.

The ideal final in prospect would have matched Portuguese against Czechs but the Greeks had other ideas, beating the Czechs on the silver goal rule and then tarnishing the dreams of Portugal's so-called golden generation in the final.

Thus the finals ended as they had begun, with a Greek defeat of Portugal. The only difference was the scoreline. The opening match in Oporto in Group A had seen Portugal lose 2-1 to Rehhagel's Greek surprises.

Spain, with skipper Raul badly out of form, opened in positive mode with a single-goal victory over an injury-hit Russia but were then held 1-1 by Greece before losing the Iberian derby 1-0 to Portugal. The hosts managed to recover their self-belief with a 2-0 win over Russia and saw off the overly cautious Spaniards with a second-half winner from substitute Nuno Gomes. Portugal thus topped the group ahead of Greece who suffered their only defeat of the finals by 2-1 to the already-eliminated Russians.

France and England came through from Group B in that order, although it could have been the way around after their opening duel when Zinedine Zidane scored twice in stoppage time – once from a free kick, once from a penalty – to turn impending defeat into a 2-1 win. In what turned out to be a vital turning point, David Beckham had missed a second-half penalty.

Euro sensation Wayne Rooney scored England's third goal against Croatia.

Switzerland's one survivor from Euro 96, Johann Vogel, was sent off in a goalless draw with unadventurous Croatia who raised their game next time out to frighten misfiring France.

England had re-entered the qualifying fray by demolishing the Swiss 3-0 with a double from Wayne Rooney who struck two more superb goals in the 4-2 defeat of Croatia which lifted Sven-Goran Eriksson's men into the quarter-finals. Eriksson conceded afterwards that Rooney had made the most explosive competition impact since Pele in the 1958 World Cup.

Group C produced a most dramatic climax which was horribly painful for Italy. They thought they had reached the quarter-finals when Antonio Cassano struck a stoppage-time winner against Bulgaria only to find that Denmark and Sweden, almost as late, had fashioned the 2-2 draw which condemned them to an early exit.

Italy, while squealing with hilarious irony about suspicions of a Nordic fix, had only themselves to blame – starting with the opening goalless draw against Denmark from which Francesco Totti drew a three-match ban afer spitting at Christian Poulsen. They then played superbly for half the next match against Sweden but, reverted to suicidal type, substituted forwards with defenders, and conceded both the initiative and a spectacular late equalizer.

Veteran manager Karel Bruckner's impressive Czech Republic topped Group D with a game to spare and were also the only team with a 100 per cent record after the group stage. Holland slipped through as runners-up. The Czechs, having struggled to open with a 2-1 comeback win over outsiders Latvia, then seized top spot and a certain quarter-finals place by memorably overcoming Holland 3-2 in Aveiro, in the finest match of the finals.

The end of the first phase added up to eight nations out of the competition (Spain, Russia, Croatia, Switzerland, Italy, Bulgaria, Germany and Latvia) and four managers out of a job – Iñaki Saez (Spain), Otto Baric (Croatia), Giovanni Trapattoni (Italy), Plamen Markov (Bulgaria) and Rudi Voller (Germany).

Portugal opened the quarter-finals in dramatic fashion. They harnessed the momentum provided by victory over Spain to defeat England on penalties despite falling behind after only two minutes to Michael Owen. England's heads went down when Rooney broke a bone in his foot on 23 minutes. Ashley Cole played with enormous tenacity to stifle Ronaldo but Portugal were well worth an equalizer even though they had to wait until eight minutes from time for

Eusebio fights back the tears as Greek skipper Theo Zagorakis and his men celebrate their shock victory in Lisbon.

striker Helder Postiga to head past David James in the England goal.

England thought they had won it in the last minute but Sol Campbell's headed goal from Beckham's right wing corner was contentiously ruled out by Swiss referee Urs Meier. As England's attack began to stutter into life in extra time, so Portugal took the lead superbly through Rui Costa. This time it was England's turn to hit back through Lampard after John Terry headed back a Beckham corner.

Unfortunately, England's captain remained out of luck with his penalties. He launched the shootout sequence by firing high over the bar for a third successive failure. Rui Costa missed Portugal's third kick, but when the duel went to sudden death Aston Villa's Darius Vassell saw England's seventh penalty saved by Ricardo. The goalkeeper then extended his hero's status by waving away Nuno Valente and converting the winning kick.

Holland also benefited from a shootout to defeat Sweden 5-4 after a goalless draw. Arjen Robben struck the decisive first Dutch kick in sudden death after yet another Aston Villa player – Swedish skipper Olof Mellberg – had seen his effort superbly saved by Fulham's Edwin Van der Sar.

The Nordic rout was completed when Denmark collapsed 3-0 to the Czech Republic for whom Milan Baros struck twice in three minutes around the hour to add to an earlier gift header for Jan Koller. Baros, with five goals, would subsequently be hailed as the finals' top scorer.

The last shred of Big Five credibility was wiped out when Greece toppled holders France 1-0. Rehhagel had demanded that his men perform like the heroes of ancient Greece and Charisteas entered the pantheon with a decisive 64th-minute 'free' header. It was the first time Greece had beaten France in seven meetings dating back

to 1958. "News of what we have done tonight is going round the world from here to New York, down to Rio de Janeiro and back up to Los Angeles," said Rehhagel jubilantly. French boss Jacques Santini did not even offer the injury absence of Patrick Vieira by way of excuse as he prepared to start his Premiership career at Tottenham earlier than expected.

The Greeks continued to defy logic, hierarchy and tradition in the semi-finals, defeating the Czechs on the silver goal rule in Oporto. The Czechs were handicapped by a knee injury which forced the first-half departure of Nedved. Greek sweeper Traianos Dellas loped forward in the last second of the first half of extra time to head home the match-winning corner.

The bitter irony for the Czechs was

that from July 1, that very day, the silver goal had been outlawed by the International Board, surviving only here because this one tournament crossed the law change deadline.

The tournament thus ended, as it had begun, with Greece facing Portugal. The hosts had made harder work than they should of scrambling through 2-1 against Holland on strikes from Ronaldo and Maniche, who curled in the finest goal of the finals.

The abiding mystery of the match was how such a pedestrian Dutch side had managed to progress so far. But that was nothing compared with the mystery of how Greece managed to upstage the giants of European soccer and come through to take the crown with their final fling at the hosts' expense.

THE FINAL

2004 (Portugal)

PORTUGAL 0 (0)
GREECE 1 (0)
Charisteas 56

Estadio Da Luz, 62,865

GREECE: Nikopolidis; Kapsis, Dellas; Seitaridis, Zagorakis, Katsouranis, Basinas, Fyssas; Charisteas, Giannakopoulos (Venetidis 75); Vryzas (Papadopoulos 80).
PORTUGAL: Ricardo; Miguel (Paulo Ferreira 42), Ricardo Carvalho, Jorge Andrade, Nuno Valente; Costinha (Rui Costa 60); Figo, Deco, Maniche, Ronaldo; Pauleta (Nuno Gomes 73).

TOP SCORER
5 **BAROS** (Czech Republic)

EURO 2008

Spain, for so many years Europe's most frustrating national team, finally turned a long, long corner in triumphing in Vienna.

In winning the 2008 European Championship by defeating Germany 1-0, they apologised in style for years of under-performing at World Cups and European Championships.

Spain were worthy winners of their first major prize since 1964. They won all their six games - albeit the quarter-final against Italy thanks to two fine penalty saves by Iker Casillas – and were far better winners in the final than the scoreline suggested.

A first-half goal from Fernando

Torres brought Spain a second European title 44 massive years after their one and only and rewarded their first appearance in a final since defeat by hosts France in 1984. Victory provided belated fulfilment for a country which had to rely for international jewels on the club glories of Real Madrid and Barcelona.

Overall Euro 2008 generated a lot of soccer fun. It had some excellent soccer, some gripping drama – mostly involving Turkey –

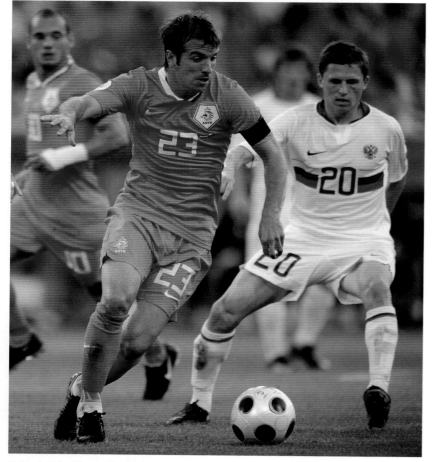

Holland's Rafael Van der Vaart takes on Russia's Igor Semshov in a Euro 2008 quarter-final match.

and a modicum of awful, unambitious soccer; it had some outstanding goals and superb saves.

An intriguing factor was the selection of the diligent, perceptive Barcelona midfielder Xavi Hernandez as official player of the tournament. But the destination of that accolade underlined a dearth of outstanding centre-forward play. Co-hosts Austria and Switzerland as well as Greece, Croatia, France and even Italy suffering from their strikers' poor form and finishing and the goal average was a disappointing 2.48 per game.

The jury remained out on co-hosting. European federation UEFA worked hard to produce a tournament which ran together as seamlessly as possible between Austria and Switzerland considering the different legal systems and different currencies.

The snag is that co-host countries have, by virtue of their modest size, only modest national teams. Any major sports event needs national, host momentum. That demands either that the host public believe their team can win or that they can at least go beyond the group stage. But middle-nation soccer nations such as Austria and Switzerland cannot generate that belief or thus excitement or momentum.

In Switzerland, even in Basel on match days, the casual visitor would have been in ignorance that a major soccer event was taking place. In Austria the practical staging of matches in Innsbruck and Salzburg left a lot to be desired and it took the Greek fans to awaken Salzburg to the event. Klagenfurt was just too small and too distant to catch even a minor

fever except on match days. The stadia were the minimum size to meet UEFA's organisational standards and accounted for the modest 37,076 average attendance.

UEFA also blundered in applying the flawed concept of making mutual results the first factor to split teams level on points. Thus concluding matches in several groups were unnecessarily "dead" – which would not have been the case had goal difference been the first factor. A return to goal difference might also amend attitudes to goal scoring. It was disappointing to see the top-scorer award being carried off by a player, Spain's David Villa, who managed "only" four goals.

All in all, however, it was perfectly understandable that UEFA president Michel Platini should have declared himself, on the eve of the final, "a very happy president."

Portugal topped Group A ahead of Turkey who owed their progress to two late goals from Nihat Kahveci which converted a prospective 2-1 defeat against the Czech Republic into a 3-2 win. Co-hosts Switzerland slid out despite beating the already-qualified Portuguese by 2-0 in the concluding outing.

Croatia made an impressive start to the finals by winning all their three games in Group B, including a 2-1 victory over Germany who finished runners-up. Co-hosts Austria went the same eliminatory way as Switzerland, managing only one goal in their three games – and that was a penalty converted by Ivica Vastic in a 1-1 draw with fellow failures Poland.

Group C was the most dramatic with Holland magnificent and Italy fighting back in gritty fashion after collapsing 3-0 against the Dutch in the first match. France were a major disappointment. They were held goalless by Romania, were thrashed 4-1 by Holland then fell apart 2-0 against Italy. Remarkably manager Raymond Domenech, despite contentious choices of personnel

Spain's players celebrate after their 1-0 victory over Germany in the 2008 European Championship Final.

and tactics, somehow escaped the sack on his return home.

Romania were one of two teams whose unambitious approach shamed their presence at the finals. The other culprits were Sweden in Group D which was won commandingly by Spain. Russia qualified as runners-up despite losing 4-1 to Spain in their opener. Captain Andrei Arshavin returned from suspension just in time to inspire a last-match 2-0 win over Sweden which lifted them into the last eight.

The knockout stages brought more drama and upset. Portugal, with Cristiano Ronaldo a disappointment, went down 3-2 to fast-starting Germany while Holland surprisingly fell 3-1 to Arshavin-inspired Russia in extra time. Shootouts decided the other two ties. Spain, thanks to the shootout agility of captain Iker Casillas, overcame jinx rivals Italy 4-2 after a goalless draw while Turkey beat Croatia 3-1 after a 1-1 stalemate.

The Croats could not believe their ill fortune. They thought they had reached the semi-finals when Mario Klasnic broke the deadlock in the last minute of extra time – only for Semih Senturk to punish their celebratory lack of concentration with an instant equalizer. Semih was also one of the Turks' match-winning penalty takers.

Turkey's luck ran out, however, against Germany in the semi-finals. Much of Europe missed the drama, after a thunderstorm wiped out TV pictures of the Germans grabbing a 3-2 win after three goals in the last 11 minutes.

Spain used a comparatively easy 3-0 win over Russia as their springboard to an ultimate victory which happily justified their status as pre-final favourites. They had won all their five games (albeit one on penalties) compared with the Germans' four, lost none compared with Germany's one and outscored

their opponents by 11-10. They had also conceded fewer goals, three compared with six.

Everything went according to plan in the first half. Torres first headed against a post and then struck what proved the winner on 33 minutes after Philipp Lahm allowed the Liverpool striker to accelerate around behind him and slide a shot beyond advancing keeper Jens Lehmann.

Desperate situations demand desperate measures. Germany brought on striker Kevin Kuranyi for midfielder Tomas Hitzlsperger and piled forward. The gamble nearly paid off when the superb Michael Ballack thumped a volley just wide of Casillas's right-hand post and then threw in a cross which forced the keeper to fly left to deny the leaping Kuranyi.

Spain would once have caved in. But this team, under Luis Aragones, in his last game as national coach, were made of sterner stuff. They resisted superbly and might even have scored again only for midfielder Marcos Senna to arrive just too late in front of an open goal. Senna thumped the turf in frustration. But he did not have long to wait before making history as first Brazilian-born player to win a European Championship.

His impressive contribution, as midfield anchor, to Spain's winning effort from first game to final was appropriate. After all, it was long since time that a foreigner gave something back to the national team of a country in which imported stars have traditionally stolen the local boys' thunder.

THE FINAL

2008 (Austria & Switzerland)
SPAIN 1 (1)
GERMANY 0 (0)
Torres 33

Erst-Happel-Stadion, 51,428
SPAIN: Casillas; Sergio Ramos, Puyol, Marchena, Capdevila; Senna; Iniesta, Xavi, Fabregas (Xabi Alonso 63), David Silva (Santi 66); Torres (Guiza 78).
GERMANY: Lehmann; Friedrich, Mertesacker, Metzelder, Lahm (Jensen 46); Frings, Hitzlsperger (Kuranyi 57); Schweinsteiger, Ballack, Podolski; Klose (Gomez 78).

TOP SCORER
4 **VILLA** (Spain)

COPA AMERICA

The South American Championship is the oldest running international competition in the world. Contested by CONMEBOL, it is 50 years older than its European equivalent.

The first tournament was not an official championship (it was instead an "extraordinario") in 1910. Argentina decided to arrange a tournament involving themselves, Uruguay, Brazil and Chile. Brazil withdrew before the tournament began, but on May 29, 1910, Uruguay beat Chile 3-0 in the very first South American Championship match in Buenos Aires.

Almost 40,000 crowded into the Gimnasia ground to see the great rivals, Argentina and Uruguay, battle it out for the inaugural title, but they were to be disappointed. The fans burned one stand and the match was abandoned before it started. A day later a rearranged match was staged at Racing Club's ground, where only 8,000 saw Argentina win 4-1.

The second tournament, in 1916, was organized to celebrate Argentina's centenary as an independent country. Argentina and Uruguay again clashed in the "decider", with the Uruguayans avenging their defeat of six years

previously. Three years later the 1919 tournament still stands out as one of the most important in the history of the event. The Brazilian club Fluminense had built a 20,000-capacity stadium for the finals which are considered a watershed in the history of soccer in Brazil. It had been viewed, until then, to be a sport favoured by the upper classes in their private clubs. Suddenly, soccer became the people's game.

Brazil reached the final by defeating Chile 6-0 and Argentina 3-1. Uruguay beat Chile 2-0 and Argentina 3-2. The final ended in a 2-2 draw so a replay was ordered. Brazil's hero was centre-forward Arthur Friedenreich. But the stars of the game were the goalkeepers – 16-year-old Saporiti from Wanderers of Montevideo for Uruguay and Marcos Carneiro de Mendoca from host club Fluminense for Brazil. The 90 minutes failed to produce a goal. Neither did the 30 minutes' extra time. So the teams chose to play on

until one of them scored – the first "golden goal" in international soccer history. The teams had played a further 13 minutes – taking the match duration to two hours 13 minutes – when Saporiti could only parry a header from Neco and Friedenreich volleyed into the net.

Between 1916 and 1959 the tournament was held, on average, every two years in one country. Uruguay won six of the first 11 tournaments. Argentina then gained the upper hand winning 11 of the 18 tournaments from the 1920s to the 1950s.

Argentina's greatest era in the competition began in 1955 in Chile. The hosts believed they could win for the first time but they lost the concluding match 1-0 to the Argentines.

The Argentines should have won again in 1956, but complacency set in and they lost the decider – and thus their crown – to hosts Uruguay.

The following year's championship, in Lima, Peru, in 1957, remains one of the fondest memories of Argentine soccer. They sent a team featuring one of the great inside forward trios in South American history – Humberto Maschio, Antonio Valentin Angelillo and Sivori. No-one could withstand them. Argentina opened with an 8-2 destruction of Colombia; Maschio scored four goals, Angelillo two. They beat Ecuador 3-0 (Angelillo two and Sivori); beat Uruguay 4-0 (Maschio two, Angelillo and Sanfilippo); beat Chile 6-2 (Angelillo two, Maschio two, Sivori and Corbatta); and beat Brazil 3-0 (Angelillo, Maschio and Cruz). The Argentines lost their last match by 2-1 to hosts Peru, but they didn't care. The

Brazil's Julio Baptista celebrates scoring in their 3-0 victory over Argentina in 2007.

crown was already theirs. Not only that, but Argentina were the hot South American tip to win the World Cup the following year in Sweden.

A South American team did win in Stockholm, but not Argentina. They flopped. The reason was simple: within weeks of the Triumph of Lima, Maschio, Angelillo and Sivori had all been lured away to Italy. Ever afterwards they were known bitterly, after the popular film of the day, as the "Angels With Dirty Faces".

Ironically Argentina did pip Brazil to win the next title, in 1959. But the tournament was marred by another pitched battle. No fewer than ten players needed treatment in hospital before the match could continue.

Brazil won 3-1 with a hat-trick from Paulo Valentim. But they failed to win the title after drawing 1-1 with hosts Argentina in the last match. Argentina took the title instead.

Brazil's first four victories were all on

Omar Sivori scores another goal on Argentina's route to 1957 championship success in Peru.

home soil but it was unlucky that, when they were at their peak in the 1960s, only two tournaments were staged.

After an experiment with a two-leg knock-out format, the competition returned to a finals system in 1987 in Argentina – with old rivals Uruguay winning. Brazil hosted the 1989 event and won their first title in 40 years, and Argentina won in 1991.

In 1993, in Ecuador, the tournament underwent another face-lift. Mexico and the United States were invited to take part as guests, and three first round groups produced eight quarter-finalists. Mexico, almost spoiled the party by reaching the Final, where they lost 2-1 to Argentina. Mexico and the USA were invited again in 1995 in Uruguay and this time it was the US turn to embarrass their hosts, reaching the semi-finals before losing 1-0 to Brazil. But Brazil lost in the Final to hosts Uruguay, 5-3 in a penalty shoot-out. Brazil made up for lost time by claiming the Cup in 1997 and 1999.

Colombia won at home in 2001 with a 1-0 Final victory over invitees Mexico. Brazil, victims of quarter-final giant-killing by Honduras, made amends by taking the 2004 title on a penalty shootout against Argentina. Brazil's takeover of the tournament was interrupted by Colombia who, in 2001, scored a 1-0 victory in the final over invitees Mexico. However Brazil made amends for their shock quarter-finals upset by Honduras by regaining the cup in 2004 and retaining it in 2007.

The South American confederation, by now, had decided to settle the event on a four-year calendar basis in the year after a World Cup.

Brazil defeated Argentina on penalties in the 2004 final and struggled a little in their opening group in Venezuela in 2007, losing their opening match 2-0 to Mexico. They caught light, however, in the knockout stages, thrashing Chile 6-1, edging old rivals Uruguay on penalties after a 2-2 draw then wiping out Argentina 3-0 in the final. Robinho, the new starlet from Pele's old club Santos, ended the tournament as its six-goal top scorer.

COPA AMERICA FINALS

1910	Buenos Aires
1st Argentina, 2nd Uruguay*	
1916	Buenos Aires
1st Uruguay, 2nd Argentina*	
1917	Montevideo
1st Uruguay, 2nd Argentina	
1919	Rio de Janeiro (play-off)
Brazil 1, Uruguay 0 Att: 28,000	
1920	Vina del Mar
1st Uruguay, 2nd Argentina	
1921	Buenos Aires
1st Argentina, 2nd Brazil	
1922	Rio de Janeiro (play-off)
Brazil 3, Paraguay 1 Att: 20,000	
1923	Montevideo
1st Uruguay, 2nd Argentina	
1924	Montevideo
1st Uruguay, 2nd Argentina	
1925	Buenos Aires
1st Argentina, 2nd Brazil	
1926	Santiago
1st Uruguay, 2nd Argentina	
1927	Lima
1st Argentina, 2nd Uruguay	
1929	Buenos Aires
1st Argentina, 2nd Paraguay	
1935	Lima
1st Uruguay, 2nd Argentina*	
1937	Buenos Aires (play-off)
Argentina 2, Brazil 0 Att: 80,000	
1939	Lima
1st Peru, 2nd Uruguay	
1941	Santiago
1st Argentina, 2nd Uruguay*	
1942	Montevideo
1st Uruguay, 2nd Argentina	
1945	Santiago
1st Argentina, 2nd Brazil*	
1946	Buenos Aires
1st Argentina, 2nd Brazil*	
1947	Guayaquil
1st Argentina, 2nd Paraguay	
1949	Rio de Janeiro (play-off)
Brazil 7, Paraguay 0 Att: 55,000	
1953	Lima (play-off)
Paraguay 3, Brazil 2 Att: 35,000	
1955	Santiago
1st Argentina, 2nd Chile	
1956	Montevideo
1st Uruguay, 2nd Chile*	
1957	Lima
1st Argentina, 2nd Brazil	

1959	Buenos Aires
1st Argentina, 2nd Brazil*	
1959	Guayaquil
1st Uruguay, 2nd Argentina	
1963	Bolivia
1st Bolivia, 2nd Paraguay	
1967	Montevideo
1st Uruguay, 2nd Argentina	
1975	Bogota (1st leg)
Colombia 1, Peru 0 Att: 50,000	
	Lima (2nd leg)
Peru 2, Colombia 0 Att: 50,000	
	Caracas (play-off)
Peru 1, Colombia 0 Att: 30,000	
1979	Asuncion (1st leg)
Paraguay 3, Chile 0	
	Santiago (2nd leg)
Chile 1 Paraguay 0 Att: 55,000	
	Buenos Aires (play-off)
Paraguay 0, Chile 0 Att: 6,000	
(Paraguay won on goal difference)	
1983	Montevideo (1st leg)
Uruguay 2, Brazil 0 Att: 65,000	
	Salvador (2nd leg)
Brazil 1, Uruguay 1 Att: 95,000	
1987	Buenos Aires
Uruguay 1, Chile 0 Att: 35,000	
1989	Brazil
1st Brazil, 2nd Uruguay	
1991	Chile
1st Argentina, 2nd Brazil	
1993	Guayaquil
Argentina 2, Mexico 1 Att: 40,000	
1995	Montevideo
Uruguay 1, Brazil 1	
(Uruguay 5-3 on pens). Att: 58,000	
1997	La Paz
Brazil 3, Bolivia 1 Att: 45,000	
1999	Asuncion
Brazil 3, Uruguay 0 Att: 30,000	
2001	Bogota
Colombia 1, Mexico 0 Att: 52,000	
2004	Lima
Brazil 2, Argentina 2 Att: 72,000	
(Brazil 4-2 on penalties)	
2007	Maracaibo
Brazil 3, Argentina 0 Att: 40,000	

NOTES
Details of finals or championship play-offs have been given where applicable. All other tournaments, played on a league basis, only first and second are listed. * unofficial "extraordinarios" tournaments.

OLYMPIC GAMES

Soccer has featured officially at the Games since 1908, but until the Samaranch "revolution", the amateur ethos seemed at odds with senior soccer, which had long been mostly professional.

Trouble erupted as far back as the 1920s, when the four British Associations withdrew from FIFA in a row over broken time payments to players to compensate for loss of income from their regular jobs while they were away playing soccer.

Soccer was first played at the Olympics in 1896, when a scratch tournament involving select teams from Denmark, Athens and Izmir was organized. (The only recorded result was a 15-0 victory for the Danish XI against the Izmir XI.) In Paris in 1900, soccer was again included as a demonstration sport, with Upton Park FC, representing England, beating France 4-0 in the only game played. In 1904 in St Louis, three North American teams entered a demonstration event

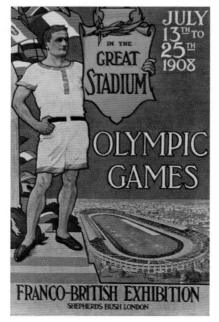

Soccer's first official Olympics, in 1908.

which was won by Galt FC from Ontario representing Canada.

Soccer finally arrived as an accepted Olympic sport with the 1908 Games in London. The England amateur team (not a United Kingdom team), containing many of the best players in the country, won the title, beating Denmark 2-0 in the Final at the White City Stadium. Vivian Woodward, one of the outstanding players of the day, scored the second goal at the White City, and led the England side four years later in Stockholm. Denmark, the best amateur side on the continent, were again England's Final opponents, and again they ended up with the silver medal. Berry, Walden and Hoare (twice) scored for England in a 4-2 win against a Danish side which contained Nils Middelboe, later to play for Chelsea – one of Woodward's clubs.

The 1920 Games in Antwerp were marked by the bad-tempered Final between Belgium and Czechoslovakia. Trailing by two goals, the Czechs felt the referee was favouring the home side and walked off the pitch before the game had ended.

In 1924 the Games returned to Paris and a South American nation, Uruguay, appeared for the first time. The Uruguayans brought with them dazzling ball skills which most Europeans had never seen before. They fielded a side containing some of the greats of Uruguayan soccer: Nasazzi, Andrade, Vidal, Scarone, Petrone, Cea and Romano, and Switzerland were beaten 3-0.

Four years later Uruguay returned,

along with their great rivals Argentina, to take part in the 1928 Amsterdam Games. They met in the Final and Uruguay won after a replay.

Uruguay's successes in 1924 and 1928 helped spark the launch of the World Cup but were, oddly, the last time South America struck gold for well over 70 years. No soccer was played in 1932 and Europe then took control both sides of the war with Italy winning in 1936 and Sweden in London in 1948.

The Swedes, featuring the famous "Grenoli" trio forward line of Gunnar Gren, Gunnar Nordahl and Nils Liedholm (all of whom later joined Milan), beat Yugoslavia 3-1 at Wembley, with Gren scoring twice. Yugoslavia reached the Final again in Helsinki in 1952, but they came up against Hungary's "Magic Magyars". Ferenc Puskas and Zoltan Czibor scored in Hungary's 2-0 win.

The period from 1952 to 1976 was dominated by the "state amateurs" from the Eastern bloc where all players, officially "state amateurs" but indirectly professional, were allowed to compete; in the West, players were openly professional and thus ineligible.

A qualifying series was introduced for the 1956 Melbourne Games. The Soviet Union won gold, beating Yugoslavia 1-0 in the Final in front of 120,000 at Melbourne Cricket Ground.

Yugoslavia made it fourth time lucky in Rome, beating the Danes, 3-1, in the Final. Hungary clinched a hat-trick of titles when they beat Czechoslovakia in 1964 in Tokyo and Bulgaria in 1968 in Mexico City; Poland ended the Hungarians' run by beating

Argentina's Lionel Messi holds off Nigeria's Victor Obinna in the 2008 Olympic Final.

them 2-1 in the Final in Munich in 1972; and East Germany made it seven in a row for Eastern Europe when they beat Poland 3-1 in Montreal in 1976.

FIFA changed the rules for the 1980 tournament, preventing any European or South American who had played in a World Cup qualifier from taking part. Countries from Eastern European had a last hurrah in Moscow, where Czechoslovakia

beat East Germany 1-0. But the new eligibility ruling, even if only an unsatisfactory compromise, did break the monopoly in 1984, when France won gold in Los Angeles.

The 1988 tournament in Seoul featured a host of top professional players and many emerging youngsters yet to play in the World Cup. Ironically, the Soviet Union again struck gold, beating Brazil 2-1 in the Final.

For 1992, the rules were changed again to restrict teams to players aged 23. Hosts Spain won a superb final, beating Poland 3-2 with goals from Kiko (two) and Abelardo. They were unable to hang on to their medals, however, four years later at the Atlanta Olympics.

Yet none of the soccer matches were played in Atlanta itself – a discourtesy which grated with FIFA, particularly after the world body had bent the rules again to permit each nation to field three over-age players. The hope of Olympic president Juan Antonio Samaranch was that this would encourage mainstream nations to send a handful of star names whose presence would contribute promotional support to US soccer. In fact, it was not a mainstream nation who carried off gold at all but Nigeria who made history as the first African winners, beating Argentina 3-2 in the Final.

Cameroon emulated their example four years later in Sydney, winning a penalty shoot-out against Spain, before Argentina restored the status quo with a first Olympic triumph of their own in Athens in 2004. Eight of the 18-man squad who beat Paraguay 1-0 went on to the World Cup finals in 2006 though only one, defensive midfielder Javier Mascherano, was retained for the gold medal defence in Beijing in 2008.

Argentina were favourites from the outset with a team bossed in midfield by the Juan Roman Riquelme and electrified in attack by Leo Messi and the Atletico Madrid striker Sergio Aguero. They won all their six games, with their most satisfying win being seeing off Brazil by 3-0 in the semi-finals. They then beat Nigeria 1-0 in a heat-draining final.

WOMEN'S WORLD CUP

The Women's World Championship, as it is known officially, is one of the newest international competitions in the game.

The Women's World Cup – though that is not quite its official title – was launched in 1991 as a further plank in FIFA's bid to make soccer more user-friendly to a United States audience ahead of the men's World Cup finals three years later.

The reasoning was perfectly obvious: the United States has shown a far greater commitment and enthusiasm for organized women's soccer than any other country. Appropriately, the

Americans were winners of the inaugural women's event that year in China. The US, led by an outstanding player in Michelle Akers-Stahl, beat Norway 2-1 in the Final.

Norway took their revenge four years later in Sweden. This time they boasted the outstanding player in the tournament in Helge Riise. The impact she made in her native land can be assessed from the fact that Egil Olsen, coach to the men's national team,

included her among his three nominations in the annual FIFA Footballer of the Year award. In the 1995 final the Norwegians defeated Germany 2-0 in Stockholm. Riise scored the first goal in front of a crowd of more than 17,000 fans.

A year later, in 1996, women's soccer was included in the Olympic Games for the first time, largely thanks to pressure exerted by the American soccer community because the Games were being staged in Atlanta. A world record crowd for a women's soccer match saw the US beat China 2-1 in the final in Athens, Georgia.

Further evidence of the respect being won by the women's game came in 1997 with an invitation to top Canadian referee Sonia Denoncourt to referee top-level men's league matches in Brazil, one of the most testing soccer arenas in the world.

Two more years and the Women's World Cup hit the international headlines as never before. The United States was a natural choice as host and crowds turned out in nationalistic excitement. When the men's finals were staged in the US in 1994 it was always known that the host team would not be among the big players. But the women's tournament was a different matter.

The confidence of American coach Tony Di Cicco was fully justified. Mia Hamm, Foudy and Kristine Lilly scored the goals in the opening 3-0 win over Denmark; Hamm, Lilly, Akers, Cindy Parlow, Tiffany Milbrett (two) and an own goal swept Nigeria aside 7-1. The Americans were through to the quarter-finals even before they strolled past South Korea

3-0 in the last group match.

Germany, Norway, China and Sweden were the only nations capable of testing the hosts. The Germans were disposed of 3-2 in the quarter-finals though only after the US hit back twice from being behind 1-0 and 2-1. Brandi Chastain made her first, but not last, headlines by scoring an own goal to give Germany the lead on five minutes then scoring the 49th-minute equaliser for 2-2. Joy Fawcett claimed the winner on 66 minutes. The 2-0 semi-final defeat of an overawed Brazil was simple by comparison.

China came through to the final from the other side of the draw, inspired by the nimble, dynamic Sun Wen – a regular runner-up behind one or other of the Americans down the years in the FIFA Women's World Player of the Year awards.

The final was staged amid an all-American expectation in the Rosebowl in Pasadena, where the men's final had been staged in 1994. Like that final, this one also ended goalless and went to penalties. Liu Ying failed with the third Chinese kick and victory was the Americans when Chastain converted their fifth. Chastain, famously, whipped off her shirt in victorious delight. For better or worse, the subsequent pictures earned her more worldwide fame than any of her goals.

China's international status in the women's game earned the right to host the 2003 World Cup. Unfortunately, the SARS epidemic in the early summer forced FIFA to transfer the finals back to the US. But all was not well with the women's game. On

Germany's Birgit Prinz dribbles the ball to score against Brazil in the 2008 Olympics.

September 16, three weeks after the conclusion of its third season and two days before the start of the World Cup, the Americans' own professional league, WUSA, collapsed because of a fatal lack of adequate sponsorship.

FIFA president Sepp Blatter, who had once declared that "soccer in the 21st century will be feminine" was baffled, saying: "Of course, I regret it whenever a league shuts down but I am especially surprised at the timing of the announcement just before the World Cup which would given the game in the States new impetus."

The league declared 387 employees redundant. At least 50 of them were already poised to kick off the World Cup – including 19 Americans, seven Chinese, six Norwegians, six Canadians, four Australians, three Germans, two Brazilians, two French and one Swede.

The writing was on the wall as far as US world domination was concerned. Germany scored 13 goals in Group C and hit another seven against Russia in the quarter-finals to earn a semi showdown with their American hosts. Ironically, Maren Meinert, Prinz and captain Bettina Wiegmann drew on all their WUSA experience to score the goals which sent the US out 3-0.

Sweden beat Canada 2-1 in the other semi-final and took the lead in the final through Hanna Ljungberg, whose power had raised speculation of a transfer to Italian men's soccer with Perugia. Ljungberg struck three minutes before half-time but a minute after the break Germany were level.

No further goals sent the match into extra time which had lasted just eight minutes when German reserve defender Nia Kunzer headed the golden goal winner.

China, having lost the 2003 finals at short notice through ill health, were obvious hosts for 2007 when the anticipation for the event was caught up with preparations for the Olympic Games a year further forward in Beijing. The Chinese expected to make amends for two runners-up places by capitalising victoriously on host advantage but the event did not run to plan.

Instead Germany became the first nation to win a second consecutive Cup after dominating, literally, from start to finish. They defeated Brazil 2-0 in the final to climax a campaign which they had launched in devastating fashion by humiliating Argentina 11-0. Prinz, now by far the finest European women's player, scored a hat-trick. It was both the largest win and the highest scoring match in the history of the Women's World Cup but the negative aspect was in the inmplication that the women's game was not developing worldwide at the pace some people had expected.

Not surprisingly Germany topped Group A ahead of England for whom star forward Kelly Smith scored twice in both a 2-2 draw with Japan and a 6-1 thrashing of Argentina. The United States and North Korea came through from Group B, Norway and Australia from Group C then the fancied pairing of Brazil and China from Group D. Brazil's Marta underlined her status as the world's top player by scoring a hat-trick against New Zealand and two more in a 4-0 win over China. Attacking partner Christiane scored the other two goals.

England's World Cup campaign was ended decisively, 3-0, in the quarter-finals by the United States. They were joined in the semi-finals by Brazil and Germany and also, surprisingly, by Norway. The Norwegians threw a domestic pall over the tournament by defeating China 1-0 in Wuhan and were then comprehensively outplayed 3-0 by Germany in the semi-finals. Far more of a surprise was Brazil's 4-0 rout of the US in the other semi-final.

Marta and Christiane each scored twice apiece once more but could not weave the same old magic in the final against the Germans. Captain Prinz and midfield soldier Simone Laudehr scored the goals.

Brandi Chastain in the most famous winning pose in the history of women's soccer after her penalty decider against China in 1999.

OLYMPIC GAMES WOMEN'S TOURNAMENT

2000 SYDNEY	
NORWAY 3 (Espeseth 44, R Gulbrandsen 78, Mellgren 102 golden goal)	
USA 2 (Milbrett 5, 90)	
2004 ATHENS	
USA 2 (Tarpley 39, Wambach 112)	
BRAZIL 1 (Pretinha 73) (after extra time)	
2008 BEIJING	
BRAZIL 0	
USA 1 (Lloyd 96) (after extra time)	

WOMEN'S WORLD CUP FINALS

1995 STOCKHOLM, SWEDEN	
Norway 2 (Riise 37, Pettersen 41)	
Germany 0	
1999 PASADENA, USA	
United States 0	
China 0	
aet, United States won 5-4 on pens	
2003 LOS ANGELES, USA	
Germany 2	
(Meinert 46, Kunzer 98 golden goal)	
Sweden 1 (Ljungberg 41)	
2007 SHANGHAI	
Germany 2 (Prinz 52, Laudehr 86)	
Brazil 0	

OTHER INTERNATIONAL COMPETITIONS

FIFA UNDER-17 WORLD CHAMPIONSHIP

FIFA has, as one its central missions, the encouragement of soccer at grass roots level, and the Under-17 (Junior) and Under-20 (Youth) World Championships are crucial elements of that process. The Under-17 World Championship in particular has shown that skilful soccer is not confined to Europe and South America. Of the 13 tournaments held so far, Africa has won five times and Asia once. However, European nations have frequently sent only reserve squads because of a conflict of dates with domestic league demands.

FIFA WORLD UNDER-17 CUP FINALS

1989	**SAUDI ARABIA 2-2 SCOTLAND** (Saudi Arabia won 5-4 on penalties)
1991	**GHANA 1-0 SPAIN**
1993	**NIGERIA 2-1 GHANA**
1995	**GHANA 3-2 BRAZIL**
1997	**BRAZIL 2-1 GHANA**
1999	**BRAZIL 0-0 AUSTRALIA** (Brazil won 8-7 on penalties)
2001	**FRANCE 3-0 NIGERIA**
2003	**BRAZIL 1-0 SPAIN**
2005	**MEXICO 3-0 BRAZIL**
2007	**NIGERIA 0-0 SPAIN** (Nigeria won 3-0 on pens)
2009	**SWITZERLAND 1-0 NIGERIA**

FIFA WORLD UNDER-20 CUP

This cup reflects the gap between Europe and South America and the rest of the world which exists from this level up. The reasons for this are too numerous to list, but socio-economic problems and the strong club base in Europe and South America are important factors. It was 30 years before Ghana recorded a first success for Africa.

FIFA WORLD UNDER-20 CUP FINALS

1981	**WEST GERMANY 4-0 QATAR**
1983	**BRAZIL 1-0 ARGENTINA**
1985	**BRAZIL 1-0 SPAIN**
1987	**YUGOSLAVIA 1-1 WEST GERMANY** (Yugoslavia won 5-4 on penalties)
1989	**PORTUGAL 2-0 NIGERIA**
1991	**PORTUGAL 0-0 BRAZIL** (Portugal won 4-2 on penalties)
1993	**BRAZIL 2-1 GHANA**
1995	**ARGENTINA 2-0 BRAZIL**
1997	**ARGENTINA 2-1 URUGUAY**
1999	**SPAIN 4-0 JAPAN**
2001	**ARGENTINA 3-0 GHANA**
2003	**BRAZIL 1-0 SPAIN**
2005	**ARGENTINA 2-1 NIGERIA**
2007	**ARGENTINA 2-1 CZECH REPUBLIC**
2009	**GHANA 0-0 BRAZIL** (Ghana won 4-3 on penalties)

AFRICA CUP OF NATIONS

The Africa Cup of Nations is the blue riband event of African soccer, and the tournament is as old as the Confederation of African Football itself. Held every two years in a nominated country, the tournament has grown from humble beginnings to embrace the whole continent.

The first finals took place in Khartoum in 1957 and involved only Sudan, Egypt and Ethiopia. South Africa were initially due to take part,

AFRICA CUP OF NATIONS FINALS

1957	**EGYPT 4-0 ETHIOPIA**
1959	**1ST EGYPT, 2ND SUDAN**
1962	**ETHIOPIA 4-2 EGYPT** (aet)
1963	**GHANA 3-0 SUDAN**
1965	**GHANA 3-2 TUNISIA** (aet)
1968	**CONGO KINSHASA (ZAÏRE) 1-0 GHANA**
1970	**SUDAN 1-0 GHANA**
1972	**CONGO 3-2 MALI**
1974	**ZAÏRE 2-2 ZAMBIA** (aet)
	ZAÏRE 2-0 ZAMBIA (replay)
1976	**1ST MOROCCO, 2ND GUINEA**
1978	**GHANA 2-0 UGANDA**
1980	**NIGERIA 3-0 ALGERIA**
1982	**GHANA 1-1 LIBYA** (aet) (Ghana won 7-6 on penalties)
1984	**CAMEROON 3-0 NIGERIA**
1986	**EGYPT 0-0 CAMEROON** (aet) (Egypt won 5-4 on penalties)
1988	**CAMEROON 1-0 NIGERIA**
1990	**ALGERIA 1-0 NIGERIA**
1992	**IVORY COAST 0-0 GHANA** (aet) (Ghana won 11-10 on penalties)
1994	**NIGERIA 2-1 ZAMBIA**
1996	**SOUTH AFRICA 2-0 TUNISIA**
1998	**EGYPT 2-0 SOUTH AFRICA**
2000	**CAMEROON 2-2 NIGERIA** (aet) (Cameroon won 4-3 on penalties)
2002	**CAMEROON 0-0 SENEGAL** (aet) (Cameroon won 3-2 on penalties)
2004	**TUNISIA 2-1 MOROCCO**
2006	**EGYPT 0-0 IVORY COAST** (aet) (Egypt won 4-2 on penalties)
2008	**EGYPT 1-0 CAMEROON**
2010	**EGYPT 1-0 GHANA**

and were scheduled to play Ethiopia in the semi-final, but would only send either an all-black team or an all-white team. The CAF insisted on a multi-racial team, South Africa refused and withdrew, and, until readmitted to the CAF in 1992, they took no further part in African or international soccer.

Egypt won the first tournament and the same three nations took part in the second, which Egypt hosted in 1959. Ethiopia hosted the third tournament in 1962, where Tunisia and Uganda took part for the first time.

Ghana and Nigeria joined for the 1963 tournament, held in Ghana, with two groups of three producing the two finalists – Ghana and Sudan. The hosts won 3-0 and went on to become the dominant force in African soccer.

Two years later, in Tunisia, the Ghanaians won again, this time beating the hosts 3-2 after extra time.

The tournament had by now grown from its original three to 18 entrants, and a qualifying tournament was introduced to produce eight finalists, with the hosts and holders qualifying for the final round automatically.

In 1972, in Yaounde, Zaire's neighbours Congo won the title, beating Mali 3-2 in the Final. But Zaire returned in 1974 to beat Zambia in the Final. Morocco won in 1976 in Ethiopia, and surprisingly, it remains Morocco's only African title thus far.

Nigeria won their first African Nations Cup title on home soil in 1980 and the 1982 tournament in Libya saw the return of Ghana to the African throne. The two-overseas-players rule, which had become impractical with so many of them earning a living in Europe, was abolished, and nations could choose their best line-ups again, and Cameroon emerged for their only victory in the 1984 finals.

In 1986 Egypt hosted the tournament, which was marked by incidents on and off the field. After a

Egypt's Mohamed Aboutrika celebrates his African Nations Cup-winning penalty against Ivory Coast.

very dull 0-0 draw the hosts won the Final, 5-4 on penalties, to the delight of the 100,000 crowd.

Cameroon recovered by winning the 1988 title in Morocco and a crowd of 50,000 saw them win 1-0 with a goal after 55 minutes.

In 1992 a new name was added to the list of winners: the Ivory Coast. The tournament was expanded to 12 teams. The Final finished goalless and, in one of the most amazing penalty shoot-outs ever seen, the Ivory Coast won 11-10.

Winners in 1996, South Africa were again finalists in 1998. Ajax forward Benni McCarthy was voted star player and was joint top-scorer with seven goals. But he failed to score in the final and South Africa lost 2-0 to Egypt.

That victory was the first of the Pharaohs' four in a 12-year spell which included a hat-trick in 2006, 2008 and 2010. But it was also significant, in a negative way, that the 2006 final was goalless and one single goal was sufficient in both the succeeding two finals. African players were being exported in droves but they brought home defensive rigour and safety-first attitudes which compromised the Cup's entertainment value.

ASIAN CUP

The Asian Cup for national teams started in 1956 and, until the 1980 tournament, was dominated by South Korea and Iran. Since then Kuwait and Saudi Arabia have enjoyed success, reflecting the shift of power in Asian soccer towards the Arab states, extended by Iraq's sensational win in 2007.

ASIAN GAMES

The first Asian games were organized by India in 1951, and six countries brought teams for the soccer tournament. Since then the Asian Games soccer tournament has expanded to include most of the continent, and is effectively the region's second continental championship.

CONCACAF 'GOLD CUP' CHAMPIONSHIP

The Central American Championship has been contested, under various formats and with varying numbers of participants, since 1941. Costa Rica have the most outstanding record, with 10 victories, including three in a row between 1960 and 1963. In 1991 Mexico and the United States were joint hosts for what was now

Iraq's captain Younis Mahmoud celebrates winning the AFC Asian Cup in 2007.

upgraded as the CONCACAF Gold Cup. The United States beat Honduras on penalties in that final but Mexico dominated the rest of the 1990s, winning three times in a row. Canada were surprise winners in 2000 before regional giants US and Mexico took over – winning the next five cups between them

CONFEDERATIONS CUP

Sponsor pressure to squeeze every last drop of value out of the four-year contracts with FIFA led to the launch of the Confederations Cup in 1992. The purpose was to bring together all the regional title-holders midway between World Cups. Controversially, it just deepened the world fixture quagmire with tragic consequences. The Cameroon captain, Marc-Vivien Foe, collapsed and died during a semi-final against Colombia at the 2003 event in France. FIFA then decided to stage the event only once every four years instead of every two and use it as a World Cup warm-up for the hosts.

ASIAN CUP FINALS	
1956	SOUTH KOREA 2-1 ISRAEL
1960	SOUTH KOREA 3-0 ISRAEL
1964	ISRAEL 2-0 INDIA
1968	IRAN 3-1 BURMA
1972	IRAN 2-1 SOUTH KOREA
1976	IRAN 1-0 KUWAIT
1980	KUWAIT 3-0 SOUTH KOREA
1984	SAUDI ARABIA 2-0 CHINA
1988	SAUDI ARABIA 0-0 SOUTH KOREA
	(Saudia Arabia won 4-3 on penalties)
1992	JAPAN 1-0 SAUDI ARABIA
1996	SAUDI ARABIA 0-0 UAE
	(Saudi Arabia won 4-2 on penalties)
2000	JAPAN 1-0 SAUDI ARABIA
2004	JAPAN 3-1 CHINA
2007	IRAQ 1-0 SAUDI ARABIA

ASIAN GAMES FINALS	
1951	INDIA 1-0 IRAN
1954	TAIWAN 5-2 SOUTH KOREA
1958	TAIWAN 3-2 SOUTH KOREA
1962	INDIA 2-1 SOUTH KOREA
1966	BURMA 1-0 IRAN
1970	BURMA 0-0 SOUTH KOREA
1974	IRAN 1-0 ISRAEL
1978	NORTH KOREA 0-0 SOUTH KOREA
1982	IRAQ 1-0 KUWAIT
1986	SOUTH KOREA 2-0 SAUDI ARABIA
1990	IRAN 0-0 NORTH KOREA
	(Iran won 4-1 on penalties)
1994	UZBEKISTAN 4-2 CHINA
1998	IRAN 2-0 KUWAIT
2002	IRAN 2-1 JAPAN
2006	QATAR 1-0 IRAQ

NOTE The trophy was shared in 1970 and 1978

CONCACAF GOLD CUP WINNERS			
1941	COSTA RICA	1977	MEXICO
1943	EL SALVADOR	1981	HONDURAS
1946	COSTA RICA	1985	CANADA
1948	COSTA RICA	1989	COSTA RICA
1951	PANAMA	1991	USA
1953	COSTA RICA	1993	MEXICO
1955	COSTA RICA	1996	MEXICO
1957	HAITI	1998	MEXICO
1960	COSTA RICA	2000	CANADA
1961	COSTA RICA	2002	USA
1963	COSTA RICA	2003	MEXICO
1965	MEXICO	2005	USA
1967	GUATEMALA	2007	USA
1969	COSTA RICA	2009	MEXICO
1971	MEXICO		
1973	HAITI		

FIFA CONFEDERATIONS CUP WINNERS	
1992	ARGENTINA
1995	DENMARK
1997	BRAZIL
1999	MEXICO
2001	FRANCE
2003	FRANCE
2005	BRAZIL
2009	BRAZIL

EUROPEAN CHAMPIONS LEAGUE CUP

The UEFA Champions League, originally the European Champions Club Cup, is not only the most lucrative club event in the world but has become the most prized trophy in world club soccer.

Reputations have been made and broken over the five decades since the competition began, and it has always had an aura of romance and glamour about it, some say even more so than national team competition.

The idea came, typically, from the French. Gabriel Hanot, a former international and then editor of the French daily sports paper L'Equipe, was angered by English newspaper claims that Wolverhampton Wanderers were the champions of Europe because they had beaten Honved and Moscow Spartak in friendlies.

Hanot decided to launch a competition to find the real champions of Europe and, in 1955, invited representatives of 20 leading clubs to Paris to discuss the idea. The meeting was attended by 15 clubs and it was agreed that the competition should begin in the 1955–56 season. FIFA supported the idea and consequently UEFA approved the tournament and took over its administration.

Eligibility was restricted to the champions of each country plus the holders after the first series, to play home and away on a knock-out basis, and the result decided by the aggregate score – except in the Final, which was a one-off match played at a neutral venue. Drawn ties used a play-off to produce a winner until 1967, when a new method was introduced, whereby the team scoring most away goals progressed. In the event of a draw even on away goals, a toss of a coin decided the winner until 1971, when penalty kicks were introduced.

Sixteen teams entered the first tournament, though several were not really champions, merely replacements for teams who could not, or would not, take part. Chelsea, the English champions, stayed away on the short-sighted advice of the notoriously aloof Football League, while Hibernian, who had finished fifth, represented Scotland.

By a fortunate coincidence, just as the competition was launched, Real Madrid were blossoming into one of the greatest club sides the world has ever seen. In the Final, fittingly played in Paris, Real faced a Stade de Reims side containing the legendary Raymond Kopa, who joined Real the following season. Despite leading twice, Reims could not cope with Real's deadly forwards, Alfredo Di Stefano, Hector Rial and Francisco 'Paco' Gento, and lost 4–3.

Real went on to win the Cup for the next four years running, a feat which is unlikely to be matched in the modern game. Fiorentina (1957), Milan (1958), Reims again (1959) and Eintracht Frankfurt (1960) were all beaten in successive finals, with the match against Frankfurt being arguably the best final ever. In front of 135,000 fans at Hampden Park in Glasgow, Real thrashed the West German champions 7–3, with Ferenc Puskas, the "galloping major" of the great Hungarian team of the 1950s, scoring four goals and Di Stefano a hat-trick.

Real's run came to an end the next season in the second round, beaten by deadly rivals Barcelona, who went on to contest the Final with Portugal's Benfica – the newly emerging kings of Europe. Benfica contained the bulk of the Portuguese national side and would go on to play in five Finals during the 1960s, and win two of them. The first, against Barcelona, was won even without Eusebio, the Mozambique-born striker.

Eusebio was in the line-up the following year, though, when Benfica faced Real Madrid, and he scored twice as Benfica won 5–3 despite Puskas scoring another hat-trick for Real. In 1963, the Lisbon Eagles appeared in their third consecutive Final, but lost 2–1 to Italy's Milan.

Milan's victory was the first of three for the city of Milan in the mid-1960s, as their city rivals Internazionale emerged to win the trophy in 1964 and 1965. Coached by the legendary Helenio Herrera, Inter fielded a host of international stars including Italy's Giuliano Sarti, Tarcisio Burgnich, Giacinto Facchetti and Sandro Mazzola,

Real Madrid's Juan Santisteban (left) foils Reims' Roger Piantoni in Stuttgart in 1959.

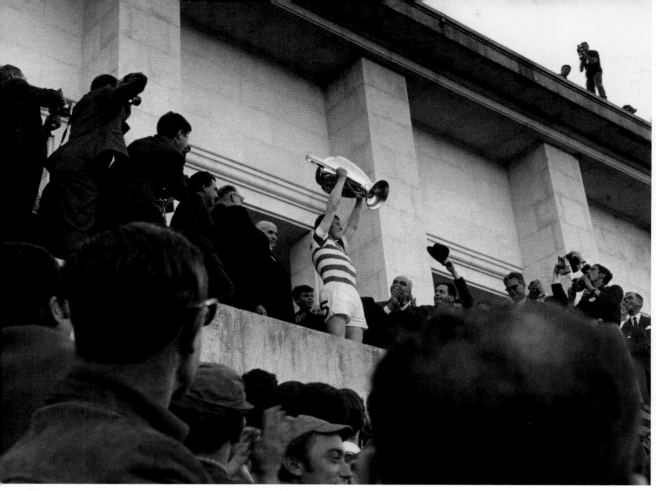

Lisbon's Estadio Nacional rises to Celtic's Billy McNeill after the historic comeback victory over Internazionale.

Jair from Brazil plus the Spaniard Luis Suarez. Their Final victims were Real Madrid and Benfica.

Real's sixth triumph, in 1966, marked the end of an era in the European Cup. For the first 11 years of its existence, the Cup had only been won by clubs from Latin countries – Spain, Portugal and Italy – and of the first 22 finalists, 18 were from these three countries. Now the power-base of European club soccer shifted from the Mediterranean to northern Europe – Britain, Holland and Germany to be precise. The 1967 Final paired Inter with Scotland's Celtic. The Scots, under the guiding hand of the great Jock Stein, won everything open to them that season, rounding off with a fine 2-1 win over the Italians in Lisbon. The breakthrough had been made, and Manchester United consolidated the position by becoming England's first winners the following season.

Benfica were the unfortunate losers again in the Final, at Wembley, where Matt Busby's side won 4-1 after extra time with goals by Bobby Charlton, George Best and a young Brian Kidd.

Milan regained the trophy in 1969, with a 4-1 demolition of Ajax in Madrid, but it was the last Latin success in the Cup for 17 years as Holland, Germany and then England dominated during the 1970s and early 1980s.

Feyenoord of Rotterdam were the first Dutch winners, in 1970, when they narrowly defeated Celtic 2-1 after extra time in Milan. Feyenoord's great rivals, Ajax, maintained Holland's position the following season when they beat Panathinaikos of Greece 2-0 at Wembley. It was the first of three consecutive titles for the Amsterdam club, which contained the bulk of the thrilling Dutch "total football" side of the 1970s. Johan Cruyff was the star of the show, and his departure in 1973

for Barcelona saw Ajax cede European command to Bayern Munich. Stars such as Franz Beckenbauer, Sepp Maier, Gerd Müller, Paul Breitner, Georg Schwarzenbeck and Uli Hoeness went on to form the core of the West German side which won the European Championship in 1972 and the World Cup in 1974. Bayern needed a replay to dispose of Atletico Madrid in the first of their three wins, Hoeness and Müller scoring two each in a 4-0 win after a 1-1 draw in Brussels. In 1975 they beat Leeds United 2-0 in a hotly-disputed match in Paris, after which distraught Leeds supporters trashed the stadium. Bayern's hat-trick came with a 1-0 win over France's Saint-Etienne in Glasgow.

Then, in 1977, Liverpool clinched the first of six consecutive English victories with a 3-1 win over Germany's Borussia Mönchengladbach, veteran defender Tommy Smith scoring the decisive second goal. Liverpool, under

Barcelona goalkeeper Andoni Zubizarreta and the rest of the team celebrate with the European Cup for the first time in 1992.

Bob Paisley, retained the trophy at Wembley the following year with a win over Belgium's Club Brugge. Kenny Dalglish, signed from Celtic to replace the Hamburg-bound Kevin Keegan, scored the only goal.

In 1979 a cruel twist of fate drew Liverpool with Brian Clough's Nottingham Forest in the first round. Forest had come up from the Second Division to win the title in successive seasons, and they out-fought Liverpool to win 2-0 on aggregate. In the Final, against Swedish outsiders Malmo, Britain's first million-pound footballer, Trevor Francis, scored the only goal in a very tight game. Forest retained the Cup in 1980, ironically against Hamburg, who included Keegan in their side.

Liverpool returned for their third triumph the following season with a 1-0 win over Real Madrid in Paris, and Aston Villa became the fourth English winners in 1982, when they beat Bayern Munich 1-0 in Rotterdam. Hamburg broke the English monopoly in 1983 by beating Juventus 1-0, but it was only a brief respite. Liverpool, the

most successful side in the history of English soccer, returned for the 1984 Final and, against all the odds, beat AS Roma in Rome. After a 1-1 draw, Liverpool won 4-2 on penalties.

The period of English dominance was about to end, however, and the 1985 Final at the Heysel Stadium in Brussels will always be remembered, not for the soccer, but for the appalling loss of life. Before the game, against Juventus, a group of English hooligans charged at the Italian fans behind one of the goals. A safety wall collapsed and 39 people, mostly Italian, lost their lives in the crush. Two weeks previously, 53 supporters had died in a fire at Bradford City's Valley Parade ground, leaving the image of English soccer at its lowest point ever.

Juventus won a meaningless game 1-0 with a Michel Platini penalty. More significantly, Liverpool were banned from European competitions indefinitely, while all English clubs were banned for five years. The ban took some of the gloss off the Cup because, without the English clubs,

who had such a fine record in the competition, winning it was less satisfactory. Meanwhile the hooligan problem still remained.

Shootout success paid off twice in three years - for Steaua Bucharest against Terry Venables's Barcelona and for PSV Eindhoven against Benfica - before Milan reclaimed the trophy. Two years in a row they rewarded media magnate Silvio Berlusconi's investment in the Dutch triumvirate of Ruud Gullit, Marco Van Basten and Frank Rijkaard.

Berlusconi and other director of the big clubs were instrumental then in sparking the evolution towards the present Champions League. They threatened a breakaway super league if UEFA did not provide them with the guarantee of mini-league income. They got their way before Barcelona put a gloss on the saga by winning the cup for the first time. An extra-time rocket from Ronald Koeman edged out Sampdoria at Wembley..

Then, in 1993, came the biggest scandal the competition has ever

seen. After 37 long years, the French drought in the European Cup seemed to have ended. Marseille beat Milan 1-0 in Munich, with a goal by centre-back Basile Boli, but the celebrations were cut short when it emerged that Marseille officials had allegedly paid three Valenciennes players to "take it easy" in a league game shortly before the Final. Chaos ensued, but in the end, Marseille were banned from Europe and stripped of their French title and the right to play São Paulo in the World Club Cup. Marseille's outspoken owner – socialist, millionaire and politician Bernard Tapie – was ultimately punished with a jail term.

The format changed slightly again for the 1994 tournament, with the re-introduction of semi-finals for the winners and runners-up of the two Champions League groups. But nothing could stop Milan, their 4-0 defeat of Barcelona was a stunning display.

Yet more tinkering with the format followed in 1994-95 as UEFA sought a compromise with the bigger clubs' desire for a TV-bankrolled European League.

The holders and top seven seeded teams went through directly to the Champions League, which was expanded to 16 teams in four groups of four; the eight other teams came from a preliminary round involving the teams ranked eight to 23 in the seeding list. All the other "minnow" national champions were off-loaded into an expanded UEFA Cup as the price of progress.

The first redeveloped Champions League Cup Final - as it was rebranded - was won by Ajax of Amsterdam, duly succeeded by Juventus, Borussia Dortmund and a revived Real Madrid.

Another revivalist tour de force was achieved by Manchester United in 1999. Two goals in injury time from substitutes Teddy Sheringham and Ole Gunnar Solskjaer turned what looked like a sure 1-0 defeat by Bayern Munich into a win. United became the first English club to achieve the treble of European Cup, domestic league and F.A. Cup in the same season.

In Europe, United's rule lasted not even a year. In both 2000 and 2001 they lost in the quarter-finals to the eventual winners, first Real Madrid, yet again, and then Bayern Munich. Valencia set an unhappy record in those two years by becoming the first club to lose finals in successive seasons.

Spain remained a dominant force, however, with history repeating itself to uncanny effect in 2002. Real Madrid returned to Hampden Park, scene of their most glorious triumph in 1960, to claim a record-extending ninth crown after a 2-1 win over German opposition again in the shape of the tough Bayer Leverkusen. Zinedine Zidane volleyed a winning goal as spectacular as anything pastmasters Di Stefano or Puskas had produced in their day.

The intensity of modern soccer mitigated against the sort of domination Madrid had established back in the 1950s. Thus they fell in the 2003 semi-finals to Juventus who then lost the first all-Italian final in a penalty shootout to Milan at Old Trafford.

Welcome proof that financial muscle was not everything then followed in 2004 when Milan, Madrid and runaway Premiership leaders Arsenal all tumbled in the quarter-finals. Roman Abramovich's newly-enriched Chelsea fell in the semis and modest Porto duly outgunned first-time finalists Monaco 3-0.

Modest Porto made headlines in 2004 for their ambitious and outspoken coach Jose Mourinho. He immediately left for newly Russian-enriched Chelsea but, though they ended the next Premier season a massive 37 points ahead of Liverpool it was Rafa Benitez and his men who made the season memorable. Losing 3-0 at half-time to Milan, they stormed back for a 3-3 draw and shootout triumph which turned skipper Steven Gerrard and Jerzy Dudek into Anfield legends.

The increasing power of the Premier League was now making itself irresistibly felt in the Champions League. Every subsequent final saw an English presence. Not that the English sides had everything their own way once they got there.

In 2006 Arsenal reached the final for the first time and faced Barcelona in the Stade de France. This could have been the perfect homecoming for the Gunners' French manager Arsene Wenger. Unfortunately, Arsenal began disastrously when goalkeeper Jens Lehmann became the first player sent off in a Champions' final for bringing down Samuel Eto'o. Arsenal did manage to snatch an unlikely lead through Sol Campbell but they succumbed 2-1 ultimately to fatigue and superior weaponry.

A further beating for Premiership soccer followed the next year when Liverpool lacked, this time, the necessary comeback fire and lost 2-1 to vengeful Milan in Athens. Veteran striker Pippo Inzaghi struck both goals as the Italians wrapped up a seventh Champions' crown and a fifth for their magnificent captain, Paolo Maldini.

He was now 38, however, and ageing legs as much as anything cost Milan their crown the following season. That suited the English contingent who provided three of the four semi-finalists for the second season in a row. Chelsea beat Liverpool and Manchester United saw off Barcelona to set up the first all-English final in the competition's history.

Manchester United, as in 1999, conjured up the spirit of good fortune right at the death to win on penalties after a 1-1 draw. Chelsea, who had Didier Drogba sent off in extra time, were blue indeed as captain John Terry fluffed their decisive spot-kick.

The following year saw Barcelona cruise through the knockout stage to reach the final by crushing Lyon and Bayern Munich then edging Chelsea with a late goal from Andres Iniesta. Manchester United, similarly decisive, outplayed Jose Mourinho's Internazionale then Porto and subsequently English rivals Arsenal.

The only semi-final snag for United was having midfielder Darren Fletcher sent off and thus suspended from the final. His absence proved crucial as Barcelona triumphed 2-0 with goals from Samuel Eto'o and Lionel Messi.

Manchester United won their second Champions League in 2008 following a tense penalty shoot-out.

UEFA CHAMPIONS LEAGUE 2010

Jose Mourinho continued to write the script as Internazionale regained European pre-eminence by snatching back the Champions Cup they had had last won in 1965.

Victory over Bayern Munich in Madrid not only secured a historic treble – Inter had already won the Italian league and cup – but fulfilled destiny for president Massimo Moratti. Father Angelo had been president when Inter first won the European Cup in the mid-1960s.

Only one cloud spoiled the Spanish sunshine: Mourinho, having guided Inter to European glory quit immediately after the game to stay on in Madrid with Real.

The campaign began with UEFA president Michel Platini increasingly concerned about the financial fragility of many clubs as well as the increasing prevalence of match-fixing. FK Pobeda of Macedonia were barred for eight years from European competition for manipulating a 2004 Champions League qualifier against Pyunik of Armenia while German police cracked down on a Europe-wide betting and match-fixing ring.

At least Platini had the consolation of witnessing a positive reorganization of the qualifying system. His wish to open up the group stage to more clubs from mid-ranking nations meant a revised qualifying system whose success was represented by group stage debuts for Standard Liege (Belgium), APOEL (Cyprus), Wolfsburg (Germany), Debrecen (Hungary), AZ Alkmaar (Netherlands), Unirea Urziceni (Romania) Rubin Kazan (Russia) and Zurich (Switzerland).

None made it any further though Rubin Kazan went out with their heads held high after springing a major surprise in winning 2-1 away to reigning champions Barcelona in Group F. The all-conquering Catalans had carried off, in glorious attacking style, all six titles on offer in 2009. But the defeat by the Russians offered an early reminder of the fleeting nature of soccer invincibility.

Intriguingly in the same group, bearing in mind later events, Barcelona drew goalless away to Mourinho's Inter and won 2-0 back in Camp Nou. The clubs knew each other well, apart from the Mourinho connection; during the summer they had swapped strikers with Cameroon's Samuel Eto'o quitting Barcelona for Inter and Sweden's Zlatan Ibrahimovic heading the opposite way.

Honours were ultimately shared as Barcelona headed the group with Inter their runners-up.

Elsewhere Bordeaux and Bayern Munich edged out Juventus in Group A while the knockout stage also beckoned Manchester United and CSKA Moscow (Group B), Real Madrid and Milan (Group C), Chelsea and Porto (Group

Internazionale striker Diego Milito runs away in celebration after scoring one of his two Champions League final goals against Bayern Munich.

In 2010 Jose Mourinho got his 'special' hands on the Champions League trophy for the second time.

could give of their best after two days on the road. They scored first in Milan but lost 3-1 to goals from Sneijder, Maicon and Milito; Inter then held out superbly, despite the early contentious expulsion of Thiago Motta, to lose 'only' 1-0 in Camp Nou. In six games against Mourinho teams Barcelona's Leo Messi, world and European player of the year, had yet to score once.

Defeat was doubly painful for Barcelona. Not only had they lost their European crown but they had forfeited the chance to secure another in the home of old rivals Real Madrid.

The final matched Inter against a Bayern side back on the climactic stage for the first time since they beat Valencia in a penalty shootout in 2001. They had not been considered likely finalists this time but, after barely surviving a stuttering start to the season, coach Louis Van Gaal had turned spirit and fortunes around. Fellow Dutchman Arjen Robben made the difference out on the pitch. He scored decisive late away goals against both Fiorentina in the second round and Manchester United in the quarter-finals.

The Old Trafford recovery – Bayern conceded two goals in the first seven minutes to fall behind on aggregate – was in the best traditions of unlikely German comebacks. As United goalkeeper Edwin Van der Sar said ruefully: "Germans teams are never beaten until they are in the bus on the way to the airport."

Robben would further enhance his star status with the first-leg winner in a comfortable 4-0 aggregate dismissal of Lyon in the semi-finals. Lyon had earlier seen off a Real Madrid side for whom the massive expenditure of £85m on Portugal flyer Cristiano Ronaldo from Manchester United and £55m on Brazil playmaker Kaka from Milan proved worthless.

Madrid's only connection with the final was to provide the venue and a touch of history. The showdown in the Estadio Santiago Bernabeu was the

first played on a Saturday, a switch from the usual midweek date spurred by Platini's love of the old cup traditions and wish to hand the final an even higher, weekend-dominating profile than it already boasted.

Bayern missed suspended French forward Franck Ribery, even appealing in vain to the Court of Arbitration for Sport before conceding his absence; Inter's presence was shadowed by a Madrid media frenzy concerning Mourinho's expected imminent switch from Inter to Real.

The script was entirely his own: Inter's victory, secured by two goals from Milito, duly rewarded president Massimo Moratti with the trophy for the first time since the presidential days of his father oil baron father Angelo in 1964 and 1965.

Inter had won the treble of Champions League plus domestic league and cup; Bayern had to be satisfied with 'merely' the German domestic double. They dominated possession but were outgunned on the counter-attack. Eto'o thus won his third Champions League and Mourinho carried off his second with a different club . . . to remain as special as ever.

D), Fiorentina and Lyon (Group E), Sevilla and Stuttgart (Group G) plus Arsenal and Olympiacos (Group H).

Inter kicked off the knockout stage against Chelsea, the club at which Mourinho had first defined himself as The Special One.

They had fallen to English opposition in Manchester United the previous season and Chelsea caught the backlash. As Mourinho said later: "Instead of crying I had asked myself a lot of questions about why weren't we strong enough to defeat United?"

His conclusions had meant the arrival of Lucio to shore up central defence, Dutch playmaker Wesley Sneijder in midfield and reliance in attack on the sheer hard work and cohesive talents of Gabriel Milito.

Mourinho's tactical acumen provided the platform for acclaimed

victories both home and away. The Stamford Bridge clash was an emotional return with which Mourinho coped far better than his old Stamford Bridge pupils under one-time Milan boss Carlo Ancelotti.

CSKA Moscow were edged by single-goal victories both home and away in the quarter-final to bring Mourinho back up against Barcelona.

Crucially, in all the circumstances, the first leg was in the Stadio Meazza at San Siro just as a cloud of volcanic ash spewed out by the erupting Eyjafjallajoekull in Iceland grounded flights across western Europe.

Barcelona thus had to travel to Milan by bus.

Coach Pep Guardiola and his players denied any negative influence but it was hard for Barcelona fans to believe that highly-tuned and toned athletes

EUROPA LEAGUE

When UEFA was formed in 1954, FIFA vice-president Ernst Thommen devised a European competition to test teams from trade fair cities. It evolved from Fairs Cup to UEFA Cup and is now the Europa League.

Peter Lorimer thumps a trademark free kick past Partizan keeper in Leeds' 2-1 win in 1967.

The original title was the cumbersome International Inter-Cities Fairs Cup and the first 'edition' was equally cumbersome – taking three years to complete between 1955 and 1958 when Barcelona crushed a London XI 2-2, 6-0 in the final.

The second tournament, 1958-60, drew 16 entrants, mostly club sides, and was played on a straight home-and-away knock-out basis. Barcelona, strengthened by the arrivals of Hungary's Sandor Kocsis and Zoltan Czibor, retained the trophy without losing a match. Their opponents were again English, but this time it was Birmingham and not London who made it to the Final. A 0-0 draw on a terrible pitch in Birmingham set Barcelona up for the 4-1 return win, with goals by Eulogio Martinez, Czibor (two) and Luis Coll.

Barcelona's attempt to win a hat-trick of Fairs Cups ended in the second round of the 1960-61 tournament, at the unlikely hands of Scotland's Hibernian. The Edinburgh side only took part because Chelsea withdrew, but, having beaten Lausanne in the first round, they surprised everybody by beating the holders in the next round. Birmingham again made it the Final, where they faced Italy's Roma, who needed a third match to beat Hibs in the semi-finals. This extended semi-final meant that the Final itself was held over until the following season, by

which time Roma had added to an already impressive line-up.

Birmingham did well to force a 2-2 draw at home, but were beaten 2-0 in Rome in the return... their second successive defeat in the Final.

The organizers had decided to allow three teams per country to enter the 1961-62 tournament, which had an entry of 28, and now the Spanish showed their dominance. Barcelona and Valencia reached the Final, with Valencia powering to a 7-3 aggregate victory over their countrymen. Valencia held on to the trophy the following season, beating Dinamo Zagreb 4-1 on aggregate in the Final, but were thwarted in their hat-trick bid by another Spanish side, Zaragoza. The 1964 Final was played as a one-off match in Barcelona, where goals by Juan Manuel Villa and Marcelino secured a 2-1 win for Zaragoza.

The 1965 competition attracted 48 entries, and for the first time the Cup left Latin Europe, and headed east. Hungary's Ferencvaros fought their way through from the first round, with victories over Spartak Brno, Wiener Sport-Club, Roma, Athletic Bilbao and Manchester United, to face Juventus in the Final. The Italians, having safely negotiated the two opening rounds, were given a bye in the quarter-finals as the organizers sought to balance the numbers. This, coupled with

the fact that the Final (again a one-off match) was in Turin, seemed to give Juve a definite advantage. But Ferencvaros produced a defensive formation that surpassed even the Italians' catenaccio, and a single goal by Matos Fenyvesi after 74 minutes was enough.

The 1966 tournament returned to the two-game format for the Final, but the earlier rounds were marked by violence. Chelsea were pelted with rubbish in Rome, Leeds and Valencia fought a battle which resulted in three dismissals, and Leeds then had Johnny Giles sent off in the semi-final against Real Zaragoza. The Spanish again emerged triumphant, as Barcelona and Real Zaragoza met in the Final. A goal by Canario in the first leg at the Nou Camp gave Zaragoza the edge, but a hat-trick by the teenager Pujol in the return sealed a 4-2 victory for the Catalans, who won the trophy for the third time on a 4-3 aggregate.

The tournament was now moving into an era of English dominance. Leeds reached the 1967 Final, where

they lost to Dinamo Zagreb, but they made amends the following season by beating Ferencvaros 1-0 on aggregate in the Final, after going unbeaten in previous rounds. This was the first of six consecutive victories by English clubs during the late 1960s and early 1970s.

In 1971 the Cup returned to Leeds, who beat Juventus. The first leg of the Final, in Turin, was abandoned at 0-0 because of heavy rain, and in the re-arranged fixture the Leeds team forced an excellent 2-2 draw. Juve were more threatening in the return, but could only manage a 1-1 draw, which meant Leeds won on away goals. Both sides were unbeaten in the tournament, and it was most unfortunate for the Italians to play 12 matches, without defeat, and still not win the Cup.

UEFA then took over full command of the competition to herald a largely northern European era with victories by Tottenham Hotspur (over Wolverhampton Wanderers), Liverpool (twice) and Ipswich Town, Holland's Feyenoord and PSV Eindhoven as well as Germany's

Borussia Monchengladbach (twice) and Eintracht Frankfurt. Juventus were brief Latin interlopers in 1977, beating a Bilbao side who featured the future Spanish federation president and FIFA vice-president Angel Maria Villar.

IFK Gothenburg became the first Swedish winners of a European trophy when they beat Hamburg in 1982, and they went on to win again in 1987, beating Dundee United. Between those two victories, Anderlecht and Real Madrid dominated the competition. Anderlecht beat Benfica 2-1 on aggregate to win the 1983 competition, and they returned to the Final the following year against Tottenham. Both legs produced 1-1 draws, and after extra time produced no winner, Tottenham took the Cup on penalties, reserve goalkeeper Tony Parks saving the decisive kick.

Tottenham's defence of the trophy in 1985 ended in the quarter-finals, where they were narrowly beaten 1-0 on aggregate by Real Madrid. The Spaniards, aided by the German Uli Stielike and the Argentinian Jorge Valdano, went on to beat Hungary's Videoton 3-1 in the Final. Real retained the trophy the following season with a far more impressive demolition of West Germany's Köln. A 5-1 win in Madrid was followed by a 2-0 defeat in Germany, but Real kept the trophy with a 5-3 aggregate margin.

Following Gothenburg's second success in 1987, the Cup was won on penalties for the second time when Bayer Leverkusen and Español contested the Final. Español won the first leg 3-0 at home and looked all set for Spain's ninth victory, but Bayer levelled the aggregate score in the second leg, and then won 3-2 on penalties.

From 1989, until 1999, the UEFA Cup was dominated by Italian clubs, with 14 out of 22 finalists coming from Serie A. In 1989 Napoli, led by Diego Maradona, beat Stuttgart;

Juventus and Fiorentina contested an all-Italian Final in 1990, with Juventus winning 3-1 at home and on aggregate; in 1991 Internazionale narrowly beat Roma 2-1; in 1992 Torino lost to Ajax – who were completing a hat-trick of European trophy wins – but only on away goals after 2-2 and 0-0 draws; and in 1993 Juventus won the again against Borussia Dortmund.

Internazionale overcame Austrians Salzburg to win in 1994, 1-0 in both games. In 1994-95, Juventus and Parma were first and second for most of the Serie A season, and reached both the UEFA and domestic Cup finals. In the UEFA Cup it was the newcomers who prevailed 2-1 on aggregate, with ex-Juventus player Dino Baggio scoring both goals.

The system of entry into the UEFA Cup, based on past performances, ensured that the more successful countries, such as Italy, Germany, Spain and England, received four entrants. However, as more countries joined UEFA, it had to expand the tournament with a preliminary round in mid-July. The rebuilt UEFA-Intertoto Cup was used as a qualifying event for 1995-96. French club Bordeaux entered that way and went all the way to the final – beating Milan in a shock quarter-final – before losing with honour to Bayern Munich. Jürgen Klinsmann scored 15 goals in the tournament, a record for a European club competition.

The Cup stayed in Germany in 1997 when historic Schalke from the Ruhr, appearing in a European final for the first time, defeated Internazionale on penalties in Milan. Inter bounced back a year later to beat their fellow Italians of Lazio 3-0 in the Parc des Princes in Paris. UEFA's decision to abandon the two-leg format in favour of a single-match final was vindicated by a superb display from Inter while Parma maintained Italy's pre-

eminence in 1999. A year later Galatasaray made history by becoming the first Turkish club to reach a European final and the first to win a European trophy – thanks to a shootout victory over Arsenal in Copenhagen after a 0-0 draw.

Liverpool defeated outsiders Alaves 5-4 in 2001 in a sensational

Glory for Borussia's Berti Vogts in 1975.

1958
LONDON SELECT XI 2-2 BARCELONA
BARCELONA 6-0 LONDON SELECT XI
1960
BIRMINGHAM CITY 0-0 BARCELONA
BARCELONA 4-1 BIRMINGHAM CITY
1961
BIRMINGHAM CITY 2-2 ROMA
ROMA 2-0 BIRMINGHAM CITY
1962
VALENCIA 6-2 BARCELONA
BARCELONA 1-1 VALENCIA
1963
DINAMO ZAGREB 1-2 VALENCIA
VALENCIA 2-0 DINAMO ZAGREB 0
1964
REAL ZARAGOZA 2-1 VALENCIA
1965
FERENCVAROS 1-0 JUVENTUS
1966
BARCELONA 0-1 REAL ZARAGOZA
REAL ZARAGOZA 2-4 BARCELONA
1967
DINAMO ZAGREB 2-0 LEEDS UTD
LEEDS UTD 0-0 DINAMO ZAGREB
1968
LEEDS UTD 1-0 FERENCVAROS
FERENCVAROS 0-0 LEEDS UTD
1969
NEWCASTLE 3-0 UJPEST DOZSA
UJPEST DOZSA 2-3 NEWCASTLE
1970
ANDERLECHT 3-1 ARSENAL
ARSENAL 3-0 ANDERLECHT
1971
JUVENTUS 2-2 LEEDS UTD
LEEDS UTD 1-1 JUVENTUS
(Leeds won on away goals)

Atletico Madrid celebrate after beating Fulham in the 2010 UEFA Europa final.

Final in Dortmund. Manager Gerard Houllier's side thus completed a unique treble – for an English club – in carrying off the two domestic cups plus a European trophy.

More "golden oldies" followed their example: in 2002 Feyenoord defeated Borussia Dortmund at home in Rotterdam, then FC Porto became the first Portuguese winners of the UEFA Cup, at the expense of Celtic of Scotland. Porto were the first team to triumph with a "silver goal" – UEFA's new but short-lived method of deciding games in extra-time.

But the pre-eminence now of the all-conquering Champions League had robbed the UEFA Cup of its earlier glamour. Europe's major clubs, gathered together under the banner of G-14, had forced the European federation to open up the elite competition to up to three and four teams per country and this was all at the expense of the secondary competition.

Indeed, the gap in class between the two was such that, most of the time, it was one of the clubs who had been "relegated" out of the Champions League group stage in mid-season which went on to win the UEFA Cup; something of a triumphant cuckoo in the international club soccer nest.

Initially, the strength in depth of the Spanish league carried the UEFA Cup day. Valencia, under the sagacious managership of Rafa Benitez, defeated Marseille in the 2004 final – albeit the French were furious at the first-half expulsion of keeper Fabien Barthez by Italian referee Pierluigi Collina which virtually decided the game and the destination of the medals.

Then Sevilla won twice in a row in 2006 and 2007. They were worthy winners each time under coach Juande Ramos whose sudden emergence as a cup-winning manager subsequently earned him a step across into the English Premier League with Tottenham (with whom he also won the League Cup before the Anglo-Spanish experiment collapsed).

First time around Sevilla, appearing in their first final, beat fellow newcomers in Middlesbrough. But the Spanish outfit had far too much worldly wisdom and won 4-0 with goals from Brazilian Luis Fabiano, Italian Enzo Maresca (two) and Mali's Frederic Kanoute.

The next year was much tighter. This time Sevilla needed penalties and the heroics of keeper Andres Palop before they finally saw off the challenge of Espanyol at Hampden Park. Espanyol thus lost the final in a shootout just as they had to Leverkusen nearly 20 years earlier.

However, a new wind of change was blowing in from the east to threaten western Europe's command. Finally, well over a decade since Soviet sport had been thrown into near-bankrupt chaos by the collapse of communism, with its state funding guarantees, the Russians were back. And, as it proved, not only the Russians.

The new generation of millionaire oligarchs had come to understand soccer's value as the new opium of the people, as a modern Karl Marx might have recast his dismissal of religion. Hence an investment in foreign players and coaches which brought Russian clubs two trophies in four season. First CSKA Moscow scored an outstanding victory over hosts Sporting Clube in Lisbon in 2005 and then Zenit St Petersburg outsmarted Rangers far more conclusively than the 2-0 scoreline suggested in the City of Manchester Stadium in 2008.

The revival of club power among the former Soviet nations was underlined in the last season of the UEFA Cup in 2008-09 when Shakhtar Donetsk, from Ukraine, defeated Germany's injury and suspension-weakened Werder Bremen 2-1 after extra-time.

Both clubs had been parachuted into the UEFA Cup at the halfway stage after finishing only third in their groups in the Champions League but that did not spoil Shakhtar's pride at having become the first Ukrainian club to win a European prize since the country gained independence at the start of the 1990s.

The miners' club from the Donetsk basin had reached the final by defeating domestic rivals Kiev Dynamo, who had just deposed them as national champions, in the semis. They seized early command in the final through Luiz Adriano, one of five Brazilians in their squad. However Bremen, who had also beaten fellow countrymen in Hamburg in the semis, hit back within nine minutes through Naldo.

Appropriately then, it took yet another Brazilian to resolve the deadlock when Jadson shot home nine minutes before the end of extra-time. Shakhtar thus became last winners of the UEFA Cup.

2010 EUROPA LEAGUE

Atletico de Madrid wrote a chapter in both their own and European soccer's history by defeating Fulham in the first final of the Europa League.

The competition had been known previously as the UEFA Cup and, before that, as the Fairs Cup. Victory for Atletico, after extra-time, was only their third in the international club arena. No wonder two-goal match-winner Diego Forlan, his team-mates, club officials, directors and fans celebrated long into the Hamburg night.

Ironically, Hamburg's own club had expected to have been playing in the final themselves in their own home stadium until a painful but decisive semi-final defeat by Fulham. Instead the nearest they came to enjoying their own party was in seeing 'old boy' Tomas Ujfalusi collecting a winner's medal from Michel Platini, UEFA's president.

Platini must have been pleased to see such a positive conclusion to the first season of the rebranded Europa League.

The Fairs and UEFA Cups – until latter years – had been two-leg knockout competitions. Then the first round of the UEFA Cup was converted into a group stage at the urging of clubs who wanted a more secure income stream. Yet the initial system was complex with groups of five teams who played each other only once, home or away depending on the luck of the draw. That made it virtually impossible for fans to work out group prospects.

The Europa League was built on the clearer foundation provided by groups of four clubs. Additional attention was secured, also, by

Platini's success in persuading the law-making International Board to use the Europa League as a test centre for the experiment with two additional goal-line officials.

Fulham, skilfully managed by Roy Hodgson on their first-ever foray into Europe, had reached the final with notable victories over holders Shakhtar Donetsk, Juventus, Wolfsburg and, of course, Hamburg. In the final they played with determination and vigour but, ultimately, lacked a crucial extra ingredient of class and international experience.

Atletico went ahead in the 31st minute after a sweeping move between Jose Antonio Reyes, Simao Sabrosa and 'Kun' Aguero set up Forlan to score. But it was a lead they held for only six minutes. Then Bobby Zamora bulldozed his way across the penalty box and Zoltan Gera's cross was volleyed home by Simon Davies.

Fulham's hopes of forging ahead were reduced in the second half after Zamora was forced off by a long-standing achilles injury. They went close a couple of times only to see Atletico rally in extra time. Five minutes from the end Aguero wriggled in the from the left and Forlan flicked home his low cross.

Fulham manager Hodgson put on a brave face in defeat, saying: "It's been a great competition and we can only say great things about it. The new format is much more interesting because it's much closer to that of the Champions League. UEFA should be congratulated on having two such outstanding competitions which will continue to attract and entertain their public."

UEFA CUP FINALS

1972
WOLVERHAMPTON W 1-2 TOTTENHAM HOTSPUR
TOTTENHAM HOTSPUR 1-1 WOLVERHAMPTON W

1973
LIVERPOOL 3-0 BORUSSIA MÖNCHENGLADBACH
BORUSSIA MÖNCHENGLADBACH 2-0 LIVERPOOL

1974
TOTTENHAM HOTSPUR 2-2 FEYENOORD
FEYENOORD 2-0 TOTTENHAM HOTSPUR

1975
B. MÖNCHENGLADBACH 0-0 TWENTE ENSCHEDE
TWENTE ENSCHEDE 1-5 B. MÖNCHENGLADBACH

1976
LIVERPOOL 3-2 CLUB BRUGGE
CLUB BRUGGE 1-1 LIVERPOOL

1977
JUVENTUS 1-0 ATHLETIC BILBAO
ATHLETIC BILBAO 2-1 JUVENTUS
(Juventus won on away goals)

1978
BASTIA 0-0 PSV EINDHOVEN
PSV EINDHOVEN 3-0 BASTIA

1979
RED STAR BELGRADE 1-1 B. MÖNCHENGLADBACH
B. MÖNCHENGLADBACH 1-0 RED STAR BELGRADE

1980
B. MÖNCHENG'BACH 3-2 EINTRACHT FRANKFURT
EINTRACHT FRANKFURT 1-0 B. MÖNCHENG'BACH

1981
IPSWICH 3-0 AZ 67 ALKMAAR
AZ 67 ALKMAAR 4-2 IPSWICH

1982
IFK GOTHENBURG 1-0 HAMBURG SV
HAMBURG SV 0-3 IFK GOTHENBURG

1983
ANDERLECHT 1-0 BENFICA
BENFICA 1-1 ANDERLECHT

1984
ANDERLECHT 1-1 TOTTENHAM HOTSPUR
TOTTENHAM HOTSPUR 1-1 ANDERLECHT
(aet, Tottenham won 4-3 on penalties)

1985
VIDEOTON 0-3 REAL MADRID
REAL MADRID 0-1 VIDEOTON

1986
REAL MADRID 5-1 KÖLN
KÖLN 2-0 REAL MADRID

1987
IFK GOTHENBURG 1-0 DUNDEE UNITED
DUNDEE UNITED 1-1 IFK GOTHENBURG

1988
ESPAÑOL 3-0 BAYER LEVERKUSEN
BAYER LEVERKUSEN 3-0 ESPAÑOL
(aet, Leverkusen won 3-2 on penalties)

1989
NAPOLI 2-1 STUTTGART
STUTTGART 3-3 NAPOLI

1990
JUVENTUS 3-1 FIORENTINA
FIORENTINA 0-0 JUVENTUS

1991
INTERNAZIONALE 2-0 ROMA
ROMA 1-0 INTERNAZIONALE

1992
TORINO 2-2 AJAX
AJAX 0-0 TORINO
(Ajax won on away goals)

1993
BORUSSIA DORTMUND 1-3 JUVENTUS
JUVENTUS 3-0 BORUSSIA DORTMUND

1994
SALZBURG 0-1 INTERNAZIONALE
INTERNAZIONALE 1-0 SALZBURG

1995
PARMA 1-0 JUVENTUS
JUVENTUS 1-1 PARMA

1996
BAYERN MUNICH 2-0 BORDEAUX
BORDEAUX 1-3 BAYERN MUNICH

1997
SCHALKE 1-0 INTERNAZIONALE
INTERNAZIONALE 1-0 SCHALKE
(aet, Schalke won 4-1 on penalties)

1998
INTERNAZIONALE 3-0 LAZIO

1999
PARMA 3-0 MARSEILLE

2000
GALATASARAY 0-0 ARSENAL
(aet, Galatasaray won 4-1 on penalties)

2001
LIVERPOOL 5-4 ALAVES
(Liverpool won on golden goal)

2002
FEYENOORD 3-2 BORUSSIA DORTMUND

2003
FC PORTO 3-2 CELTIC 2
(Porto won on silver goal)

2004
VALENCIA 2-0 MARSEILLE 0

2005
CSKA MOSCOW 2-1 SPORTING CLUB LISBON

2006
SEVILLA 4-0 MIDDLESBROUGH

2007
SEVILLA 2-2 ESPANYOL
(aet, Sevilla won 3-1 on penalties)

2008
ZENIT ST PETERSBURG 2-0 RANGERS

2009
SHAKHTAR DONETSK 2-1 WERDER BREMEN
(aet)

2010 Europa League
ATLETICO DE MADRID 2-1 FULHAM (aet)

CLUB WORLD CUP

The original World Club Cup was merely a challenge between the champions of Europe and South America. Now FIFA has opened up the tournament to clubs from every region.

Henri Delaunay, the general secretary of UEFA first suggested the idea of a challenge match between the champions of Europe and South America in a letter to CONMEBOL, the South American Confederation, in 1958. His idea provided the impetus for them to launch the Copa Libertadores (the South American Club Cup) because, at that stage, South America had no championship for its clubs

Before 1980, matches in the World Club Cup, or Intercontinental Club Cup as it is sometimes known, were played on a home and away basis, and up until 1968 the result was decided by points, not the aggregate score. This meant that if the clubs won one match each or both were drawn, a decider had to be played.

Despite these tortuous rules, the competition got off to a flying start in 1960, when Real Madrid met Penarol of Uruguay. Madrid had just won their fifth European Cup in a row, with a 7-3 demolition of Eintracht Frankfurt, while Penarol had become the first winners of the Copa Libertadores. The first leg, in Montevideo, produced a 0-0 draw, but in the return two months later Real Madrid pounded the Uruguayans 5-1. The Real forward line was one of the best ever, and contained Del Sol, Di Stefano, Gento and Puskas, who scored twice. A combined attendance of 200,000 watched.

In 1961 it was Penarol's turn to chalk up five goals, this time against the emerging Portuguese eagles, Benfica. However, a solitary Coluna goal in the first leg meant a decider was necessary, and Penarol only just managed to win 2-1 at home against a Benfica side bolstered by a young Eusebio, who was specially flown in.

Benfica represented Europe again in 1962, but this time they ran headlong into Brazil's Santos... and Pele. Santos became one of only four sides to retain the trophy when they beat Milan in 1963.

The next two editions were contested by Internazionale of Italy and Independiente of Argentina, with Inter winning on both occasions.

It was back to South America In 1966, as Penarol won for the third time, beating Real Madrid 2-0 in both legs. From this encouraging start, the World Club Cup ran into severe problems in the late 1960s and early 1970s, largely owing to different styles of play and behaviour.

The 1967 series paired Argentina's Racing Club with Scotland's Celtic. Feelings in Argentina were still running high over their 1966 World Cup quarter-final elimination by England, and the matches degenerated into a bad-tempered farce. It was all square after two matches and the decider, in Montevideo, was doomed before it began. Celtic lost their composure under extreme provocation and had four men sent off. Racing had two men sent off but won 1-0.

The next team to represent South America - for three years running - were Estudiantes de La Plata of Argentina. At home in 1968 they battered Manchester United, who had Nobby Stiles sent off and Bobby Charlton taken off with a shin injury. Under the competition's revised rules, the Argentinians completed a 2-1 aggregate win.

The following year, Milan came off even worse than United. After winning 3-0 at home, Milan were savaged in Buenos Aires, where Nestor Combin had his nose broken and Pierino Prati was kicked in the back while receiving treatment. Milan held on to win 4-2 on aggregate. Three Estudiantes players were imprisoned after the game.

Estudiantes did not learn their lesson, and things were as bad in 1970 when they played Feyenoord, who came out on top after drawing the first leg in Buenos Aires. The following year their countrymen, Ajax, went a step further by refusing to play against Nacional of Uruguay. Panathinaikos, beaten finalists in the European Cup, were appointed by UEFA to replace Ajax, but lost 3-2 on aggregate.

European champions Manchester United celebrate their 1-0 win over South American champions LDU Quito in the 2008 World Club Cup.

After such violent clashes, the value of the competition came into question as a string of European championa declined to play, Thus, in 1980s the format of the World Club Cup was changed. The two-legged tie was replaced by a single game at the National Stadium in Tokyo at the behest of Japanese officials dreaming of the prospect of, one far-off day, hosting the World Cup finals. The car manufacturer Toyota underwrote the costs as sponsor.

The event regained much of its credibility though the cool temperatures, hard pitches – first in Tokyo and then in Yokohama – inspired little memorable soccer. European clubs won 13 times against 12 successes for South America in the years before FIFA stepped in. The world governing body, envious at the sums being raised by UEFA through club soccer, launched its own Club World Championship in 1999.

The first such event, won by Corinthians of Sao Paulo in Brazil, proved a false start because of financial problems. However, in 2005, FIFA then used the 'old' World Club Cup, its December fixture slot and Japanese venue, as a foundation for a revamped Club World Cup which featured all the champion clubs from the game's six geographical regions.

Opening up the event did not disturb the overall balance of power. All five subsequent final matches have matched opposition from Europe and South America. Sao Paulo and Internacional from Brazil won the first two under the new system but command shifted back to Europe for the subsequent three years.

The victory path set by Milan and Manchester United – defeating LDU of Ecuador despite the expulsion of Nemanja Vidic – was followed by Barcelona. However, in a new tournament 'home' of Abu Dhabi in 2009, Leo Messi and Co needed extra-time before seeing off his fellow Argentine countrymen from Estudiantes de La Plata.

WORLD CLUB CUP FINALS

From 1960 to 1979 the World Club Cup was decided on points, not goal difference. Since 1980 it has been a one-off match in Japan.

1960	**PENAROL 0-0 REAL MADRID**
	REAL MADRID 5-1 PENAROL
	Real Madrid won 5-1 on aggregate
1961	**BENFICA 1-0 PENAROL**
	PENAROL 5-0 BENFICA
	PENAROL 2-1 BENFICA (play-off)
1962	**SANTOS 3-2 BENFICA**
	BENFICA 2-5 SANTOS
	Santos won 8-4 on aggregate
1963	**MILAN 4-2 SANTOS**
	SANTOS 4-2 MILAN
	SANTOS 1-0 MILAN (play-off)
1964	**INDEPENDIENTE 1-0 INTERNAZIONALE**
	INTERNAZIONALE 2-0 INDEPENDIENTE
	INTER. 1-0 INDEPENDIENTE (play-off)
1965	**INTERNAZIONALE 3-0 INDEPENDIENTE**
	INDEPENDIENTE 0-0 INTERNAZIONALE
	Internazionale won 3-0 on aggregate
1966	**PENAROL 2-0 REAL MADRID**
	REAL MADRID 0-2 PENAROL
	Penarol won 4-0 on aggregate
1967	**CELTIC 1-0 RACING CLUB**
	RACING CLUB 2-1 CELTIC
	RACING CLUB 1-0 CELTIC (play-off)
1968	**ESTUDIANTES 1-0 MANCHESTER UTD 0**
	MANCHESTER UTD 1-1 ESTUDIANTES
	Estudiantes won 2-1 on aggregate
1969	**MILAN 3-0 ESTUDIANTES**
	ESTUDIANTES 2-1 MILAN
	Milan won 4-2 on aggregate
1970	**ESTUDIANTES 2-2 FEYENOORD**
	FEYENOORD 1-0 ESTUDIANTES
	Feyenoord won 3-2 on aggregate
1971	**PANATHINAIKOS 1-1 NACIONAL**
	NACIONAL 2-1 PANATHINAIKOS
	Nacional won 3-2 on aggregate
1972	**INDEPENDIENTE 1-1 AJAX**
	AJAX 3-0 INDEPENDIENTE
	Ajax won 4-1 on aggregate
1973	**INDEPENDIENTE 1-0 JUVENTUS**
1974	**INDEPENDIENTE 1-0 ATLETICO MADRID**
	ATLETICO MADRID 2-0 INDEPENDIENT
	Atletico Madrid won 2-1 on aggregate
1975	not played
1976	**BAYERN MUNICH 2-0 CRUZEIRO**
	CRUZEIRO 0-0 BAYERN MUNICH
	Bayern won 2-0 on aggregate

1977	**BOCA JUNIORS 2-2 B. MÖNCHENGLADBACH**
	B. MÖNCHENGLADBACH 0-3 BOCA JUNIORS
	Boca Juniors won 5-2 on aggregate
1978	not played
1979	**MALMÖ 0-1 OLIMPIA**
	OLIMPIA 2-1 MALMÖ
	Olimpia won 3-1 on aggregate
1980	**NACIONAL 1-0 NOTTINGHAM FOREST**
1981	**FLAMENGO 3-0 LIVERPOOL**
1982	**PENAROL 2-0 ASTON VILLA**
1983	**GREMIO 2-1 HAMBURG SV**
1984	**INDEPENDIENTE 1-0 LIVERPOOL**
1985	**JUVENTUS 2-2 ARGENTINOS JUNIORS**
	(aet, Juventus won 4-2 on penalties)
1986	**RIVER PLATE 1-0 STEAUA BUCHAREST**
1987	**FC PORTO 2-1 PENAROL** (aet)
1988	**NACIONAL (URU) 2-2 PSV EINDHOVEN**
	(aet, Nacional won 7-6 on penalties)
1989	**MILAN 1-0 NACIONAL** (aet)
1990	**MILAN 3-0 OLIMPIA**
1991	**RED STAR BELGRADE 3-0 COLO COLO**
1992	**SÃO PAULO 2-1 BARCELONA**
1993	**SÃO PAULO 3-2 MILAN**
1994	**VELEZ SARSFIELD 2-0 MILAN**
1995	**AJAX 0-0 GREMIO**
	(aet, Ajax won 4-3 on penalties)
1996	**JUVENTUS 1-0 RIVER PLATE**

1997	**BORUSSIA DORTMUND 2-0 CRUZEIRO**
1998	**REAL MADRID 2-1 VASCO DA GAMA**
1999	**MANCHESTER UNITED 1-0 PALMEIRAS**
2000	**BOCA JUNIORS 2-1 REAL MADRID**
2001	**BAYERN MUNICH 1-0 BOCA JUNIORS**
2002	**REAL MADRID 2-0 OLIMPIA ASUNCION**
2003	**BOCA JUNIORS 1-1 MILAN**
	(Boca won 3-1 on penalties)
2004	**FC PORTO 0-0 ONCE CALDAS**
	(Porto won 8-7 on penalties)
2005	**SÃO PAULO 1-0 LIVERPOOL**
2006	**INTERNACIONAL 1-0 BARCELONA**
2007	**MILAN 4-2 BOCA JUNIORS**
2008	**MANCHESTER 1-0 LDU QUITO**
2009	**BARCELONA 2-1 ESTUDIANTES DE LA PLATA**
	(aet)

Carles Puyol enjoyed a special 2009, lifting the Club World Cup, as well as every other competition entered by Barcelona. With the national team in 2010, Puyol tasted more glory.

OTHER MAJOR CLUB COMPETITIONS

EUROPEAN CUP-WINNERS' CUP

When Lazio held aloft the Cup-Winners' Cup after beating Mallorca at Villa Park, Birmingham in May 1999 they were also celebrating the end of an era – UEFA had decided that the tournament should be scrapped to make way for its expansion of the Champions League and the UEFA Cup. Yet the Cup-Winners' Cup had earned a distinguished place in the history of the game since its launch in the 1960-61 season.

The 1961 final saw Fiorentina beat Rangers and the success of the first tournament encouraged more clubs to get involved, and 23 entered the second in 1961-62. Fiorentina's impressive defence took them all the way again where they met Atletico Madrid in the Final. The match, in Glasgow, produced a 1-1 draw, and when the replay took place – four months later – Atletico won with a 3-0 win.

In the 1963 competition Atletico faced Tottenham in Rotterdam and Jimmy Greaves and Terry Dyson both scored twice as Tottenham won 5-1 to become the first English winners of a European trophy.

Tottenham's reign ended in the second round in 1964, and Portugal's Sporting Lisbon went on to win the Cup against MTK Budapest.

The Cup-Winners' Cup had established itself on the European scene, and 30 clubs entered in 1965. West Ham United, essentially novices in Europe, emulated Tottenham's success by beating TSV Munich 1860 at Wembley. The following year, featured another England–West Germany Final, this time involving Liverpool and Borussia Dortmund; the Germans won.

In 1969 the original draw was abandoned after Soviet troops entered Czechoslovakia, and a new draw, keeping East and West apart, was made. Most Eastern countries were against the idea and withdrew, but the Czechs remained ... and Slovan Bratislava collected the trophy.

For the following three years the Cup stayed in Britain as Manchester City, Chelsea and Rangers all won.

The Rangers victory, however, was marred by ugly scenes in and around the Nou Camp stadium in Barcelona. The lunatic fringe of their supporters invaded the pitch and the team, having done so well to win, were banned for a year and were consequently unable to defend their title.

Leeds United almost made it four in a row for Britain in 1973 when they faced Milan in the Final in Salonika. Milan scored after five minutes through Chiarugi and Norman Hunter and Riccardo Sogliano were sent off for fighting.

Milan reached the Final again the following year, but lost to FC Magdeburg, who became the only East German winners of a European trophy. Kiev Dynamo kept the trophy behind the Iron Curtain with their first win, by beating Ferencvaros 3-0 in Basle in 1975. Belgium's Anderlecht then emerged as the competition's specialists with three successive appearances in the final – of which they won the first and the third. In 1976 they beat West Ham, lost to Hamburg in 1977, and beat FK Austria in Paris.

The 1979 tournament produced the highest-scoring Final ever as Barcelona beat Fortuna Dusseldorf 4-3 in Basle. Valencia retained the Cup for Spain the following season in the first European Final to be decided on penalties. A

Tottenham become the first English club to win a European trophy.

EUROPEAN CUP-WINNERS' CUP FINALS		
1961	**RANGERS 0-2 FIORENTINA**	
	FIORENTINA 2-1 RANGERS	
	Fiorentina won 4-1 on aggregate	
1962	**ATLETICO MADRID 1-1 FIORENTINA** (aet)	
	ATLETICO MADRID 3-0 FIORENTINA	
1963	**TOTTENHAM HOTSPUR 5-1 ATLETICO MADRID**	
1964	**SPORTING LISBON 3-3 MTK BUDAPEST** (aet)	
	SPORT. LISBON 1-0 MTK BUDAPEST (replay)	
1965	**WEST HAM UNITED 2-0 TSV MUNICH 1860**	
1966	**BORUSSIA DORTMUND 2-1 LIVERPOOL** (aet)	
1967	**BAYERN MUNICH 1-0 RANGERS** (aet)	
1968	**MILAN 2-0 HAMBURG SV**	
1969	**SLOVAN BRAT'A 3-2 BARCELONA**	
1970	**MANCHESTER CITY 2-1 GORNIK ZABRZE**	
1971	**CHELSEA 1-1 REAL MADRID** (aet)	
	CHELSEA 2-1 REAL MADRID (replay)	
1972	**RANGERS 3-2 MOSCOW DYNAMO**	
1973	**MILAN 1-0 LEEDS UNITED**	
1974	**FC MAGDEBURG 2-0 MILAN**	
1975	**KIEV DYNAMO 3-0 FERENCVAROS**	
1976	**ANDERLECHT 4-2 WEST HAM UTD**	
1977	**HAMBURG SV 2-0 ANDERLECHT**	
1978	**ANDERLECHT 4-0 FK AUSTRIA**	
1979	**BARCELONA 4-3 FORTUNA DÜSSELDORF** (aet)	
1980	**VALENCIA 0-0 ARSENAL**	
	(aet, Valencia won 5-4 on pens)	
1981	**DYNAMO TBILISI 2-1 CARL ZEISS JENA**	
1982		**BARCELONA 2-1 STANDARD LIÈGE**
1983		**ABERDEEN 2-1 REAL MADRID** (aet)
1984		**JUVENTUS 2-1 FC PORTO**
1985		**EVERTON 3-1 RAPID VIENNA**
1986		**KIEV DYNAMO 3-0 ATLETICO MADRID**
1987		**AJAX 1-0 LOKOMOTIVE LEIPZIG**
1988		**MECHELEN 1-0 AJAX**
1989		**BARCELONA 2-0 SAMPDORIA**
1990		**SAMPDORIA 2-0 ANDERLECHT** (aet)
1991		**MANCHESTER UTD 2-1 BARCELONA**
1992		**WERDER BREMEN 2-0 MONACO**
1993		**PARMA 3-1 ANTWERP**
1994		**ARSENAL 1-0 PARMA**
1995		**REAL ZARAGOZA 2-1 ARSENAL**
1996		**PARIS SG 1-0 RAPID VIENNA**
1997		**BARCELONA 1-0 PARIS SG**
1998		**CHELSEA 1-0 STUTTGART**
1999		**LAZIO 2-1 MALLORCA**

disappointing 0-0 draw in Brussels was decided when Graham Rix missed Arsenal's fifth penalty in the shoot-out, giving Valencia a 5-4 victory.

In the 1981 competition, Welsh Cup winners Newport County, then in the English Fourth Division, caused a sensation by knocking out the holders Valencia in the second round. Newport then lost in the quarter-finals to Carl Zeiss Jena, who went on to contest the Final with Dynamo Tbilisi, who had destroyed West Ham in the quarter-finals. Tbilisi won 2-1 to clinch the Soviet Union's second Cup.

Barcelona won for the second time in four years in 1982, Real Madrid spurned the chance to match their Catalan rivals the next year, when they lost to Aberdeen and Juventus became the third Italian side to win the Cup when they beat FC Porto in 1984.

Everton won it the following season and in 1986 Kiev Dynamo won their second title with an outstanding 3-0 win over Atletico Madrid. Ajax appeared in the next two finals: in 1987 they beat Lokomotive Leipzig, but the following season lost to European debutants Mechelen, in the final.

Barcelona collected their third Cup-Winners' Cup in 1989 and in 1991 Manchester United went all the way to the Final and won 2-1. The match provided Welsh striker Mark Hughes - dumped by Barcelona three years before - with sweet revenge as he scored both United's goals.

In 1992 Werder Bremen beat Monaco, and then Parma completed a remarkable ten-year transition from the Italian Third Division to European trophy-winners in 1993, when they beat Antwerp 3-1 at Wembley.

Arsenal beat Parma 1-0 in 1994, but lost 2-1 to a freak 120th minute goal to Spain's Zaragoza the next season.

Zarargoza's attempt to become the first club to retain the cup faltered in their 1996 quarter-finals against compatriots La Coruña, who fell to Paris Saint-Germain. PSG became only the second French club to win a European trophy when they beat Rapid Vienna 1-0 in the Final. The unwritten law which prevents holders from retaining the cup was again evident in 1997, when PSG fell 1-0 to Barcelona in Rotterdam. A penalty from Ronaldo separated the teams on paper though Barcelona were superior on the day.

The same could not be said of Chelsea when they beat Stuttgart the following year in Stockholm. Vialli was back in his new role as Chelsea player-manager, but it was Gianfranco Zola who scored a superb winner. Chelsea continued the odd tradition of failing to hold onto the trophy, defeated by European newcomers Mallorca who were themselves beaten by Lazio, winning their first European trophy.

EUROPEAN SUPER CUP

The European Super Cup is played annually between the winners of the European Cup and the European Cup-Winners' Cup. Its status has been upgraded with a switch to Monaco as a neutral, single-venue final. It serves as a formal curtain-raiser to the mainstream European international club season.

MITROPA CUP

The Mitropa Cup was an important competition in the inter-war period, and was the forerunner of the European Cup. Created by Hugo Meisl, the Mitropa Cup (shortened form of Mittel Europa) was restricted to clubs from Austria, Italy, Hungary, Czechoslovakia, Switzerland, Romania and Yugoslavia. The competition, involving the champions of each country, was suspended between 1939 and 1950 and lost much of its status once the European Cup got under way in 1955. From 1980 entry was restricted to the Second Division champions of each country, and it was abandoned in 1992.

INTERTOTO CUP

The event, dating back to the 1960s for summer football pools purposes, was relaunched in 1995. The offer of three places in the UEFA Cup failed to attract the best efforts of some nations, such as Italy, Spain and England, but Bordeaux went all the way to the 1996 UEFA Cup Final.

LATIN CUP

The Latin Cup was western Europe's top club event in the early 1950s. Played between the champions of France, Spain, Italy and Portugal, it ended in 1957.

EUROPEAN SUPER CUP WINNERS	
1975	KIEV DYNAMO
1976	ANDERLECHT
1977	LIVERPOOL
1978	ANDERLECHT
1979	NOTTINGHAM FOREST
1980	VALENCIA
1982	ASTON VILLA
1983	ABERDEEN
1984	JUVENTUS
1986	STEAUA BUCHAREST
1987	FC PORTO
1988	MECHELEN
1989	MILAN
1990	MILAN
1991	MANCHESTER UNITED
1992	BARCELONA
1993	PARMA
1994	MILAN
1995	AJAX
1996	JUVENTUS
1997	BARCELONA
1998	CHELSEA
1999	LAZIO
2000	GALATASARAY
2001	LIVERPOOL
2002	REAL MADRID
2003	MILAN
2004	VALENCIA
2005	LIVERPOOL
2006	SEVILLA
2007	MILAN
2008	ZENIT ST PETERBURG
2009	BARCELONA

MITROPA CUP WINNERS			
1927	SPARTA PRAGUE	1967	SPARTAK TRNAVA
1928	FERENCVAROS	1968	RED STAR BELGRADE
1929	UJPEST DOZSA	1969	TJ INTERNACIONAL
1930	RAPID VIENNA	1970	VASAS BUDAPEST
1931	FIRST VIENNA	1971	CELIK ZENICA
1932	BOLOGNA	1972	CELIK ZENICA
1933	FK AUSTRIA	1973	TATABANYA
1934	BOLOGNA	1974	TATABANYA
1935	SPARTA PRAGUE	1975	WACKER INNSBRÜCK
1936	FK AUSTRIA	1976	WACKER INNSBRÜCK
1937	FERENCVAROS	1977	VOJVODINA
1938	SLAVIA PRAGUE	1978	PARTIZAN BELGRADE
1939	UJPEST DOZSA	1980	UDINESE
1951	RAPID VIENNA	1981	TATRAN PRESOV
1955	VOROS LOBOGO	1982	MILAN
1956	VASAS BUDAPEST	1983	VASAS BUDAPEST
1957	VASAS BUDAPEST	1984	SC EISENSTADT
1959	HONVED	1985	ISKRA BUGOJNO
1960	VASAS BUDAPEST	1986	PISA
1961	BOLOGNA	1987	ASCOLI
1962	VASAS BUDAPEST	1988	PISA
1963	MTK BUDAPEST	1989	BANIK OSTRAVA
1964	SPARTAK SOKOLOVO	1990	BARI
1965	VASAS BUDAPEST	1991	TORINO
1966	FIORENTINA		

LATIN CUP WINNERS	
1949	BARCELONA
1950	BENFICA
1951	MILAN
1952	BARCELONA
1953	STADE DE REIMS
1955	REAL MADRID
1956	MILAN
1957	REAL MADRID

COPA LIBERTADORES (SOUTH AMERICAN CLUB CUP)

This is South America's premier club event, but has had a long history of problems both on and off the pitch.

The competition was started in 1960 after a proposition from UEFA that the champions of South America should play against the European champions for the world title. A South American Champion Clubs Cup had been organized by Chile's Colo Colo as early as 1948, but the competition, won by Brazil's Vasco da Gama, was a financial disaster and was not staged again. But UEFA's success with the European Cup prompted CONMEBOL to consider giving the competition another chance, and the lucrative carrot of the World Club Cup swayed the balance in favour of trying again.

The first two competitions were won by Penarol, and almost passed unnoticed. Alberto Spencer scored in both those victories, against Olimpia and Palmeiras, and he remains top scorer in the Copa Libertadores with over 50 goals.

In the following year, 1962, the format of the competition changed as more teams entered. The home-and-away knock-out method was replaced by groups, played for points, up until the Final. Penarol appeared in the Final against Santos, and the first of many unsavoury incidents which have scarred the Copa Libertadores occurred. The first leg, in Montevideo, passed peacefully with a 2-1 win for Santos, but the second leg took three and a half hours to complete because of suspensions after both referee and a linesman were knocked unconscious by missiles thrown from the crowd. In the end Santos – starring Pele – won a play-off easily enough by 3-0.

The 1966 tournament involved no fewer than 95 games. Penarol, the winners, playing 17 games to win the title. With ever-increasing disruption caused to domestic championships, Argentina joined Brazil in a boycott in 1969, prompting CONMEBOL to streamline the competition slightly by reducing the number of group matches. Boca Juniors won the trophy for Argentina in 1977 and again in 1978, but in 1979 Olimpia of Paraguay broke the Argentina-Uruguay-Brazil domination of the competition. Olimpia's breakthrough marked a new era for the competition, which became more even and more open.

Uruguay came back into contention with wins by Nacional (1980 and 1988) and Penarol (1982 and 1987), but no Uruguayan club has won the Copa Libertadores since 1988.

In 1989 Nacional of Medellin won the trophy for Colombia for the first time, and they returned the following year to win again. In 1992 São Paulo beat Newell's Old Boys, of Argentina, to win Brazil's first Copa Libertadores for almost a decade.

The Copa Libertadores is now a more respectable event which features the top clubs from not only South America but also Mexico. Such is the excitement that it is worth putting up with the constantly changing format.

In the new century Boca Juniors re-established Argentine command by winning four times in eight seasons. However the financial pressure on leading clubs from both Argentina and Brazil to sell their best players to European outfits levelled the balance of the playing field.

Thus the twin giants' hegemony was interrupted by Olimpia of Paraguay, Once Caldas from Colombia and LDU of Quito. In 2004 Once Caldas were competing in the Copa for only the third time while LDU, in 2008, were the first Ecuadorian club ever to land the crown. They triumphed in the two-leg final thanks to a penalty shootout defeat of Brazil's Fluminense.

An echo of history resounded in 2009 when Estudiantes de La Plata regained the cup for the first time since their hat-trick of titles at the end of the 1960s. Guiding light in their final victory over Brazil's Cruzeiro was playmaker Juan Sebastian Veron . . . son of 1960s hero Juan Ramon Veron.

Cuauhtemoc Blanco of Mexico's America is buried by Penarol defenders.

COPA LIBERTADORES WINNERS

The first series was held in 1960, with home & away matches on a knock-out basis. The final is played over two legs, with games won, not goal difference, deciding.

1960	**PENAROL**
1961	**PENAROL**
1962	**SANTOS**
1963	**SANTOS**
1964	**INDEPENDIENTE**
1965	**INDEPENDIENTE**
1966	**PENAROL**
1967	**RACING CLUB**
1968	**ESTUDIANTES**
1969	**ESTUDIANTES**
1970	**ESTUDIANTES**
1971	**NACIONAL** (Uruguay)
1972	**INDEPENDIENTE**
1973	**INDEPENDIENTE**
1974	**INDEPENDIENTE**
1975	**INDEPENDIENTE**
1976	**CRUZEIRO**
1977	**BOCA JUNIORS**
1978	**BOCA JUNIORS**
1979	**OLIMPIA** (Paraguay)
1980	**NACIONAL** (Uruguay)
1981	**FLAMENGO**
1982	**PENAROL**
1983	**GREMIO**
1984	**INDEPENDIENTE**
1985	**ARGENTINOS JUNIORS**
1986	**RIVER PLATE**
1987	**PENAROL**
1988	**NACIONAL** (Uruguay)
1989	**ATLETICO NACIONAL**
1990	**OLIMPIA** (Paraguay)
1991	**COLO COLO**
1992	**SÃO PAULO**
1993	**SÃO PAULO**
1994	**VELEZ SARSFIELD**
1995	**GREMIO**
1996	**RIVER PLATE**
1997	**CRUZEIRO**
1998	**VASCO DA GAMA**
1999	**PALMEIRAS**
2000	**BOCA JUNIORS**
2001	**BOCA JUNIORS**
2002	**OLIMPIA** (Paraguay)
2003	**BOCA JUNIORS**
2004	**ONCE CALDAS**
2005	**SÃO PAULO**
2006	**INTERNACIONAL**
2007	**BOCA JUNIORS**
2008	**LDU QUITO**
2009	**ESTUDIANTES DE LA PLATA**

CONCACAF CHAMPIONS CUP

The premier club competition for the Central American and Caribbean regions has been contested since 1962, albeit on a confused basis because it does not always end within the "proper" calendar year. Clubs from Mexico and Costa Rica have dominated.

AFRICAN CHAMPIONS LEAGUE

The competition was launched originally in the early 1960s as the African Champions Cup largely at the behest of ambitious clubs in Francophone Africa eager to copy the European model. Quickly the event's popularity grew, attracting entries from all of Africa though financial and transport problems have proved a long-term headache for organisers. The importance of a stable economy has been signalled by the increasing successes of northern African clubs since the event was transformed – again, copying Europe – into the African Champions League.

ASIAN CHAMPIONS LEAGUE

Asia's own club championship was first contested in 1967 when Hapoel Tel-Aviv were winners before Israel was expelled from the confederation. Success was then spread around the region with South Korean clubs winning five times in seven years at the turn of the century. Urawa and Gamba have since demonstrated the increasing power of Japan's J.League.

OCEANIA CHAMPIONS CUP

This was launched only in the 1990s to take advantage of the place on offer to Oceania's champions at FIFA's new Club World Championship. Although the competition resumed in 2005, it is uncertain what the future holds for the event in the long term after the Football Federation of Australia quit the Oceania confederation to join its Asian counterpart.

CONCACAF CHAMPIONS CUP

1962	GUADALAJARA CD (Mexico)
1963	RACING CLUB (Haiti)
1964	Not completed
1965	Not completed
1966	Not contested
1967	ALIANZA (El Salvador)
1968	TOLUCA (Mexico)
1969	CRUZ AZUL (Mexico)
1970	CRUZ AZUL (North)
	DEPORTIVO SAPRISSA (Central)
	TRANSVAAL (Caribbean)
1971	CRUZ AZUL (Mexico)
1972	OLIMPIA (Honduras)
1973	TRANSVAAL (Surinam)
1974	MUNICIPAL (Guatemala)
1975	ATLETICO ESPANOL (Mexico)
1976	AGUILA (El Salvador)
1977	AMERICA (Mexico)
1978	UNIV GUADALAJARA (North)
	COMUNICACIONES (Central)
	DEFENCE FORCE (Caribbean)
1979	DEPORTIVO FAS (El Salvador)
1980	UNAM (Mexico)
1981	TRANSVAAL (Surinam)
1982	UNAM (Mexico)
1983	ATLANTE (Mexico)
1984	VIOLETTE (Haiti)
1985	DEFENCE FORCE (Trinidad)
1986	LD ALAJUELENSE (Costa Rica)
1987	AMERICA (Mexico)
1988	OLIMPIA (Honduras)
1989	UNAM (Mexico)
1990	AMERICA (Mexico)
1991	PUEBLA (Mexico)
1992	AMERICA (Mexico)
1993	DEP. SAPRISSA (Costa Rica)
1994	CARTAGINES (Costa Rica)
1995	DEP. SAPRISSA (Costa Rica)
1996	Not completed
1997	CRUZ AZUL (Costa Rica)
1998	DC UNITED (USA)
1999	NECAXA (Mexico)
2000	LOS ANGELES GALAXY (USA)
2001	Not completed
2002	PACHUCA (Mexico)
2003	TOLUCA (Mexico)
2004	LD ALAJUELENSE (Costa Rica)
2005	DEP. SAPRISSA (Costa Rica)
2006	AMERICA (Mexico)
2007	PACHUCA (Mexico)
2008	PACHUCA (Mexico)
2009	ATLANTE (Mexico)
2010	PACHUCA (Mexico)

AFRICAN CHAMPIONS LEAGUE

1964	ORYX DOUALA (Cameroon)
1966	STADE ABIDJAN (Ivory Coast)
1967	TP ENGLEBERT (Zaïre)
1968	TP ENGLEBERT (Zaïre)
1969	AL ISMAILI (Egypt)
1970	ASANTE KOTOKO (Ghana)
1971	CANON YAOUNDE (Cameroon)
1972	HAFIA CONAKRY (Ghana)
1973	AS VITA KINSHASA (Zaïre)
1974	CARA BRAZZAVILLE (Congo)
1975	HAFIA CONAKRY (Ghana)
1976	MC ALGIERS (Algeria)
1977	HAFIA CONAKRY (Ghana)
1978	CANON YAOUNDE (Cameroon)
1979	UNION DOUALA (Cameroon)
1980	CANON YAOUNDE (Cameroon)
1981	JE TIZI-OUZOU (Algeria)
1982	AL AHLY (Egypt)
1983	ASANTE KOTOKO (Ghana)
1984	ZAMALEK (Egypt)
1985	FAR RABAT (Morocco)
1986	ZAMALEK (Egypt)
1987	AL AHLY (Egypt)
1988	EP SETIF (Algeria)
1989	RAJA CASABLANCA (Morocco)
1990	JS KABYLIE (Algeria)
1991	CLUB AFRICAIN (Tunisia)
1992	WYDAD CASABLANCA (Morocco)
1993	ZAMALEK (Egypt)
1994	ESPERANCE (Tunisia)
1995	ORLANDO PIRATES (S Africa)
1996	ZAMALEK (Egypt)
1997	RAJA CASABLANCA (Morocco)
1998	ASEC ABIDJAN (Ivory Coast)
1999	RAJA CASABLANCA (Morocco)
2000	HEARTS OF OAK (Ghana)
2001	AL AHLY (Egypt)
2002	ZAMALEK (Egypt)
2003	ENYIMBA (Nigeria)
2004	ENYIMBA (Nigeria)
2005	AL-AHLY (Egypt)
2006	AL-AHLY (Egypt)
2007	ETOILE SAHEL (Tunisia)
2008	AL-AHLY (Egypt)
2009	T P MAZEMBE (DR Congo)

OCEANIA CHAMPIONS LEAGUE CUP WINNERS

1987	ADELAIDE CITY (Aus)
1999	SOUTH MELBOURNE (Aus)
2001	WOLLONGONG CITY WOLVES (Aus)
2002-2004	Not contested
2005	SYDNEY FC (Aus)
2006	AUCKLAND CITY (NZ)
2007	WAITAKERE UNITED (NZ)
2005	WAITAKERE UNITED (NZ)
2009	AUCKLAND CITY (NZ)

ASIAN CHAMPIONS LEAGUE

1967	HAPOEL TEL-AVIV (Israel)
1969	MACCABI TEL-AVIV (Israel)
1970	TAJ (Iran)
1971	MACCABI TEL-AVIV (Israel)
1972-1985	Not contested
1986	DAEWOO ROYALS (S Korea)
1987	FURUKAWA (Japan)
1988	YOMIURI (Japan)
1989	AL-SAAD (Qatar)
1990	LIAONING (China)
1991	ESTEGHLAL (Iran)
1992	AL HILAL (S Arabia)
1993	PAAS (Iran)
1994	THAI FARMERS BANK
1995	THAI FARMERS BANK
1996	ILHWA CHUNMA (S Korea)
1997	POHANG STEELERS (S Korea)
1998	POHANG STEELERS (S Korea)
1999	JUBILO IWATA (Japan)
2000	AL HILAL (S Arabia)
2001	SUWON BLUEWINGS (S Korea)
2002	SUWON BLUEWINGS (S Korea)
2003	AL AIN (UAE)
2004	AL ITTIHAD (S Arabia)
2005	AL ITTIHAD (S Arabia)
2006	JEONBUK HYUNDAI (S Korea)
2007	URAWA RED DIAMONDS (Jap)
2008	GAMBA OSAKA (Japan)
2009	POHANG STEELERS (S Korea)

AFRICAN CAF CUP

1992	SHOOTING STARS (Nigeria)
1993	STELLA ABIDJAN (Ivory Coast)
1994	BENDEL INSURANCE (Nigeria)
1995	ETOILE DU SAHEL (Tunisia)
1996	KAWKAB MARRAKECH (Morocco)
1997	ESPERANCE (Tunisia)
1998	CS SFAXIEN (Tunisia)
1999	ETOILE DU SAHEL (Tunisia)
2000	JS KABYLIE (Algeria)
2001	JS KABYLIE (Algeria)
2002	JS KABYLIE (Algeria)
2003	RAJA CASABLANCA (Morocco)
2004	HEARTS OF OAK (Ghana)
2005	FAR RABAT (Morocco)
2006	ETOILE DU SAHEL (Tunisia)
2007	CS SFAXIEN (Tunisia)
2008	CS SFAXIEN (Tunisia)
2009	STADE MALIEN (Mali)

PART 3:

THE SOCCER NATIONS

It was soccer's fortune that it developed internationally when the world was adjusting to the concept of the power & authority of the nation state. FIFA was created out of the need to offer nation states an international sporting platform within the soccer family.

In Britain the nationalistic pride associated with English and Scots gave rise to the first international fixture. But the British "arrangement" with its four associations – England, Scotland, Wales and Northern Ireland – remains an anomaly within world soccer.

Indeed, the revision of FIFA's governing statutes in 2003 enshrined the maxim that future membership had to be restricted only to associations representing states as recognized formally by the United Nations.

International soccer has held a firm line over eligibility. National associations, for example, which wish to maintain the right to vote within FIFA Congress must not only pay membership fees regularly but also compete consistently within the authority's international competitions.

Political interference is also frowned on. FIFA has suspended various associations around the world from time to time when governments have sought too much control over local soccer bodies.

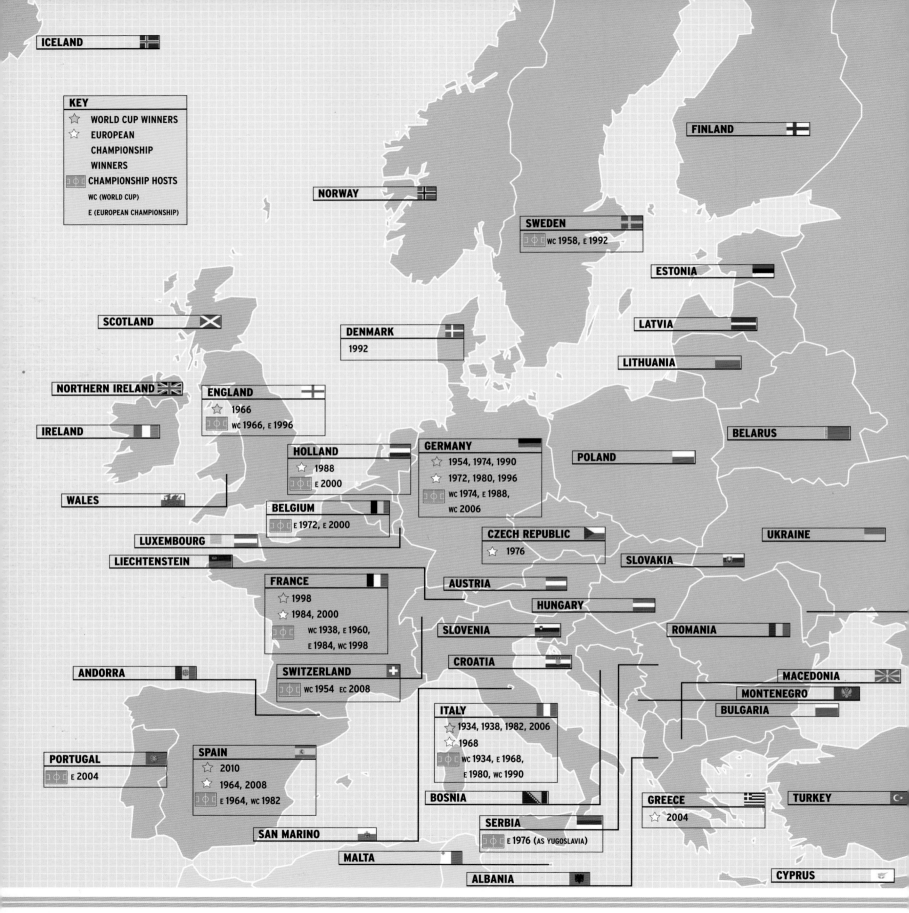

ICELAND

KEY
★ WORLD CUP WINNERS
☆ EUROPEAN CHAMPIONSHIP WINNERS
CHAMPIONSHIP HOSTS
WC (WORLD CUP)
E (EUROPEAN CHAMPIONSHIP)

FINLAND

NORWAY

SWEDEN
WC 1958, E 1992

ESTONIA

DENMARK
1992

LATVIA

SCOTLAND

LITHUANIA

NORTHERN IRELAND

ENGLAND
★ 1966
WC 1966, E 1996

BELARUS

IRELAND

GERMANY
★ 1954, 1974, 1990
☆ 1972, 1980, 1996
WC 1974, E 1988, WC 2006

POLAND

HOLLAND
☆ 1988
E 2000

WALES

BELGIUM
E 1972, E 2000

CZECH REPUBLIC
☆ 1976

UKRAINE

LUXEMBOURG

LIECHTENSTEIN

SLOVAKIA

FRANCE
★ 1998
☆ 1984, 2000
WC 1938, E 1960, E 1984, WC 1998

AUSTRIA

HUNGARY

ROMANIA

SLOVENIA

ANDORRA

MACEDONIA

SWITZERLAND
WC 1954 EC 2008

CROATIA

MONTENEGRO

BULGARIA

ITALY
★ 1934, 1938, 1982, 2006
☆ 1968
WC 1934, E 1968, E 1980, WC 1990

PORTUGAL
E 2004

SPAIN
★ 2010
☆ 1964, 2008
E 1964, WC 1982

BOSNIA

GREECE
☆ 2004

TURKEY

SAN MARINO

SERBIA
E 1976 (AS YUGOSLAVIA)

MALTA

ALBANIA

CYPRUS

EUROPE

It is in Europe where the matches, sponsorships and television rights raise over 85 per cent of world soccer's estimated wealth.

Although FIFA was established in Paris in 1904 the need for a quasi-independent European federation had become inevitable by the time of the creation in 1954 of UEFA (the Union of European Football Associations). The first formal international match on the Continent had been played between Austria and Hungary in 1902 and central Europe had also seen the launch of the Mitropa Cup, the forerunner of today's hugely successful European club competitions. France, in particular, were leaders in founding FIFA and bringing the vision of a World Cup to reality and, later, launching the European competitive structures which are so familiar, and so avidly followed, today.

Now with some 53 members, UEFA began with just 30 and is operated from a base in Switzerland in Nyon near Geneva. The current President is former France star Michel Platini who heads the executive committee of 16. At least half of the executive stands for election every two years and it is this committee which oversees the regulation of the Union's regulations via a series of sub-committees. UEFA had its problems, not least an uneasy relationship with FIFA, but it can console itself with the fact that it controls the richest club competition in the world in the form of the Champions League.

Trix and Flix, the 2008 European Championship mascots, show-off the tournament trophy.

RUSSIA
★ 1960

KAZAKHSTAN

MOLDOVA

AZERBAIJAN

GEORGIA

ARMENIA

ENGLAND

England gave soccer to the world. First organized on the playing fields of England's public schools in the 1860s, it was nicknamed 'soccer', to distinguish it from Rugby Football, or 'rugger'.

The Football Association
Founded: 1863
FIFA: 1905-1920, 1924-1928, 1946
World Cup: 1966
Olympics: 1908, 1912 (as Great Britain)

The FA Cup was introduced in 1871, the first tournament in the world, and was fundamental to the development of the game – pitting the established amateur sides of the south against the burgeoning professional outfits of the north. A year later, the very first international match was played between England and Scotland in Glasgow and in 1888 the Football League was formed in order to organize what was, by now, a largely professional game, based mostly in the industrial north.

As the century closed, the British Championship, played between England, Scotland, Wales and Ireland, was the zenith of world soccer and before the First World War, England and Scotland were well above the rest of the world and, as Great Britain, won Olympic gold in 1908 and 1912.

The inter-war period, however, was a time of increasing isolation as the rest of the world warmed to the game and although the FA had joined FIFA in 1905, they took a disdainful attitude to it and withdrew in 1920 and 1928.

Even after the Second World War, England's superiority complex did not change, despite an ignominious 1-0 defeat by the United States in the 1950 World Cup, which was dismissed as a fluke. However in 1953, Hungary's "Magical Magyars" came to Wembley and destroyed English arrogance forever with a 6-3 victory. Further defeats at the 1954, 1958 and 1962 World Cup finals confirmed that the rest of the world had caught up.

The challenges presented by the new order were spectacularly answered in 1966, when England's "wingless wonders" won the World Cup on home soil. Alf Ramsey moulded his side around the outstanding talents of goalkeeper Gordon Banks, captain Bobby Moore, and the Charlton brothers Bobby and Jack. In doing so, he created a system that worked with the players at his disposal, and instilled a team spirit and an understanding that has proved difficult to match.

The 1966 success was the springboard from which English club sides launched an unprecedented assault on the three European competitions, winning trophy after trophy between 1964 and 1985. Conversely, as the clubs prospered the national side suffered. Failure to qualify for the 1974 and 1978 finals confirmed England's slump. From then on, the English team have been inconsistent: there were dismal performances at the 1988 and 1992 European Championship finals and, worse, the failure to qualify for the 1994 World Cup finals, brought the structure of the English game under scrutiny. There were signs of hope, although the team seemed to be dogged by bad luck: England went out of the 1986 World Cup finals in Mexico after Diego Maradona's infamous 'Hand of God' goal, and lost to Germany on penalties in both the semi-final of Italia 90 and Euro 96 – which was held in England and created soccer fever throughout the country. From 1996, the national team's performances slowly improved, although the same bad luck struck again at France 98, when England reached the second round but lost on penalties to old foes Argentina.

The experiment with a first foreign manager saw England, under the Swede Sven-Goran Eriksson, reach the quarter-finals in the 2002 and 2006 World Cups. Steve McClaren's managerial failure in the Euro 2008 qualifiers brought recourse to another foreigner in Fabio Capello but only further disappointment with defeat by Germany in the 2010 World Cup second round.

Meanwhile, the domestic game had changed dramatically after the appalling loss of life at Bradford (1985) and Hillsbrough (1989). An enforced modernization of stadia was followed by an astonishing cash surge from successive Sky TV contracts and a boom in attendances. Suddenly the new Premier League was considered the richest in Europe and the most popular with fans around the world.

The downside was that the league title race became a preserve of only the rich such as Manchester United, Chelsea, Arsenal and Liverpool.

England welcomes Europe to Wembley in 1996 before the clash with Switzerland.

Seats empty rapidly in Munich as the margin of World Cup qualifying defeat stares German fans in the face.

RECENT INTERNATIONAL RESULTS

Date	Opponent	Score	
02.09.06	ANDORRA	5-0	ECQ
06.09.06	MACEDONIA	1-0	ECQ
07.10.06	MACEDONIA	0-0	ECQ
11.10.06	CROATIA	0-2	ECQ
15.11.06	HOLLAND	0-1	
07.02.07	SPAIN	0-1	
24.03.07	ISRAEL	0-0	ECQ
28.03.07	ANDORRA	3-0	ECQ
01.06.07	BRAZIL	1-1	
06.06.07	ESTONIA	3-0	ECQ
01.06.07	BRAZIL	1-1	
06.06.07	ESTONIA	3-0	ECQ
22.08.07	GERMANY	1-2	
08.09.07	ISRAEL	3-0	ECQ
12.09.07	RUSSIA	3-0	ECQ
13.10.07	ESTONIA	3-0	ECQ
17.10.07	RUSSIA	1-2	ECQ
16.11.07	AUSTRIA	1-0	
21.11.07	CROATIA	2-3	ECQ
06.02.08	SWITZERLAND	2-1	
26.03.08	FRANCE	0-1	
28.05.08	USA	2-0	
01.06.08	TRIN. & TOBAGO	3-0	
20.08.08	CZECH REPUBLIC	2-2	
06.09.08	ANDORRA	2-0	WCQ
10.09.08	CROATIA	4-1	WCQ
11.10.08	KAZAKHSTAN	5-1	WCQ
15.10.08	BELARUS	3-1	WCQ
19.11.08	GERMANY	2-1	
11.02.09	SPAIN	0-2	
28.03.09	SLOVAKIA	4-0	
01.04.09	UKRAINE	2-1	WCQ
06.06.09	KAZAKHSTAN	4-0	WCQ
10.06.09	ANDORRA	6-0	WCQ
12.08.09	HOLLAND	2-2	
05.09.09	SLOVENIA	2-1	
09.09.09	CROATIA	5-1	WCQ
10.10.09	UKRAINE	0-1	WCQ
14.10.09	BELARUS	3-0	WCQ
14.11.09	BRAZIL	0-1	
03.03.10	EGYPT	3-1	
25.05.10	MEXICO	3-1	
30.05.10	JAPAN	2-1	
12.06.10	UNITED STATES	1-1	WC
18.06.10	ALGERIA	0-0	WC
23.06.10	SLOVENIA	1-0	WC
27.06.10	GERMANY	1-4	WC

*ENGLAND SCORE SHOWN FIRST

SCOTLAND

Scotland has a proud soccer playing heritage and, for such a small country, it has been a remarkable story, which began in 1873.

Scottish Football Association
Founded: 1873
FIFA: 1910–20, 1924–28, 1946

The Scottish FA was founded in 1873, and still retains a permanent seat on the law-making international board. Scotland was also the venue for the world's first international match on November 30 1872, when Scotland and England drew 0-0. The rivalry has continued ever since, sharpened by the fact that many of England's most successful club sides have contained or been managed by Scots: Bill Shankly at Liverpool, Matt Busby at Manchester United, Alex Ferguson also at United and George Graham at Arsenal, while the players include Alex James, Denis Law, Kenny Dalglish and Billy Bremner. This continual draining of talent would

have withered many countries, but the Scottish League survives, thanks mainly to the two great Glasgow clubs, Celtic and Rangers. These two have dominated the domestic scene unlike any other country in Europe.

Scottish club soccer was at its peak in the 1960s, with Celtic winning the European Cup in 1967 – the first British side to do so – and reaching the final again in 1970. The Glasgow monopoly was briefly threatened by Aberdeen (European Cup-Winners Cup winners in 1983) and Dundee United (UEFA finalists in 1987), but the Old Firm, with Celtic breaking Rangers' hold on the championship in 1998, still rule the roost. As for the national side, having entered the World Cup for the first time in 1950, they qualified for the finals in 1970, 1974,

1978, 1982, 1986, 1990 and 1998. They also reached the European finals in 1992 and 1996. Once in the finals, however, the Scots appear incapable of going beyond the first round. In seven World Cups they have always got the plane home after the opening stage.

The revolutionary appointment of a foreigner to replace Craig Brown as national coach, Germany's Berti Vogts, was unsuccessful and Scotland failed to reach any finals in the new century. Walter Smith instigated a resurgence and successor Alex McLeish lifted Scotland to a best-ever 14th in the FIFA world rankings in May 2007. But the rapid turnover of managers continued with McLeish leaving and then successor George Burley being replaced by Craig Levein after the failure to qualify for the 2010 World Cup finals.

Archie Gemmill wheels away after his goal against Holland which gave Scotland vain hope of reaching the 1978 World Cup second round.

RECENT INTERNATIONAL RESULTS		
09.10.04 NORWAY	0-1	WCQ
13.10.04 MOLDOVA	1-1	WCQ
17.11.04 SWEDEN	1-4	
26.03.05 ITALY	2-0	WCQ
04.06.05 MOLDOVA	2-0	WCQ
08.06.05 BELARUS	0-0	WCQ
17.08.05 AUSTRIA	2-2	
03.09.05 ITALY	1-1	WCQ
07.09.05 NORWAY	2-1	WCQ
08.10.05 BELARUS	0-1	WCQ
12.10.05 SLOVENIA	3-0	WCQ
12.11.05 USA	1-1	
01.03.06 SWITZERLAND	1-3	
11.05.06 BULGARIA	5-1	
13.05.06 JAPAN	0-0	
02.09.06 FAROE ISLANDS	6-0	ECQ
06.09.06 LITHUANIA	2-1	ECQ
07.10.06 FRANCE	1-0	ECQ
11.10.06 UKRAINE	0-2	ECQ
24.03.07 GEORGIA	2-1	ECQ
28.03.07 ITALY	0-2	ECQ
30.05.07 AUSTRIA	1-0	
06.06.07 FAROE ISLANDS	2-0	ECQ
22.08.07 SOUTH AFRICA	1-0	
08.09.07 LITHUANIA	3-1	ECQ
12.09.07 FRANCE	1-0	ECQ
13.10.07 UKRAINE	3-1	ECQ
17.10.07 GEORGIA	0-2	ECQ
17.11.07 ITALY	1-2	ECQ
26.03.08 CROATIA	1-1	
30.05.08 CZECH REPUBLIC	1-3	
20.08.08 N. IRELAND	0-0	
06.09.08 MACEDONIA	0-1	WCQ
10.09.08 ICELAND	2-1	WCQ
11.10.08 NORWAY	0-0	WCQ
19.11.08 ARGENTINA	0-1	
28.03.09 NETHERLANDS	0-3	WCQ
01.04.09 ICELAND	2-1	WCQ
29.05.09 ESTONIA	1-0	
06.06.09 AZERBAIJAN	1-0	WCQ
12.08.09 NORWAY	0-4	WCQ
05.09.09 MACEDONIA	2-0	WCQ
09.09.09 HOLLAND	0-1	WCQ
10.10.09 JAPAN	0-2	
14.11.09 WALES	0-3	
03.03.10 CZECH REPUBLIC	1-0	

* SCOTLAND SCORE SHOWN FIRST

WALES

The FA of Wales was formed in 1876, and 31 years later, in 1907, they won the British Championship for the first time.

Football Association of Wales
Founded: 1876
FIFA: 1910-20, 1924-28, 1946

Wales qualified for the World Cup finals in 1958 through a 'lucky losers' play-off and surprised even themselves by reaching the quarter-finals with a fine team led by 'Gentle Giant' John Charles. However that proved to be the first and last time they reached the final tournament of any major international competition.

The closest they came subsequently was in the Euro 2004 qualifiers when they lost a play-off to Russia despite an appeal after it emerged that a Russian player had failed a dope test after the first leg.

The major Welsh clubs play competitively in the English league system without top-level success. However Cardiff City did become the only non-English club ever to win the FA Cup when they beat Arsenal in the 1927 Final. Against the odds, as a second tier club they returned to the Final in 2008 but lost to Portsmouth.

In the formative years of the Welsh Cup the village of Chirk figured prominently. Between 1886 and 1894 Chirk played in six finals, winning five.

In modern times the FA of Wales has conceded growing power to a revamped League of Wales. Cardiff and Swansea were granted special dispensation to continue playing in English league competition but forfeited right of entry into the Welsh Cup and thus access to Europe.

'Gentle giant' John Charles above England's Don Howe and Billy Wright.

NORTHERN IRELAND

The story of Irish soccer runs parallel to that of mainland Britain, with the founding of the Irish Football Association in November 1880.

Irish Football Association
Founded: 1880
FIFA: 1911-20, 1924-28, 1946

The Irish Cup was launched in 1880 by the pioneering J. M. McAlery. By the turn of the century Dublin was hosting the finals. In 1905 Shelbourne became the first Dublin side to win the trophy, but in the season of 1911-12 a serious split parted the Dubliners from Belfast. The Belfast clubs withdrew their support and organized a new Irish

Cup, with a trophy made of gold.

Meanwhile Ireland was heading for political division, and that was formalized in soccer by a split within the game's administration. The Irish Football Association continued to run the game in the North while the new Football Association of Ireland controlled soccer in the Irish Free State, now the Republic of Ireland.

On the international front, Northern Ireland's most memorable year was 1957, when they beat England 3-2 at

Wembley for the first time and also qualified, for the first time, for the World Cup Finals in Italy.

There was more World Cup glory in 1982 and 1986 under Billy Bingham. In 1982, Northern Ireland created a sensation by defeating hosts Spain 1-0. In the 1986 finals in Mexico Pat Jennings played in his 119th international game - then a world record - on his 41st birthday. Northern Ireland have not returned to a major finals tournament since then.

Gerry Armstrong's goal shocks goalkeeper Luis Arconada and 1982 World Cup hosts Spain.

RECENT INTERNATIONAL RESULTS			
3.10.04	AUSTRIA	3-3	WCQ
26.03.05	ENGLAND	0-4	WCQ
30.03.05	POLAND	0-1	
04.06.05	GERMANY	1-4	
03.09.05	AZERBAIJAN	2-0	WCQ
07.09.05	ENGLAND	1-0	WCQ
08.10.05	WALES	2-3	WCQ
12.10.05	AUSTRIA	0-2	WCQ
15.11.05	PORTUGAL	1-1	
01.03.06	ESTONIA	1-0	
21.05.06	URUGUAY	0-1	
26.05.06	ROMANIA	0-2	
16.08.06	FINLAND	2-1	
02.09.06	ICELAND	0-3	ECQ
06.09.06	SPAIN	3-2	ECQ
07.10.06	DENMARK	0-0	ECQ
11.10.06	LATVIA	1-0	ECQ
06.02.07	WALES	0-0	
24.03.07	LIECHTENSTEIN	4-1	ECQ
28.03.07	SWEDEN	2-1	
22.08.07	LIECHTENSTEIN	3-1	ECQ
08.09.07	LATVIA	0-1	ECQ
12.09.07	ICELAND	1-2	ECQ
17.10.07	SWEDEN	1-1	ECQ
17.11.07	DENMARK	2-1	ECQ
21.11.07	SPAIN	0-1	ECQ
06.02.08	BULGARIA	0-1	
26.03.08	GEORGIA	4-1	
20.08.08	SCOTLAND	0-0	
06.09.08	SLOVAKIA	1-2	WCQ
20.10.08	CZECH REPUBLIC	0-0	WCQ
11.10.08	SLOVENIA	0-2	WCQ
15.10.08	SAN MARINO	4-0	WCQ
19.11.08	HUNGARY	0-2	
11.02.09	SAN MARINO	3-0	WCQ
28.03.09	POLAND	3-2	WCQ
01.04.09	SLOVENIA	1-0	WCQ
06.06.09	ITALY	0-3	
12.08.09	ISRAEL	1-1	
05.09.09	POLAND	1-1	WCQ
14.10.09	CZECH REPUBLIC	0-0	WCQ
14.11.09	SERBIA	0-1	
03.03.10	ALBANIA	0-1	
26.05.10	TURKEY	0-2	
30.05.10	CHILE	0-1	

*NORTHERN IRELAND SCORE SHOWN FIRST

REPUBLIC OF IRELAND

The Irish Republic developed as an independent international soccer entity after partition and the creation of the Irish Free State in the early 1920s.

Football Association of Ireland
Founded: 1921
FIFA: 1923

They competed in the World Cup qualifiers of 1934 and 1938, and the clubs founded before partition lived on and gained new strength. However, many old links survived. Several players appeared for both Irelands, and the first foreign nation to beat England in England was the Irish Republic, 2-0 in September 1949.

Almost all the best players raised in the Republic were quickly sold to English and Scottish clubs. It was not until an Englishman, Jack Charlton, who was prepared to take advantage of the parental qualification loophole, became manager, that the Republic gained international prestige.

Charlton brought organization and discipline to the side. By 1988 he had proved his worth, leading them to their first appearance in the European Championship Finals, where they beat England 1-0 in their opening game.

Two years later the Irish were at the World Cup Finals. A second round victory on penalties over Romania took the Irish to the quarter-finals where hosts Italy proved too strong.

Charlton's men were back at the finals in 1994 and beat Italy 1-0, before falling to Holland in the second round. Holland repeated their 2-0 victory in the qualifying play-off for the 1996 European Championship.

Steve Staunton (left) and Terry Phelan (right) help Ray Houghton hail his 1994 strike against Italy.

It was the end of the road for Charlton. His former defensive mainstay, Mick McCarthy, succeeded him as manager. McCarthy rebuilt the team and guided them to the 2002 World Cup. However, their performance was overshadowed by a clash between McCarthy and skipper Roy Keane. Keane was sent home, and McCarthy himself did not survive much longer. At least he had guided them to a major finals, more than successors Brian Kerr, Steve Staunton and Giovanni Trapattoni have managed to do.

FRANCE

England gave the game to the world, but the French organized it into a structured sport, and gained their reward in 1998.

Fédération Française de Football
Founded: 1918
FIFA: 1904
World Cup: 1998
European Championship: 1984, 2000
Olympics: 1984

France's 3-0 victory over Brazil in the 1998 World Cup Final, on home soil, was long overdue. They French had been prime movers behind the creation of FIFA, UEFA, the World Cup and European club cups but had had little to show for it in terms of silverware. Not until the 1950s when Reims twice reached the European Cup Final did fortunes pick up. Their stars were Raymond Kopa and Just Fontaine, the latter finishing as record 13-goal top scorer when France took third place at the 1958 World Cup.

International club success proved elusive until 1993, when Marseille beat Milan 1-0 to win the Champions Cup. France went wild, but only briefly. Within a month Marseille had been engulfed by a match-fixing scandal that prevented them defending the Cup, prompted their relegation and brought suspensions and legal action against players and officials, including president Bernard Tapie.

On the international front, Michel Platini arrived in the 1970s and transformed France into one of Europe's most attractive sides. Platini, a midfielder with immense skill, vision and grace, inspired France to reach the final stages of three World Cups (1978, 1982 and 1986) and win the 1984 European Championship. Platini was nine-goal top scorer and captain and would, in due course, progress to become president of UEFA.

Before then the greatest day in Les Bleus' history saw the historic World Cup triumph over Brazil with two goals from playmaker Zinedine Zidane. Two years later France achieved the double by winning the European title on a golden goal against Italy. The Italians took revenge however with a shootout win over France in the 2006 World Cup Final.

Hopes of a revival in 2010 in South Africa were rudely shattered by internal divisions which sparked a row between coach Raymond Domenech and striker Nicolas Anelka then a players' training-ground strike.

Michel Platini shoots France ahead from a free kick in the 1984 European final against Spain.

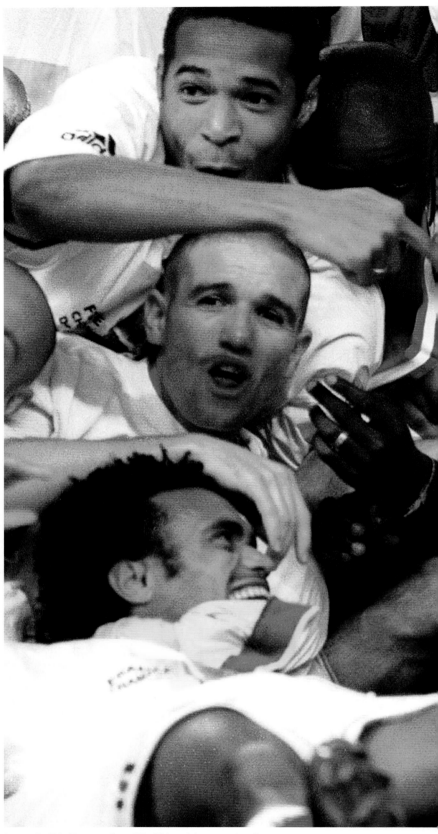

France thrill to the sensation of World Cup victory over Brazil.

GERMANY

Despite political divisions, post-war Germany has remained among the best sides in Europe. Since the country was reunified in 1990, the team is stronger than ever.

Deutscher Fussball-Bund
Founded: 1900
FIFA: 1904-46, 1950
World Cup: 1954, 1974, 1990 (West Germany)
European Championship: 1972, 1980 (both West Germany), 1996
Olympics: 1976 (East Germany)

Since the Second World War, Germany have enjoyed a record of success unparalleled in the history of the European game. Yet Germany's pre-war record was quite poor, with third place at the 1934 World Cup the peak of their achievement. The war brought division of the country and in 1948, East Germany, under the Soviets, formed its own association, league and national side.

The East Germans, with their state-sponsored emphasis on individual rather than team sports, never matched the success of their country-men on the other side of the Berlin Wall. In fact, half a century of East German soccer only produced two successes of note: Olympic gold in Montreal in 1976 and a 1-0 victory over West Germany, in the only match ever played between the two sides, at the 1974 World Cup finals.

While the East floundered, the West flourished. Banished from FIFA in 1946, they were readmitted in 1950 as West Germany and won the World Cup just over four years later. That victory, engineered by coach Sepp Herberger, was all the more amazing because their Final opponents were the "Magical Magyars", whose 3-2 defeat was only their second loss in five years. From then on the Germans grew in stature. In the World Cup, they were semi-finalists in 1958, quarter-finalists in 1962 and then runners-up in 1966.

The 1970s seemed to belong to Bayern Munich and West Germany. Bayern won a hat-trick of European Cups in 1974, 1975 and 1976 and provided the nucleus of the national side that won the European Championship in 1972, the World Cup in 1974 and, after finishing second in 1976, the European Championship again in 1980. Franz Beckenbauer single-handedly revolutionized the sweeper's role into one of attack as well as defence and Gerd Müller was the closest thing to a scoring machine yet seen. In 62 internationals, he scored an incredible 68 goals.

The 1970's sides were replaced by new stars of the world game in the 1980s and 90s: Lothar Matthäus, Karl-Heinz Rummenigge, Rudi Völler, Jürgen Klinsmann, Thomas Hässler and Matthias Sammer. Following the World Cup success and German reunification in 1990, they capitalized on their new-found resources by securing victory in Euro 96 with a 2-1 defeat of the Czech Republic.

An ageing team crashed 3-0 to Croatia in the quarter-finals of the 1998 World Cup and then suffered the humiliation of a first round exit from Euro 2000. National pride was assuaged however at subsequent World Cups when Germany surprised themselves by finishing runners-up in 2002 and then reaching the last four in 2006, as hosts, and again in 2010 after dramatic victories over England and Argentina.

West Germany line up against East Germany for the one and only time - in the 1974 World Cup.

Pierre Littbarski and captain Lothar Matthäus share World Cup delirium in 1990.

RECENT INTERNATIONAL RESULTS

02.06.07	**SAN MARINO**	**6-0**	ECQ
06.06.07	**SLOVAKIA**	**2-1**	ECQ
22.08.07	**ENGLAND**	**2-1**	
08.09.07	**WALES**	**2-0**	ECQ
12.09.07	**ROMANIA**	**3-1**	
13.10.07	**REP. OF IRELAND**	**0-0**	ECQ
17.10.07	**CZECH REPUBLIC**	**0-3**	ECQ
17.11.07	**CYPRUS**	**4-0**	ECQ
21.11.07	**WALES**	**0-0**	ECQ
06.02.08	**AUSTRIA**	**3-0**	
26.03.08	**SWITZERLAND**	**4-0**	
27.05.08	**BELARUS**	**2-2**	
31.05.08	**SERBIA**	**2-1**	
08.06.08	**POLAND**	**2-0**	EC
12.06.08	**CROATIA**	**1-2**	EC
16.06.08	**AUSTRIA**	**1-0**	EC
19.06.08	**PORTUGAL**	**3-2**	EC
25.06.08	**TURKEY**	**3-2**	EC
29.06.08	**SPAIN**	**0-1**	ECF
20.08.08	**BELGIUM**	**2-0**	
06.09.08	**LIECHTENSTEIN**	**6-0**	WCQ
10.09.08	**FINLAND**	**3-3**	WCQ
11.10.08	**RUSSIA**	**2-1**	WCQ
15.10.08	**WALES**	**1-0**	WCQ
19.11.08	**ENGLAND**	**1-2**	
11.02.09	**NORWAY**	**0-1**	
28.03.09	**LIECHTENSTEIN**	**4-0**	WCQ
01.04.09	**WALES**	**2-0**	WCQ
29.05.09	**CHINA**	**1-1**	
02.06.09	**UAE**	**7-2**	
12.08.09	**AZERBAIJAN**	**2-0**	WCQ
05.09.09	**SOUTH AFRICA**	**2-0**	
09.09.09	**AZERBAIJAN**	**4-0**	WCQ
10.10.09	**RUSSIA**	**1-0**	WCQ
14.10.09	**FINLAND**	**1-1**	WCQ
18.11.09	**IVORY COAST**	**2-2**	
03.03.10	**ARGENTINA**	**0-1**	
13.05.10	**MALTA**	**3-0**	
29.05.10	**HUNGARY**	**3-0**	
03.06.10	**BOSNIA-HERZ**	**3-1**	
13.06.10	**AUSTRALIA**	**4-0**	WC
18.06.10	**SERBIA**	**0-1**	WC
23.06.10	**GHANA**	**1-0**	WC
27.06.10	**ENGLAND**	**4-1**	WC
03.07.10	**ARGENTINA**	**4-0**	WC
07.07.10	**SPAIN**	**0-1**	WC
10.07.10	**URUGUAY**	**3-2**	WC

* GERMANY SCORE SHOWN FIRST

HOLLAND

World Cup exploits leave no room for doubt about Dutch status among the leading nations in international soccer.

Koninklijke Nederland Voetbalbond (KNVB)
Founded: 1889
FIFA: 1904
European Championship: 1988

The Dutch were early devotees of soccer, partly owing to the country's close proximity to Britain, and they were among the continent's leading amateur sides in the early 1900s. Indeed they reached the semi-finals of four consecutive Olympic Games from 1908 to 1924 ... but lost them all. Third place in 1908 and 1912 was their best result. The 1920s marked a move away from amateurism in other countries, and Dutch soccer entered a decline that lasted until the 1960s. Up until that decade, internationals were mostly played against European neighbours, especially Belgium, and first-round defeats in the 1934 and 1938 World Cups did little to encourage them to venture further afield.

The lowest point came just after the Second World War, when a dismal sequence of results, with just one victory in over five years, prompted modernization of the domestic game. So, in 1957, a national league was created and professionalism was introduced in an attempt to staunch the flow of Dutch players to abroad. The main beneficiaries of the reorganization were Ajax of Amsterdam, Feyenoord of Rotterdam and PSV Eindhoven – the "big three" who have dominated Dutch soccer ever since.

The big breakthrough came in 1970 when Feyenoord won the European Cup. It was the beginning of a golden era for Dutch soccer in which Ajax won a hat-trick of European Cups (1971,

Holland line up before the 1978 World Cup Final against Argentina.

Marco Van Basten's goals fired Holland to victory in the European Championships in 1988.

1972, 1973), Feyenoord and PSV both won the UEFA Cup, and Holland reached two consecutive World Cup Finals.

The generation of Dutch players who emerged in the 1970s was among the finest the modern game has seen. Ajax led the way, providing the backbone of the national side with hugely talented players such as Arie Haan, Johan Neeskens, Ruud Krol, Wim Suurbier and, of course, Johan Cruyff, arguably the best player of his day. Along with the Feyenoord duo of Wim Van Hanegem and Wim Jansen, they formed the nucleus of a side that was unfortunate to lose the 1974 and 1978 World Cup Finals to the host nations, West Germany and Argentina respectively. Coach Rinus Michels was the architect of the success with his "total football" system, which involved moulding highly his skilled players into a team unit, with the

Date	Team	Score	Comp
02.06.07	SOUTH KOREA	2-0	
06.06.07	THAILAND	3-1	
22.08.07	SWITZERLAND	1-2	
08.09.07	BULGARIA	2-0	ECQ
12.09.07	ALBANIA	1-0	ECQ
13.10.07	ROMANIA	0-1	ECQ
17.10.07	SLOVENIA	2-0	ECQ
17.11.07	LUXEMBOURG	1-0	ECQ
21.11.07	BELARUS	1-2	ECQ
06.02.08	CROATIA	3-0	
26.03.08	AUSTRIA	4-3	
24.05.08	UKRAINE	3-0	
29.05.08	DENMARK	1-1	
01.06.08	WALES	2-0	
09.06.08	ITALY	3-0	EC
13.06.08	FRANCE	4-1	EC
17.06.08	ROMANIA	2-0	EC
21.06.08	RUSSIA	1-3	EC
20.08.08	RUSSIA	1-1	
06.09.08	AUSTRALIA	1-2	
10.09.08	MACEDONIA	2-1	WCQ
11.10.08	ICELAND	2-0	WCQ
15.10.08	NORWAY	1-0	WCQ
19.11.08	SWEDEN	3-1	
11.02.09	TUNISIA	1-1	
28.03.09	SCOTLAND	3-0	WCQ
01.04.09	MACEDONIA	4-0	WCQ
06.06.09	ICELAND	2-1	WCQ
10.06.09	NORWAY	2-0	WCQ
12.08.09	ENGLAND	2-2	
05.09.09	JAPAN	3-0	
09.09.09	SCOTLAND	1-0	WCQ
10.10.09	AUSTRALIA	0-0	
14.11.09	ITALY	0-0	
18.11.09	PARAGUAY	0-0	
03.03.10	UNITED STATES	2-1	
26.05.10	MEXICO	2-1	
01.06.10	GHANA	4-1	
05.06.10	HUNGARY	6-1	
14.06.10	DENMARK	2-0	WC
19.06.10	JAPAN	1-0	WC
24.06.10	CAMEROON	2-1	WC
28.06.10	SLOVAKIA	2-1	WC
02.07.10	BRAZIL	2-1	WC
06.07.10	URUGUAY	3-2	WC
11.07.10	SPAIN	0-1	WCF

* HOLLAND SCORE SHOWN FIRST

emphasis on interchangeability and with every player being totally comfortable in possession.

As the total football side broke up, though, the Dutch slipped into a malaise, failing to qualify for both the 1982 and 1986 World Cup finals. But a revival was soon to follow, spearheaded by a new generation of players at Ajax and PSV. PSV won the European Cup in 1986, while Ajax won the European Cup-Winners Cup in 1987, the UEFA Cup in 1992 (making them only the third side to complete a treble of all three European trophies) and the Champions Cup again in 1995 – remaining unbeaten in all 11 games. To add to that, Ruud Gullit, Frank Rijkaard, Marco van Basten and Ronald Koeman, once again under Rinus Michels' guidance, triumphed in the 1988 European Championship.

That remains Holland's only trophy. They were semi-finalists in the 1998 World Cup and Euro 2000 (which they co-hosted with Belgium) then lost a third World Cup Final 1-0 to a late extra-time goal against Spain in South Africa in 2010. Holland, for whom five-goal tournament joint top scorer Wesley Sneijder was outstanding, were furious with English referee Howard Webb who yellow-carded eight of their players and sent off Johnny Heitinga.

ITALY

The first 30 years of Italian soccer were chaotic and complicated, with various regional leagues and the industrial cities of the north - Milan and Turin - competing for power.

Federazione Italiana Giuoco Calcio
Founded: 1898
FIFA: 1903
World Cup: 1934, 1938, 1982, 2006
European Championship: 1968
Olympics: 1936

The Italian association finally settled in Rome in 1929, and a national league was formed in 1930, providing the boost the game needed and leading to unmatched success in the 1930s.

Under legendary coach Vittorio Pozzo, Italy lost only seven games during the decade, winning the World Cup in 1934 and 1938 and the 1936 Olympic title in between to confirm their superiority. The 1930s also saw the beginnings of a trend for Italian clubs to import foreign players to gain an advantage in the league. The best-known stars of this era were Luisito Monti and Giuseppe Meazza.

After the war Torino were the dominant side, winning four consecutive titles, and providing virtually all of the national team. But, returning from Lisbon, Torino's plane crashed into the Superga Hill outside Turin killing all on board, including ten internationals. Unsurprisingly, this led to a decline for both Torino and Italy during the 1950s.

Many blamed the national team's failure on the number of foreign imports - led by Milan with their Swedish trio of Gunnar Gren, Gunnar Nordahl and Nils Liedholm. The importation of foreigners was banned in 1964, which hampered the clubs making headway in Europe, but it allowed a new generation of Italian players to develop, and they won the 1968 European Championship.

The 1950s and 1960s had seen the development of the sterile defensive system of catenaccio. Even so, Milan and Inter won the European Cup three four times between them in the 1960s and the national side finished runners-up to a marvellous Brazil side in the 1970 World Cup.

A progressive lifting of the imports ban saw Juventus, inspired by Frenchman Michel Platini, dominate the first half of the 1970s while the national side, captained by 40-year-old goalkeeper Dino Zoff, grafted out a third World Cup victory in 1982.

A subsequent Milan revival, financed by millionaire businessman and politician Silvio Berlusconi, brought European Cup successes for a side led by Ruud Gullit and Marco Van Basten under the guidance of Arrigo Sacchi. He progressed to national coach and led Italy to the 1994 World Cup Final which they lost to Brazil after shootout misses by Franco Baresi and Roberto Baggio.

The agonizing manner of the Azzurri exits from major tournaments when they lost on a golden goal to France in the final of Euro 2000 but they turned the tables by defeating the French in the 2006 World Cup Final. This was Italy's fourth triumph, only one fewer than Brazil.

Italy's success came against the domestic backdrop of a match-fixing scandal which created a power vacuum on which Inter capitalized to win five successive league titles and - under coach Jose Mourinho - the Champions League. That success did not carry over into the 2010 World Cup: Italy, to general astonishment, crashed out in the initial group stage.

Italy's captain Fabio Cannavaro leads the World Cup Cup-winning party in Berlin in 2006.

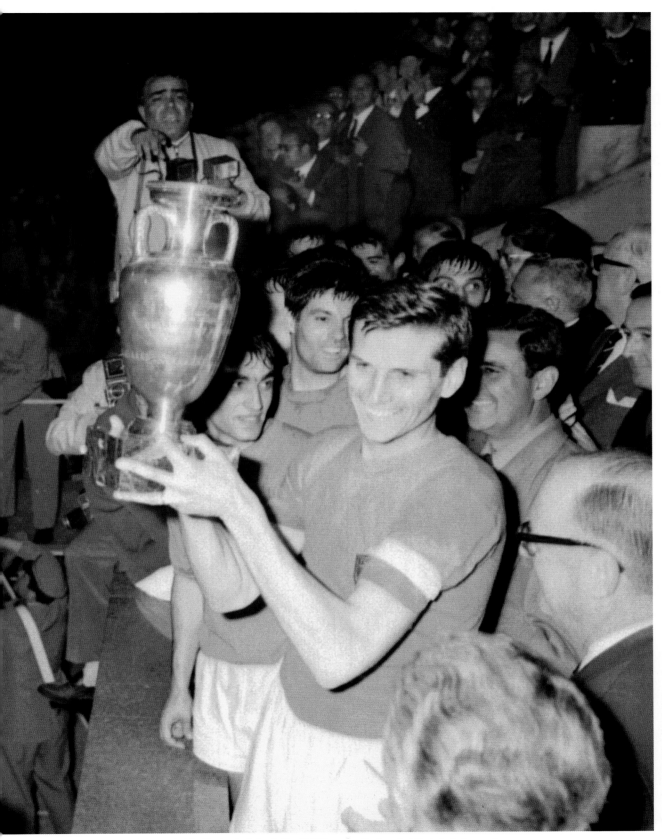

Second time lucky for Giacinto Facchetti after hosts Italy win the 1968 European final against Yugoslavia in a replay.

SPAIN

Spain buried their reputation as international under-achievers by following Euro 2008 success with a first World Cup triumph in South Africa

Real Federacion Española de Futbol
Founded: 1913
FIFA: 1904
European Championship: 1964
Olympics: 1992

Until then Spanish soccer's reputation had been based largely on the exploits of its clubs, particularly Real Madrid and Barcelona, and the successes of the national side in the second half of the 20th century.

Thus the national team's triumph in winning the European Championship in 2008 was long-overdue since Spain had gone 44 years without landing a major title. Subsequently they embarked on a world record-breaking unbeaten run, establishing themselves, along the way, as early favourites to go on and win the 2010 World Cup in South Africa.

Soccer first gained a foothold in the Basque country of Northern Spain through migrant British workers in the 1890s. Indeed, Spain's oldest club, Athletic Bilbao, still retains its English title to this day. The game spread very quickly and was soon popular in Madrid, Barcelona and Valencia. The various regional organizations were brought together in 1913 when the Real Federacion Española de Futbol was formed. In 1920 the national side made their debut, with a 1-0 win over Denmark and, until the Spanish Civil War, Spain's record was quite good. They reached the quarter-finals of the 1928 Olympics, and the 1934 World Cup finals – losing to Italy both times. Star of the side was goalkeeper Ricardo Zamora.

The Civil War and the Second World War halted internationals for almost a decade. But the domestic league grew stronger as the rivalry between Real Madrid, the 'Royal' club, and Barcelona, the Catalan people's club, intensified, especially in the 1950s, as both clubs began importing foreign talent.

Real had Alfredo Di Stefano and Ferenc Puskas, while Barca had the Hungarian trio of Kubala, Kocsis and Czibor. Real Madrid won the first five European Cups (1956-60), heralding the 1960s as a decade of huge success at club and national level. Barcelona won the Fairs Cup, now the UEFA Cup, in 1959, 1960 and 1966; Valencia won it in 1962 and 1963, Real Zaragoza in 1964. Meanwhile Atletico Madrid won the European Cup-Winners Cup in 1962, and Real Madrid won the European Cup again in 1966.

The national side also saw success with qualification for the 1962 and 1966 World Cup finals and a European Championship victory in 1964. A side containing Luis Suarez, possibly the greatest Spanish soccer player ever, and one of comparatively few Spaniards to play in Italy (with Internazionale), beat the Soviet Union 2-1 in Madrid to clinch Spain's first major trophy.

A subsequent ban on foreign imports, intended to enhance the national team, backfired. Over the next 30 years the best Spain achieved was in finishing runners-up in the 1984 European Championship and in reaching the World Cup quarter-finals in 1986. An easing of import restrictions saw stars such as Johan Cruyff of Holland and Diego Maradona of Argentina at Barcelona as well as West Germany's Gunter Netzer and Paul Breitner at Real Madrid grace the club scene. But the clubs never reclaimed their overwhelming initial domination of the international scene despite occasional success.

Madrid won the UEFA Cup twice in succession in the mid-1980s while Barcelona twice picked the Cup-winners Cup and then finally laid their Champions Cup jinx, now with Cruyff as coach, in 1992.

That same year Spain also won Olympic gold in Barcelona but national team success remained elusive even while Real Madrid regained old glories by winning three Champions League crowns around the turn of the millennium.

A dramatic change of fortune was on the way, however, courtesy of a core of outstanding home-grown players from Barcelona such as Xavi,

Emilio Butragueno (right) and his Spanish World Cup hopefuls await the challenge of Algeria in the first round in Mexico.

Fernando Torres scoring the winning goal of the Euro 2008 Final, Spain's first international honours for 44 years.

Andres Iniesta and Carles Puyol.

Spain collected their first major trophy in 44 years when, under veteran coach Luis Aragones, they beat Germany with a Fernando Torres goal in the final of Euro 2008. Barcelona then underlined their own power by winning a unique clean sweep of all six available trophies in 2009 – including the Champions League and Club World Cup.

No fewer than eight of their players – including newly-acquired David Villa – were in the squad as Spain secured their long-overdue first World Cup triumph in South Africa in 2010. Remarkably, new coach Vicente Del Bosque's men did so despite scoring only eight goals in their seven games. Five of those fell to Villa, making him the tournament's joint top scorer. Spain made history as the first team to win the World Cup despite having lost their opening game (against Switzerland).

OTHER EUROPEAN COUNTRIES

Albania

Federata Shqiptare Futbollit
Founded: 1930
FIFA: 1954

Soccer in Albania started at the beginning of the twentieth century, but progress was hampered by first, the ruling Turks and, second, Mussolini's annexation in 1939. The Communist take-over in 1944, under Enver Hoxha, promised a new dawn – but it was a short-lived period of hope for Albanian soccer.

Throughout the 1950s, Albania was in isolation, and between 1954 and 1963 they played only one international – against East Germany. Some progress was made in the 1960s, with Albania gaining entry to both the World Cup and the European Championship, but the isolationist cloak which shrouded the country for so long has ensured that its soccer playing prospects remain as poor as those of its economy.

Andorra

Federacio Andorrana de Futbol
Founded: 1996
FIFA: 1996

Armenia

Football Federation of Armenia
Founded: 1922
FIFA: 1992

Austria

Österreichischer Fussball-Bund
Founded: 1904
FIFA: 1905

Until the 1960s, Vienna was arguably the focal point of continental European soccer in the first half of the twentieth century. Britons living in Vienna provided Austrian soccer's early impetus and, in 1902, Austria beat Hungary 5-0 at the Prater in what has become the world's second oldest regular international fixture after England vs Scotland. The inter-war period was Austria's most successful era when, from 1931 to 1934 the "Wunderteam" – led by Matthias Sindelar – scored 101 goals in 30 matches. They seemed certain favourites for the 1934 World Cup, but defeat in the semi-final to hosts Italy ended their hopes. Austria's chances in the 1938 event were destroyed by the German occupation, and from March 1938 'Austrian' soccer ceased to exist.

A new side came together in the 1950s, led by Ernst Ocwirk and Gerhard Hanappi, which looked set for World Cup success in 1954. But Germany again beat them in the semi-final, 6-1. A poor showing in 1958 in Sweden marked the start of a long decline, with the low point coming in 1991 with defeat to the Faroe Islands – playing their first ever competitive match – in a European Championship qualifier.

Austria, who last qualified for the World Cup in 1998, were disappointing first round flops in co-hosting Euro 2008.

Azerbaijan

Azarbaycan Futbol Federasiyalari Assosiasiyasi
Founded: 1993
FIFA: 1994

The Azeris made their independent international debut in the 1996 European Championship but, because of civil war, were forced to play their initial home games in Turkey rather than in their national stadium which is named after Tofik Bakhamorov, the linesmen who ruled in England and Geoff Hurst's favour in the 196 World Cup Final.

Belarus

Belarus Football Federation
Founded: 1992
FIFA: 1992

Belgium

Union Royale Belge des Sociétés de Football-Association
Founded: 1895
FIFA: 1904

Belgian soccer has taken a long time to develop. With an association formed in 1895 and the second-oldest league outside Great Britain, it was natural for the Belgians to be a driving force behind the formation of FIFA and one of only four European sides to go to Uruguay for the first World Cup in

Bulgaria's Yordan Lechkov topples World Cup holders Germany in New Jersey in 1994.

1930. But the strictly amateur nature of the domestic game severely hindered progress. Amateurism was discarded in 1972 and the national side immediately improved. From 1972 to 1984, Belgium reached the last eight of four successive European Championships, reaching the Final in 1980 when they lost to West Germany. The class of 1980 represented Belgium for almost a decade and contained many of their most celebrated players, including goalkeeper Jean-Marie Pfaff, full-back Eric Gerets and striker Jan Ceulemans. Their finest hour came at the 1986 World Cup finals, where they reached the semi-finals. Belgium made history as co-hosts of the 2000 European Championship but have missed out on major events since reaching the second round of the 2002 World Cup.

Bosnia-Herzegovina

Nogometni Savez Bosne I Herzegovine
Founded: 1991
FIFA: 1992

Bosnia made history as UEFA's 50th member nation.

Bulgaria

Bulgarski Futbolen Solus
Founded: 1923
FIFA: 1924

Bulgarian soccer has been sliding steadily from grace at both national team and domestic level since they finished a best-ever fourth in the 1994 World Cup finals in the United States when they knocked out defending Cup-holders Germany along the way. Occasional disappointing appearances followed in occasional World Cup and Euro tournament finals while the domestic game struggled to cope with an increasing wave of hooligan violence.. Like many Eastern Bloc countries Bulgaria made little impact in international soccer until the Communists had taken over in 1944 and completely reorganized the domestic game. A rigid style of passing play was imposed on the national side, making Bulgaria very difficult opponents and one of Europe's top sides during the 1960s and 1970s.

However, this system discouraged individual flair and flexibility – and although they qualified for five finals between 1962 and 1990, they did not win one of their matches! But this period did produce one of Bulgaria's greatest players, Georgi Asparoukhov, who scored 19 goals in 50 games before dying, with teammate Nikola Kotkov, in a car crash in 1971.

There followed progression beyond the group round of the World Cup in Mexico in 1986, and then success in 1994, when Bulgaria qualified with a last-gasp 2-1 victory over France, then eliminated defending Cup-holders Germany 2-1 in the quarter-finals on their way to finishing fourth. Hristo Stoichkov, a Champions Cup-winning hero with Barcelona, emerged as one of the world's finest players, with fellow striker Emil Kostadinov and midfielders Yordan Lechkov and Krasimir Balakov not far behind. However, the succeeding generation of players has proved nowhere near as talented or successful.

Croatia

Croatian Football Federation
Founded: 1991
FIFA: 1992

Until 1991 Croatia did not even exist as a country, and they were not recognized by FIFA until a year later. But since then their impact on the world stage has been huge. They reached the quarter-finals of Euro 96, beating Italy on the way, and then stormed to third place in France with players such as Zvonimir Boban, Davor Suker and Robert Prosinecki (all World Youth Cup-winners with Yugoslavia in 1987) proving

themselves as some of the most technically gifted in the game. Suker scored six goals in France to win the Golden Boot. No such luck in 2002 and 2006, though Croatia did reach the quarter-finals of Euro 2008.

Cyprus

Cyprus Football Association
Founded: 1934
FIFA: 1948

Cypriot soccer developed in the 1930s thanks to British colonial encouragement. Independent FIFA membership came in 1948 but Cyprus remain one of Europe's minnows. Their 2-0 win over the Faroe Islands in 1992 was their first in competition for nearly 20 years.

Czech Republic

Cesko Moravsky Fotbalovy Svaz
Founded: 1993
FIFA: 1994
European Championship: 1976
(as Czechoslovakia)
Olympics: 1980 (as Czechoslovakia)

From the time Czechoslovakia came into existence in 1918, the Czechs were at the forefront of European soccer. They were runners-up in both the 1920 and 1964 Olympic Games, and won the tournament in 1980, in Moscow. They were finalists at the 1934 World Cup with a side containing Antonin Puc, Frantisek Planicka, the finest pre-war goalkeeper, and Oldrich Nejedly.

The Communist take-over after the war led to the usual reorganization of the domestic game, which hindered rather than helped as clubs like Sparta and Slavia Prague had been doing very well as professional sides. The army team Dukla Prague rose to prominence and provided the basis of the 1960's Czech side that was among the best in the world. Josef Masopust, Czechoslovakia's most famous player, led the side to third place in the inaugural European Championship in 1960, and to the 1962 World Cup Final, which was lost to Brazil. Czechoslovakia's biggest success came at the 1976 European Championship

when, with stars such as goalkeeper Ivo Viktor, defender Anton Ondrus, Antonin Panenka, in midfield, and Zdenek Nehoda, in attack, they beat West Germany in the Final.

The political split in 1994 with Slovakia proved no handicap for the new Czech Republic national team. They finished runners-up – albeit only on a golden goal – to Germany in Euro 96 and were beaten unluckily on the short-lived silver goal method by Greece in the semi-finals of Euro 2004. Injuries in attack and midfield upset their prospects in the finals of both the 2006 World Cup and Euro 2008.

Denmark

Dansk Boldspil-Union
Founded: 1889
FIFA: 1904
European Championship: 1992
Olympics: 1906

Denmark was one of the first countries in continental Europe to take up soccer and has some of the oldest clubs in the world. But their rigid adherence to amateurism meant that Denmark was left behind when most of the rest of Europe adopted professionalism.

Denmark has enjoyed its greatest success at the Olympics. Winners in 1906 and runners-up in 1908 and 1912, the Danes produced some outstanding players – notably Nils Middelboe, who played so well for Chelsea. A period of decline occurred during the inter-war years, but qualification for the 1948 and 1960 Olympics sparked hopes of a revival. However, the amateur nature of the domestic game, together with a rule that barred foreign-based players from the national side, stifled progress.

The 1970s prompted great chances for Danish soccer as a flood of

Michael Laudrup lays claim to being Denmark's greatest-ever player.

players – such as Allan Simonsen – left Denmark to join clubs in Western Europe. The rule barring 'exported' players such as Michael Laudrup, Preben Elkjaer, Jesper Olsen, Morten Olsen and Soren Lerby from the national side was lifted in 1976 and undoubtedly helped the Danish side develop. These players formed the nucleus of the 1980's "Dinamite" side that reached the 1984 European Championship semi-finals and the 1986 World Cup second round.

In the late 1980s the league was restructured and a new generation of players – including Michael Laudrup's brother, Brian – emerged to propel Denmark to a surprise European Champions title in 1992. That success was all the more remarkable as they were eleventh-hour replacements for the expelled Yugoslavs. Denmark were also impressive in France 98, reaching the quarter-finals. Building a new team after the Laudrup brothers retired proved challenging and the best the Danes have managed since was reaching the World Cup second round in 2002.

Estonia
Estonian Football Federation
Founded: 1921
FIFA: 1923

Estonia, like Baltic neighbours Lithuania and Latvia, ceased to exist after 1940 when the Soviet Union took over. However, Estonia never withdrew from FIFA, their membership was merely put on ice, and in 1992 they came back into the fold. The hand-to-mouth survival of the national game was illustrated in 1996 when Estonia became embroiled in controversy over the suitability of hired floodlights for a World Cup-tie against Scotland and refused to turn up for the match in Tallinn. The match was awarded to Scotland, but then FIFA reconsidered and ordered a replay on neutral territory, in Monaco, which finished 0-0.

Faroe Islands
Fotboltssamband Foroya
Founded: 1979
FIFA: 1988

Soccer has been played on these tiny islands since before the Second World War, with a league starting in 1942 and a cup competition in 1967. But owing to the Faroes' remoteness and lack of grass pitches, competitive matches against overseas opponents were few and far between.

The Faroes entry into the 1992 European Championship, however, was spectacular. A 1-0 win over Austria in their first competitive match made headlines across Europe and stimulated development of the domestic game.

Finland
Suomen Palloliito Finlands Bollofoerbund
Founded: 1907
FIFA: 1908

Soccer lags well behind ice hockey, athletics, winter sports and motor rallying in terms of popularity in Finland. Prior to the 1970s, national team outings were confined to other Nordic countries, and even though Finland have regularly entered the World Cup and European Championship since then, success has been scarce. However, the Finns did almost qualify for the 1980 European Championship finals and from time to time have given one of their rivals a severe fright. In 1995 star forward Jari Litmanen, with Ajax, became the first Finnish soccer player to be a Champions Cup-winner.

Georgia
Football Federation of Georgia
Founded: 1992
FIFA: 1992

Georgia seceded, in soccer terms, from the old Soviet Union, in the late 1980s. Their latent strength had been underlined by the success of top club Dynamo Tbilisi in winning the 1981 Cup-Winners Cup. But they struggled to establish themselves in international competition at all levels after the final collapse of the Soviet empire.

Greece
Fédération Hellénique de Football
Founded: 1926
FIFA: 1927
European Championship: 2004

Greek soccer's development in the first half of the twentieth century was severely hampered by civil war and the unstable political climate in the Balkans. These factors, linked to the 'Olympian' adherence to the amateur spirit of the game, meant that a national league was not formed until 1960, and full professionalism arrived as late as 1979. Consequently, success for Greek sides at national and club level has been rare. The clubs, centred on Athens and Salonica have so far failed to win a single European trophy. Panathinaikos went closest to breaking that duck when they reached the 1971 European Cup Final, which they lost to Ajax. Panathinaikos also made it to the 1996 UEFA Champions League semi-final and a famous first-leg victory away to Ajax Amsterdam.

The national side had consistently failed to make an impression until 2004. Qualification for the 1980 European Championship was the first time the Greeks had qualified for any finals tournament, and it was another 13 years before they tasted success again. Coach Alketas Panagoulias – the man behind the 1980 success – returned to guide Greece through to the 1994 World Cup finals for the first time, where they lost all three games. It was all change in the 2004 European Championships, however, when, led by German coach Otto Rehhagel, they defied all the odds to emerge as winners with a highly disciplined performance. Rehhagel stepped down after, in 2010, leading Greece back to the World Cup.

Hungary
Magyar Labdarugo Szovetseg
Founded: 1901
FIFA: 1906
Olympics: 1952, 1964, 1968

Hungary will always be renowned for the "Magical Magyars" side of the 1950s. This side lost only one international in five years before failing in the 1954 World Cup. The forward line of Laszlo Budai, Sandor Kocsis, Nandor Hidegkuti, Zoltan Czibor and Ferenc Puskas – the greatest player of his era – terrorized opposition defences and scored 173 goals during this time. In 1953, they became the first non-British side to beat England at home.

Yet this was not the first outstanding

Greece's captain Theodoras Zagorakis (centre) celebrates winning the European Championship in 2004.

History in the making: Ferenc Puskas (left) and his Hungarians prepare to demolish England at Wembley in 1953.

side Hungary had produced. Hungarian clubs, notably MTK Budapest, who won ten consecutive titles (1914-25), dominated European soccer in the inter-war period, winning five Mitropa Cups in the 1930s. The national side, containing players such as Gyorgy Sarosi and Gyula Zsengeller reached the World Cup Final in 1938, where they lost to Italy.

The Hungarian uprising of 1958 broke up the "Magical" side, but by the 1960s another had emerged. The new stars were Florian Albert and Ferenc Bene, who led Hungary to the 1962 and 1966 World Cup quarter-finals and Olympic gold in 1964 and 1968. Despite some successes for the clubs, particularly Ujpest who won nine titles in eleven years, the 1970s marked the beginning of a decline for the national side. Regular recent failure to qualify for the World Cup finals followed poor performances at the 1978, 1982, and 1986 tournaments.

Iceland
Knattspyrnusamband Island
Founded: 1947
FIFA: 1929

Although one of Europe's "minnow" nations, Iceland are often capable of producing an upset. In the 1994 World Cup qualifiers they beat Hungary home and away and finished five points above them in the group! They played their first international in 1946, against Denmark, and have only entered the World Cup and European Championship regularly since the 1970s. Iceland has produced several outstanding players in recent years, notably Asgeir Sirgurvinsson and Petur Petursson. They also made history in 1996 when a father and son, Arnor and Eidur-Smari Gudjohnsen, both played in a friendly against Estonia. Eidur Godjohnsen later enhanced the status of Icelandic players by starring with Chelsea and Barcelona.

Israel
Hitachdut Lekaduregel Beisrael
Founded: 1928
FIFA: 1929
Asian Championship: 1964

Despite the fact that the state of Israel was not founded until 1948, a soccer association had been formed in the former Palestine some 20 years earlier. Palestine played only a handful of international matches before the national side was revived as Israel in 1949. At first only World Cup matches or friendlies were played, as Israel was surrounded by hostile Arab nations, all of whom were members of the Asian Federation and who refused to play the Israelis. In the 1958 World Cup, for instance, Israel's opponents all withdrew, forcing FIFA to order them to play-off against Wales for a finals place. Similar withdrawals disrupted the Asian Championships, which Israel hosted and won in 1964 - their only honour.

In 1976, Israel were thrown out of the Asian Confederation on political grounds. They led a nomadic existence, as associate members of Oceania, until they were formally accepted into UEFA in 1991. The national side and clubs subsequently became regular entrants in European competitions though their progress has been restricted by security problems that have often prevented matches taking place in Israel itself.

Kazakhstan
Football Association of the
Republic of Kazakhstan
Founded: 1914
FIFA: 1994

A former Soviet state, Kazakhstan "went independent" first into the Asian Football Confederation, then transferred to UEFA in 2002.

Latvia
Football Association of Latvia
Founded: 1921
FIFA: 1923

Latvia were the strongest of the Baltic sides before the Second World War, but still represented easy pickings for European opponents – France hammered them 7-0 at the 1924 Olympics. Despite this, Latvia only narrowly failed to qualify for the 1938 World Cup finals. Occupied, and wiped off the political map of Europe by the Soviet Union in 1940, Latvia continued playing full internationals until 1949. They returned to competition in 1993. A decade later they shocked Turkey in a play-off to qualify for the finals of the 2004 European Championship but collected only one point.

Liechtenstein
Liechtensteiner Fussball-Verband
Founded: 1933
FIFA: 1974

With a population of just 27,000, it is remarkable that Liechtenstein has a national side at all. They made unsuccessful attempts to qualify for the 1988 and 1992 Olympic Games, before entering the competitive mainstream in the 1996 European Championship qualifying round. Liechtenstein's few clubs compete in regional Swiss leagues.

Lithuania

Lithuanian Football Association
Founded: 1921
FIFA: 1923

Lithuania were FIFA members between 1923 and 1940, at a time when the Baltic nations were among the weakest in Europe. They lost their first international 5-0 at home to Estonia in 1923, and they made an unsuccessful bid to qualify for the 1924 Olympic tournament. The Soviets took over in 1940, but Lithuania continued playing until 1949, by which time they were the strongest of the Baltic states. Lithuania played their first World Cup match since 1937 in 1992, and now the country has its own national league.

Luxembourg

Fédération Luxembourgeoise de Football
Founded: 1908
FIFA: 1910

Luxembourg made a minor slice of history in the 2010 World Cup: this was the first time, in 16 vain qualifying attempts, that they had not finished bottom of their preliminary group. This time around they finished above Moldova. Thus the Grand Duchy has to look back to 1964 for any significant international progress when they reached the quarter-finals of the European Championship. Though Luxembourg has a domestic league their most notable players end up with clubs in France or Belgium of Holland.

Macedonia (Former Yugoslav Republic of)

Football Association of the Former Yugoslav Republic of Macedonia
Founded: 1908
FIFA: 1994

One of the Balkan states that gained independence in the 1990s,

Portugal's exciting Cristiano Ronaldo, who, in 2009, became the world's most expensive footballer.

Macedonia have failed to emulate the success of neighbours Slovenia or even threaten qualification in a major event.

Malta

Malta Football Association
Founded: 1900
FIFA: 1959

Malta, as a British colony, took up soccer early. The Malta FA was affiliated to the Football Association in London until 1959, when they decided to go their own way and join FIFA. They entered the 1960 Olympic qualifiers, in the African section, but made no headway. Malta have never qualified for the World Cup or the European Championship finals.

Moldova

Moldavian Football Federation
Founded: 1993
FIFA: 1994

Moldova marked their competitive 'arrival' on the international soccer scene only after the collapse of the Soviet Union, and they defeated Wales 3-2 in a 1996 European Championship qualifying tie in the capital, Chisinau.

Montenegro

Football Association of Montenegro
Founded: 2006
FIFA: 2007

Soccer playing independence followed the country's political split from Serbia in 2006.

Norway

Norges Fotballforbun
Founded: 1902
FIFA: 1908

Norway, once a European minnow, upset the form book in the 1994 World Cup qualifiers, easily winning their group ahead of Holland, England and Poland - and they have continued to progress ever since. They also beat Brazil 2-1 in a group-stage match in France in 1998 before losing to Italy in the second round. It has been an incredible rise up the national rankings for the Scandinavian side, thanks largely to the fact that most of their senior players are based abroad. Many have been in England (such as Chelsea's Tore Andre Flo, Manchester United's Ole Gunnar Solskjaer and Henning Berg and Tottenham's Steffen Iversen). At Euro 2000, Iversen scored to beat Spain, but it was their only goal of the finals.

Poland

Polski Zwiazek Pilki Noznej
Founded: 1919
FIFA: 1923
Olympics: 1972

The Polish state was created in 1921 and Poland made their debut the same year against Hungary. Despite reaching the 1938 World Cup finals, the pre-war record was poor, but the post-war Communist take-over brought great change. Clubs became attached to government bodies and new ones were formed - notably Gornik Zabrze, who reached the European Cup-Winners Cup Final in 1969.

In 1972 Poland won the gold medal at the Munich Olympics. This side contained Wlodzimierz Lubanski, their top scorer, Kazimierz Deyna, capped 102 times, and Robert Gadocha. For the 1974 World Cup finals, this trio was joined by Gregorz Lato, Poland's most capped player (104 times), with Jan Tomaszewski in goal. Poland finished third and this team stayed together, reaching the World Cup finals again in 1978. There was more success at the 1982 finals when, with an outstanding Zbigniew Boniek, Poland reached the semi-finals. The subsequent collapse of Communism led also to the collapse of state subsidies, forcing clubs to sell star players abroad to the detriment of the national team. They proved first-round failures at the World Cups of both 2002 and 2006 but will hope to do better as co-hosts of the 2012 European finals.

Portugal

Federacao Portuguesa de Futebol
Founded: 1914
FIFA: 1926

The Portuguese Football Association was founded in 1914 as the result of a merger between the associations of Lisbon and Oporto - the two cities that have utterly dominated domestic soccer. The Lisbon duo of Benfica and Sporting Lisbon, along with their rivals FC Porto from Oporto, are among the most famous names in world club soccer. The League Championship, set up in 1935, has only ever been won by these three, apart from 1948 (won by Belenenses) and 2001 (Boavista).

Portugal's greatest era was in the 1960s, when Benfica won the European Cup twice (1961 and 1962) and reached a further three finals. The bulk of this Benfica side formed the nucleus of the national team, which was then at its peak. The most famous of them was Mozambique-born Eusebio, who was arguably the best player of the 1966 World Cup when Portugal finished third. Fellow Mozambican Mario Coluna and Angola-born José Aguas were other 'adopted' players in an impressive side which also included the Benfica quartet Costa Pereira, in goal, Germano, in defence, and Cavem and José Augusto on the wings.

Portugal sparked revival signs in the 1980s as Porto won the Champions Cup and Benfica reached the finals of both the Champions Cup and UEFA Cup. The youngsters then won the World Youth Cups of 1989 and 1991 and star graduate Luis Figo would later be crowned both World and European Player of the Year. Porto, under bright young coach Jose Mourinho, won the UEFA Cup and Champions League in 2003 and 2004 to spark a renewal of confidence in the national team. The emergence of outstanding attacker Cristiano Ronaldo saw Portugal revive to finish runners-up, as hosts, at Euro 2004 and then finish fourth in the 2006 World Cup.

Romania

Federatia Romana de Fotbal
Founded: 1908
FIFA: 1930

Romania embraced soccer before most of her Balkan neighbours, mainly owing to the influence of the country's sovereign, King Carol, who was a soccer fanatic. He was determined that Romania should enter the first World Cup where they were beaten by Uruguay in the first round. They also entered the 1934 and 1938 tournaments, but could not progress beyond the first round, despite the presence of Iuliu Bodola, their top scorer to this day. The Communists took over in 1944 and, as elsewhere, reorganized the domestic game. Two of the clubs created in Bucharest, Steaua, the army team, and Dinamo, the police team, have dominated Romanian soccer ever since – and in 1986 Steaua became the first team from behind the Iron Curtain to win the European Cup.

On the international front, Romania enjoyed a brief upsurge with qualification for the 1970 World Cup, and a quarter-final finish in the 1977 European Championship. They reached three World Cups in a row, 1990–98 and qualified for the Euro 96 and 2000 finals, too. However, despite the inspiration of Gheorghe Hagi, they did not have the best of luck. In 1990 and 1994 Romania were eliminated after penalty shoot-outs and in 1998, they topped their first round group, but lost 1-0 to Croatia in the second round. They reached the quarter-finals at Euro 2000 but were first-round failures in 2008.

Russia

Russian Football Federation
Founded: 1922 (as Soviet Union)
FIFA: 1922 (as Soviet Union)
European Championship: 1960 (as Soviet Union)
Olympics: 1956, 1988 (as Soviet Union)

Russia's soccer history is inextricably entwined with that of the former Soviet Union. By the start of the twentieth century, leagues had been formed in most of the cities of the Russian empire, notably in what was then the capital, St Petersburg.

In 1912, an all-Russian soccer union was created and a championship was introduced. In the same year 'Tsarist Russia' entered the Stockholm Olympics but went out in the first round to Finland, and then lost 16-0 to Germany in the consolation tournament that followed. After the Revolution, Russia took on the guise of the Soviet Union. The Communists reorganized soccer from top to bottom, with the emphasis on teamwork rather than individual flair. Moscow, now the Soviet capital, became the main soccer centre with five great workers' clubs: Dynamo (electrical trades), Spartak (producers co-operatives), Torpedo (car manufacturers), Lokomitive (railways) and CSKA (the army).

In the 1950s the national side began to venture outside the country. They won the 1956 Olympic Games and reached the quarter-finals of the 1958 World Cup at their first attempt. This side contained some of Soviet soccers greatest names, including Igor Netto, Valentin Ivanov, Nikita Simonyan and the great goalkeeper Lev Yashin. In 1960 they won the very first European Championship,

FC Porto revel in the club's second Champions Cup triumph, in Gelsenkirchen in 2004.

but this remains the only major triumph either the Soviet Union or Russia has ever had. During the 1960s, the Soviets lost the Final of the European Championship in 1964 and 1972, and reached the semi-finals in 1968. In the World Cup, they reached the quarter-finals in 1962 and went the semi-finals in 1966.

During the 1970s Oleg Blokhin emerged as the Soviet Union's greatest-ever player, but the national side was in decline until, in 1988, they reached the European Championship Final. The Soviet sides of 1986 and 1988 were arguably the best since the 1960s, but were composed mainly of Dynamo Kiev players. Despite Moscow's, and therefore Russia's, dominance of Soviet soccer, the only Soviet sides to win European club competitions were not Russian. Kiev, in the Ukraine, won the European Cup-Winners Cup in 1975 and 1986 and Dynamo Tbilisi, from Georgia, won the same tournament in 1981.

In September 1991 the Soviet Union began to disintegrate with the 15 former republics gaining independence and joining the Asian or European confederations. Russia, picking up where the Soviet Union had left off, reached the World Cup finals in 1994 and 2002. However they failed disappointingly to qualify in 2006 and 2010 despite reaching the Euro 2008 semi-finals inbetween under Dutch coach Guus Hiddink.

San Marino
Federazione Sammarinese Giuoco Calcio
Founded: 1931
FIFA: 1988
Located entirely within Italy, the Most Serene Republic of San Marino is one of the smallest nations ever to enter the international arena. Its population is just 24,000.

Serbia (formerly Yugoslavia)
Fudbalski Savez Srbije I Crne Gore
Founded: 1919
FIFA: 1919
Olympic Games: 1960
Serbia is the country to emerge from the fragmentation of the former Yugoslavia. In 2003 the country became Serbia and Montenegro and then, in 2006, Serbia alone.

Yugoslavia had been nicknamed the "Argentina of Europe" for its apparent production line of talented players who were exported all over Europe, starting with Ivan Bek who starred in the Yugoslav team who reached the semi-finals of the inaugural World Cup in 1930.

Later Yugoslavia were Olympic winners in 1960 and World Cup semi-finalists two years later while top clubs such as Red Star and army club Partizan from Belgrade achieved notable success in the European Cup: Partizan were runners-up in 1966 and Red Star the first Slav champions in 1991.

The outbreak of civil strife saw Yugoslavia barred from competing in the 1992 European finals but, as Serbia, they returned to reach the last eight in 2000. They were disappointing first-round failures however in the 2010 World Cup finals.

Slovakia
Slovak Football Association
Founded: 1993
FIFA: 1994

Slovakia were always poor relations in the former Czechoslovakia and, after the political split in the mid-1990s, it took them 17 years to find their international soccer feet. Then they not only reached the finals of the World Cup in 2010 for the first time but eliminated holders Italy on their way to reaching the second round. Three-goal Robert Vittek was briefly the tournament's joint top scorer.

Most notable achievement by a Slovak club was Slovan Bratislava's victory in the European Cup-winners Cup in 1969, before the national split.

Slovenia
Nogometna Zveza Slovenije
Founded: 1991
FIFA: 1992
Slovenia were the first newly-independent country to emerge from the fragmentation of the former Yugoslavia at the start of the 1990s. For a small new nation their international progress has been remarkable. They first joined the elite at the finals of Euro 2000 then reached the subsequent World Cup only to lose their nerve when an initial 3-1 defeat by Spain prompted a row between coach Srecko Katanec and star forward Zlatko Zahovic. They returned to the finals in South Africa in 2010 and were in sight of reaching the second round for the first time until narrowly losing their last group game by 1-0 to England.

Sweden
Svensk Fotbollforblundet
Founded: 1904
FIFA: 1904
Olympics: 1948
Since the 1920s Sweden have been Scandinavia's top national side and have a deserved reputation for producing quality players. An Association was formed in 1904 and they joined FIFA the same year. Gothenburg was, and still is, the centre of Swedish domestic soccer and the National League, instituted in 1925, has been dominated by Gothenburg's

Henrik Larsson reels away in celebration after scoring for Sweden.

clubs, Orgryte, IFK and GAIS, along with AIK and Djurgardens of Stockholm. Sweden's national side made their debut in 1908 and entered the first four Olympic tournaments, with mixed success. This era, however, produced the country's greatest striker, Sven Rydell, who scored 49 goals in 43 games. Sweden were at their best in the late 1940s when they boasted one of the most famous forward lines in history: Gunnar Gren, Gunnar Nordahl and Nils Liedholm sparked Sweden to Olympic gold in 1948 and were signed by Milan.

Swedes were regularly bought by European clubs but were then barred from the national side by the strictly amateur rules of the association. Despite this handicap, Sweden finished third in the 1950 World Cup, with Nacka Skoglund the new star. The professional ban was lifted in time for the 1958 World Cup finals, which Sweden hosted, and with all their players available they reached the Final. A decline followed in the 1960s, but Sweden qualified for all three World Cup finals in the 1970s, with Björn Nordqvist clocking up a record 115 appearances between 1963 and 1978. The clubs too began to make an impact, and Malmö reached the European Cup Final in 1979. IFK Gothenburg enjoyed the greatest success, though, winning the UEFA Cup twice – as part-timers, because Sweden had not yet introduced full professionalism. Sweden's first appearance in the European Championship finals came in 1992, by virtue of being hosts, but they were beaten in the semi-finals by Germany. They finished third in the 1994 World Cup and reached the second round in both 2002 and 2006. They started brightly at Euro 2004 before losing to Holland in the quarter-finals.

Switzerland
Schweizerischer Fussballverband
Founded: 1895
FIFA: 1904
The Swiss, as host to the headquarters of both FIFA and UEFA, have always

Turkey overcome shock outsiders Senegal to reach the 2002 World Cup semi-finals.

had a role in the forefront of world and European soccer. The British influence in the early days remains clear in the club names such as Grasshopper (Zurich) and Young Boys (Bern).

The national side was a power as early as the inter-war years. They were runners-up at the 1924 Olympics and World Cup quarter-finalists in both 1934 and 1938. The most famous names of this era were the Abegglen brothers, Max and André, who scored over 60 goals between them. The man responsible for this success was Karl Rappan. He devised the "Swiss Bolt" system, which involved using a free man at the back as a sort of libero, and under Rappan, the Swiss reached the finals of four of the first five World Cups played after the war. Their best performance was in 1954 when, as hosts, they reached the quarter-finals.

Nothing comparable was achieved for another 40 years before Switzerland were revitalized under the management of Englishman Roy Hodgson. They then surprised themselves again by reaching the second round of the 2006 World Cup.

Here a penalty shootout defeat by Ukraine meant the Swiss became the first team ever eliminated without having conceded a goal. However their own attacking failures led to first-round exits from Euro 2008 – which they co-hosted with Austria – and the 2010 World Cup.

Turkey
Turkiye Futbol Federasyono
Founded: 1923
FIFA: 1933
Turkey's third place finish at the 2002 World Cup underlined their rapid rise up Europe's soccer ladder. With a population of 55 million, a fiercely competitive and well-attended league and plenty of talented players, one World Cup finals appearance in 1954 always appeared a pretty sorry return. Then, in the mid-1990s, the TV and commercial revolution financed change and development. The big three Istanbul clubs – Galatasaray, Besiktas and Fenerbahce – began buying foreign players, with Gala importing Romania's Gica Popescu and Gheorghe Hagi, plus

Brazil's 1994 World Cup-winning goalkeeper Claudio Taffarel. They helped inspire domestic stars, such as striker Hakan Sukur, to raise their game and the international profile of Turkish soccer.

The national team reached the European Championship finals in 1996 and 2000 – when Galatasaray also carried off the UEFA Cup to become the first Turkish club to land a European trophy. The national team then topped that by securing third place at the 2002 World Cup.

Ukraine
Football Federation of Ukraine
Founded: 1992
FIFA: 1992
Ukraine, and top club Kiev Dynamo, had been powers within the Soviet system before its collapse. But they struggled to establish an identity after independence in 1992, with the domestic game hampered by corruption and criminality. Finally, the national team not only reached the World Cup finals for the first time in 2006 but reached the quarter-finals before losing to Italy.

VENEZUELA
- CA 2007

COLOMBIA
- 2001
- CA 2001

ECUADOR
- CA 1947, CA 1993

PERU
- 1939, 1975
- CA 1927, CA 1939, CA 1953, CA 1957, CA 2004

BRAZIL
- 1958, 1962, 1970, 1994, 2002
- 1919, 1922, 1949, 1989, 1997, 1999, 2004
- CA 1919, CA 1922, CA 1949, WC 1950, CA 1989, CA 1997, CA 1999, CA 2004, CA 2007

BOLIVIA
- 1963
- CA 1963, CA 1997

PARAGUAY
- 1953, 1979
- CA 1999

CHILE
- CA 1920, CA 1926, CA 1955, WC 1962, CA 1991

ARGENTINA
- 1978, 1986
- 1921, 1925, 1927, 1929, 1937, 1947, 1955, 1957, 1959, 1991, 1993
- CA 1921, CA 1925, CA 1929, CA 1937, CA 1959, WC 1978, CA 1987

URUGUAY
- 1930, 1950
- 1917, 1920, 1923, 1924, 1926, 1942, 1967, 1983, 1987, 1995
- CA 1917, CA 1923, CA 1924, WC 1930, CA 1942, CA 1967, CA 1995

KEY
- ☆ WORLD CUP WINNERS
- ☆ COPA AMERICA WINNERS
- CHAMPIONSHIP HOSTS
- WC (WORLD CUP)
- CA (COPA AMERICA)

SOUTH AMERICA

Geographical and communications problems in the early years of international soccer led to South America going its own way in terms of regional administration.

Indeed, South America should be credited as the model for the other five continental confederations.

The Confederacion Sudamericana de Futbol, known for ease of use as CONMEBOL, was founded in 1916. The moving spirit was the Uruguayan official Hector Gomez who had started trying to enthuse other South Americans in his concept in 1912.

Four years later what is often considered the first official South American championship was staged in Buenos Aires. The Argentine federation undertook the organization as its own means of celebrating the country's centenary of independence. Gomez duly sailed across the river Plate from Montevideo to convene what was CONMEBOL's founding meeting with colleagues from Argentina, Brazil and Chile.

Paraguay joined in 1917, Peru in 1924, Bolivia in 1925, Ecuador in 1927, Colombia in 1940 and Venezuela in 1952. In the northern regions of South America disputes reigned over whether countries fell into the remit of CONMEBOL or of a fledgling Central American confederation. Colombia, for example, switched alliegiance from Central to South in 1940. However Guyana and Surinam had always looked culturally and socially towards the Caribbean and thus duly became members of CONCACAF.

CONMEBOL grew in importance after the launch of the Copa Libertadores in 1960 at the behest of the continent's big clubs who wanted their own equivalent to Europe's Champions Club Cup – and the lucrative opportunity to cross swords in what would become the so-called World Club Cup.

Remarkably, given the political turbulence in the region, CONMEBOL has remained surprisingly stable under the long-term leadership provided over the past two decades by Peru's Teofilo Salinas Fuller and then Paraguay's Nicolas Leoz.

Uruguayan fans get behind the 'Celeste' in typically colourful fashion ahead of the 1999 South American Championship final against Brazil.

ARGENTINA

This country consistently produced some of the most technically gifted and hard-working players in the world.

Asociacion del Futbol Argentino
Founded: 1893
FIFA: 1912
World Cup: 1978, 1986
South American Championship: 1910, 1921, 1925, 1927, 1929, 1937, 1941, 1945, 1946, 1947, 1955, 1957, 1991, 1993

Of the South American nations, Argentina are one of the most consistently successful.

The British brought soccer to Argentina in the 1860s, and although, at first, it was exclusive to the British residents in Buenos Aires, by the turn of the century numerous clubs had been formed.

The Argentine Football Association was founded in 1891 by an Englishman, Alexander Hutton, and a league was formed the same year. Although the championship was not a truly national competition, as it contained only clubs from Buenos Aires, La Plata, Rosario and Santa Fé, their intense rivalry of ensured that Argentina had a vibrant domestic scene from the outset.

The national side also made an early start, and in 1901 a representative side played neighbouring Uruguay in the first international match to be staged outside Great Britain. The seeds were sown for a rivalry that has grown into one of the most enduring and intense derby matches in the world.

Professionalism was adopted in 1931, and River Plate and Boca Juniors soon emerged as dominant forces. River's side of the 1940s was the greatest of them all, containing a forward line of Muñoz, Moreno, Pedernera, Labruna and Loustau, which became known as La Maquina – "the machine."

The national side were runners-up to Uruguay in the 1928 Olympics and met their deadly rivals again two years later in the 1930 World Cup Final. Although they lost 4-2,

Maradona salutes after his brilliant solo goal against England in the 1986 World Cup quarter-final.

the impressive Argentine side was plundered by Italian agents – starting a draining process that continues today. To avoid a repeat, a third-rate side went to the 1934 tournament, and Argentina did not make a serious attempt on the World Cup again until the 1950s. Indeed, the 1950s saw the birth of an exceptional side, with another famous forward line of Corbatta, Maschio, Angelillo, Sivori and Cruz.

Little progress was made in the 1960s and 1970s, despite Independiente and Estudiantes dominating the Libertadores Cup, and Argentina had to wait until 1978 for their first World Cup success. On

Argentina prepare to fly to London for their first senior international against England.

Date	Opponent	Score	Comp
02.07.07	COLOMBIA	4-2	CA
05.07.07	PARAGUAY	1-0	CA
08.07.07	PERU	4-0	CA
11.07.07	MEXICO	3-0	CA
15.07.07	BRAZIL	0-3	CA
22.08.07	NORWAY	1-2	
11.09.07	AUSTRALIA	1-0	
13.10.07	CHILE	2-0	WCQ
17.10.07	VENEZUELA	2-0	WCQ
17.11.07	BOLIVIA	3-0	WCQ
20.11.07	COLOMBIA	1-2	WCQ
06.02.08	GUATEMALA	5-0	
26.03.08	EGYPT	2-0	
04.06.08	MEXICO	4-1	
08.06.08	USA	0-0	
15.06.08	ECUADOR	1-1	WCQ
18.06.08	BRAZIL	0-0	WCQ
20.08.08	BELARUS	0-0	
06.09.08	PARAGUAY	1-1	WCQ
10.09.08	PERU	1-1	WCQ
11.10.08	URUGUAY	2-1	WCQ
15.10.08	CHILE	0-1	WCQ
19.11.08	SCOTLAND	1-0	
11.02.08	FRANCE	2-0	
28.03.09	VENEZUELA	4-0	WCQ
01.04.09	BOLIVIA	1-6	WCQ
20.05.09	PANAMA	3-1	
06.06.09	COLOMBIA	1-0	WCQ
10.06.09	ECUADOR	0-2	WCQ
12.08.09	RUSSIA	3-2	
05.09.09	BRAZIL	1-3	WCQ
09.09.09	PARAGUAY	0-1	WCQ
30.09.09	GHANA	3-0	
10.10.09	PERU	2-1	WCQ
14.10.09	URUGUAY	1-0	WCQ
14.11.09	SPAIN	1-2	
26.01.10	COSTA RICA	3-2	
10.02.10	JAMAICA	2-1	
03.03.10	GERMANY	1-0	
05.05.10	HAITI	4-0	
24.05.10	CANADA	5-0	
12.06.10	NIGERIA	1-0	WC
17.06.10	SOUTH KOREA	4-1	WC
22.06.10	GREECE	2-0	WC
27.06.10	MEXICO	3-1	WC
03.07.10	GERMANY	0-4	WC

* ARGENTINA SCORE SHOWN FIRST

home soil, and with a side containing only one overseas-based player, Mario Kempes, Argentina deservedly won the tournament. They did so again in Mexico in 1986, when the side was led by Diego Maradona – who ranks as one of the greatest players the world has ever seen despite his drug abuse problems.

Maradona, defying injury and virtually on one leg, led Argentina to the World Cup Final in 1990 and a bad-tempered defeat by Germany. He was then sensationally banished from the 1994 finals after failing a dope test when Argentina, without him, fell in the second round. The furthest progress since then has been the quarter-final stage at which Argentina fell in 1998, in 2006 and then again in 2010 – this time with Maradona back as coach, despite having had minimal experience at the job. Impressive early on, with Leo Messi in fine form, they collapsed almost inexplicably against Germany.

BRAZIL

Brazil are the most famous team in the world game. They have won more World Cups than anyone else and consistently produce players to impress spectators everywhere.

Confederaçao Brasileira de Futebol
Founded: 1914
FIFA: 1923
World Cup: 1958, 1962, 1970, 1994, 2002
South American Championship: 1919, 1922, 1949, 1989, 1997, 1999, 2004, 2007

Brazilian soccer has a romantic air about it that sets it apart from other nations. Between 1958 and 1970 they won the World Cup three times, with a team packed full of star players, including arguably the greatest in history – Pele. Brazil remains the only country to have competed in every World Cup finals tournament and the only five-time winner.

Brazilian soccer developed at the end of the nineteenth century, prompted by migrant British workers, and leagues were established in Rio de Janeiro and São Paulo by the turn of the century. The vast size of Brazil meant that a national league was impractical and until the 1970s these leagues dominated domestic soccer. The 'classic' Rio derbies between Flamengo, Fluminense, Botafogo and Vasco da Gama regularly attracted massive crowds to the 200,000-capacity Maracana Stadium.

The national team were a little slower out of the blocks, and their first real international was not played until 1914 with a visit to Buenos Aires. In 1916 Brazil entered the South American Championship, but this event has not been a rewarding one for the Brazilians, who have won it only eight times.

The World Cup, however, was another matter and brought a Brazilian golden age between 1950 and 1970. In 1950 they lost the final to Uruguay in front of their own shocked fans but in 1958 the advent 17-year-old Pele and Garrincha brought victory over the hosts in Sweden. In 1962, in Chile, an almost identical team triumphed again, this time over Czechoslovakia,

In 1966 a side in transition fell in the first round. However the newcomers Tostao, Gerson and Jairzinho were present in Mexico four years later when Brazil clinched a hat-trick of World Cups, earning them the right to keep the Jules Rimet Trophy in perpetuity.

The 1970 side is considered as among the best ever with Pele at his peak.Yet it was 24 years before they again scaled the World Cup-winning heights – and even then they needed a penalty shootout to defeat Italy after a drab goalless Final in Pasadena.

Ironically, in the 1994 qualifiers, Brazil lost to Bolivia, their first defeat ever in a World Cup qualifier, and scrambled through in an unconvincing fashion. But, having won the title, they set about building a new, more attractive, side under coach Mario Zagallo. The emergence of Ronaldo, together with the flair of Rivaldo, Cafu and Roberto Carlos, ushered in a new era. Brazil were favourites to win the World Cup again in 1998 but fell to hosts France in a Final shrouded in controversy after Ronaldo suffered a convulsive fit on the morning of the game. Four years later, he made impressive amends by scoring both goals in the 2–0 Final victory over Germany in Yokohama. Ronaldo was also the tournament's eight-goal top scorer and thus equalled Pele's Brazilian record of 12 goals in 14 finals appearances. Cafu became the first player to appear in the Final of three consecutive World Cups. Both were past their best when Brazil lost their crown in Germany in 2006 – though Ronaldo did score the three goals which established him as the World Cup's 15-goal all-time record marksman.

Brazil could have used his attacking prowess in 2010. Having won the Confederations Cup in South Africa in 2009 they returned a year later, managed by 1994 World Cup winning former captain Dunga, with an unnecessarily and fatally over-cautious approach. To fan fury back home, they took a quarter-final lead against Holland then gave away two poor second-half goals, had midfielder Felipe Melo sent off, and went out. Unsurprisingly, Dunga paid the price with his job. Sole consolation was the knowledge that, as hosts in 2014, not only will they not have to qualify but will be favourites to make title-winning amends.

Back: Carlos Alberto, Brito, Piazza, Felix, Clodoaldo, Everaldo; front: Jairzinho, Rivelino, Tostao, Pele, Paolo Cesar.

Ronaldo collects the World Cup prize his two goals against Germany earned in Yokohama in 2002.

OTHER SOUTH AMERICAN COUNTRIES

Bolivia

Federacion Boliviana de Futbol
Founded: 1925
FIFA: 1926
South American Championship: 1963

Since their first international outing in 1926, Bolivia have been the perennial whipping boys of South American soccer - until recently. In the 1994 World Cup qualifiers the Bolivians finished a close second in Group B to qualify for the finals for the first time in 40 years, recording a notable 2-0 victory over Brazil along the way and knocking out Uruguay and Ecuador in the process. Before that, apart from World Cup qualification in 1930 and 1950, the 1963 South American Championship victory, played at home, was the only success of note.

Chile

Federacion de Futbol de Chile
Founded: 1895
FIFA: 1912

Chile were among the five South American nations who caused a stir at the 2010 World Cup finals by all reaching the second round. Unfortunately their own campaign ended there in a decisive 3-0 defeat by Brazil. History thus repeated itself: the previous time Chile had reached the second round they had also fallen to Brazil, in 1998. Thus their most successful World Cup remains the 1962 tournament when Chile hosted the finals and finished third.

At club level their most successful outfit on the international stage has been Colo-Colo who won the Copa Libertadores in 1991.

Colombia

Federacion Colombiana de Futbol
Founded: 1924
FIFA: 1936
South American Championship: 2001

Colombia's history has been dominated by years of internal disputes, disruptions and turbulence. The most notorious came in 1950, shortly after professionalism was introduced, when a break-away league outside FIFA jurisdiction, the DiMayor, was formed and Colombian sides began importing players from all over South America and from Britain. The huge salaries on offer led to the four years of its existence being known as the "El Dorado" period. The bubble burst in 1954, with readmission to FIFA.

The national side made their debut as late as 1938, and results at first were poor. Between 1949 and 1957 no internationals were played at all, and thereafter outings were infrequent. It was a huge surprise, then, when Colombia qualified for the 1962 World Cup in Chile. In 1965 another breakaway federation was formed and confusion reigned once more. FIFA had to intervene and effectively ran Colombian soccer up until 1971, when the present administration was installed. A new league structure was introduced in 1968, careful controls on the number of foreign imports were implemented, and the national side soon benefited. In 1989 Nacional Medellin won the Libertadores Cup, the country's first victory, and a year later the national side, coached by Francisco Maturana, qualified for the 1990 World Cup finals. In the 1994 World Cup qualifiers, Argentina were thrashed 5-0 in Buenos Aires and this performance led a number of people to consider the Colombians a good bet to win the whole competition. But at USA 94, Colombia's efforts foundered on poor morale, not helped by death threats against players and coach Maturana. Worst of all, after their surprise first-round elimination, defender Andres Escobar - who had scored an own goal in the shock 2-1 defeat by the USA - was shot dead in Medellin. Drug and gambling cartels undermined much of the good work achieved by outstanding players such as Carlos Valderrama.

Carlos Valderrama has been a mainstay of the Colombian national side for years. Here they are playing the USA.

Ecuador

Asociacion Ecuatoriana de Futbol
Founded: 1925
FIFA: 1926

Ecuador made history by reaching the second round of the 2006 World Cup in Germany. Here they lost only 1-0 to England via a David Beckham free kick. This was the first time Ecuador had progressed so far on only their second appearance at the finals, following a first-round elimination four years earlier in Korea and Japan. Players such as central defender Ivan Hurtado and striker Agustin Delgado earned their nation a new footballing respect. This was maintained when LDU Quito won the Copa Libertadores in 2008 and finished runners-up in the Club World Cup.

Paraguay

Liga Paraguaya de Futbol
Founded: 1906
FIFA: 1921
South American Championship: 1953, 1979

Paraguay's progress the last four World Cups has raised the country's international profile and the domestic game's self-confidence. Their inspiration was charismatic goalkeeper Jose Luis Chilavert who scored more than 60 goals in club and national team soccer from penalties and free kicks. In 1998, 2002 and 2006, Paraguay reached the second round and, in 2010, they appeared in the quarter-finals for the first leg, losing only 1-0 to Spain. They have also won the Copa America in 1953 and 1979. On the club front, Olimpia remain Paraguay's most successful side at international level, winning the Copa Libertadores in 1979, 1990 and 2002 and finishing runners-up on three occasions.

Peru

Federacion Peruana de Futbol
Founded: 1922
FIFA: 1924
South American Championship: 1939, 1975

Soccer in Peru has always been dominated by Lima, and the national association was founded there in 1922. The local Lima League was the strongest in the country and, until a national championship was introduced in 1966, the winners were considered national champions. Lima's clubs, Alianza, Universitario and Sporting Cristal, have dominated at home, but none have achieved success in the Libertadores Cup. Sadly in 1964, 300 spectators died in a riot, and in 1988, the Alianza team was wiped out in a plane crash.

Peru's international debut came in the South American Championship of 1927, and they won the event at home in 1939. Their World Cup record was poor, however, until the 1970s, when a generation of notable players came together and made the decade the country's most successful ever. Stars of the 1970s side were the highly eccentric and entertaining goalkeeper Ramon "El Loco" Quiroga, Hector Chumpitaz and midfield maestro Teofilo Cubillas, the greatest Peruvian player of all time. Coached by Brazilian World Cup winner Didi, this side reached the quarter-finals of the 1970 World Cup, won the 1975 South American Championship, and qualified for the 1978 World Cup, where they fell in the second round. Peru qualified for the World Cup again in 1982, but the side was past its best. Since then, Peru have slipped back into their role of the "middle-men" of South American soccer. Political instability in the country has not helped.

The first winners of the World Cup: Uruguay 1930.

Uruguay

Asociacion Uruguaya de Futbol
Founded: 1900
FIFA: 1923
World Cup: 1930, 1950
South American Championship: 1916, 1917, 1920, 1923, 1924, 1926, 1935, 1942, 1956, 1959, 1967, 1983, 1987, 1995.
Olympics: 1924, 1928

Before the Second World War, Uruguay were undoubtedly the best team in the world. Today they are no longer a world power, but they can still be dangerous opponents. Montevideo dominates the domestic scene and, as it is located just across the River Plate estuary from Buenos Aires, the two cities can rightly claim to be the centre of South American soccer. Montevideo's two great clubs, Penarol and Nacional, have dominated Uruguayan soccer, winning more than 80 championships between them. The clubs have both enjoyed great success in the Libertadores Cup; Penarol winning it five times, Nacional three. Both clubs have also won the World Club Cup.

The national side dominated world soccer in the first half of this century, but has faded since the 1950s. Early successes in the South American Championship were followed by victory in the 1924 Olympics in Amsterdam. Uruguay repeated the success in 1928 and two years later, as the host nation, swept to victory in the first World Cup. The side of the 1920s and 1930s contained many of Uruguay's all-time greats: skipper Jose Nasazzi, the midfield "Iron Curtain" of Jose Andrade, Lorenzo Fernandez and Alvarez Gestido, and outstanding forwards Hector Castro, Pedro Cea and Hector Scarone. In 1950 Uruguay beat Brazil 2-1 in the World Cup Final in Brazil. The side contained strikers Juan Schiaffino, Uruguay's greatest player, and Omar Miguez, Victor Andrade, Roque Maspoli in goal and Obdulio Varela in defence. However, they failed to defend their crown in 1954 when they were defeated in the semi-final.

Subsequent World Cups proved largely disappointing despite the effort of stars such as Fernando Morena and Enzo Francescoli. Finally, in 2010, the inspiration of forwards Diego Forlan and Luis Suarez lifted Uruguay back into the last four for the first time in 40 years.

Venezuela

Federacion Venezolana de Futbol
Founded: 1926
FIFA: 1952

Venezuela is the weakest of the ten South American countries, but this is hardly surprising because the national sport is baseball. Originally members of CONCACAF, they made their international debut in 1938 and switched to CONMEBOL in 1958. The national record national record is poor with only a handful of victories to celebrate in both the World Cup qualifying competition and Copa America, even though they enter both consistently. The clubs are weak too, and three Libertadores Cup semi-finals are the best they have managed. A professional league was finally set up in 1956, but Venezuela have a long way to go if they are even to catch up with the other South American minnows.

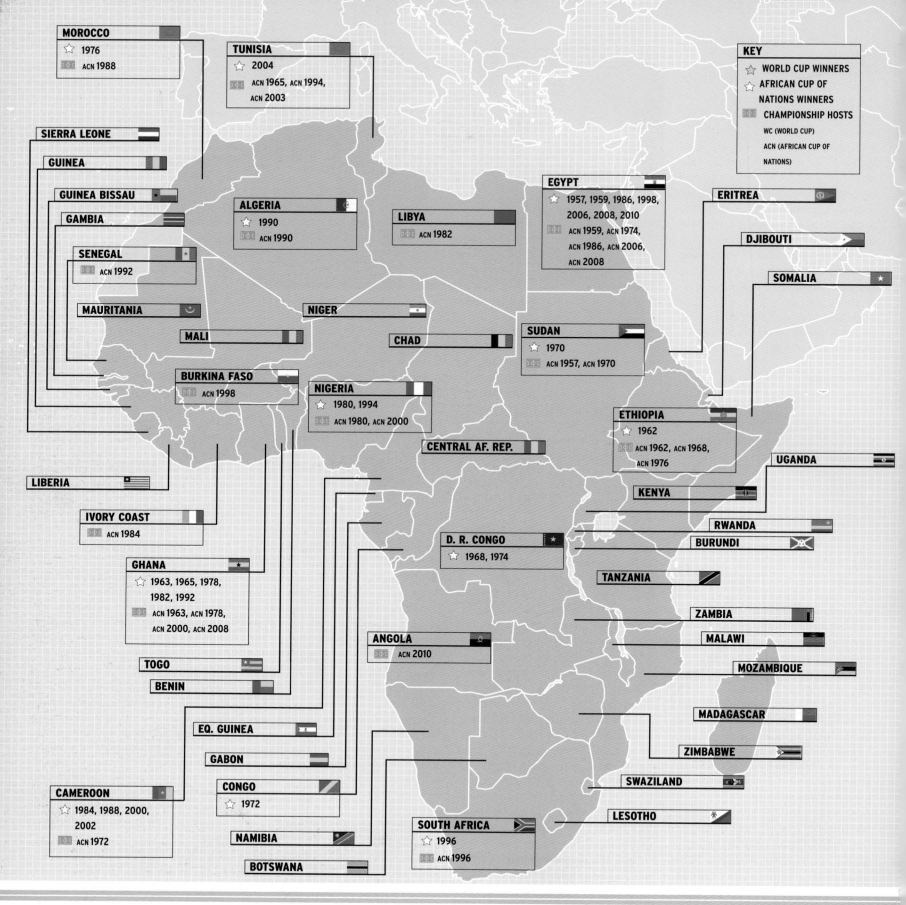

KEY
- ☆ WORLD CUP WINNERS
- ☆ AFRICAN CUP OF NATIONS WINNERS
- CHAMPIONSHIP HOSTS
  WC (WORLD CUP)
  ACN (AFRICAN CUP OF NATIONS)

MOROCCO
- ☆ 1976
- ACN 1988

TUNISIA
- ☆ 2004
- ACN 1965, ACN 1994, ACN 2003

SIERRA LEONE

GUINEA

GUINEA BISSAU

GAMBIA

ALGERIA
- ☆ 1990
- ACN 1990

LIBYA
- ACN 1982

EGYPT
- ☆ 1957, 1959, 1986, 1998, 2006, 2008, 2010
- ACN 1959, ACN 1974, ACN 1986, ACN 2006, ACN 2008

ERITREA

DJIBOUTI

SOMALIA

SENEGAL
- ACN 1992

MAURITANIA

NIGER

MALI

CHAD

SUDAN
- ☆ 1970
- ACN 1957, ACN 1970

BURKINA FASO
- ACN 1998

NIGERIA
- ☆ 1980, 1994
- ACN 1980, ACN 2000

ETHIOPIA
- ☆ 1962
- ACN 1962, ACN 1968, ACN 1976

UGANDA

LIBERIA

CENTRAL AF. REP.

KENYA

IVORY COAST
- ACN 1984

GHANA
- ☆ 1963, 1965, 1978, 1982, 1992
- ACN 1963, ACN 1978, ACN 2000, ACN 2008

D. R. CONGO
- ☆ 1968, 1974

RWANDA

BURUNDI

TANZANIA

ZAMBIA

TOGO

BENIN

ANGOLA
- ACN 2010

MALAWI

MOZAMBIQUE

EQ. GUINEA

MADAGASCAR

GABON

ZIMBABWE

CONGO
- ☆ 1972

SWAZILAND

CAMEROON
- ☆ 1984, 1988, 2000, 2002
- ACN 1972

LESOTHO

SOUTH AFRICA
- ☆ 1996
- ACN 1996

NAMIBIA

BOTSWANA

AFRICA

Africa has supplied a steady stream of outstanding players to the game for years but it is only in the past two decades that its strength and potential has been recognized.

The reason lies in the continent's history of colonial control. For many years outstanding soccer players either were unable to gain access to the international stage or were lured away to Europe to play representative soccer for the colonial powers.

One of the first great African exports was the Moroccan-born inside forward Larbi Ben Barek who played for France between 1938 and 1954. Even greater was Just Fontaine, also born and brought up in Morocco, who scored a record 13 goals for France at the 1958 World Cup finals. Three years later Mozambique-born Eusebio da Silva Ferreira exploded onto the club stage with Benfica in Portugal.

The exodus of African players to Europe gathered pace throughout the second half of the 20th century and became a flood following the Bosman judgment which relaxed player import restrictions in many European countries. Players from top African nations even transferred behind the old iron curtain to Russia, Romania and Poland – and Nigerian-born Emannuel Olisadebe led Poland's attack at the 2002 World Cup finals.

The African confederation was created in Libson in 1956 during the FIFA Congress. Egypt, Ethiopa, South Africa and Sudan were the founding members who created CAF and the African Nations Cup.

Soon afterwards, the South African association was barred because of the country's racially-segregated apartheid policies, although its eventual return to the fold was sealed by the successful staging of Africa's first World Cup in 2010.

CAF has worked hard to try to keep politically onside with Europe although clubs fail to appreciate the fact when their best African players are whisked away to the Nations Cup in January every two years.

South African bid leaders Irving Khoza (left) and Danny Jordaan (right) join Nelson Mandela at the party to acclaim the securing of 2010 World Cup hosting rights.

AFRICA

Algeria
Fédération Algérienne de Football
Founded: 1962
FIFA: 1963
African Nations Cup: 1990
The French brought soccer to Algeria in the late 1880s and, within 40 years, major clubs founded include future African champions Mouloudia Challia. The World Cup finals have been a disappointment, however. Algeria were squeezed out controversially by Germany and Austria in 1982 and failed to make an impact in 2010, when they finished bottom of the group.

Angola
Federacao Angolana de Futebol
Founded: 1977
FIFA: 1980
In the old Portuguese colonial days, all Angola's went to Lisbon and Porto to earn fame and fortune. Then, after independence, a long civil war restricted the country's sporting development. Finally they made their World Cup finals debut in 2006, finishing a creditable third in their group. Angola's subsequent 2010 hosting of the Africa Cup of Nations was marred, however, by an armed attack on the Togo team by secessionist rebels.

Benin
Fédération Beninoise de Football
Founded: 1968
FIFA: 1969

Botswana
Botswana Football Association
Founded: 1970
FIFA: 1976

Burkina Faso
Fédération Burkinabe de Football
Founded: 1960
FIFA: 1964

Burundi
Fédération de Football du Burundi
Founded: 1948
FIFA: 1972

Cameroon
Fédération Camerounaise de Football
Founded: 1960
FIFA: 1962
Olympic Games: 2000
African Nations Cup: 1984, 1988, 2000, 2002
Cameroon have made by far the biggest impact of all the African nations to have reached the World Cup finals. In 1982, they drew their three first round games – against Italy (eventual winners), Poland (third) and Peru – but were eliminated. They qualified again in 1990, beating reigning champions Argentina in the opening match before reaching the quarter-finals where they lost in extra time to England. As a result of these performances FIFA granted Africa a third berth at the 1994 finals. This time, the "Indomitable Lions" were disappointing, torn apart by internal strife. Administrative, managerial and financial problems also contributed to their inability to progress beyond the finals first round in 1996, 2002 and 2010. However Cameroon could take pride, inbetween, in becoming the only the second African nation to win the Olympic title. Cameroon, four times African champions, added Games gold on emulating Nigeria by defeating Spain in a penalty shootout after a 2-2 draw.

The greatest player in Cameroon history is striker Roger Milla, a veteran of the 1982, 1990 and 1994 World Cups and the 1976 and 1990 African Footballer of the Year. Cameroon have won the African Nations Cup four times, but the Ivory Coast beat them to a place in the 2006 World Cup finals.

Cape Verde Islands
Federacao Cabo-Verdiana de Futebol
Founded: 1982
FIFA: 1986

Central African Republic
Fédération Centrafricaine de Football
Founded: 1937
FIFA: 1963

Chad
Fédération Tchadienne de Football
Founded: 1962
FIFA: 1988

Comoros Islands
Federation Comorienne de Football
Founded: 1975
FIFA: Provisional

Congo
Fédération Congolaise de Football
Founded: 1962
FIFA: 1962
African Nations Cup: 1972

Congo DR
Federation Congolaise de Football-Association (FECOFA)
Founded: 1919
FIFA: 1962
African Nations Cup: 1968, 1974
Then known as Zaire, the Congolese won the African Nations Cup twice in six years between 1968 and 1974 – the year in which they also became the first black African side to qualify for the World Cup finals. Since then, however, their best performances have been restricted to the African Nations Cup.

Djibouti
Federation Djiboutienne de Football
Founded: 1977
FIFA: 1994

Egypt
All Ettihad el Masri Li Korat el Kadam
Founded: 1921
FIFA: 1923
African Nations: 1957, 1959, 1986, 1998, 2006, 2008, 2010
Egypt were one of the four founder members of the Confédération Africaine de Football and the first north Africans to join FIFA, in 1923. Given this 20-year start on most of their neighbours, it is no surprise that Egypt became one of the great African powers, winning the first two Nations Cups in 1957 and 1959. Egypt finished fourth in the 1928 Olympics and entered the World Cup in 1934. Olympic semi-finalists again in 1964, Egypt entered only one of the World Cups played between 1938 and 1970. A revival in the 1970s saw them finish third in the African Nations Cup in

Algeria's Ali Fergani (left) greets Nigeria's Christian Chukwu before their 1980 Nations Cup.

1970 and 1974, fourth in 1976 and reach the Olympic quarter-finals in 1984. They have won the Africa Cup of Nations a record seven times.

Allied to this success at national level, Egyptian clubs are among the most powerful in Africa. Well organized, wealthy and well supported, Egypt's clubs, led by Cairo rivals Al Ahly and Zamalek, have won the African club cups repeatedly.

Equatorial Guinea
Federacion Equatoguineana de Futbol
Founded: 1976
FIFA: 1986

Eritrea
Eritrean National Football Federation
Founded: 1996
FIFA: 1998

Ethiopia
Yeithiopia Football Federechin
Founded: 1943
FIFA: 1953
African Nations Cup: 1962

Gabon
Fédération Gabonaise de Football
Founded: 1962
FIFA: 1963

Gambia
Gambia Football Association
Founded: 1952
FIFA: 1966

Ghana
Ghana Football Association
Founded: 1957
FIFA: 1958
African Nations Cup: 1963, 1965, 1978, 1982
Ghana achieved independence in 1957 and the Black Stars quickly established themselves as a powerful force in African soccer. They won the Nations Cup at first attempt in 1963, retained the trophy two years later and were runners-up in the following two events. In 1982 Ghana became the first nation to win the Cup four times and they also achieved notable successes in FIFA's

Egypt parade their fifth African Cup of Nations after winning as hosts in 2006.

world youth cups. Surprisingly, it was not until 2006 that they reached the senior World Cup finals for the first time. They reached the second round both then and in 2010. Here, however, Africa's only surviving hope in the continent's 'home' championship ran out of luck. Striker Gyan Asamoah missed a penalty against Uruguay with the last kick of extra time and they lost the subsequent shootout.

Guinea
Fédération Guinéenne de Football
Founded: 1959
FIFA: 1961

Guinea-Bissau
Federaçao de Football da Guinea-Bissau
Founded: 1974
FIFA: 1986

Ivory Coast
Fédération Ivoirienne de Football
Founded: 1960
FIFA: 1960
African Nations Cup: 1992
The Ivory Coast are one of Africa's great soccer enigmas. Off the field, they have a stable government and a

healthy economy; on it the Ivory Coast has a well-organized league – advantages which many African countries do not enjoy – and yet success at international level eluded them until 1992 when "The Elephants" won the African Nations Cup, defeating Ghana on penalties in the final. They had previously been semi-finalists three times without going further.

Greater European experience – partly thanks to the availability of Belgium's Beveren as a 'feeder' club – helped the Ivoriens develop an outstanding national team by 2005-06. Led fearlessly by Chelsea striker Didier Drogba and stiffened in defence by Arsenal's Kolo Toure, they finished runners-up in the Africa Cup of Nations. They considered themselves unlucky not to progress beyond the first round in both the 2006 and 2010 World Cup finals.

Kenya
Kenya Football Federation
Founded: 1932
FIFA: 1960

Lesotho
Lesotho Sports Council
Founded: 1932
FIFA: 1964

Liberia
Liberia Football Association
Founded: 1936
FIFA: 1962

Libya
Libyan Arab Jamahiriya Football Federation
Founded: 1962
FIFA: 1963
Libya emerged as one of the most ambitious of African countries off the pitch at the turn of the millennium when the Gadaffi family decided to use soccer as an alternative form of international diplomacy. Saad Gadaffi, son of the Libyan leader, was involved first by taking a stake in the Italian automotive giant Fiat and then in persuading Italy's top clubs to stage their season's curtain-raising Supercup in the Libyan capital, Tripoli. In 2003 Saad Gadaffi signed to play for the Serie A club Perugia but he left the club after being suspended for failing a dope test.

Madagascar

Fédération Malagasy de Football
Founded: 1961
FIFA: 1962

Malawi

Football Association of Malawi
Founded: 1966
FIFA: 1967

Mali

Fédération Malienne de Football
Founded: 1960
FIFA: 1962

Mali are one of the emerging forces in a tipping of the balance within African soccer. In 2002 they finished runners-up, as hosts, in the African Nations Cup and two years later they reached the semi-finals. Mali were one of several African countries who benefited from a change in player eligibility rules: in their case it offered them the chance to select the then Tottenham striker Frédéric Kanouté. Although his father was from Mali, he had been barred from the national team because of an Under-21 appearance with France.

Mauritania

Fédération de Football de la République de Mauritanie
Founded: 1961
FIFA: 1964

Mauritius

Mauritius Football Association
Founded: 1952
FIFA: 1962

Morocco

Fédération Royale Marocaine de Football
Founded: 1955
FIFA: 1956
African Nations Cup: 1976

Morocco were possibly the unluckiest side at the 1998 World Cup finals in France. The Africans thought they had qualified for the second stage after a tremendous 3-0 victory over Scotland. But as the players celebrated on the pitch they were unaware that Norway had beaten Brazil to snatch second spot in the group. Despite that the Moroccans did plenty to confirm their emergence as a world force. They first qualified for the World Cup finals in 1970 when they gave West Germany a fright before losing 2-1 in the second round. They qualified again in 1986 and won their first round group ahead of England, Poland and Portugal, before losing to the Germans again. They won the 1976 African Nations and in 1994 reached the World Cup finals again.

Moroccan domestic clubs have also enjoyed repeated success. FAR Rabat won the Champions Cup in 1985, Raja Casablanca repeated the trick in 1989, followed by Wydad Casablanca in 1992. Morocco has also sent a stream of outstanding players to French soccer - notably Larbi Ben Barek, the so-called "Black Pearl" and later Marrakech-born Just Fontaine who scored a record 13 goals for France in the 1958 World Cup finals in Sweden.

Mozambique

Federacao Moçambicana de Futebol
Founded: 1975
FIFA: 1978

Namibia

Namibia Football Federation
Founded: 1992
FIFA: 1992

Niger

Fédération Nigérienne de Football
Founded: 1967
FIFA: 1967

Nigeria

Nigeria Football Association
Founded: 1945
FIFA: 1959
Olympic Games: 1996
African Nations Cup: 1980, 1994

Nigeria, with a huge population and over 500 registered clubs, emerged in the 1990s as one of the most powerful nations in Africa - reaching the second round of the World Cup in 1994 and 1998. It was about time the seniors caught up because Nigeria's youth teams had led the international way for years. In 1985 they won the World Under-17 Championship - the first African side to win a FIFA world tournament; in 1989, Nigeria were runners-up in the World Under-20 Championship; and in 1993 the "Green Eaglets" won their second Under-17 title. A World Cup breakthrough came in 1994 when Nigeria nearly sprang one of the greatest of all upsets, topping their first-round group - ahead of Argentina, Bulgaria and Greece - nearly eliminating eventual finalists Italy in the second round.

In 1996 they became the first African nation to win the Olympic tournament, beating favourites Brazil in the semi-final and Argentina in the final. Not surprisingly, there was plenty of expectation when Nigeria qualified for France 98. They again reached the second round, but lost 4-1 to Denmark.

They did not even go that far in 2002, finishing bottom of their first round group. Between World Cups, in the 2000 Nations Cup, despite host advantage, they lost on penalties to Cameroon in the Final. Nigeria didn't qualify for the 2006 World Cup and lost to the Ivory Coast in that year's African Cup of Nations. In 2010 there was again disappointment in both the African Cup of Nations, a semi-final defeat to Ghana, and the World Cup, a first round exit.

Nigeria's Samson Siasia leads the dance class after scoring against Argentina.

Réunion
Ligue de la Réunion
Founded: 1985
FIFA: Associate member

Rwanda
Fédération Rwandaise de Football Amateur
Founded: 1972
FIFA: 1976

Sao Tome And Principe
Federacion Santomense de Futebol
Founded: 1975
FIFA: 1986

Senegal
Fédération Sénégalaise de Footballs
Founded: 1960
FIFA: 1962

Senegal came from nowhere in international terms in sensational style at the 2002 World Cup when a team led by El Hadji Diouf and Khalil Fadiga beat holders France 1-0 in the Opening Match and went on to reach the quarter-finals before losing on a golden goal to Turkey. That good work went to waste when they failed to qualify in both 2006 and 2010

Seychelles
Seychelles Football Federation
Founded: 1976
FIFA: 1986

Sierra Leone
Sierra Leone Amateur Football Association
Founded: 1923
FIFA: 1967

Somalia
Somalia Football Federation
Founded: 1951
FIFA: 1961

South Africa
South African Football Association
Founded: 1892
FIFA: 1952 (suspended 1964-76), 1992
African Nations Cup: 1996

South Africa, not even back in international soccer two decades after the collapse of apartheid, made history as first African hosts of the

Senegal's Khalil Fadiga baffles French defender Frank Leboeuf.

World Cup finals in 2010. A courageous decision by FIFA was rewarded with an fanatically-supported and controversy-free event, at least as far as the organization was concerned. The only local disappointment was that South Africa's own national team made unwanted history as the first host side not to progress beyond the first round.

At least international projection of the finals taught the rest of the world about the country's passion for soccer which had been most popularly evidenced for years locally by the fierce club rivalry of Soweto's Kaizer Chiefs and Orlando Pirates. At national team level South Africa had also won the 1996 Africa Cup of Nations.

Sudan
Sudan Football Federation
Founded: 1936
FIFA: 1948
African Nations Cup: 1970

Swaziland
National Football Association of Swaziland
Founded: 1964
FIFA: 1976

Tanzania
Football Association of Tanzania
Founded: 1930
FIFA: 1964

Togo
Fédération Togolaise de Football
Founded: 1960
FIFA: 1962

Togo shocked African soccer by reaching the World Cup finals for the first time in 2006 but their campaign was a disaster. Unwisely they had sacked coach Stephen Keshi after a poor African Nations Cup outing and his successor, German Otto Pfister, staged a brief walk-out during the finals in a row over unpaid bonuses. Not surprisingly, Togo lost all three games, scored only one goal and finished bottom of their group.

Tunisia
Fédération Tunisienne de Football
Founded: 1956
FIFA: 1960
African Nations Cup: 2004

Tunisia, relying largely on home-grown players, underlined the country's soccer prowess by reaching the World Cup finals three times in a row in 1998, 2002 and 2006. Scoring goals proved a problem on all three occasions however as they managed a total of only four goals and twice finished bottom of their group. In between, however, French manager Roger Lemerre gave fans plenty to celebrate by guiding them to victory as hosts in the 2004 African Nations

Cup. Tunisia beat neighbours Morocco 2-1 in the final. Their hero was four-goal striker Francileudo Santos who had been born in Brazil, had played in France and was granted citizenship only weeks before the tournament began.

Uganda
Federation of Uganda Football Associations
Founded: 1924
FIFA: 1959

Zambia
Football Association of Zambia
Founded: 1929
FIFA: 1964

Zambia's national side have been semi-finalists in the African Nations Cup three times since 1974, and pulled off a remarkable victory over Italy in the 1988 Olympics in Seoul. The star was Kalusha Bwalya, who became a top professional with PSV in Holland. Sadly, Zambia will always be remembered for the plane crash in April 1993 that wiped out the entire national squad – bar the five overseas-based professionals who were not travelling with them. Astonishingly, the Zambians rebuilt their squad around their five exports, and went on to reach the 1994 African Nations Cup Final. They only missed out on the World Cup finals after losing their last qualifying game 1-0 in Morocco.

Zimbabwe
Zimbabwe Football Association
Founded: 1950
FIFA: 1965

Zimbabwe won independence as recently as 1983 and have been making steady progress ever since. They went within one game of reaching the 1994 World Cup finals, but lost the group match 3-1 to Cameroon. England-based Bruce Grobbelaar (Liverpool) and Peter Ndlovu (Coventry City) were the key men. The progress has rather halted and Zimbabwe have not come close to qualifying for a World Cup since then.

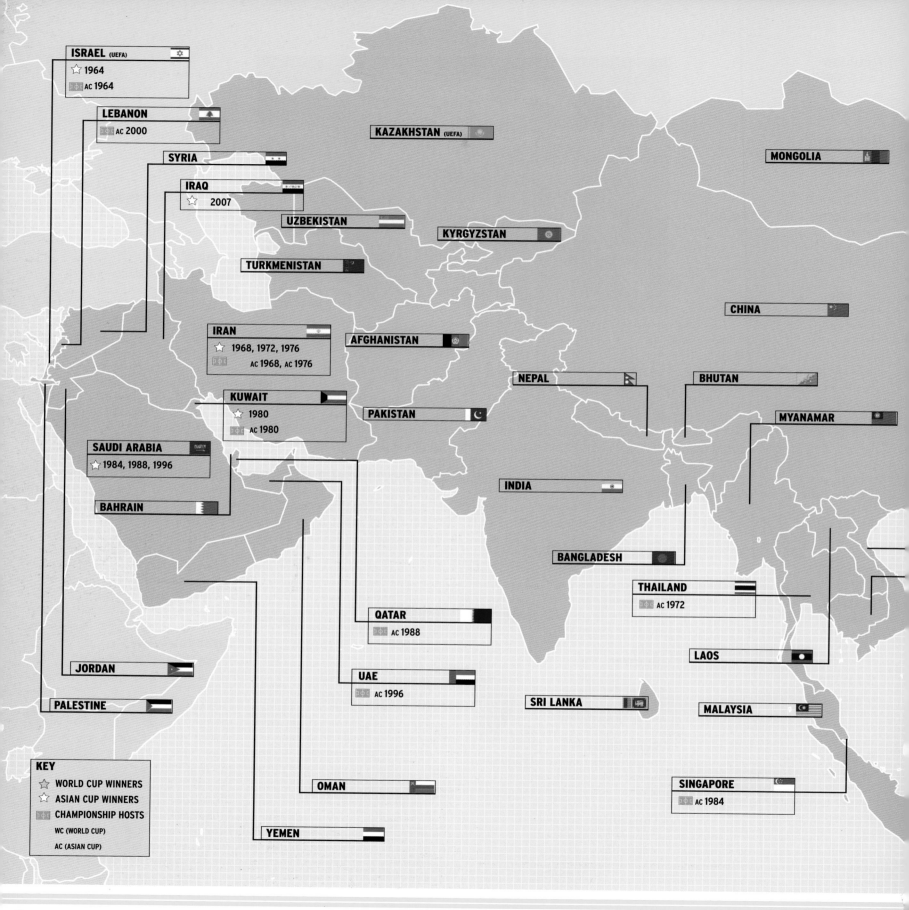

ISRAEL (UEFA)
☆ 1964
AC 1964

LEBANON
AC 2000

SYRIA

IRAQ
☆ 2007

KAZAKHSTAN (UEFA)

MONGOLIA

UZBEKISTAN

KYRGYZSTAN

TURKMENISTAN

CHINA

IRAN
☆ 1968, 1972, 1976
AC 1968, AC 1976

AFGHANISTAN

NEPAL

BHUTAN

KUWAIT
☆ 1980
AC 1980

PAKISTAN

MYANAMAR

SAUDI ARABIA
☆ 1984, 1988, 1996

INDIA

BAHRAIN

BANGLADESH

THAILAND
AC 1972

QATAR
AC 1988

LAOS

JORDAN

UAE
AC 1996

SRI LANKA

MALAYSIA

PALESTINE

KEY
☆ WORLD CUP WINNERS
☆ ASIAN CUP WINNERS
CHAMPIONSHIP HOSTS
WC (WORLD CUP)
AC (ASIAN CUP)

OMAN

SINGAPORE
AC 1984

YEMEN

ASIA

Asian soccer's regional confederation was founded in the same year as Europe's: 1954.

Originally it had nine members: Hong Kong, India, Indonesia, Japan, Malaysia, Philippines, Singapore, South Korea and South Vietnam. More members followed as regional independence movements prospered. Nationalist China (now Taiwan or Chinese Taipei) joined in 1955, Israel in 1956 followed by other eastern and southern Asian nations and then the Middle Eastern and Gulf states in the 1960s and 1970s.

The more members who signed up, however, meant more political problems, largely concerning Israel – which was eventually forced out into the administrative wilderness before finally finding a new home within Europe and UEFA in the early 1990s.

Asia's status within world soccer took a major leap forward with the return of PR China to the FIFA fold at the behest of president Joao Havelange and then in a first Asian hosting of the World Cup finals in 2002.

A model Mount Fuji arises to greet the 2002 World Cup finalists in Yokohama.

NORTH KOREA

SOUTH KOREA
☆ 1956, 1960
AC 1960 WC 2002

JAPAN
☆ 1992, 2000, 2004
AC 1992 WC 2002

HONG KONG
AC 1956

TAIWAN

VIETNAM

CAMBODIA

PHILIPPINES

BRUNEI

AUSTRALIA
☆ 1980, 1996, 2000

INDONESIA

ASIA

Afghanistan
The Football Federation of the National Olympic Committee
Founded: 1922
FIFA: 1948

Australia
Australia Soccer Federation
Founded: 1961
FIFA: 1963
Oceania Cup: 1980, 1996, 2000
** Geographically in Oceania but now a member of the Asian confederation (See page 143)

Bahrain
Bahrain Football Association
Founded: 1951
FIFA: 1966

Bangladesh
Bangladesh Football Federation
Founded: 1972
FIFA: 1974

Bhutan
Bhutan Football Federation
Founded: 1960
FIFA: Associate member

Brunei
Brunei Amateur Football Association
Founded: 1959
FIFA: 1969

Cambodia
Federation Khmere De Football Association
Founded: 1933
FIFA: 1953

China
Football Association of the People's Republic of China
Founded: 1924
FIFA: 1931-58, 1979

China's long-awaited arrival at the World Cup finals finally came in 2002 under veteran World Cup specialist, coach Bora Milutinovic. Disappointingly, they lost all three games, conceding nine goals overall against Costa Rica, Brazil and Turkey.

Despite slow World Cup progress, in 1913 China had taken part in the first international match on Asian soil when they met the Philippines in Manila, in the Far Eastern Games. International success subsequently eluded them however and their best honours achievement to date remains runners-up spot at the 1984 Asian Cup.

Political complications concerning nationalist Taiwan had much to do with China's failure to emerge from the shadows and live up to expectations for the most populous nation on earth. A side containing only Hong Kong players took part in the 1954 Asian Games, calling themselves China. The Chinese FA protested that it was the legitimate ruling body and subsequently withdrew from FIFA in 1958. It was not until Brazilian Joao Havelange took over as FIFA president in 1974 that negotiations were launched and ultimately brought their re-admission to the world governing body.

Guam
Guam Soccer Association
Founded: 1975
FIFA: Associate member

Hong Kong
Hong Kong Football Association
Founded: 1914
FIFA: 1954

China's outstanding women's team commit themselves to what will prove a 1-0 victory over Russia at their 2003 World Cup.

Soccer has been played in Hong Kong since the 1880s. The Hong Kong Shield - an early knock-out competition - was launched in 1896, a soccer association was founded in 1914 and affiliated to the Football Association in London a year later. The sport reached its peak in the colony in the 1970s. The league's top clubs became fully professional and imported a string of veteran players from England and continental Europe. The national team competed regularly in international events after first entering the World Cup in 1974. Special dispensation from FIFA means Hong Kong continues to exist as an independent soccer entity, despite having been reintegrated formally into mainland China in 1997.

India

All India Football Federation

Founded: 1937

FIFA: 1948

India's only successes at international level have come in the Asian Games, which they won in 1951 and 1962. They finished third at the 1956 Olympics, but since then the national side's record has been poor, despite massive enthusiasm for soccer in this huge, heavily-populated country. The annual Nehru Cup tournament, featuring guest European and South American national sides or selections, is a popular event, though India have never won it. The Calcutta League - the best in the country - is dominated by India's most famous clubs, Mohammedan Sporting, East Bengal and Mohun Bagan.

Indonesia

All Indonesia Football Federation

Founded: 1930

FIFA: 1952

Indonesia briefly threatened a surprise on the global stage when the federation launched a bid to host the World Cup in 2018 or 2022. This was later scrapped in the spring of 2010.

Hamid Estili writes his name into Iranian soccer history with their first goal against the United States at France 98.

Iran

Football Federation of the Islamic Republic of Iran

Founded: 1920

FIFA: 1948

Asian Cup: 1968, 1972, 1976

Iran emerged as a major Asian power in the 1960s, and they were the continent's most successful side in the 1970s. They claimed a hat-trick of Asian Championships, in 1968, 1972 and 1976 - winning every game they played in the tournament over an eight-year period. They also won the gold medal at the 1974 Asian Games and qualified for the 1978 World Cup finals, where they held Scotland to a 1-1 draw. They missed out on qualification for USA 94, but set a then World Cup record by beating the Maldives 17-0 in a qualifying match in June 1997 and

ultimately made it to the finals in France. A 2-1 victory in Lyon in the politically-sensitive match against the USA was undoubtedly the highlight, along with the performances of impressive forward Ali Daei and midfielder Mehdi Mahdavikia. They missed out in 2002, disappointed in the first round of the Finals in 2006 and failed to qualify again in 2010.

Iraq

Iraqi Football Association

Founded: 1948

FIFA: 1951

Asian Cup: 2007

The 1970s witnessed a shift in the balance of power in Asian soccer towards the Arab states, and Iraq were at the forefront of this movement. They won the Asian

Games gold medal in 1982 and four years later qualified for the World Cup finals in Mexico, where they put up creditable performances. Iraq were thrown out of FIFA and suspended from international soccer in 1991 because of the invasion of Kuwait, but were soon re-admitted to the international fold - and almost qualified for the 1994 World Cup finals. Their most noted player was striker Ahmed Radhi. The second Gulf War meant Iraqi's soccer administration had to be rebuilt all over again but the national team not only quickly resumed international duty but secured a shock victory in the 2007 Asian Cup beating Saudi Arabia 1-0 in the final.

Japan's Hidetoshi Nakata battles for the ball with Kaka of Brazil in the 2006 World Cup.

Japan
The Football Association of Japan
Founded: 1921
FIFA: 1929-45, 1950
Asian Cup: 1992, 2000

Japan earned enormous respect both on and off the pitch for their co-hosting, alongside South Korea, of the 2002 World Cup finals. The organization was almost perfect and the national team, coached by Philippe Troussier, reached the second round for the first time in their history before losing narrowly by 1-0 to Turkey. With a sound professional foundation in the professional J.League, the Japanese national team went on from strength to strength. Stars such as Hidetoshi Nakata and Junichi Inamoto shone though Japan fell in the World Cup first round in Germany in 2006. But a demonstration of the country's increasing power was that, without them in 2010, they reached the second round on foreign soil for the first time. A team with outstanding

new players such as forward Keisuke Honda and goalkeeper Eiji Kawashima fell only in a penalty shootout after a goalless extra-time draw with Paraguay.

Soccer had always taken a back seat in Japan's sporting hierarchy until the federation decided, in the early 1990s, to launch its ambitious bid to be the first Asian hosts of the World Cup. That campaign included the launch of the first professional championship, the J.League, in 1993, with a string of new clubs backed by private sponsors and local authorities. Foreign star veterans such as Zico of Brazil, Gary Lineker of England, Italy's Toto Schillaci and Pierre Littbarski of Germany were signed to help promote the league and "sell" it to the Japanese population. A failure to qualify for the 1994 World Cup finals in the USA was only a temporary setback and Japan duly qualified for the following finals in 1998, by which time they had also been confirmed as co-hosts for the 2002 tournament.

Jordan
Jordan Football Association
Founded: 1949
FIFA: 1958

Kuwait
Kuwait Football Association
Founded: 1952
FIFA: 1962
Asian Cup: 1980

Kyrgyzstan
Football Association of Kyrgyzstan
Founded: 1992
FIFA: 1994

Laos
Fédération de FootBall Lao
Founded: 1951
FIFA: 1952

Lebanon
Fédération Libanaise de Football
Founded: 1933
FIFA: 1935

Macao
Associacao de Futebol de Macau
Founded: 1939
FIFA: 1976

Malaysia
Persuatuan Bolasepak Malaysia
Founded: 1933
FIFA: 1956

Maldives
Football Association of Maldives
Founded: 1983
FIFA: 1986

Myanmar
Myanmar Football Federation
Founded: 1947
FIFA: 1947

Nepal
All Nepal Football Association
Founded: 1951
FIFA: 1970

North Korea
Football Association of the Democratic People's Republic of Korea
Founded: 1945
FIFA: 1958

North Korea's national side has consistently lived in the shadow of its much more successful neighbours from the South, but in 1966 the North made headlines around the world by beating Italy 1-0 in the first round of the World Cup. Pak Do Ik will forever be remembered as the man who scored the most famous goal in North Korean soccer history. Then, in an incredible quarter-final against Portugal, the North Koreans went 3-0 ahead after 22 minutes. But the dream faded almost as dramatically, as Portugal won 5-3.

Some 44 years later the North Koreans returned to the finals, in South Africa but with a far less dramatic effect. A hard-working team lost only 2-1 to Brazil in their opening game but that appearance was deceptive. They crashed 7-0 to Portugal with no hint of a 1966 repeat and 3-0 to Ivory Coast.

Oman

Oman Football Association
Founded: 1978
FIFA: 1980

Pakistan

Pakistan Football Federation
Founded: 1948
FIFA: 1948

Palestine

Palestinian Football Federation
Founded: 1928 then 1962
FIFA: 1998

Philippines

Philippine Football Federation
Founded: 1907
FIFA: 1928

Qatar

Qatar Football Association
Founded: 1960
FIFA: 1970

The enormous wealth of the tiny Gulf state was finally put to work on behalf of sport in general and soccer in particular in the early 2000s. A professional league was launched with the promotional help of veterans including the likes of Gabriel Batistuta and Fernando Hierro. The QFA also earned a significant international profile with an audacious and technologically imaginative bid to host the 2022 World Cup.

Saudi Arabia

Saudi Arabian Football Federation
Founded: 1959
FIFA: 1959
Asian Cup: 1984, 1988, 1996

Saudi Arabia is one of the most powerful nations within the Asian region and, with untold oil-based wealth on tap, could dominate at both national team and club level if a wider exchange of coaching and playing talent were possible.

First honours came with two Asian championship wins in the 1980s and constriction of the notable King Fahd Stadium in Riyadh to host the inaugural FIFA Confederations Cup in 1993. That commitment to the game was rewarded with four successive appearances at the World Cup finals of 1994- when Saeed Al-Owairan scored the goal of the tournament – 1998, 2002 and 2006.

Singapore

Football Association of Singapore
Founded: 1892
FIFA: 1952

South Korea

Korea Football Association
Founded: 1928
FIFA: 1948
Asian Cup: 1956, 1960

South Korea underlined their status as Asia's top soccer nation by reaching the semi-finals of the 2002 World Cup finals, which they co-hosted, with Japan.

They had made their mark first on the international stage by qualifying for the finals in Switzerland in 1954. They were eliminated in the first round but capitalized on the experience by winning the initial two Asian Championships in 1956 and 1960.

For 20 years the Korean game stood still until the creation of a pro league was rewarded with appearances at the finals at the finals of seven successive World Cups between 1986 and 2010. Key players in the late 1990s had been powerful central defender Hong Myung-bo, and German-based Cha Bum-kun, whose son would later emulate him as a World Cup footballer.

A decisive step forward came in 1996 when the Korean federation persuaded FIFA to award Korea co-hosting rights with Japan to the 2002 finals. The Koreans owed their success to positive memories of the 1988 Olympics in Seoul, their World Cup pedigree, plus an aggressive campaign in the corridors of power.

Dutch coach Guus Hiddink was appointed national coach at the start of 2001 and worked a minor miracle, albeit with virtually full-time access to his players in the months before the finals. Fired by the passionate supporters, Korea defeated Poland 2–0, played out a 1–1 with the United States then beat Portugal 1–0 to progress beyond the group stage. Victories over Italy and Spain earned them a place in history as the only Asian nation to reach the World Cup semi-finals. They then finished fourth after losing 3-2 to Turkey in the third-place playoff.

Sri Lanka

Football Federation of Sri Lanka
Founded: 1939
FIFA: 1950

Syria

Association Arabe Syrienne de Football
Founded: 1936
FIFA: 1937

Taiwan

Chinese Taipei Football Association
Founded: 1936
FIFA: 1954

Tajikistan

Football Federation of Tajikistan
Founded: 1991
FIFA: 1994

Thailand

Football Association of Thailand
Founded: 1916
FIFA: 1925

Turkmenistan

Football Federation of Turkmenistan
Founded: 1992
FIFA: 1994

United Arab Emirates

United Arab Emirates Football Association
Founded: 1971
FIFA: 1972

With only 25 registered clubs and 3,400 players, the United Arab Emirates caused a big surprise when they qualified for the 1990 World Cup finals. The UAE were beaten in all three of their matches.

Uzbekistan

Football Federation of Uzbekistan
Founded: 1946
FIFA: 1994

Uzbekistan had never been able to boast any sort of representation at the World Cup finals until 2010 in South Africa. This was when Ravshan Irmatov made history on being appointed, by FIFA, to referee the Opening Match between the hosts and Mexico.

Vietnam

Association de Football de la République du Vietnam
Founded: 1962
FIFA: 1964

Yemen

Republic of Yemen Football Association
Founded: 1962
FIFA: 1980

Hands across the pitch... as South Korea hail their World Cup dismissal of Italy.

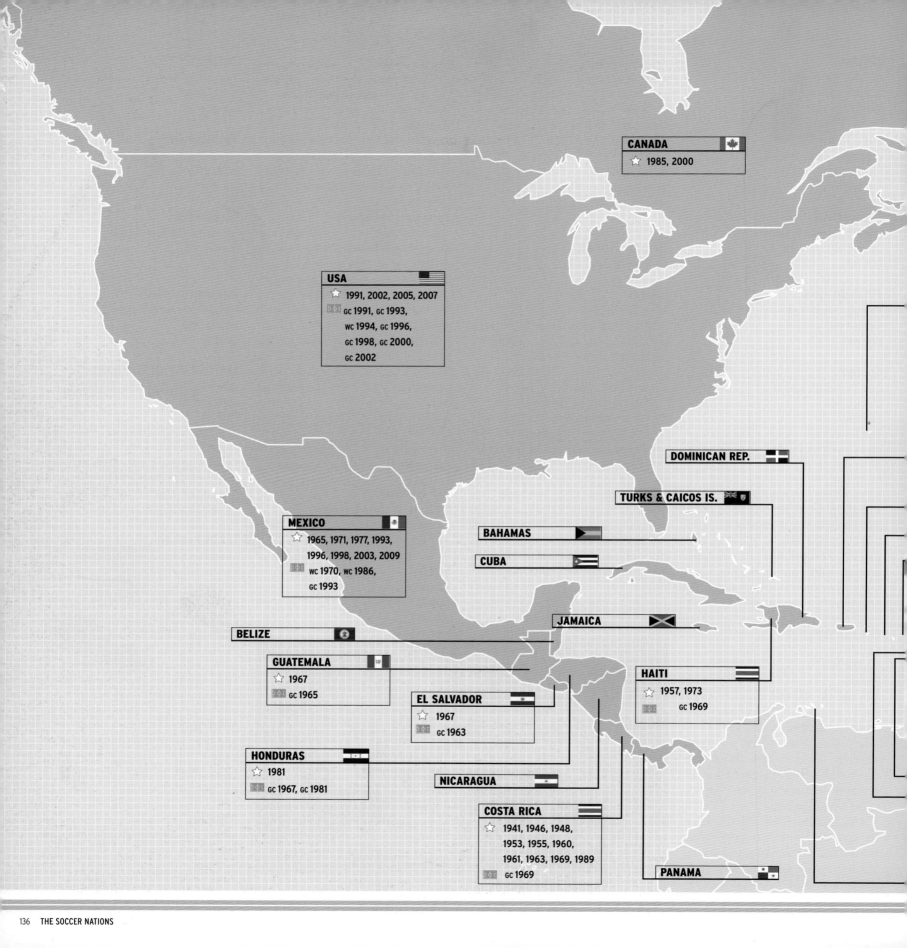

CANADA
⭐ 1985, 2000

USA
⭐ 1991, 2002, 2005, 2007
GC 1991, GC 1993,
WC 1994, GC 1996,
GC 1998, GC 2000,
GC 2002

DOMINICAN REP.

TURKS & CAICOS IS.

MEXICO
⭐ 1965, 1971, 1977, 1993,
1996, 1998, 2003, 2009
WC 1970, WC 1986,
GC 1993

BAHAMAS

CUBA

BELIZE

JAMAICA

GUATEMALA
⭐ 1967
GC 1965

HAITI
⭐ 1957, 1973
GC 1969

EL SALVADOR
⭐ 1967
GC 1963

HONDURAS
⭐ 1981
GC 1967, GC 1981

NICARAGUA

COSTA RICA
⭐ 1941, 1946, 1948,
1953, 1955, 1960,
1961, 1963, 1969, 1989
GC 1969

PANAMA

NORTH & CENTRAL AMERICA

KEY

☆ WORLD CUP WINNERS
☆ CCCF/CONCACAF
CHAMPIONSHIP/
GOLD CUP WINNERS
▦ CHAMPIONSHIP HOSTS
WC (WORLD CUP) GC (GOLD
CUP/CHAMPIONSHIP)

CONCACAF covers the whole of North and Central America and the Caribbean.

It is a huge space but international successes have been few for the millions in this federation. The USA alone boasts hundreds of millions of potential soccer players, but the vast majority of them are interested in sports with equipment rather different from the simplicity of what you need for a basic soccer match.

The huge influence of the USA, both economically and culturally, has meant that traditional USA ballsports have sometimes been pursued in countries that would originally have gone for the "global game".

Many central American nations may appear little more than a statistical dot in the world game's atlas, but CONCACAF (the North and Central American Federation) is very quickly learning how to capitalize on the commercial value of soccer. Income is being used profitably for coaching schemes and administrative improvements. "American" soccer is much more now than merely those nations which have done well in the World Cup: Mexico's double staging of the World Cup finals in 1970 and 1986 proves the point. So, of course, did USA 94. Building on that base, the US national team surprised many to reach the quarter-finals of the 2002 World Cup in Japan and South Korea.

Soccer's home town... Pasadena hosts the 1994 World Cup Final between Brazil and Italy.

BERMUDA

PUERTO RICO

US VIRGIN IS.

BRITISH VIRGIN IS.

ANGUILLA

ANTIGUA

DOMINICA

ST. LUCIA

BARBADOS

ST. VINCENT

GRENADA

TRINIDAD & TOBAGO
▦ GC 1971

MONTSERRAT

ST KITTS & NEVIS

SURINAM

GUYANA

NETHERLANDS ANTILLIES

NORTH AND CENTRAL AMERICA

The United States' display in the 2010 World Cup, where they reached the second round after finishing ahead of England in their group, ended the perception of the US as a non-soccer country.

United States

United States Soccer Federation
Founded: 1913
FIFA: 1913
CONCACAF Championship: 1991, 2002, 2005, 2007

In 1869, two leading colleges – Rutgers and Princeton – played each other on Rutgers' New Jersey campus, basing the game on the new FA rules. Rutgers took the game 6–4, but were trounced 8–0 in the return at Princeton. Alas, the University authorities were not delighted by this diversion from studies, and they managed to ban the third and deciding game. But the games had proved very popular with the students, and for a short while, it looked as though soccer would become the autumn sport in the colleges. But this did not happen. By 1877 soccer had vanished from college fields. Americans did not want to play sports imported from England. Cricket had been replaced by baseball, and the colleges soon abandoned soccer for rugby, which, in turn was Americanized into gridiron football.

Soccer, now bearing a seemingly 'un-American' label, faded into the background, but did not disappear thanks to the efforts of European immigrants – British, German and Irish mostly. A national side entered the 1924 and 1928 Olympics and then travelled to Uruguay for the first World Cup in 1930. 3–0 wins over both Belgium and Paraguay put the Americans into the semi-finals, where

Cosmos duo Giorgio Chinaglia and Pele turn revolutionaries for soccer's sake in the North American Soccer League in the mid-1970s.

they were taken apart 6–0 by the Argentines who had mauled them in the Olympics two years earlier.

By the outbreak of the Second World War, soccer in the US was still very much a minor sport. Attempts to start a pro league, or to capture the interest of the American public or media, had all ended in failure. And because it was played and controlled largely by immigrant groups from Europe it had an image problem: it was widely seen as a foreign sport. This led to unfavourable comparisons with the home-grown sports of baseball and gridiron football. There was even a hint that playing soccer was somehow unpatriotic.

Nothing much changed in the immediate post-war years although soccer was no longer limited to the north-east, but was now played all over the United States with St Louis emerging as the sport's new capital. But important changes were on the way, brought about by the war and advancing technology. The war had brought waves of new European immigrants to the US – and their passion for soccer injected dynamism into the game in the New York area.

Admittedly, it was unashamedly ethnic soccer. Teams now proudly bore names such as Philadelphia Ukrainians or Brooklyn Italians or the German-Hungarians of New York. But they drew good crowds. It was those same fans who responded when the advent of air travel made it easier for foreign teams to tour the US. In 1948 England's Liverpool played Djurgardens of Sweden at the stadium of the Brooklyn Dodgers baseball team. It was billed as the first-ever meeting of two foreign teams on American soil and more than 18,000 turned out to celebrate the occasion.

Then, seemingly out of the blue, came an event that should have given soccer in the US a tremendous boost. It started with the US qualifying for the 1950 World Cup in Brazil. The team of part-timers included a lively assortment of professions: a carpenter, a teacher, a machinist ... and an undertaker. In Brazil they pulled off one of the greatest sporting upsets when they beat England 1-0.

It was all change in 1967 with the founding of the North American Soccer League. The NASL featured corporate-backed teams that enabled the clubs to pay huge wages and attract top foreign stars such as Pele, Franz Beckenbauer, Johan Cruyff and George Best. But support and television levels reached nothing like the levels most backers had expected and the NASL imploded in 1984.

The US qualified for the 1990 World Cup finals but in Italy, however, the Americans' international naivety was exposed as they lost all three matches. Fortunately, they did not have to qualify in 1994: they were hosts. The USSF hired World Cup managerial specialist Bora Milutinovic who fashioned a team that proved not only exceptionally awkward to beat but, in 1991, they won their first major honour, the CONCACAF Championship. Milutinovic benefited from the unique creation of "Team America" on to which he grafted a number of players with experience of club soccer in Europe. They produced one of the shocks of the finals when they defeated Colombia in the group stage and lost only 1-0 to Brazil in the second round.

The 1995 Copa America, under a new coach – Steve Sampson – proved this success was no fluke as the US reached the semi-finals after defeating Argentina 3-0. But Sampson lost the plot at the 1998 World Cup finals when the US were eliminated in the first round in France. Sampson was replaced by top domestic club coach Bruce Arena who proved admirably skilled in the tactical manipulation of his super-fit players and proved his worth when he guided them to the quarter-finals of the 2002 World Cup – their best placing since they had reached the semi-finals of the inaugural tournament back in 1930.

Subsequent World Cup exits in the first round in 2006 and second round in 2010 did nothing to retard the progress and expansion of Major League Soccer. Launched in 1996, this was the first outdoor elite national league since the demise of NASL. Much of the glitz of the NASL may be missing, but MLS does have one big advantage: as well as stars from

Landon Donovan is the star man of the US national team.

around the world, the league boasts top home-grown internationals. Some – notably outstanding forward Landon Donovan – even preferred to stay and play in MLS rather than build a career in Europe.

Meanwhile, a new phenomenon exploded noisily on the scene: women's soccer. There is a huge irony here: for the very thing that held the men's game back for so long – college soccer – is what gave the American women their lead over the rest of the world. In no other country has the sport been given the attention and the backing that it receives in the American colleges. It greatly benefits from the government's Title IX regulations, which make it an offence not to provide equal sports opportunities for men and women.

The staging of the 1999 Women's World Cup – enhanced by the victory of the US team – proved a stunning success, with huge crowds and high television ratings. Many felt that the enthusiasm owed more to feminism and patriotism than to any devotion to soccer but the US went on to win three of the first four Olympic women's titles and, after one false start, launch a women's professional league.

Los Angeles Galaxy celebrate winning the MLS Cup in 2005.

Anguilla
Anguilla Football Association
Founded: 1996
FIFA: 1996

Antigua and Barbuda
Antigua Football Association
Founded: 1928
FIFA: 1970

Aruba
Arubaanse Voetbal Bond
Founded: 1932
FIFA: 1988

Bahamas
Bahamas Football Association
Founded: 1967
FIFA: 1968

Barbados
Barbados Football Association
Founded: 1910
FIFA: 1968

Belize
Belize National Football Association
Founded: 1980
FIFA: 1986

Bermuda
Bermuda Football Association
Founded: 1928
FIFA: 1962

British Virgin Islands
British Virgin Islands Football Association 1974
Founded: 1974
FIFA: 1996

Canada
Canadian Soccer Association
Founded: 1912
FIFA: 1912
Olympics: 1904 (Galt FC of Ontario)
CONCACAF Championship: 2000

Soccer in Canada has struggled to establish itself for two main reasons. First, the enormous size of the country makes a coherent structure difficult to implement and consequently a true, national league was only set up in 1987. Second, the sport trails badly in popularity behind ice hockey, baseball, gridiron and basketball – the big North American sports. Soccer took hold in Canada at the turn of the century, and in 1904 Galt FC from Ontario entered the St Louis Olympic Games. Soccer was only a demonstration sport, but Galt won the event.

In the 1970s, following in the tradition of many of Canada's ice hockey and baseball clubs who play in the North American leagues, three Canadian clubs, from Vancouver, Toronto and Edmonton, played in the North American Soccer League. Canada had to wait until 2000 to secure their first international trophy when they beat Colombia in the final of the CONCACAF Gold Cup,

Canada bring the Gold Cup home for the first time in 2000.

the regional championship. English-based goalkeeper Craig Forrest, then of West Ham, was voted Player of the Tournament.

Cayman Islands
Cayman Islands Football Association
Founded: 1992
FIFA: 1992

Costa Rica
Federacion Costarricense de Futbol
Founded: 1921
FIFA: 1921
CONCACAF Championship: 1941, 1946, 1948, 1953, 1955, 1960, 1961, 1963, 1969, 1989

Costa Rica have made enormous progress since the late 1980s, as their performances at the World Cup demonstrated. The breakthrough came in 1990 under Bora Milutinovic when Costa Rica marked their finals debut by beating Scotland and Sweden to reach the second round where they lost to Brazil. They narrowly failed to reach the second round in 2002 and had the honour and glamour of sharing the opening match in 2006 though they lost 4-2 to hosts Germany. They have always been one of the better teams in the region, having won nine CONCACAF Gold Cups. Top clubs Deportivo Saprissa and LD Alajuelense have both won the CONCACAF club championship.

Cuba
Asociacion de Futbol de Cuba
Founded: 1924
FIFA: 1932

Dominica
Dominica Football Association
Founded: 1970
FIFA: 1994

Dominican Republic
Federacion Dominicana de Futbol
Founded: 1953
FIFA: 1958

El Salvador
Federacion Salvadorena de Futbol
Founded: 1935

FIFA: 1938
CONCACAF Championship: 1943

El Salvador's biggest claim to soccer fame is the 1969 "Football War" with Central American neighbours Honduras. The countries met in a World Cup qualifying group and rioting followed both matches, especially after the second game when El Salvador forced a play-off. El Salvador won it and, as tension mounted, the army invaded Honduras on the pretext of protecting expatriate Salvadorean citizens. The World Cup match was more an excuse than a cause for the war, but the conflict cost 3,000 lives before it was settled. El Salvador have qualified for the World Cup finals twice, losing all three games in 1970 and again in 1982 – which included a 10-1 thrashing by Hungary.

Grenada
Grenada Football Association
Founded: 1924
FIFA: 1976

Guatemala
Federacion Nacional de Futbol de Guatemala
Founded: 1926
FIFA: 1933
CONCACAF Championship: 1967

Guyana
Guyana Football Association
Founded: 1904
FIFA: 1968

Haiti
Fédération Haitienne de Football
Founded: 1904
FIFA: 1933
CONCACAF Championship: 1957, 1973

Honduras
Federacion Nacional Automana de Futbol
Founded: 1935
FIFA: 1946
CONCACAF Championship: 1981

Honduras, like neighbouring El Salvador, is a country that has been plagued by insurgency and guerrilla warfare. Indeed, the two went to war in 1969, over the outcome of a

All smiles for the captains of Honduras and El Salvador before a World Cup qualifier... in 1982.

soccer match [See El Salvador]. Honduras have twice reached the World Cup finals, finishing bottom of their group without a win in both 1982 and 2010.

Jamaica
Jamaica Football Federation
Founded: 1910
FIFA: 1962

Jamaica have made incredible strides in the past decade. In 1998, having qualified for their first-ever World Cup finals under Brazilian coach Rene Simoes, the Reggae Boyz went on a world tour and found they had fans all over the world – especially in England. It was a carnival wherever they played, although they went out in the first round in France.

Mexico
Federacion Mexicana de Futbol Asociacion
Founded: 1927
FIFA: 1929
CONCACAF Championship: 1963, 1971, 1977, 1993, 1996, 1998, 2003, 2009

Mexico dominate central America to such an extent that over the past 20 years the national team and clubs have sought more testing competition in South American competitions such as the Copa America and Copa Libertadores. That has also helped maintain their remarkable World Cup record of having appeared in 13 of the 18 finals tournaments. They almost certainly missed out on one other, in 1990, through a suspension imposed by FIFA for having breached Youth Cup age limit rules. Mexico's finest World Cups were in 1970 and 1986 when they reached the quarter-finals. After the finals' expansion to 32 teams they reached the second round in both 2006 and 2010 only then to lose on both occasions to Argentina.

Mexico, eight-time CONCACAF Championship winners, have also twice reached the final of the South American Championship as guests. Along the way, Mexico launched new stars on the world stage such as colourful goalkeeper Jorge Campos, record international Claudio Suarez and forward Cuauhtemoc Blanco.

Montserrat
Montserrat Football Association
Founded: 1995
FIFA: 1996

Netherlands Antilles
Nederlands Antiliaanse Voetbal Unie
Founded: 1921
FIFA: 1932

Nicaragua
Federacion Nicaraguense de Futbol
Founded: 1931
FIFA: 1950

Panama
Federacion Nacional de Futbol de Panama
Founded: 1937
FIFA: 1938
CONCACAF Championship: 1951

Puerto Rico
Federacion Puertorriquena de Futbol
Founded: 1940
FIFA: 1960

Saint Kitts and Nevis
St Kitts and Nevis Football Association
Founded: 1992
FIFA: 1992

Saint Lucia
St Lucia National Football Association
Founded: 1988
FIFA: 1988

St Vincent & Grenadines
St Vincent and the Grenadines Football Federation
Founded: 1988
FIFA: 1988

Surinam
Surinaamse Voetbal Bond
Founded: 1920
FIFA: 1929

Trinidad and Tobago
Trinidad and Tobago Football Association
Founded: 1906
FIFA: 1963

In 2006 the 'Soca Warriors' became only the second Caribbean nation (after Jamaica) to reach the World Cup finals after a dramatic victory over Bahrain in an intercontinental play-off. Veteran Dutch coach Leo Beenhakker plotted a respectable campaign in Germany which saw a team starring former Manchester United veteran Dwight Yorke open with a surprise goalless draw against Sweden.

Turks and Caicos
Turks and Caicos Island Football Association
Founded: 1961
FIFA: 1999

United States Virgin Islands
USVI Soccer Federation
Founded: 1992
FIFA: 1998

Mexico's Manuel Negrete celebrates scoring against Bulgaria in 1986, one of the World Cup's greatest goals.

OCEANIA

Oceania is the poor relation of international soccer. Only Australia has significant mainstream potential and it defected to the Asian Confederation in 2006.

South America has proved that a small membership need not be a hindrance to power. However, international achievement is also necessary and here Oceania has fallen down. Australia and New Zealand have made only fleeting appearances at the World Cup finals, victims of a vicious circle. Oceania nations fail on the big stage hence their path back is not eased.

The confederation was founded in 1965 but Australian ambitions have upset the boat. Australia quit briefly in 1973 when it sought to join the Asian confederation mainstream. The Australians duly returned to the fold but finally, despite remaining geographically in Oceania, they transferred into the Asian federation in 2005. Oceania's image had not

been enhanced in 2000 when its long-serving president, Charles Dempsey, walked out on the FIFA executive in the midst of its deliberations over hosting rights to the 2006 World Cup. Dempsey's departure set off a political chain reaction which led to Germany pipping South Africa by one vote. Finally, in 2001, that same FIFA executive did, eventually, vote for

Oceania to receive a single guaranteed place at the World Cup finals. However, that guarantee was rescinded two years later when Oceania was the victim of another power battle this time inspired by South American concerns at the loss of a place of their own. Australia's departure into the Asia confederation has weakened Oceania's status further.

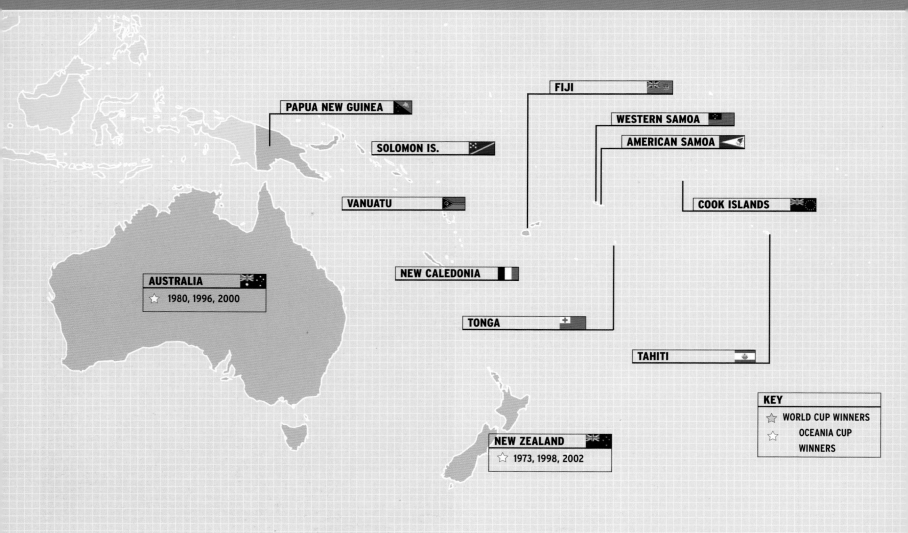

PAPUA NEW GUINEA

FIJI

WESTERN SAMOA

AMERICAN SAMOA

SOLOMON IS.

VANUATU

COOK ISLANDS

AUSTRALIA
⭐ 1980, 1996, 2000

NEW CALEDONIA

TONGA

TAHITI

NEW ZEALAND
☆ 1973, 1998, 2002

KEY
⭐ WORLD CUP WINNERS
☆ OCEANIA CUP WINNERS

American Samoa

American Samoa Football Association
Founded: 1975
FIFA: Associate member
American Samoa set a soccer record when they lost a 2001 World Cup qualifier 31–0 to Australia.

Australia

Australia Soccer Federation (Asia Confederation)
Founded: 1961
FIFA: 1963
Oceania Cup: 1980, 1996, 2000
Soccer has struggled to gain a foothold down-under, with Aussie rules and both codes of rugby being the soccer sports of choice. The need for fresh competitive impetus was one of the reasons Australia quit the Oceania confederation to join Asia in 2006. The Socceroos competed first at the World Cup finals in 1974 but missed out, one step short, in the inter-continental play-offs for 1994, 1998 and 2002. Dutch coach Guus Hiddink guided them not only safely through to Germany in 2006 but to the second round. This meant it was a major disappointment when they crashed out at the group stage four years later in South Africa.

Cook Islands

Cook Islands Football Federation
Founded: 1971
FIFA: 1994

Fiji

Fiji Football Association
Founded: 1938
FIFA: 1963

New Caledonia

Federation Neo-Caledonienne de Football
Founded: 1960
FIFA: Provisional member

New Zealand

New Zealand Football Association
Founded: 1938
FIFA: 1963
Oceania Cup: 1973, 1998, 2002
New Zealand took advantage of Australia's defection from Oceania to qualify for the 2010 World Cup where they failed bravely after drawing all their three group games.

Papua New Guinea

Papua New Guinea Football Association
Founded: 1962
FIFA: 1963

Samoa

Samoa Football (Soccer) Federation
Founded: 1968
FIFA: 1986

Solomon Islands

Solomon Islands Football Federation
Founded: 1988
FIFA: 1988

Tahiti

Fédération Tahitienne de Football
Founded: 1938
FIFA: 1990

Tonga

Tonga Football Association
Founded: 1970
FIFA: 1994

Vanuatu

Vanuatu Football Federation
Founded: 1934
FIFA: 1988

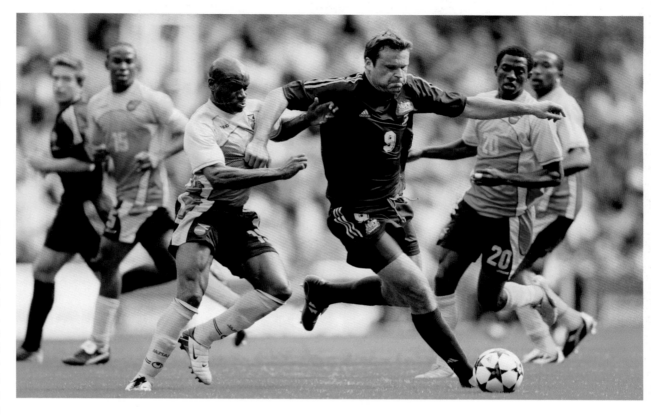

Australian striker Mark Viduka in typically forceful action for the Socceroos against Jamaica (above) and New Zealand play China in a 1981 World Cup qualifier (below).

PART 4:

THE GREAT PLAYERS

These are the men who have delighted fans over the years not merely with their achievements but with their personalities on the pitch and occasionally off it. They draw spectators who are attracted beyond an attachment to a club or a national team.

A comparative handful of players qualify for the status of true greatness. Achievement alone is not enough. Indeed, the trophy potential has expanded down the years. Until the 1930s a player had 'only' domestic league and cup and a small number of national team friendlies in which to establish his fame.

Even the World Cup did not envelop the entire global game until the 1950s. But this was also the decade which opened up the potential of fame and fortune via the European club competitions. Simultaneously, the allure of the heroes from the first half of the 20th century was overshadowed by 'modern' players whose talents

were able to sparkle around the world via the medium of television. The appreciation of greatness has been skewed by the technological developments which brought the first colour television World Cup in 1970 and then the communications revolution wrought by the internet at the turn of the 21st century.

Andre "Trello" Abegglen

National team: Switzerland
Born: March 7, 1909
Club(s): Etoile Rouge, Cantonal, Grasshoppers, Sochaux (Fr), Servette, La Chaux-de-Fonds

Abegglen was the first great Swiss player to make his mark on the world stage. He and brother Max, nicknamed Xam, were inside-forward stalwarts together at the Grasshoppers club of Zurich. Trello scored 30 goals in 52 internationals for Switzerland between 1927 and 1943. He starred at the 1934 and 1938 World Cup finals and won three Swiss championships, two with Grasshoppers and one after moving on to Servette of Geneva. Brother Max played 68 times for Switzerland and was top scorer at the 1924 Olympic Games.

Anthony "Tony" Adams

National team: England
Born: October 10, 1966
Club(s): Arsenal

As a boy Adams had always dreamed of playing for Arsenal and his dream came true at 15. He made his league debut at 17 and his England debut in 1987 against Spain. Adams missed the 1990 World Cup finals in Italy, but went on to display enormous strength of character as he became captain of both Arsenal and England, after serving a prison sentence for a motoring offence and winning a battle against alcohol addiction. He went on to captain Arsenal to three League championships and to victories in two Finals of the FA Cup – the 1998 triumph securing the league and cup double – the League Cup and European Cup-Winners Cup. He played 66 times for England between 1987 and 2001.

Ademir Marques de Menezes

National team: Brazil
Born: November 8, 1922
Club(s): FC Recife, Vasco da Gama, Fluminense, Vasco da Gama

Ademir was the seven-goal leading scorer at the 1950 World Cup finals,

Tony Adams puts heart and soul into winning another tackle for England.

when he played centre-forward for Brazil. The inside-forward trio of Ademir, Zizinho and Jair da Rosa was considered one of the greatest in Brazil's history. Ademir scored 32 goals in 37 internationals and he began his impressive career as an outside-left. He had a powerful shot with both feet and was a Rio state league champion six times: five times with Vasco da Gama and once with Fluminense. It was said that Brazilian coaches created 4-2-4 because Ademir's ability made it necessary for opposing teams to play with an extra central defender.

José Pinto Carvalho dos Santos Aguas

National team: Portugal
Born: November 9, 1930
Club(s): Benfica, FK Austria (Aus)

Aguas was captain and centre-forward of Benfica when they succeeded Real Madrid as champions of Europe in 1961. Legend has it that he was a famous lion-hunter in his native Angola before Benfica persuaded him he could enjoy a more lucrative existence hunting goals. He flew to Portugal in 1950 and scored more than 250 goals for Benfica, finishing top league scorer five times. In 1960–

61 he was also top scorer, with 11 goals, in the European Cup and collected the trophy after the final victory over Barcelona. In 1963 he joined FK Austria but later returned to Portugal to work as a coach.

Florian Albert

National team: Hungary
Born: September 15, 1941
Club(s): Ferencvaros

Albert was the first great player to emerge in Hungary after the dissolution of the great team of the early 1950s. He was a farmer's son whose family moved to Budapest. His talent was quickly recognized by the youth coaches of Ferencvaros and he made his international debut at 17 – just a few days after passing his major school examinations – in a 3-2 win over Sweden in Budapest. Centre-forward Albert was three times the leading scorer in the Hungarian league and four times a league championship winner with Ferencvaros. His most memorable display was in Hungary's 3-1 win over Brazil at the 1966 World Cup finals, and he was voted European Footballer of the Year the following year.

Ivor Allchurch

National team: Wales
Born: October 16, 1919
Club(s): Swansea, Newcastle United (Eng), Cardiff, Swansea

Slim, elegant, creative and a natural scorer, in the first quarter-century after the Second World War, Ivor the Golden Boy had just about everything an inside-forward needs – except luck. He was fated to play in mediocre club teams throughout his long career and, apart from the 1958 World Cup, even his excellent work for his country went largely to waste. He won 68 caps spread over 16 years, and scored 23 goals – records which stood until the 1990s. His 251 league goals in nearly 700 appearances emphasized his excellent finishing.

Luigi Allemandi

National team: Italy
Born: November 18, 1903
Club(s): Juventus, Internazionale, Roma

Allemandi was a left-back and one of the outstanding personalities in Calcio in the inter-war years. He played 25 times for his country and would have made more appearances but for a match-fixing scandal, when he was accused of having accepted a bribe from a director of Torino to fix a match while playing for Juventus in 1927. The matter did not emerge until a year later when Allemandi, despite reports identifying him as one of the best players on the field, was found guilty and suspended for life. By now he was playing for Internazionale, who challenged the ban on his behalf and had it quashed. In 1929 Allemandi returned to Italy's team for a match against Czechoslovakia, and he went on to win a World Cup medal in 1934.

Alpay Ozalan Fehmi

National team: Turkey
Born: May 29, 1973
Club(s): Besiktas, Altay, Fenerbahce, Aston Villa (Eng)

Alpay, a central defender or defensive midfielder, starred for Turkey at the finals of both the European Championship in 2000 and the World Cup two years later, when they finished a best-ever third. He had made his name at home with Besiktas, with whom he won the championship and the cup twice, before he transferred to Aston Villa for £10.5 million after Euro 2000. However, he never quite adjusted to England or English soccer. Villa released him after his tormenting of David Beckham during the high-tension European qualifier against England in Istanbul in October 2003.

José Altafini

National teams: Brazil and Italy
Born: August 27, 1938
Club(s): Palmeiras, São Paulo, FC, Milan, Napoli, Juventus, Chiasso (Swz)

Altafini was a subject of confusion and admiration throughout his career. A direct, aggressive centre-forward, he began with Palmeiras of Sao Paulo, where he was known by the nickname of Mazzola because of his resemblance to the Italian star of the late 1940s. He played at the 1958 World Cup and was immediately signed by Milan. The Italians insisted on reverting to Altafini's own name and he played for his 'new' country at the 1962 World Cup finals. A year later Altafini scored a record 14 goals in Milan's European Cup success, including two goals in the final victory over Benfica at Wembley. After falling out with Milan he joined Omar Sivori in inspiring a Napoli revival, then became a 'super sub' with Juventus before playing out his career in Switzerland. He is now a TV soccer analyst in Italy.

Alessandro Altobelli

National team: Italy
Born : November 28, 1955
Club(s): Brescia, Internazionale

Altobelli was an outstanding attack leader who never hesitated to let his emotions flow – he once slapped a team-mate across the face for missing an open goal. Altobelli joined Internazionale of Milan in 1977 and was a member of Italy's fourth-placed European Championship squad in 1980. He became a national hero two years later when he stepped into the 1982 World Cup Final as tenth-minute substitute for injured Francesco Graziani and scored one of Italy's title-winning goals. Altobelli scored 25 goals in the 61 internationals between his debut against Belgium in 1980 and farewell against Russia in 1988.

Amancio Amaro Varela

National team: Spain
Born: October 12, 1939
Club(s): Deportivo La Coruña, Real Madrid

In 1962 Real Madrid, seeking a replacement for Italy-bound Luis Del Sol, bought outside-right Amancio from his hometown club, Real Deportivo La Coruña. Coach Miguel Muñoz changed his position, playing him first in midfield and then as a striker. His outstanding technique and acceleration brought him a string of honours. He played 42 times for Spain between 1964 and 1971, was ten times a Spanish league champion with Madrid and four times a cup-winner. In 1968 he was honoured with selection for a World XI against Brazil, but the highlight of his career was winning the European Nations Championship with Spain in 1964 at his own club's Estadio Bernabau in Madrid.

Amarildo Tavares Silveira

National team: Brazil
Born: June 29, 1939
Club(s): Botafogo, AC Milan, Fiorentina (It)

Amarildo, an attacking inside-left whose slight appearance disguised a wiry frame, burst onto the international scene at the 1962 World Cup finals after Pele was injured. He had not expected to play when he was called in to deputize for O Rei in a decisive group match against Spain. Brazil recovered from a goal down to win 2-1, thanks to two late strikes from Amarildo, and in the Final against Czechoslovakia he proved decisive, once more scoring with a snap shot which deceived the goalkeeper on the near post. A year later Amarildo was bought by Milan, and he enjoyed a successful career in Italy with both Milan and Fiorentina, with whom he won the championship in 1969. Amarildo stayed in Italy after his retirement and joined Fiorentina's youth coaching staff.

Manuel Amoros

National team: France
Born: February 1, 1961
Club(s): Monaco, Marseille, Lyon

Amoros played both right- and left-back in the outstanding French national team of the 1980s. Born in Nimes of Spanish parents, he excelled at both soccer and rugby, but Monaco persuaded him to concentrate on soccer. Amoros played for France at youth and Under-21 levels before a surprise, and successful, promotion to the senior team at the 1982 World Cup finals, in which France finished fourth. He won a European Championship medal in 1984, despite

Alessandro Altobelli made a decisive contribution even as substitute.

missing most of the tournament after being sent off in the opening match against Denmark. Amoros held the French record of 82 caps until the late 1990s.

Pietro Anastasi

National team: Italy
Born: April 7, 1948
Club(s): Varese, Juventus

Anastasi made headlines in the summer of 1968 when, apart from helping Italy win the European Championship, he was sold from Varese to Juventus for a then world record fee of £500,000. The deal had already been agreed when Anastasi scored a decisive goal against Yugoslavia in the replayed final. Injury kept him out of the 1970 World Cup but he played in all of Italy's three games at the finals four years later. He totalled eight goals in 25 international appearances between 1968 and 1975 and was a European Champions Cup runner-up with Juventus, to Ajax, in 1973.

José Leandro Andrade

National team: Uruguay
Born: November 20, 1898
Club(s): Bella Vista, Nacional

Andrade was an old-fashioned wing-half in the 2-3-5 tactical system, which served much of the world for the first half of the century. He was a stalwart of the great Uruguayan teams of the 1920s and 1930s, winning gold medals at the Olympic Games soccer tournaments of both 1924 and 1928. Injury then threatened to end his career but Andrade was recalled, because of his vast experience, for the inaugural World Cup finals which Uruguay won on home ground in 1930. He played 41 times for his country before retiring in 1933. Andrade's nephew, Victor Rodriguez Andrade, was in the Uruguayan World Cup winning side of 1950 and was never once booked or sent off.

Giancarlo Antognoni

National team: Italy
Born: April 1, 1954
Club(s): Astimacombi, Fiorentina, Luzern (Swz)

In the 1970s and early 1980s Antognoni was considered by Italian fans to be the successor to Milan's Gianni Rivera as the Golden Boy of Italian soccer. A graceful, wonderfully intuitive midfield general, Fiorentina bought Antognoni for £750,000 from Fourth Division Astimacombi, when he was still a teenager in 1972. He went straight into the Fiorentina team and made the first of his 73 appearances for Italy in late 1974. Antognoni was a regular transfer target for Italy's richest clubs but remained faithful to Fiorentina until he eventually wound down his career in Switzerland. Sadly, Antognoni missed Italy's victory over West Germany in the 1982 World Cup Final after suffering a gashed ankle in the semi-final defeat of Poland.

Osvaldo Ardiles

National team: Argentina
Born: August 3, 1952
Club(s): Huracan, Tottenham Hotspur (Eng), Paris S-G (Fr), Tottenham Hotspur (Eng), Queens Park Rangers (Eng)

Ardiles combined legal and soccer studies in the mid-1970s, when he earned his initial reputation as midfield general of Argentina under manager Cesar Luis Menotti. Hardly had Ardiles collected his winners' medal at the 1978 World Cup when he and national teammate Ricardo Villa were the subjects of a remarkable transfer to Tottenham Hotspur. Ardiles cost Spurs £300,000, which made him one of the greatest bargains of modern soccer history. His outstanding playing career included Tottenham's FA Cup success of 1981 and their UEFA Cup triumph of 1984. He returned to White Hart Lane as manager in the summer of 1993, but lasted little more than a year.

Andrei Arshavin

National team: Russia
Born: May 29, 1981
Clubs(s): Zenit St Petersburg, Arsenal (Eng)

Arshavin came comparatively late to international headlines. He was already in his mid-20s when his perceptive attacking play, from either wing, earned him star status in Russia. He captained Zenit to their 2008 UEFA Cup win and would have made an even greater impact in Russia's run to the Euro semi-finals had he not missed the first two games through suspension. Linked immediately with a move to Spain, Arshavin had to wait until the following January before joining Arsenal. Made an early impact by scoring all their goals in a remarkable 4-4 draw at Liverpool.

Luis Artime

National team: Argentina
Born: December 2, 1938
Club(s): Atlanta, River Plate, Independiente, Palmeiras (Br), Nacional (Uru), Fluminense (Br)

Artime was a centre-forward in the traditional Argentine mould: powerful, aggressive and prolific. He scored 47 goals in two teenage seasons with minor Buenos Aires club Atlanta to earn a move in 1961 to River Plate, with whom he will always be most closely linked. He concluded his stay there, which included 66 league goals, by leading Argentina's attack at the 1966 World Cup finals. Artime then joined Independiente, scoring 44 goals in 18 months, before moving on to Palmeiras and then to Nacional of Montevideo, with whom he was top Uruguayan league marksman three years in a row. He also scored 24 goals for Argentina.

Georgi Asparoukhov

National team: Bulgaria
Born: May 4, 1943
Club(s): Botev Plovdiv, Spartak Sofia, Levski Sofia

"Gundi" Asparoukhov remains one of the most outstanding yet tragic players in Bulgaria's history. A tall, direct centre-forward, he scored 19 goals in 49 internationals before he was killed in a car crash, aged 28, in 1971. Asparoukhov led Bulgaria's attack in the World Cup finals of 1962, 1966 and 1970 and scored 150 goals in 245 league games for his only senior club, Levski Sofia. Portuguese club Benfica tried to sign him in 1966 after

Osvaldo Ardiles made history with Argentina and then Tottenham.

he impressed in a European Cup tie. But Asparoukhov did not want to move because he had all he wanted in Bulgaria – including his favourite Alfa Romeo sports car which, ultimately, proved the death of him.

Augusto José Pinto de Almeida

National team: Portugal
Born: April 13, 1937
Club(s): Barreirense, Benfica

Jose Augusto was originally a centre-forward, and had already made his debut for Portugal in this position when Benfica bought him, from local club Barreirense, in 1959 on coach Bela Guttmann's recommendation. Guttmann then successfully converted him into an outside-right. Augusto was considered, after Frenchman Raymond Kopa, as the best 'thinking' player in Europe and appeared in five European Cup finals. He was a winner in 1961 and 1962 and a loser in 1963, 1965 and finally in 1968 against Manchester United, by which time he was an attacking midfield player. Augusto was a key member of the Portugal side which finished third at the 1966 World Cup, and later coached both Benfica and Portugal.

Roberto Baggio

National team: Italy
Born: February 18, 1967
Club(s): Fiorentina, Juventus, Milan, Bologna, Internazionale, Brescia

Roberto Baggio became the world's most expensive soccer player when Juventus bought him from Fiorentina on the eve of the 1990 World Cup finals for £8 million. His transfer provoked three days of riots in the streets of Florence by angry fans and he proved his worth by scoring a glorious World Cup goal against Czechoslovakia. He then helped Juventus win the 1993 UEFA Cup and was voted World Player of the Year in 1994, despite missing a penalty in the World Cup Final shoot-out against Brazil. He made up for that error in the 1998 finals, bravely volunteering

Roberto Baggio cost Juventus a then world record £8m in 1990.

to take a penalty against Chile and also scoring in a shoot-out against France. He won the title with Juventus in 1995 and again with Milan in 1996 before "going provincial" with Bologna and Brescia.

Alan Ball

National team: England
Born: May 12, 1945
Club(s): Blackpool, Everton, Arsenal, Southampton

Ball, son of a former professional player and manager of the same name, was one of the hardest-working heroes of England's 1966 World Cup triumph. He made his name with Blackpool, collected a league championship medal with Everton in 1970 then later moved to Arsenal for what was then their record fee of £220,000. Later Ball moved on to Southampton before returning to Blackpool as player-manager. His determination to remain within the game saw him take up a variety of managerial appointments, including Stoke City, Manchester City, Southampton and Portsmouth.

Michael Ballack

National team: Germany
Born: September 26, 1976
Club(s): Chemnitz, Motor Karl-Marx-Stadt, Bayer Leverkusen, Bayern Munich, Chelsea (Eng), Bayer Leverkusen

Ballack became the new hero of German soccer after leading the national team, surprisingly, to the 2002 World Cup Final. Suspension cost him an appearance in the defeat by Brazil, after which Bayern bought him from Bayer Leverkusen. Ballack had also just led Leverkusen to the Champions League Final (where they lost 2-1 to Real Madrid) and to runners-up status in the German league and cup. After winning two 'doubles' with Bayern and captaining Germany to the 2006 World Cup semi-finals and 2008 Euro final, he launched a four-year stint at Chelsea.

Gordon Banks

National team: England
Born: December 20, 1937
Club(s): Leicester, Stoke

A product of the prolific Chesterfield goalkeeper academy, Banks went on to undying fame with England. He set all kinds of goalkeeping records, including 73 caps, 23 consecutive internationals, and seven consecutive clean sheets, a run eventually ended by Eusebio's penalty in the 1966 World Cup semi-final. His withdrawal through illness the night before the 1970 quarter-final probably cost England the match, even though they did go 2-0 up. He was a loser in two FA Cup Finals with Leicester and, unluckiest of all, he lost an eye in a car crash when he still had years left to play. Perhaps only Shilton has equalled him as a goalkeeper for England.

Franceschino "Franco" Baresi

National team: Italy
Born: May 8, 1960
Club(s): Milan

Baresi was perhaps the greatest in a long line of outstanding Italian sweepers. He began as an attacking midfielder with Milan in the late 1970s and was kept waiting for an international opportunity because of the dominance of Juventus' Gaetano Scirea. Finally, in 1987, Baresi secured

Gabriel Batistuta played for both Argentina's top clubs.

a place in the national team and simultaneously provided the defensive foundation on which coach Arrigo Sacchi built Milan's all-conquering club team. Although Dutchmen Ruud Gullit and Marco Van Basten were granted much of the glory, discerning observers recognized the enormous influence of Baresi.

John Barnes

National team: England
Born: November 7, 1963
Club(s): Watford, Liverpool

Barnes was an England regular, mainly on the left wing, for 13 years from 1983. But the moment which defined his ability and overshadowed all his efforts for clubs and country was the dramatic goal against Brazil in Rio's Maracana Stadium in June 1984. Barnes strode through the Brazilian ranks from the halfway line to unleash a shot which shocked all Brazil and inspired England to their only away win to the five-times world champions. It was by far the most amazing of his 11 goals in his 79 internationals. At Liverpool, Barnes won the league once, FA Cup twice and League Cup once.

Fabien Barthez

National team: France
Born: June 28, 1971
Club(s): Marseille, Monaco, Manchester United (Eng), Marseille

Barthez created his own "soccer fashion" with his short-sleeved goalkeeper shirts. But far more significant have been his career achievements thus far. He won the Champions Cup with Marseille in controversial circumstances in 1993 and then cemented his personal reputation with Monaco, before moving to Manchester United as successor to Peter Schmeichel. Simultaneously Barthez was one of the most charismatic members of the France team who won the 1998 World Cup as hosts and the 2000 European Championship in Holland and Belgium.

Yildiray Basturk

National team: Turkey
Born: December 24, 1978
Club(s): Bochum (Ger), Bayer Leverkusen (Ger)

Basturk was one of the most successful products to emerge for Turkey from the émigré community in Germany. He turned professional with Bochum in

1997 and cost Bayer Leverkusen £4 million in 2001. It proved money well spent as he starred in their remarkable 2001-02 season. Bayer, under Klaus Toppmoller, finished runners-up in the German league and cup as well as in the European Champions League Final to Real Madrid. He then played in all seven of Turkey's games at the World Cup finals in South Korea and Japan in 2002, where they finished third.

Gabriel Batistuta

National team: Argentina
Born: February 1, 1969
Club(s): Newells Old Boys, River Plate, Boca Juniors, Fiorentina (It), Roma (It), Internazionale (It), Al-Arabi (Qtr)

Batistuta was long underrated by Argentine fans who are used to centre-forwards with a more refined technical style. But he was top-scorer with six goals when Argentina won the 1991 South American Championship, a performance that earned him a transfer to Italy. Fiorentina pulled out of the imminent purchase of compatriot Diego Latorre, so impressed were they by Batistuta's international explosion. Nicknamed "Batigol" in Florence, he endeared

himself to the fans when he insisted on staying with Fiorentina following their shock relegation in 1992 – and scored the goals which brought them back up to Serie A at the first attempt. In 2000 he was sold to Roma and scored 20 goals to inspire only the third league title in their history.

Jim Baxter

National team: Scotland
Born: September 29, 1939
Club(s): Raith Rovers, Glasgow Rangers, Sunderland (Eng), Nottingham Forest (Eng), Glasgow Rangers

Baxter's skill quickly established him as an Ibrox idol after Rangers signed him in June 1960. An attacking left-half, he won three Scottish leagues, three Scottish Cups and four League Cups. His profile was enhanced by selection for FIFA's World XI against England at the FA's centenary in 1963. A leg fracture disrupted his career in December 1964 and on recovery he moved south with Sunderland and then Nottingham Forest. Baxter's greatest moments were Scotland's Wembley triumphs over England by 2-1 in 1963 and by 3-2 in 1967.

Bebeto
Full name: Jose Roberto Gama de Oliveira

National team: Brazil
Born: February 16, 1964
Club(s): Flamengo, Vasco da Gama, Deportivo La Coruña (Sp), Vitoria Bahia, Gremio, Botafogo, Vasco da Gama, Jubilo Cerezo (Jpn)

Striker Bebeto could have made an impact long before winning the 1994 World Cup with Brazil but for a weak temperament and bad luck with injuries. He was predictably nicknamed the "New Zico" after exploding into Brazilian soccer with Flamengo in 1982 when the real thing was on World Cup duty. He starred when Flamengo won the Rio championship in 1986 and was the club's top scorer four years in a row. His transfer in 1989 to Rio rivals Vasco caused enormous controversy which dissipated after he scored six goals in Brazil's Copa America triumph

FRANZ BECKENBAUER
Born to win

"Kaiser Franz" is the only man in soccer who can boast that he has lifted the World Cup as both captain, in 1974, and manager, in 1990.

Throughout his career, Franz Beckenbauer has had the sort of luck that only a player of his genius deserves. Fate smiled on him through his illustrious playing days and on into management when, in his first appointment at any level, he took West Germany to the final of the World Cup in Mexico in 1986 and four years later went one better with victory in Italy.

No other player has ever had a career that reached such tangible heights. His honours include the World Cup in 1974 (runner-up in 1966), the European Championship in 1972 (runner-up 1976), the World Club Cup (1976), the European Cup (1974, 1975, 1976), the European Cup-Winners' Cup (1967), as well as the West German league and cup. He was also a runner-up in the UEFA Cup with Hamburg and a runner-up in the Super Cup with Bayern. With New York Cosmos, Beckenbauer also won the NASL Soccer Bowl in 1977, 1978 and 1980. He was also the first German to reach 100 international appearances.

However, Beckenbauer's innovative strength was in the revolutionary role of attacking sweeper which, with the encouragement of Bayern Munich coach Tschik Cajkovski, he introduced in the late 1960s.

Within a year of making his league debut with Bayern as an outside-left, Beckenbauer was promoted into the senior national team. Later he was voted German Footballer of the Year and European Footballer of the Year.

Out on the pitch he was graceful and elegant, combining an athlete's physique with a computer-like brain for the game which saw gaps before they had opened and goal opportunities for which opposing defences had not prepared.

Beckenbauer spent almost all his senior career with Bayern Munich as attacking sweeper. Many critics said he was wasting his talent, but Beckenbauer, in an increasingly crowded modern game, found that the sweeper role provided him with time and space in which to work his magical influence on a match. He was a sort of puppet master, standing back and pulling the strings which earned West Germany and Bayern Munich every major prize.

Not that Beckenbauer shied away from an attacking opportunity when it presented itself and, from midfield, he scored the goal which inspired West Germany's revival against England in the 1970 World Cup quarter-final.

After leaving Bayern, Beckenbauer spent four years with the New York Cosmos and then had a spell at Hamburg. During his time in the United States of America he won many friends and admirers.

He returned to Germany as national coach and, despite a lack of experience, mastermind the 1990 success which made him the only man to captain and tehn manage World Cup-winners.

The Midas touch remained secure as Beckenbauer rose up the political ladder. He led Germany's hosting of the 2006 World Cup, becoming a German federation vice-president and a member of the executive committees of both FIFA and UEFA.

Franz Beckenbauer was a winner as player, captain, coach and president.

1945	1959	1964	1966	1972	1976	1986	1993
Born on September 11 in Munich	Joined Bayern Munich youth section	Made his Bayern debut in a 4-0 win away to St Pauli in Hamburg	Starred in midfield, on the losing side, for West Germany in the 4-2 World Cup Final defeat by England	Captained West Germany to European Championship victory over the Soviet Union in Brussels	Completed a record 103 appearances for West Germany before transferring to the New York Cosmos in the North American Soccer League	Guided an average side to the World Cup Final, where they lost 3-2 to Argentina	After a short spell as coach of Olympique Marseille, Beckenbauer returned to Bayern as executive vice-president

1955	1962	1965	1967	1974	1984	1990	1994
Began playing for the schoolboy team, FC 1906 Munich	Gave up a job as a trainee insurance salesman to sign full-time with Bayern	Made his national team debut in a 2-1 World Cup qualifying win in Sweden	Captained Bayern Munich to victory over Glasgow Rangers in the European Cup-Winners Cup Final	Captained Bayern Munich to victory in the European Cup Final and then West Germany to victory in the World Cup Final against Holland	Appointed national manager of West Germany in succession to Jupp Derwall	Became the first man to captain and then manage a World Cup-winning team as West Germany beat Argentina	Guided Bayern to the league title, first as manager then as club president

DAVID BECKHAM
A roller-coaster ride

David Beckham has transformed himself from English pariah to English soccer icon – and built a new career with Real Madrid after 12 years with Manchester United. He has also become one of the most famous sportsmen on the planet with a commercial profile that few can match. His brand appeal was one of the factors that persuaded Madrid to pay more than £20 million for him in the summer of 2003.

However, it was Beckham's soccer that first made him famous. He is one of England's few world-class players of the last generation. He won the European Champions League Cup and every prize in the English game with Manchester United before his move to the Estadio Santiago Bernabeu.

But just five years earlier, Beckham was the most hated man in English soccer and was blamed for causing England's 1998 World Cup exit when he was sent off for a rash flick at Diego Simeone in the second round match against Argentina in St Etienne.

He answered his critics with his performances. In 1998-99, he was one of United's driving forces as they won the Champions League, the Premiership crown and the FA Cup and was short-listed for both World

and European Player of the Year awards. Beckham's ability to whip in accurate crosses under the tightest marking created a host of goals for Dwight Yorke, Andy Cole and Ruud van Nistelrooy at United. He also

proved a deadly free-kick exponent and, as captain of England, his stoppage time free-kick against Greece clinched England's automatic qualification for the 2002 World Cup and completed his transformation

from national villain to national hero. In fact, his national status was such that when he was injured just weeks before the World Cup finals, the same newspapers that had encouraged people to throw darts at his image four years earlier, now printed pictures of his foot for the nation to kiss to help it convalesce.

During his final season with Manchester United, with five Premiership title medals in his trophy cabinet, Beckham's relationship with mentor Sir Alex Ferguson cooled and he was dropped to the bench for the Champions League quarter-final second leg against Madrid; he came on to score twice in United's 4-3 win.

Beckham quit United in 2003 for Real Madrid who capitalized financially on his iconic status but did not win league silverware until just before his departure for Los Angeles Galaxy four years later.

In the meantime Beckham had quit as England captain after the 2006 World Cup quarter-final exit. He interrupted his MLS stint with loan spells to Milan to keep fit ahead the 2010 World Cup but an Achilles injury ultimately shattered his dream of being the first England player to appear in four World Cups.

David Beckham makes his Spanish presence felt for Real Madrid.

1975	1989	1993	1996	1998	2001	2003	2007
Born in Leytonstone, London on May 2	Signs associate forms with Manchester United on his 14th birthday	Signs professional contract with United	With United wins first Premiership and FA Cup double. Makes England debut in 3-0 World Cup qualifying win	Scores first England goal in World Cup finals against Colombia. Sent off against Argentina at Saint-Etienne in second round	Wins another Premiership medal and skippers England to famous 5-1 win in Germany then converts free kick against Greece to clinch qualification for 2002 World Cup finals	Wins his sixth Premiership title with United then moves to Real Madrid for £20 million. Awarded OBE for services to soccer	Signs for LA Galaxy of MLS. His form returns and he wins both England recall and La Liga title

1986	1992	1995	1997	1999	2002	2008
Wins Bobby Charlton Soccer Skills Tournament at Old Trafford	Now a trainee, helps United win FA Youth Cup. Makes senior debut in League Cup	League debut in February on loan, then Premiership debut for United at home to Leeds	Wins second Premiership and voted PFA Young Player of the Year	Finishes runner-up in the FIFA World Player of the Year poll and second in the European Footballer of the Year for his role in United's treble win	Carried off in United's Champions League quarter-final with metatarsal injury. Scores England's penalty winner against Argentina in World Cup finals match	Signs up to play for Milan in the MLS off-season. Reaches the milestone, of 100 England caps.

that year. Bebeto moved to Deportivo in 1993 and scored three times in Brazil's World Cup triumph the following year. He repeated that number four years later but this time collected only a silver medal after Brazil lost the Final to hosts France.

Igor Belanov

National team: Soviet Union
Born: September 25, 1960
Club(s): Dynamo Kiev, Borussia Mönchengladbach (Ger)

Belanov hit a career peak in 1986 when his starring role at the World Cup earned him the European Footballer of the Year award. Yet he was lucky to have made the squad, owing much to his working relationship at Kiev with new national boss Valeri Lobanovsky. He repaid Lobanovsky's faith with a string of sensational performances. Belanov scored in the initial 6-0 thrashing of Hungary, then scored a superb hat-trick in the 4-3 second-round defeat by Belgium. Belanov vindicated his "arrival" among the international superstars by helping the Soviets finish European runners-up in 1988. Later he moved to Switzerland and became involved in the game as a sponsor.

Miodrag Belodedici

National team: Romania
Born: May 20, 1964
Club(s): Steaua Bucharest, Red Star Belgrade (Yug), Valencia (Sp), Valladolid (Sp), Villarreal (Sp)

Belodedici was the first man to win the Champions Cup with two clubs: Steaua in 1986 and Red Star in 1991. Born in a small village on the Serb border, he was brought up in Romania and starred as sweeper in Steaua's 1986 Champions Cup win over Barcelona. He made his Romania debut against China in 1984 but then sought asylum in Yugoslavia in 1988. After diplomatic wrangling he joined Red Star and was invited to play again for Romania in 1990. He refused, fearing possible recriminations, but, after the collapse of the Ceascescu regime, he was happy to make a comeback in 1992.

Dennis Bergkamp's trademark curving shots have netted him goals for club and country alike.

Ferenc Bene

National team: Hungary
Born: December 17, 1944
Clubs: Kaposzvar, Ujpest Dozsa

Bene was a versatile attacker who played centre-forward for Ujpest Dozsa but usually outside-right for Hungary because of the presence of Florian Albert. Bene was first capped in 1962 but did not make much impact on the international scene until two years later when he was top scorer with 12 goals in Hungary's victory at the Tokyo Olympics. Bene was the Hungarian league's leading scorer three times and he won the championship four times with Ujpest. In the 1966 World Cup Bene was an outstanding member of the Hungarian team which scored a 3-1 victory over Brazil. Hungary fell in the quarter-finals, but Bene had scored in all four matches.

Dennis Bergkamp

National team: Holland
Born: May 10, 1969
Clubs: Ajax Amsterdam, Internazionale (It), Arsenal (Eng)

Bergkamp, a youth product of Ajax, was such a natural that he made his European club debut the day after sitting his school examinations. Bergkamp starred for Holland at the 1992 European Championship finals, and Internazionale beat Barcelona, Juventus and Milan to his £8 million signature the following spring. Bergkamp never settled in Italy, and in 1995 he was transferred to Arsenal for £7.5 million, playing key roles in their league and cup doubles in 1998 and 2002. He was also one of the stars of the World Cup finals in France in 1998, helping Holland to fourth place and was influential when Holland reached the semi-finals in the European Championships in 2000.

Giuseppe Bergomi

National team: Italy
Born : December 22, 1963
Club(s): Internazionale

Bergomi was a rock-solid fullback then central defender and long-time captain of both club and country. Yet he was rejected by AC Milan as a youngster and had to switch to Inter to find success across the city. He made his Italy debut at 18 as a substitute in a 1-0 defeat to East Germany in April 1982. Just over two months later he helped Italy win the World Cup by defeating West Germany 3-1 in Madrid. Bergomi was a one-club man who set a record of 117 appearances in the European club competitions, which stood until early 2002 when it was overtaken by Paolo Maldini of local rivals Milan.

Orvar Bergmark

National team: Sweden
Born: November 16, 1930
Club(s): Orebro, AIK Solna, Roma (It)

Bergmark was one of the great European full-backs of the 1950s and early 1960s. He began with Orebro in 1949 as a centre-forward but quickly converted to full-back and made his debut in that position for Sweden in 1951. He was voted best right-back at the 1958 World Cup finals, in which his steady play helped the hosts reach the Final against Brazil. Bergmark also had a spell in Italy with Roma before retiring with a then record 94 caps. As manager he guided Sweden to the 1970 World Cup finals. One of his players then was Tommy Svensson, who would emulate him as World Cup boss in 1994.

George Best

SEE PAGE 154

Roberto Bettega

National team: Italy
Born: December 27, 1950
Club(s): Juventus

Bettega enjoyed a remarkable rise from supporting Juventus on the terraces as a boy to the ranks of star striker and then on to senior management. As a striker Bettega starred with Juve for more than a decade. For a big man, he was surprisingly skilful on the ground and deadly in the air, scoring one spectacularly famous goal against England in a World Cup qualifier. Bettega overcame illness early in his career and later a serious knee injury to score 19 goals in 42 appearances for Italy between 1975 and 1983. With Italy he shared a fourth-place World Cup finish in 1978.

GEORGE BEST
Soccer star to media idol

The story of the brilliant maverick from east Belfast is a tale of wasted genius. Best was the most gifted British player of his generation, but following the retirement of Manchester United's legendary boss Sir Matt Busby in 1969, he drifted into drinking, missed training and, after a game at Queens Park Rangers, he walked out of Manchester United on New Years Day 1974 at the age of just 26. He preferred to enjoy the high life, often fuelled by alcohol. He later admitted: "I spent a lot of money on booze, birds and fast cars. The rest I just squandered. I was born with a great gift and sometimes that comes with a self-destructive streak. Just as I wanted to outdo everyone when I played, so I wanted to outdo everyone when we were out on the town."

One often-repeated story sums up Best's rise and fall. He was in bed with Miss World in a plush hotel suite, cash was strewn across the room. Best ordered vintage champagne from room service. The waiter immediately recognized him and said, "George, George... where did it all go wrong?"

Best attempted several comebacks, most notably with Fulham in 1976, but they always petered out as the lure of the girls and drink proved too attrac-tive. He turned out briefly for Dunstable, Cork Celtic, Los Angeles Aztecs, Fort Lauderdale, Hibernian, San Jose, Bournemouth and Brisbane Lions (Australia) before hanging up his boots in 1983.

A year later he received a short prison sentence for drink-driving and an assault on a policeman. He built a new career in the 1990s as an after-dinner speaker and Sky Sports soccer pundit. But his drink problems contin-ued and he eventually needed a life-saving liver transplant in 2002.

Best at his peak was a force of na-ture. He was incredibly skilful, fast, two-footed and brave. He could tackle fiercely, he had an eye for gaps that others never saw – and he could con-jure goals out of nothing. Nearly 40 years afterwards, his dribbling spec-taculars are still shown on British TV, as is the outrageous lob he scored against Tottenham and the six goals he netted in one FA Cup tie against Northampton.

George Best hit the heights on the pitch then plumbed the depths off it.

He stood out, even in a team that included such greats as Bobby Charlton and Denis Law. He scored 136 goals in 361 appearances for United after making his debut against West Bromwich as a 17-year-old in 1963, and he was an inspiration as United won the championship in 1965, then reached the European Champions Cup semi-finals the following season. He destroyed Benfica almost single-handedly in the quarter-final second leg in Porto; United won 4-1.

Best was in devastating form again as United won the title once more in 1967. A year later, he was voted Footballer of the Year and European Footballer of the Year as United be-came the first English team to win the European Cup.

For years Best had shouldered massive expectations when he played for unfashionable Northern Ireland. Now similar pressures were heaped on him to keep United at the top and it was too much for Best to bear. However, he still finished United's top scorer for four successive seasons. At the start of the 1971–72 season, it seemed, briefly, that Best might inspire a resurgent United to a title challenge. Instead, it was the last hurrah of his declining career.

1946	1963	1965	1967	1968	1970	1976	1984	2006
Born in Belfast on May 22	Signs as professional and makes senior debut against West Bromwich Albion	Gains first championship medal	Gains second title medal	Voted Footballer of the Year and European Footballer of the Year	Scores six goals in FA Cup tie at Northampton	Attempts comeback with Fulham	Jailed for three months for drink-driving and assaulting a police officer	Dies aged 59 and 100,000 mourners line the route of his funeral in Belfast

1961	1964	1966	1974	1983	2005
Joins Manchester United as an apprentice	The Best-Law-Charlton trio play together for United for the first time in a 4-1 win at West Bromwich	Nicknamed "O Beatle" by Portuguese press after performance in victory over Benfica	Quits United after game against Queens Park Rangers. Top class ca-reer is effectively over	Quits soccer after final comeback attempts with Bournemouth and Brisbane Lions (Australia)	Died after losing fight with alcoholism and liver damage

Franz "Bimbo" Binder

National team: Austria
Born: December 1, 1911
Club(s): St Polten, Rapid Vienna

Binder was a prolific marksman, either from centre-forward or inside-forward, and is popularly considered to have been the first European player to have topped 1,000 goals in his first-class career. When he retired in 1950 to manage his old club Rapid, Binder claimed career figures of 1,006 goals in 756 games. He was Rapid's greatest player in the 1930s and played 20 times for Austria before being selected nine times for Greater Germany after the Anschluss of 1938. Binder's greatest achievement for Rapid was in the 1941 Greater German championship play-off when he scored a hat-trick against Schalke in Rapid's victory.

Laurent Blanc

National team: France
Born: November 19, 1965
Club(s): Ales, Montpellier, Napoli (It), Nimes, Saint-Etienne, Auxerre, Barcelona (Sp), Internazionale (It), Manchester United (Eng)

Blanc developed into one of the finest central defenders in Europe after starting out as an attacking midfielder. That was the role in which he made his France debut in 1989 against the Irish Republic. He was Montpellier's top marksman with 18 goals in 1986–87. Blanc was a European Under-21 champion in 1988 and won the French Cup in 1990 with Montpellier. Following this success, he had a spell in Italy, returned to Auxerre, then extended his international experience with Barcelona, Internazionale and Manchester United. He missed the 1998 World Cup Final through suspension but played in the European Championship win over Italy in 2000. He graduated to national coach in 2010 after a league title-winning stint with Bordeaux.

Danny Blanchflower

National team: Northern Ireland
Born: February 10, 1926
Club(s): Barnsley (Eng), Aston Villa (Eng), Tottenham Hotspur (Eng)

A tactically astute play-maker, Danny Blanchflower was one of the major forces in Northern Ireland's valiant 1958 World Cup side and Tottenham's excellent team of the early 1960s. The league and cup double was followed by the FA Cup the following season, and the European Cup-Winners' Cup in 1963, with Blanchflower's cerebral approach blending perfectly with the more robust forays of the other wing-half, Dave Mackay. In the days when few sportsmen appeared on TV, Blanchflower was a media darling, always entertaining and forthright in speech or in print. As so often with gifted players, his foray into management, with Chelsea, was an anti-climax. He died in 1993.

Dirk "Danny" Blind

National team: Holland
Born: August 1, 1961
Club(s): Racing Club Souburg, Sparta Rotterdam, Ajax

Blind became Ajax's defensive cornerstone after making his name as a right-back with Sparta Rotterdam. With Ajax, he won 16 titles including five Dutch championships, three Dutch Cups and three Dutch Super Cups. He also won the UEFA Cup in 1992, the Champions Cup and World Club Cup in 1995 and the European Super Cup in 1996. He not only played but also captained Ajax to their 1995 Champions Cup victory over Milan. However his luck ran out in the Cup-Winners' Cup and he missed Ajax's Final victory in 1987 through injury and was sent off in their 1988 defeat by Mechelen.

Northern Ireland's Danny Blanchflower was the modern game's first media darling.

Oleg Blokhin

National team: Soviet Union
Born: November 5, 1952
Club(s): Dynamo Kiev, Vorwärts Steyr (Aus)

Blokhin was originally an outside-left, but, according to his friend, Olympic sprint champion Valeri Borzov, he could have been a star sprinter. Certainly he used his pace to electric effect and his key role in Kiev's European Cup-Winners' Cup triumph of 1975 earned him the accolade of European Footballer of the Year. Blokhin played in the World Cup finals of 1982 and 1986, having by then become the first Soviet player to top a century of international appearances. By the time Blokhin, now a central striker, was "freed" to move west with Vorwärts Steyr of Austria, he had totalled a Soviet record 39 goals in a further record 109 internationals. After retiring he turned to coaching and in 2006 guided Ukraine to the quarter-finals on their first appearance in the World Cup finals.

Steve Bloomer

National team: England
Born: January 20, 1874
Club(s): Derby, Middlesbrough, Derby

England's most famous player before the First World War, Bloomer established long-lasting records: his 352 league goals were not equalled until the 1930s; his 28 goals for his country, in only 23 games, were not surpassed until the 1950s. Bloomer was of medium height and slightly built, and was often the target for unscrupulous defenders with heavy boots and desperate intent. But he survived, thanks to agility and a sharp brain, through 22 years until the start of the First World War when he was in his 41st year. Born at Cradley Heath in the West Midlands' "Black Country", he was, nevertheless, a Derby player throughout his career, apart from a four-year spell with Middlesbrough. In later years he coached Derby players and did odd jobs at the ground.

Zvonimir Boban

National team: Yugoslavia and Croatia
Born: October 8, 1968
Clubs: Dynamo Zagreb (Yug/Cro), Bari, Milan (It)
Boban first made a name as a member of the former Yugoslavia team which won the 1987 World Youth Cup. He became Dynamo Zagreb's youngest-ever captain at 18 and was hailed a local hero after he came to the defence of Croat fans being manhandled by police at a high-tension match against Red Star Belgrade, for which he was given a six-month suspension. It cost him a place with Yugoslavia at the 1990 World Cup finals. His brilliant ball control, astute passing and explosive free kicks were noticed in Italy, however, and Milan snapped him up for £8 million. He won four championships at the San Siro and a European Cup, playing a major part in the 4-0 final victory over Barcelona in 1994. But the highlight of his career was captaining fledgling country Croatia to third place in the 1998 World Cup finals in France.

Hristo Bonev

National team: Bulgaria
Born: February 3, 1947
Club(s): Lokomotive Plovdiv, CSKA Sofia
Bonev was Bulgaria's outstanding personality of the 1970s, guiding them to the finals of the World Cup in West Germany. He was also their only marksman there, scoring the equalizing goal in a 1-1 draw with Uruguay. As a boy Bonev idolised the centre-forward Gundi Asparoukhov who became his teammate on the day of his debut against West Germany in 1967. Bonev was subsequently voted domestic Footballer of the Year and was one of the youngest players selected for the farewell match to the Soviet goalkeeper, Lev Yashin, in 1971. Winner of 100 caps, he later became national coach.

Rainer Bonhof

National team: West Germany
Born: March 29, 1952
Club(s): SuS Emmerich, Borussia Monchengladbach
Bonhof was the energetic midfielder who manager Helmut Schon called on in the middle of the 1974 World Cup to put a new spark into midfield. He achieved not only that task but made the winning goal against Holland in the Final. But for injuries Bonhof would have played many more than 48 times for West Germany between 1970 and 1978. Apart from the World Cup, he was also a European Championship runner-up in 1976. At club level he won four German titles, one German Cup and a UEFA Cup with Borussia Mönchengladbach. He later turned to coaching – first on the staff of the DFB and then as Under-21 manager of Scotland under old Borussia and Germany teammate Berti Vogts.

Zbigniew Boniek

National team: Poland
Born: March 3, 1956
Club(s): Zawisza Bydgoszcz, Widzew Lodz, Juventus (It), Roma (It)
Boniek must be considered the greatest Polish soccer player of all time. He was the product of the soccer generation that followed the outstanding side of the mid-1970s, but his talents shone in World Cups and in European club competition with Juventus. Boniek made his name with Widzew Lodz and his hat-trick against Belgium in the 1982 World Cup finals persuaded Juventus to pay £1.1 million for him – then a record for a Polish player. Boniek scored Juve's winner in the 1984 European Cup-Winners' Cup Final defeat of FC Porto and he was a member of the side which won the European Cup a year later, playing the Final against Liverpool in the shadow of the Heysel disaster. Boniek scored 24 goals in 80 internationals.

Roberto Boninsegna

National team: Italy
Born: November 13, 1943
Club(s): Internazionale, Prato, Potenza, Varese, Cagliari, Internazionale
Boninsegna, a dangerous attack leader despite being short and stocky, scored nine goals in 22 games for Italy between 1967 and 1974. He learned his attacking game alongside Gigi Riva at Cagliari. Then, in the 1970 World Cup Final against Brazil, it was Boninsegna's determination and shooting accuracy which fleetingly put Italy on level terms. On returning home he was sold by Cagliari back to Internazionale, who had given him away as a teenager thinking he would not make the grade. He scored 24 goals in 28 games to lead Inter to the championship in his first season back.

Giampiero Boniperti

National team: Italy
Born: July 4, 1928
Club(s): Momo, Juventus
Boniperti was the original golden boy of Italian soccer. He enjoyed a meteoric rise: within a few months of being signed by Juventus from minor club Momo in July 1946, he was promoted to the Italian national team and made his debut in a 5-1 defeat by Austria in Vienna. Originally a centre-forward, Boniperti later switched to inside-forward and played on the right wing for FIFA's World XI against England in 1953 (scoring twice in a 4-4 draw). Boniperti won five Italian league titles with Juventus, for whom he played a record 444 league games. He was considered a father figure in the Charles/Sivori team of the late 1950s and scored eight goals in 38 internationals. On retiring from the game he took up a business career, which eventually turned full circle when he became a hugely successful president of Juventus in the 1970s and early 1980s, under the Agnelli family's patronage.

Maxime Bossis

National team: France
Born: June 26, 1955
Club(s): Nantes, Racing Club of Paris
Bossis was a no-nonsense left-back and later central defender in the French team which offered so much entertainment in the 1980s. He was discovered by Nantes in 1973, staying until 1985 when he was transferred to the newly reformed Racing Club of Paris in the second division. He held his national team place despite self-imposed relegation and led Racing into the top flight in his first season. Bossis missed the decisive penalty in the 1982 World Cup semi-final shoot-out against West Germany. But his consolation was to win the European title in Paris two years later.

Liam Brady brought winning class and vision to the Arsenal midfield.

Jozsef Bozsik

National team: Hungary
Born: September 28, 1929
Club(s): Kispest, Honved

Bozsik will always be remembered as right-half of the wonderful Hungarian national team of the early 1950s. A team-mate of Ferenc Puskas with Kispest and then Honved, Bozsik was the midfield brains, but he could also score spectacular goals, including one from 30 yards in the historic 6-3 win over England at Wembley in 1953. Bozsik made his debut for Hungary against Bulgaria in 1947, returned home – unlike teammates Puskas, Kocsis and Czibor – after the 1956 revolution and combined a career as a footballer with that of an MP. In 1962 he scored a goal against Uruguay in a friendly to mark his 100th and last game for his country. Bozsik was also a member of Hungary's victorious side at the 1952 Helsinki Olympics.

Liam Brady

National team: Republic of Ireland
Born: February 13, 1956
Club(s): Arsenal (Eng), Juventus (It), Sampdoria (It), Internazionale (It), Ascoli (It), West Ham (Eng)

Brady was already an Irish schoolboy international when he joined Arsenal as an apprentice in 1971. Two years later he made his first-team debut and became the club's key player and a regular full international. He guided Arsenal to three successive Cup Finals in 1978, 1979 – when he created the winner against Manchester United – and 1980. He was Footballer of the Year several times in both England and Ireland before transferring to Italy in 1980 where he was a league champion with Juventus. He returned to England with West Ham in 1987.

Raymond Braine

National team: Belgium
Born: April 28, 1907
Club(s): Beerschot, Sparta Prague (Cz), Beerschot

Braine was considered the greatest Belgian player until the advent of Paul Van Himst in the 1960s. In 1922 he made his league debut for Beerschot at the age of 15 and was chosen, that same year, for a Belgian XI against Holland. The English club Clapton Orient of London tried to sign him in 1928 but could not obtain a work permit for him to come to England, so instead he turned pro in Czechoslovakia with the great Sparta Prague club. The Czechs wanted him to take citizenship and play for them in the 1934 World Cup, but Braine preferred to represent Belgium – and did so at the 1938 World Cup after returning home to Beerschot. Braine's centre-forward talents earned him selection for Western Europe against Central Europe in 1938, and then for Europe against England that same year. He won 54 caps for Belgium.

Rune Bratseth

National team: Norway
Born: March 19, 1961
Club(s): Rosenborg Trondheim, Werder Bremen (Ger)

Bratseth was the defensive commander of Norway's 1994 World Cup campaign having previously masterminded Werder Bremen's victory in the 1992 Cup-Winners' Cup. He is considered one of Norway's most complete players of all time, and he began his career with Rosenborg Trondheim but did not turn even part-time professional until he moved to Germany in 1986. He cost Bremen only £65,000 but was twice nominated as the best foreigner in the Bundesliga. He made his Norway debut in a 2-1 win over Grenada in the Caribbean in 1986. When he finally quit soccer in Germany, he returned home to an administrative post back home in Rosenborg.

Andreas Brehme

National team: West Germany
Born: November 9, 1960
Club(s): Kaiserslautern, Bayern Munich, Internazionale (It), Zaragoza (Sp), Kaiserslautern

Brehme earned his niche in history by converting Germany's match-winning penalty against Argentina in the 1990

Billy Bremner was captain and driving force for Leeds under Don Revie.

World Cup Final. He was already based in Italy with Inter. He quit the national team after the 1992 European Championships but was recalled by national coach Berti Vogts for the 1994 World Cup. Brehme was one of the world's most effective left-backs, despite spending much of his time supporting attack. Two years later he left for Zaragoza before returning to captain his first club, Kaiserslautern, to a remarkable league title triumph.

Paul Breitner

National team: West Germany
Born: September 5, 1951
Clubs: Bayern Munich, Real Madrid (Sp), Eintracht Braunschweig, Bayern Munich

Breitner was a flamboyant virtuoso left-back when Helmut Schon brought him into the West German national team in 1971-72. He was a key member of the Bayern-dominated side which included greats like Franz Beckenbauer, Sepp Maier, Uli Hoeness and Gerd Muller. Breitner displayed his big-match temperament by nervelessly converting the penalty which brought West Germany level in the 1974 World Cup Final against Holland. A soccer intellectual, Breitner considered he was being stifled at Bayern and transferred to Real Madrid where he moved forward to midfield. A falling-out with the German soccer authorities caused him to miss the 1978 World Cup, but he returned to his national team in 1982 and again scored in the Final - only this time it was the Germans' consolation in their defeat by Italy on his old home ground in Madrid.

Cafu made history by appearing in three successive World Cup Final matches.

Billy Bremner

National team: Scotland
Born: December 9, 1942
Club(s): Leeds United (Eng), Hull (Eng), Doncaster (Eng)

Bremner made his debut for Leeds aged 17 as a winger partnered by Don Revie, a man nearly twice his age. Later, as a midfielder, Bremner and manager Revie were key figures as Leeds emerged from decades of mediocrity to be a force feared throughout the game. Bremner's fierce tackling, competitive spirit and selflessness made him a winner of various medals, though the list of second places was much longer. He was not a prolific scorer, but a useful one, providing the winner in each of three FA Cup semi-finals. He also won 55 caps, including three at the 1974 World Cup finals, when the Scotland national team was eliminated, unbeaten, after three matches.

Gianluigi Buffon

National team: Italy
Born: January 28, 1978
Club(s): Parma, Juventus

Buffon, nephew of 1960s international goalkeeper Lorenzo Buffon, was hailed by most observers as the outstanding keeper of the 2006 World Cup finals. He made his name with Parma, making his debut at 17 and was a European under-21 winner with Italy while still a teenager. Buffon was a reserve with the seniors at the 1998 World Cup and then missed Euro 2000 through injury. But his subsequent sale to Juventus in 2001 generated a world record fee for the position of £30 million and Buffon went on to help win four league titles and make the Italy goalkeeping place his own. He missed the first half of the 2005-06 season with a shoulder injury but was back, better than ever, as a World Cup-winner in Germany.

Emilio Butragueño

National team: Spain
Born: July 22, 1963
Club(s): Castilla, Real Madrid, Celaya (Mex)

Butragueño, nicknamed "The Vulture", was once considered not good enough by Real Madrid's youth coaches. Real's nursery club, Castilla, had second thoughts and Butragueño became "leader" of Madrid throughout the 1980s. His close ball control and marksmanship helped Real Madrid win the UEFA Cup in 1985 and 1986, and in both years Butragueño won the Prix Bravo as Europe's best young player. He made a scoring debut for Spain in 1984, and in 1986 became a World Cup sensation when he scored four in Spain's five-goal thrashing of well-fancied Denmark in the second round of the finals in Mexico. Butragueño wound down his career in Mexico but later returned to Madrid in a senior administrative role.

Antonio Cabrini

National team: Italy
Born: October 8, 1957
Club(s): Atalanta, Juventus

Cabrini was hailed, almost overnight, as the "new Facchetti" when, after having appeared in only 22 games at left-back for Juventus, he was granted international stardom by national manager Enzo Bearzot at the 1978 World Cup finals in Argentina. Four years later Cabrini made a luckless piece of history for himself when, against West Germany, he became the first man ever to miss a penalty in a World Cup Final. However, Cabrini did win almost every honour in professional soccer, along with 73 caps between 1978 and 1987 and a decade of service with Juventus.

Cafu
Full name: Marcos Evangelista de Moraes

National team: Brazil
Born: June 7, 1970
Club(s): Sao Paulo, Zaragoza (Sp), Palmeiras, Roma (It), AC Milan (It)

Attacking right-back Cafu celebrated the climax of his career as captain of Brazil when they won the World Cup for a record fifth time against Germany in Yokohama, Japan, in 2002. It was also his 111th appearance for his country and repeated his share in the 1994 success and made amends for the Final defeat by France in Paris in 1998. He is the only man to have played in three successive World Cup Finals. Cafu, who made his name with home-city Sao Paulo, lined up briefly for Zaragoza in Spain then had two years back in Brazil with Palmeiras before winning a Serie A title with Roma. He then added to his honours while winding down at Milan.

Jose Antonio Camacho

National team: Spain
Born: June 8, 1955
Club(s): Real Madrid

Defence has never been Real Madrid's greatest strength but Camacho came as near as any of the club's modern defenders to putting that right. Originally a combative left-back Camacho raced up through the youth ranks in the mid-1970s and later served club and country in central defence and also at right-back. He was nearly lost to the game through a knee ligament injury which cost him a place at the 1978 World Cup as well as 18 months of his career. But he made a remarkable recovery to total a then record 81 caps. Later Camacho coached Spain to the quarter-finals of the 2002 World Cup before returning to the club game with Benfica and, twice briefly, Madrid.

Rodion Camataru

National team: Romania
Born: June 22, 1958
Club(s): U. Craiova, Dyn. Bucharest, Charleroi (Bel)

Camataru was a bluff, determined centre-forward who scored more than 300 goals in Romanian league soccer before transferring to Belgium towards the end of his career. In 1986-87 he won the Golden Boot as Europe's top league marksman, albeit in controversial circumstances. Camataru totalled 44 goals but many were scored in a string of 'easy' matches towards the season's end, and revelations after the collapse of the Communist regime cast doubt on the matches' integrity – not that this detracted from Camataru's abilities.

Sulzeer "Sol" Campbell

National team: England
Born: September 18, 1974
Club(s): Tottenham Hotspur, Arsenal, Portsmouth

Central defender Campbell, from Newham in East London, progressed up through the youth ranks at Tottenham to establish himself as a defensive cornerstone, club captain and an England regular. He also helped Tottenham win the League Cup in 1999 and played for England at youth, Under-21 and B level before transferring controversially to neighbours and old enemy Arsenal in 2001. Campbell's contract had expired so he left on a free transfer, which rubbed salt into Tottenham's wounds, but he could not resist the far greater opportunity of club success. A year later Campbell was the proud winner of the league and cup double and was then one of England's successes in their run to the quarter-finals of the 2002 World Cup.

Claudio Caniggia

National team: Argentina
Born: January 9, 1967
Club(s): River Plate, Verona (It), Atalanta (It), Roma (It), Benfica (Por), Boca Juniors, Dundee (Sco), Rangers (Sco)

Caniggia was one of the most intriguing stars of the 1994 World Cup, having only just completed a 13-month drugs suspension in Italy. He scored on his return to international duty in a 3-0 win over Israel, but was injured when Argentina lost to Romania in USA 94. Caniggia began with River Plate, moving to Italy in 1988. His play was one of Argentina's few redeeming features at the 1990 World Cup, when he scored the quarter-final winner against Brazil and semi-final equalizer against Italy. Caniggia missed the final through suspension and, without him, Argentina had nothing to offer in attack. Ten years later, he revived his career in remarkable fashion in Scotland, but fitness problems kept him on the sidelines at the 2002 World Cup after he was back in the squad.

Fabio Cannavaro

National team: Italy
Born: September 13, 1973
Club(s): Napoli, Parma, Internazionale, Juventus, Real Madrid (Spa), Juventus, Al-Ahli (Dubai)

Cannavaro made the classic progression up through the youth system ranks to establish himself as one of Italy and Europe's most reliable central defenders. His composure was clear in one of his very first senior internationals when he marked Alan Shearer out of the game in a World Cup qualifying tie against England at Wembley. Cannavaro rose via home-town Napoli, Parma, Inter and Juventus to captain Italy to World Cup victory in 2006. He was voted world and European player of the year then gained more league title success in Spain with Real Madrid.

Eric Cantona

National team: France
Born: May 24, 1966
Club(s): Martigues, Auxerre, Marseille, Bordeaux, Montpellier, Nimes, Leeds (Eng), Manchester United (Eng)

Eric Cantona's career was a mixture of glorious success and disciplinary muddle. Born in Marseille, he was

Eric Cantona came out of premature retirement to star in English soccer.

discovered by Auxerre and sold to Marseille for £2 million in 1988. Two months later he scored on his international debut. Banned for a year from the national team for insulting coach Henri Michel, he then bounced to Bordeaux, Montpellier and Nimes before quitting after a shouting match with a disciplinary panel. He relaunched his career in England – and won the championship five times – in 1992 with Leeds and four times in five years with Manchester United. An incident with a hooligan cost him a seven-month ban from soccer, but he returned all the hungrier for success. He was voted Footballer of the Year and then, as captain, sealed United's 1996 double by scoring the FA Cup Final winner against Liverpool.

Antonio Carbajal

National team: Mexico
Born: June 7, 1929
Club(s): España, Leon

Carbajal set a record at the 1966 World Cup in England as the only man then to have appeared in five finals tournaments. A tall, agile goalkeeper, he played for Mexico in Brazil in 1950, in Switzerland in 1954, in Sweden in 1958 and in Chile in 1962. The 1966 finals provided an appropriate retirement point since Carbajal had made his international debut at the 1948 London Olympics. He turned professional with Leon in 1948 and played for them until his retirement in 1966. Later he was presented with governing body FIFA's gold award for services to the world game.

Careca
Full name: Antonio de Oliveira Fulho

National team: Brazil
Born: October 5, 1960
Club(s): Guarani, São Paulo, Napoli (It), Hitachi (Jap), Santos

Careca was one of the outstanding spearheads in the world game throughout the 1980s and early 1990s. Born in Brazil's Campinas state, he helped unrated Guarani win the 1987–88 national championship and was later sold to São Paulo. Careca missed the 1982 World Cup after being injured in training on the eve of the finals. He made superb amends with five goals in Mexico in 1986, was voted Brazil's Sportsman of the Year and was subsequently transferred to Italy's Napoli. His attacking partnership with Diego Maradona lifted Napoli to the 1989 UEFA Cup and 1990 Italian league titles.

Johnny Carey

National team: Ireland and Republic of Ireland
Born: February 23, 1919
Club(s): Manchester United (Eng)

Johnny Carey was one of the early all-purpose players and was equally at home playing at full-back, wing-half, inside-forward and even as deputy goalkeeper. He was a calming influence, short on pace but long on perception. At £200 to a Dublin junior club he was one of the all-time best transfer bargains. He captained Manchester United in the early post-war years, winning league and cup once each and narrowly missing several more. He earned 37 caps and led the Rest of Europe selection against Great Britain in 1946. Carey later managed Blackburn (twice),

Roberto Carlos is usually in the Real line-up.

Everton – until he was sacked in the back of a taxi when they were lying fifth in the table – Orient and Nottingham Forest.

Roberto Carlos
Full name: Roberto Carlos da Silva

National team: Brazil
Born: April 10, 1973
Club(s): Palmeiras, Internazionale (It), Real Madrid (Sp), Fenerbahce (Tur)

Roberto Carlos earned fame not so much for his defensive skills and pace but for the remarkable ferocity of his free kicks, very much in the Brazilian national tradition. He made his name winning the Brazilian national championship with Palmeiras in 1993 and 1994. He scored a memorable, swerving free kick goal in a pre-World Cup tournament in France in 1993 which helped secure a transfer to Internazionale of Milan. However, his attacking style did not suit Serie A and he moved to Real Madrid in Spain, helping them to win the Champions League in 1998, 2000 and 2002 and the World Club Cup in both 1998 and 2002. In 2002 Roberto Carlos was also a key member of Brazil's World Cup-winning team in Korea and Japan. It was a mystery to many that his outstanding achievements on the pitch were not rewarded with the accolade of FIFA World Player of the Year.

Amadeo Carrizo

National team: Argentina
Born: June 12, 1926
Club(s): River Plate, Alianza (Peru), Millonarios (Col)

Carrizo set a string of longevity records in a goalkeeping career which lasted from the mid-1940s to the mid-1960s. A dominant character with great personality, Carrizo played 520 Argentine league matches over 21 seasons until he was 44. He won five league championships with River Plate in the early 1950s and played

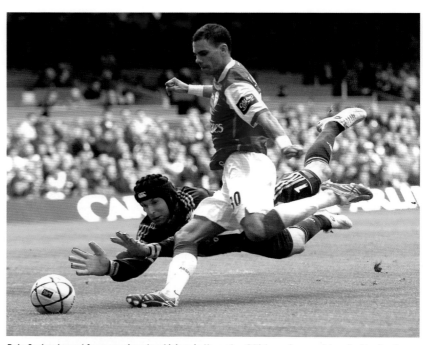

Petr Cech returned from a serious head injury in November 2006 wearing special protective headgear.

in the 1958 World Cup finals in Sweden. Carrizo was blamed for Argentina's 6-1 defeat by Czechoslovakia but was recalled two years later with great success when Argentina beat England and Brazil to win the 1960 "Little World Cup" in Brazil. After parting company with River Plate he played on in Peru and Colombia before returning home to coach youth teams.

Casillas
Full name: Iker Casillas Fernandez

National team: Spain
Born: May 20, 1981
Club(s): Real Madrid

Casillas ranks among the most remarkable goalkeeper-captains in soccer history after leading Spain to victory in both Euro 2008 and then the 2010 World Cup when he was also hailed as top keeper after conceding just two goals in seven games. He also contributed mightily to Spain's success by saving a crucial penalty at 0-0 in the quarter-final against Paraguay. Remarkably the Real Madrid star was still only 29. He first made headlines in Spain's World

Youth Cup win in 1999 then made a sensational, match-saving substitute's appearance in Madrid's 2002 Champions League win over Leverkusen. He first signaled his penalty-stopping prowess at the subsequent World Cup as well as in the Euro and World Cup double.

Petr Cech

National team: Czech Republic
Born: May 20, 1982
Club(s): Viktoria Plzen, Chmel Blsany, Sparta, Rennes (Fr), Chelsea (Eng)

Cech signed for Chelsea when Claudio Ranieri was manager but, by the time he arrived, Jose Mourinho had taken over – and the coach quickly offered thanks to his predecessor. Previously with Rennes, Cech was voted into the Euro 2004 all-star squad after the Czechs reached the semi-finals. The following season he set an English Premiership record of not conceding a goal in 1,025 minutes in the first of Chelsea's back-to-back title-winning campaigns. But he missed three months with a skull fracture the following season – a key factor in Chelsea's slip to second.

Jan Ceulemans

National team: Belgium
Born: February 28, 1957
Club(s): Lierse, Club Brugge

Ceulemans was the central pillar of Belgium's national team throughout the 1980s, first as a striker and then as a midfield general. He began with Lierse and cost Brugge a then record domestic fee of £250,000 in the summer of 1978. In 1980 he scored 29 of their 76 goals in a league title win and was voted Footballer of the Year for the first time. A year later Ceulemans was poised to join Milan but his mother persuaded him to stay in Belgium, a decision which he never regretted. Ceulemans played with distinction in the Belgian team which finished fourth at the 1986 World Cup finals in Mexico. In 96 internationals – a Belgian record – he scored 26 goals.

Bum Kun Cha

National team: South Korea
Born: May 21, 1953
Club(s): Darmstadt, Eintracht Frankfurt, Bayer Leverkusen (all West Germany)

Thanks to his record at the peak of the European game in West Germany's Bundesliga, Cha ranks as South Korea's finest player. He was a popular fixture from 1978, when he arrived at Darmstadt, until his retirement in 1986 after appearing at his first and only World Cup finals. Cha, who won the UEFA Cup with both Eintracht Frankfurt (1980) and Bayer Leverkusen in 1988 – when he scored one of the goals against Español – was mystifyingly ignored by his country after moving to Germany. Despite that, he still laid claim to 55 goals in 121 international appearances and was voted Asian Player of the Century. He used his time in Europe well to gain the appropriate coaching qualifications and subsequently managed South Korea at the 1998 World Cup finals in France. His son, Cha Doo-ri, helped the co-hosts reach the semi-finals four years later.

Stéphane Chapuisat

National team: Switzerland
Born: June 28, 1969
Club(s): FC Malley, Red Star Zurich, Lausanne, Bayer Uerdingen (Ger), Borussia Dortmund (Ger), Grasshopper

Chapuisat, one of Switzerland's finest strikers, was son of a former international, Pierre-Albert Chapuisat, who earned notoriety in his day as a sharp-tempered defender. Son Stéphane, by contrast, not only played his soccer at the other end of the pitch but also had a far more even temperament. Chapuisat moved to Germany in 1991 with Uerdingen and transferred to Dortmund a year later. His starring role at the 1994 World Cup finals led to a Footballer of the Year accolade. In 1997, after recovering from injury, he led Dortmund to both the European Champions Cup and World Club Cup. In due course he returned to Grasshopper and helped Switzerland reach the finals of Euro 2004.

John Charles

National team: Wales
Born: December 27, 1931
Club(s): Leeds (Eng), Juventus (It), Leeds (Eng), Roma (It), Cardiff

Known as the "Gentle Giant", John Charles allied great skill to an awesome physique, and was good enough to set a Leeds record of 42 goals in one season as a centre-forward while also playing as a dominant central defender for his country. He was one of the first British exports to Italy, in 1957, and probably the best. The £67,000 fee, a record for a British player, bought Juventus a man who became a legend and helped to win the Serie A title three times in five years, as he scored 93 times in 155 games. He became a non-league manager, publican and shopkeeper. He died in 2004.

Bobby Charlton

SEE PAGE 162

Jose Luis Chilavert

National team: Paraguay
Born: July 27, 1965
Club(s): Sportivo Luqueno, Zaragoza (Sp), Velez Sarsfield (Arg), Strasbourg (Fra), Penarol (Uru), Velez Sarsfield (Arg)

Paraguayan goalkeeper Chilavert emerged as one of the most powerful personalities of South American soccer in recent years, with his aggressive approach carrying his influence way beyond his own penalty area. After playing in Paraguay and in Spain, he achieved his greatest success in Argentina with Velez Sarsfield – scoring a record 62 goals from free kicks and penalties. His most famous free kick goal was struck against Argentina in the 1998 World Cup qualifiers. Chilavert's larger-than-life personality helped earn him awards such as the 1997 South American Footballer of the Year and World Goalkeeper of the Year. He had a short spell in France in Strasbourg but walked out after a contract row and returned to South America to help Penarol win the 2003 Uruguayan championship.

Igor Chislenko

National team: Soviet Union
Born: January 4, 1939
Club(s): Torpedo Moscow, Moscow Dynamo

Chislenko was only 5ft 7ins but, in the 1960s, he was one of Europe's most dynamic outside or inside rights. Having started his career with the Torpedo Moscow youth section, he transferred to Dynamo at 17 and played 300 league games, winning two Soviet league titles.

Goalkeeper Jose Luis Chilavert scored more than 50 goals from set pieces.

SIR BOBBY CHARLTON
The gentleman midfielder

Bobby Charlton, throughout the world, is probably the most famous English player to ever thrill a crowd. His name is synonymous with some of the greatest moments of the English game, but also with the highest traditions of sportsmanship and integrity.

Long after he had finished playing Charlton's reputation worked wonders in breaking down the tightest security at World Cups and European Championships. It only needed a player or manager to glance out and see Charlton arriving for barred doors and gates to be flung open. Today's heroes may possess a string of fan clubs and millions in Swiss banks, but they still recognize magic.

The delight with which much of the English public took in Manchester United's success in the inaugural Premier League in 1992–93 may be partly explained by the respect in which Bobby Charlton is held for reasons which transcend "mere" soccer.

Soccer was always in the Charlton blood. Bobby and World Cup-winning brother Jackie were nephews of that great Newcastle United hero of the 1950s, Jackie Milburn. They began in the back streets of Ashington in the north-east of England, and Charlton fulfilled every schoolboy's dream when, at 17, he was signed by Manchester United.

Matt Busby had invested more time and determination than any other manager in seeking out the finest young talents in the country. Not only Charlton, but Duncan Edwards, Eddie Colman, David Pegg and many more had been singled out for the Old Trafford treatment: turned from boys into young footballing men under the tutelage of assistant Jimmy Murphy, and then released to explode into the league.

Bobby Charlton won World Cup and European Cup within two years of each other.

This was the philosophy behind the Busby Babes, the team of youngsters who took the league by storm in the mid-1950s and brought a breath of optimistic fresh air into an austere post-war England. The sense of that spirit being lost added to the nation's grief when United's plane crashed in the snow and ice at the end of a runway in Munich on their way home from a European Cup quarter-final in Belgrade in February 1958.

Charlton had established his first-team potential the previous season. He was initially an inside-right, later switched to outside-left with England, and finally settled as a deep-lying centre-forward, using his pace out of midfield and thunderous shot to score some of the most spectacular goals English soccer has ever seen. One such goal marked his England debut against Scotland, another broke the deadlock against Mexico in the 1966 World Cup finals, and dozens of them inspired Manchester United's post-Munich revival. The European Cup victory at Wembley in 1968, when he captained United and scored twice, was a highly emotional moment.

Then, as now, Sir Bobby – ennobled in 1994 – has been a perfect ambassador for the game.

1937	1958	1966		1970		1973
Born on October 11 in Ashington, County Durham	Survived the Munich air crash to play in another FA Cup Final	Starred for England in the World Cup victory, scoring goals against Mexico and Portugal along the way to help earn him the European Footballer of the Year award		Played his record 106th and last international for England in the 3-2 defeat by West Germany at the World Cup finals in Mexico		Moved to Preston for two years as player-manager before becoming a director at Old Trafford

	1957	1963		1968		1994
	Played in the FA Cup Final at 19	Played in his third FA Cup Final, and was at last on the winning side as United beat Leicester City 3-1		Scored two of the goals as Manchester United finally won the European Cup, defeating Benfica 4-1 after extra time at Wembley		Received a knighthood

Chislenko, also a useful ice hockey player, appeared at the World Cups of 1962 and 1966 as well as in the European Championship in between. He was the best Soviet forward in the 1966 World Cup and their prospects of reaching the Final disappeared when he was sent off during the semi-final against West Germany.

Cristian Chivu
National team: Romania
Born: October 26, 1980
Club(s): CSM Resita, Universitatea Craiova, Ajax (Hol), Roma (It)

Chivu is one of European soccer's most talented central defenders but he made the wrong sort of impact after joining Ajax as an 18-year-old – being sent off twice in his first month and four times in his first year. Chivu quickly adjusted to the style of the Dutch game and became not only the rock of the Ajax defence but also their captain. Coach Ronald Koeman, himself a former central defender, provided the support which helped Chivu develop an international reputation. Roma, surprisingly, won the £9 million transfer race for him in the spring of 2003 – though Ajax at one stage threatened to recall Chivu after the Italian club struggled to keep up the payments.

Hector Chumpitaz
National team: Peru
Born: April 12, 1944
Club(s): Sporting Cristal

Chumpitaz, a powerful, inspirational centre-back, starred for Peru in the World Cup finals of both 1970 and 1978. On the first occasion he was a promising youngster, on the second an experienced, resilient organizer of an otherwise fragile defence. Chumpitaz played all his senior career with Sporting Cristal of Lima and appeared around 100 times for his country between his debut in 1966 and the six-goal thrashing by Argentina which controversially

Ray Clemence maintained an England goalkeeping rivalry with Peter Shilton.

ended Peru's 1978 World Cup campaign. Earlier claims that he played 147 full internationals have been discounted, Peru having played only 110 matches in that time.

Ray Clemence
National team: England
Born: August 5, 1948
Club(s): Scunthorpe, Liverpool, Tottenham Hotspur

Clemence was one of Bill Shankly's most astute signings. He cost a mere £15,000 from third division Scunthorpe but went on to win a string of honours with Liverpool and play 61 times for England between 1973 and 1984. He would have won many more caps but for the rivalry with Peter Shilton. Clemence was one of five players who appeared in all Liverpool's first three Champions Cup-winning sides. In 1970-71, when he missed only one game, Liverpool conceded a miserly record-equalling low of 24 goals in a 42-match league campaign. Clemence moved to Tottenham for £300,000 in 1981.

Ashley Cole
National team: England
Born: December 20, 1980
Club(s): Arsenal, Crystal Palace, Arsenal, Chelsea

Cole became one of the few English players to hold down a regular place in Arsenal's cosmopolitan side under Arsene Wenger. He joined the North London side as a trainee and turned professional in November 1998. Cole had a spell on loan to Crystal Palace in the spring of 2000 but then returned to Highbury to take over at left-back from veteran Nigel Winterburn. He rapidly established himself as an England regular at World Cups and Euro finals while moving, controversially, to Chelsea and setting a record in 2010 by claiming his sixth FA Cup winner's medal.

Mario Esteves Coluna
National team: Portugal
Born: August 6, 1935
Club(s): Deportivo Lourenço Marques, Benfica

Coluna was midfield general of Benfica's outstanding club side of the 1960s and the Portuguese national team which reached the World Cup semi-finals in 1966. Born in Mozambique, he held the local long-jump record when he was lured away by Benfica to play soccer in 1954. Originally a centre-forward, he was converted to inside-left and then midfield by Benfica and won 73 caps for Portugal. In both of Benfica's European Cup Final victories of 1961 and 1962, he scored with typically spectacular long-range efforts. Coluna later turned to coaching and became sports minister in his native Mozambique.

Gianpiero Combi
National team: Italy
Born: December 18, 1902
Club(s): Juventus

Combi was goalkeeper and captain of the Italian team which won the 1934 World Cup, thus pre-dating Dino Zoff in that dual role by nearly 50 years. Combi was considered Italy's best goalkeeper until Zoff came along. He started unpromisingly, beaten seven times by Hungary in Budapest in his first international in 1924, and did not gain a regular place in Italy's team until the Paris Olympics of 1928. He was goalkeeper in Juventus' four consecutive league title successes of 1931 to 1934, the year when he retired – immediately after captaining Italy to victory over Czechoslovakia in the World Cup Final in Rome. That was Combi's 47th international.

Bruno Conti
National team: Italy
Born: March 13, 1955
Club(s): Roma, Genoa, Roma

Wingers made a comeback on the tactical scene thanks to Bruno Conti's displays at the 1982 World Cup. Italy's right-winger proved a crucial influence in increasing the momentum of their campaign, which took them past Argentina, Brazil and Poland to victory over West Germany in the Final. Conti had struggled to make an impression in the early years of his career but was rescued by Swedish coach Nils Liedholm, who brought Conti back from a loan spell with Genoa and turned him into one of the most consistently effective creative players in Calcio. Conti scored five goals in 47 internationals between his debut against Luxembourg in 1980 and the second round defeat by France at the 1986 World Cup.

Henri "Rik" Coppens

National team: Belgium
Born: April 29, 1930
Club(s): Beerschot, Charleroi, Crossing Molenbeek, Berchem, Tubantia

Coppens was the enfant terrible of Belgian soccer in the 1950s: a centre-forward or occasional outside-left of great goal-scoring talent, but one who carried his aggression over into his dealings with team-mates, clubs and other officials. Coppens began with Beerschot as a ten-year-old, and on his debut at 16 in a crucial relegation match he scored twice and made Beerschot's two other goals. Three times he was the league's leading scorer and he ended his career with a then record total of 217 goals. He once scored six goals in a game against Tilleur. Altogether Coppens played 47 times for Belgium.

Alberto Da Costa Pereira

National team: Portugal
Born: December 12, 1929
Club(s): Benfica

Da Costa Pereira was another of Portugal's great discoveries in the African colonies. He was born in Nacala, Portuguese East Africa, and joined Benfica in 1954. He was a tower of strength in their biggest triumphs, though prone to the odd unpredictable error when the pressure was off. Da Costa Pereira won seven league titles with Benfica and played in four European Cup Finals – the victories of 1961 and 1962 and the defeats of 1963 and

Ashley Cole was a quarter-finalist at both the 2002 World Cup and Euro 2004.

1965. In the latter game against Internazionale, on a quagmire of a pitch in Milan, Da Costa Pereira was injured early in the game and had to leave the game. He retired soon after to take up coaching. Costa Pereira played 24 times for Portugal, but is not to be confused with the José Pereira who kept goal at the 1966 World Cup.

Alessandro Costacurta

National team: Italy
Born: April 24, 1966
Club(s): Monza, AC Milan

Costacurta took over as Italy's defensive anchor after the international retirement of the great Franco Baresi. He not only played a central role in the successes of the great Milan side of the late 1980s but was still there winning a Champions League medal as late as 2002. Costacurta made his international debut in Arrigo Sacchi's first game in charge – a 1-1 European Championship draw with Norway in November 1991. Sadly, ill-timed suspensions meant that he missed both Milan's 1994 Champions

Cup Final victory over Barcelona and also Italy's 1994 World Cup Final clash with Brazil.

Teofilo Cubillas

National team: Peru
Born: March 8, 1949
Club(s): Alianza, Basel (Swz), FC Porto (Port), Alianza, Fort Lauderdale Strikers (US)

Cubillas was a key figure in Peru's greatest international successes – their appearances at the 1970 and 1978 World Cup finals – in which he scored a total of ten goals. A powerfully-built inside-left, he forged an ideal partnership with the more nimble Hugo Sotil in 1970 then, in 1978, he emerged as an attacking director. Cubillas also packed a very powerful shot, scoring a memorable goal against Scotland in the 1978 finals. He was not particularly successful in Europe, where he grew homesick. But in Peru he remained a legend after 38 goals in 88 internationals and an appearance for the World XI in a 1978 Unicef charity match.

Zoltan Czibor

National team: Hungary
Born: August 23, 1929
Club(s): Ferencvaros, Csepel, Honved, Barcelona (Sp), Español (Sp)

Czibor played outside-left in the great Hungarian team of the early 1950s. He had great pace and a powerful shot, both of which he used to great effect in 43 internationals before he moved to Spain following the Hungarian Revolution of 1956. Czibor and team-mate Sandor Kocsis were both persuaded to sign for Barcelona by Ladislav Kubala and enjoyed five more years in the international spotlight, reaching a climax when Barcelona, most unluckily, lost to Portuguese club Benfica in the 1961 European Cup Final. Czibor had a short spell with neighbours Español before he retired and eventually returned home to live in Hungary.

JOHAN CRUYFF
The total footballer

Johan Cruyff stands out as not merely the greatest Dutch soccer player but one of the greatest of all time, a status for which he owes much to his mother. She worked as a cleaner at Ajax and persuaded the club coaching staff to take Johan into their youth section when he was still only 12. A 25-year succession of trophies and awards at the highest level followed.

Cruyff made his first-team debut at 17, his goal-scoring international debut at 19 and went on to inspire Ajax and Holland through most of their golden 1970s. This was the era of 'total football', a concept first described as "the whirl" in the early 1950s by the Austrian expert Willy Meisl.

He saw the day when every player in a team would possess comparable technical and physical ability and would be able to interchange roles at will.

Cruyff was "the whirl" in action. Nominally he played centre-forward. But his idea of centre-forward was about as orthodox as the squad number 14 he wore at Ajax. He was also to be found meandering through midfield and out on the wings, using his nimble, coltish pace to seriously unhinge defences.

Single-handed, he pulled Internazionale of Italy apart in the 1972 European Cup Final and scored both goals in Ajax's win.

Barcelona won the race for Cruyff's signature – but after the close of the Spanish federation's autumn deadline. However, such was the magnitude of the transfer that the federation bent their own regulations so that Cruyff could play immediately.

When Cruyff arrived in Barcelona, the Catalans were struggling down the table. By the season's end they were champions, Cruyff's triumphant progress having included a spectacular

Johan Cruyff was the embodiment of Ajax and Holland's 'total football.'

5–0 victory away to deadly rivals Real Madrid. It was at the end of his first season with Barcelona that Cruyff's career reached its international zenith. At the 1974 World Cup finals Holland took their total football through round after round. No-one could handle the mercurial Cruyff, who inspired victories over Uruguay and Bulgaria in the first round, then provided two goals to lead the way against Argentina in the second. The last group match was against Brazil: the old masters against the new. Cruyff scored Holland's second goal in a 2–0 victory which signalled a new era. The final, of course, ended in defeat at the hands of West Germany.

Cruyff retired from international soccer and headed west. He played in the NASL but, late in 1981, returned to Holland to win the championship twice more with Ajax and once with old rivals Feyenoord.

Cruyff's move into management, typically, aroused new controversy as he had never obtained the necessary qualifications. Not that it mattered: he guided Ajax to the Cup-winners' Cup in 1987, and again in 1989, after retracing his steps to Barcelona. His innovations caused as much fuss as the total football of his playing days.

1947	1963	1969	1973	1978	1984	1992
Born on April 25 in Amsterdam	Signed his first Ajax contract at 16 on the recommendation of coach Vic Buckingham, then marked his debut with a goal	First European Cup Final appearance with Ajax, but Milan won 4-1 in Madrid	Sold by Ajax to Barcelona for a world record fee of £922,000	Retired from the national team before the World Cup finals, and left Barcelona to play in America with Los Angeles Aztecs and Washington Diplomats	Went back to Ajax, this time as technical director	Managed Barcelona to their long awaited victory in the European Cup Final, where they beat Sampdoria 1-0 at Wembley

1959	1966	1971	1974	1981	1987	1996
Enrolled by his mother in the Ajax youth section	Made his debut for Holland in a 2-2 draw against Hungary and scored a last-minute equalizer in the first of his 48 internationals	Won the first of three successive European Cups. He was also voted European Footballer of the Year, the first of three such accolades	Captained and inspired Holland to reach the 1974 World Cup Final in Munich, where they lost 2-1 to hosts West Germany	Returned to Europe to play for minor club Levante in Spain, then to Holland with Ajax and, finally, Feyenoord	Guided Ajax to victory in the European Cup-Winners' Cup as a parting gift before being appointed coach to Barcelona	Left Barcelona after a record seven years in charge – including four league championships

KENNY DALGLISH
King of the Kop

Kenny Dalglish is the most decorated man in British soccer. He won 26 major trophies as a player and manager after gaining a record 102 caps for Scotland and scoring 30 goals, a record he shares with Denis Law. Dalglish enjoyed a glittering career as a player with Celtic and Liverpool, then proved himself as a manager with Liverpool and Blackburn Rovers.

Ironically Dalglish, a Glasgow Rangers fan as a boy, had a trial for Liverpool as a 15-year-old. He played for one of their youth teams against Southport reserves, but headed back to Scotland and heard no more. Instead, the former Scotland schoolboy right-half was snapped up by Celtic in July 1967 and signed professional a year later. Legendary manager Jock Stein handed him his first team chance in October 1969.

Dalglish could play with equal facility as a striker or an attacking midfield player. He began as a forward at Celtic, continued up front after replacing Kevin Keegan at Liverpool, then dropped into a deeper role later in his career when he created a host of goals for Ian Rush. He had a deft touch, an eye for a pass and a sure touch in front of goal. He was also one of the world's best at shielding the ball

under the tightest marking. The Arsenal center-half David O'Leary recalls: "It was so hard to get the ball off him. He crouched over it, legs and elbows spread out. Whichever angle you came at him, you were likely to find his backside in the way."

Kenny Dalglish won every club prize in both Scotland and England.

Dalglish made his Scotland debut in November 1971. He played in three World Cup finals – 1974, 1978 and 1982. He missed the 1986 tournament through injury. However, he showed only glimpses of his best form in any of them.

By contrast Dalglish was peerless at club level. He won every honour in the Scottish game and played in the 1974 European Cup semi-finals for Celtic against Atletico Madrid. But he wanted a bigger challenge and none came bigger than succeeding Kevin Keegan who joined Hamburg after the 1977 European Cup Final. Dalglish said: "I had to know if I could make it somewhere other than Celtic. I didn't want to go through the rest of my life wondering what might have been."

Dalglish scored 30 goals in his first season in England – including Liverpool's winner in the 1978 European Cup Final at Wembley. The following year he netted 25 times. Liverpool won the championship with a record points total and he was voted Footballer of the Year.

Dalglish inspired Liverpool to European Champions Cup victories in 1981 (against Real Madrid) and in 1984 against Roma. He helped Liverpool win the title again in 1980 then three in a row between 1982 and 1984. They won the League Cup four years running. He was Footballer of the Year in 1983.

He became player-manager at Anfield, managed Blackburn Rovers, Newcastle United, and was later director of operations at Celtic.

1951	1967	1972	1978	1983	1986	1989	1995	1996	1998
Born on March 4 in Dalmarnock, Glasgow	Joins Celtic and develops in their nursery side Cumbernauld Utd	Wins Scottish title medal and Scottish Cup winner's medal	Scores Liverpool's winner in Champions Cup Final against Brugge	Champion & League Cup winner again. Voted Footballer of the Year and PFA Player of the Year	Steers Liverpool to double of championship and FA Cup. Retires from international soccer	Guides Liverpool to FA Cup Final win over Everton after Hillsborough	Guides Blackburn Rovers to Premiership title	Leaves Blackburn Rovers	Leaves Newcastle United in August

1966	1974	1977	1979	1984	1988	1991	1997	1999
Plays for Scotland schoolboys as an attacking right-half	Wins Scottish title medal, and Scottish Cup winner's medal. Appears in World Cup	Wins fourth Scottish championship medal and third Scottish Cup-winner's medal. Moves to Liverpool for £440,000	Voted Footballer of the Year	Wins fifth championship, third European Cup and fourth League Cup. Awarded MBE	Steers Liverpool to another championship and retires from playing	Quits as Liverpool boss, later returning to management with Blackburn Rovers	Succeeds Kevin Keegan as Newcastle United boss	Returns to Celtic for one season as Director of Operations

Rinat Dassayev

National team: Soviet Union

Born: June 13, 1957

Clubs: Spartak Moscow, Sevilla (Sp)

Dassayev was rated the world's top keeper at the end of the 1980s. Born in Astrakhan, he was nicknamed the "new Yashin" after helping the Soviet Union win bronze at the 1980 Olympics in Moscow. He was voted domestic player of the year shortly after. With only two goals conceded, he was the top keeper in the 1982 World Cup qualifiers and enhanced his reputation in Spain in the finals and then again in Mexico four years later. Dassayev made his Spartak debut comparatively late at the age of 22 and his senior international debut just four months after that against East Germany. Dassayev was goalkeeper coach to the Russian national team at the 2004 European Championship.

Edgar Steven Davids

National team: Holland

Born: March 13, 1973

Clubs: Schellingwoude (Amsterdam), Ajax, Milan, Juventus (It), Barcelona, Inter (It), Tottenham (Eng), Ajax

Davids, nicknamed "Pitbull" for his aggressive style of play, snapped into action with Ajax in 1991. He won the Dutch league in 1994 and 1995 as well as the Dutch Cup in 1993 and Supercup in 1993, 1994 and 1995. He also helped Ajax win the World Club Cup, European Champions Cup and European Supercup in 1995 and the UEFA Cup in 1992. He was beaten to a place in Holland's 1994 World Cup squad by Rob Witschge but forced his way back for the European finals in 1996. A move to Milan was marred by a serious leg break before he joined Juventus with whom he has twice been a Champions League runner-up. Davids fell out with Juventus and was loaned to Barcelona in early 2004. Later he maintained his itinerant soccer lifestyle with further moves to Internazionale and then into the Premiership, with Tottenham.

Deco
Full name: Anderson de Souza

National team: Portugal

Born: August 27, 1977 (Brazil)

Clubs: Alverca, Salgueiros, Porto, Barcelona (Sp)

Deco was born in Brazil but moved to Portuguese soccer at the age of 19. He soon caught the eye of Jose Mourinho who utilised him as playmaker of the Porto side who won the league title and UEFA Cup in 2003 and Champions League in 2004. Simultaneously and amid controversy, Deco obtained Portuguese citizenship and celebrated his debut for the national team by scoring the winning goal in a friendly against Brazil. After helping guide hosts Portugal to runners-up spot at Euro 2004 he was sold by Porto to Barcelona, with whom he won Spanish and Champions Leagues, before a less successful spell with Chelsea.

Bill 'Dixie' Dean

National team: England

Born: January 22, 1907

Clubs: Tranmere, Everton, Notts Co.

Anybody who begins his international career by scoring more than once in his first five consecutive matches (two, three, two, two, three respectively) deserves a place in the Hall of Fame. Curly-topped Bill Dean was 20 at the time, and still only 21 when he scored his record 60 league goals in one season for Everton, scoring two, four and three in the last three games of the season. Overall, he scored 18 goals in 16 England appearances, 47 in 18 of the other representative matches which were so popular in pre-television days, 28 in 33 Cup ties (one in the 1933 Wembley win), and 379 in 438 League games.

Alessandro Del Piero

National team: Italy

Born: November 9, 1974

Clubs: Padova, Juventus

Del Piero was another of the "boy wonders" regularly thrown up by Italian soccer. He made his league

Edgar Davids was one of Europe's most aggressive midfielders.

debut for Juventus in September 1993 then celebrated his first full league season with a hat-trick against Parma. He made his international debut in a 4-1 European qualifying win over Estonia in 1995 and has been kept busy by club and country ever since. Del Piero struggled to defy both injuries and the suspicion of some coaches that he was a luxury player. Yet he was a key squad member for the 2006 World Cup win and converted one of the crucial penalties in the shootout win over France.

Luis Del Sol
Full name: Luis del Sol Cascajares

National team: Spain

Born: April 6, 1935

Clubs: Betis, Seville, Real Madrid, Juventus, Roma Del Sol was inside-right in the legendary Real Madrid forward line which won the 1960 European Cup against Eintracht Frankfurt at Hampden. A neat, aggressive midfielder, he had been a wing-half at his home-town club Betis of Seville, when the Madrid management decided that the great Brazilian, Didi, was not fitting in well enough alongside Alfredo Di Stefano. Del Sol was hurriedly bought in the middle of the 1959-60 season and ran his legs off in support of veterans Di Stefano and Puskas. In 1962 Madrid sold Del Sol to Juventus to raise the cash in a vain attempt to buy Pele from Santos. Del Sol was a pillar of the Italian League through eight seasons with Juventus and two with Roma before his retirement and return to Spain.

Marcel Desailly

National team: France
Born: September 7, 1968
Clubs: Nantes, Marseille, Milan, Chelsea, Quatar SC
Desailly grew up into France's record international with well over 100 appearances to his credit. Yet he was born in Accra, Ghana, and moved to France with his family as a child. Apart from becoming captain of France, he is the only player to have won the Champions Cup with two different clubs in successive seasons – with Marseille against Milan in 1993 then with Milan against Barcelona a year later. Desailly won the Italian League in 1994 and 1996 before joining Chelsea. He was rock solid at the heart of the French defence for the World Cup and European double of 1998 and 2000. He announced his retirement from international soccer in 2004.

Kazimierz Deyna

National team: Poland
Born: October 23, 1947
Clubs: Starogard, Sportowy Lodz, Legia Warsaw, Manchester City (Eng), San Diego (US)
Poland's emergence as a world power in the early 1970s owed a huge debt to the skilled grace of Deyna, their midfield fulcrum. Deyna played centre midfield, supported by workers such as Maszczyk and Kasperczak, and was constantly creating openings for strikers Lato and Gadocha. He earned a domestic reputation in helping army club Legia win the league in 1969 and was promoted into the national squad when the Legia coach, Kazimierz Gorski, was appointed manager of Poland. Deyna won an Olympic gold medal with Poland in Munich in 1972 then returned to the Olympiastadion two years later to celebrate Poland's best-ever third-place finish at the World Cup. He was never quite the same player after moving abroad, first to England and then to the United States, where he died in a car crash. Deyna scored 38 goals in 102 internationals.

Marcel Desailly was European club champion two years in a row with different clubs.

Didi
Full name: Waldyr Pereira

National team: Brazil
Born: October 8, 1928
Clubs: FC Rio Branco, FC Lencoes, Madureiro, Fluminense, Botafogo, Real Madrid (Sp), Valencia (Sp), Botafogo
The success of Brazil's 4-2-4 system, revealed in all its glory internationally at the 1958 World Cup, rested heavily on the creative talent of Didi, one of the greatest of midfield generals. Teammates said he could "make the ball talk", and drop it on a coin from any distance, any angle. Didi was the first to perfect the "dead leaf" free kick, with which he scored a dozen of his 31 goals in 85 appearances for Brazil. He won the World Cup in 1958 and 1962 and counted a spell in between with Real Madrid – where he failed to settle – as the only failure of his career.

El Hadji Ousseynou Diouf

National team: Senegal
Born: January 15, 1981
Clubs: Rennes (Fr), Sochaux (Fr), Lens (Fr), Liverpool (Eng), Bolton (Eng), Sunderland (Eng), Blackburn (Eng)
Diouf was one of the new heroes thrown up by Senegal's success at the 2002 World Cup finals. Like most of his teammates he is a product of the French domestic game though his father had also been a Senegalese international. El Hadji made his own national team debut in 2000 and two years later was named African Footballer of the Year twice in succession. He earned the original award with his eight-goal haul in leading Senegal to the World Cup finals for the first time. He was then a key figure in their shock opening match victory over France and subsequent progress to the quarter-finals.

Domingos Antonio Da Guia

National team: Brazil
Born: November 19, 1912
Clubs: Bangu, Vasco da Gama, Nacional (Uru), Boca Juniors (Arg), Flamengo, Corinthians, Bangu

Domingos was a full-back of the old school, as much a pivoting central defender as a marker in the old-fashioned 2-3-5 formation. His talents earned him transfers all round South America, and he remains more of a legend in Uruguay and Argentina than he is in Brazil. The Uruguayans nicknamed him the "Divine Master". Domingos made his debut for Brazil in 1931, was a key member of the team which reached the 1938 World Cup semi-finals, and did not retire until 1948. By this time he had returned to his original club, Bangu. His contemporary centre-forward Leonidas da Silva once said no defender ever "read a game" better than Domingos.

Roberto Donadoni

National team: Italy
Born: September 9, 1963
Clubs: Atalanta, Milan
Donadoni, an attacking midfielder with right wing tendencies, came into the Italian reckoning after the 1986 World Cup and stayed for a decade, albeit scoring only five goals in his 63 appearances. Most important of those games was the 1994 World Cup Final when Italy lost on penalties to Brazil after a 0-0 draw. Donadoni was more fortunate at club level. He missed Milan's 1989 Champions Cup win through suspension but collected a string of honours in his 13 years with the club including the 1994 treble of Champions Cup, European Supercup and World Club Cup.

Landon Donovan

National team: United States
Born: March 4, 1982
Clubs: San Jose Earthquakes, Bayer Leverkusen (Ger), San Jose Earthquakes, LA Galaxy
Landon Donovan has established himself beyond doubt as the most outstanding United States player of the modern era after he became the third-youngest player ever called up, ahead of a friendly against Argentina in June 1999. In the event he did not play and had to wait until October

ALFREDO DI STEFANO
Champion of champions

Alfredo Di Stefano is reckoned by many to be the greatest soccer player of all time. His greatness lay not only in his achievement in leading Madrid to victory in the first five consecutive European Cup Finals – and inspiring a great breakthrough in international soccer – but also because no other player so effectively combined individual expertise with an all-embracing ability to organize a team to play to his command.

Today he is a wealthy elder statesman of soccer, but he was born in Barracas, a poor suburb of the Argentine capital of Buenos Aires, and learned his soccer first in the tough streets of the city, then out on the family farm. This was where he built up the stamina that became legendary across the world in later years.

Di Stefano's grandfather emigrated to Argentina from Capri and his father had played for the leading Buenos Aires club River Plate, but abruptly ended his career when professionalism was introduced. Young Alfredo – nicknamed "El Aleman" (the German) , because of his blond hair – made his River Plate debut at outside-right on August 18, 1944. However, Di Stefano was determined to follow the example of his hero, Independiente's free-scoring Paraguayan centre-forward, Arsenio Erico, and become a centre-forward himself. So he learned his trade while on loan to Huracan, then returned to River Plate, replacing the great Adolfo Pedernera to make up part of River's famous forward line nicknamed "La Maquina" (the Machine), for the remorseless consistency with which they took opposing defences apart.

He transferred his prowess into the national team when they won the 1947 South American Championship.

However, in 1949, Argentine players went on strike and the clubs locked them out and completed their fixtures with amateur players. Meanwhile, the star professionals were lured away to play in the pirate league that had been set up in Colombia. Playing for Millonarios of Bogota, the so-called "Blue Ballet", Di Stefano was the star of stars and when Colombia was reintegrated into FIFA, Millonarios went on one last world tour... where he was spotted by Real Madrid.

Madrid agreed a fee with Millonarios and thus nearly outflanked rivals Barcelona, who had sealed a deal with Di Stefano's old club, River Plate. A Spanish soccer court ruled that Di Stefano should play one season for each. But after making a quiet start to the season Barcelona, unimpressed, sold out their share in Di Stefano to Madrid. Four days later he scored a hat-trick in a 5-0 win against... Barcelona. A legend was born.

Madrid were Spanish champions in Di Stefano's first two seasons and European Cup-winners in his next five. He scored in each of Madrid's European Cup Finals, including a hat-trick against Frankfurt in 1960 in a 90-minute spectacular which has become one of the most admired soccer matches of all time.

Di Stefano was "total football" personified before the term was invented. One moment he was defending in his own penalty area, the next organizing midfield, the next scoring from the edge of the opponents' six-yard box. As Miguel Muñoz, long-time Madrid colleague as player and coach, once said: "The greatness of Di Stefano was that, with him in your side, you had two players in every position."

Alfredo Di Stefano covering back in defensive mode for Real Madrid against Milan.

1926	1942	1944	1947	1953	1960	1964
Born Alfredo Stefano Di Stefano Lauhle on July 4 in a poor suburb of Buenos Aires	Left Los Cardales after a row with the coach, to join his father's old club, River Plate	Transferred on loan to Huracan, for whom he scored the winner in a league game against River Plate	Already an international, won the South American Championship with Argentina	Moved to Spain where he joined Real Madrid	Scored a hat-trick in Real's legendary 7-3 victory over Eintracht Frankfurt in the European Cup Final at Hampden Park, Glasgow	Left Madrid for one last season as a player with Espanol of Barcelona, before becoming a coach in both Argentina and Spain

1940	1943	1946	1949	1956	1963	2000
Hinted at things to come by scoring a hat-trick in 20 minutes for his first youth team, Los Cardales	Made his debut for River Plate, playing as a right-winger, aged 17, against Buenos Aires rivals San Lorenzo	Returned to River Plate to succeed the great Adolfo Pedernera at centre-forward in an attack nicknamed La Maquina (the Machine)	Lured away, during the famous Argentine players' strike, to play in a pirate league outside of FIFA's jurisdiction in Colombia	Inspired Madrid to the first of five successive European Cup victories and made his national team debut for Spain	Kidnapped – and later released unharmed – by urban guerrillas while on tour with Real Madrid in Venezuela	Appointed honorary president of Real Madrid

2000 for his first game and first goal against Mexico. The Californian's pace and versatile attacking talent secured a transfer to Leverkusen but he did not enjoy the European experience and returned to San Jose. He then starred in the US team who reached the quarter-finals of the World Cup in 2006 and second round in 2010.

Didier Drogba

National team: Ivory Coast
Born: March 11, 1978
Clubs: Levallois, Le Mans, Guingamp, Marseille (all France), Chelsea (Eng)

Drogba has been twice top scorer in the Premier League with Chelsea and twice African Footballer of the Year. Drogba, born in the Ivory Coast but brought up in France by an uncle, had been a slow starter in the lower leagues before exploding to fame – and fortune – in leading Marseille to the 2004 UEFA Cup Final. Drogba scored 19 league goals, was voted Player of the Year and thus cost Chelsea a then club record of £24million. He took his fine form into the 2006 World Cup and Ivory Coast's finals debut. His 2010 finals campaign was spoiled by an arm fracture on the eve of action in South Africa.

Dunga
Full name: Carlos Bledorn Verri

National team: Brazil
Born: October 31, 1963
Clubs: Vasco da Gama, Pisa (It), Fiorentina (It), Pescara (It), Stuttgart (Ger), Jubilo Iwata (Jpn), Internacional

Dunga, one of the most controversial of modern Brazilian players, obtained the ultimate revenge over his critics when he lifted the World Cup after the victory over Italy in the 1994 Final. Dunga was severely criticized because, as a defensive midfield player, he was strong and keen in the tackle but slightly slow and relatively clumsy on the ball when compared with his compatriots. But he possessed a strong shot in both feet and 1994 World Cup boss Carlos

Ivorian Didier Drogba starred in the 2006 World Cup and won the Premiership Golden Boot in 2007.

Alberto Parreira considered Dunga's tactical discipline vital to his strategy. He captained Brazil to a runners-up finish at France 98 and was unsuccessful again as national coach in the 2010 finals

Dragan Dzajic

National team: Yugoslavia
Born: May 30, 1946
Clubs: Red Star Belgrade, Bastia (Fr), Red Star Belgrade

The British press baptized Dzajic the "Magic Dragan" after his left-wing skills helped take England apart in the semi-finals of the 1968 European Nations Championship. Dzajic had pace, skill and intelligence and was perhaps the greatest soccer hero to have emerged in post-war Yugoslavia. He was five times a national champion, four times a cup-winner and earned selection for a variety of World and European XIs on five occasions. Dzajic remained an outside-left throughout

his career in which he scored 23 goals in 85 internationals, never needing to fade back into midfield like so many wingers who lose the edge on their talent. He retired in 1978 and became general manager of his original club, Red Star.

Duncan Edwards

National team: England
Born: October 1, 1936
Club: Manchester United

Edwards was a giant who is still revered by generations who never saw him play. Comparatively few did, for his career was brief, but his awesome power and genuine all-round skill, as creator as well as destroyer, made him a man apart. At club level, Edwards was the outstanding discovery among Manchester United's Busby Babes. Sometimes he seemed to be a team in himself, as at Wembley in 1957, when ten men fought bravely in a vain effort against an Aston Villa side set on

depriving United of a merited cup and league double. Having won 18 England caps, Edwards was looking forward to playing a starring role in the 1958 World Cup. His death in the Munich Air Disaster robbed England of one its finest ever players.

Samuel Eto'o

National team: Cameroon
Born: March 10, 1981
Clubs: Real Madrid, Legranes, Mallorca, Barcelona (all Sp), Internazionale (It)

Eto'o is one of the finest of Africa's modern soccer exports. He is the 16-goal all-time top scorer in the African Nations Cup and, in 2008-09, became the fourth-highest marksman in the history of Barcelona. Ironically, Eto'o was discovered as a young teenager by Real Madrid but could never make a breakthrough and joined Barcelona in 2004 after a successful loan spell at Mallorca. He was La Liga's 26-goal leading scorer in 2005-06 when he also scored for Barcelona in their Champions League victory over Arsenal. Three times Africa's No1, he was also a winner against Manchester United in 2009 and then, with Italy's Inter, against Bayern Munich in 2010.

Cesc Fabregas Erico

National team: Spain
Born: May 4, 1987
Clubs: Barcelona, Arsenal (Eng)

Known as Cesc in Spain and Fabregas in England, Arsenal's young club captain and playmaker was a teenage "steal" from Barcelona. He was spotted while starring for Spain at the World Under-17s in Finland in 2003 and signed in the following September. When Cesc made his debut on October 23, 2003, in a League Cup tie at home to Rotherham he became Arsenal's youngest ever first-team player at 16 years 177 days. Shortly afterwards he also became the club's youngest-ever competitive goalscorer. He was rapidly promoted into Spain's national squad though he was

EUSEBIO
Soccer ambassador

Eusebio, the greatest Portuguese footballer in history, did not, in fact, come from Portugal. Born and brought up in Mozambique, then still one of Portugal's African colonies, Eusebio was the first African player to earn a worldwide reputation.

The big Portuguese clubs such as Benfica, Sporting and Porto financed nursery teams in Mozambique and Angola and unearthed a wealth of talent for Portuguese soccer and the Portuguese national team.

The young Eusebio, ironically, was a nursery product not of Benfica but of their great Lisbon rivals, Sporting. But when Sporting summoned him to Lisbon for a trial in 1961, he was virtually kidnapped off the plane by Benfica officials and hidden away until Sporting, having all but forgotten about him, lost interest.

Bela Guttmann, a veteran Hungarian, was coach of Benfica at the time and had a high regard for the potential offered by Mozambique and Angola. The nucleus of the Benfica team which Guttmann had guided to European Cup victory that year came from Africa and Eusebio would prove to be the greatest of them all.

Guttmann introduced him to the first team at the end of the 1960-61 season. He was a reserve when Benfica went to France to face Santos of Brazil – inspired by Pele – in the famous Paris Tournament. At half-time Benfica were losing 3-0. Guttmann, with nothing to lose, sent on Eusebio. Benfica still lost, but Eusebio scored a spectacular hat-trick and outshone even Pele. He was still only 19.

A year later Eusebio scored two cannonball goals in the 5–3 victory Benfica ran up against Real Madrid in the European Cup Final in Amsterdam. In 13 seasons he helped Benfica win the league seven times and the Cup twice; he was European Footballer of the Year in 1965; top scorer with 9 goals in the 1966 World Cup; scorer of 38 goals in 46 internationals and the league's leading scorer seven times.

Soccer was Eusebio's life and when the North American Soccer League offered him the chance of a lucrative extension to his career, he flew west to play for the Boston Minutemen, the Toronto Metros-Croatia, and finally Las Vegas Quicksilver.

Benfica's faithful had mixed feelings about his self-imposed exile in North America, but controversy was soon forgotten when he returned to Lisbon to take up appointments as television analyst, assistant coach and the honoured public face of Benfica.

Fans around the world took Eusebio to their hearts not only because of his ability but because of the sportsmanlike way he played the people's game. At Wembley in 1968 Eusebio very nearly won the European Cup Final for Benfica against Manchester United in the closing minutes of normal time, but he was foiled by the intuition of Alex Stepney. In response Eusebio patted Stepney on the back, applauding a worthy opponent.

A statue of Eusebio in action now dominates the entrance to the Estadio da Luz. A a film made about his life was subtitled Sua Majestade o Rei... His Majesty the King.

Eusebio shoots Benfica into the lead in the 1963 Champions Cup Final.

1942
Born Eusebio Da Silva Ferreira on January 25 in Lourenço Marques, Mozambique

1952
Joined the youth teams of Sporting (Lourenço Marques), a nursery team for the Portuguese giants

1961
Sporting tried to bring Eusebio to Lisbon, but he was "kidnapped" on arrival by Benfica. In the autumn, with barely a dozen league games to his name, he made his debut for Portugal

1962
Scored two thundering goals as Benfica beat Real Madrid 5-3 in a classic European Cup Final in Amsterdam

1965
Voted European Footballer of the Year

1966
Crowned top scorer with nine goals as Portugal finished third in the World Cup finals in England, where he was nicknamed the "new Pele" and the "Black Panther"

1969
Won the Portuguese championship medal for the seventh and last time with Benfica before winding down his career in Mexico and Canada

1992
A statue in his honour was unveiled at the entrance to Benfica's Estadio da Luz in Lisbon

2004
Acts as ambassador for soccer and watches Portugal reach the Final at home in the European Championship

mostly a high-class and highly-effective substitute in both the triumphs at Euro 2008 and in Spain's first-ever World Cup victory two years later.

Giacinto Facchetti

National team: Italy
Born: July 18, 1942
Clubs: Trevigliese, Internazionale

Full-back was never a romantic role until the emergence of Facchetti in the early 1960s. He had been a big, strapping centre-forward with his local club in Treviso when he was signed by Inter and converted into a left-back by master coach Helenio Herrera. The rigid man-to-man marking system perfected by Herrera permitted Facchetti the freedom, when Inter attacked, to stride upfield supporting his forwards. Facchetti scored 60 league goals, a record for a full-back in Italy, including ten in the 1965–66 season. But his most important goal came in the 1965 European Cup semi-final when he burst through in the inside-right position to score the winner against Liverpool. Facchetti later switched to sweeper, from where he captained Italy in the 1970 World Cup Final. He would surely have taken his total of 94 caps to 100 but for an injury he suffered shortly before the 1978 World Cup finals.

Rio Ferdinand

National team: England
Born: November 8, 1978
Clubs: West Ham, Bournemouth, West Ham, Leeds, Manchester United

Ferdinand was acclaimed as one of the classiest central defenders for years when he emerged at local club West Ham in the late 1990s. Similar praise was lavished on him at the 2002 World Cup, where he also claimed a crucial goal against Denmark in the second round. Weeks later he was sold by Leeds to Manchester United for a British record £30 million. Ferdinand, nephew of centre-forward Les Ferdinand, helped United win the Premiership in his first season. He anchored United not only to more domestic success but also to Champions League glory after bouncing back from an eight-month dope test ban.

Giovanni Ferrari

National team: Italy
Born: December 6, 1907
Clubs: Alessandria, Juventus, Ambrosiana-Inter

Only two members of Italy's 1934 World Cup-winning side were retained by manager Vittorio Pozzo for the ultimately successful 1938 defence – Giuseppe Meazza was one and Ferrari the other. A hard-working inside-forward he scored 14 goals for Italy in 44 internationals between his debut in a 4-2 win over Switzerland in 1930 and his farewell in a 1-0 win over France in late 1938. "Gioanin" won a record successive league titles with Juventus between 1931 and 1935 and then further championships with Ambrosiana-Inter in 1940 and Bologna in 1941. He later managed Italy's ill-starred campaign at the 1962 World Cup in Chile.

Tom Finney

National team: England
Born: April 5, 1922
Club: Preston North End

Moderate in height, thin and fair, Finney was nondescript in appearance, but a player whose versatility was matched by his skill. "Grizzly and strong" was the description applied to him by Bill Shankly, who played wing-half behind winger Finney at Preston – "Grizzly" in the sense of bear-like power rather than miserable attitude, for he always had a generous word for opponents as well as a rock-like solidity that belied his frame. Finney was genuinely two-footed, brave as they come, and in his later years a deep-lying centre-forward along Hidegkuti lines. Lack of support left him bereft of honours at club level, but a 12-year England career, with 76 caps and a then-record 30 goals, earned him a belated knighthood.

Just Fontaine
SEE PAGE 174

Diego Forlan

National team: Uruguay
Born: May 19, 1979
Clubs: Independiente (Arg), Manchester Utd (Eng), Villarreal (Sp), Atletico de Madrid (Sp)

Forlan emulated his father when he starred for Uruguay at the 2010 World Cup in South Africa. Father Pablo had played in the 1974 finals and a grandfather had played for Independiente in Argentina where Diego began his professional career after playing youth soccer for Penarol in his native Uruguay. A two-year spell with Manchester United proved disappointing but Forlan more than made up after moving to Spain. Here he was twice the Liga top scorer and he scored Atletico de Madrid's winning goal in their Europa League Final victory over Fulham in May 2010. Weeks later he scored five goals in leading unfancied Uruguay to fourth place at the World Cup and carried off the 'best player' award.

Karlheinz Förster

National team: West Germany
Born: July 25, 1958
Club: Stuttgart

Förster, at his peak of efficiency, was one of the most effective central defenders in world soccer. He made his debut for West Germany as a substitute against Brazil in 1978 then made rapid progress to help win the European Championship against Belgium two years later. He played all the Germans' matches in the World Cup run-up campaigns in both 1982 in Spain and in

Giacinto Facchetti set a goalscoring record for Italian fullbacks.

LUIS FIGO
The golden galactico

Luis Figo carries the pressure of having been the first "Galactico" in the empire-building strategy of the Real Madrid president Florentino Perez. But he has been far more than a pawn in the war between Madrid and Barcelona: Figo has also had to carry the weight of expectation of the fans in his native Portugal.

Figo was recognized as one of Europe's outstanding talents when he was a teenager. He joined top Lisbon outfit Sporting Clube of Portugal at 11, was a European Champion at under-16 level in 1989 in Denmark and a World Youth Cup-winner in 1991 against Brazil in Lisbon. Coach Carlos Queiroz saw Figo as a star of the so-called "golden generation" as he proved when Portugal reached the finals of the European Under-21 Championship in France in 1994.

By the time Parma and Juventus came calling, Figo was an established international with four goals in 23 matches. Both Italian clubs claimed his signature and the row went to FIFA for arbitration. The world authority ruled both agreements invalid and banned Figo from a move to Italy for two years. That suited Barcelona who jumped in at high speed to snap him up for a bargain £1.5 million.

He said later: "It was like destiny. When I had decided I wanted to leave Sporting Lisbon the possibility of joining Barcelona was non-existent. But if they had been bidding from the start then I would have signed for them with my eyes shut."

Figo arrived in Barcelona in the days of Johan Cruyff but enjoyed his success under successors Bobby Robson and Louis Van Gaal. That meant winning the Cup-winners Cup, Spanish Cup and European Supercup in 1997, the league and cup double in 1998 and league again in 1999.

On the international stage Figo, who had made his Portugal debut in 1991, starred in the run to the quarter-finals of Euro 96 and semi-finals of Euro 2000. Then, after defeat by France, Figo starred in an even more sensational transfer drama.

Figo had already recognized that, if he were to achieve all his ambitions, he needed a higher-profile club stage. Fiorentino Perez, a millionaire property developer, won the Real Madrid presidential elections by promising to sign Figo – which he did for a then world record fee of £35 million. It was a brave move by Figo, which cast him in the role of ultimate hate figure for the Barcelona faithful. He was pelted with missiles from the crowd on returning to the Nou Camp to play for Madrid; on one occasion that included a pig's head.

In trophy terms, however, the collection of titles, cups and personal awards proved that Figo had made the right move. After pulling on the all-white of Madrid he won the Champions League, World Club Cup and Spanish league and was hailed as both FIFA World Player of the Year and as European Footballer of the Year.

Later Figo moved on to Italy's Internazionale while taking his Portugal tally to a record 127 matches – including runners-up spot as hosts in 2004 and a fourth-place finish at the subsequent 2006 World Cup in Germany.

Luis Figo was one of the few to transfer with success from Barcelona to Real Madrid.

1975
Born Luis Filipe Madeira Caeiro Figo on November 14 in Lisbon

1986
Joined Sporting Clube de Portugal youth section, aged 11

1989
Helped Portugal win the World Youth Cup

1991
Won the World Youth Cup again under Carlos Queiroz, against Brazil in Lisbon in the Final. Made his Sporting league debut and his senior Portugal debut

1994
Appointed Sporting's youngest-ever captain and led them to domestic cup success

1995
Centre of transfer controversy after signing contracts with both Parma and Juventus joined Barcelona instead

1997
Under Bobby Robson, helped Barcelona win the European Cup-Winners Cup, Spanish Cup and European Super Cup

1998
Captained Barcelona to first of two successive league titles under Louis Van Gaal

2000
Led Portugal to semi-finals of European Championship finals in Holland and Belgium. Collected hate mail by the sackful from furious Barcelona fans after transferring to Real Madrid for a world record £37 million.

2001
Followed up by winning FIFA World Player of the Year

2002
Won his first Champions League with Real Madrid, beating Bayer Leverkusen

2006
Quit international soccer after leading Portugal to the 2006 World Cup semi-finals

JUST FONTAINE
Gallic goal machine

France boast a unique World Cup hat-trick. Jules Rimet was the driving force behind the event's creation, Lucien Laurent scored the first goal and no-one will ever come close to equalling – never mind overtaking – Just Fontaine's record of 13 goals in a finals tournament in 1958.

The Fontaine story was a remarkable one because of the elements of coincidence which provided him with one glorious summer. He really was a shooting star because nothing he had done before and nothing he did afterwards approached his achievements in the 1958 World Cup in Sweden.

Fontaine was not even born in France but in Marrakech, Morocco, then under French rule, on August 18, 1933. Discovered and brought to France by Nice, Fontaine was later bought by Reims – then the top club in France – as replacement for Raymond Kopa when he joined Real Madrid in 1956. It was surprising that Fontaine was even taken along for the 1958 World Cup finals; he had played only twice for France and had missed most of the 1957–58 season because of knee trouble. Not until the middle of February 1958 was Fontaine back on duty with Reims.

Indeed, he went to the World Cup finals expecting to be reserve to Reims teammate René Bliard, but Bliard was injured on the eve of the finals and Fontaine took his opportunity in record-breaking style. He owed the majority of his goals to Kopa's creative work alongside him: a hat-trick against Paraguay, two against Yugoslavia, one against Scotland, two against Northern Ireland, one in the semi-final defeat by Brazil and a further four against West Germany.

He could have had more. Fontaine recalls: "I even let someone else take a penalty in our last match because in those days there was no golden boot or financial prizes such as players can earn now. Nobody made a fuss of it all at the time, nobody said: 'Here, you take this penalty'."

But the man whose goals nearly won his country the World Cup could not manage it single-handed. Fontaine never fails to acknowledge the debt he owed Kopa in 1958 for so many slide-rule passes through flat, open, "old-fashioned" defences.

The following season, 1958–59, Fontaine was the ten-goal top scorer in the Champions Cup. Reims reached the final again and, once again, lost to Real Madrid. French consolation was that, after the match, Reims negotiated the transfer return of Kopa.

Sadly Fontaine had to retire in 1961 after breaking his leg for a second time. He had been twice top league scorer and totalled 27 goals in 20 internationals. Later he was president of the French Players' Union and also, briefly, national manager. But his fame rests today on a record-breaking achievement which earned far less attention in 1958 than it would have done today. Fontaine says: "In those days centre-forwards were expected to score a lot of goals. It went with the No 9 shirt. But I was helped enormously in that we played with five forwards. Now it is a miracle if you find a team playing with three. The media pressure was much less then too, which is another burden for players such as Ronaldo nowadays...

"In 1958, no-one knew me. And, by the time they did know me, it was all over."

Just Fontaine triumphant after scoring a record 13 goals in the 1958 World Cup.

1933	1951	1954	1956	1958	1961	1962	2004
Born on August 18 in Marrakech, Morocco	Transferred to top Moroccan club, USM Casablanca	Was Nice's 17-goal top scorer in his first season and wins the Cup	Won league title with Nice and signed for Reims	Scored the first of his 27 goals for France in a 2-2 draw with Spain in March at the Parc des Princes in Paris. Crowned league top scorer for the first time with 34 goals	Suffered a second leg fracture	Confirms his retirement because of the leg injuries	Nominated as top French footballer of the past 50 years by the French federation in a UEFA survey

1949	1953	1956	1957	1960	1961	1967
Signed part-time with local club AC Marrakech	Brought to French soccer by Nice	Made the first of his 20 appearances for France in a 2-1 defeat by Hungary in the Stade de Colombes in Paris	Recorded his finest domestic season with 30 goals for Reims	Broke a leg for the first time in league match against Sochaux in March. Crowned league top scorer again with 28 goals in another of Reims' league title-winning campaigns.	Elected first president of the newly formed French Players' Union	Had a four-month spell as manager of France

1986 in Mexico. Förster, whose brother Bernd played alongside him in defence for both club and country, was voted West Germany's Footballer of the Year in 1982.

Enzo Francescoli

National team: Uruguay
Born: November 12, 1961
Clubs: Wanderers, River Plate (Arg), Matra Racing (Fr), Marseille (Fr), Cagliari (It), Torino (It), River Plate (Arg)

Francescoli followed in a long line of Uruguayan superstars, starting with the heroes of the 1920s and 1930s and continuing through Schiaffino, Goncalves and Rocha. He began with a small club, Wanderers, and then moved to River Plate after the Agentinian club outbid Uruguayan giants Penarol and Nacional. Francescoli was top scorer in the Argentine league and voted South American Footballer of the Year before transferring to France with Racing in 1986. Even Francescoli's 32 goals in three seasons were not enough to save Racing from financial collapse. He scored 11 goals in Marseille's championship season of 1989-90 before moving first to Italy, then back to River Plate to wind down his career.

Trevor Francis

National team: England
Born: April 19, 1954
Clubs: Birmingham City, Nottingham Forest, Manchester City, Sampdoria (It), Atalanta (It), Rangers (Scot), Queens Park Rangers, Sheffield Wednesday

Francis secured his place in British soccer history as the first £1 million footballer when he was sold by Birmingham City to Nottingham Forest in 1979. The fee prompted controversy but Forest were rewarded when, a few months later, Francis scored their Champions Cup Final winning goal against Malmo. At Birmingham Francis had been nicknamed "Superboy" after establishing himself at 16 and he would later take his attacking talents

to Manchester City and on to Italy. He played in all England's five ties at the 1982 World Cup and totalled 12 goals in 52 games for his country.

Arthur Friedenreich

National team: Brazil
Born: July 18, 1892
Clubs: Germania, Ipiranga, Americao, Paulistano, São Paulo FC, Flamengo

Friedenreich was the first great Brazilian footballer and the first player officially credited with more than 1,000 goals. His overall total was 1,329. The son of a German father and a Brazilian mother, Friedenreich was also significant as the first black player to break through the early racial/cultural barriers in Brazilian soccer. Nicknamed "the Tiger", Friedenreich began playing senior soccer at 17 and did not retire until 1935, when he was 43. He scored eight goals in 17 internationals for Brazil between 1914 and 1930. His first representative appearance for Brazil was in a 2-0 win against the English club Exeter City on July 21, 1914, when he lost two teeth in a collision.

Paulo Futre

National team: Portugal
Born: February 28, 1966
Clubs: Sporting Lisbon, FC Porto, Atletico Madrid (Sp), Benfica, Marseille (Fra), Reggiana (It), Milan (It), West Ham United (Eng), Atletico Madrid (Sp)

Futre was only 17 when he made his international debut and his star continued to shine brightly after FC Porto snatched him away from Sporting Lisbon to inspire their European Cup victory of 1987. A few weeks later Futre was signed by Atletico Madrid as the first major coup in the controversial presidency of Jesus Gil. Futre survived all the tempests at Atletico until the start of 1993, when he forced his sale home to Benfica. However, financing the deal proved beyond even Benfica. They sold him to Marseille, who also had to sell him after only a few months to resolve their own cash

Garrincha owed his initial World Cup success to his team-mates' player power.

crisis. Reggiana of Italy paid £8 million to become Futre's fourth club in a year – but he was never the same player after tearing knee ligaments in his first game.

Garrincha
Full name: Manoel Francisco dos Santos

National team: Brazil
Born: October 28, 1933
Clubs: Pau Grande, Botafogo, Corinthians, AJ Barranquilla (Col), Flamengo, Red Star Paris (Fr)

Garrincha ranked alongside Pele in Brazilian soccer in the 1960s. Born in poverty, childhood illness left his legs badly twisted and the surgeons who carried out corrective surgery thought he would do well merely to walk, let alone turn out to be one of the quickest and most dangerous right-wingers of all time. Yet it took a players' deputation to persuade manager Vicente Feola to include him in the 1958 World Cup side in Sweden. Once in, Garrincha was there to stay and was the dominant personality at the 1962 finals after

the early injury to Pele. Sadly, his private life was chaotic and he died prematurely of alcohol poisoning.

Paul Gascoigne

National team: England
Born: May 27, 1967
Clubs: Newcastle, Tottenham Hotspur, Lazio (It), Rangers (Scot), Middlesbrough, Everton, Burnley, Gansu Tianma (Ch)

Gascoigne's career was blighted by his own indiscipline and misfortune with injuries. A powerful midfielder with a deft touch, he was England's star of the 1990 World Cup. He was memorably inconsolable when his second yellow card ruled him out of a possible Final. Gascoigne left Newcastle for Spurs and led them to the 1991 FA Cup Final, where he suffered a bad knee injury making a rash tackle. After missing a year through injury he signed with Lazio but played only 42 games in three seasons. He moved to Rangers in 1995, where he won two league titles and was Footballer of the Year in 1996. He joined Middlesbrough in

1998, helping them to win promotion. But "Gazza's" England career ended when he was omitted from the 1998 World Cup squad because of a lack of fitness.

Tommy Gemmell

National team: Scotland
Born: October 16, 1943
Clubs: Celtic, Nottingham Forest (Eng)

A big and sometimes clumsy full-back who became a folk hero because of his goals. He scored eight in European matches for his club, a remarkable record for a defender, and two of them were in European Cup Finals. Gemmell crashed one past Internazionale to equalize when Celtic won in 1967, and also scored against Feyenoord when they lost in 1970. His extroverted style of play was well suited to upsetting foreign defences during Celtic's greatest years, but he also collected a large haul of domestic honours before a final fling at Forest.

Paul Gascoigne's great talent was marred by injury and indiscipline.

Claudio Gentile

National team: Italy
Born: September 27, 1953
Clubs: Varese, Juventus

Gentile's fearsome reputation has extended far beyond the end of his career. His ability to man-mark opposing forwards was legendary. At the 1982 World Cup finals in Spain he famously tracked Argentina's Diego Maradona into anonymity in their second-round duel. Gentile was originally a full-back when Juventus signed him from Varese in 1973 but soon switched to central defence and was a key figure in Italy's 1982 World Cup win. With Juventus he won all three major European club competitions and a string of domestic honours as well as 71 caps between 1975 and 1984. Later Gentile succeeded former Italy and Juventus teammate Marco Tardelli as coach of the national under-21 team.

Francisco Gento

National team: Spain
Born: October 22, 1933
Clubs: Santander, Real Madrid

Real Madrid's great team of the 1950s and 1960s was more than "just" Di Stefano and Puskas. Tearing great holes in opposing defences was outside-left Gento, whose pace earned him the nickname of "El Supersonico". Gento began with Santander and was considered a player with pace but little else when Madrid signed him in 1953. Fortunately, he found a marvellous inside-left partner in José Hector Rial, who tutored Gento in the arts of the game. Gento is the only man to have won six European Cup medals. He scored 256 goals in 800 games for Madrid, with whom he won Spanish championship medals on 12 occasions. He played 43 times for Spain despite the challenging rivalry of Enrique Collar, an outstanding left-winger with Atletico Madrid.

Dudu Georgescu

National team: Romania
Born: September 1, 1950
Clubs: Progresul Bucharest, RCM Resita, Dynamo Bucharest

Georgescu, a strong, brave centre-forward, was just too early to share in Romania's international emergence at the World Cups and European Championships. However, he made an international mark of his own through his remarkable marksmanship. This twice earned him the Golden Boot as Europe's leading league scorer. The first award was for his 33 goals in the Romanian Championship in 1974-75 and then he ran up a remarkable 47 in the 1976-77 season – each time for Dynamo Bucharest. Georgescu was domestic top scorer four years in a row and also claimed 21 goals in 44 internationals.

Eric Gerets

National team: Belgium
Born: May 18, 1954
Clubs: Standard Liege, Milan (It), PSV Eindhoven (Hol)

Gerets joined Standard as a teenage centre-forward but it was only after being converted to right-back that he made his mark in both domestic and international soccer. He was outstanding in the Belgian side which finished runners-up at the 1980 European Championship and then captained Standard in their Cup-winners Cup Final defeat by Barcelona in 1982. He joined Milan a year later but was suspended over a Belgian domestic scandal. He moved on to PSV Eindhoven with whom he won the Champions Cup in 1988.

Luis de Figueiredo Germano

National team: Portugal
Born: January 18, 1933
Clubs: Benfica

Germano was one of the world's finest central defenders in the early 1960s but was unfortunate with injuries. Even so, he earned high praise for his role in organizing Benfica's defence while Eusebio & co were grabbing greater attention with their goal-scoring exploits. Injury cost Germano his place at the heart of Portugal's defence at the 1966 World Cup. He won the Champions Cup twice with Benfica in 1961 and 1962 but third time proved unlucky. He even had to go in goal in the 1965 final after Costa Pereira was injured in the 1-0 defeat by Internazionale in Milan.

Steven Gerrard

National team: England
Born: May 30, 1980
Clubs: Liverpool

Gerrard quickly announced himself as a world-class midfielder after striding through from the Liverpool youth academy in the wake of Michael Owen. Gerrard played for England at youth and under-21 level and quickly forced his way into Kevin Keegan's squad for

Euro 2000, though he made only one appearance as a substitute. Unluckily for both himself and England, Gerrard missed the subsequent World Cup through injury. He helped Liverpool to their magnificent five trophies in 2001 – League Cup, FA Cup, UEFA Cup, Charity Shield and European Supercup – and futher enhanced his formidable international reputation by the manner in which he inspired Liverpool's legendary comeback from 3-0 down to beat Milan in the 2005 Champions League Final.

Ryan Giggs

National team: Wales
Born: November 29, 1973
Club: Manchester United

Giggs was called the "new George Best" for his ability to outwit opposing defenders. The son of a rugby league player, he became Wales' youngest-ever international when he faced West Germany in October 1991 at 17 years 321 days. United manager Sir Alex Ferguson was fiercely protective of Giggs and his youthful talent subsequently helped United win the league championship repeatedly (on a record 11 occasions), four FA Cups, three League Cups. He has been twice a European club champion while overtaking Sir Bobby Charlton's club appearances record.

Johnny Giles

National team: Rep Ireland
Born: January 6, 1940
Clubs: Home Farm, Manchester United (Eng), Leeds United (Eng), West Bromwich Albion (Eng), Vancouver Whitecaps (Can), Shamrock Rovers

Giles was the outstanding figure in Republic of Ireland international soccer before the advent of Jack Charlton – his former Leeds teammate in the late 1960s and early 1970s. Giles, born in Dublin, joined Manchester United originally as an orthodox outside right but converted into a midfield general on moving to Elland Road. He was the creative fulcrum of Don Revie's Leeds machine

Ryan Giggs won the league title eight times in his first 11 seasons.

before moving into player-managership with both West Bromwich Albion and the Irish Republic. He lost out later to Charlton and subsequently became a perceptive newspaper soccer columnist.

Alain Giresse

National team: France
Born: September 2, 1952
Clubs: Bordeaux, Marseille

Giresse emerged as one of the smallest of World Cup heroes at the heart of the French midfield in Spain in 1982. Among other things Giresse contributed a memorable goal in the dramatic semi-final against West Germany. He further enhanced his reputation in the 1984 European

Championship success, helped Bordeaux to the Champions Cup semi-finals in 1985 and then France to third place in the World Cup in Mexico the following year. Giresse played more than 500 league games for Bordeaux before transferring, briefly, to Marseille after the 1986 World Cup finals.

Sergio Javier Goycochea

National team: Argentina
Born: October 17, 1963
Clubs: River Plate, Millonarios (Col), Racing Club, Brest (Fr), Cerro Porteno (Par), River Plate, Deportivo Mandiyu

Goycochea earned fame at the 1990 World Cup finals when he stepped into the action during Argentina's match against the Soviet Union after Nery

Pumpido had broken a leg. Goycochea's heroics in the penalty shoot-out victories over Yugoslavia and Italy subsequently took Argentina to the Final. Yet he had not played a competitive game over the previous six months because of the domestic unrest in Colombia, where he had been contracted to Millonarios of Bogota. After the 1990 World Cup finals Goycochea signed for the ambitious French provincial club, Brest. They soon went bankrupt, however, and he returned to Argentina.

Jimmy Greaves

National team: England
Born: February 20, 1940
Clubs: Chelsea, AC Milan (It), Tottenham Hotspur, West Ham

Greaves was an instinctive goalscorer, whose speed in thought and deed made up for lack of size and power. His 44 goals in 57 full internationals included two hauls of four goals and four threes, and his 357 goals in league games (all First Division) included three fives. An unhappy interlude in Italy did little to mar his scoring ability, and he gave wonderful value for money until his closing chapter with West Ham. By then drink had taken a grip, and his overcoming of that blight to become a popular television pundit set an inspiring example to others in the same position.

Harry Gregg

National team: Northern Ireland
Born: October 25, 1932
Clubs: Dundalk, Doncaster (Eng), Manchester United (Eng), Stoke (Eng)

Genial, popular Gregg won his first cap after only nine Football League games for Second Division Doncaster and had established himself as Ireland's first choice before the fateful 1957-58 season. Hardly had he left Yorkshire for Manchester United when, as a survivor of the Munich air crash, he became a hero by helping to rescue some of the injured. Later that year he performed well in helping his club to the FA Cup Final, where they lost 2-0 to Bolton, and the Irish to the quarter-final of the World Cup in Sweden. Injury kept him out of United's FA Cup-winning side in 1963.

John Greig

National team: Scotland
Born: September 11, 1942
Clubs: Glasgow Rangers

A 16-year spell of hard labour in defence and midfield brought Greig a record 496 League appearances for Rangers and a considerable number of honours, although Celtic were the dominant team in Scotland for a large part of that time. He was Footballer of the Year in 1966, the season in which he scored a spectacular goal against Italy in a World Cup qualifier, and won 44 caps, often as skipper. Greig also played in two European Cup-Winners Cup finals, losing in 1967 and winning in 1972. Later, he had a spell as manager at Ibrox.

Gunnar Gren

National team: Sweden
Born: October 31, 1920
Clubs: IFK Gothenburg, AC Milan (It), Fiorentina (It), Orgryte, GAIS Gothenburg

Gren, nicknamed "the Professor", claimed Italian attention when he was a member of the gold medal-winning team at the Olympic Games in London in 1948. His nickname stemmed both from his premature baldness and his astute inside-forward play. Milan won the transfer race and Gren forged, with fellow Swedes Nordahl and Liedholm, the legendary "Gre-No-Li" trio who took Italian soccer by storm. In 1955, after a spell with Fiorentina, he returned home to Sweden and, at 37, helped the hosts to the Final of the 1958 World Cup. That was the last of Gren's 57 internationals. Later he returned to IFK Gothenburg – with whom he had won the Swedish championship in 1942 – as manager of the souvenir shop.

Arend "Arie" Haan

National team: Holland
Born: November 16, 1948
Clubs: Ajax, Anderlecht (Bel)

Haan came to prominence in midfield with Ajax's triple European club champions. He appeared as a substitute against Panathinaikos in the 1971 Final but was a regular starter alongside the likes of Neeskens and Muhren in the victories of 1972 and 1973. Then he switched effectively into central defence when Holland finished World Cup runners-up in 1974. Haan moved back into midfield in Argentina in 1978 when he struck a spectacular long-range goal against Italy. He achieved further international club success in the Cup-Winners Cup after transferring to Anderlecht. He later entered management including an appointment as boss of China in 2003.

Gheorghe Hagi

National team: Romania
Born: February 5, 1965
Clubs: FC Constanta, Sportul Studentesc, Steaua Bucharest, Real Madrid (Sp), Brescia (It), Barcelona (Sp), Galatasaray (Tur)

Hagi was always destined for stardom. He played for Romania's youth team at 15, was a top-flight league player at 17, an international at 18, and a year later was appearing in the 1984 European Championship finals. In 1985 he hit 20 goals and in 1986 he managed 31, after scoring six in one match. Steaua Bucharest virtually stole Hagi from neighbours Sportul without a transfer fee – an escapade approved by the Steaua-supporting ruling Ceaucescu family. After the 1990 World Cup Hagi played in Spain then Italy – returning briefly to Barcelona after inspiring Romania to reach the quarter-finals of the 1994 World Cup and the second round in 1998. Red cards marred both Hagi's international swansong at Euro 2000, and Galatasaray's UEFA Cup Final victory a month earlier.

Gheorghe Hagi inspired Romania's international rise in the 1990s.

Hakan Sukur

National team: Turkey
Born: September 1, 1971
Club(s): Sakaryaspor, Bursaspor, Galatasaray, Torino (It), Galatasaray, Internazionale (It), Parma (It), Galatasaray

Hakan Sukur was the standard-bearer for Turkey's emerging national team in the decade from the mid-1990s. A rangy, intelligent centre-forward, he made his name domestically as Galatasaray's top scorer for three successive seasons between 1993 and 1995. He helped Turkey win the 1993 Mediterranean Games and was top scorer in the qualifying competition for Euro 96 when Turkey reached the finals for the first time. Torino bought him for £3 million but he quickly grew homesick and was sold back to Galatasaray for the same fee. Later he tried his luck again in Italy after leading Galatasaray to the first Turkish club success in Europe in the 2000 UEFA Cup. He played in all Turkey's matches at the 2002 World Cup and scored their opening goal after a record 11 seconds in the third-place play-off defeat of co-hosts South Korea.

Helmut Haller

National team: West Germany
Born: July 21, 1939
Club(s): BC Augsburg, Bologna (It), Juventus (It), BC Augsburg.

Haller earned himself a reputation while still a teenager as an inside-forward in West Germany in the late 1950s, before the advent of full-time professionalism and the Bundesliga. The Italian club Bologna gambled on his youth and were superbly rewarded: in 1963 Haller's partnership with the Dane Harald Nielsen brought Bologna their first league title in more than 20 years. Later Haller played with further success for Italian giants Juventus before returning to Augsburg. He will be remembered above all for his outstanding contribution to West Germany's 1966 World Cup campaign.

RUUD GULLIT
The player who had it all

Ruud Gullit was the forward or attacking midfielder who sparked Milan's all-conquering side of the late 1980s and the Holland team who won the 1988 European Championship. Gullit was an individualist, instantly recognizable by his flowing dreadlocks. He was never afraid to challenge authority, even if it damaged his career - as Holland coach Dick Advocaat and Milan's Fabio Capello discovered.

At 17 Gullit made his debut for Haarlem and joined Feyenoord in 1982, starring in their championship win two years later. In 1985, he joined PSV Eindhoven where he blossomed to become one of the most coveted talents in Europe. In 1987 he was voted World and European Player of the Year. He dedicated the awards to the then-jailed African National Congress leader Nelson Mandela. He cost a world record £6.5 million fee when he moved from PSV to Milan in the summer of 1987. He inspired Milan to their first championship for a decade in 1988, scoring nine goals from midfield. He became the first Holland captain to lift a major trophy after his side won the European Championship in West Germany. A year later, Gullit netted the first two goals as Milan beat Steauea Bucharest 4-0 to win the European

Ruud Gullit talked the game almost as well as he played it in Holland, Italy and England.

Cup for the first time since 1969. He had made a rapid recovery from a knee injury to play, but knee knocks were beginning to take their toll. He played in the World Cup finals in 1990, but knee trouble continued to bother him. There was talk of dressing room tension between him and Italy centre-back Franco Baresi and the Dutchman was also at loggerheads with new coach Capello. He spent the 1993–94 season with Sampdoria, scoring 16 goals in a free role - his best return in Serie A - lifting Sampdoria to fourth place and victory in the Italian Cup Final. Gullit had announced his international retirement in 1992 for "personal reasons", but counted himself in and out for years. He returned briefly to Milan, but completed a full transfer to Sampdoria.

His glory days were clearly behind him when he joined Chelsea in 1995. Gullit took over as manager and made another little piece of history. He became the first foreign coach to manage an FA Cup-winning side when Chelsea beat Middlesbrough in the 1997 Final. A spell at Newcastle went awry after Gullit dropped local hero Alan Shearer for a local derby before he returned home to coach Holland's juniors and then Feyenoord.

1962	1978	1982	1985	1987	1989	1993	1995	1997	2003
Born in Amsterdam	Signed for Haarlem	Moved from Haarlem to Feyenoord	Moved from Feyenoord to PSV Eindhoven	Won another Dutch title medal, voted World, European and Dutch Footballer of the Year and joined Milan for world record £6.5m	Gained first of two successive European Champions Cup medals	Won third Serie A championship medal	Joined Chelsea	Steered them to FA Cup Final success	Became Holland youth coach

1970	1981	1984	1986	1988	1992	1994	1996	1998
Joined junior club Meerboys then DWS Amsterdam	Made Holland debut against Switzerland	Won Dutch championship and Dutch Cup winner's medals	Won championship medal and voted Footballer of the Year	Landed Serie A title and captained Holland to European Championship win	Collected second Serie A title medal	Collected Italian Cup with Sampdoria	Appointed Chelsea player-manager	Left Chelsea in February, was appointed manager of Newcastle United in August but stayed barely a year

Kurt Hamrin

National team: Sweden
Born: November 19, 1934
Clubs: AIK Solna, Juventus (It), Padova (It), Fiorentina (It), Milan (It), Napoli (It), Caserta (It)

Hamrin ranks close behind Matthews and Garrincha among the great outside-rights of the modern game. He was a quick, darting attacker, who was not only nimble and clever but one of the most successful goal-grabbers in the history of the Italian League. Hamrin disappointed Juventus and they sold him off after only one year. Once he had adjusted, however, Hamrin proved an irresistible one-man strike force with Fiorentina, with whom he scored 150 goals in nine seasons and won the European Cup-Winners' Cup in 1961. At 34, while with Milan, he added a European Cup winners' medal to his collection.

Gerhard Hanappi

National team: Austria
Born: July 9, 1929
Clubs: Wacker, Rapid Vienna

Hanappi was one of the most versatile players to be found anywhere in the world in the 1950s. He played mainly wing-half or occasionally inside-forward for his long-time club, Rapid, but also lined up at centre-forward and at full-back in the course of winning 93 caps for Austria. He would have topped a century had it not been for a row with officialdom. Hanappi, an architect by profession, designed a new stadium for Rapid that was named in honour of his memory, after his premature death in 1980. Hanappi was Austrian champion and Austrian Cup-winner once each with Wacker then national champion six times and Austrian Cup-winner once again with Rapid. He played for FIFA's World XI against England in 1953.

Eddie Hapgood

National team: England
Born: September 27, 1908
Clubs: Bristol Rovers, Kettering, Arsenal

Hapgood was small for a left-back, but as tough as teak. He was an inspiring captain who led England in 21 of his 30 games during the 1930s, with 13 more during the war. In his teens he was an amateur with Bristol Rovers, but was allowed to leave and was with non-league Kettering when Arsenal recruited him. He went on to earn five championship medals and played in three FA Cup Finals, winning two. His first international was against Italy in Rome; his first as captain was also against Italy but on his club ground in the infamous "Battle of Highbury" – when he returned to play on after an opponent's elbow had smashed his nose. After retirement he managed Blackburn and Watford.

Ernst Happel

National team: Austria
Born: June 29, 1925
Clubs: Rapid Vienna, 1st FC Vienna, Racing Club of Paris (Fr)

Happel was a redoubtable centre-back with Rapid and Austria in the 1950s, and his 51-cap playing career reached a climax at the 1958 World Cup finals. He possessed a powerful shot and once scored a hat-trick, with free-kicks and a penalty in an early European Cup tie against Real Madrid. After retiring, Happel became one of Europe's most successful coaches, taking Feyenoord to the World Club Cup and European Cup in 1970. He was also manager of Holland when they reached the World Cup Final in Argentina in 1978. He achieved further success in guiding outsiders Hamburg to victory in the 1983 European Champions Cup.

Hasan Sas

National team: Turkey
Born: August 1, 1976
Clubs: Ankaragucu, Galatasaray

Hasan Sas, a mobile and nippy forward or attacking midfielder, was quick to make his mark after joining Galatasaray in 1999. A year later he was helping them beat Arsenal in the UEFA Cup Final and then going on to make his national team debut. Hasan was one of the outstanding players on view at the 2002 World Cup finals when he scored for Turkey in their initial 2-1 defeat by Brazil in the group stage and then again in the victory over China. He was subsequently voted Turkish Footballer of the Year.

Hasan Sas (right) was outstanding for Turkey at the 2002 World Cup finals.

Johnny Haynes

National team: England
Born: October 17, 1934
Clubs: Fulham, Durban City (SA)

Like Tom Finney, Haynes won nothing in nearly two decades with one club. However, he was the hub of many an England team in a 56-cap career, hitting long passes through a needle's eye and scoring a surprising number of goals with an incredibly powerful shot that belied his comparatively slight frame. As England's first £100-a-week player he was often unjustly criticized, but he earned every penny in the service of Fulham (generally struggling) and England (frequently rampant). He was England captain from 1960 until he was involved in a serious car accident in 1962. During that period, in successive games, England won 5-2, 9-0, 4-2, 5-1, 9-3 and 8-0. The 9-3 result was a slaughter of Scotland, perhaps the best performance of his era. His career might have added up differently if Milan had persisted in their bid for him or if, after his accident, a record-breaking bid from Tottenham Hotspur had succeeded. He ended his playing career in South Africa, winning a championship medal with Durban City.

Willie Henderson

National team: Scotland
Born: January 24, 1944
Clubs: Rangers, Sheffield Wednesday (Eng)

If "Wee Willie" had performed throughout his career as he did in his first few years, he would have been perhaps the greatest ever Scottish player. Despite persistent foot trouble and far from perfect eyesight, he had won all four domestic honours – League, Scottish Cup, League Cup and international cap – before his 20th birthday. By then Rangers had sold international winger Alex Scott to Everton in order to make room for the kid. Henderson went on to play in 29 internationals and captivate fans with his wizardry, but his career was marred by discontent, and gradually petered out in disappointment

THIERRY HENRY
Speeding Eurostar

A chance meeting with his old boss rescued Thierry Henry's career and set him on the road to become one of the world's greatest strikers. The former Monaco star's career had stalled after his move to Juventus in January 1999 when he was consigned to the bench or used, sparingly, as a left winger. Then he bumped into Arsene Wenger and started the chain of events that saw him hailed as an Arsenal great. Henry said: "Things weren't working out for me at Juventus, when I met Arsene on a plane and told him I wanted to play for him again. He was the man who launched my pro career at Monaco and he was the man who re-launched it at Arsenal."

Wenger had watched Henry develop from his early days at France's Clairefontaine National Academy. He signed the teenager for Monaco and handed him a senior debut at 17. Henry had been one of the great hopes of French soccer and by the time he was 21, he had won a championship medal and reached the Champions League semi-finals – and scored three goals to help France win the 1998 World Cup.

Wenger was looking for a striker to replace Nicolas Anelka who had joined Real Madrid and he decided to back Henry's talent and rebuild his

confidence. It is often said that Wenger converted Henry from a left winger to a central striker. In fact, Wenger was more subtle; he encouraged Henry to start in his favoured position, then cut inside to beat defenders with his pace.

Henry is a different operator from other great strikers. The likes of Van Nistelrooy, Shevchenko, Ronaldo and Raul play through the middle and pop up in the box. All score regularly from close range. All score with headers. Henry rarely scores those "little" goals. His trademark strike is spectacular. He dribbles in from the left at speed, leaves a defender or two in his wake, then unleashes a low, curling right foot shot. His finishing with his left is handy too; he has the close control to tie markers in knots and he can be lethal with free kicks from 30 yards.

His goals propelled Arsenal to the Premiership title in 2002 and 2004 and towards FA Cup wins in 2002, 2003 and 2005. His first contract extension took him up to 2007 and then, after massive speculation, he committed himself to the Gunners until 2010.

Finishing as the Premiership top scorer in 2002, 2004, 2005 and 2006, Henry also surpassed Ian Wright's club goals record of 184 and had totalled more than 200 for the north London club by the end of the 2005-06 season. Henry ended term in style: scoring a hat-trick – and the concluding penalty – in a win over Wigan in Arsenal's last competitive match there before the club's move to a new stadium at Ashburton Grove.

Henry was voted Footballer of the Year a record three times before quitting Arsenal for Barcelona. He was later mired in World Cup controversy after a handball incident ahead of what proved a disastrous 2010 finals campaign.

Thierry Henry won the 2004 and 2005 Golden Boot as the top league marksman in Europe.

1977	1993	1996	1998	2000	2001	2006
Born Essonne, Paris on August 17	Transferred to Monaco	Helped France win European Youth Championship and is voted France's Young Player of the Year	Reached Champions League semi-finals with Monaco. Collected World Cup winner's medal after scoring three goals	Scored 27 goals in all competitions in first season with Arsenal. Won Euro 2000 with France after golden goal defeat of Italy	Arsenal's top scorer with 24 goals. On losing side in the FA Cup Final against Liverpool. Helped Arsenal reach Champions League quarter-finals	Double runner-up at international level with Arsenal in the Champions League and then with France at the World Cup in Germany

1992	1994	1997	1999	2002	2007
Joined FC Versailles after leaving Clairefontaine National Academy	Made top division debut two weeks after his 17th birthday	Signed first pro contract with Monaco and won the championship – scoring nine goals in 36 games. Made senior France debut	Sold to Juventus in January but played only 16 games and joined Arsenal in August for £11 million	Collected Premiership and FA Cup winner's medals with Arsenal 'double' squad. Premiership top scorer – for the first of four times – with 22 goals.	Joined Barcelona in 2007 and helped them win La Liga and the Champions League in 2009.

Glenn Hoddle was the most naturally talented English midfielder of his generation.

Nandor Hidegkuti

National team: Hungary
Born: March 3, 1922
Clubs: Herminamezo, MTK Voros Lobogo

Hidegkuti was the man whose tactical tricks provided the strategical fulcrum for the great Hungarian team of the early 1950s. He marked his national team debut in 1945 by scoring twice but did not gain a regular place until he helped Hungary win Olympic Gold in Helsinki in 1952. Hidegkuti then took over the deep-lying centre-forward role, which opened up goal-scoring gaps for team-mates Puskas and Kocsis. Not that Hidegkuti lost his eye for goal. He totalled 39 goals in his 68 internationals including a hat-trick in the legendary 6-3 win over England at Wembley in 1953.

Fernando Ruiz Hierro

National team: Spain
Born: March 23, 1968
Clubs: Malaga, Valladolid, Real Madrid, Al Rayyan (Qtr), Bolton (Eng)

Hierro graduated to iconic status at Real Madrid after joining in 1989 from Valladolid. Yet he had only been given a chance at Valladolid because his elder brother was at the club. Captain Hierro's greatest match for Madrid was probably the 1998 Champions League Final when his sure-footed tackling inspired victory over Juventus – the first of Hierro's Champions League successes in five seasons. Hierro's eye for goal from midfield and defence meant that, briefly, he was Spain's top international marksman with 29 goals in 89 appearances. He retired from the national team after the 2002 World Cup then quit Spanish soccer altogether in 2003 on being released by Real Madrid 24 hours after captaining them to yet another league title win.

Glenn Hoddle

National team: England
Born: October 27, 1957
Clubs: Tottenham Hotspur, Monaco (Fr), Swindon, Chelsea

Hoddle's playing exploits in the 1980s and early 1990s, when his remarkable talents lit up English soccer, meant he remains an icon at Tottenham even after his spell as manager ended abruptly in the autumn of 2003.

Hoddle played more than 500 matches in midfield for Spurs, winning the UEFA Cup and FA Cup before collecting a league title in France with Monaco under Arsene Wenger. He returned to English soccer successfully as player-manager with Swindon and then Chelsea before taking over England in 1996. Hoddle led England to the second round of the 1998 World Cup before being forced to quit amid controversy over his personal beliefs.

Uli Hoeness

National team: West Germany
Born: January 5, 1952
Clubs: Ulm, Bayern Munich

Hoeness has achieved success as both player and administrator. He burst onto the West German game when the national team won the 1972 European Championship. Remarkably, Hoeness had been a professional for barely two years. Hoeness was an attacking inside-forward who had also proved an overnight sensation with Bayern Munich, with whom he won the European Champions Cup to add to the 1974 World Cup and 1972 European titles. Knee trouble forced an early end to Hoeness's career so he 'transferred' smoothly to the administration to become one of German soccer's most powerful executives.

Myung Bo Hong

National team: South Korea
Born: February 12, 1969
Clubs: Korea University, Sangmoo, Pohang Steelers, Bellmare Hiratsuka (Jpn), Kashiwa Reysol (Jpn), Pohang Steelers

Veteran defender Hong joined the rarefied ranks of players who have appeared in four World Cup finals tournament when he captained co-hosts South Korea on their remarkable 2002 adventure. Hong had been one of the Koreans' outstanding players in the finals in 1990, 1994 – when he scored a superb goal against Germany – and 1998. Injury cost him his place in Korea's team towards the end of 2001 and he was warned by coach Guus Hiddink

that reputation alone would not earn him a recall. He thus worked hard to regain not merely form but also fitness and led Korea, sensationally, to the 2002 World Cup semi-finals. Hong made the first of his 135 international appearances against Norway in February 1990 and the last against Brazil in November 2002.

Geoff Hurst

National team: England
Born: December 8, 1941
Clubs: West Ham United, Stoke City

A big man who was made for the big occasion, the strong and deceptively fast Hurst was frequently mundane in West Ham's toils through their League programmes. But when needed in the big events, he was out of the traps like a greyhound. He scored the remarkable total of 46 goals in the League Cup, 23 in the FA Cup (including a fluke in the 1964 Final) and three in the 1966 World Cup Final, when he appeared virtually from nowhere to put the trophy on the nation's sideboard with his hat-trick against West Germany. Years later, the feat also earned him a knighthood. Like so many big-name players, he failed to achieve similar success in management despite the opportunity of a spell in charge at Londoners Chelsea.

Ivan Hurtado

National team: Ecuador
Born: August 16, 1974
Club(s): Emelec, Celaya (Mex), UNAL (Mex), Puchaca (Mex), Barcelona Guayaquil, Al Arabi (Qtr)

Hurtado, a former striker turned dominant central defender, set a South American record in the run-up to the 2006 World Cup when he reached a total of 57 appearances in qualifying matches. His selection for the finals then extended his own and Ecuador's record of international appearances beyond 130. Hurtado played the bulk of his club career in Mexico and first achieved international recognition as one of the corner stones of the Ecuador side who reached the World Cup finals for the first time in 2002.

Sami Hyypia

National team: Finland

Born-:-October 7, 1973

Clubs: MyPa-47, Willem II (Hol), Liverpool (Eng), Bayer Leverkusen (Ger)

Hyypia wasted no time making his mark at Anfield. Having begun his career with MyPa-47 in Finland, he turned full-time professional with Dutch club Willem II of Tilburg whom he captained in 1999 to a Champions League qualifying place. Hyypia then signed for Liverpool where he formed a solid central defensive partnership with Stephane Henchoz. Hyypia was one of Liverpool's most consistent players in 2000-01 when they won the League Cup, FA Cup and UEFA Cup. Remarkably, he was never shown either a yellow or red card.

Filippo Inzaghi

National team: Italy

Born-: August 9, 1973

Clubs: Piacenza, Leffe, Verona, Piacenza, Parma, Atalanta, Juventus, Milan

Inzaghi has collected a hatful of both goals and honours after his career got off to a stuttering start. He began with hometown Piacenza in Serie B and went on loan to Leffe in the third division and Verona in Serie B before returning to Piacenza. He was sold to Parma in 1995 but made little impression and was given away to Atalanta. Here Inzaghi sprang to goalscoring life with 24 goals in the 1996-97 season to earn a summons to

Jairzinho scored in Brazil's every match on their way to 1970 World Cup glory.

play for Italy and then subsequent big-money transfers to Juventus and then Milan - with whom he won the 2003 and 2007 Champions League.

Denis Irwin

National team: Republic of Ireland

Born: October 31, 1965

Clubs: Leeds United (Eng), Oldham Athletic (Eng), Manchester United (Eng), Wolves (Eng)

Irwin proved a bargain signing for Manchester United when they paid Oldham £650,000 for him in June 1990. The Republic of Ireland full-back brought a touch of steel to United's defence but also contributed significantly to their revival with his goals from free kicks and penalties. Irwin scored 18 goals in more than 500 senior competitive appearances and collected a vast range of 16 honours at domestic and international level topped off by the 1999 treble of Champions League, Premiership and FA Cup.

Valentin Ivanov

National team: Soviet Union

Born-: November 19, 1934

Clubs: Moscow Torpedo

Denis Irwin was United's penalty king.

Ivanov, a skilful inside-right who could both make goals and take them, played for Torpedo for the whole of his career. He scored a then club record of 124 league goals in 287 matches. He also scored a then record 26 goals for the Soviet Union with whom he won the Olympic Games title at Melbourne in 1956. Ivanov played in the 1958 and 1962 World Cup finals and was four-goal joint top scorer at the latter tournament. He also helped the Soviet Union win the first European Championship in 1960. His son, also Valentin, refereed the stormy Portugal v Holland World Cup duel in 2006.

Jairzinho
Full name: Jair Ventura Filho

National team: Brazil

Born: December 25, 1944

Clubs: Botafogo, Marseilles (Fr), Cruzeiro, Portuguesa (Ven)

Jairzinho was the heir to Garrincha's glory, both with Botafogo and with Brazil. He moved from his hometown of Caxias to sign professional with Botafogo at 15, and played in the same

Brazil squad as his hero at the 1966 World Cup. Four years later Jairzinho made history by scoring in every game in every round of the World Cup on the way to victory. He scored seven goals, including two in Brazil's opening win over Czechoslovakia and one in the defeat of Italy in the Final. He tried his luck in Europe with Marseille but returned home after disciplinary problems to win yet another trophy, the South American Club Cup, with Cruzeiro at the age of 32.

Alex James

National team: Scotland

Born: September 14, 1901

Clubs: Raith Rovers, Preston (Eng), Arsenal (Eng)

Eight international caps were a meagre reward for the outstanding inside-forward of the 1930s. James began his career as a fiery attacking player (he was sent off twice in successive matches at Raith), but changed his style to fit Arsenal manager Herbert Chapman's "W" formation. He scored only 26 League goals in eight years at Highbury, but made countless others with his astute passing from deep to the flying wingers or through the middle. Despite his superb display in the 5-1 rout of England by the "Wembley Wizards", James was often thought too clever by the selectors, though not by fans; at club level he won six major medals and undying fame.

Pat Jennings

National team: Northern Ireland
Born: June 12, 1945
Clubs: Newry Town, Watford (Eng), Tottenham Hotspur (Eng), Arsenal (Eng)

A goalkeeper with character and charm to match his size, Jennings even bowed out of soccer in a big way by winning his 119th international cap for Northern Ireland on his 41st birthday – and in a World Cup, too. Only defeat by Brazil marred the occasion. By then Jennings had appeared in well over 1,000 senior matches in a 24-year career, four of them in FA Cup finals. He won with Tottenham Hotspur in 1967 and Arsenal in 1979, lost with Arsenal in 1978 and 1980. Jennings also scored a goal with a clearance from hand during the 1967 Charity Shield against Manchester United. He remains one of Britain's finest ever goalkeepers.

Jimmy Johnstone

National team: Scotland
Born: September 30, 1944
Clubs: Celtic, San José (US), Sheffield United (Eng), Dundee, Shelbourne (Ire)

Johnstone was a remarkably talented winger, but infuriatingly inconsistent, as shown by the fact that his 23 caps were spread over 12 years. Small and nippy, he was an old-style "tanner-ball dribbler" and nicknamed "the Flea". He won 16 winners' medals with Celtic, the club where he started his career – one in the European Cup, eight in the Scottish League, three in the Scottish Cup and four in the Scottish League Cup. Johnstone also earned a reputation for occasional wayward behaviour, on the field and off, but his courage was never in doubt, as many a far bigger opponent found to his cost.

He was particularly effective in the 1966–67 season, when Celtic won every competition they entered, culminating in the European Cup Final defeat of Internazionale in Lisbon.

Robert Jonquet

National team: France
Born: May 3, 1925
Clubs: Reims, Strasbourg

Jonquet, one of the greatest French central defenders, began in Paris with minor clubs Chatenay-Malabry and SS Voltaire. But at 17 he signed out-of-town for Reims with whom he made his name. Cool under pressure, Jonquet first earned international attention with a resolute display as France drew 2-2 with England at Highbury in 1951. His domestic achievements added up to five league titles and two French Cups. He was centre-back for Reims in their Champions Cup Final defeats by Real Madrid in 1956 and 1959.

Juanito
Full name: Juan Gomez Gonzalez

National team: Spain
Born: November 10, 1954

Clubs: Malaga, Burgos, Real Madrid
Juanito, a nimble and aggressive winger-turned-striker, was a favourite with fans but not officials at Madrid in the early 1980s. He was banished as a teenager by Atletico Madrid for squabbling with referees and was also suspended from European competition for three years (later commuted) for a similar incident. In between he starred at the 1978 and 1982 World Cup finals and was a Champions Cup runner-up with Madrid in 1981.

Oliver Kahn

National team: Germany
Born: June 15, 1969
Clubs: Karlsruhe, Bayern Munich

Kahn was voted top player at the 2002 World Cup at which Germany finished runners-up. Originally making his name with Karlsruhe, he joined Bayern in 1994 and subsequently won the European Champions League as well as the German League and Cup. Kahn, who has twice been voted Footballer of the Year, was a member of the German squad at the 1994 World Cup finals in the United States but did not make his international debut until a year later in a 2-1 win

over Switzerland in Bern. He became national No 1 after the 1998 World Cup and graduated to captaincy of both club and country. He was replaced controversially by Jens Lehmann for the 2006 World Cup despite having just won two successive league and cup doubles with Bayern.

Sotiris Kaiafas

National team: Cyprus
Born: December 18, 1949
Clubs: Omonia Nicosia

Centre-forward Kaiafas was the hero of Omonia Nicosia in the 1970s and ranks as perhaps the greatest footballer ever produced by Cyprus. In 1975-76 he became the first and last Cypriot player to win the Golden Boot as European's leading league scorer with 39 goals. Kaiafas was top league marksman eight times in 11 years including four years in a row from 1979. His goals contributed decisively to Omonia winning the championship nine times in those 11 years.

Kaka

SEE PAGE 185

Roy Keane

National team: Republic Ireland
Born: August 10, 1971
Clubs: Cobh Ramblers, Nottm Forest (Eng), Manchester Utd (Eng), Celtic (Scot)

Keane ranks among Old Trafford legends for captaining Manchester United aggressively to sustained success, particularly between 1998 and 2005. He won 11 domestic trophies with United but unluckily missed the 1999 Champions League victory over Bayern Munich through suspension. Keane's fortright style led him, famously, to label a section of United's crowd as the "prawn sandwich brigade." At national team level he also had a falling-out with then manager Mick McCarthy on the eve of the 2002 World Cup finals in Korea and Japan. Later he moved into management with mixed results at Sunderland and Ipswich.

Republic of Ireland and Manchester United midfielder Roy Keane was a successful no-nonsense enforcer.

KAKA
Grace and goals

Kaka's career has been outstanding enough but a remarkable extra factor in his success is the fact that Ricardo Ezecson dos Santos Leite was almost paralysed as an 18-year-old, after fracturing his spine when he toppled from a swimming pool's diving board.

He recovered not only to play professional soccer with his local club Sao Paulo but blossom into one of the finest players of his era, meandering gracefully and intelligently between midfield and attack, linking the constructive play then finding space in the penalty box to score a steady stream of goals.

Kaka made his debut on the grand stage as a member of Brazil's triumphant World Cup-winning squad in South Korea and Japan in 2002 though he played only 25 minutes. His form and style had already alerted Milan who swooped early the following year to buy him for £5.5m.

Kaka's vision, poise on the ball and prolific strike-rate from a support-striker role made him an icon among supporters at the Stadio Meazza in San Siro and one of his greatest admirers was an important one in club president and owner Silvio Berlusconi.

Outstanding performances as Milan reached Champions League Final in 2005 were forgotten after the Rossoneri conceded a three-goal half-time lead to remarkably resurgent Liverpool and ultimately lost in a penalty shootout.

Then further disappointment

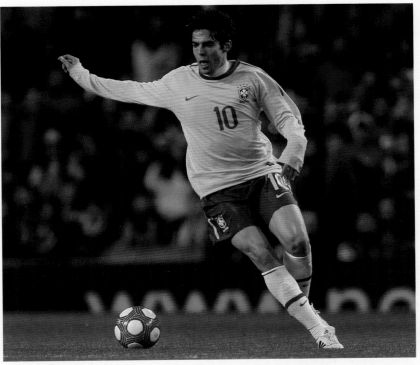

Kaka provided flair and skill in an otherwise less than flamboyant Brazilian squad coached by Dunga.

followed the next year when Kaka was a key member of the Brazilian side who, under Carlos Alberto Parreira, fell to France and thus lost their world champions' crown in the quarter-finals of the 2006 World Cup finals.

Kaka was spared much of the criticism thrown the way of coach and team-mates and raised his profile further in 2007 when he masterminded Milan's revenge victory over Liverpool in another Champions League Final showdown in Athens. Milan won 2-1 and Kaka set up both their goals for Pippo Inzaghi. His reward was not only a winner's medal but subsequent acclaim as international federation FIFA's World Footballer of the Year in 2007.

Reports that Milan were heading for financial problems sparked speculation that Kaka might be sold and Milan stood firm before being unable to resist Real Madrid when they offered a then world record £50m in 2009.

Kaka's initial Spanish campaign was a frustrating one as he missed significant chunks of the action through injury and it was questionable whether he was fully fit when he joined up with Brazil's squad for the World Cup finals in South Africa.

The previous summer Kaka had been outstanding when Brazil won the Confederations Cup.

Back in South Africa, however, saw Brazil unable to find the same winning rhythm, and both his and his country's campaign ended in defeat by Holland in the quarter-finals.

1982	2000	2002	2004	2008
Born Ricardo Ezecson dos Santos Leite on April 22 in Brasilia	Told he would never play again after injuring his back in a swimming pool accident	Member of Brazil's World Cup-winning squad in Korea and Japan	Became youngest ambassador of the United Nations' World Food Programme	Named by *Time* magazine among the world's 100 most influential people

1997	2001	2003	2007	2009
Turned professional with Sao Paulo	Won first senior title, in Rio-Sao Paulo Torneo, with Sao Paulo	Sold to Milan by Sao Paulo for £5.5m	Voted World and European Player of the Year; 10-goal Champions League top scorer	Sold to Real Madrid for £50 million; voted best player at the Confederations Cup

Kevin Keegan was a European winner with Liverpool and loser with Hamburg.

Kevin Keegan

National team: England
Born: February 14, 1951
Clubs: Scunthorpe, Liverpool, Hamburg (Ger), Southampton, Newcastle

Keegan, the only British player to win the European Footballer of the Year award twice, cost Liverpool a bargain £35,000 when he was signed from Scunthorpe United in 1971. He was an overnight success, first in his original position of outside-right, then as a free-ranging attacking raider. Keegan won two league titles with Liverpool, leaving for German club Hamburg after the Reds' triumph in the European Cup Final of 1977. He was a European Cup Final loser with Hamburg against Nottingham Forest in 1980 before breathing new life into Southampton and then Newcastle. Management roles followed with Newcastle, Fulham and Manchester City as well as short ill-fated spell with the England national team. He resigned after a 0-1 loss to Germany in the last game at Wembley Stadium.

Jack Kelsey

National team: Wales
Born: November 19, 1929
Clubs: Arsenal (Eng)

"Big Jack" won 43 caps in goal for Wales and played for Britain against the Rest of Europe in 1955. That was a fine record, considering he had been beaten five times on his debut for Arsenal in 1951. Kelsey then went on to be first choice for 11 years until a spinal injury, in a collision with Vava of Brazil, forced him to retire. He remained a familiar figure at Highbury as manager of the club shop, with a fund of reminiscences about his time in the game. He was powerful enough to withstand the challenges of an age when keepers were not well protected, and agile enough to make many remarkable stops, helped by rubbing chewing gum into his palms.

Mario Alberto Kempes

National team: Argentina
Born: July 15, 1952
Clubs: Instituto Cordoba, Rosario Central, Valencia (Sp), River Plate, Hercules (Sp), Vienna (Aut), Austria Salzburg (Aut)

Kempes, an aggressive young striker with legs like tree trunks, had his first taste of World Cup soccer in West Germany in 1974. He swiftly earned a transfer to Spain with Valencia, where he developed into such a threat to opposing defences that he was the only foreign-based player recalled to join the hosts' World Cup squad under Cesar Luis Menotti in 1978. His addition proved decisive: Kempes was the event's top scorer with six goals, including two in the 3-1 defeat of Holland in the Final. Strangely, he was never able to scale those heights again, despite playing once more for Argentina in the 1982 finals in Spain, where he should have felt at home.

Harry Kewell

National team: Australia
Born: September 22, 1978
Clubs: Leeds United (Eng), Liverpool (Eng), Galatasaray (Tur)

An injury and suspension-jinxed star of Australia's 2006 and 2010 World Cup campaigns, Kewell never played as a pro back home. Instead the Sydney-born forward flew directly from the famed Australian Academy of Sport to England in December 1995 to sign for Leeds United. After a few fleeting appearances in his first two years he established himself with five goals in 29 games in 1997–98 and was one of the stars of the team that, guided by David O'Leary, reached the semi-finals of the Champions League in 2001. He followed up with 11 goals in 2002 and 16 in 2003 but was then sold to Liverpool for £6 million in the fire sale that followed Leeds United's relegation and collapse to the brink of financial disaster.

Ove Kindvall

National team: Sweden
Born: May 16, 1943
Clubs: Norrkoping, Feyenoord (Hol), Norrkoping

Kindvall scored 126 goals in five seasons in Holland with Feyenoord after being vastly underrated on his arrival from hometown Norrkoping. Three times he was top scorer in the

Harry Kewell was an academy award-winner.

Dutch league and he also scored the extra-time winner against Celtic in the Champions Cup Final in the San Siro, Milan, in 1970. A few months later Kindvall also scored in Feyenoord's World Club win over Estudiantes de La Plata. Kindvall led Sweden's attack at the 1970 and 1974 World Cups.

Jürgen Klinsmann

National team: Germany
Born: July 30, 1964
Clubs: Stuttgart Kickers, VfB Stuttgart, Internazionale (It), Monaco (Fr), Tottenham Hotspur (Eng), Bayern Munich, Sampdoria (It), Tottenham Hotspur (Eng)

Jürgen Klinsmann needed little time before breaking through as the German league's top scorer and the country's Footballer of the Year during his first Bundesliga spell with VfB Stuttgart, whom he also led to the UEFA Cup Final in 1989. He then spent three successful years at Internazionale in Italy before moving to France with Monaco and then to England with Tottenham (where he spent two spells) before returning to Germany and Bayern Munich in July 1995. A year later Bayern won the UEFA Cup with Klinsmann contributing a European club competition record of 15 goals in a season. He was a World Cup and European title-winner in 1990 and 1996 respectively then later made a remarkable managerial debut in guiding hosts Germany to the semi-finals of the 2006 World Cup.

Miroslav Klose

National team: Germany
Born: June 9, 1978
Clubs: Kaiserslautern, Werder Bremen, Bayern Munich

Klose's four goals for third-placed Germany in the 2010 World Cup placed him second, one goal behind 15-goal Ronaldo, as the event's all-time top scorer. Polish-born Klose started with Kaiserslautern and was always determined to play international soccer for Germany. He even scored the winning goal in both of his first two internationals – against Albania and Greece in World Cup qualifying matches in March 2001. Klose was the Lauterers' top scorer in both 2001 and 2002 and also helped them reach the 2001 UEFA Cup semi-finals. He exploded on the World Cup finals with a hat-trick of headers against Saudi Arabia in the 2002 finals and followed up by finishing five-goal top scorer with hosts Germany in 2006.

Patrick Kluivert

National team: Holland
Born: September 1, 1976
Clubs: Schellingewoude, Ajax, Milan (It), Barcelona, Newcastle United (Eng), Valencia (Sp)

Centre-forward Kluivert is, to many experts, the finest natural Dutch talent since Johan Cruyff. A product of the noted Ajax junior system, he made a sensational debut at 18 in a 3-0 win over old rivals Feyenoord in the 1994 Dutch Supercup. Another Supercup success fell his way in 1995 as well as Dutch league crowns in 1995 and 1996. He also scored the goal with which Ajax beat Milan to win the Champions Cup in Vienna in 1995 and helped them win the 1995 World Club Cup and European Supercup. The following year, Kluivert scored both goals in the 2-0 defeat of the Republic of Ireland in the Euro 96 qualifying play-offs. He took advantage of the Bosman ruling to transfer fee-free to Milan in 1997, but

Kluivert was the ultimate teenage superstar.

his career in Italy was overshadowed by a court case resulting from a fatal car crash in Holland. It took a further move to Spain with Barcelona before he fulfilled his goal-grabbing potential.

Sandor Kocsis

National team: Hungary
Born: September 30, 1929
Clubs: Ferencvaros, Honved, Young Fellows (Swz), Barcelona (Sp)

Kocsis was an attacking inside-right for Honved and Hungary in the early 1950s. He and fellow inside-forward Puskas pushed forward while the nominal centre-forward withdrew towards midfield, creating gaps for the others to exploit. Kocsis did so to the extent of 75 goals in 68 internationals. He was three times the Hungarian league's top scorer, as well as the leading marksman, with 11 goals, at the 1954 World Cup finals. After the Hungarian Revolution of 1956 Kocsis decided to stay abroad and joined Barcelona with further success, winning the Fairs Cup in 1960. A year later Kocsis was on the losing side with Barcelona at the European Cup Final against Benfica in Bern.

Ivan Kolev

National team: Bulgaria
Born: November 1, 1930
Clubs: CDNA/CSKA Sofia

Kolev was the first great Bulgarian footballer, often compared for control and vision with Hungarian contemporary Ferenc Puskas. Kolev, who could play outside- or inside-left, spent his whole career with the Bulgarian army club, variously known as CDNA and then CSKA Sofia. He scored 25 goals in 75 internationals and led Bulgaria on their first appearance at a major soccer tournament in the 1952 Helsinki Olympic Games. He won the Bulgaria championship on 11 occasions and the Cup four times.

Ronald Koeman

National team: Holland
Born: March 21, 1963

Club(s): Groningen, PSV Eindhoven, Barcelona (Sp)
Koeman was admired not only as one of the world's best sweepers but as one of the finest free-kick experts. It was from a dead-ball opportunity that he thundered in Barcelona's winner in the 1992 Champions Cup, a trophy he also won with PSV Eindhoven in 1988. Koeman and brother Erwin began with their father's old club, Groningen and were later both members of the Holland side that won the 1988 European title. That same year Ronald also won the treble of Champions Cup, Dutch league and Cup. He joined Barcelona in 1989, winning four Spanish league titles as well as the Champions Cup.

Jürgen Kohler

National team: West Germany
Born: October 6, 1965
Clubs: Jahn Lambsheim, Waldhof-Mannheim, Koln, Bayern Munich, Juventus (It), Borussia Dortmund

Kohler was perhaps the best man-marking stopper in European soccer in the 1990s. He made his name with Waldhof-Mannheim then Koln – who sold him to Bayern for a then defender's record of £1 million in 1989. He was sold on to Juventus in 1991 for £5 million, then another world record for a defender. A World Cup winner in 1990 he was, with Juventus, a UEFA Cup winner in 1993 and Italian League champion in 1995. He returned to Germany in the summer of 1995 with Borussia Dortmund whom he helped beat his old Juventus teammates in the 1997 Champions League Final.

Raymond Kopa

National team: France
Born: October 13, 1931
Clubs: Angers, Reims, Real Madrid (Sp), Reims
Born Kopaszewski, the son of an immigrant Polish miner, Kopa gained an added incentive to escape from a mining future when he damaged a hand in a pit accident as a teenager. He was spotted by Angers and then sold on to Reims in 1950. Originally a right-winger, Kopa soon switched to a

creative centre- or inside-forward role. He led Reims to the first European Cup Final in 1956, being transferred afterwards to their conquerors on the day, Real Madrid. Kopa starred in midfield for third-placed France at the 1958 World Cup, and returned to Reims a year later as European Footballer of the Year. He played 45 times for France but his playing career ended amid controversy over his outspoken espousal of the cause of freedom of contract.

Johannes "Hans" Krankl

National team: Austria
Born: February 14, 1953
Clubs: Rapid Vienna, Barcelona (Sp), 1st FC Vienna, Barcelona (Sp), Rapid Vienna, Wiener Sportclub

For Krankl everything happened in 1978. He scored 41 goals for Rapid Vienna, to win the Golden Boot as Euorpe's leading league marksman, and starred for Austria at the World Cup finals in Argentina. He joined Barcelona and inspired their victory in the 1979 European Cup-Winners' Cup.

Frank Lampard, a formidable goalscoring midfielder.

Serious injury in a car crash interrupted Krankl's career in Spain and he went home to Austria briefly. Later he returned to Rapid, becoming general manager after retiring. Krankl scored 34 goals in 69 internationals and was top league scorer four times in Austria and once in Spain. He later became national team manager.

Ruud "Rudi" Krol

National team: Holland
Born: March 24, 1949
Clubs: Ajax, Napoli (It)

Krol was one of the pillars of the Dutch "total football" revolution. He played left-back for Ajax in their three Champions Cup victories between 1971 and 1973 and was a World Cup runner-up against West Germany in Munich in 1974 and then again against Argentina in Buenos Aires in 1978. Krol's pace, intelligence and recuperative powers meant he was ideally suited to the inter-changing system developed by the Dutch under innovative coach Rinus Michels. Later Krol impressed Italian soccer with his imaginative interpretation of the sweeper's role while at Napoli.

Ladislav Kubala

National teams: Czechoslovakia, Hungary, Spain
Born: June 10, 1927
Clubs: Ferencvaros (Hun), Bratislava (Cz), Vasas Budapest (Cz), Barcelona (Sp), Español (Sp), FC Zurich (Swz), Toronto Falcons (Can)

One of the ironies of 1950s soccer was that Hungary created a great team without one of their very greatest players. Centre- or inside-forward Kubala had escaped to the West after having played international soccer for both Czechoslovakia and Hungary in the late 1940s. In exile in Italy, Kubala formed a refugees' team called Pro Patria that played exhibition tours and provided him with the springboard to join Spain's Barcelona. There Kubala was Spanish champion five times and twice won the Fairs Cup. He also gained international recognition with a third country, winning 19 caps for Spain to

add to his seven for Czechoslovakia and three for Hungary. He left Barcelona after the 1961 European Cup Final defeat by Benfica, but later returned to coach both Barcelona and the Spanish national team.

Angel Amadeo Labruna

National team: Argentina
Born: September 26, 1918
Clubs: River Plate, Platense, Green Cross (Chile), Rampla Juniors (Uru)

Labruna remains one of the greatest Argentine soccer personalities of all time. Not only was he a great inside-left, but he earned longevity records by playing with River Plate for 29 years and won a reputation as a South American Stanley Matthews by playing on until he was 41. At the 1958 World Cup finals in Sweden, Labruna was recalled at the age of 40 to complete an international career which brought him 17 goals in 36 games for Argentina. Labruna began with River Plate when he was 12 and won nine league championships. In the late 1940s he was a member of the legendary Maquina, or "Machine", forward line. In 1986 Labruna was coach when River at last won the South American Club Cup.

Frank Lampard

National team: England
Born: June 20, 1978
Club(s): West Ham United, Chelsea

Lampard, whose father (also Frank) was a West Ham stalwart and then coach, has been one of the most consistently outstanding midfielders in the Premiership since moving from East to West London with Chelsea in 2001. Lampard cost £11 million but has more than repaid the outlay with a stream of goals from midfield in Chelsea's Premier title-winning seasons in 2005, 2006 and 2010. His efforts efforts earned player of the year awards in 2005 from England fans and the Football Writers' Association. Lampard made his England debut in a 2-1 win over Belgium in October 1999, scored

Henrik Larsson won a Premiership winner's medal with Manchester United aged 35.

three goals at the finals of Euro 2004 in Portugal but failed, crucially, to find the net in the World Cup finals efforts of both 2006 and 2010.

Henrik Larsson

National team: Sweden
Born: September 20, 1971
Clubs: Helsingborgs, Feyenoord (Hol), Celtic (Scot), Barcelona (Sp), Helsingborgs, Manchester United (Eng)

Larsson was a winger rather than an out-and-out striker when he made his debut for Sweden against Finland in October 1993, soon after transferring to Dutch giants Feyenoord from Helsingborgs. The following year he helped unheralded Sweden finish a surprising third at the World Cup finals in the United States and also inspired Feyenoord to two Dutch Cup successes before being sold to Celtic in 1997. A serious leg injury in 1999-2000 threatened his career but he returned just in time to play for Sweden at the European Championship finals. The next season he scored a remarkable 53 goals all-in and led Celtic to the Scottish treble of League, League Cup and SFA Cup. He then moved to Barcelona and played a key role in the 2006 Champions League success. He returned to Helsingborgs, but enjoyed one last hurrah during a loan spell at Manchester United.

Grzegorz Lato

National team: Poland

Born: April 8, 1950

Clubs: Stal Mielec, Lokeren (Bel), Atlante (Mex)

Lato was a Polish phenomenon, an outstanding striker who later proved equally influential when he moved back into midfield. He made his debut for Poland against Spain in 1971 and won an Olympic gold medal in Munich a year later. Lato became a fixture in the senior national team in 1973, after impressing manager Kazimierz Gorski, and he went on to score 46 goals in 104 internationals – a Polish record – including seven goals at the 1974 World Cup finals where he was top scorer. After leading Poland's attack at the 1978 World Cup finals, Lato moved to Belgium, and he ended his career in Mexico.

Brian Laudrup

National team: Denmark

Born: February 22, 1969

Clubs: Brondbyernes, Bayer Uerdigen (Ger), Bayern Munich (Ger), Fiorentina (It), Milan (It), Glasgow Rangers (Scot), Chelsea (Eng), FC Kobenhavn, Ajax (Hol)

Brian, Michael's younger brother, maintained the pride of the Laudrup family to great effect – starting with a Danish Cup win with Brondby in 1989. He then starred in the 1992 European Championship triumph when his brother would not play after a row with coach Richard Moller Nielsen over which position suited Brian best. Spells in Germany and Italy followed before a move to Scotland with Rangers reignited his career. He was the first foreigner to be voted Scotland's Footballer of the Year and was Player of the Year a record three times in Denmark.

Michael Laudrup

National team: Denmark

Born: June 15, 1964

Clubs: Brondbyernes, Lazio (It), Juventus (It), Barcelona (Sp), Real Madrid (Sp), Vissel Kobe (Jap), Ajax (Hol)

Michael and brother Brian are sons of a former Danish international, Finn Laudrup. Michael, as a teenager, attracted scouts from all Europe's top clubs but finally chose Juventus, who loaned him to Lazio before recalling him to replace Poland's Zbigniew Boniek. With Juventus, Laudrup won the World Club Cup before moving on to win the European Cup with Barcelona. He starred at the 1986 World Cup finals before falling out with Denmark's national manager Richard Moller Nielsen and thus missing the 1992 European Championship triumph. But he was back for the 1998 World Cup finals in France and was named in the FIFA team of the tournament before retiring.

Denis Law

National team: Scotland

Born: February 22, 1940

Clubs: Huddersfield (Eng), Manchester City (Eng), Torino (It), Manchester United (Eng), Manchester City (Eng)

Denis Law and Jimmy Greaves were born within four days of each other, and spent several years as rival scorers and supreme entertainers. Law, of medium height and slim in build, had a lion's heart and a salmon's leap, scoring many spectacular headed goals. He was also an incisive passer of the ball, and a fierce competitor. Suspensions and injury cost him many more goals. He was European Footballer of the Year in 1964, won two league titles and the 1963 FA Cup, and scored 30 goals in 55 internationals, but missed United's European Cup victory in 1968 through knee trouble.

Tommy Lawton

National team: England

Born: October 6, 1919

Clubs: Burnley, Everton, Chelsea, Notts County, Brentford, Arsenal

One of the first players to realize what his market value was – and to work at getting it – Lawton made frequent moves at a time when there was rarely any percentage for a transferred player. Lawton was a star from his dubbin-smothered toe-caps

Denis Law was the only Scot to win the European Footballer of the Year crown.

to his glistening centre parting. He got a hat-trick on his senior debut aged 16, was the First Division top scorer two years in a row, won a title medal aged 19, scored 23 goals in 22 full internationals, and goals by the dozen during the Second World War. Lawton was still frightening foes deep into his 30s and pulling in fans everywhere he went.

Leonidas da Silva

National team: Brazil

Born: November 11, 1910

Clubs: Havanesa, Barroso, Sul Americano, Sirio Libanes, Bomsucesso, Nacional (Uru), Vasco da Gama, Botafogo, Flamengo, São Paulo

Leonidas was Brazil's 1930s superstar, although he played only 23 times for his country. He was the inventor of the overhead bicycle kick, which was unveiled to the international game when he scored twice on his international debut against Uruguay in 1932. The Uruguayans were so impressed he was immediately signed by the top club, Nacional. Later he returned home with Vasco da Gama and was top scorer at the 1938 World Cup with eight goals, including four in a 6-5 victory over Poland. Unfortunately, an overconfident management rested Leonidas from the semi-final against Italy, wanting to keep him fresh for the Final... and they lost.

Billy Liddell

National team: Scotland

Born: January 10, 1922

Club: Liverpool (Eng)

An accountant, Justice of the Peace and youth worker, Liddell the player is still revered as one of the greatest players in Liverpool's history, which is saying a great deal. Liddell missed six years on war service and spent his whole career with one club. Apart from the championship in 1947 and a cup final defeat three years later,

Gary Lineker was six-goal top scorer at the 1986 World Cup finals in Mexico, including a hat-trick against Poland in the last of the group matches.

Liverpool achieved little during Liddell's 15 years there, but he set club records with 492 league appearances and 216 goals.

Nils Liedholm

National team: Sweden
Born: October 8, 1922
Clubs: Norrköping, Milan (It)

Liedholm originally played at inside-forward, he later moved back to wing-half and finally, in his veteran years, became one of the best sweepers of all time. He began with Norrkoping, winning two championship medals and playing 18 times for his country. After helping Sweden win the 1948 Olympic title from outside-left, he moved to Italy. There Liedholm formed Milan's celebrated trio with Gunnar Gren and Gunnar Nordahl and he scored 60 goals in 367 league games. At the end of his career Liedholm captained hosts Sweden to runners-up spot at the 1958 World Cup finals.

Gary Lineker

National team: England
Born: November 30, 1960
Clubs: Leicester, Everton, Barcelona (Sp), Tottenham Hotspur, Nagoya Grampus 8 (Jap)

All sorts of records fell to this unassuming son of a market trader, who accepted good and bad with the smiling sincerity that, allied to his skill, made him such a popular figure. This was never more evident than in the desperate days when serious illness struck his first-born son. He went within one goal of England's 49-goal scoring record, ten coming in World Cup final stages, was top First Division marksman with three different clubs, scored a hat-trick for Barcelona against Real Madrid, and won the FA Cup despite missing a penalty. Lineker retired after two injury-plagued seasons in Japan, and immediately became a popular tv broadcaster.

Jari Litmanen

National team: Finland
Born: February 20, 1971
Clubs: Reipas Lahti, HJK Helsinki, MyPa, Ajax (Hol), Barcelona (Sp), Liverpool (Eng), Ajax (Hol)

Litmanen achieved history when he helped Ajax win the Champions Cup Final against Milan in 1995. He thus became the first Finnish player to lay hands on European club soccer's most prestigious trophy. Litmanen had left Finland for Holland and Ajax in 1992 and scored 91 goals in 159 games before following his mentor, Louis Van Gaal, to Barcelona in 1999. Injuries and then the departure of Van Gaal kept him on the sidelines however and he was delighted to transfer to Liverpool, his boyhood favourites. However, a wrist injury suffered playing for Finland in a World Cup qualifier pushed him back in the queue for places and he returned to Ajax in 2002.

Pierre Littbarski

National team: Germany
Born: April 16, 1960
Clubs: Hertha Zehlendorf, Köln, Racing Paris (Fr), Köln, JEF United (Jap)

Littbarski, an outside-right who later took his dribbling skills back into midfield, shot to prominence by hitting two goals on his debut for West Germany in a World Cup qualifier against Austria in 1981. He joined Koln, the club with which he is most associated, in 1978, played in the 1982 and 1986 World Cup Finals and finally achieved victory in Italy in 1990. Before heading out to Japan to wind down his career, Littbarski described his career ambition as "scoring a goal after beating all ten outfield players, dribbling round the goalkeeper and putting the ball in the net with a back-heel".

Bixente Lizarazu

National team: France
Born: December 9, 1969
Clubs: Bordeaux, Athletic Bilbao (Sp), Bayern Munich (Ger), Marseille

Lizarazu has won almost every major prize in the game with both clubs and country. He rose through the youth ranks at Bordeaux to become an under-21 international, before being promoted to the senior team, making his debut against Finland in 1992 and going on to win the World Cup and European Championship. An attacking left wing-back, he scored nine goals in the 1993–94 French League campaign before moving to Athletic Bilbao and then on to Bayern Munich with whom he won the treble of Champions League, World Club Cup and German Bundesliga in 2001.

Wlodzimierz Lubanski

National team: Poland
Born: February 28, 1947
Clubs: GKS Gliwice, Gornik Zabrze, Lokeren (Bel), Valenciennes (Fr), Quimper (Fr), Lokeren (Bel)

Lubanski ranks among Poland's finest players despite being plagued by injury. He emerged with the miners' club, Gornik, in the mid-1960s, taking over the mantle of inspiration with both club and country from Ernest Pol. Lubanski was four times top league marksman in Poland and captained his country to the 1972 Olympic Games victory in Munich. The following year he suffered a serious thigh injury in a World Cup qualifier against England and missed the finals in which Poland finished third. He returned to national team duty at the 1978 finals in Argentina, before winding down his career in Belgium and France.

Ally McCoist

National team: Scotland
Born: September 24, 1962
Clubs: St Johnstone, Sunderland (Eng), Glasgow Rangers, Kilmarnock

A lively striker who survived a disastrous spell in England to become a hugely successful and popular player back in his homeland, McCoist started at St Johnstone, who earned a club record £400,000 when selling him to Sunderland in 1981. After 56 games and only eight goals, he was sold to Rangers, and began a decade of almost constant medal-collecting

Sammy McIlroy was commitment personified as both player and manager.

as the club dominated the Scottish game. He won the Golden Boot as Europe's leading league marksman and recovered from a broken leg to smash the legendary Bob McPhail's record of 233 league goals for Rangers. His one disappointment was being left out of Scotland's 1998 World Cup finals squad.

Paul McGrath

National team: Republic of Ireland
Born: December 4, 1959
Clubs: Manchester United (Eng), Aston Villa (Eng), Derby Co (Eng)

English-born McGrath was a fine player whose career was dogged by bad luck and – on occasions – lack of self-discipline. Born in Middlesex of Irish parentage, McGrath made troubled progress through Manchester United's junior ranks and on into the senior squad, with injuries and authority combining to hinder him. But manager Ron Atkinson kept faith and took McGrath with him when he moved to Villa. As a club player one FA Cup win in 1985 – he performed heroically for ten-man United – was poor reward for his

talents. As an international for the Republic of Ireland, his considerable skill and total commitment made him a folk hero among the Irish fans during European Championship and World Cup campaigns.

Jimmy McIlroy

National team: Northern Ireland
Born: October 25, 1931
Clubs: Glentoran, Burnley (Eng), Stoke (Eng), Oldham (Eng)

If Danny Blanchflower was the key man of the Irish World Cup campaign in 1958, Jimmy McIlroy was only a little way behind him. His unhurried, elegant work at inside-forward proved ideal for the tactics devised by team manager Peter Doherty. Altogether McIlroy played 55 games for his country, to go with more than 600 at club level, earning a Championship medal with the attractive young Burnley squad in 1960, and a runners-up medal in the FA Cup two years later – against Blanchflower's Spurs. He later enjoyed a brief but brilliant combination with Stanley Matthews at Stoke.

Sammy McIlroy

National team: Northern Ireland
Born: August 1, 1954
Clubs: Manchester United (Eng), Stoke (Eng), Manchester City (Eng)

Another valuable midfielder, like his namesake, but of a totally different type. Sammy McIlroy's all-action style was in complete contrast to Jimmy's deliberate method, but was ideally suited to the hurly-burly of the modern game. It earned him 88 games for his country, spread over 15 years, but only five goals. He also played in three FA Cup Finals with United, losing to Southampton in 1976 and Arsenal in 1979, beating Liverpool in 1977. He later turned to management, guiding Macclesfield up into the Football League before undertaking a three-year stint as Northern Ireland boss. Back in club soccer with Morecambe, he took them up into the Football League.

Billy McNeill

National team: Scotland
Born: March 2, 1940
Clubs: Celtic

The nickname "Caesar" suited McNeill. In both size and style he was a big man, and was the hub of the Celtic defence during their great days of the 1960s. He won a host of domestic medals and, in 1967, as captain of Celtic, he became the first Briton to lift the European Cup, the most coveted prize in club soccer. He was educated at a rugby-playing school, but made up for a late introduction to soccer with years of splendid service and a club record number of appearances. McNeill's international debut was in the 9–3 mauling by England in 1961, but he recovered to gain 28 more caps. McNeill was later manager of his old club (twice), as well as Aston Villa and Manchester City.

Paul McStay

National team: Scotland
Born: October 22, 1964
Clubs: Celtic

This product of Hamilton played for his country as a schoolboy, at youth level, in the Under-21 team and then in the full national squad. He made his senior debut against Uruguay in 1983 and plied his creative midfield trade to such good effect that he made 76 appearances, becoming Celtic's most capped player. McStay's loyalty to Celtic was admirable, and he gave good value for his high earnings in a period when his club was overshadowed by Rangers. He sadly missed the 1996 European Championships through injury and retired from professional soccer in 1997.

Josef "Sepp" Maier

National team: West Germany
Born: February 28, 1944
Clubs: TSV Haar, Bayern Munich

Maier's career peaked in 1974 when he won the European Cup with Bayern Munich and the World Cup with West

Germany on his home ground, the Olympistadion in the Bavarian capital. He was noted, apart from his goalkeeping talent, for his trademark long shorts, outsized gloves and a love of tennis. Maier even opened a tennis school thanks to the money he earned in a 19-year career with Bayern from 1960 to 1979. Maier played 473 league matches, including a run of 422 consecutive games. He made his international debut in 1966, and he was the No. 3 goalkeeper in West Germany's World Cup squad in England. However, he soon became first-choice and was a member of West Germany's European Championship-winning side against the Soviet Union in Brussels in 1972. Maier won the European Cup three times with Bayern as well as the World Club Cup in 1976.

Roy Makaay
National team: Holland
Born: March 9, 1975
Clubss: Vitesse Arnhem, Tenerife (Sp), Deportivo La Coruna (Sp) Bayern Munich (Ger), Feyenoord
Bayern splashed a club record £12 million in the summer of 2003 to buy Dutch striker Makaay from Spanish club Deportivo La Coruna. He had earned that valuation with 29 goals in Spain the previous season, which also secured him the prize of the Golden Boot as the leading marksman in mainstream European league action. Makaay made a slow start to his new career in Germany but then he opened up by helping Bayern to win the league and cup double and successive seasons. International club soccer was particularly important for Makaay given that competition for places in the Holland side restricted his opportunities with his national team.

Paolo Maldini
SEE PAGE 193

Diego Maradona
SEE PAGE 194

Silvio Marzolini
National team: Argentina
Born: October 4, 1940
Clubs: Ferro Carril Oeste, Boca Juniors
To many experts, and not only Argentines, Marzolini is the finest full-back of the modern era. He was a left-back who could tackle and intercept with the best of them but also displayed the technique and virtuoso skill of a forward when he had the opportunity to go on a foray into attack. At only 13 Marzolini won the Buenos Aires youth title with Ferro Carril Oeste and became a First Division regular at 19. In 1960 he was bought by Boca Juniors, winning the league title in 1962, 1964 and 1965. He played in the World Cup finals of 1962 and 1966 – where he rose above all the unpleasant mayhem of the quarter-final defeat by England. After retirement he enjoyed some success as a TV and film actor before he returned to Boca as coach and took them to the league title in 1981. He was forced to retire because of a heart condition.

Josef Masopust
National team: Czechoslovakia
Born: February 9, 1931
Clubs: Union Teplice, Dukla Prague, Crossing Molenbeek (Bel)
Masopust is the only man from the old Czechoslovakia to have won the European Footballer of the Year award, which he collected in 1962 after an outstanding World Cup campaign in Chile – Pavel Nedved from the Cech Republic has subsequently been awarded it. Czechoslovakia finished runners-up to Brazil, and Masopust scored the opening goal in the Final, which they ultimately lost 3-1. Originally an inside-forward, Masopust made his name as a left-half but was essentially more of an old-fashioned centre-half, preferring a central position in midfield, both for Czechoslovakia and the army club Dukla.

Marco Materazzi
National team: Italy
Born: August 19, 1973
Clubs: Perugia, Carpi, Everton (Eng), Perugia, Internazionale
Materazzi was always considered a support player, a cog in the engine room, until the 2006 World Cup. Injury to Alessandro Nesta saw him promoted to Italy's starting line-up from the substitutes' bench but the Final began disastrously when he conceded the penalty from which France went ahead. The central defender made amends by heading Italy's equaliser and was then at the centre of the defining controversy when his remarks provoked Zinedine Zidane's headbutt and expulsion. Materazzi also had the last word, converting Italy's second spot-kick in their shoot-out victory. Simultaneously, his defensive qualities served Internazionale well in their four league and two cup triumphs between 2006 and 2009.

Lothar Matthäus
National team: West Germany
Born: March 21, 1961
Clubs: Borussia Monchengladbach, Bayern Munich, Internazionale (It), Bayern Munich, New York-New Jersey MetroStars (US)
Matthäus was Germany's outstanding leader from midfield – and, later, sweeper – from the early 1980s. His career reached its zenith in 1990 when he was not only West Germany's World Cup-winning captain in Rome, but also voted Player of the Tournament by the world's media. Matthäus was a substitute for West Germany's 1980 European Championship-winning side and only established himself in 1986, when he scored a magnificent winner against Morocco in the World Cup second round on the way to defeat by Argentina in the Final. He began with Borussia, joined Bayern for £650,000 in 1984 and moved to Italy with Inter in 1988 for £2.4 million. Injury kept him out of Euro 1992, but he won the 1996

Marco Matterazzi will be forever remembered for his parts in the 2006 World Cup Final, good and bad.

PAOLO MALDINI
His father's son

For almost 50 years Milan have boasted a Maldini in the ranks. It is a remarkable record of family consistency and a rare feature when a son emerges out of the shadow of his father to become an ever greater and more successful footballer. But that is the case with Paolo Maldini.

His father, Cesare, was captain the first time Milan won the European Champions Cup in 1963. Both against Steaua Bucharest in Barcelona in 1989 and then again against Benfica in Vienna in 1990, Milan's left-back was Cesare's son, Paolo. No prouder spectator sat up in the stands on those two May evenings than young Paolo's father. He was, naturally, afforded much of the credit for his son's success. Yet, as Paolo has readily confessed, there were no favours along the way. If anything, his father worked him harder than the rest of the Milan youth team before Cesare was lured away by the Italian federation to manage the under-21s.

Italian soccer, remarkably considering its defensive reputation, has developed some of the finest attacking full-backs in the history of the modern game and the younger Maldini has scored more than 40 goals for club and country.

Maldini made his Milan debut away to Udinese in January 1985, at the age of 16 – staggering in Italy – and his national team debut as a substitute in the goalless draw against Yugoslavia in March 1988. Three months later he was starring for Italy at the European finals in West Germany.

Italy fell in the semi-finals but it

was obvious that a fine team was being created and that Maldini would be a fixture for more than a decade to come. Maldini junior had represented his country a then record 126 times by the time he finally called a halt to his Azzurri career after the controversial World Cup second round exit in Korea and Japan in 2002.

In 1990 Maldini was a key member of the Italian side who finished third at 'their own' World Cup after losing on penalties to Argentina in the semi-finals. Four years later he went even closer and lost in the Final on penalties. Penalties again proved unlucky in 1998 when Italy went out to hosts France in Paris. Then, at the 2000 European Championship, Italy led 1-0 as the Final entered its closing seconds in Rotterdam... only for France to grab a stoppage-time equalizer and then a winner in extra time.

Club honours continued to accrue and Maldini junior was a Champions Cup winner in 1989, 1990, 1994, 2003 and 2007. In 2003 Maldini captained Milan to victory on English soil just as his father had done 40 years earlier.

Maldini played more than 500 league matches for Milan, set a record for European club appearances and collected six league titles as well as two World Club Cups and three European Supercups.

As Paolo has said: "My father taught me everything. From the moment I first remember seeing a picture of him holding the European Cup I wanted to copy his success. I wanted to do it for myself; but I owed it to him."

Paolo Maldini gets his hands on the Champions League trophy for the fifth time at Athens in 2007.

1968	1985	1989	1992	1998	2002	2003	2007
Born on June 26	Made his Serie A debut in a 1-1 draw away to Udinese on January 20	Helped Milan to win the World Club Cup, European Champions Cup and European Supercup	Won second Serie A scudetto with Milan – the first of four in five seasons	Another penalties failure, this time in the quarter-finals of the World Cup against hosts France	Retired from the Italian national team after winning record-setting 126th cap in the World Cup second round defeat by co-hosts South Korea on a golden goal	Captained Milan to sixth Champions League Cup triumph over Juventus in the first all-Italian final. Finished on the winning side after a penalty shoot-out	Won his fifth – Milan's seventh – Champions League title with defeat of Liverpool

1980	1988	1990	1994	2000
Joined Milan's mainstream youth section – with father Cesare as coach	Made his Azzurri debut, under coach Azeglio Vicini, in a 1-1 draw away to Yugoslavia on March 31	Won another Champions Cup and European Supercup and helped Italy finish third at their own hosting of the World Cup	Won a third Champions Cup and later rewarded with an award as World Player of the Year from London magazine *World Soccer* - one of the few defenders to take any major international soccer prize. Outstanding left-back at the 1994 World Cup finals in which Italy finished runners-up to Brazil after a penalty shoot-out	Captain of the Italian national team who lost the Euro 2000 Final to France in Rotterdam on a golden goal. The game was Maldini's 111th international, one short of coach Dino Zoff's old record

DIEGO MARADONA
The people's favourite

Diego Maradona was not only the world's greatest player throughout the 1980s and early 1990s. He was also the most controversial and the most enigmatic. His admirers in Argentina, where he knew the early glory days with Argentinos Juniors and Boca Juniors, considered him little less than a god, and the tifosi in Italy, where he triumphed with Napoli, worshipped his bootlaces. So did all of Argentina after Maradona reached the zenith of his career, captaining his country to victory in the 1986 World Cup finals in Mexico.

Argentina fans remember most clearly his goal against England when he collected the ball inside his own half and outwitted five defenders and goalkeeper Peter Shilton before gliding home one of the greatest goals in the history of the World Cup. Maradona provided a repeat against Belgium in the semi-finals, then, in the final against West Germany, his slide-rule pass sent Jorge Burruchaga away to score the dramatic winner. Maradona's great ability made his subsequent fall all the greater.

His love affair with Italian soccer went sour after the 1990 World Cup, when Argentina defeated their hosts on penalties in the semi-final in Maradona's adopted home of Naples. The following spring a dope test showed cocaine traces. He was banned from Italian and then world soccer for 15 months, returned to Argentina and was arrested there for cocaine possession. Even his 1994 World Cup comeback ended in the shameful ignominy of dope-test failure and a new 15-month

Diego Maradona remained an Argentine icon even after his fall from grace.

international playing ban. That was not the end of Maradona and the World Cup, however. He reappeared, despite virtually no coaching experience, in 2009 to bring Argentina through a rocky World Cup qualifying campaign and on to the quarter-finals a year later in South Africa.

Maradona had made his league debut as a 15-year-old in 1976 then his Argentina debut at 16 but he was omitted from the finals squad in 1978 and did not make his World Cup debut until 1982 in Spain. Here he also succumbed to World Cup pressures for the first time in being sent off for an awful lunge at Brazil's Batista.

By then Maradona had been sold by Argentinos Juniors to Boca Juniors for a domestic record £1m and on to Barcelona for a world record £2m.

It says much for the magical technique of his left foot that, despite all the negative vibes, Maradona continued to entrance the game. In 1984 Napoli paid another world record, this time £5 million, to end Maradona's injury-battered two-year stay with Barcelona. Within weeks Napoli sold a staggering 70,000 season tickets. Two Italian League championships and one UEFA Cup success were the reward for the fans.

1960	1977	1980	1984	1987	1990	1992	1994
Born on October 30 in Lanus, Buenos Aires	Made international debut at 16 for Argentina	Sold to Boca Juniors for £1 million, a record for a teenager	Sold to Napoli for a third world record, now £5 million	Led Napoli to their first-ever Italian league title plus victory in the Italian Cup	Led Argentina back to the World Cup Final, where they were defeated 1–0 by West Germany	Made a disappointing comeback with Sevilla in Spain	Banned for 15 months again after a positive drugs test during the World Cup

	1976	1982	1986	1988	1991	1993	1995
	Made league debut at 15 for Argentinos Juniors	Sold to Barcelona for another world record £3 million, then out of the game for four months following reckless a tackle on him	Inspired Argentina to victory at the World Cup finals in Mexico: was unanimous choice as Player of the Tournament	Won his only European prize as Napoli beat Stuttgart in the UEFA Cup Final	Failed a dope test and was banned for 15 months	Sacked by Sevilla and began a second comeback in Argentina with Newells Old Boys	Returned to playing with Boca Juniors after coaching stints with Deportivo Mandiyu and Racing Avellaneda

SIR STANLEY MATTHEWS
The wizard of dribble

Stanley Matthews was the first great player of the modern era. There will be cases made for Billy Wright, Bobby Charlton, Bobby Moore and others but none dominated his particular era as long as the barber's son from Hanley in the Potteries area of the English Midlands.

Matthews was nicknamed "the Wizard of Dribble" and the magic of his talent and reputation survived until the closing days of his career when he returned to his original club, Stoke City, and inspired them to win promotion out of the Second Division. That achieved, at the climax of the longest first-class career of any player, he decided to retire, at the age of 50. Later, however, Matthews insisted that he could – and should – have played for several more years.

Matthews went out in a style befitting one of the legends of the game. Among the other great players who turned out for his testimonial match at Stoke were Di Stefano, Puskas and Yashin. Always keen to put back into soccer as much, if not more, than he had taken out in terms of fame and glory, Matthews became general manager of another Potteries club, Port Vale. But the role was too restrictive, and Matthews left after 18 months to take coaching and exhibition courses around the world, in particular Africa.

In the 1930s and 1940s Matthews was without rival as the greatest outside-right in the world. Opposing left-backs feared their duels with him as Matthews brought the ball towards them, feinted one way and accelerated clear another. His adoring public desperately wanted to see him crown his career with an FA Cup winner's medal. That dream was denied by Manchester United in 1948 and Newcastle United in 1951. But in 1953 – a remarkable year for English sport with England reclaiming cricket's Ashes trophy from Australia and the veteran jockey Sir Gordon Richards winning the Derby – the 38-year-old Matthews tried again.

When Blackpool were 3-1 down to Bolton with time running out, it seemed Matthews was destined never to claim that elusive prize. But Matthews took over, ripping the Bolton defence to shreds and providing not only the inspiration for Blackpool's climb back to equality, but also the cross from which Bill Perry shot the winning goal. Blackpool scored twice in the last three minutes.

But Matthews was, like many of the game's greatest players, a personality and an inspiring example for all youngsters. His knighthood was appropriate recognition for a 33-year career, completed without a single booking, in which he had graced the game as the First Gentleman of Soccer. Tributes poured in from all over the world after his death in February 2000.

Sir Stanley Matthews was never booked or sent off in a career which lasted 33 years.

1915	1934	1948	1955	1961	1965
Born on February 1 in Hanley, Stoke-on-Trent	Made debut for England in 4-0 win over Wales in Cardiff	Played a key role in one of England's greatest victories – 4-0 over Italy in Turin, and voted Footballer of the Year	One of his many summer exhibition tours took him to Mozambique, where among the ball boys mesmerized at a match in Lourenço Marques was Eusebio	Returned to Stoke for a mere £2,800 and, despite his 46 years, inspired their successful campaign to get back into the First Division	His knighthood was the first ever for a soccer player and came at the end of his 33-year career in soccer

1932	1946	1953	1957	1965	2000
Turned professional with local club Stoke City	Sold to Blackpool for £11,500	Sealed his place among soccer's legends by inspiring Blackpool's FA Cup Final comeback against Bolton	Played the last of 84 games for England (including wartime internationals) in a 4-1 World Cup qualifying victory over Denmark in Copenhagen	Retired after a star-spangled Farewell Match at Stoke's Victoria Ground featuring the likes of Di Stefano, Puskas and Yashin	The soccer world mourns the death of Sir Stanley Matthews

UEFA Cup with Bayern Munich and the 1997 league title. He then made a shock international return, aged 37, for the 1998 World Cup finals. Matthaus continued his international career right on into the 2000 European Championship, commuting from his temporary home in the US. He earned a then world record 150 caps.

Alessandro "Sandro" Mazzola

National team: Italy
Born: November 7, 1942
Clubs: Internazionale

Sandro Mazzola was the son of Valentino, the skipper of Torino and Italy who was killed in the 1949 Superga air disaster when Sandro was six. To escape comparisons, he launched his soccer career with Inter rather than Torino, and made his debut in a 9-1 defeat by Juventus – when Inter fielded their youth team in protest at the Italian federation's decision to order an earlier game to be replayed. In 1962-63 Mazzola, a striking inside-forward, scored ten goals in 23 games as Inter won the league title. In both 1964 and 1965 he won the European Cup and World Club Cup, scoring in the victories over Real Madrid and Benfica. Mazzola reverted to midfield to help Italy win the 1968 European Championship and was outstanding when Italy reached the World Cup Final in Mexico in 1970.

Valentino Mazzola

National team: Italy
Born: January 26, 1919
Clubs: Teresoldi, Alfa Romeo, Venezia, Torino

Mazzola was an inside-left who was born in Milan where he played for Tresoldi and then the Alfa Romeo works side. In 1939 he was bought by Venezia where he struck up a remarkable inside-forward partnership with Ezio Loik – with whom he moved to Torino in 1942. Mazzola captained and inspired Torino to five consecutive league championship victories in 1943 and 1946-49. Before he could celebrate

the fifth title, however, Mazzola and 17 of his Torino colleagues were killed in the 1949 Superga air disaster. Mazzola had been the league's top scorer in 1947, and made his international debut for Italy against Croatia in Genoa in 1942. He scored four goals in 12 internationals and would almost certainly have been the captain for Italy's World Cup defence in Brazil in 1950.

Giuseppe Meazza

National team: Italy
Born: August 23, 1910
Clubs: Internazionale, AC Milan, Juventus, Varese, Atalanta

Only two Italian players won the World Cup in 1934 and 1938: Giovanni Ferrari was one, inside-forward partner Meazza was the other. Meazza was considered the most complete inside-forward of his generation, able both to score goals and create them. Born in Milan, Meazza made his debut with Inter at 17 and scored a then league record 33 goals in 1928-29. He spent a decade with Inter before crossing the city to play for rivals AC Milan in 1938, playing wartime soccer with Juventus and Varese and retiring in 1947 after two seasons with Atalanta. Meazza marked his international debut by scoring twice in a 4-2 win over Switzerland in Rome in 1930 and, later the same year, scored a hat-trick in a 5-0 defeat of Hungary. In all, his international goal haul was an impressive 33 in 53 matches.

Joe Mercer

National team: England
Born: August 9, 1914
Clubs: Everton, Arsenal

"Your legs wouldn't last a postman his morning round" was Dixie Dean's description of Mercer's skinny legs. But Joe played for a quarter of a century on his odd-shaped pins before breaking one of them and going into management. He won a league title with Everton and two with Arsenal after they had gambled on his durability when he was 32 and had

two dodgy knees. He also won a cup final with the Gunners in 1950 and lost one two years later, when he captained a ten-man team (Arsenal had a player carried off injured and no substitutes were allowed at the time) to a narrow defeat. Mercer repeated his league and Cup success as manager of Manchester City, and had a brief spell as England caretaker manager between Alf Ramsey and Don Revie.

Billy Meredith

National team: Wales
Born: July 30, 1874
Clubs: Manchester City (Eng), Manchester United (Eng), Manchester City (Eng)

Meredith won his first medal in a dribbling contest at the age of ten, and played his last senior game – a losing FA Cup semi-final – when nearly 50. He was a rugged individual,

originally a miner, and a strong union man, often involved in off-field rows with officialdom. On the field he was rarely in trouble, plying his trade down the right wing with enviable skill and consistency. He won 48 caps (scoring 11 goals) spread over 25 years, with five lost to the First World War, and played around 1,000 first-team matches, in spite of missing a complete season after being involved in a match-fixing scandal.

Lionel Messi

SEE PAGE 197

Michel

Full name: José Miguel Gonzalez Maria del Campo
National team: Spain
Born: March 23, 1963
Clubs: Castilla, Real Madrid, Celaya (Mex)

Billy Meredith tormented not only opponents but also club and FA officials.

LIONEL MESSI
The Magician

Lionel Messi went, with Argentina, into the 2010 World Cup finals in South Africa hailed as the finest footballer in the world. The fact that their campaign ended at the hands of Germany in the quarter-finals was not down to any failure on his behalf. He was still ranked among the player of the tournament candidates a week later when he and his team-mates had long since flown home.

Despite being born in the Argentine city of Rosario, Messi has been at the Catalan club since the age of 13. His move to Europe, from Newell's Old Boys, was aided by Barcelona's agreement to pay for growth hormone treatment.

Messi made his league debut in 2004-05 and won a double of Spanish league and Champions League in 2006. The next season was even more sensational, including a hat-trick against the old enemy of Real Madrid.

Prodigious dribbling skills helped land him with a 'new Maradona' label but, unlike previous pretenders such as Ariel Ortega and Andres D'Alessandro, the description seems to suit Messi perfectly.

His Barcelona goal against Getafe in April 2007, a winding solo run from the halfway line, was uncannily similar to Diego Maradona's legendary second goal against England at the 1986 World Cup.

Going from strength to strength, Messi was Barcelona's most inspirational player when the Catalan club achieved a unique feat in the calendar year of 2009 by winning all six major trophies available to them – the Champions League, Spanish

The world's best player in 2009, diminutive Lionel Messi made Barcelona and Argentina exciting to watch.

league and cup and supercup, UEFA Supercup and Club World Cup.

Messi also, remarkably, contributed not only with his eel-like runs and inch-perfect passes but by heading Barcelona's second, decisive goal against Manchester United in the Champions League showdown in Rome's Stadio Olimpico.

Messi had already guided Argentina to victory in the Olympic Games soccer tournament in Beijing in 2008. Now he was expected by fans back in Buenos Aires to spark a similar outcome in the 2010 World Cup.

Qualifying had turned out to be a closer shave than anyone expected with contributing only four goals even though he ended the year hailed as FIFA World Player of the Year and European Footballer of the Year.

Messi was top scorer in the Spanish league with 34 goals as Barcelona retained their domestic crown. He was also eight-goal leading marksman in the Champions League but here Barcelona lost their crown, losing to eventual winners Internazionale in the semi-finals.

That may have been an bad omen for the World Cup. Messi was outstanding but failed to score a goal as Argentina fell short once more.

1987	2000	2005	2007	2008	2010
Born on June 24 in Rosario	Moved to Barcelona as a 13-year-old	Six-goal top scorer and winning captain of Argentina in World Youth Cup	Scored a Maradona-type solo goal against Getafe in a Spanish cup-tie	Won Olympic Games gold in Beijing	Top scorer in both Spanish league and Champions League

1997	2003	2006	2009
Joined children's section of Newell's Old Boys	Made Barcelona debut in a friendly against Porto aged 16 years 145 days	Youngest Argentina debutant in the World Cup finals, at 18	Voted World Player and also European Footballer of the Year after a six-trophy clean sweep with Barcelona

Michel was one of European soccer's classic midfield operators in the 1980s and early 1990s. He made his debut with Castilla, the nursery team of Real Madrid, and was promoted to the senior outfit in 1984. A year later he starred in the UEFA Cup Final defeat of Videoton, scoring Madrid's first goal and making the other two in their 3-0 first leg win in Hungary. Michel made his Spain debut in 1985 and was unlucky to be denied a goal against Brazil at the 1986 World Cup finals when a shot was cleared from behind the line, but he scored a hat-trick against South Korea in Italy in 1990.

Predrag Mijatovic

National team: Yugoslavia
Born: January 19, 1969
Clubs: Buducnost Titograd, Partizan Belgrade, Valencia (Sp), Real Madrid (Sp), Fiorentina (It)

Mijatovic arrived late on the international stage after conflict in the former Yugoslavia saw his country barred from the World Cup and European Championship in the mid-1990s on security grounds. He had established a goal-scoring reputation with Buducnost and then Partizan Belgrade, which transferred effectively to Spain with Valencia and Real Madrid. He won the Spanish League in 1997 with Madrid and then scored the poacher's goal that won the 1998 Champions League Final against Juventus. In the 1998 World Cup qualifiers, Mijatovic wasthe European zone top scorer with 14 goals.

Roger Milla

National team: Cameroon
Born: May 20, 1952
Clubs: Leopard Douala, Tonnerre Yaounde, Valenciennes (Fr), Monaco (Fr), Bastia (Fr), Saint-Etienne (Fr), Montpellier (Fr)

Centre-forward Milla – real name Miller – delighted crowds at the 1990 World Cup with his celebratory dances around the corner flags. His goals, especially the winner against Colombia, made him the first player to become African Footballer of the Year for a second time. Milla played

The legendary Roger Milla playing in Cameroon's defeat of Argentina in the World Cup of 1990.

most of his club soccer in France, winning the Cup there in 1980 with Monaco and in 1981 with Bastia. He was first voted African Footballer of the Year in 1976. In 1994, he became the oldest player to appear in the World Cup finals at the age of 42.

Milos Milutinovic

National team: Yugoslavia
Born: February 5, 1933
Clubs: FK Bor, Partizan Belgrade, OFK Belgrade, Bayern Munich (Ger), Racing Paris (Fr), Stade Français (Fr)

Milutinovic, a powerful, aggressive centre-forward, was head of a famous dynasty of soccer players which has included Bora Milutinovic, coach to a record five different nations at the World Cup finals. Milos began with FK Bor, made his debut for Yugoslavia in 1951 and, the same year, transferred to Belgrade with army club Partizan. He scored 183 goals in 192 games before controversially moving to neighbours OFK, then to Germany with Bayern Munich and finally settling in France. Milutinovic proved a huge success with Racing Paris before injury forced his retirement in 1965. He scored 16 goals in 33 internationals between 1953 and 1958.

Severino Minelli

National team: Switzerland
Born: September 6, 1909
Clubs: Kussnacht, Servette, Grasshopper

Minelli was a steady, reliable right-back with great positional sense who played a then record 79 times for Switzerland during the inter-war years. In 1930 he made his national team debut while simultaneously winning his first league championship medal with Servette of Geneva. In the next 13 years he won another five league medals as well as eight cup finals with Grasshopper of Zurich. Minelli was a key figure in the verrou or "bolt" defence introduced by fellow-countryman Karl Rappan, and played to great effect for Switzerland in the World Cups of both 1934 and 1938. One of his finest games was Switzerland's 2-1 defeat of England in Zurich in May 1938.

Kazuyoshi "Kazu" Miura

National team: Japan
Born: February 26, 1967
Clubs: Santos (Bra), Yomiuri, Genoa (It), Kawasaki Verdy, Kyoto Purple Sanga, Vissel Kobe

Miura was the first major Japanese star of the modern era. Thrilled by soccer as a kid he dared to take

himself off to Brazil as a teenager where he volunteered to sign up for Santos, Pele's old club. Ironically he made his debut in Japan for a Brazilian League select in the Kirin Cup in 1986. Four years later Miura returned home to join all-powerful Yomiuri. His skills and leadership earned him the Asian Footballer of the Year award in 1993 when he also joined Genoa and became the first Asian player to score a goal in Serie A. The launch of the professional J.League then lured him home to play for Yomiuri Verdy again. Unfortunately for Miura, the Japanese soccer take-off had come just too late. He scored 14 goals in the early qualifying rounds of the 1998 World Cup but lost form and was among the three players dropped from the 25-man pre-finals squad.

Luisito Monti

National team: Argentina and Italy
Born: January 15, 1901
Clubs: Boca Juniors, Juventus (It)

Monti was an old-style attacking centre-half in the late 1920s and early 1930s. He was notable for a rugged, ruthless style but was also one of the great achievers of the inter-war years. Monti won an Olympic Games silver

BOBBY MOORE
National treasure

Bobby Moore assured his place in soccer history when he became the first, and only, England skipper to lift the World Cup after extra time victory over West Germany on that July afternoon in 1966.

He won a then-record 108 caps, captained his country 90 times and built a lasting reputation as England's finest centre back. When he died from cancer, aged 51, in 1993, soccer's greats lined up to pay tribute.

Pele said: "The world has lost one of its greatest players. He was my friend as well as the best defender I ever played against." Old adversary Franz Beckenbauer called Moore "a true gentleman," and twenty six years after his final league appearance, England's fans voted Moore "the best player of the last 50 years" in an FA poll.

Nowadays, the top Premiership and European clubs would contest auctions to sign him. But he played before freedom of contract and the Bosman ruling. Sometimes he held out for improved terms. Before the 1966 World Cup he was in dispute with West Ham over an extra £10 a week. Yet he spent nearly 18 years with the club he joined as an amateur after leaving school in 1956.

Moore's quality and maturity soon shone through. He broke into the England youth team in 1957 and captained them to runners-up place in the European Youth Championships the following year. He made his first team debut at 17, then graduated through the England under-23s to win

Bobby Moore earned special praise from his greatest opponent, Pele.

his first full cap as a 21-year-old. Walter Winterbottom made him England skipper. Alf Ramsey was happy to continue the arrangement.

Ramsey and the West Ham manager Ron Greenwood both saw Moore as their leader on the pitch. He skippered West Ham to victory in the 1964 FA Cup final and the Cup-Winners' Cup final a year later.

Moore's influence was crucial in the World Cup final. He rallied England after Helmut Haller's early goal. His free kick set up England's equalizer for Geoff Hurst. Then, with England ahead 3-2 as extra time ticked away, Jack Charlton and Nobby Stiles urged Moore to make one last clearance. Instead he picked out Hurst with a 40-yard pass and the striker ran on to complete his hat-trick.

Moore was just as imposing at the Mexico finals in 1970. The sight of Moore and Pele swopping shirts after England's game against Brazil, is an enduring image of the tournament.

Moore's form was even more impressive given his preparation for the finals: he was held in the eve of the competition on a (subsequently discredited) charge of shoplifting at the England squad's hotel.

He reached his 100 caps against Scotland in 1972 but time was taking the edge off Moore's pace. He played his final game for England in a 1-0 defeat by Italy in 1973. A few months later, he moved to Fulham – and played for them on the losing side against West Ham in the 1975 FA Cup final.

1941	1962	1964	1966	1972	1974	1977	1993
Born April 12 in Barking, a few miles from the West Ham stadium	Makes full England debut in friendly against Peru	Captains West Ham to FA Cup Final win over Preston and is voted Footballer of the Year	Captains England to World Cup victory over West Germany	Wins 100th cap for England, against Scotland	Joins Fulham in £25,000 transfer	Plays last game for Fulham, against Blackburn Rovers	Announces that he is suffering from cancer. He dies nine days later

1958	1963	1965	1967	1973	1975	1984-86
Makes West Ham full debut at 17 in First Division game against Manchester United	Captains England for first time in friendly against Czechoslovakia	Captains West Ham to victory over TSV 1860 Munich in the European Cup-Winners' Cup final at Wembley	Awarded OBE	Makes last of 108 England appearances in friendly against Italy	Plays for Fulham against West Ham in FA Cup Final	Manages Southend United for two years

medal in 1928 when Argentina lost to Uruguay in Amsterdam and was again on the losing side against the same opponents at the first World Cup Final two years later. In 1931 Juventus brought Monti to Italy. At first he looked slow and vastly overweight, but a month's lone training brought him back to fitness and, little more than a year later, he made his debut for Italy in a 4-2 win over Hungary in Milan. Monti was not only a key figure in the Juventus side which won four successive league titles in the 1930s, but he also played for Italy when they first won the World Cup, defeating Czechoslovakia in Rome in 1934.

Bobby Moore
SEE PAGE 199

Juan Manuel Moreno
National team: Argentina
Born: August 3, 1916
Clubs: River Plate, España (Mex), River Plate, Universidad Catolia (Chile), Boca Juniors, Defensor (Uru), FC Oeste, Medellin (Col)
Many Argentines consider Moreno to have been the greatest footballer of all time. An inside-right for most of his career, Moreno began with River Plate's youth teams and was a league championship winner in 1936. He won four league titles with River and was a member of the legendary forward line of the late 1940s, together with Muñoz, Pedernera, Labruna and Loustau. Moreno played for Mexican team España between 1944 and 1946, returned to River for two more years, then wandered off again to ply his trade in Chile, Uruguay and Colombia. He scored an impressive 20 goals in 33 internationals.

Stan Mortensen
National team: England
Born: May 26, 1921
Club(s): Blackpool, Hull, Southport
As fast over ten yards as any English forward, with the finishing skill to round off the openings his pace created, Mortensen scored four times in a 10-0 win over Portugal

(away!) in his first international, and his goal in his last England game was his 23rd in 25 appearances. That was against the 1953 Hungarians, a few months later he became the first man to score a hat-trick in a Wembley Cup Final: his third, after two defeats. Morty loved the FA Cup, scoring in each of Blackpool's first 12 post-war rounds in the tournament and finishing with 28 Cup goals as well as 225 in the league.

Alan Morton
National team: Scotland
Born: April 24, 1893
Clubs: Queen's Park, Glasgow Rangers
"The Wee Blue Devil" was a left-winger with elusive dribbling skill and a waspish shot who had a 20-year career and gained nine championship medals and three for the Scottish Cup. He was a mining engineer who spent several seasons with the amateurs at Queen's Park, before becoming the first signing for new Rangers manager, William Struth, who remained in charge for 34 years. Morton played well over 500 games for Rangers and is reputed never to have appeared in the reserves. He was always very much the gentleman, often appearing for matches in a bowler hat and carrying an umbrella.

Coen Moulijn
National team: Holland
Born: February 15, 1937
Clubs: Xerxes, Feyenoord
Moulijn was perhaps Holland's first post-war superstar. A brilliant outside-left, he played 38 times for Holland between his debut in a 1-0 defeat by Belgium in Antwerp in 1956 and his last game, a 1-1 World Cup qualifying draw against Bulgaria, in October 1969. That may have been Moulijn's last international, but his final and greatest achievement came the following May when Feyenoord beat Celtic in the European Cup Final in 1970. Moulijn helped Feyenoord go on

Hidetoshi Nakata was the first Japanese player to 'make it' in Europe.

to beat Estudiantes de La Plata in the World Club Cup and retired in 1972 with five league championships to his name. At the insistence of the Dutch federation, Feyenoord had inserted a clause in Moulijn's contract that he should never be sold abroad.

Gerd Muller
SEE PAGE 200

Hans Peter "Hansi" Muller
National team: West Germany
Born: July 27, 1957
Clubs: Stuttgart, Internazionale (Italy)
Muller was just the sort of imaginative midfielder to bring variation to the West German national team in the early 1980s. Unfortunately the consequences of a knee injury upset his international career prospects. He thus made the last of his 42 appearances for his country in 1983 when still only 26. Muller had made his debut in a 1-0 defeat by Brazil in the spring of 1978. He played in the World Cup finals later that year and helped win the 1980 European title. In the 1982 World Cup he played as a substitute in the Final defeat by Italy.

Hidetoshi Nakata
National team: Japan
Born: January 22, 1977
Clubs: Bellmare Hiratsuka, Perugia (It), Roma (It), Parma (It), Bologna (It), Fiorentina (It), Bolton Wanderers (Eng)
Nakata ranks as the finest Japanese player of the modern era although he ended the 2002 World Cup still not having reached 50 international appearances for his country. This was largely due to the fact that, although he made his debut in 1997, European club commitments restricted his availability. Nakata was outstanding for Japan on their World Cup debut in 1998 and he contributed impressively on their way to the second round in 2002. His European experiences proved erratic, however: despite some success with Perugia he then helped Roma win the 2001 Italian league. But his form slipped, perhaps because he had the World Cup in mind, after his transfer to Parma in the summer of 2001. Further transfers did not diminish his status back home though he retired from national team soccer after the 2006 World Cup.

GERD MULLER
Germany's record-holder

Gerd Müller's nickname said it all. He was "Der Bomber" and he exploded a record haul of goals in the Bundesliga for Bayern Munich and for the West German national team in the late 1960s and early 1970s.

Yet Müller was anything but the ideal build for one of the greatest goal poachers in the history of the world: he was not the archetypal tall, lean, long-striding centre-forward. Quite the reverse: he was short, stocky and muscular with a low centre of gravity which gave him the edge over defenders who towered head and shoulders over him at corners, free kicks and in the attacking build-up.

His appearance fooled Yugoslav coach Tschik Cajkovski when he joined Bayern on the personal say-so of president Wilhelm Neudecker. "I'm not putting that little elephant into my team of thoroughbreds," he told Neudecker – who then pulled rank. The subsequent results justified the judgement of president rather than coach.

In 62 internationals for West Germany, Müller scored 68 goals, a national record, which included four goals in a match four times despite playing at the height of soccer's most defensive era. That was merely an extension of his club standard with Bayern. Müller ran up 365 goals in 427 league appearances between 1965 and 1979 – a goals total almost 150 beyond his nearest challenge in the Bundesliga history books. Of course, those goals meant that the honours also came thick and fast. Müller won the European Cup-winners Cup with Bayern in 1967 and the Champions Cup in 1974, 1975 and 1976. Indeed, many Bayern fans with long memories claim it was only because Müller had been sidelined by injury in 1977 that Bayern failed to make it four.

On four occasions Müller led Bayern to victory in the West German league and, on four occasions, the cup. He was European Footballer of the Year in 1970 – after claiming a top-scoring ten goals at the World Cup finals in Mexico – and Germany's Player of the Year in both 1967 and 1969.

"He scores 'little' goals," said Helmut Schön, for years Müller's national team manager. Meaning that Müller's specific talent lay in finishing off moves from close range in and around the six-yard box.

Müller quit the national team after the World Cup win and left German soccer altogether in 1979 when he went to play in the North American Soccer League. But fading glory and boredom turned Müller, almost surreptitiously, into an alcholic. He said: "I did not realize what was happening ... Then, they came along and saved me from it."

"They" were Müller's old teammates Beckenbauer and Hoeness, who had stuck with the club and risen to president and general manager respectively. They brought Müller back to Munich, supported him through treatment and put him to work with Bayern's youngsters.

Gerd Muller was 10-goal top scorer at the 1970 World Cup finals in Mexico.

1945	1966	1968	1970	1973	1974	1976	1979
Born on November 3 in Nordlingen	Won the German Cup with Bayern and made West Germany debut in a 2-0 win away to Turkey in October	Footballer of the Year again	Again top scorer in the Bundesliga with 38 goals and also top-scored with 10 goals at the World Cup.	Bundesliga champion again	Scored twice as Bayern beat Atletico Madrid 4-0 to become the only club to win the Champions Cup in a replay. World Cup winner with West Germany	Collected a third Champions Cup-winner's medal with Bayern against Saint-Etienne in Glasgow	Moved to USA: 40 goals in 80 games over three years with Fort Lauderdale Strikers in the NASL

1963	1967	1969	1972	1975	1978
Joined Bayern Munich from TSV Nordlingen	Won the German Cup again and secured his first European prize as Bayern beat Rangers 1-0 to win the Cup-Winners' Cup	Top-scorer in the league with 30 goals in Bayern's first Bundesliga triumph. Footballer of the Year for a third year in succession.	Ended his finest domestic season with a top-scoring 40 goals for champions Bayern. Wins European Championship with West Germany	Again a Champions Cup winner with Bayern against Leeds in Paris	Retired from German soccer

José Nasazzi

National team: Uruguay
Born: May 24, 1901
Clubs: Lito, Roland Moor, Nacional, Bella Vista

Nasazzi was one of the great captains in soccer history. He led Uruguay to their victories in the 1924 and 1928 Olympic Games and then to the 1930 World Cup. Nasazzi was nicknamed "the Marshall" for his organizational ability at the heart of defence from right-back, though he also played occasionally at centre-half and at inside-forward. Nasazzi was also a South American champion on four occasions in his 15-year, 64-game international career and was a key member of the Nacional team which dominated the championship in 1934.

Pavel Nedved

National team: Czech Republic
Born: August 30, 1972
Clubs: Sparta Prague, Lazio (It), Juventus (It)

Playmaker Nedved became only the second Czech player to be hailed as European Footballer of the Year in 2003. The award underlined his status as the finest player to emerge since the Czech Republic split with Slovakia at the start of the 1990s. Nedved's achievements in Italy with Lazio and Juventus were matched by his inspirational leadership of his country. Several times domestic Footballer of the Year, Nedved made his Czech debut in a 3-1 win in the Irish Republic in June 1994 and was still impressing in the European Championships of 2004. At club level he won three Czech League titles with Sparta and two in Italy. Nedved was also a member of the Lazio side who won the last European Cup-Winners Cup in 1999. Juventus blamed his absence through suspension for their shootout defeat by Milan in the 2003 Champions League Cup Final at Old Trafford.

Johan Neeskens

National team: Holland
Born: September 15, 1951
Clubs: Haarlem, Ajax, Barcelona (Sp), New York Cosmos (US)

Neeskens was an aggressive, sharp-tackling midfielder who fitted perfectly into the "total football" pattern set by Ajax and Holland in the early 1970s. Neeskens provided the steel which supported the more technical gifts of team-mates Cruyff, Keizer and Van Hanegem. He scored 17 goals in 49 internationals and earned a place in history by converting the first-ever World Cup Final penalty against West Germany in Munich in 1974. With Ajax, Neeskens won a hat-trick of victories in the European Cup, the Dutch league and the Dutch Cup. In 1974 he moved to Barcelona, with whom he won the Spanish Cup in 1978 and the European Cup-Winners Cup in 1979.

Zdenek Nehoda

National team: Czechoslovakia
Born: May 9, 1952
Clubs: TJ Hulin, TJ Gottwaldov, Dukla Prague, SV Darmstadt (W Ger), Standard Liège (Bel), FC Grenoble (Swz)

Nehoda, a skilled, mobile, general of a centre-forward, was the first – and last – Czechoslovak player to go anywhere close to a century of caps. He scored 31 goals in 90 internationals, of which the highlight was the European Championship victory over West Germany in Belgrade in 1976. Nehoda was three times a champion of Czechoslovakia with the army club, Dukla Prague, twice a domestic cup-winner and was twice voted his country's Footballer of the Year, in 1978 and 1979. Nehoda's international reputation also earned him selection for a Europe XI against Italy in 1981.

Oldrich Nejedly

National team: Czechoslovakia
Born: December 13, 1909
Clubs: Zebrak, Rakovnik, Sparta Prague

Nejedly played inside-left for the Sparta club which dominated the Mitropa Cup for much of the 1930s and for the Czechoslovak national team which reached the 1934 World Cup Final. His skills were described as "pure as Bohemian crystal", and his partnership with outside-left Antonin Puc was one of the best of its kind in Europe in the inter-war years. Nejedly scored twice in the defeat of Germany in the semi-finals but could make no headway against Italy in the Final. Nevertheless he was the World Cup's top scorer with five goals. A broken leg against Brazil in 1938 ended Nejedly's dream of revenge over Italy. He scored 28 goals in 4 internationals and was chosen for Central Europe against Western Europe in 1937.

Alessandro Nesta

National team: Italy
Born: March 19, 1976
Clubs: Lazio, AC Milan

Nesta came up through the ranks at Lazio with whom he achieved European success even before his sale to AC Milan in 2002. He was first a ball boy with Lazio then an apprentice who made headlines for the wrong reason when his training ground tackle resulted in a broken leg for newly-arrived Paul Gascoigne. He made his league debut in 1994 and was called up late by Italy, in emergency, for Euro 96 in place of injured Ciro Ferrara. He won the Italian League, two Italian Cups and the last European Cup-Winners' Cup with Lazio before moving to Milan in 2002 with whom he won the Champions League.

Igor Netto

National team: Soviet Union
Born: September 4, 1930
Clubs: Spartak Moscow

Netto was a left-half in the 1950s who captained the Soviet Union from 1954 to 1963, leading by example and winning what was then a record 57 caps with four goals. Netto led the Soviets to victory in the 1956 Olympic Games in Melbourne, but injury kept

Pavel Nedved was voted European Footballer of the Year in 2003.

him out of all but one match at the 1958 World Cup finals. In 1962 he played in all four games when the Soviets reached the quarter-finals in Chile. Altogether he scored 37 goals in 367 league games for Spartak, with whom he stayed throughout his playing career, winning five Soviet titles.

Günter Netzer

National team: West Germany
Born: September 14, 1944
Clubs: Borussia Mönchengladbach, Real Madrid (Sp), Grasshopper (Swz)

In the late 1960s and 1970s, West Germany had a surfeit of outstanding midfield generals. Netzer was at his best in the West German side that won the 1972 European Championship, forging a marvellously refined partnership with sweeper Beckenbauer behind him. He lost his place in the national team to Wolfgang Overath after transferring to Real Madrid, and never regained it on a permanent basis, although he made an occasional appearance. He was twice West German champion with Borussia, twice Spanish champion with Real Madrid, and a cup-winner once in each country and once West German Footballer of the Year. Later, as manager of Hamburg, he masterminded their championship win in 1989.

Gary Neville was one of the key figures in Manchester United's modern success story.

Gary Neville

National team: England
Born: February 18, 1975
Club: Manchester United

Neville and versatile brother and fellow international Phil were two of the stalwarts of the "Beckham era" youth side at Manchester United, which provided a home-grown foundation for the decade-long stream of triumphs which started under Sir Alex Ferguson in the mid-1990s. Neville turned professional in 1992 and had become a regular at right-back – and occasionally in the centre of defence – three years later. He missed only a handful of matches for both club and country over the succeeding years, which included a share in the "treble" success of 1999 and appearances for England at the World Cups of 1998 and 2006 as well as the European Championships of 2000 and 2004.

Thomas Nkono

National team: Cameroon
Born: July 20, 1955
Clubs: Tonnerre Yaounde, Español (Sp), Hospitalet (Sp)

Nkono was the goalkeeping star of the Cameroon side that first reached the World Cup finals, in Spain in 1982, then the quarter-finals eight years later in Italy. In between, Nkono became the first Cameroonian to appear in a European club final when he starred in Español's run to the 1988 UEFA Cup Final. He played for the World XI against Brazil in the match staged in Milan in October 1993 to celebrate Pele's 50th birthday. Then he turned out for the Italia 90 team in Peter Shilton's testimonial at White Hart Lane, the following December. Nkono, a former African Footballer of the Year, attended his last World Cup in the United States in 1994, but did not get a game.

Gunnar Nordahl

National team: Sweden
Born: October 19, 1921
Clubs: Degerfors, Norrköping, AC Milan (It), Roma (It)

Nordahl was the most famous of five First Division brothers. He was born in Hornefors in northern Sweden and scored 77 goals in 58 games with local Degerfors. Next came 93 goals in 92 games, which brought Norrköping four championships in a row. A fireman by training, Nordahl gave that up in 1948 when, after Sweden's Olympic Games victory in London, he was lured away to Milan. There Nordahl formed the central spearhead of the "Gre-no-li" trio (with Gunnar Gren and Nils Liedholm). He was the Italian League's leading scorer five times, and by the time he retired in 1957 he had totalled 225 goals in 257 Italian League matches.

Bjorn Nordqvist

National team: Sweden
Born: October 6, 1942
Clubs: IFK Hallsberg, Norrkoping, PSV Eindhoven (Hol), IFK Gothenburg, Minnesota Kicks (US), Orgryte

Nordqvist was, at one time, the world record international – having won 115 caps in the 1970s and early 1980s. He also played in three World Cups, in 1970, 1974 and 1978, and, with Norrkoping, was twice champion of Sweden and once cup-winner. Having taken the professional plunge in 1974, Nordqvist immediately won the Dutch league with PSV Eindhoven and later tried his luck briefly with Minnesota in the North American Soccer League. Despite his century of caps, Nordqvist had to wait a year between his 1963 debut against Finland and his second game against Norway in September, 1964.

Ernst Ocwirk

National team: Austria
Born: March 7, 1926
Clubs: FK Austria, Sampdoria (It)

Ocwirk, nicknamed "Clockwork" by the British for his consistent creativity in midfield, was the last of the old-fashioned attacking centre-halves – a role for which he was ideally suited, with both technical and physical strengths. Ocwirk began with FK

Austria of Vienna, made his debut for his country in 1947 and appeared at the 1948 Olympic Games in London. Three years later he was back at Wembley, captaining an Austrian side which thoroughly deserved a 2-2 draw against England. In 1953 the stopper centre-back had taken over throughout Europe and Ocwirk was selected at wing-half in the Rest of the World team which drew 4-4 with England in a match played to celebrate the 90th anniversary of the Football Association. In 1956, at the advanced age of 30, he undertook an Italian adventure with Sampdoria with whom he spent five seasons before returning for one last campaign with FK Austria. Later he coached FKA to league titles in 1969 and 1970.

Morten Olsen

National team: Denmark
Born: August 14, 1949
Clubs: Vordingborg, Brugge (Bel), Anderlecht (Bel)
Olsen, a thoughtful midfield general, but even better as a highly-organized and commanding sweeper, was a key figure in Denmark's international revival. He won 102 caps between 1970 and 1989 when he guided the "Danish dynamite" to the semi-finals of the European Championship in 1984 and the second round of the World Cup in Mexico in 1986. At club level he won three Belgian League championships and one UEFA Cup with Anderlecht before retiring to launch a high-profile coaching career with Brondby, Koln, Ajax and Denmark.

Anton Ondrus

National team: Czechoslovakia
Born:-March 27, 1950
Club: Slovan Bratislava
Ondrus was the ideal successor to Jan Popluhar at the centre of defence with both Slovan Bratislava and Czechoslovakia. Tall and strong, his intuitive reading of the game made up for a slight lack of pace. He was twice a Czechoslovak champion and once a Cup-winner with Slovan in the years

Wolfgang Overath played all his senior career with Koln, later taking over as president.

before Slovakia split away from the Czech Republic. In 1976 he was at the heart of defence as the Czechoslovaks beat first Holland then West Germany on penalties to win the European Championship in Belgrade. As captain, it was Ondrus who had the honour of raising the Henri Delaunay trophy.

Viktor Onopko

National team: Russia
Born: October 14, 1969
Clubs: Stakhanovets, Dynamo Kiev, Shakhtyor Donetsk, Spartak Moscow, Oviedo (Sp), Alania Vladikavkaz
Onopko, first a left-back then an all-controlling left-side midfielder, emerged as an international figure just as Russian soccer was going through its biggest-ever upheaval. In one 12-month period he played international soccer for the Soviet Union in late 1991, then for the Commonwealth of Independent States in the 1992 European Championship finals, and finally for the newly-

independent Russian national team in the 1994 World Cup. Onopko was Footballer of the Year in 1992 and 1993 and won three Russian league titles with Spartak before joining Oviedo.

Raimundo Orsi

National team: Argentina and Italy
Born: December 2, 1901
Clubs: Independiente, Juventus (It)
Vittorio Pozzo, Italy's manager in the 1920s and 1930s, had no hesitation in picking imported South Americans such as Orsi for his team. "If they can die for Italy," said Pozzo, "they can play soccer for Italy." Orsi played outside-left for Argentina in the 1928 Olympic Final against Uruguay before switching, amid controversy, to Juventus. He spent six months kicking his heels before finally making his Juventus debut. Within four months he was playing for Italy and scored twice on his debut in a 6-1 win over Portugal in November 1929. Orsi was one of the exceptional players who won five successive league titles with Juventus in the early 1930s. For good measure, he scored Italy's all-important equalizer on the way to an extra-time victory over Czechoslovakia in the 1934 World Cup Final.

Wolfgang Overath

National team: West Germany
Born: September 29, 1943
Club: Köln
Overath, an old-style inside-left and then a left-footed midfield general, was one of the most admired members of the West German sides which featured in starring roles at the World Cups of 1966, 1970 and 1974. Overath played his entire senior club career for Köln and scored 17 goals in 81 internationals between 1963 and 1974. He was selected for the World XI that played Brazil in Rio de Janeiro in 1968 and he was a World Cup runner-up in 1966, scored the goal against Uruguay, which earned West Germany third place in 1970, and won a personal duel to oust Gunter Netzer as midfield commander for the World Cup victory

of 1974. Overath then retired from the national team. The latter years of Overath's Köln career were sadly marred by disagreements with opinionated coach Hennes Weisweiler.

Marc Overmars

National team: Holland
Born: March 29, 1973
Clubs: Go-Ahead Eagles, Willem II, Ajax, Arsenal (Eng), Barcelona (Sp)
Overmars was a highly-successful anachronism in 1990s soccer. Thirty years after Sir Alf Ramsey was thought to have killed off wingers, he was still using his pace and skill to take on full-backs – on either the right or left wing – head for the byline and cross to devastating effect. Overmars began with Go-Ahead Eagles of Deventer and Ajax signed him from Willem II in 1992. He scored his first international goal after just four minutes with the first kick of his debut against Turkey in February 1993. Two months later, Overmars scored twice in Ajax's 6-2 victory over Heerenveen in the Dutch Cup Final. He took England apart in a World Cup qualifier at Wembley in 1993 and did the same to Real Madrid – twice – in the UEFA Champions League 18 months later. Overmars transferred to Arsenal in 1997 and climaxed his first season in England by helping inspire the Gunners to the league and FA Cup double. The Gunners sold him to Barcelona where he continued to outwit defenders until injury forced his premature retirement aged 31.

Michael Owen

National team: England
Born: December 14, 1979
Clubs: Liverpool, Real Madrid (Sp), Newcastle Utd, Manchester Utd
Owen is one of England's most prolific strikers, with 40 goals in 89 internationals over a decade after his goal-scoring debut against Chile and before injury wreaked havoc with his career. He was Liverpool's top scorer for seven successive seasons

and a key figure in the treble season of 2000-01 when he was hailed as European Footballer of the Year after winning the UEFA Cup, FA Cup and League Cup. He scored 118 goals in 216 league games before moving to Real Madrid in 2004 then back to English soccer with Newcastle. Injury at the 2006 World Cup cost Owen a year out of soccer and, after his Tyneside spell ended in relegation, he moved on a free transfer to Manchester United. Injury again hampered his bid to gain both a regular starting role and an England World Cup recall.

Antonin Panenka

National team: Czechoslovakia
Born: December 2, 1948
Clubs: Bohemians Prague, Rapid Vienna (Aut)
Panenka was a throw-back in style, a languid, skilled, dreamer of a midfield general who might have appeared more at home in the central European game of the 1930s than in the increasing hurly-burly of international soccer in the 1970s. He spent most of his career in the Czech shadows with Bohemians, from which the national manager, Vaclav Jezek, rescued him for the 1976 European Championship finals. Panenka was influential in midfield and struck the decisive blow in the Final when his penalty shot, stroked so deliberately past Sepp Maier, brought Czechoslovakia their shoot-out triumph. Later he spent several successful years in Austria with Rapid Vienna. Panenka's 65 caps included helping Czechoslovakia finish third, this time after a penalty shoot-out against Italy, in the 1980 European Championship.

Jean-Pierre Papin

National team: France
Born: November 5, 1963
Clubs: Valenciennes, Club Brugge (Bel), Marseille, AC Milan (It), Bayern Munich (Ger), Bordeaux
Papin was one of the outstanding strikers of the game. He began his career with Valenciennes and played in Belgium with Brugge before returning to France to become captain and the attacking inspiration of Marseille. Papin was top scorer in the French league for four successive seasons before joining Milan in the summer of 1992. A year later he found himself appearing as a substitute for Milan against Marseille in the Final of the European Cup, which the French club won 1-0. That was Papin's second European Cup Final defeat, for he had been on the losing side in a penalty shoot-out when Red Star Belgrade beat Marseille in Bari in 1991. His consolation came, however, as he was voted European Footballer of the Year later that year. Injuries upset his career after a 1994 transfer to Bayern Munich in Germany.

Daniel Passarella

National team: Argentina
Born: May 25, 1953
Clubs: Sarmiento, River Plate, Fiorentina (It), Internazionale (It)
Passarella belongs to that select band of heroes who can claim to have received the World Cup as winning captain. His moment of triumph came in the River Plate stadium – his own home club ground – in 1978. Passarella thoroughly deserved the honour, since he had guided, controlled and commanded Argentina from the defence. Time and again Passarella powered up into midfield to serve Ardiles and Kempes, while his vicious free-kicks and strength in the air at corners added to the pressure on opposing defences. He ended his career as a goalscoring defender with Fiorentina and Inter in Italy, before returning to River Plate as coach. He later guided Argentina to the quarter-finals of France 98 after taking over the national side.

Adolfo Pedernera

National team: Argentina
Born: November 15, 1918
Clubs: River Plate, Atlanta, Huracan, Millonarios (Col)
Pedernera was a great centre-forward turned rebel. He made his debut for River Plate in 1936 and won five league championships in 11 years. In the late 1940s Pedernera led the legendary Maquina, or "Machine", attack with Munoz, Moreno, Labruna and Loustau. River sold him, perhaps prematurely, to Atlanta and he joined Huracan just before the Argentine players' strike of 1948. Millonarios of Bogota, from the pirate Colombian league, signed up Pedernera not merely as a player but as "liaison officer" to lure away other top Argentines, including his centre-forward successor at River Plate, Alfredo Di Stefano. Later Pedernera returned to Argentina as coach of Gimnasia y Esgrima, Boca Juniors, Huracan and Independiente. He played 21 times for Argentina.

Pele

SEE PAGE 206

Emmanuel Petit

National team: France
Born: September 22, 1970
Clubs: Monaco, Arsenal (Eng), Barcelona (Sp), Chelsea (Eng)
Petit made an instant impact as a teenager with Monaco. He was a French Cup runner-up at 18 in 1989 only three months after his first team debut in his favourite midfield role. His international debut followed not long afterwards in a 0-0 draw against Poland in August 1990. Petit then transferred to Arsenal and proved such an effective member of their championship-challenging team that he earned a France recall for the 1998 World Cup. He celebrated the event by scoring France's third goal in the Final win over Brazil after dashing the full length of the pitch. Petit helped France win Euro 2000 before his club career entered a lengthy period of instability after being sold to Barcelona then coming back to the Premiership at Chelsea.

Daniel Passarella was a ferocious captain of Argentina's World Cup-winning side in 1978.

PELE
Simply the best

Pele remains one of those great examples and inspirations of world sport: a poor boy whose talent lifted him to the peaks of achievement, fame and fortune... yet who, amidst all that, retained his innate sense of sportsmanship, his love of his calling and the respect of teammates and opponents alike. His father Dondinho had been a useful player in the 1940s, but his career had been ended prematurely by injury. He was his son's first coach and his first supporter.

Most Brazilian soccer players are known by nicknames. Pele does not know the origin of his own tag, he recalls only that he did not like it and was in trouble at school for fighting with class-mates who called him Pele. Later it became the most familiar name in world sport.

Pele's teenage exploits as a player with his local club, Bauru, earned him a transfer to Santos at the age of 15. Rapidly he earned national and then international recognition. At 16 he was playing for Brazil; at 17 he was winning the World Cup. Yet it took pressure from his teammates to persuade national manager Vicente Feola to throw him into the action in Sweden in 1958.

Santos were not slow to recognize the potential offered their club by Pele. The directors created a sort of circus, touring the world, playing two and three times a week for lucrative match fees. The income from this gave the club the financial leverage to buy a supporting cast which helped turn Santos into World Club Cup champions twice. But the pressure on Pele was reflected in injuries, one of which restricted him to a peripheral role in the 1962 World Cup finals. Brazil, even without him, went on to retain the Jules Rimet Trophy.

In 1966 Pele led Brazil in England. But referees were unprepared to give players of skill and creativity enough protection. One of the saddest images of the tournament was Pele, a raincoat around his shoulders, leaving the pitch after being kicked out of the tournament by Portugal. Brazil, this time, did not possess the same strength in depth as in 1962, and crashed out.

Four years later Pele took his revenge in the most glorious way. As long as the game is played, his performance in the 1970 World Cup finals will be revered as the apotheosis of a great player at his very best, achieving the rewards he deserved.

It says everything about Pele's transcending genius that he was the one man able to set light soccer in the US in the 1970s. Although the North American Soccer League eventually collapsed, soccer was by that stage firmly established as a grass-roots American sport. Without Pele's allure that could never have happened and the capture of host rights for the 1994 finals would never have been possible.

Pele rose from poverty to become the greatest personality in world soccer history.

1940	1956	1958	1970	1977	1994
Born Edson Arantes do Nascimento on October 21 in Tres Coracoes	Transferred to big-city club Santos and made league debut at 15	Became youngest-ever World Cup winner, scoring two goals in the Final as Brazil beat Sweden 5-2	Inspired Brazil to complete historic World Cup hat-trick in Mexico	Retired again after lifting Cosmos to their third NASL championship	Appointed Brazil's Minister for Sport

1950	1957	1962	1975	1982
Began playing with local club Bauru, where his father was a coach	Made debut for Brazil, at 16, against Argentina	Missed the 1962 World Cup win because of injury in the first round, but compensated by winning the World Club Cup with Santos	Ended an 18-month retirement to play for Cosmos of New York in the dramatic, short-lived North American Soccer League	Presented with FIFA's Gold Medal Award for outstanding service to the worldwide game

Roger Piantoni

National team: France
Born: December 26, 1931
Clubs: Nancy, Reims

Piantoni was one of the last great European inside-forwards, before the "old" positions were wiped out by the advent of the 4-2-4 and 4-3-3 formations, with their new roles and terminology. Piantoni, who was born at Etain, in the Meuse, built his reputation with Nancy and transferred to Reims in 1957. He played in the World Cup finals of 1958 - when France finished third - and in the European Cup Final of 1959 (which Reims lost to Real Madrid). Piantoni played 38 times for France, having made a scoring debut in a 1-1 draw against the Irish Republic in Dublin in 1952. He also scored in his last international, nine years later, against Finland. Piantoni's left-wing partnership, for Reims and France, with outside-left Jean Vincent was famed throughout the continent.

Silvio Piola

National team: Italy
Born: September 29, 1913
Clubs: Pro Vercelli, Lazio, Torino, Juventus, Novara

Piola was a tall, strong, athletic, aggressive centre-forward who scored 30 goals in 24 internationals between his debut against Austria in 1935 - when Piola scored both Italy's goals in a 2-0 win - and his last game, a 1-1 draw against England in 1952. Piola, a World Cup-winner in 1938 when he scored twice in the 4-2 Final defeat of Hungary, would have collected even more goals and won more caps had it not been for the war years. As it was he played on until he was 43 in a prolific career which included his fair share of controversy - such as the goal he later admitted he punched against England, nearly 50 years before Maradona's Hand of God repetition. Piola scored six goals in Pro Vercelli's 7-2 win over Fiorentina in 1933-34.

Pirri
Full name: Jose Martinez Sanchez

National team: Spain
Born: March 11, 1945
Club: Real Madrid

Pirri epitomized the spirit of Spanish soccer during his 15 extraordinary years with Real Madrid between 1964 and 1979. He began as a goal-grabbing inside-forward, then shifted back successively to midfielder and central defender in a glittering career which brought honours flooding in - eight Spanish championships, three Spanish Cups and the European Cup in 1966. Pirri played 44 times for Spain between 1966 and 1978 and was twice selected for Europe XIs, first against Benfica in 1970, then against South America in 1973. After retiring, Pirri completed his studies to qualify as a doctor and was appointed to the Real Madrid medical staff.

Frantisek Planicka

National team: Czechoslovakia
Born: June 2, 1904
Clubs: Slovan Prague, Bubenec, Slavia Prague

Planicka was Central Europe's finest goalkeeper of the 1930s, a great personality as well as an outstanding and courageous player in the World Cups of both 1934 - when Czechoslovakia lost the Final 2-1 to Italy - and 1938. In the latter competition, long before the days of substitutes, Planicka played the last half of the quarter-final draw against Brazil despite the pain of a broken arm. Planicka won more than almost anyone in the history of the Czechoslovak game. He was a domestic league champion nine times with the great Slavia club, and won the cup six times and the Mitropa Cup - forerunner of today's European club competitions - in 1938. Planicka played 74 times for his country between 1925 and 1938.

Michel Platini

SEE PAGE 208

Svatopluk Pluskal

National team: Czechoslovakia
Born: October 28, 1930
Clubs: Dukla Prague, Bohemians

Pluskal, originally a right half and later a second central defender, was an ideal foil for Josef Masopust, his half-back partner with club and country. He joined the army club UDA Prague, later Dukla, in his teens and stayed until he was 35 when he moved to neighbours Bohemians for one last season. His height and strength in the tackle helped Czechoslovakia reach the 1962 World Cup Final in which they lost 3-1 to Brazil in Chile. A year later his achievements earned him selection for the FIFA World XI, which played England to mark the centenary of the Football Association.

Ernst Pol

National team: Poland
Born: November 3, 1932
Clubs: Legia Warsaw, Gornik Zabrze

Pol was the first great Polish player of the post-war era. He played centre- or inside-forward and scored 40 goals in 49 internationals - then a Polish record - between 1950 and 1966. He was a complete player, with ball-control, good passing and tactical ability and an accurate shot. Pol won the Polish championship twice with the army club Legia, then five times with Gornik, the Silesian miners' club. He once scored five goals in an international against Tunisia in 1960, and had the consolation of scoring a marvellous individual strike for Gornik in their 8-1 thrashing by Tottenham in the European Cup in 1961. It was Pol's ill fortune that Eastern European players were not allowed transfers to the professional west.

Anton "Toni" Polster

National team: Austria
Born: March 10, 1964
Clubs: Simmering, FK Austria, Torino (It), Ascoli (It), Sevilla (Sp), Logrones (Sp), Rayo Vallecano (Sp), Koln (Ger)

Polster was one of European soccer's most outstanding league marksmen for a decade and with eight clubs in four different countries. He first made his mark when he was runner-up in the Golden Boot competition for Europe's top league goalscorer in 1986-87. Polster scored 39 goals for FK Austria only to find his total overtaken, amid controversy, by Romania's Rodion Camataru. Polster moved to Italy with Torino and Ascoli before rediscovering his shooting boots in Spain with Sevilla, Logrones and Rayo Vallecano.

Jan Popluhar

National team: Czechoslovakia
Born: September 12, 1935
Clubs: Slovan Bratislava, Lyon (Fr), Brno

Popluhar began with Slovan as a right-back and then converted to centre-half in time to make the Czechoslovak squad at the 1958 World Cup finals. A reserve then, he had graduated to full command of his defence four years later when he was a pillar of the side who finished runners-up to Brazil. Popluhar played 63 times for his country, played for FIFA's World XI against England in 1963, was voted domestic Footballer of the Year in 1965 and anchored Slovan's victory over Barcelona in the 1969 Cup-Winners' Cup Final. He retired when he was almost 37.

Ferenc Puskas

SEE PAGE 209

Helmut Rahn

National team: West Germany
Born: August 16, 1929
Clubs: Altenessen, Olde 09, Sportfreunde Katernberg, Rot-Weiss Essen, Koln, Enschede (Hol), Meiderich, SV Duisburg

Rahn's shooting power from outside-right was immense, as Hungary found to their cost in the 1954 World Cup Final. Rahn struck the equalizer at 2-2 and then the winner with only a couple of minutes remaining. Yet Rahn, enfant terrible of the German game, might not have even been in Europe: shortly before the finals he

MICHEL PLATINI
Soccer for life

Michel Platini has gone on to more great things since his playing days. He became, successively, French national manager, joint president of the 1998 World Cup organizing committee, special counsellor to FIFA president Sepp Blatter, then president of UEFA and vice-president of FIFA.

But his enduring legend owes everything to his brilliance on the pitch, largely in the early 1980s, when he rivalled Diego Maradona for the unofficial crown of world No. 1. Few players have made a greater international impact at varying levels within the game. His popularity has endured in both his native France, where he was voted the No. 1 Sports Personality of his generation, as well as in Italy where he was voted the greatest player ever for Juventus.

Platini's first joust on the World Cup stage was in Argentina in 1978. Four years later he inspired France to fourth place in Spain after feeling the pain of a shoot-out defeat in the semi-final against West Germany in Seville. After the finals Platini was sold to Juventus for whom he converted the penalty kick which brought the club their long-awaited first European Champions Cup victory in 1985 – although the match itself was overshadowed by the Heysel Stadium tragedy.

The following year Platini guided France back to the semi-finals of the World Cup, this time in Mexico. France defeated Brazil in the tournament's finest match in the quarter-finals. France progressed, nevertheless, only to fall 2-0 to the Germans in the semis. 'I have such bad memories of the Germans,' said Platini years later. 'They are so competitive. You have to beat them out of sight even to get to a penalty shoot-out.'

Platini was three times European Footballer of the Year before retiring to concentrate on commercial interests and TV work. He was persuaded to become national manager and then entered the corridors of power.

His first-team debut, at 17 for Nancy-Lorraine was memorable for the wrong reason: he was carried off with a broken leg. But he returned and burst onto the domestic and international scene in 1975 in some style.

Internazionale made an initial offer but were foiled by the Italian federation's import restrictions so Platini signed for Saint-Etienne. The Italian move went through, eventually, in 1982 when Platini transferred to Juventus. He was Serie A's leading scorer in each of his first three seasons and nipped back to France to captain and inspire Les Bleus to their 1984 European Championship victory. Platini scored in all their five matches, collected nine goals in all including two hat-tricks and the opening goal in the 2-0 victory over Spain in the Final in the Parc des Princes. Then he stepped forward, as captain, to raise the trophy named after fellow Frenchman Henri Delaunay.

Michel Platini was a popularity poll winner in both Italy and his native France.

1955	1976	1979	1982	1984	1986
Born on June 21 in Joeuf	Scored from a free kick on his France debut, a 2-2 draw against Czechoslovakia – the first of a record 41 goals in 72 games. Captained France to the quarter-finals of the Olympic Games soccer tournament in Montreal	Transferred to Saint-Etienne	Sold to Juventus	Guided Juventus to Italian League title and European Cup-Winners' Cup. Again Serie A top scorer with 20 goals and European Footballer of the Year. Captained France to victory as hosts in the European Championship and was also the tournament's nine-goal leading scorer	Italian champion for a second time with Juventus. Captained France to third place at the World Cup in Mexico

1972	1978	1981	1983	1985	2007
Broke his leg on his league debut with Nancy-Lorraine	Scored the cup final winner for Nancy-Lorraine against Nice. Made his World Cup finals debut in Argentina	French champion with Saint-Etienne	Won Italian Cup and top-scored in Serie A with 16 goals. Champions Cup runner-up and voted European Footballer of the Year.	Scored penalty winner for Juventus in Champions Cup Final against Liverpool and won the European Supercup and World Club Cup. Top marksman in Serie A with 18 goals and European Footballer of the Year again, the only player to win it three years in a row	Twenty years after retiring, recorded a mighty off-pitch victory by winning election for President of UEFA

FERENC PUSKAS
The Hungarian hot shot

Ferenc Puskas was one of the very greatest players of all time - a symbol of the legendary "Magic Magyars" who dominated European soccer in the early 1950s and stand as perhaps the greatest team never to have won the World Cup.

Puskas's father was a player and later coach with the local club, Kispest. At 16 Ferenc was a regular at inside-left, terrorizing opposing goalkeepers with the power of his shooting. He rarely used his right foot but then his left was so lethal that he seldom needed it. At 18 he was in the national team, too. His brilliance had much to do with the decision to convert Kispest into a new army sports club named Honved, that formed the basis of the national side.

For four years Hungary, built around goalkeeper Gyula Grosics, right-half Jozsef Bozsik and the inside-forward trio of Sandor Kocsis, Nandor Hidegkuti and Puskas, crushed all opposition. They also introduced a new tactical concept. The inside-forwards, Kocsis and Puskas, formed the spearhead of the attack, with Hidegkuti a revolutionary deep-lying centre-forward. Hungary won the 1952 Olympic title before ending England's record of invincibility against continental opposition with a stunning 6-3 triumph at Wembley.

Early the following year, Hungary thrashed England again, 7-1 in Budapest. No wonder they were overwhelming favourites to win the 1954 World Cup in Switzerland. But Puskas presented a problem. He had been injured in an early round game against West Germany and was a hobbling spectator at training before the Final, against these same West Germans, in Berne. Could his great left foot withstand the strain? Puskas thought so and decided to play, thus taking one of the most controversial gambles in the game's history. After only 12 minutes the gamble appeared to be paying off when Hungary led 2-0. However, they lost 3-2, their dominance finally ended in the one match which mattered most.

It was eight long years before Puskas would return to the World Cup finals. Then, in Chile in 1962, his trusty left foot was doing duty for Spain, because Puskas had, in the meantime, defected to the West, joining Real Madrid. Honved had been abroad when the Hungarian Revolution of 1956 erupted. Puskas and several team-mates decided to stay in the West. He made an attempt to sign for several Italian clubs, but they thought him too old. How wrong they were was underlined when Puskas developed, at Madrid, a new career to emulate his first in brilliance.

Four times Puskas was the Spanish league's top scorer and his partnership with the Argentine centre-forward, Alfredo Di Stefano, was one of the greatest of all time. They hit perfection together on the famous night when Madrid thrashed Eintracht Frankfurt 7-3 in the European Cup Final before a record 135,000 crowd at Hampden. Di Stefano scored three goals, Puskas four. The Spanish fans loved him.

In 1966 he finally retired. His future was secure, thanks to business investments which included a sausage factory near Madrid. In the course of time he was able to visit his native Hungary, where he was celebrated once more as a national hero. Hardly surprising. After all, how many can boast 83 goals in 84 games for their country? In 2002, the Nep Stadium itself was renamed in Puskas's honour.

In his Hungarian army club days at Honved, Puskas had been known as the "Galloping Major".

1927	1945	1952	1954	1958	1962	1993
Born on April 2 in Budapest	Made international debut for Hungary against Austria	Captained Hungary to victory over Yugoslavia in the final of the Olympic Games soccer tournament in Helsinki	Played despite injury, amid controversy, in the World Cup Final which Hungary lost 3-2 to West Germany in Berne - their first defeat for four years	Signed for Real Madrid by his old manager at Honved, Emil Oestreicher	Played in the World Cup finals in Chile, this time for his adopted country of Spain	Achieved his greatest success as a trainer, guiding outsiders Panathinaikos of Athens to the European Cup Final (they lost 2-0 to Ajax at Wembley)

1943	1948	1953	1956	1960	1966	2006
Made his debut for his father's old club, Kispest	Transferred with the entire Kispest playing staff to the new army club, Honved, and top-scored with 50 goals in the League championship	Earned a place in history by inspiring Hungary's historic 6-3 victory over England at Wembley	Stayed in western Europe when the Hungarian Revolution broke out while Honved were abroad to play a European Cup tie against Bilbao	Scored four goals for Madrid in their famous 7-3 demolition of Eintracht Frankfurt in the European Cup Final at Hampden Park, Glasgow	Retired and turned to coaching	Died on November 17, aged 79

had been on a South American tour with Rot-Weiss Essen and was discussing a foreign transfer to Nacional of Uruguay when German national coach Sepp Herberger sent a telegram to summon him home. Rahn unfortunately could not repeat the World Cup miracle in 1958 but still totalled 21 goals in 40 international matches.

Antonio Ubaldo Rattin

National team: Argentina
Born: May 16, 1937
Club: Boca Juniors

Rattin was a midfield pillar with club and country in the 1950s and 1960s. He made his league debut in 1956 and played 14 inspiring seasons with Boca Juniors, setting a club record of 357 league appearances and winning five championships. Rattin was also a key figure in the Boca side – along with Silvio Marzolini and Angel Rojas – which lost narrowly to Pele's Santos in the final of the South American Club Cup in 1963.

Born in the Tigre delta outside Buenos Aires, Rattin played 37 times for Argentina. His most unfortunate game is, however, the one for which he is best remembered. This was the 1966 World Cup quarter-final against England at Wembley, when Rattin's refusal to accept the expulsion given to him by the German referee Kreitlein very nearly provoked a walk-off by the entire Argentine team. Rattin always insisted he was an innocent victim of questionable circumstances.

Raul

SEE PAGE 211

Thomas Ravelli

National team: Sweden
Born: August 13, 1959
Clubs: Oster Vaxjo, IFK Gothenburg, Tampa Bay (US)

Ravelli and twin brother Andreas, a midfielder, were both internationals, but Thomas was by far the most successful – with what was a world record number of 143 caps. Goalkeeper

Thomas' parents emigrated to Sweden from Austria, and Thomas made his reputation with Oster Vaxjo. In 1989 he joined IFK Gothenburg, Sweden's leading club, as successor to Tottenham Hotspur-bound Erik Thorstvedt. Early in his career, Ravelli's temperament was considered suspect: for example, he was sent off for dissent during a 2-0 defeat in Mexico in November 1983. Ravelli learned his lesson to inspire Sweden to reach the semi-finals of both the European Championship in 1992 and, two years later, the World Cup. In June 1995 he overtook Peter Shilton's total of 125 international caps, and was briefly world record-holder. His ambition to play club soccer outside Sweden was fulfilled in the US.

Rustu Recber

National team: Turkey
Born: May 10, 1973
Clubs: Antalyaspor, Fenerbahce, Barcelona (Sp)

Goalkeeper Rustu did not establish himself as first choice for Turkey until 1996 – just in time to play in all Turkey's three games on their first appearance in the European Championship finals. He established a reputation for physical power and inspiring leadership and had won more than 60 caps by the time he starred in Turkey's third place finish at the 2002 World Cup.

Rob Rensenbrink

National team: Holland
Born: July 3, 1947
Clubs: Anderlecht, Portland Timbers (US), Toulouse (Fr)

Rensenbrink, a goal-scoring left-winger, was born in Amsterdam but spent the majority of his career in Belgian soccer. Anderlecht benefited from his loyalty and his goals, most notably in the European Cup-Winners' Cup victories of 1976 and 1978. Rensenbrink scored twice in each victory over first West Ham United and then FK Austria. Later Rensenbrink had a brief spell in the North American Soccer League with Portland before ending his career back in Europe with

French club Toulouse. He was a member of the Dutch side who finished runners-up in both the 1974 and 1978 World Cups. In 1974 he was withdrawn because of injury after the first half of the Final defeat by West Germany; in 1978 he shot against the post against hosts Argentina – who went on to win 3-1 in extra time.

Claudio Reyna

National team: United States
Born: July 20, 1973
Clubs: Bayer Leverkusen (Ger), Wolfsburg (Ger), Glasgow Rangers (Sco), Sunderland (Eng), Manchester City (Eng), Red Bull New York

Reyna was one of the most impressive playmakers on view at the 2002 World Cup, regaining his verve and command after a mixed-up club career. As a teenager he had been one of the most successful soccer players in US college history, leading the University of Virginia to a hat-trick of NCAA titles between 1991 and 1993. He was then called directly into the US squad, preparing to host the 1994 World Cup, after which he moved to Europe with Bayer Leverkusen. Twelve years later he was back in Germany, playing for his country at the 2006 World Cup. In between, Reyna became the first American to captain a European club while with Wolfsburg, was a Scottish champions during five seasons with Rangers and then moved south with Sunderland and Manchester City.

Jose Hector Rial

National team: Argentina and Spain
Born: October 14, 1928
Clubs: San Lorenzo (Arg), Independiente Santa Fe (Col), Nacional (Ur), Real Madrid (Sp), Union Española (Chile), Español (Sp), Marseille (Fr)

Rial was four times a European Champions Cup-winner with Real Madrid. A centre-forward or inside-left, he was considered the virtual equal of Di Stefano when he fled Argentine soccer at the end of the 1940s to star in the pirate league of Colombia. Later he played briefly in Uruguay before joining

Madrid just after Di Stefano. Rial scored twice in Madrid's inaugural Champions Cup Final victory over Reims in 1956. His guiding influence also enabled Madrid to get the best out of the left-winger, Francisco Gento. Rial played five times for Spain in the mid-1950s.

Franck Ribery

National team: France
Born: April 7, 1983
Club(s): Boulogne, Ales, Brest, Metz, Galatasaray (Tur), Marseille, Bayerh Munich (Ger)

Ribery shot to worldwide fame with his sparkling performances on the right wing for France in their run to luckless runners-up spot in the 2006 World Cup finals. His performances in Germany and then subsequent back in the Bundesliga with Bayern – as a league champion in 2008 – suggested his temperament was finally adjusting to the demands of fame. This was a welcome change after earlier career storms which had included a walk-out from Turkish club Galatasaray. By the summer of 2009 he had emerged as one of the most highly-coveted of European soccer players.

USA's Claudio Reyna

RAUL
Made in Madrid

Raul Gonzalez Blanco is a rare talent in a European soccer world dominated by big-money transfers and the fall-out from the Bosman judgment – a home-grown kid who has played all his senior career for his home-town club. Real Madrid's superstar skipper has proved, in a cash-conscious era, that home-town loyalty still counts. He is also proof that the post-Bosman open market in foreign players need not shut the door on local talent.

In the spring of 1998 Raul celebrated a century of appearances for Madrid at the age of 20. But he has remained very much the electrician's son from a working-class suburb of the Spanish capital.

Raul always excels against Atletico Madrid. It's revenge. He played for them as a kid until volatile president Jesus Gil scrapped the youth section. Raul switched to Real with results Atletico have regretted ever since.

At 17 he was plucked from Real's third team and dropped in at the Primera Liga deep end. The man behind that decision, the then coach Jorge Valdano, stood by him after a poor debut, and was rewarded when Raul scored a fine goal... against none other than local rivals Atletico.

Raul led Madrid to four Spanish league titles in 1995, 1997, 2001 and 2003, to the European Champions League in 1998, 2000 and 2002 and the World Club Cups in 1998 and 2002. In 1999 he was also the first Spanish player to be the Primera Liga's top-scorer for seven years.

His form for Spain has been similarly electrifying, though end results have been comparatively disappointing. In March 1999, he scored seven goals in the space of four days for his country – four in a 9–0 thrashing of Austria and a hat-trick in a 6–0 victory over San Marino. He also scored 11 goals in the qualifying competition for Euro 2000 after Spain recovered from a shock first-game defeat by Cyprus.

At club level, however, the records have kept on tumbling. League marksmanship primacy at Real Madrid belongs to Alfredo Di Stefano. The legendary Argentine totalled 216 Liga goals between 1953 and 1964. Raul, by the time he was still only 26, had overtaken Hugo Sanchez's total of 164 to move into third place behind Di Stefano and Carlos Santillana (186). Along the way Raul also overtook Di Stefano's 49-goal record in the Champions Cup.

Not only has Raul piled up the achievements, he has the potential for far more, according to Valdano, his first Madrid coach and later sports director in the Galactico era when Raul was joined at Madrid by the likes of Luis Figo, Zinedine Zidane, Ronaldo and David Beckham. "I have admired his ability ever since I first saw him here as a teenager," says Valdano. "Very few players can decide a match with their own individual ability. The remarkable thing about Raul is that he can do this, time and again, and even when he is having a bad day. His only rival will be history."

Raul set all manner of Real Madrid records before reaching his mid-20s.

1977	1991	1994	1997	1999	2002	2004	2007
Born in Madrid on June 27	Scored 65 goals with the Atletico 13-year-olds	Transferred to Real Madrid's nursery team and was almost immediately promoted again to the seniors, making his debut on October 29 in a 3-1 defeat by Zaragoza	Won first league title, under Italian coach Fabio Capello	Leading scorer in La Liga	Completed Champions League hat-trick and then added European Supercup and World Club Cup. Helped Spain reach World Cup quarter-finals	Became Real Madrid's third all-time leading marksman in the Spanish league, overtaking Hugo Sanchez's 164-goal tally	Was Real's captain as he won his fifth La Liga title

1990	1992	1995	1996	1998	2000	2003
Joined the Atletico Madrid youth section	Joined Real after Atletico cut back their youth system	Ended season as champion of Spain, still only 17	Completed first full season and scored 19 goals. Finished runner-up with Spain in the European under-21s and made senior debut in October against the Czech Republic	Champions League and World Club Cup winner	Champions League winner a second time and European Championship quarter-finalist with Spain	Won his fourth Spanish league title. Scored goal in Euro qualifier against Ukraine to extend record as Spain's all-time leading marksman

Frank Rijkaard

National team: Holland

Born: September 30, 1962

Clubs: Ajax, Sporting Lisbon (Por), Zaragoza (Sp), AC Milan (It), Ajax

Rijkaard was one of the most admired and versatile players of the 1990s at both club and international level. He turned professional under Johan Cruyff at Ajax in 1979 and made his Holland debut at 19 despite Ajax's protests that he was "too young". Rijkaard had brief spells in Portugal and Spain before committing the key years of his career to Milan with whom he won the World Club Cup and the European Cup twice apiece. Rijkaard played in midfield for Milan, but usually in central defence for Holland, with whom he won the 1988 European Championship. Following Milan's defeat by Marseille in the 1993 European Cup Final he returned to Ajax, and was vital to their 1995 European Cup and Dutch title-winning teams. He managed Holland at Euro 2000

then guided Barcelona to 2006 Champions League success.

Juan Roman Riquelme

National team: Argentina

Born: June 24, 1978

Club(s): Argentinos Juniors, Boca Juniors, Barcelona (Sp), Villarreal (Sp), Boca Juniors

Riquelme followed the same path as Diego Maradona – beginning with Argentinos Juniors and then swiftly being snapped up by Boca. Initially a winger, his deft control and perfect passing style quickly saw him converted into midfield playmaker. He starred in Boca's successes in 2000 in winning both the Copa Liberadores and the World Club Cup. But he struggled initially after moving to Spain with Barcelona whose then coach, Louis Van Gaal, thought Riquelme lacked pace. That did not matter to Villarreal – whom Riquelme inspired first to qualify for the Champions League then to reach the 2006 semi-finals – or for Argentina. Riquelme was outstanding in the qualifiers and was seen at his

best in the finals in the 6-0 thrashing of Serbia and Montenegro in Gelsenkirchen in the first round.

Luigi Riva

National team: Italy

Born: November 7, 1944

Clubs: Legnano, Cagliari

Riva, orphaned in childhood, was adopted by all Italy after shooting the Azzurri to the 1970 World Cup Final. He built a teenage reputation with third division Legnano as a left-winger and joined Cagliari in 1963. Riva's formidable left foot fired them out of the shadows and to league title success in 1970. He was top league scorer three times, including the 1969-70 season when he hit 21 goals in 28 games. He scored 35 goals in 42 internationals including Italy's 1970 World Cup run when he scored three times in the quarter and semi-final wins over Mexico and West Germany.

Rivaldo
Full name: Vitor Borba Ferreira

National team: Brazil

Born: April 19, 1972

Clubs: Mogi-Mirim, Corinthians, Palmeiras, Deportivo La Coruña (Sp), Barcelona (Sp), Milan (It), Cruzeiro, Olympiakos (Gr), AEK (Gr), Budyonkor (Uzb), Washington Phoenix (US)

Rivaldo joined Barcelona for a club record fee of £16 million from Spanish rivals Deportivo La Coruña in the summer of 1997 to replace fellow Brazilian Ronaldo. Rivaldo was generally used wide on the wing but he felt most at home playing just behind the strikers. He was Brazil's best forward when they finished runners-up at the 1998 World Cup and was the top-scoring inspiration of their Copa America win in 1999. In the same year Rivaldo led Barcelona to the Spanish league and Cup double despite an uneasy relationship with coach Louis Van Gaal. His achievements were duly rewarded as he was named World and European Player

of the Year. His five goals helped to propel Brazil to another World Cup triumph in 2002.

Roberto Rivelino

National team: Brazil

Born: January 1, 1946

Clubs: Corinthians, Fluminense

Rivelino was originally the deep-lying left-winger who filled the Zagallo role in Brazil's World Cup-winning side of 1970. He was not quick, but was possessed of a superb technique, which made him a perpetual danger with his banana-bending of free-kicks and corners. Rivelino later moved into centre midfield and was influential in the third-place finish of 1978. Rivelino is credited unofficially with the fastest goal in soccer history: scored in three seconds with a shot from the starting pass after he noticed the opposing goalkeeper still concentrating on his pre-match prayers.

Gianni Rivera

National team: Italy

Born: August 18, 1943

Clubs: Alessandria, AC Milan

The "Bambino d'Oro", the Golden Boy: that was Rivera in the early 1960s. As a creative inside-forward, he had the lot: skill, pace and a deft shot, plus the rare natural gift of grace. Rivera in full flight was soccer poetry in motion. Milan paid Alessandria £65,000 for a half-share in the 15-year-old Rivera and signed him "for real" in 1960. In 16 years with the "Rossoneri" he was twice a winner of the World Club Cup, the European Cup and the Italian league, as well as three times an Italian Cup-winner and once European Footballer of the Year, in 1969. Rivera became a controversial figure, however, as successive national managers struggled to build teams around him. He played only the last six minutes of the 1970 World Cup Final – although his Italy career produced 14 goals in 60 games. On retiring Rivera turned his hand to politics and became a member of the Italian parliament.

Frank Rijkaard tackles Soviet striker Oleg Protassov into touch.

Bryan Robson leads out England against Scotland in one of his 90 internationals.

Arjen Robben

National team: Holland

Born: January 23, 1984

Clubs: Groningen, PSV Eindhoven, Chelsea (Eng), Real Madrid (Sp), Bayern Munich (Ger)

Robben's pace and power off right or left wing earned him a transfer to Premier League Chelsea when he was still only 20. He won two league titles but, after a number of injury problems, sought a new start in Spain. He stayed barely a year at Real Madrid before finding a happier haven at Bayern Munich whom he fired to the Champions League Final in 2010. The disappointment of defeat by Internazionale was followed by another when Holland lost in the World Cup Final after Robben missed two clear chances.

Bryan Robson

National team: England

Born: January 11, 1957

Clubs: West Bromwich Albion, Manchester United, Middlesbrough

A considerable part of English soccer in the 1980s was played to the accompaniment of breaking bones, many of them Robson's. Despite this, he won an impressive list of honours, with 90 caps (often as captain), three FA Cup medals, European Cup-Winners Cup in 1991, and the inaugural Premier League championship in 1992-93. Robson was an inspiring, driving force in midfield and a believer in the value of an early strike: three of his England goals were in the first minute. He broke a leg twice as a

teenager with West Bromwich Albion, and then broke the transfer fee record when Manchester United bought him for £1.5 million. He moved into management in 1994, immediately leading Middlesbrough into the Premier League.

Romario da Souza Faria

National team: Brazil

Born: 29 January, 1966

Clubs: Vasco da Gama, PSV Eindhoven (Hol), Barcelona (Sp), Flamengo, Valencia (Sp), Flamengo, Vasco da Gama, Al Saad (Qtr), Fluminense, Vasco da Gama, Fluminense

Romario was arguably the finest attacker in the world game in the 1990s. Discovered by Vasco da Gama, he was still a teenager when he began to establish a reputation

for controversy after being banished from Brazil's World Youth Cup squad for flouting a hotel curfew. After starring at the 1988 Seoul Olympics, he was transferred to PSV Eindhoven. There he clashed with coaches and teammates, yet still managed a total of 98 league goals in five seasons to earn a £3 million sale to Barcelona in 1993. Simultaneously, Romario was recalled for USA 94 by Brazil after almost a year in the wilderness and he scored five crucial goals for his national team in their World Cup triumph.

Ronaldinho
Full name: Ronaldo Assis de Moreira

National team: Brazil

Born: March 21, 1980

Clubs: Gremio Porto Alegre, Paris Saint-Germain (Fr), Barcelona (Sp), Milan (It)

Ronaldinho was described as "the most difficult player I have ever come across" by the French coach Luis Fernandez. The then Paris Saint-Germain boss was referring to the Brazilian forward's wayward behaviour off the pitch. But dozens of defenders would go on to echo his comments for very different reasons. Ronaldinho was as much a star of Brazil's 2002 World Cup win as Ronaldo and Rivaldo. He contributed a decisive, controversial floated goal in the win over England in the quarter-finals – following which he was then sent off. A year later Barcelona splashed £21m on him and were rewarded with Champions League success in 2006 before club and player fell out and he moved on to Milan.

Ronaldo

SEE PAGE 214

RONALDO
Brazil's new beginning

Zico and Tostao were admirers who provided a perfect recommendation for Ronaldo, the Brazilian striker whose natural talent raised comparisons with the incomparable Pele. Zico described Ronaldo as "equally cool and ruthless as the great goalscorers".

Ronaldo Luiz Nazario de Lima grew up playing soccer the traditional way, on the streets and wasteland in the working class district of Bento Ribeiro, on Rio's west side. He was offered a trial with Flamengo but they would not send the bus fare his family could not afford. So Ronaldo went to Sao Cristovao, a small second-division club. There he was spotted by Jairzinho, like Tostao a 1970 World Cup hero. He recommended Ronaldo to provincial giants Cruzeiro.

At 18, a lack of experience meant Ronaldo was never in the running for a starting role at the 1994 World Cup in the United States. But a chance to show his prowess came in Brazil's final warm-up against Iceland. Ronaldo scored one goal and created the other two in a 3-0 win.

Coach Carlos Alberto Parreira sat him on the bench "for the experience" throughout the campaign but that did not deter PSV Eindhoven, weeks later, from paying £6 million for him.

After 42 goals in 45 games and two seasons he went. Barcelona paid £12.5 million, then a club record, to introduce Ronaldo to Spanish soccer.

The combination of the fiercely proud Catalans, a budding superstar and an English manager in Bobby Robson could have proved a Babel-like disaster. Instead it was a triumph: Barcelona won the European Cup-Winners' Cup, Spanish Cup and Supercup and finished league runners-up. Ronaldo top-scored with 34 goals and added the penalty winner in the Cup-Winners' Cup Final against Paris Saint-Germain.

Mysteriously, Barcelona and Ronaldo fell out immediately after this and he was sold to Internazionale for £19.5 million. His initial Italian season added a further 25 goals plus a UEFA Cup medal to his honours list. Then came the World Cup in France. Ronaldo scored against Morocco, Chile (two) and Holland in the semis to lead Brazil to the Final against their French hosts. Then, on match day, he suffered a convulsive fit. Roommate Roberto Carlos summoned help and Ronaldo was taken to a nearby hospital. Doctors pronounced him fit and well and he was whisked off to the Stade de France, arriving little more than an hour before kick-off. Ronaldo proceeded to play in zombie-like fashion as Brazil crashed to a 3-0 defeat.

Ronaldo was injured for much of the next four years but then produced a top-scoring eight-goal campaign to inspire Brazil's record-extending fifth World Cup win. Four years later, in Germany, Ronaldo forgot a controversial spell with Real Madrid long enough to claim three more goals for a finals record aggregate of 15, one more than Gerd Muller.

Ronaldo was an eager World Cup pupil who eventually became the tournament's master.

1976	**1994**	**1996**	**1998**	**2000**	**2003**	**2007**
Born on February 22 in Rio de Janeiro	Spotted by old World Cup hero Jairzinho and recommended to Cruzeiro. Scored 12 goals in 14 games to earn a place in Brazil's World Cup-winning squad	Scored "only" 12 goals in 13 games in an injury-interrupted season then joined Barcelona for a club record £12.5m. FIFA World Player of the Year	Scored 25 Serie A goals and won the UEFA Cup with Inter. Finished World Cup runner-up amid controversy in France	Injured again on his comeback in the Italian Cup Final	Scored Madrid's winner in the World Club Cup Final and top scorer in Spanish league with 23 goals to win the first league title of his career	Transferred from Real Madrid to AC Milan

1992	**1995**	**1997**		**1999**	**2002**	
Signed for local club Sao Cristovao	Rewarded PSV Eindhoven for a £6.5m outlay with 30 goals in 32 games	Scored the Cup-Winners' Cup Final winning goal for Barcelona. Was also the Liga's leading marksman with 34 goals in 37 games before forcing his £19.5m sale to Internazionale. Won FIFA World Player award again and European Footballer of the Year award for the first time		Suffered first serious knee injury	Scored seven goals in ten games in comeback season with Inter – and six goals in seven games to lead Brazil to their record fifth World Cup triumph. Needed a police escort to the airport when he quit Inter for Real Madrid. Voted FIFA World Player of the Year for a third time and European Footballer of the Year for a second time	

Cristiano Ronaldo

National team: Portugal
Born: February 5, 1985
Club: Nacional, Sporting Clube, Manchester United (Eng), Real Madrid (Sp)

Ronaldo, named after former US president Ronald Reagan, was discovered at 16 in his native Madeira by Sporting of Lisbon. Liverpool delayed bidding and Manchester United pounced after their stars were impressed in a pre-season friendly in 2003. United manager Sir Alex Ferguson paid £12million, a remarkable fee for a teenager. Initially Ronaldo's selfishness on the ball infuriated fans and, occasionally, even his team-mates. But he quickly developed judgment, confidence with his left foot and power in the air. All those qualities inspired United to a double Premier League win, a Champions League win, and saw Ronaldo voted Footballer of the Year as well as World and European player of the year. Injury problems did not deter Real Madrid from paying a world record £80m for him in July 2009. He hit 26 goals in his first Spanish season but had a poor World Cup as Portugal went out in the second round.

Wayne Rooney

National team: England
Born: October 24, 1985
Club: Everton (Eng), Manchester United (Eng)

Rooney was still earning an apprentice's £80-a-week when he first hit the headlines with a brilliant first Premiership goal against Arsenal in October 2001. Born in Croxteth, three miles from Goodison Park, Rooney was only nine when he was spotted by Everton scout Bob Pendleton and ran up 99 goals in his last season with the Copplehouse Boys Club. He became England's youngest international at 17, years 111 days against Australia at West Ham in February 2003 and England's youngest goal scorer against Macedonia the following September. He exploded onto the international

Wayne Rooney exploded onto the international scene at Euro 2004.

scene at the 2004 European Championships, scoring four goals in as many games before falling to injury. Further injury and then a red card against Portugal upset his 2006 World Cup by which time he had secured a £20million move to Manchester United which led on to a Premier League hat-trick and Champions League success in 2008.

Paolo Rossi

National team: Italy
Born: September 23, 1956
Clubs: Prato, Juventus, Como, Lanerossi Vicenza, Perugia, Juventus, AC Milan

Paolo Rossi's story is more fantastic than fiction. As a teenager Juventus gave him away because of knee trouble. Later, when they tried to buy him back, they were outbid by Perugia, who paid a world record £3.5 million. Rossi, a star already at the 1978 World Cup, was then banned for two years for alleged involvement in a betting-and-bribes scandal. Juventus finally got him back, and he was only three matches out of his ban when Italy took him to the 1982 World Cup finals, where he top-scored with six goals and

collected a winner's medal from the Final victory over West Germany.

Manuel Cesar Rui Costa

National team: Portugal
Born: March 29, 1972
Clubs: Fafe, Benfica, Fiorentina (It), AC Milan (It)

Rui Costa's contribution to Portuguese soccer was recognized when the country's oldest youth tournament was renamed in his honour. He had been an outstanding youngster as a World Youth Cup-winner in 1991. With Benfica, Rui Costa won the Portuguese Cup in 1993 and league in 1994. He was then sold to Italy's Fiorentina and later joined Milan with whom he added the Champions League to his honours role in 2003.

Karl-Heinz Rummenigge

National team: West Germany
Born: September 25, 1955
Clubs: Lippstadt, Bayern Munich, Internazionale (It), Servette (Swz)

Rummenigge will go down as one of the greatest bargains in the history of German soccer. Bayern Munich paid Lippstadt just £4,500 for their young, blond right-winger in 1974 and sold him a decade later for more than £2

million. In between Rummenigge had won the World Club championship and the European Cup and had twice been hailed as European Footballer of the Year. The former bank clerk developed into a central striker as he progressed. Injuries reduced his effectiveness and controversy lingered over whether manager Jupp Derwall was right to start with his injured captain in the 1982 World Cup Final defeat by Italy.

Ian Rush

National team: Wales
Born: October 20, 1961
Clubs: Chester (Eng), Liverpool (Eng), Juventus (It), Liverpool (Eng), Leeds United (Eng), Newcastle United (Eng)

Rush was the goal-scorer supreme in modern British soccer, but he would have been a great player even if he had never hit a net. His off-the-ball running and excellent passing were bonuses to go with his acutely developed finishing ability. Rush was only 18 when Liverpool paid £300,000 to get him and in two spells at Anfield, he broke scoring records for club, country and FA Cup Finals (five goals in three winning appearances).

Cristiano Ronaldo played a pivotal role in Manchester United's 2007 Premiership title run.

Matthias Sammer

National team: Germany
Born: September 5, 1967
Clubs: Grodlitz, Einheit Dresden, Dynamo Dresden (all East Germany), Stuttgart, Internazionale (It), Borussia Dortmund

Sammer made history in 1996 when he became the first player from the former East Germany to win the European Footballer of the Year award, recognition for his guiding role in the united Germany's European Championship victory. Sammer's father, Klaus, had starred with Dresden and East Germany and had barely retired before his son followed the same path. In 1990 he led Dresden to the GDR league and cup double. Then, after the collapse of the Berlin Wall, Sammer moved west, first with Stuttgart and then Dortmund. Playing as a sweeper, he anchored their disciplined Champions League win over Juventus in 1997.

Hugo Sanchez

National team: Mexico
Born: June 11, 1958
Clubs: UNAM, Atletico Madrid (Sp), Real Madrid (Sp), America, Rayo Vallecano (Sp)

Hugo Sanchez was top league goal-scorer in Spain five seasons in a row in the late 1980s and early 1990s. His 230 plus goals in Spain left him second overall and underlined his claim to be considered one of the great strikers of the modern game. Each one of Sanchez's goals was followed by a celebratory somersault, taught him originally by a sister who was a gymnast in Mexico's team for the 1976 Olympics in Montreal – at which Sanchez made his international soccer debut. Despite a World Cup finals debut as far back as 1978, he totalled only around 50 games for Mexico – his absences caused by club commitments in Spain or disputes with Mexican soccer bureaucracy.

Leonel Sanchez

National team: Chile
Born: April 25, 1936
Club: Universidad de Chile

Leonel Sanchez was the outstanding left-winger in South America in the late 1950s and early 1960s – perhaps not as fast as Pepe of Brazil or as intelligent a player as Zagalo of Brazil, but far more forceful when it came to making his presence felt in the penalty box. Sanchez was a star of the Chilean side which finished third as hosts in the 1962 World Cup, but he also featured in controversy: earlier in the tournament he somehow escaped punishment from the match referee for a punch which flattened Humberto Maschio in the so-called "Battle of Santiago" against Italy. Sanchez played 106 times for Chile, though only 62 of those appearances may be counted as full internationals. He was seven times national champion with "U", his one and only club.

José Emilio Santamaria

National team: Uruguay and Spain
Born: July 31, 1929
Clubs: Nacional, Real Madrid (Sp)

Santamaria was a ruthless centre-back whose finest years were spent at Real Madrid in the 1950s and early 1960s, closing down the defensive gaps left by great attacking colleagues such as Di Stefano, Puskas and Gento. Santamaria was first called up at 20 by Uruguay but missed the 1950 World Cup finals because his club, Nacional, refused to let him accept the inside-forward spot allocated to him in the squad bound for Brazil. Four years later Santamaria was one of the stars of the 1954 World Cup, this time in his traditional place in the centre of defence. Madrid brought him to Europe in 1957 and, having played 35 times for Uruguay, he collected another 17 caps in the service of Spain, including the 1962 World Cup. He was a World Club championship and triple European Cup winner with Real Madrid and later managed hosts Spain at the 1982 World Cup finals.

Santillana, Full name: Carlos Alonso Gonzalez

National team: Spain
Born: August 23, 1952
Clubs: Santander, Real Madrid

Santillana, despite not being the tallest of centre-forwards, was one of the best headers of a ball in the modern game. He joined Madrid in 1971 from Santander, following a path trod by a previous Real hero, Francisco Gento. He overcame serious kidney and eye injuries to become one of Madrid's most prolific marksmen. He was a European club runner-up in the Champions Cup (1981) and Cup-Winners' Cup (1983) and a runner-up with Spain to France at the 1984 European Championship. He also led Spain's attack at the 1978 and 1982 World Cups and 1980 European finals.

Djalma Santos

National team: Brazil
Born: February 27, 1929
Clubs: Portuguesa, Palmeiras, Atletico Curitiba

Djalma Santos is considered a cornerstone of the Brazil side that won the World Cup in 1958 and 1962 and lost it in 1966. Yet, in Sweden in 1958, he was brought in only for the Final because manager Vicente Feola considered his acute soccer brain and positional sense would make him more effective against Swedish left-winger Skoglund than regular right-back Nilton Di Sordi. In due course he became the first Brazilian player to reach an official century of international appearances, though he was well past his best when – to even his own surprise – he was recalled by Feola for the 1966 World Cup finals in England. He played for the World XI against England in 1963 in the FA Centenary match.

Nilton Santos

National team: Brazil
Born: May 16, 1927
Club: Botafogo

Nilton Santos was a left-back and, though no relation to Brazil partner Djalma Santos, was equally outstanding. Nilton Santos played 83 times for his

Matthias Sammer was the most successful star to emerge from East German soccer.

country between 1949 and 1963, having made his Brazil debut just a year after signing for his only club, Botafogo of Rio. He loved nothing more than powering forward in support of attack, a tactic which surprised the opposition and owed everything to the new freedom afforded wing-backs by the advent of 4-2-4. Santos was a World Cup-winner in 1958 and 1962 and was immensely respected by teammates and officials. He led the player delegation which, in Sweden in 1958, crucially persuaded coach Vicente Feola to call up his Botafogo teammate, the match-winning right-winger Garrincha.

Gyorgy Sarosi

National team: Hungary
Born: September 12, 1912
Club: Ferencvaros

Sarosi, one of the world's greatest soccer players between the wars, died in 1993 in his adopted home of Genoa, Italy, aged 81. Sarosi was born in Budapest, where he played both at centre-forward and centre-half for FTC (Ferencvaros), scoring 349 goals in 383 games. He won the Hungarian championship eight times, the cup once and the Mitropa Cup once. In internationals Sarosi scored 42 goals in 75 appearances, and captained Hungary to the 1938 World Cup Final. Doctor, lawyer and magistrate, he made his debut for Hungary in a 3-2 defeat by Italy in Turin in November 1931. When the Communists took over in Hungary in 1947, Sarosi fled to Italy, where he coached Padova, Lucchese, Bari, Juventus (winners of the 1952 championship), Genoa, Roma, Bologna and Brescia. He also coached Lugano in Switzerland.

Dejan Savicevic

National team: Yugoslavia
Born: September 15, 1966
Clubs: Buducnost Titograd, Red Star Belgrade, Milan (It)

Savicevic was one of Europe's outstanding attackers of the 1990s but had an uphill task making his talent

tell. After starring at the 1990 World Cup, he returned to Italy a year later to help Red Star win the Champions Cup in Bari and then the World Club crown. As Yugoslavia fell apart, so Savicevic "escaped" via a transfer to Milan. However he spent as much time on the sidelines as on the pitch because of foreign player restrictions and knee trouble. Eventually, he was able to express his talent to the full in Milan's 4-0 win over Barcelona in the 1994 Champions Cup Final.

Hector Scarone

National team: Uruguay
Born: June 21, 1898
Clubs: Sportsman, Nacional, Barcelona (Sp), Ambrosiana-Internazionale (It), Palermo (It)

Scarone was Uruguay's inspiring inside-forward in their greatest era of the 1920s and early 1930s. He won Olympic gold medals in Paris in 1924 and Amsterdam in 1928 – in between playing in Spain for Barcelona – and was top scorer at both the 1926 and 1927 South American Championships. He then led Uruguay to victory at the inaugural World Cup finals on home soil in Montevideo in 1930. Inevitably, his talents drew more offers from Europe, but he insisted on waiting until after the World Cup before returning, this time to Italy with Ambrosiana-Inter. In the early 1950s he went back to Spain as coach to Real Madrid before making a playing comeback in Uruguay with Nacional and retiring finally at 55 – a South American – and probably a world – record.

Juan Alberto Schiaffino

National team: Uruguay and Italy
Born: July 28, 1925
Clubs: Penarol, Milan (It), Roma (It)

When he was a boy, "Pepe" Schiaffino always wanted to play centre-forward, but youth coaches with Penarol of Montevideo, his first club, considered him too thin and fragile. They switched him to inside-forward and, at 20, he was playing for Uruguay at the South American Championship and top-scoring with 19 goals in Penarol's

Peter Schmeichel was inspirational in Denmark's 1992 European title win.

league-winning side. In World Cup terms, Schiaffino peaked in 1950 when he scored Uruguay's equalizer at 1-1 on the way to their shock victory over Brazil. After starring again at the finals in 1954, he was sold to Milan for a world record £72,000, and is regarded as one of the greatest players ever to have graced Calcio. He wound down his career with Roma, after narrowly failing to lead Milan to victory over Real Madrid in the 1958 European Cup Final, when, despite Schiaffino's fine solo goal, they lost 3-2 to the Spanish club.

Salvatore "Toto" Schillaci

National team: Italy
Born: December 1, 1964
Clubs: Messina, Juventus, Internazionale, Jubilo Iwata (Jap)

Schillaci was Italy's unheralded hero at the 1994 World Cup. He only just

squeezed into the squad but came off the substitutes' bench to become the tournament's six-goal top scorer. Yet the previous season had been his first in Serie A after joining Juventus from the minor Sicilian club, Messina. Schillaci made his Italy debut in a 1-0 win over Switzerland before the World Cup. But his form lost its edge after the finals and he only regained confidence when he joined Internazionale. In 1994, he became the first top-name Italian player to join Japan's newly-formed J.League.

Peter Schmeichel

National team: Denmark
Born: November 18, 1963
Clubs: Hvidovre, Brondbyerenes (Den), Manchester United (Eng), Sporting Clube (Por), Aston Villa (Eng), Manchester City (Eng)

Schmeichel very nearly came to England in 1987, after Newcastle sent spies to watch him. Although he was then considered too inexperienced for the English First Division, Manchester United bought him for a bargain £800,000 in 1991. He was a hero of Denmark's astonishing triumph at the 1992 European Championship finals in Sweden, his saves at crucial moments against Holland in the semi-final and Germany in the Final helping to win him the accolade of the World's Best Goalkeeper. With Manchester United, he won the English league and Cup double in 1994 and 1996 and the fabulous "treble" – adding European Cup glory in 1999.

Karl-Heinz Schnellinger

National team: West Germany
Born: March 31, 1939
Clubs: Duren, Koln, Mantova (It), Roma (It), Milan (It)

Schnellinger, a left-back who later played in most other defensive positions, was to be found at the heart of the international action throughout the 1960s. He stood out not merely for his blond hair and bulky frame but for his power, pace and will to win. He made his World Cup finals debut at 19 in Sweden and was a key member of the West German sides which reached the quarter-finals (1962), the Final (1966) and third place (1970) over the next 12 years. His injury-time goal in the 1970 semi-final with Italy, which forced extra time, typified his fighting spirit. Roma took him to Italy but had to sell him to Milan to overcome a cash crisis. Their loss was Milan's gain as Schnellinger's steel lifted them to victory in the 1969 European Cup. This was the peak of a career which also earned success in the German and Italian championships and the Italian Cup, three selections for World XIs and four for Europe Selects. He was West German Footballer of the Year in 1962.

Paul Scholes

National team: England
Born: November 16, 1974
Club: Manchester United

Salford-born Scholes may have lacked the charisma of a Beckham or Giggs but few players brought as much to the Manchester United table at the turn of the millennium. Versatile Scholes could work his way tirelessly in and around midfield or play further forward as support to the likes of Ruud van Nistelrooy. Scholes had won 66 caps before his international retirement in 2004 including appearances at the 1998 and 2002 World Cups and European Championship in between. In the 2002–03 season he proved especially effective at club level with his 13-goal contribution to United's Premiership success including a hat-trick in an eight-goal thriller against Newcastle.

Viliam Schroiff

National team: Czechoslovakia
Born: August 2, 1931
Club: Slovan Bratislava

Schroiff played 39 times for the former Czechoslovakia in a 12-year international career. A couple of costly slips in the 1962 World Cup Final, when the Czechs finished runners-up to Brazil, did not mar his status as the best keeper at the tournament. Schroiff made his national team debut as substitute goalkeeper in a 5-1 home defeat in Prague by the all-conquering Hungary of Puskas and Kocsis in 1953. He was not recalled for another two years but then secured No. 1 status right through until 1965 when the Czechoslovaks failed in their bid to reach the World Cup finals in England.

Bernd Schuster

National team: West Germany
Born: December 22, 1959
Clubs: Koln, Barcelona (Sp), Real Madrid (Sp), Atletico Madrid (Sp)

Schuster lists among the few who have played for the three traditional giants of the Spanish game. He burst onto the international scene with some superb displays in West Germany's European title win in Italy in 1988. Then with Koln, he nearly joined New York Cosmos the next

Enzo Scifo preferred to play for Belgium despite Italian enticements.

year but when that move collapsed, he moved to Barcelona instead. He concentrated on club soccer after falling out with the German national team set-up and thus won "only" 21 caps. He won the Spanish league with Barcelona in 1984 but was a Champions Cup Final loser against Steaua Bucharest the following year.

Vincenzo "Enzo" Scifo

National team: Belgium
Born: February 19, 1966
Clubs: Anderlecht, Internazionale (It), Bordeaux (Fr), Auxerre (Fr), Torino (It), Monaco (Fr), Anderlecht, Charleroi

Born in Belgium of Italian parents, Scifo joined Anderlecht as a teenager after scoring hatfuls of goals at junior level for La Louvière. In 1984 he chose Belgian citizenship in time to play for his country at the European Championship finals in France. His Latin technique and vision earned an almost instant transfer to Italy, but he was too inexperienced to cope with the challenge of running Inter's midfield. A spell in France and appearances at the 1986 and 1990 World Cups (and later the 1998 finals, too) revived Italian interest and he joined Torino. Scifo schemed their

way to the 1992 UEFA Cup Final, which they lost out to Ajax.

Gaetano Scirea

National team: Italy
Born: May 25, 1953
Clubs: Atalanta, Juventus

Scirea the Sweeper was "the sweeper with charm", a skilled, graceful performer very different to the sort of ruthless "killers" employed by many of the top Italian clubs in the 1960s and 1970s. Scirea began with Atalanta as an inside-forward and later became the defensive cornerstone of the great all-conquering Juventus side of the 1980s. His central defensive partnership with Claudio Gentile was one of the most effective in the international game, as they proved when Italy won the World Cup in Spain in 1982. Scirea's sustained brilliance – he was seven times Italian champion with Juventus in 11 years – thwarted the international ambitions of Milan's Franco Baresi.

Sadly, soon after his retirement from playing the game, Scirea was killed in a car crash in Poland while visiting on a scouting mission for Juventus.

David Seaman

National team: England
Born: September 19, 1963
Clubs: Leeds, Peterborough, Birmingham City, Queens Park Rangers, Arsenal, Manchester City

Seaman was the only member of the England squad who reached the 2002 quarter-finals to have been a part of the squad that reached the semi-finals in 1990 – albeit as a reserve. For most of the subsequent years, however, he was barely challenged as his country's No. 1 goalkeeper. Seaman made his international debut against Saudi Arabia in November 1988 and his secure presence earned him a string of honours at club level with Arsenal including the Premier League and FA Cup double in both 1998 and 2002 and an assortment of other league, FA Cup and League Cup successes. Only in Europe was his record unbalanced, with Arsenal winning the Cup-winners Cup in 1994 (against Parma) but losing the 1995 final (against Zaragoza) and also the 2000 UEFA Cup Final (against Galatasaray).

Clarence Clyde Seedorf

National team: Holland
Born: April 1, 1976
Clubs: AS'80 (Almere), Real Almere, AS'80, Ajax, Sampdoria (It), Real Madrid (Sp), Internazionale (It), Milan (It)

Almost every competition Seedorf has graced has brought him success. With Ajax he was voted Young Player of the Year in Holland in 1993 and 1994, he won the championship in 1994 and 1995, the Cup in 1993, the Dutch Supercup in 1993 and 1994 and then the ultimate prize – the European Champions Cup in 1995. That proved one of his last matches for the club since he rejected advice to stay another year or two in Amsterdam and decided to try his luck in Italy with Sampdoria. He admitted later that he had been, perhaps, too young and inexperienced for the Italian challenge. But he learned fast and regained his status as one of Europe's outstanding creative forces after transferring to

Real Madrid at coach Fabio Capello's behest in the summer of 1996. He won the Spanish league title in his first season and the UEFA Champions League Cup – again – in his second.

Uwe Seeler

National team: West Germany
Born: November 5, 1936
Club: Hamburg

Seeler, son of a former Hamburg player, was so much the central figure in West German soccer in the 1960s and early 1970s that the fans used his name – "Uwe, Uwe" – as their chant at international matches.

He made his full senior debut in a 3-1 defeat by England at Wembley in 1954 when still only 18. Seeler captained West Germany in their World Cup Final defeat at Wembley in 1966, but gained a measure of revenge by scoring a remarkable back-headed goal when Germany won 3-2 in extra time in the dramatic 1970 quarter-final. He scored 43 goals in 72 internationals and he and Pele are the only men to score in four World Cups. Seeler played for Hamburg throughout his career from 1952 to 1971, loyally rejecting a string of offers from Italy and Spain.

Alan Shearer proved a prolific marksman for Southampton, Blackburn and Newcastle.

Dragoslav Sekularac

National team: Yugoslavia
Born: November 10, 1937
Clubs: Red Star Belgrade, TSV 1860 Munich (Ger), Karlsruhe (Ger), St Louis (US), OFK Belgrade

Sekularac was one of the creative geniuses of European soccer in the late 1950s and early 1960s. An inside-forward, his dribbling talents and eye-of-the-needle passing created many goals for attacking partners such as Bora Kostic and he was a star member of the Red Star side which drew 3-3 with Manchester United on the eve of the Munich air disaster. Sekularac's Achilles heel was a quick temper which brought him into repeated conflict with officials, administrators and teammates. After playing in the United States, he turned to coaching.

Alan Shearer

National team: England
Born: August 13, 1970
Clubs: Southampton, Blackburn Rovers, Newcastle United

Shearer exploded into international soccer with a record 13 goals in 11 matches for the under-21s and then collected a superb goal on his senior national team debut against France at Wembley in February 1992. Unfortunately, a serious knee injury cost Shearer a potentially lethal place alongside Gary Lineker in England's attack at the European Championship finals in 1992. That same summer Blackburn signed Shearer for £3.3 million and he was their joint top scorer with 22 goals in his first season at Ewood Park. Following that, he became the only player in English soccer history to score 30 or more goals in three consecutive seasons, and this record helped Blackburn win their first Premier League title in 81 years in 1995. As the top scorer at Euro 96 with five goals, Shearer was transferred to Newcastle in 1996 for £15 million. Home at last, Shearer won nothing in terms of trophies but secured legendary status among fans as his 206 goals took him past Jackie Milburn's club record tally.

Edward "Teddy" Sheringham

National team: England
Born: April 2, 1966
Clubs: Millwall, Aldershot, Millwall, Nottingham Forest, Tottenham Hotspur, Manchester United, Tottenham Hotspur, Portsmouth, West Ham

Few strikers have offered as much committed service to the top-level English game in the modern era. Sheringham started out in the hard knocks school of south London and climaxed his apprenticeship at Millwall by scoring 33 goals in 46 games in 1990-91. After that it was top-flight soccer at Forest, Tottenham, Old Trafford and Tottenham again. His Manchester United spell brought Sheringham three league titles, one FA Cup and one Champions League. He also snatched the equalizing, last-minute goal which set up United's dramatic victory over Bayern Munich in Barcelona. Sheringham was an England regular between 1993 and 2002 when he bowed out as a substitute in the World Cup quarter-final defeat by Brazil.

Andriy Shevchenko

National team: Ukraine
Born: September 29, 1976
Clubs: Dynamo Kiev, Milan (It), Chelsea (Eng)

Shevchenko finally made his international mark when he converted the decisive penalty that brought Milan a shoot-out victory over Juventus in the 2003 Champions League Final. Until then, he had missed out on the big occasions because of the Ukraine national team's repeated failures in qualifying tournaments. Not that Shevchenko was at fault. His prolific marksmanship meant he was five times a Ukraine champion with Kiev before transferring to Milan in 1999. He was twice top scorer in Serie A and finally achieved his longed-for World Cup breakthrough when Ukraine, on their first appearance, reached the 2006 quarter-finals in Germany. By then Shevchenko had already agreed to quit Milan for a controversial Premiership experience with Chelsea.

Andriy Shevchenko struggled to make an impact in his first season at Chelsea after leaving Milan.

Peter Shilton

National team: England
Born: September 18, 1949
Clubs: Leicester, Stoke, Nottingham Forest, Southampton, Derby, Plymouth Argyle, Bolton Wanderers, West Ham United, Leyton Orient

Shilton was only 20 when first capped, and nearly 41 when he made his 125th and last appearance for England during the 1990 World Cup. That was his 17th game in such competitions, a record for a Briton. He conceded only 80 international goals, every one of them a dreadful blow to such a perfectionist. Shilton's pursuit of personal fitness and elimination of error were renowned throughout the game. He played in an FA Cup Final with Leicester, who lost, when he was 19, but never appeared in another. Only with his move to Forest, and

their brief dominance of England and Europe, did club honours flow. Following a brief and controversial spell as player manager at Plymouth Argyle, Shilton went on to play league soccer well into his 40s and made a record-breaking 1,000th league appearance with Leyton Orient.

Diego Pablo Simeone

National team: Argentina
Born: April 28, 1970
Clubs: Velez Sarsfield, Pisa (It), Sevilla (Sp), Atletico Madrid (Sp), Internazionale (It), Lazio (It), Atletico Madrid (Sp)

Simeone was the hard-man midfielder who not only became Argentina's record international, but also was notoriously involved in the incident which saw England's David Beckham sent off in the 1998 World Cup second-

round tie in Saint-Etienne. Simeone enjoyed a much-travelled career after making his name with the Buenos Aires club Velez Sarsfield. He moved to Italy initially with Pisa in 1990 then played in Spain with Sevilla and Atletico Madrid before returning to Serie A in 1997 with Internazionale, with whom he won the UEFA Cup. He moved on to Lazio but missed a significant portion of the 2001-02 season through ligament damage. He was better in time for the World Cup finals but was unable to save Argentina from first round failure.

Nikita Simonian

National team: Soviet Union
Born: October 12, 1926
Clubs: Kirilia Sovietov, Spartak Moscow

Simonian, one of the few Armenian soccer players to have succeeded in the Soviet game, was small for a centre-forward but skilful and quick – talents which brought him a then record 142 goals in 265 league matches in the 1950s. Three times he was leading scorer in the Soviet Supreme League, and his 1950 haul of 34 goals set a record that was not overtaken until the emergence of Oleg Protasov in the 1980s. Simonian began his career on Georgia's Black Sea coast, moved to Moscow with Kirilia Sovietov, or "Wings of the Soviet" and, three years later in 1949, joined Spartak. He won the league four times, the cup twice and scored 12 goals in 23 internationals before retiring. Later he was coach to Spartak, then joint manager of the Soviet national team at the 1982 World Cup finals in Spain.

Allan Simonsen

National team: Denmark
Born: December 15, 1952
Clubs: Vejle, Borussia Monchengladbach (W Ger), Barcelona (Sp), Charlton (Eng), Vejle

Simonsen was the waif-like forward who inspired Denmark's emergence in the early 1980s. Sadly, Simonsen broke an ankle in the opening match of the 1984 European Championship finals against France. At club level he shone first with Borussia Monchengladbach. He was three times champion of Germany, once German Cup-winner and twice UEFA Cup-winner. He also inspired Borussia to reach the 1977 European Champions Cup Final where they lost to Liverpool. Later, after moving on, he won the Spanish Cup and Cup-Winners' Cup with Barcelona. Simonsen scored 20 goals in 54 games for Denmark.

Agne Simonsson

National team: Sweden
Born: October 19, 1935
Clubs: Orgryte, Real Madrid (Sp), Real Sociedad (Sp), Orgryte
The Swedish team which reached the 1958 World Cup Final on home soil leaned heavily on foreign-based veterans but they, in turn, depended for the injection of a decisive attacking edge on Simonsson, the splendid centre-forward from the Gothenburg club of Orgryte. Simonsson enhanced his reputation by leading Sweden to victory over England at Wembley in 1959 and was signed the following summer by Real Madrid. They envisaged Simonsson becoming the successor to the ageing Alfredo Di Stefano, but Simonsson failed to adjust to life and soccer in Spain and, in any case, Di Stefano was not ready to go. After a spell with Real Sociedad,

Simonsen: 1977 European Footballer of the Year.

Simonsson returned to Orgryte and played again for Sweden, but never quite recovered his earlier spark.

Matthias Sindelar

National team: Austria
Born: February 18, 1903
Clubs: FC Hertha Vienna, FK Austria
Nicknamed "the Man of Paper", for his slim build, Sindelar was the very spirit of the Austrian "Wunderteam" of the 1930s as well as their centre-forward and attacking leader. Born and brought up in Kozlau, in Czechoslovakia, he was discovered by minor Viennese club Hertha in 1920, and joined neighbouring giants FK Austria a year later. Twice he won the Mitropa Cup – the inter-war forerunner of the European Cup – with FK Austria in the 1930s and added 27 goals in 43 internationals to his list of honours. Those 27 included two hat-tricks against old rivals Hungary in 1928 and the two goals which beat Italy in the newly-built Prater Stadium in Vienna in 1932. Sindelar scored in both Austria's classic matches against England in 1932 and 1936 and led Austria to the World Cup semi-finals of 1934. Depressed by the 1938 Anschluss, when Austria was swallowed up into Hitler's Greater Germany, he and his girlfriend committed suicide together in January, 1939.

Omar Enrique Sivori

National team: Argentina and Italy
Born: October 2, 1935
Clubs: River Plate, Juventus (It), Napoli (It)
Sivori was nicknamed "Cabezon" – Big Head – by his admirers in Argentina and Italy, because his technical virtuosity prompted him to humiliate and embarrass opposing defenders in the most outrageous ways. An inside-left with great talent and a quick temper, Sivori put fire into the Juventus attack of the late 1950s alongside the coolness of John Charles and the experience of veteran Giampiero Boniperti. He cost Juventus a world record £91,000 fee

and repaid them with 144 goals in eight seasons before falling out with Paraguayan coach Heriberto Herrera and sulking off to Napoli, where his partnership with Milan outcast José Altafini produced the sort of fervour seen since the 1980s for Maradona. Sivori played 18 times for Argentina, a total of nine times for Italy, and was European Footballer of the Year in 1961.

Wesley Sneijder

National team: Holland
Born: June 9, 1984
Clubs: Ajax, Real Madrid (Sp), Internazionale (It)
Sneijder is a product of the famed Ajax academy and made his first-team debut as a 17-year-old winger. Soon he graduated into midfield playmaker with an eye for goal and a particular skill at free kicks. Real Madrid paid £18m for him in 2007 but sold him on to Inter a year later and he showed them exactly what they had lost by starring in his new club's 2010 Champions League triumph in Madrid's own Estadio Bernabeu. Sneijder, unaffected unlike other stars, by a long European season, then proved a five-goal decisive factor in Holland's World Cup runners-up campaign

Ole-Gunnar Solskjær

National team: Norway
Born: February 26, 1973
Clubs: Clausenengen, Molde, Manchester United (Eng)
A classic goal poacher, Solskjær is probably Norway's most famous soccer player of all time thanks to his achievements at Manchester United. However, he was a late starter in the professional game, not making his top-flight debut until he was 22 in the lower divisions with Clausenengen from his hometown of Kristiansund. He made an immediate impact after joining Molde in 1995, scoring 20 goals to finish second in the league to Rosenborg's Harald Brattbakk. In 1996 Solskjaer was signed by United for a bargain £1.5 million. He scored on his United debut as a substitute and

ended up with 17 goals in his first season. He then struck the historic winning goal for United in the 1999 Champions League Final against Bayern Munich. Honours include winning the Premier League four times and the FA Cup once as well as the 1999 Champions League.

Graeme Souness

National team: Scotland
Born: May 6, 1953
Clubs: Tottenham Hotspur (Eng), Middlesbrough (Eng), Liverpool (Eng), Sampdoria (It), Glasgow Rangers
Souness walked out of Spurs without playing in the first team in a league game, although he did appear for them in a European tie in Iceland. Even as a teenager, he was a player who knew his own value. He developed into a world-class midfielder, winning 54 caps and a string of honours with Liverpool, where he was an influential player and captain. Despite his abrasive style, he then became a great favourite with Sampdoria in Italy, but returned to become player-manager of Rangers. His huge spending ensured a string of titles for the club in the small arena of Scottish soccer, but he was less successful after his return to Anfield, succeeding his old friend Kenny Dalglish as Liverpool boss. He was then manager of Southampton, Blackburn Rovers and Newcastle United.

Neville Southall

National team: Wales
Born: September 16, 1958
Clubs: Bury (Eng), Everton (Eng), Port Vale (Eng), Everton (Eng), Torquay (Eng), Bradford (Eng)
A fiery character, Southall played Welsh League soccer at 14 and worked as a dish-washer, hod-carrier and dustman before joining Bury. He was then 21, and shortly afterwards was signed by Everton. A moderate start and a brief loan period were forgotten after his return, when he suddenly hit the form that established him as one of the world's top goalkeepers. He won two championship

medals, two FA Cups, and one European Cup-Winners' Cup medal, and was voted Footballer of the Year in 1985. After passing the Welsh record of 73 caps, ironically he made an expensive error in the defeat that prevented his country from qualifying for the 1994 World Cup.

Jürgen Sparwasser

National team: East Germany
Born: June 14, 1948
Club: Magdeburg

Sparwasser was one of the few outstanding players produced by East Germany in its 40 years of independent soccer existence. Sweeper Hans-Jurgen Dörner and centre-forward Joachim Streich both earned a century of caps, but the most memorable achievement fell to Sparwasser at the 1974 World Cup finals. An excellent attacking midfield player, Sparwasser scored the historic goal in Hamburg which beat World Cup hosts West Germany in the first and last meeting between the two states at international level. Sparwasser's career featured 15 goals in 77 internationals and a European Cup-Winners' Cup medal after Magdeburg's victory over Milan in Rotterdam in 1974. Later he fled East Germany by taking advantage of his selection for a veterans' tournament in West Germany.

Pedro Alberto Spencer

National team: Ecuador and Uruguay
Born: December 6, 1937
Clubs: Everest, Penarol (Uru), Barcelona Guayaquil

Spencer is probably the greatest Ecuadorian player of all time. He scored a record 50-plus goals in the South American Club Cup (Copa Libertadores), though all in the service of the Uruguayan club, Penarol, who dominated the event's early years in the 1960s. Spencer helped Penarol win the World Club Cup in 1961 and 1966 and earned such status on the field that, with his business interests, he was created Ecuadorian Consul in

Montevideo. Uruguayan officials so coveted Spencer's talents that he was called up to lead Uruguay's attack against England at Wembley in 1964, and scored their only goal in a 2-1 defeat. But protests from Ecuador and other South American nations ensured that this remained his one and only appearance for the "Celeste".

Jaap Stam

National team: Holland
Born: July 17, 1972
Clubs: Pec Zwolle, Cambuur, Willem II, PSV Eindhoven, Manchester United (Eng), Lazio (It), Milan (It)

Stam came up through a string of minor clubs before joining PSV Eindhoven in January 1996 and he was soon being hailed as one of Europe's most resolute central defenders. Manchester United bought him for £12 million after Stam helped Holland finish fourth at the 1998 World Cup. After a shaky start he was a key member of the United team who won the unique treble of Champions League, Premier League and FA Cup in 1999. But weeks after the publication of a controversial ghosted auto-biography in the autumn of 2000, United suddenly sold him to Lazio. The year went from bad to worse when Stam was suspended from Italian league action after failing a dope test, but he served his ban and helped Holland reach the Euro 2004 semi-finals.

Uli Stielike

National team: West Germany
Born: November 15, 1954
Clubs: Borussia Mönchengladbach, Real Madrid (Sp)

Stielike was an aggressive but highly skilled midfielder who later switched successfully back into the sweeper's role. In the mid-1970s he was at the heart of the successful Borussia Monchengladbach team built by master coach Hennes Weisweiler then, after winning German domestic and UEFA Cup honours, he transferred to Spain with Real Madrid. The move

cost him a place at the 1978 World Cup but he was recalled four years later when the Germans lost to Italy in his adopted home of the Estadio Bernabeu. He was a Champions Cup runner-up with Borussia and Madrid.

Hristo Stoichkov

National team: Bulgaria
Born: August 2, 1966
Clubs: CSKA Sofia, Barcelona (Sp), Parma (It), Barcelona (Sp), CSKA Sofia, Kawisa Reysol (Jap), Chicago Fire (US), D.C. United (US)

Stoichkov built a reputation as one of Europe's finest marksmen after being reprieved from a six-month suspension following a controversial Bulgarian Cup Final between his army team CSKA and old Sofia rivals Levski-Spartak in 1985. Stoichkov then so impressed Barcelona they bought him for a Bulgarian record £2 million in 1990. Stoichkov rewarded coach Johan Cruyff's personal recommendation by scoring more than 60 goals in his first three seasons in league and European competition for the Catalan giants. He also led them to their long-awaited European Cup victory in 1992 and was the inspiration for Bulgaria's fourth place in the 1994 World Cup. He was European Footballer of the Year in 1994 and later became national manager.

Dragan Stojkovic

National team: Yugoslavia
Born: March 3, 1965
Clubs: Radnicki, Red Star Belgrade, Marseille (Fr), Verona (It), Nagoya Grampus Eight (Jap)

Stojkovic has turned out to be a leader both on the pitch and off it. Stojkovic left Radnicki for Red Star in exchange for a set of floodlights and "Piksi" made his international debut against France in 1983. Serious injury prevented him sharing in Red Star's 1991 Champions Cup Final win, but he recovered to spend eight seasons in Japan with Grampus Eight. Despite injuries, conflict in Yugoslavia and his own travels, Stojkovic still was able to score 15 goals in 84 internationals. Shortly after retiring as a player he was voted in as president of the Serb soccer federation.

Davor Suker

National team: Croatia
Born: January 1, 1968
Clubs: Osijek, FC Croatia Zagreb, Sevilla (Sp), Real Madrid (Sp), Arsenal (Eng), West Ham (Eng), TSV 1860 Munich (Ger)

Suker starred first in the Yugoslav team to win the World Youth Cup in 1987. He then became top league marksman with 18 goals while with Osijek to earn selection for the 1990 World Cup finals, but did not play.

Davor Suker was six-goal top scorer at the 1998 World Cup finals.

After the conflict in the Balkans he declared for Croatia and was overall top scorer in the Euro 96 qualifying competition with 12 goals in ten matches. At the finals Suker scored a memorable chipped goal against Denmark. Sevilla then sold him to Real Madrid with whom he won the Spanish league and Champions League. He was the six-goal top scorer at the 1998 World Cup finals.

Safet Susic

National team: Yugoslavia
Born: April 13, 1955
Clubs: Sarajevo, Gijon (Sp),
Paris Saint-Germain (Fr)

Susic was one of the most charismatic players of his generation. Brought up in the Bosnian town of Zavidovicima, he was discovered by Sarajevo for whom he scored 172 goals in 219 games. He was also top scorer in the Slav league with 17 goals in 1979–80. His talent drew offers from Italy, Spain and France but the federation barred all moves abroad as punishment for Yugoslavia's first-round exit at the 1982 World Cup in Spain. Eventually Susic obtained his release – spending half a season on loan to Spain's Gijon before joining Paris Saint-Germain with whom he won the French Cup.

Luis Suarez Miramontes

National team: Spain
Born: May 2, 1935
Clubs: Deportivo La Coruña, Barcelona,
Internazionale (It), Sampdoria (It)

Suarez was born and brought up in La Coruña, where he was discovered by Barcelona. At the age of 18, the Catalans insisted on buying him immediately after he had earned a standing ovation playing against Barcelona in their own Nou Camp stadium. Suarez was hailed as the greatest Spanish player of all time, a midfield general who was later the fulcrum of the Internazionale team that dominated world club soccer in the mid-1960s. Suarez's ability to turn defence into attack with one pinpoint pass suited Inter's hit-and-hold tactics

admirably. Injury prevented Suarez lining up against Celtic when Inter lost the 1967 European Cup Final in Lisbon. Later Suarez managed Spain at the 1990 World Cup finals.

Frank Swift

National team: England
Born: December 26, 1913
Club: Manchester City

Big Frank was a personality among goalkeepers, who enjoyed a joke with opponents and referees alike, but was deadly serious at stopping shots. He stood in the crowd and watched Manchester City lose the 1933 FA Cup Final, then played for them when they won a year later, fainting at the finish as nervous exhaustion overcame him. During the war his entertainment value became even greater, and he won 19 caps while in his 30s – only twice on the losing side. After his retirement he became a journalist, and was one of those killed in the Munich air crash in 1958.

Claudio Andre Mergen Taffarel

National team: Brazil
Born: May 8, 1966
Clubs: Crissiuma, Internacional Porto Alegre, Parma (It), Reggiana (It), Palmeiras, Atletico Mineiro, Parma (It), Reggiana (It), Galatasaray (Tur)

Taffarel retired in the middle of the 2003-04 season, claiming that a car breakdown on the motorway was "a sign from God" that he should not carry on in the game. His goalkeeping career certainly appeared to have been especially blessed. Taffarel first gained attention when Brazil beat Spain 1-0 after extra time in the 1985 World Youth Cup in Moscow. His next starring stop was the 1988 Olympics when he saved three penalties in the semi-final against West Germany, one in the match and two in the shoot-out. Taffarel, who started with Crissiuma then Internacional, had become a goalkeeper to follow the example of his hero, the Uruguayan Ladislao Mazurkiewicz. After the 1990 World

Lilian Thuram was equally effective at both rightback and in the centre of defence.

Cup Taffarel moved to Italy's Parma with whom he won the Cup-Winners' Cup before his form faded. Brazil boss Carlos Alberto Parreira still believed in him, however and he regained the No. 1 spot for the 1994 World Cup which Brazil won, of course, in a shoot-out. Taffarel repeated the magic for Galatasaray against Arsenal in the 2000 UEFA Cup Final.

Marco Tardelli

National team: Italy
Born: September 24, 1954
Clubs: Pisa, Como, Juventus, Internazionale

Tardelli was a utility defender or midfielder who was seen to best effect playing for Juventus and Italy in the first half of the 1980s. With both club and country Tardelli succeeded the more physical Romeo Benetti in midfield, though his Azzurri debut, against Portugal in Turin in 1976, was at right-back. Tardelli is one of the very few players to have won every

major prize in the modern domestic and European game, from the World Cup to the 1985 European Cup with Juventus. He scored six goals in 81 appearances for Italy and was voted official Man of the Match in the 1982 World Cup Final defeat of West Germany in Madrid.

Mauro Tassotti

National team: Italy
Born: January 19, 1960
Clubs: Lazio, Milan

Tassotti lacked the high profile of many of Milan's stars in the late 1980s and early 1990s. But what he lacked in image he made up for in professional commitment. Born in Rome, he had two seasons with Lazio before transferring in 1980 to Milan who were then in Serie B. Tassotti's tackling helped them up into Serie A and on to win two World Club crowns, three Champions Cups, two European Supercups and five Serie A titles. He played only seven times for Italy – his Azzurri career was ended by a long ban after a clash with Spain's Luis Enrique in the 1994 World Cup quarter-finals.

Lilian Thuram

National team: France
Born: January 1, 1972
Clubs: Monaco, Parma (It), Juventus (It), Barcelona (Sp)

Thuram has achieved much of his success in Italy in central defence yet his reputation with France has been built at full-back. Successive France managers Aime Jacquet and Roger Lemerre were able to enjoy this luxury in winning the 1998 World Cup and 2000 European Championship because of a plethora of central defensive talent. Thuram adapted superbly to right-back even scoring the two goals which beat Croatia in the the 1998 World Cup semi-final. He had switched finally to central defence by the time France finished runners-up at the 2006 World Cup. At club level he won the UEFA Cup with Parma and then Serie A titles with Juventus.

Jean Amadou Tigana

National team: France
Born: June 23, 1955
Clubs: Toulon, Lyon, Bordeaux

Tigana owed an enormous debt to France's World Cup-winning coach Aime Jacquet. Born in Bamako, Mali, as a child Tigana came to France with his family. On leaving school he worked in a spaghetti factory then as a postman to supplement his part-time earnings from soccer. Toulon signed him at 20 but gave him a free transfer, which was when Jacquet stepped in, to "rescue" Tigana for Lyon. His international career took off after his move to Bordeaux in 1981. Tigana was a regular in midfield in the World Cups of 1982 and 1986 as well as the 1984 European Championship-winning campaign. He went on to a successful time in charge of Monaco but did not fare so well at Fulham.

Fernando Jose Torres Sanz

National team: Spain
Born: March 20, 1984
Club(s): Atletico de Madrid, Liverpool (Eng)

Torres turned down a string offers to stay on with Atletico, whom he had supported as a boy before becoming their superstar. Ironically, after "El Nino" finally joined Liverpool for a club record £20m in 2007, Atletico qualified for Europe's top tournament without him. Torres had an instant impact on the Premier League, scoring 29 goals in all competitions including two successive Anfield hat-tricks.. Torres was Spain's match-winning hero in their Euro 2008 Final victory over Germany and, despite fitness and form problems, appeared as a substitute to help lay on the goal with which Spain won the World Cup against Holland two years later.

Tostao
Full name: Eduardo Goncalves Andrade

National team: Brazil
Born: January 25, 1947
Clubs: Cruzeiro, Vasco da Gama

Tostao, a small, nimble centre-forward, was already nicknamed "the White Pele" when he made his World Cup debut for Brazil at the 1966 finals in England. He scored Brazil's consolation goal in their 3-1 defeat by Hungary. It nearly became his only World Cup appearance when, in 1969, he suffered a detached retina during a South American Cup tie against Millonarios in Bogota. Tostao underwent specialist surgery in Houston and recovered to become one of the heroes of Brazil's World Cup victory in Mexico a year later. However Tostao, a qualified doctor, recognized that the longer he played on, the greater the risk of permanent injury, and retired at the age of 26 in 1973... to become an eye specialist.

Francesco Totti

SEE PAGE 225

David Trezeguet

National team: France
Born: October 15, 1977
Clubs: Paris Saint-Germain, Monaco, Juventus (It)

Trezeguet was born in France when his father was playing there but brought up in Argentina after the family went "home". He played there briefly as a teenager but turned professional in France for whom he starred at the 1997 World Youth Cup in Malaysia. A year later Trezeguet found himself thrust into the limelight at the senior World Cup. He played a part in every game except the Final win over Brazil, scoring one goal in the first round win over Saudi Arabia and then nervelessly converting one of the spotkicks in the shoot-out victory over Italy in the quarter-finals. Italy suffered at Trezeguet's hands again two years later when he struck the golden goal winner for France in the Euro 2000 Final. However, in 2006, his missed penalty condemned France to shoot-out defeat in the World Cup Final against . . . Italy.

Jorge Valdano

National team: Argentina
Born: October 4, 1955
Club(s): Newell's Old Boys, Alaves (Sp), Zaragoza (Sp), Real Madrid (Sp)

Valdano has proved a rare personality in the soccer world: an author, poet, polemicist, coach and World Cup-winning player. He was born in Las Parejas, and left Argentina for political reasons as a teenager, building his playing career in Spain. His success in winning the UEFA Cup with Real Madrid twice in the mid-1980s earned him selection for Argentina, and his positional and tactical skills were huge influences in the 1986 World Cup victory in Mexico. He was later struck down by hepatitis, struggled in vain to make a World Cup comeback in 1990 and retired to become a journalist and a successful coach with Tenerife before returning to Real Madrid as their general manager.

Tostao shrugged off eye trouble to help Brazil win the 1970 World Cup.

FRANCESCO TOTTI
Man in the middle

In Italian soccer it requires only a half-formed phrase, muttered sotto voce, to prompt an avalanche of front-page publicity. So Francesco Totti should not have been surprised by the frenzy of controversy which greeted a comment that he did not want "to end up" like Giuseppe Giannini, another former Roma captain. But there was never much chance of that.

Giannini was to Roma in the 1980s and early 1990s what Totti had become in the early years of the new millennium: the idol of the fans, a pin-up for all the girls and a personality whose popularity and fame stretched far beyond the confines of the soccer pitch. Totti was a local boy too, but there the similarities with Giannini end. Totti was born in the Rome suburb of San Giovanni and his soccer career began with a local boys' club called Fortitudo. From there, playing in midfield, he moved up a grade to Smit Trastevere and then was signed by a "serious" club called Lodigiani. Totti spent 18 months building a local reputation with such success that coach Emidio Neroni soon received offers for him. He went to AS Roma. Events moved quickly. Within 18 months Totti had played for Italy's schoolboys and the national youth

team. The following season he caught the eye of the veteran Yugoslav coach, Vujadin Boskov, in a training match. In March 1993 Boskov handed the teenage Totti his Serie A debut.

But not all Boskov's successors were as excited by Totti's wayward talent and lack of discipline. Carlo Mazzone rated Totti worth a place in attack but the Argentine coach, Carlos Bianchi, doubted Totti's commitment and at one stage a transfer to Sampdoria beckoned. In the end it was not Totti who left but

Francesco Totti has been a loyal servant to AS Roma, spending more than 15 years with the club.

Bianchi and successor Zdenek Zeman was the first coach to slip Totti into the space between midfield and the strike force. At last, with defenders uncertain how far to pursue him, Totti found the space to employ his close control and sharp acceleration to greatest advantage.

In the spring of 1996 Arrigo Sacchi called him up for a national team training camp and he celebrated a first international success the following May when Italy beat Spain.

Fabio Capello took over Roma around the same time that Dino Zoff became national coach. Both men were Totti fans. Capello appointed him club captain and developed Zeman's tactical strategy which allowed Totti freedom to roam across the breadth of attack. Zoff handed Totti a fixed place in Italy's attack and he was their outstanding player in the Final of the European Championship in 2000.

Within a year Totti had established himself as the most brilliantly consistent Italian forward in Serie A. After disciplinary problems at both the 2002 World Cup and Euro 2004 Totti finally secured a place in history as a starting member of Italy's 2006 World Cup-winning side.

1976
Born on September 27 in Rome

1983
Turned out for his first club team, San Giovanni

1989
Turned down an offer from Lazio and joined rivals Roma's youth team set-up

1993
Made Serie A debut aged 16 in a 2-0 win over Brescia

1996
Won the European Under-21 title with Italy against Spain

1998
Made Italy senior debut in a 2-0 win over Switzerland on October 10 in a European Championship qualifier

2000
Scored first goal for Italy in a 2-0 win over Portugal on April 26, some 18 months after winning his first cap. Outstanding for Italy at the European finals. Converted a crucial penalty in the semi-final shoot-out win over Holland but finished runner-up after the golden goal defeat by France in the Final

2001
Scored 13 goals in 30 games to lead Roma to their first Italian league championship in 18 years

2003
Organized a dressing-room collection to help pay wages to the Roma youth team players when the financially-stricken club could not afford to

2006
Became a World Cup winner with Italy in Germany

Van Basten's career was cut short by injury.

Carlos **Valderrama**

National team: Colombia
Born: September 2, 1961
Clubs: Santa Marta, Millonarios, Atletico Nacional, Montpellier (Fr), Valladolid (Sp), Medellin, Atletico Junior Barranquilla, Tampa Bay Mutiny (US), Miami Fusion (US)

Valderrama was voted South American Footballer of the Year in 1987 after guiding Colombia to a fine third place at the Copa America. The combination of frizzy hairstyle and all-round skill earned him the nickname of "the South American Gullit", and he shared South American Cup glory with Atletico Nacional before trying his luck in Europe with Montpellier of France and Valladolid of Spain. He failed to impress, but played well as Colombia reached the second round of the 1990 World Cup finals and rediscovered his touch after returning to Colombia in 1992. He was South American Footballer of the Year in 1994, after masterminding Colombia's sensational 1994 World Cup qualifying campaign (including a 5-0 win over Argentina). And, at the age of 36, he also played in the 1998 World Cup finals in France.

Marco **Van Basten**

National team: Holland
Born: October 31, 1964
Clubs: Ajax, AC Milan (It)

Marco van Basten contributed one of the all-time great international goals when he volleyed home a long, looping cross in the 1988 European Championship Final in Munich. That was when van Basten was just reaching his peak, one year after graduating from Ajax to Milan. Tall and angular, van Basten made his international debut at the 1983 World Youth Cup and scored 128 league goals for Ajax before joining Milan for a mere £1.5 million in 1987. With Ajax he had won the European Golden Boot (37 goals in 1985–86) and the European Cup-winners Cup, but with Milan he added even more honours – including FIFA, World and European Player of the Year awards plus World Club and European Cup medals. Sadly, ankle trouble wrecked the latter years of his career and he retired early.

Wilhelmus "Wim" **Van Hanegem**

National team: Holland
Born: February 20, 1944
Clubs: Velox, Xerxes, Feyenoord, AZ Alkmaar, Utrecht

Van Hanegem was a moody presence in midfield for Feyenoord in the 1970s. But it was a measure of his ability that he fitted into a Dutch national team built around the style and personnel of the Rotterdam club's great rivals from Ajax Amsterdam. Van Hanegem won the European Champions Cup and World Club crown with Feyenoord in 1970 and the UEFA Cup in 1974. A few weeks later he was on the losing side with Holland against West Germany in the World Cup Final. He scored six goals in 52 internationals between a 0-0 draw with Scotland in 1968 and a 1-0 win over Belgium in September 1979.

Paul **Van Himst**

National team: Belgium
Born: October 2, 1943
Clubs: Anderlecht, RWD Molenbeek, Eendracht Aalst

Van Himst, the manager who guided Belgium to the 1994 World Cup finals, is still regarded as his country's greatest player. He joined the Brussels club Anderlecht at the age of nine and, at 16, was playing centre-forward in the first team. He was to be Belgian champion eight times, a cup-winner four times, league top scorer three times and was four times Footballer of the Year. Van Himst scored 31 goals in 81 internationals between 1960 and 1979, which included the 1970 World Cup finals and a third-place finish as hosts at the 1972 European Championship. Later he coached Anderlecht to victory in the UEFA Cup before being appointed manager of Belgium after the qualifying failure in the 1992 European Championship.

Ruud **Van Nistelrooy**

National team: Holland
Born: July 1, 1976
Clubs: Den Bosch, PSV Eindhoven, Manchester United (Eng), Real Madrid (Sp), Hamburg (Ger)

Van Nistelrooy's move from Eindhoven to Manchester took 16 months, but the wait proved worthwhile for United. A serious knee injury cost him more than a year out of the game but, once the £19 million move had been confirmed in 2001, he wasted no time getting back into the scoring habit. Van Nistelrooy scored on his first team debut in the Charity Shield then added two more on his Premier League debut against Fulham. He totalled 23 league goals in his first season and 25 in his second including 15 in his last ten games to fire United to what proved his only Premier success. He did then win two league titles in Spain with Real Madrid.

Ruud Van Nistelrooy won two Golden Boots in Holland and one each in England and Spain.

Odbulio Varela

National team: Uruguay
Born: September 20, 1917
Clubs: Wanderers, Penarol

Varela was captain of the Uruguayan team which shocked Brazil by beating their hosts in Rio's Maracana stadium in the 1950 World Cup 'Final' (the deciding match of the final pool). Varela was an old-style attacking centre-half and a captain who led by example. He had made his league debut with Wanderers at 21 and had already played for Uruguay before joining local giants Penarol in 1942. Twice he won the South American Championship with Uruguay but the 1950 World Cup saw him at his zenith, driving his team forward with every confidence even after Uruguay went 1-0 down early on. Varela was outstanding again, even at 37, in the 1954 World Cup finals in Switzerland. He retired immediately afterwards and was briefly coach to Penarol.

Vava
Full name: Edvaldo Izidio Neto

National team: Brazil
Born: November 12, 1934
Clubs: Recife, Vasco da Gama, Atletico Madrid (Sp), Palmeiras, Botafogo

Vava may not have been one of the most refined of centre-forwards in soccer history, but he was one of the most effective when it mattered. Originally an inside-left, Vava was switched to the centre of attack by Brazil at the 1958 World Cup to allow Pele into the line-up. He scored twice in the 5-2 Final victory over Sweden to earn a transfer to Spain with Atletico Madrid. The hawk-nosed Vava was successful and hugely popular in Spain, but his family grew homesick. Returning home in time to regain his Brazil place for the World Cup defence in Chile in 1962, he scored another of his typically vital goals in the 3-1 Final victory over Czechoslovakia. In all, Vava scored 15 goals in 22 internationals spread over 12 years between 1952 and 1964.

Patrick Vieira was rescued from Milan's reserves for Arsenal by Arsene Wenger.

Juan Sebastian Veron

National team: Argentina
Born: March 9, 1975
Clubs: Estudiantes de La Plata, Boca Juniors, Sampdoria (It), Lazio (It), Manchester United (Eng), Chelsea (Eng), Inter (It), Estudiantes de La Plata

Veron's talent was spotted early thanks to his family background. His father, also named Juan, was a top-scoring left-winger with Estudiantes in the late 1960s who later became their youth coach. Juan junior made his debut with Estudiantes in 1994 and inspired their promotion campaign the following year to earn a transfer to Boca Juniors. He moved to Italy in 1997 with Sampdoria under Sven-Goran Eriksson. A season at Parma was followed by a summons from Eriksson to join Lazio. But Veron's two years in Rome were clouded by problems over the status of his passport and he was sold to Manchester United for £28 million in

2001. Inconsistent form ultimately saw him return home via Chelsea and Internazionale but a return to form at Estudiantes earned him the South American Footballer of the Year award.

Gianluca Vialli

National team: Italy
Born: July 9, 1964
Clubs: Cremonese, Sampdoria, Juventus, Chelsea (Eng)

Vialli scored 16 goals in 59 international appearances for Italy while simultaneously building a high-profile club career which brought him success both at home as well as in England. Born in Cremona, Vialli starred first with Sampdoria with whom he won the 1990 Cup-Winners' Cup and finished extra-time runners-up to Barcelona in the 1992 Champions Cup. He then joined Juventus with whom he finally won a Champions League medal in 1995

before embarking on his English adventure with Chelsea where he graduated to player-manager and guided them to success in the 1998 Cup-Winners' Cup. He was sacked despite building a successful team and stayed in England with Watford.

Patrick Vieira

National team: France
Born: June 23, 1976
Clubs: Cannes, Milan (It), Arsenal (Eng), Juventus (It), Internazionale (It), Manchester City (Eng)

Vieira took over as the new "leader" of Arsenal after the retirement of Tony Adams. Talented but temperamental, the Senegal-born midfielder had started out in France with Cannes. He was snapped up by Milan but injury problems prevented him making any impression. Arsene Wenger made Vieira his first signing for Arsenal and the £3 million fee soon looked a bargain. Vieira drove Arsenal to the league and Cup double in both 1998 and 2002. With France, he was a reserve for the 1998 World Cup win, but had established himself as first choice by the time of the Euro 2000 victory. He also captained Arsenal to seven league and cup victories in eight seasons.

Christian Vieri

National team: Italy
Born: July 12, 1973
Clubs: Prato, Torino, Venezia, Atalanta, Juventus, Atletico Madrid (Sp), Lazio, Internazionale (It), Milan (It), Monaco (Fr), Inter (It)

Vieri, son of a former Italian midfielder, was brought up in Australia and once named legendary cricketer Sir Donald Bradman as one of his sporting heroes. He returned home to build a remarkable soccer career of his own, although it was a comparatively long time before he was eventually recognized when he helped Juventus win the Italian Serie A title and reach the Champions League Final in 1997. He was sold that summer to Atletico Madrid and was league top scorer with 24 goals in his first and only

Spanish season. He then came back to Italy with Lazio, scoring the winning goal against Mallorca in the last Cup-Winners' Cup Final. Vieri's prolific form meant he cost a then world record £31 million when he transferred to Inter a few weeks later. However injuries to both Vieri and Ronaldo upset Inter's plans for what could have been the most prolific attacking partnership in world soccer. Injury problems also restricted Vieri's appearances for Italy so he played only 24 times (with ten goals) heading into the 2002 World Cup finals. He then scored four of Italy's five goals including the opener in their second round exit defeat against co-hosts South Korea.

Ivo Viktor

National team: Czechoslovakia
Born: May 21, 1942
Clubs: RH Brno, Dukla Prague

Viktor was probably European soccer's finest goalkeeper in the mid-1970s. He launched his league career with RH Brno after being called up for army service then transferred to Dukla when Brno were relegated. Viktor first ousted experienced Pavel Kouba then made his national team debut in a 2-2 draw with Brazil in Maracana. Later he became only the second foreign keeper to keep a clean sheet against England at Wembley. Viktor's greatest achievement was in anchoring Czechoslovakia's surprise 1976 European Championship win when they beat West Germany on penalties in the Final.

David Villa

National team: Spain
Born: December 3, 1981
Clubs: Gijon, Zaragoza, Valencia, Barcelona

Villa's five goals not only fired Spain to World Cup glory for the first time in South Africa in June/July 2010 but took him within reach of his country's national team scoring record. His goals, following his four-goal top-scoring contribution to Spain's Euro 2008 victory, lifted his tally to 43, one

fewer than Raul Gonzalez's record. At club level Villa had won 'only' the Spanish cup with both Zaragoza and Valencia. He went to South Africa knowing he would be sold to Barcelona immediately after the World Cup for a domestic record £35m.

Hans-Hubert "Berti" Vogts

National team: West Germany
Born: December 30, 1946
Club: Borussia Mönchengladbach

Vogts was a key player in the German team that won the World Cup in 1974 and finished European Championship runners-up two years later. He won 96 caps, scoring one goal in the process. But goalscoring was not his role. Instead Vogts was a full-back with a particular talent for close-marking opposing stars. He played all 14 years of his club career with Borussia, winning the UEFA Cup twice, the Bundesliga five times and German Cup once. Vogts was Footballer of the Year in 1971 and 1979 when he joined the DFB staff. He was national coach from 1990 to 1998 and later took up a similar role with Scotland.

Rudi Völler

National team: Germany
Born: April 13, 1960

George Weah used his earnings to help prop up soccer in his native Liberia.

Clubs: TSV 1860 Munich, Werder Bremen, Roma (It), Marseille (Fr), Bayer Leverkusen

Völler, with 47 goals in 90 games, was one of Germany's most competitive international players in the 1980s and 1990s. He appeared to great effect in the World Cup finals events of 1986, 1990 and – after being persuaded by manager Berti Vogts to rescind his retirement – in 1994. Völler joined Werder Bremen in 1982 and, in his first season, he was league top scorer with 23 goals, Footballer of the Year and won his first cap. He was a World Cup runner-up in 1986 and a winner in 1990. Later he became national manager, guiding Germany to the 2002 World Cup Final against all the odds, but quit after Euro 2004.

Fritz Walter

National team: Germany
Born: October 31, 1920
Clubs: Kaiserslautern

Fritz Walter and centre-forward brother Ottmar starred with Kaiserslautern in the late 1940s and early 1950s and were World Cup-winners together against hot favourites Hungary in the 1954 Final in Switzerland. Yet that triumph came late in a career which was cut in two by the war. Walter scored a hat-trick on his Germany debut in a 9-2 thrashing of Romania in July 1940. After soccer was halted Walter was called up as a paratrooper, but his wartime flying experiences led him to refuse to fly to games in later, peacetime years. On the resumption of international soccer, he was made captain by manager Sepp Herberger and success followed in the 1954 World Cup. Walter retired from the national team but was persuaded to return in 1958 when, at 37, he led his team to the semi-finals. Walter, who scored 33 goals in his 61 internationals, later wrote successful soccer books.

George Weah

National team: Liberia
Born: October 1, 1966
Clubs: Young Survivors, Bongrange, Mighty

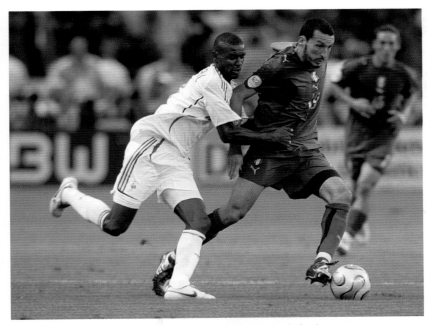
Gianluca Zambrotta was a key member of Italy's 2006 World Cup-winning team.

Barolle, Tonnerre (Cam), Monaco (Fr), Paris Saint-German (Fr), Milan (It), Chelsea (Eng), Manchester City (Eng), Marseille (Fr), Al-Jazira (UAE)
Liberian Striker Weah made history in 1995 when he became the first winner of the European Footballer poll after a rule change that opened up the award to players of any nationality. Born in Monrovia, Weah played in Cameroon with Tonnerre before moving to Monaco in 1998. He rose to stardom under Arsene Wenger to win the French championship and then moved to Paris Saint-German. Two years later he joined Milan for £3.5 million – adding the World and African player crowns to his European award. He also won the English FA Cup while on loan to Chelsea in 2000.

Xavi
Full name: Xavier Hernández i Creus
National team: Spain
Born: January 25, 1980
Club(s): Barcelona
Xavi's career reached a zenith of unprecedented success between 2008 and 2010. Barcelona's Catalan playmaker was voted best player after Spain's Euro 2008 triumph and was then a key figure in the club's unique

six-trophy clean sweep at home and abroad in 2009. In addition, he was voted man of the match after the Champions League Final victory over Manchester United in Rome. In 2010, already a world champion at club level, he added a World Cup-winner's medal to his trophy collection after Spain's dismissal of Holland in South Africa.

Ernst Wilimowski
National team: Poland and Germany
Born: June 23, 1916
Clubs: Ruch Chorzow, PSV Chemnitz (Ger), TSV 1860 Munich (Ger), Hameln 07 (Ger), BC Augsburg (Ger), Singen 04, Kaiserslautern (Ger)
Wilimowski wrote his name into World Cup history when he scored four goals against Brazil in a first-round tie in France in 1938 – yet still finished on the losing side after a 6-5, extra-time defeat. He totalled 21 goals in 22 games for Poland, where he won five league titles with Ruch Chorzow. Yet for years his name was omitted from Polish sports records – because Wilimowski, after the German invasion, continued his career with German clubs and scored a further 13 goals in eight internationals for what was then known as Greater Germany. In 1942 he scored 1860 Munich's first goal in

their 2-0 defeat of Schalke in the Greater German Cup Final.

After the war he played on in Germany with a string of regional league clubs before retiring at 37 in 1953.

Billy Wright
National team: England
Born: February 6, 1924
Club: Wolverhampton Wanderers
A lively wing-half who moved into the centre of defence and – by reading play superbly, timing tackles well and leaping to remarkable heights for a smallish man – extended his career for years and years. Two league titles and one FA Cup came his way, plus the little matter of 105 caps (out of a possible 108) in 13 seasons – with the majority as captain). He was the first player in the world to reach a century of caps, and might have had more, even at the age of 35, but ended his career at a moment's notice in response to being left out of his club side for a lesser player.

Yashin was a golden boy in 1956.

Lev Yashin
National team: Soviet Union
Born: October 22, 1929
Club: Moscow Dynamo
Yashin, rated by many as the greatest goalkeeper of all, nearly turned to ice hockey in 1953 when he tired of being reserve to Alexei "Tiger" Khomich. Then Khomich was injured and Yashin stepped in so well that, a year later, he made his Soviet national team debut in a 3-2 win over Sweden. Two years later, in 1956, Yashin kept goal for the Soviet side who won Olympic gold in Melbourne. In 1960 he inspired their inaugural European Championship win. He earned 78 caps, won the domestic league title six times and was voted European Footballer of the Year in 1963.

Gianluca Zambrotta
National team: Italy
Born: February 19, 1977
Clubs: Como, Bari, Juventus, Barcelona (Spain)
Zambrotta was hailed as arguably the world's finest wingback after his versatile contribution to Italy's 2006 World Cup triumph. But by then he was already renowned after helping the Azzurri finish runners-up in the 2000 European Championship and winning two league titles with Juventus.

Branislav "Branko" Zebec
National team: Yugoslavia
Born: May 17, 1929
Clubs: Borac, Partizan Belgrade, Red Star Belgrade, Alemannia Aachen (Ger)
Zebec was so remarkable he enjoyed two simultaneous playing careers. One saw him feared as a goal-scoring outside-left, the other saw him admired as a sure-footed central defender. He played the one role in the 1954 World Cup finals for Yugoslavia and the other in 1958. Born in Zagreb, Zebec began with Borac then transferred controversially to Partizan for whom he starred in the first-ever Champions Cup in 1955-56. Two years later he was the centre of controversy again on moving to rivals Red Star. Zebec

ZINEDINE ZIDANE
Natural born talent

Three French players had been hailed as European Footballer of the Year before Zidane. But he may lay claim to being the greatest of all.

Raymond Kopa collected his prize for inspiring Les Bleus to third place in the 1958 World Cup; Michel Platini won a hat-trick of awards in the mid-1980s; Jean-Pierre Papin was crowned for his avalanche of goals with Marseille. But great as Kopa and Platini were – Papin was a "mere" shooting star – neither won the World Cup. Zidane collected a winner's medal after the 3-0 win over Brazil in 1998, and also scored two of the goals.

His story is one to inspire the hundreds of disorientated footballing youngsters who are spirited out of Africa each year to feed the voracious appetite of European soccer. For Zidane is the son of Algerian immigrants. Hence his personal success at the 1998 World Cup was hailed as not merely a sporting but a social triumph.

Zidane's parents had arrived in France in the wake of the north African independence struggles of the late 1950s and "Zizou", a soccer-mad teenager was overlooked by Olympique Marseille, the club he idolized, and had to fight his way up with minor

neighbours Cannes instead.

At 20 he was snapped up by Bordeaux and inspired them to the UEFA Cup Final in 1996 before Juventus came calling. Zidane, won two Italian league titles, one Italian Supercup, one World Club Cup and one European Supercup.

An explosive substitute's debut in August 1994, against the Czech Republic marked his arrival on the French national team scene.

Playing against Italy in the quarter-finals of the 1998 World Cup, Zidane converted the first penalty in France's shoot-out success. Semi-final victory over Croatia prepared the stage for Zidane's match-winning display in the Final triumph over Brazil. Both his goals, unusually, were headers.

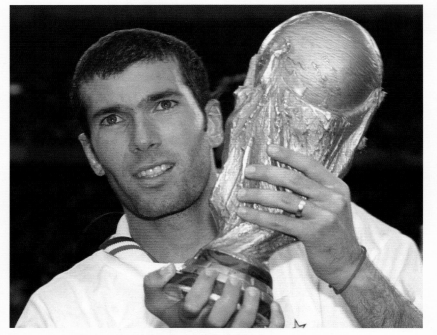

Zinedine Zidane cost Real Madrid a world record £45 million from Juventus in 2000.

Two years later Zidane was the guiding hand behind France's triumph at Euro 2000: it was Zidane who shut out the chaos at the end of extra time in the semi-final against Portugal to flick home the golden goal penalty.

The next two World Cups were not as kind. In 2002 France crashed out in the first round after Zidane missed the first two games through injury. In 2006 he scored the opening goal in the doomed Final defeat by Italy when he was sent off in extra-time in what he had said would be his very last game.

In the meantime, Zidane had found a new club kingdom. Real Madrid had spirited him away from Juventus after Euro 2000 for a world record £35 million and in Spain he raised his game to an even higher plane. With Juve, Zidane had twice been a Champions League runner-up. But Madrid changed his luck. In May 2002 Zidane volleyed one of the most masterful winning goals ever seen in the event to secure a 2-1 win over Bayer Leverkusen in the Final at Hampden Park, Glasgow.

His playing career ended contentiously with dramatic expulsion in extra time in France's defeat on penalties by Italy in the Final of the 2006 World Cup in Berlin.

1972	1992	1996	1998	2001	2003
Born June 23 in Marseille	Transferred to Bordeaux	UEFA runner-up with Bordeaux, Euro 96 semi-finalist with France then transferred to Juventus with whom he then won the World Club Cup and European Supercup	World Cup winner with France, scoring twice in the Final against Brazil. Also, with Juventus, Italian champion again and Champions League runner-up again, against Real Madrid. Voted French Sportsman of the Year, FIFA World Player of the Year and European Footballer of the Year	Won Spanish League with Madrid and Confederations Cup with France	Again a Spanish league champion and voted FIFA World Player of the Year for a record-equalling third time ahead of Arsenal's Thierry Henry and Madrid teammate Ronaldo

1988	1994	1997	2000		2002
Turned professional with Cannes, making his league debut in a 1-1 draw with Nantes	Scored twice on his national team debut in a 2-2 draw against the Czech Republic	Won the Italian League with Juventus and finished a Champions League runner-up to Borussia Dortmund	Won the European Championship with France. Sold to Real Madrid for world record £35m. Voted FIFA World Player of the Year		Won Champions League, scoring the winner against Bayer Leverkusen. Won the World Club Cup and European Supercup

enjoyed further success as a coach with Bayern Munich and Stuttgart.

Zico
Full name: Artur Antunes Coimbra

National team: Brazil
Born: March 3, 1953
Clubs: Flamengo, Udinese (It), Flamengo, Kashima Antlers (Jap)

The youngest of three professional soccer brothers, Zico was at first considered too lightweight by Flamengo. Special diets and weight training turned him into a wiry attacker who scored with one of his speciality free-kicks on his Brazil debut in 1975. Injury and tactical disagreements marred his 1978 and 1986 World Cups, so Zico was seen at his best only in Spain in 1982. He inspired Flamengo's victory in the 1981 Copa Libertadores and their demolition of European champions Liverpool in Tokyo in the World Club Cup Final. That was the start of Zico's mutual love affair with Japan which was resumed when, after a spell as Brazil's Minister of Sport, he joined Kashima Antlers and later became national coach.

Zinedine Zidane

SEE PAGE 230

Wladyslaw Zmuda

National team: Poland
Born: May 6, 1954
Clubs: Gwardia Warsaw, Slask Wroclaw, Widzew Lodz, Cremonese (It)

Zmuda, despite a deceptively low-profile role at the heart of Poland's defence, achieved a consistent World Cup record. He played in four finals tournaments, in 1974, 1978, 1982 and 1986 at which time he had played more matches at the finals (21) than any other player. Zmuda was playing his club soccer with Gwardia Warsaw when he helped Poland finish third at the 1974 World Cup. His determined attitude in clashes with authority over various club transfers did not deter successive national coaches.

Dino Zoff

National team: Italy
Born: February 28, 1942
Clubs: Udinese, Mantova, Napoli, Juventus

Zoff played a then-record 112 times for Italy, of which the 106th was the World Cup Final defeat of West Germany in Madrid in 1982. In 1973-74 he set a world record of 1,143 international minutes without conceding a goal. He won European trophies both as player and coach at Juventus, and guided Italy to the Euro 2000 Final. He quit after losing to France.

Dino Zoff emulated Gianpiero Combi as a World Cup-winning captain and goalkeeper.

Gianfranco Zola emerged from Maradona's shadow as an outstanding player in his own right.

Gianfranco Zola

National team: Italy
Born: July 5, 1966
Clubs: Nuorese, Torres, Napoli, Parma, Chelsea (Eng), Cagliari

Zola learned his trade in the shadow of Diego Maradona at Napoli – picking up all the Argentine superstar's good soccer habits. Yet it was not until his transfer to Parma that he was appreciated as an intuitive forward in his own right. Zola had an unfortunate time at Euro 96, missing a penalty after having been brought down in the decisive group match against Germany. Ironically, he regained his old confidence thanks to a transfer to England's Chelsea where he struck a brilliant winner in Chelsea's 1998 Cup-Winners' Cup Final win over Stuttgart. He later returned to London as manager of West Ham, only to be sacked in 2010 after they barely avoided relegation.

Andoni Zubizarreta

National team: Spain
Born: October 23, 1961
Clubs: Alaves, Bilbao, Barcelona, Valencia

Zubizarreta was probably the finest product of the remarkable Basque school of goalkeeping which produced internationals such as Carmelo, Iribar, Artola, Arconada and Urruti. Discovered by Bilbao in 1981 while playing for Alaves, he helped Bilbao win the league and Cup double a year later. In 1986 he cost Barcelona a then world record fee for a goalkeeper of £1.2 million but he looked worth every penny. Zubizarreta overtook Jose Camacho's record of 81 caps for Spain in a 1993 World Cup qualifier against the Republic of Ireland in Dublin, and went on to top 100 appearances for his country. He departed Barcelona for Valencia after a row with then coach Johan Cruyff.

PART 5:

THE FAMOUS CLUBS

Professionalism swept through British soccer in the 1880s and western Europe in the late 1920s. Big clubs in Spain, Italy, France and Portugal were importing star players by the turn of the 1930s. By the 1960s, Belgium, Holland and West Germany had joined in.

When they did, the balance of the European game changed again. The changes proved profound and their effect spread far beyond Europe. Increased financial power meant that the great South American clubs began to lose the ability to compete in terms of transfer fees, wages and bonuses.

The burgeoning club revolution in Europe was noted around the world. Central and North America, Africa and Asia began to develop their own high-profile international club competitions. But Europe jumped further ahead of the commercial game in the 1990s by developing the Champions League. In due course the most powerful clubs formed alliances which questioned the power of both the domestic and the international federations. The vast sums on offer for competing in the Champions League assisted the big clubs in monopolizing the transfer market and securing virtually ever-present status in Europe's most prestigious club competition.

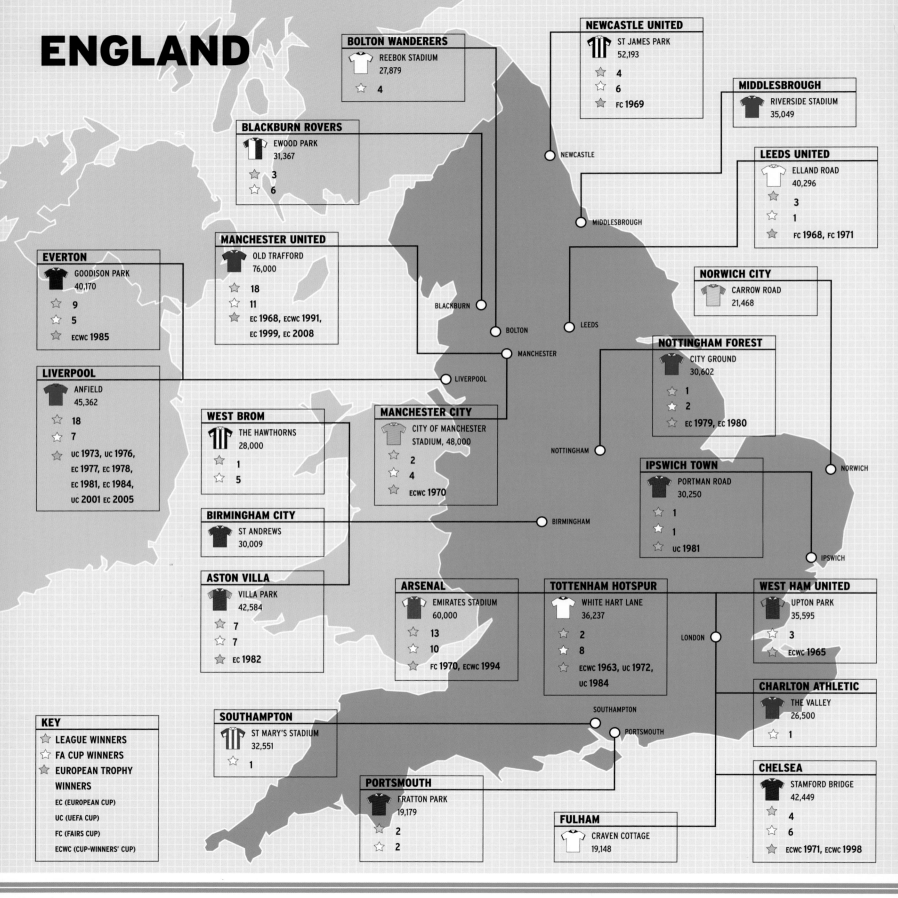

ENGLAND

NEWCASTLE UNITED
ST JAMES PARK
52,193
⭐ 4
☆ 6
⭐ FC 1969

BOLTON WANDERERS
REEBOK STADIUM
27,879
☆ 4

MIDDLESBROUGH
RIVERSIDE STADIUM
35,049

BLACKBURN ROVERS
EWOOD PARK
31,367
⭐ 3
☆ 6

LEEDS UNITED
ELLAND ROAD
40,296
⭐ 3
☆ 1
⭐ FC 1968, FC 1971

MANCHESTER UNITED
OLD TRAFFORD
76,000
⭐ 18
☆ 11
⭐ EC 1968, ECWC 1991,
EC 1999, EC 2008

EVERTON
GOODISON PARK
40,170
⭐ 9
☆ 5
⭐ ECWC 1985

NORWICH CITY
CARROW ROAD
21,468

NOTTINGHAM FOREST
CITY GROUND
30,602
☆ 1
⭐ 2
☆ EC 1979, EC 1980

LIVERPOOL
ANFIELD
45,362
⭐ 18
☆ 7
⭐ UC 1973, UC 1976,
EC 1977, EC 1978,
EC 1981, EC 1984,
UC 2001 EC 2005

WEST BROM
THE HAWTHORNS
28,000
⭐ 1
☆ 5

MANCHESTER CITY
CITY OF MANCHESTER
STADIUM, 48,000
⭐ 2
☆ 4
⭐ ECWC 1970

IPSWICH TOWN
PORTMAN ROAD
30,250
☆ 1
⭐ 1
☆ UC 1981

BIRMINGHAM CITY
ST ANDREWS
30,009

ASTON VILLA
VILLA PARK
42,584
⭐ 7
☆ 7
⭐ EC 1982

ARSENAL
EMIRATES STADIUM
60,000
⭐ 13
☆ 10
⭐ FC 1970, ECWC 1994

TOTTENHAM HOTSPUR
WHITE HART LANE
36,237
⭐ 2
⭐ 8
☆ ECWC 1963, UC 1972,
UC 1984

WEST HAM UNITED
UPTON PARK
35,595
☆ 3
⭐ ECWC 1965

CHARLTON ATHLETIC
THE VALLEY
26,500
☆ 1

SOUTHAMPTON
ST MARY'S STADIUM
32,551
☆ 1

PORTSMOUTH
FRATTON PARK
19,179
⭐ 2
☆ 2

FULHAM
CRAVEN COTTAGE
19,148

CHELSEA
STAMFORD BRIDGE
42,449
⭐ 4
☆ 6
⭐ ECWC 1971, ECWC 1998

KEY
⭐ LEAGUE WINNERS
☆ FA CUP WINNERS
⭐ EUROPEAN TROPHY
WINNERS
EC (EUROPEAN CUP)
UC (UEFA CUP)
FC (FAIRS CUP)
ECWC (CUP-WINNERS' CUP)

Map labels: NEWCASTLE, MIDDLESBROUGH, BLACKBURN, BOLTON, LEEDS, MANCHESTER, LIVERPOOL, NOTTINGHAM, NORWICH, BIRMINGHAM, IPSWICH, LONDON, SOUTHAMPTON, PORTSMOUTH

SCOTLAND

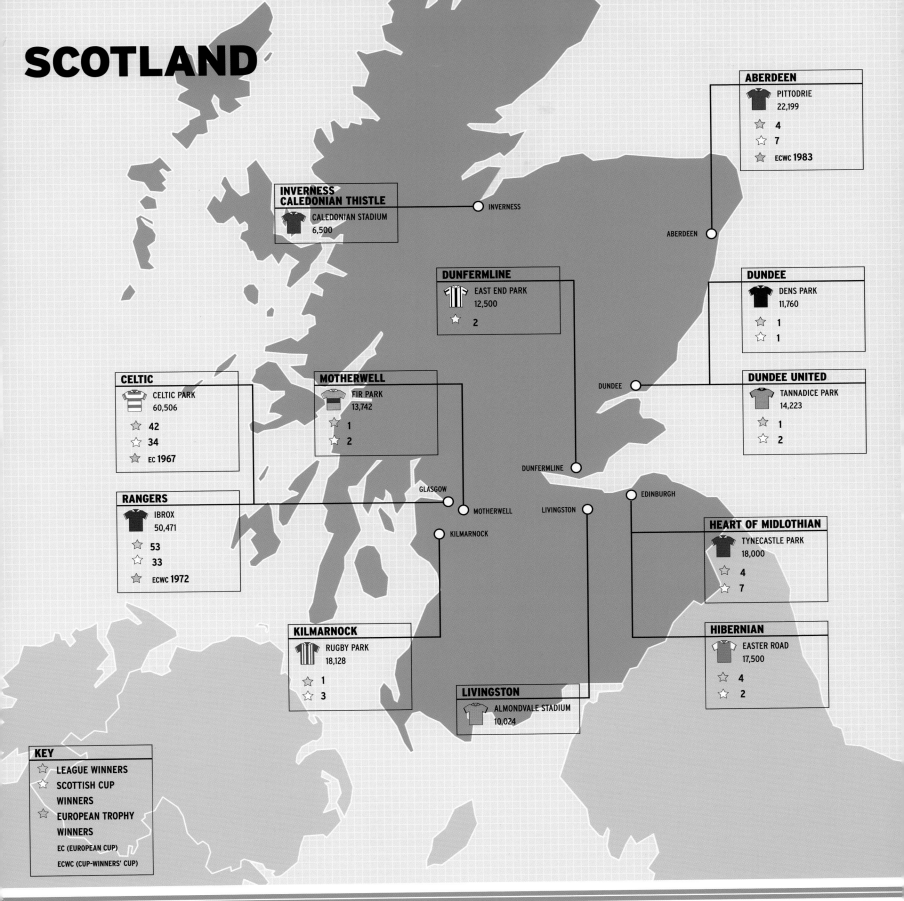

ABERDEEN
- PITTODRIE
- 22,199
- ☆ 4
- ☆ 7
- ☆ ECWC **1983**

INVERNESS CALEDONIAN THISTLE
- CALEDONIAN STADIUM
- 6,500

INVERNESS

ABERDEEN

DUNFERMLINE
- EAST END PARK
- 12,500
- ☆ 2

DUNDEE
- DENS PARK
- 11,760
- ☆ 1
- ☆ 1

CELTIC
- CELTIC PARK
- 60,506
- ☆ 42
- ☆ 34
- ☆ EC **1967**

MOTHERWELL
- FIR PARK
- 13,742
- ☆ 1
- ☆ 2

DUNDEE

DUNDEE UNITED
- TANNADICE PARK
- 14,223
- ☆ 1
- ☆ 2

RANGERS
- IBROX
- 50,471
- ☆ 53
- ☆ 33
- ☆ ECWC **1972**

GLASGOW

DUNFERMLINE

EDINBURGH

MOTHERWELL

LIVINGSTON

KILMARNOCK

HEART OF MIDLOTHIAN
- TYNECASTLE PARK
- 18,000
- ☆ 4
- ☆ 7

KILMARNOCK
- RUGBY PARK
- 18,128
- ☆ 1
- ☆ 3

HIBERNIAN
- EASTER ROAD
- 17,500
- ☆ 4
- ☆ 2

LIVINGSTON
- ALMONDVALE STADIUM
- 10,024

KEY
- ☆ LEAGUE WINNERS
- ☆ SCOTTISH CUP WINNERS
- ☆ EUROPEAN TROPHY WINNERS
  - EC (EUROPEAN CUP)
  - ECWC (CUP-WINNERS' CUP)

Arsenal

London, England
Founded: 1886
Stadium: Emirates (60,000)
Colours: Red with white sleeves/white
League: 13
FA Cup: 10
League Cup: two
European Cup-Winners' Cup: 1994
Fairs/UEFA Cup: 1970

Arsenal are one of the most famous clubs in the game – as proved by the number of teams throughout the world who adopted that illustrious title in the hope it might bring them the same glory.

The Gunners' nickname owes everything to their original foundation in south east London, at the Woolwich Arsenal munitions works. In 1913, however, they moved from south to north London in the search for a greater supporter base.

The inter-war years were sensational. Legendary manager Herbert Chapman arrived from Huddersfield Town, where he had created a highly-successful team in the early 1920s. Chapman guided Huddersfield to two successive championships before joining Arsenal in 1925. He made all the difference in London, leading Arsenal to one success after another and laying the foundations for one of the game's enduring legends. Chapman said it would take him five years to build a dominant side at Highbury. In 1930, his team won their first major honour, the FA Cup, beating his former club Huddersfield 2-0 in the final.

Until the Liverpools and Manchester Uniteds of recent years, no club had dominated a decade in English soccer as completely as Arsenal in the 1930s. Using the new and innovative stopper centre-half, they won the league championship five times, finished runners-up once, and won the FA Cup twice, again finishing runners-up once. The great players of those days – wingers Joe Hulme and Cliff Bastin, centre-forward Ted Drake, attacking

Arsenal, FA Cup-winners 1930. Back: Baker, Lambert, Preedy, Seedon, Hapgood, John. Seated: Chapman (manager), Jack, Parker, James, Whittaker (trainer).

general Alex James and immaculate full-backs George Male and Eddie Hapgood are still, today, legends of British soccer.

Chapman died in January 1934, as Arsenal were poised to win their third championship in four seasons. His work was carried on by secretary-manager George Allison, assisted by Joe Shaw and trainer Tom Whittaker.

The 1930s' aura survived both the premature death of Chapman and World War Two, so that Arsenal, now under Whittaker's guidance, won the league again in 1948 and 1953 and the FA Cup in 1950. Veteran wing-half Joe

Mercer was an inspirational captain and Jimmy Logie another midfield general in the Alex James mould.

Yet the greatest achievement of all came in 1970-71, when Arsenal became only the second English team of the 20th century to complete the celebrated double – winning both the league championship and the FA Cup in the same season. They won 1-0 at local rivals Tottenham to clinch the title in their final league game, then beat Liverpool 2-1 after extra time at Wembley. Charlie George, a north Londoner who grew up on Arsenal's doorstep, scored the Wembley winner.

A first European success had come in the Fairs Cup in 1970, when Arsenal beat Belgian club Anderlecht in the two-leg final, winning 3-0 at Highbury after losing 3-1 in Brussels. The Belgian capital was not a happy venue a decade later, when Arsenal lost the Cup-Winners' Cup Final to Spain's Valencia on a penalty shoot-out. That was Arsenal's fourth major final in three seasons, but they won only one, the 1979 FA Cup Final against Manchester United.

Great players of the modern era included England's 1966 World Cup-winner Alan Ball, "double" skipper

Front: Hulme, Bastin.

Frank McLintock, Irishmen Liam Brady, David O'Leary and Frank Stapleton and Northern Ireland's great goalkeeper Pat Jennings.

In the late 1960s and early 1970s, Arsenal were guided from midfield by George Graham, who then returned in 1986 as manager to re-ignite the flames of success. The most dramatic came in May 1989, when Arsenal became London's first league champions in 18 years thanks to a last-minute, final-match goal scored by Michael Thomas to deny Liverpool – a club he later joined – at a shocked Anfield. Two years later the wing magic

of Sweden's Anders Limpar helped inspire another championship success before Graham parted company with the club following a row over transfer "bungs" or illicit payments.

Graham had also led Arsenal to their second European success, a 1-0 win over Parma in the 1994 Cup-Winners' Cup final when centre-forward Alan Smith scored the only goal. The stars of the side were goalkeeper David Seaman and the legendary back four – Lee Dixon, Steve Bould, Tony Adams and Nigel Winterburn – who spent more than a decade together as a defensive unit.

Bruce Rioch succeeded Graham after a transfers cash scandal, but was himself replaced early in the 1996–97 season by Frenchman Arsene Wenger. Under his revolutionary leadership Arsenal turned from being one of the most dour of sides into one of the most entertaining. Wenger used to the full his contacts and knowledge of European soccer to bring in a string of new signings, most notably Frenchmen Patrick Vieira, Emmanuel Petit and Nicolas Anelka and Holland winger

Marc Overmars. His reward, with Dutchman Dennis Bergkamp outstanding, was to win the league and cup double in 1998.

For the next three years, Arsenal played second fiddle to Manchester United and their greater financial resources. They finished runners-up to United's treble-winners in 1999 and lost to them in the FA Cup semi-final.

They finished Premiership runners-up in each of the next two seasons. They also lost the UEFA Cup Final of 2000 on penalties to Galatasaray and were beaten 2-1 by Liverpool in the 2001 FA Cup Final. Wenger's shrewd work paid rich dividends in 2001-02 though. His rebuilt side, galvanised by French attackers Thierry Henry and Robert Pires, ably supported by Sweden's Freddie Ljungberg, won another league and cup double. England centre-back Sol Campbell succeeded Adams as the pillar of a rebuilt defence. Arsenal were odds-on to win another championship in 2003 after leading for most of the season. They fell away towards the end of the campaign and

United overhauled them. They had to settle for a second successive FA Cup victory, when Pires' goal beat Southampton 1-0.

There was no doubting Arsenal's Premiership mastery in 2003-04, founded on a record-equalling season-long unbeaten run. Henry found the form of his life, scoring spectacular goals almost at will. Pires was prolific from midfield and the emergence of young centre-back Kolo Toure further strengthened the defence alongside the solid Campbell. The following season saw more history as Arsenal completed a record run of 49 league games unbeaten.

Only one trophy remained elusive, the Champions League. Arsenal reached the final in 2006 but lost 2-1 to Barcelona in the Stade de France after threatening a remarkable victory despite the expulsion of goalkeeper Jens Lehmann. That summer Arsenal left cramped Highbury for an expansive new stadium in nearby Ashburton Grove but the move, while improving the club's revenue stream, brought no immediate titles or trophies.

Arsenal abandoned historic Highbury to move 'down the road' to the Emirates Stadium at Ashburton Grove in 2006.

Liverpool

England
Founded: 1892
Stadium: Anfield (45,362)
Colours: All red
Supercup: 1977, 2001, 2005
League: 18
FA Cup: seven
League Cup: seven
European Champions: 1977, 1978, 1981, 1984, 2005
UEFA Cup: 1973, 1976, 2001

Successful sportsmen the world over tell the same tale: reaching the top is tough, but not as tough as staying at the top. The enormous pressures generated by success even wore down the cogs of the Liverpool machine in the end – but only after a remarkable 28 years of unprecedented achievement. The modern adventure began in 1954 when Liverpool, with a proud history behind them, slipped into the old second division. They remained there for eight years until Bill Shankly's unrivalled enthusiasm and soccer insight guided them back to the top division in 1962. Shankly had arrived in 1959, just after the club had reached its nadir, an exit from the FA Cup at the hands of Southern League Worcester City.

In 1964 – surfing the waves of Beatlemania – Liverpool won the first of their modern championships. In the next 26 years, Liverpool were to win the league 13 times (adding up to a record 18 in all), the FA Cup five times, the League Cup four times and the league and Cup double once.

Such drive proved relentlessly successful in Europe. Shankly and successors Bob Paisley and Joe Fagan managed to create an approach which incorporated the physically-based strengths of the English game with the more technically thoughtful school of the best continental sides.

A home defeat by Red Star Belgrade, which eliminated Liverpool from the 1973-74 European Cup, convinced Shankly to change the club's style. His successor, Paisley, brought Shankly's vision to fruition in the late 1970s and early 1980s.

Five times Liverpool have won the Champions Cup and three times the UEFA Cup. They have been runners-up in the Champions Cup twice and the Cup-winners Cup once. The only occasion on which Liverpool were comprehensively put to the sword on a mainline occasion was the 1981 World Club Cup Final in Tokyo. Zico's Flamengo, from Brazil, emerged as well-deserved 3-0 winners.

Borussia Monchengladbach and Brugge suffered worst from Liverpool. Borussia were the victims of Liverpool's first UEFA Cup triumph, and the victims again in Rome in 1977 when Kevin Keegan bowed out of the Anfield scene with the club's first Champions Cup secured. Brugge were beaten by Liverpool in both the UEFA Cup Final in 1976 and the Champions Cup Final at Wembley in 1978. The winning goal second time around was scored by Kenny Dalglish, who had arrived from Celtic to fill – seamlessly – the gap left by Keegan's departure for Hamburg.

That Liverpool side incorporated stars from all over the British Isles: Goalkeeper Ray Clemence, full-back Phil Neal and midfielder Ray Kennedy were England regulars. Dalglish, assured defender Alan Hansen and tough but subtle midfielder Graeme Souness formed the Scottish contingent. Flying winger Steve Heighway played for the Republic of Ireland.

Fagan took over from Paisley and guided Liverpool to European Cup Final victory over Roma in 1984. By then, the unorthodox Zimbabwe goalkeeper Bruce Grobbelaar had succeeded Clemence. Another Ireland star, Mark Lawrenson, emerged as Hansen's centre-back partner and the prolific Wales striker Ian Rush began to partner Dalglish.

Dalglish, wherever his career may subsequently have taken him, will always be considered – at least in England – as a legend of Anfield. He

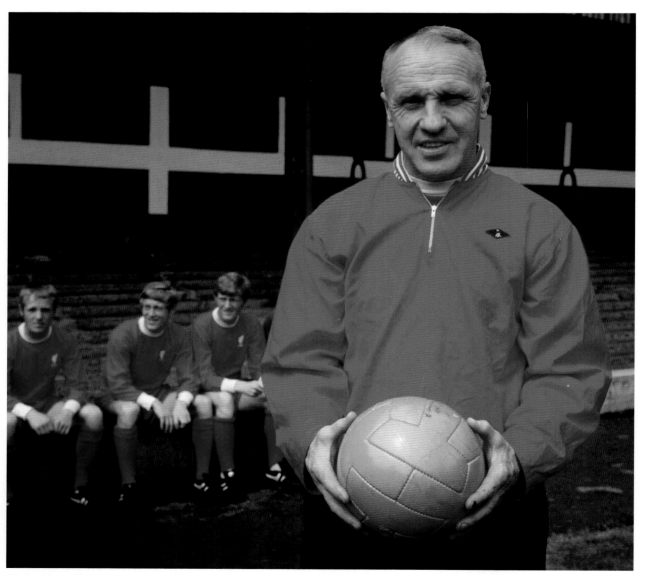

Bill Shankly was the manager whose grit and inspirational management turned Liverpool from Second Division also-rans to First Division champions.

Liverpool's players race to congratulate goalkeeper Jerzy Dudek after his penalty shoot-out saves had clinched their 2005 UEFA Champions League victory over Milan.

took over as manager in the awful wake of the Heysel tragedy in 1985 and later had to bear the burden of pain of the city after the 1989 Hillsborough disaster. At Heysel, 39 Juventus fans died; at Hillsborough 96 Liverpool fans were crushed to death.

In between, Dalglish became the only player-manager to have guided his team to the league and cup double in 1986, and there were more honours to follow. The league title trophy returned in 1988 and 1990 and the FA Cup in 1989 before Dalglish stepped out from beneath the combined stress of triumph and tragedy. A return to consistent success proved beyond successors Graeme Souness and Roy Evans and led to the appointment in sole charge of a first foreign manager in Gerard Houllier in 1998.

They failed to materialize and

French coach Gerard Houllier, who had joined Liverpool to work with Evans, was handed sole charge of team affairs in November 1998.

Houllier's first task was to restore discipline in the squad. He changed personnel and changed the culture in the Anfield dressing room. In 2001, Liverpool completed a historic cup treble. They beat Birmingham City on penalties in the League Cup Final. Owen scored two late goals as Liverpool came from behind to beat Arsenal 2-1 in the FA Cup Final. Then Houllier's side beat Alaves 4-3 in a gripping UEFA Cup Final. Wins over Roma, Porto and Barcelona en route to the final suggested that Liverpool had rediscovered the knack of beating Europe's best. Midfielder Steven Gerrard had emerged as a major influence and hopes were high

for a Liverpool resurgence. They pipped Manchester United for second place in the Premiership in 2002, despite Houllier suffering a heart attack in October 2001 which kept him out for much of the season. But Liverpool nose-dived in 2002-03. They led the Premiership early in the season, then slid down the table from November onwards. They were eliminated at the Champions League first stage and knocked out of the UEFA Cup by Celtic. League Cup Final victory over Manchester United was a mere consolation.

The outgoing Houllier's legacy was a place in the Champions League and, under successor Rafa Benitez, Liverpool capitalised dramatically.

Few fans had expected them to reach the 2005 final and even fewer thought they could win after Milan led

3-0 at half-time. But in six sensational minutes the inspiration of Steven Gerrard helped fire Liverpool level and onto victory on penalties. Sadly, there was to be no repeat in the final two years later against the same opposition, Liverpool this time losing 2-1 to the Italians in Athens.

Benitez had pledged to build a team capable of challenging for the Premier League title. Such a target appeared within reach after the arrivals of new American owners in Tom Hicks and George Gillett and major acquisitions such as top-scoring Spain striker Fernando Torres and Argentina anchor Javier Mascherano. However, the reverse happened. A second-place finish in 2009 was followed by cash problems, a slide out of the Champions League qualifying spots in 2010 and Benitez's departure.

Manchester United

England
Founded: 1878
Stadium: Old Trafford (67,650)
Colours: Red/white
League: 18
FA Cup: 11
League Cup: four
World Club Cup: 1999, 2008
European Champions Cup: 1968, 1999, 2008
Cup-Winners' Cup: 1991
Supercup: 1991

Manchester United fans may revere Sir Matt Busby as the manager who laid the most significant of foundations in the modern era. But even his achievements pale by comparison with those achieved under Sir Alex Ferguson over the past quarter of a century which established United as world champions both on the pitch and off it, in commercial terms.

Founded as Newton Heath in 1878 by railway workers the club evolved into Manchester United in 1902 but had to wait 46 more years before the spark of future greatness emerged with a dramatic 4-2 FA Cup Final victory over Blackpool.

This was the first outstanding team built by manager Busby, who had played before the war for neighbours Manchester City. He had guided United to success even though they were without a ground in the immediate post-war years, while Old Trafford was rebuilt after war damage. His second outstanding team were the so-called Busby Babes of the mid-1950s, many of whom had developed through the club's youth system. United won the championship in 1956 and 1957. In 1956-57, they defied orders and became the first English side to enter the European Champions Cup. They opened their campaign with a 10-0 thrashing of Belgium's Anderlecht and never looked back – not even in the bleak days of February 1958, after eight players, including England internationals Roger Byrne, Tommy Taylor and

Matt Busby lifts United spirits ahead of extra time in the 1968 Champions Cup Final.

Duncan Edwards, died in the Munich air disaster.

Munich deprived United of a golden generation. The legendary Real Madrid centre-forward Alfredo Di Stefano had predicted that the "Busby Babes" would be Madrid's greatest challengers for mastery in Europe. However, the sympathy felt for United after the disaster laid the foundation for the club's national, and later worldwide, fan base. It took United ten years to recover from Munich, in international terms. Thus it was in May 1968 that United's European quest was rewarded as they defeated Benfica 4-1 in extra time at Wembley. Bobby Charlton, a Munich survivor along with defender Bill Foulkes and manager Busby, scored twice to secure the club's most emotional triumph. Foulkes himself had scored the match-winner

in a dramatic semi-final against Real Madrid.

The club became synonymous with entertaining, attacking soccer as epitomized by the talents of Charlton, Denis Law and the wayward but mesmeric Northern Irishman, George Best. All three won the European Footballer of the Year award. Later came England's long-serving skipper Bryan Robson, who was still in harness in 1993 when United, under Alex Ferguson, regained the English league title for the first time in 26 years.

The years in between Busby's retirement as manager and Ferguson's arrival in 1986 were bleak. Charlton quit in the early 1970s. Injury diminished Law's sharpness. Best, a tragically wasted talent, played his last game for United at the age of 26 before

turning his back on the club. A succession of managers failed to emulate Busby's achievements. Tommy Docherty and Ron Atkinson guided the Old Trafford club to cup success, but the championship eluded them.

Ferguson, brought south from Aberdeen, managed on a knife-edge in his early days. Only an FA Cup vicory in 1990 quietened fans who had called for his dismissal. Victory in the European Cup-Winners' Cup in 1991 – United were first back, appropriately, after the five-year post-Heysel ban – proved that Ferguson was on the right lines. Events in the next five years underlined the point. Between 1993 and 1996 United won the league title three times in four seasons, including an unprecedented "double double" of league and FA Cup in 1994 and 1996. Goalkeeper Peter Schmeichel and forward Eric Cantona contributed the cosmopolitan icing to the most successful English club recipe of the 1990s.

Ferguson then pulled off a master-stroke, breaking up his title-winning squad and replacing it with a younger, even more impressive unit. As in Busby's days, the core was a remarkable group of home-grown players – Ryan Giggs, the Neville brothers, Paul Scholes and David Beckham. United were led too by another skipper with Robson's all-action qualities: hard-driving Irish midfielder Roy Keane.

United won another championship in 1997. They lost out to Arsenal the following season – but returned with a vengeance in 1999. That season they became the first – and only – English club to win the "treble" of championship, FA Cup and European Cup; an achievement that bettered even those of Busby's era. They never knew when they were beaten. They pipped Arsenal on the last day of the season to win the title. Schmeichel saved a penalty and Giggs conjured up a dramatic extra time winner against the

Gunners in the FA Cup semi-final, before United eased past Newcastle 2-0 at Wembley.

In the European Cup Final, United trailed 1-0 to Bayern Munich in Barcelona with time running out. Teddy Sheringham grabbed an equaliser. Ole Gunnar Solskjaer scored the winner in stoppage time. United dominated the Premiership for the next two seasons, until the emergence of Arsenal's "double" team in 2001-02. They gained revenge in 2002-03. Inspired by Ruud van Nistelrooy's phenomenal scoring form, they came from behind to overhaul Arsenal's lead and win their eighth Premiership title.

The subsequent six years saw United extend their title-winning and commercial reach. After falling briefly behind Arsenal again and Chelsea (twice) they secured a Premier League hat-trick between 2006 and 2009 and – just to underline their pre-eminence – defeated Chelsea, albeit on penalties – to celebrate a third Champions League Cup triumph in 2008. British record signing Rio Ferdinand anchored defence with Cristiano Ronaldo and Wayne Rooney the new heroes whose brilliance apparently vindicated the club's controversial takeover by American sports entrepreneur Malcolm Glazier.

In the spring of 2010, however, terrace concern at the club's debts manifested itself in protests against the Glazer family after the sale of Ronaldo, a failure to spend the £80m fee on new players and the loss of both Champions League and Premier League crowns.

Ole-Gunnar Solskjaer snatches United's winner against Bayern Munich in the last seconds of stoppage time in the 1999 Champions League Final in Barcelona.

Chelsea

London, England
Founded: 1905
Stadium: Stamford Bridge
(42,449)
Colours: All blue
League: four
FA Cup: six
League Cup: four
Cup-Winners' Cup: 1971, 1998
Supercup: 1998

Chelsea's trophy cabinet may appear modest compared with other domestic rivals but the west London club have been a focus of worldwide fascination since the 2003 takeover by Russian oligarch Roman Abramovich.

Chelsea should have been England's first competitors in the Champions Cup. They were invited to enter the inaugural competition in 1955-56 but withdrew on the orders of the Football League, which feared a fixtures snarl-up. The next year Manchester United did compete and thus, ironically, opened the way for Chelsea to accept an invitation into the 1968-69 Fairs Cup.

They reached the quarter-finals then and went a step further in 1966, reaching the semi-finals – beating Milan on the way in a thriller decided on the toss of a coin after a drawn play-off in San Siro – and Munich 1860 before losing to Barcelona.

Manager Tommy Docherty had brought a wind of change to English soccer with a young team featuring the likes of Peter Osgood, Bobby Tambling and Terry Venables. But it required the more pragmatic approach of Dave Sexton to steer the team to a European title.

Chelsea won the FA Cup in a memorable, if physical, replay against Leeds in 1970, to earn a shot at the Cup-Winners' Cup in which they beat Real Madrid after a replay in the Final in Athens.

Inside ten years, however, Chelsea were in grave financial difficulties and it took all the business ingenuity new chairman Ken Bates could muster to turn the club around. This he did with

John Terry lifts Chelsea's second consecutive Premiership Trophy in 2006.

such success that, in the mid-1990s, Chelsea had become London's most fashionable club to watch.

Just as in the Swinging Sixties Chelsea were a glamorous club again, attracting high-profile fans who were entertained by an imaginative transfer policy which brought in first Glenn Hoddle as player-manager then, in his wake, Ruud Gullit. The Dutchman took charge after Hoddle's departure and kept the revolution moving by importing Gianluca Vialli, Roberto Di Matteo and Gianfranco Zola.

Vialli took over as a third successive player-manager with immediate success after Gullit's controversial departure in the spring of 1998. The Italian had barely been in management more than a few weeks before he was

celebrating success in first the League Cup and then the European Cup-Winners' Cup.

He was succeeded by another Italian, Claudio Ranieri, who steered Chelsea to fourth in the Premiership in 2002-03. This was a remarkable feat because Ranieri had no money to spend – in total contrast to events after a world soccer-shattering July 2. That was the date on which everything changed in not only English but European soccer. That was the day on which Abramovich paid a staggering £140 million to buy 93 per cent of the shares and wipe out the club's massive debts.

Suddenly Chelsea had the financial power not merely to emulate Manchester United and Arsenal but to

outbid them in any transfer race.

The Blues' spending under Abramovich shocked European soccer. He bought top English, European, South American and African players plus the charismatic coach Jose Mourinho who organised Premier League title success in 2005 and 2006.

Eventually Abramovich, aspiring to a more attractive brand of soccer, tired of Mourinho's pragmatism. Avram Grant took Chelsea to the Champions League Final and Guus Hiddink to FA Cup success before Italian Carlo Ancelotti – leaning heavily on the spine of England's Frank Lampard and John Terry plus the goals of Didier Drogba – reclaimed the Premier League trophy in 2010.

Newcastle United

England
Founded: 1881
Stadium: St James' Park
(52,193)
Colours: Black and white stripes/black
League: four
FA Cup: six
Fairs Cup: 1969

Newcastle United are one of the traditional "greats" of the English game even though it is now around 50 years since they last celebrated winning one of the major domestic trophies, the FA Cup.

The northeast of England has always been a byword as a production line of soccer talent. The phrase "whistle down a pit for a player" had its origins in the manner Newcastle appeared to unearth a steady stream of outstanding players.

The Magpies duly dominated English soccer in the early years of the twentieth century. Then, with such heroes as defender Bill McCracken – the man who forced the offside law change from three defenders to two – they won the league three times and reached the FA Cup Final five times (albeit winning only once).

In the early 1950s Newcastle became the first club of the twentieth century to win the FA Cup twice in a row – beating Blackpool 2-0 in 1951 then Arsenal 1-0. Centre-forward "Wor Jackie" Milburn was one hero, left-winger Bobby Mitchell another, tough-tackling right-half Jimmy Scoular another. The full-back pairing of Dick Keith and Alf McMichael played together for the Northern Ireland team who reached the quarter-finals of the 1958 World Cup while inside-forward Ivor Allchurch reached the last eight in Sweden with Wales.

But times were changing. Newcastle's directors discovered to their cost in legal fees when their attempt to hang on to the England inside-forward George Eastham was outlawed by the courts. The club proved ill-equipped to cope with the ending of the maximum wage and slipped into the old second division.

They spent four years rebuilding before not only returning to the top flight but going on to win a European prize at first attempt. This was the 1969 Fairs Cup, which Newcastle eventually brought home to St James' Park after defeating Hungary's Ujpest Dozsa 3-0 at home then 3-2 away after being 2-0 down.

In the 1970s Newcastle found a new hero in the prolific centre-forward Malcolm Macdonald. He may have played only 14 times for England with a return of six goals but five came in one memorable match against Cyprus in April 1975. The style and persona of Supermac and the Newcastle fans idolized him. He scored a hat-trick on his debut against Liverpool – and lost four teeth in a collision with Ray Clemence – and went on to total 95 goals in 187 league games before leaving for Arsenal.

The club fell on the hard times of relegation again in the 1980s before a further cycle of revival in the 1990s – financed by Sir John Hall and inspired by the heart-on-sleeve management style of Kevin Keegan.

Keegan had already inspired one brief revival as a player and he was welcomed back as a soccer Messiah. He immediately fired Newcastle up into the promised land of the Premiership and nearly took them all the way to the title. Keegan's enthusiasm memorably boiled over during one television interview as Newcastle went 11 points clear of Manchester United. But the other United had superior staying power and Newcastle had to be satisfied with two runners-up spots and one third place during Keegan's exciting tenure.

Kenny Dalglish and Ruud Gullit were successors who never really won the hearts of the Newcastle fans and it took one of their own – former England boss Sir Bobby Robson – to lift the club into the Champions League. Robson's soccer wisdom allied to the goal-scoring leadership of veteran skipper Alan Shearer duly put Newcastle back on the European map.

Shearer later overtook Jackie Milburn's club goal record and boasted 206 by the time of his retirement in 2006. Back as manager, however Shearer was unable to save them from relegation in 2009.

They returned to the Premier League the following season managed by Chris Hughton.

Alan Shearer heads yet another goal for Newcastle, this time in the UEFA Cup against PSV Eindhoven.

Aston Villa

Birmingham, England
Founded: 1874
Stadium: Villa Park (42,584)
Colours: Claret with blue /white
League: seven
FA Cup: seven
League Cup: five
European Champions Cup: 1982
Supercup: 1982

Aston Villa means Tradition with a capital T. Few clubs anywhere in England, let alone the world, boast a timeline of success which runs right back to the pioneering days of 1874.

In the 1880s and 1890s Villa, founder members of the Football League, won five of their six championships and two of their seven FA Cups. In 1957 Villa won the FA Cup for a then record seventh time when they defeated Manchester United's Busby Babes 2–1 at Wembley.

In the early 1960s Villa drew admirers from far and wide with an attacking team managed by former England wing-half Joe Mercer and spearheaded by the England World Cup leader Gerry Hitchens. They were inaugural winners of the Football League Cup in 1961.

In the 1970s Villa suffered the humiliation of sliding down into the old Third Division. But Vic Crowe, a wing-half stalwart of both Villa and Wales in the 1960s, returned as manager to undertake a rebuilding programme. Steady progress was rewarded with the double glory of League Championship success under Ron Saunders in 1981 and then triumph in the Champions Cup a year later under former assistant, Tony Barton. The greatest moment in Villa's history was achieved with a victory over Germany's Bayern Munich.

Such standards proved impossible to maintain even with an owner/chairman as ambitious as Doug Ellis. Two League Cup wins were mere consolation before Ellis ultimately handed over to American Randy Lerner and further team rebuilding was launched under the managership of Martin O'Neill.

Everton

Liverpool, England
Founded: 1878
Stadium: Goodison Park (40,170)
Colours: Blue/white
League: nine
FA Cup: five
European Cup-Winners' Cup: 1985

Everton have lived – too long, say their fans – in the domestic and European shadow of their neighbours across Stanley Park Liverpool.

The Goodison Park club had been league founder members in 1888 and Gary Lineker and teenage superstar Wayne Rooney have been only the more recent in a long line of outstanding attackers to grace the "School of Science." Joe Parker and Bert Freeman were free-scoring forwards in the early years of the century, followed by the record-breaking Bill "Dixie" Dean in the 1920s and 30s. For an outlay of £3,000, Everton secured the 17-year-old who would total 349 league goals – a record 60 in 1927–28. He was succeeded in the No. 9 shirt, in due course, by Tommy Lawton – for many an even greater centre-forward – and then Scotland's Alex Young. Subsequent heroes included England's World Cup-winning midfield dynamo Alan Ball.

Everton hit the European heights in 1985 when they defeated Rapid Vienna in Rotterdam in the Cup-Winners' Cup Final and the talents at the disposal of manager Howard Kendall were beyond dispute. Lineker was, in 1986, not only top scorer in the World Cup finals in Mexico (with six goals) but leading marksman in the league with 30. Everton finished runners-up.

Lineker's exit for Barcelona failed to prevent Everton winning the league title a year later for the ninth time. But all they can boast for their subsequent efforts is the 1995 FA Cup win. Everton did return to Wembley in the 2009 FA Cup Final, under the revivalist managership of David Moyes, but they lost to Chelsea.

Ipswich Town

England
Founded: 1887
Stadium: Portman Road (30,250)
Colours: blue/white
League: one
FA Cup: one
UEFA Cup: 1981

At one time Ipswich was the natural stepping stone to the prowess and perils of both England management and the royal seal of approval. Both Alf Ramsey and Bobby Robson went on to national team command and knighthoods. Ramsey's achievement was to bring Ipswich out of the old Second Division in 1961 and to win the championship immediately.

Robson assumed control in 1968, established them in the First Division and guided them into European competition in nine out of ten succeeding seasons. Top European clubs such as Real Madrid, Lazio and Feyenoord came off second-best to the East Anglian club. Under Robson Ipswich won the FA Cup for the only time in their history in 1978 and three years later they followed up with the UEFA Cup. Robson's natural progression to the England job was matched by the club's decline into a yo-yo existence between the top divisions. A second brief flirtation with the Premiership ended in relegation in 2002.

Leeds United

England
Founded: 1919
Stadium: Elland Road (40,296)
Colours: All white
League: three
FA Cup: one
League Cup: one
Fairs Cup: 1968, 1971

Leeds United attained a reputation for the ultimate in disciplined, effective English soccer in the late 1960s and early 1970s under the managership of Don Revie. He instilled these qualities, plus immense pride, which made Leeds feared at home and abroad.

Yet the extent to which Leeds set the agenda in English soccer is hardly demonstrated by the trophies they won. Leeds were more often runners-up than winners: five times in the league, three times in the FA Cup, once each in the Champions Cup (in 1975), Cup-Winners' Cup (in 1973) and Fairs Cup (in 1967).

Relegation followed their golden era in 1982 and Leeds stayed down eight long years before Howard Wilkinson not only brought them back up but turned them into league champions once more. Ambition and overspending got the better of them, however, and by 2007 the club had been forced to sell their stars and tumbled down the English league ladder, saddled by massive debts.

Leeds United line up before the ill-fated 1975 Champions Cup Final in Paris.

Manchester City

England
Founded: 1894
Stadium: City of Manchester Stadium (48,000)
Colours: Sky blue/white
League: two
FA Cup: four
League Cup: two
European Cup-Winners' Cup: 1970

For the die-hard Blues fans, City have spent far too long playing second-fiddle to United in Manchester – which was why their fans so welcomed the purchase of the club by the oil-rich Abu Dhabi United Group in 2008.

The club won the FA Cup for the first time in 1904 (five years before United) but the league championship for the first time only in 1937. The most fabled of City's domestic triumphs, however, was in 1956 when they won the FA Cup Final with German goalkeeper Bert Trautmann playing with a broken neck.

Trautmann was one of City's legends along with heroes of the 1968 league championship-winning team such as right-back (and later manager) Tony Book, midfielder Colin Bell and forwards Neil Young, Mike Summerbee and Francis Lee (later club chairman).

The management team of Joe Mercer and coach Malcolm Allison worked wonders with a team who went on to win the FA Cup in 1969 and the European Cup-Winners' Cup in 1970. Young scored the winner against Leicester in the FA Cup Final and another in the 2-1 win in the European final in Vienna. A stream of big names came and went in subsequent years but with only a single League Cup to show for it – City's failures being underlined by United's successes.

A defining switch in 2003, saw the club move to the new City of Manchester Stadium. An unhappy spell under the ownership of Thai politician Thaksin Shinawatra preceded the Abu Dhabu buy-out. The new owners soon made a splash with high-price purchases of stars such as Brazil's Robinho, Arsenal striker Emmanuel Adebayor and Spain midfielder David Silva.

Nottingham Forest

England
Founded: 1865
Stadium: City Ground (30,602)
Colours: Red/white
League: one
FA Cup: two
League Cup: four
European Champions Cup: 1979, 1980
Supercup: 1979

Nottingham Forest joined illustrious company when they defeated Malmo 1-0 in Munich in 1979 to win the Champions Cup. Only Real Madrid (in the inaugural tournament in 1955-56) and Internazionale (in 1963-64) had ever won Europe's most prestigious club prize at the first attempt. Forest won it again the following year, defeating Hamburg this time by the same minimal margin, in Madrid.

Forest, when managerial legend Brian Clough took over in the mid-1970s, were a famous old club in the middle of the second division and apparently going nowhere. They came up into the top division in 1977, won the league a year later then the Champions Cup. Along the way Forest invested some of their new-found riches by turning Trevor Francis into England's first £1 million player. However, Francis stayed only two years and Clough's magic faded as Forest slipped back down the league ladder.

Tottenham Hotspur

London, England
Founded: 1882
Stadium: White Hart Lane (36,237)
Colours: White/blue
League: two
FA Cup: eight
League Cup: four
European Cup-Winners' Cup: 1963
UEFA Cup: 1972, 1984

Tottenham won the first league and FA Cup double of the 20st century in 1961 and, two years later and under the inspirational captaincy of Danny Blanchflower, became the first British side to win a European trophy. They followed their success in the Cup-winners Cup but winning reorganised UEFA Cup in 1972 and then again in 1984, after a penalty shootout victory over Anderlecht

Along the way Tottenham electrified English soccer with an innovative transfer policy which included signing Argentine World Cup-winners Osvaldo Ardiles and Ricardo Villa in 1978. German striker Jurgen Klinsmann followed in 1994 and had an enormous impact on the English game.

Occasional cup successes were no consolation for the failure, until a fourth-place finish in 2010 under Harry Redknapp, to force their way back up among the Premier League elite.

West Ham United

London, England
Founded: 1895
Stadium: Upton Park (35,089)
Colours: Claret with blue/white
FA Cup: three
European Cup-Winners' Cup: 1965

West Ham have long been known as the Football Academy, not only for the class of player they turn out but also for the class of soccer they play.

Never was that image better illustrated than on the day they won the Cup-Winners' Cup at Wembley in 1965. They defeated Munich 1860 on a night which was a credit to English soccer.

Many of West Ham's heroes that night went onto greater things. Manager Ron Greenwood would take up the same post with England and lead them to the finals of both the 1980 European Championship and the 1982 World Cup. Left-half Bobby Moore captained England to victory in the 1966 World Cup triumph, supported by Hammers Martin Peters and Geoff Hurst. Hurst, of course, made history as the only man to score a hat-trick in a World Cup Final when he put three past Hans Tilkowski.

It is an odd feature of West Ham's career in Europe that, until 2006, they had competed only in the Cup-winners Cup. In 1964-65 they competed as FA Cup holders and the following season as defending champions. However, defeat both home and away at the hands of eventual winners Borussia Dortmund ended their European commitment for nearly a decade.

After winning the FA Cup against Fulham in 1975 – this time with Moore on the losing side – West Ham returned to Europe to finish runners-up to Anderlecht in the Cup Winners' Cup. A further FA Cup win followed in 1980 and they went agonisingly close in 2006 before losing to Liverpool on penalties in Cardiff. The euphoria soon dissipated, however, amid financial concerns.

Trevor Francis justifies his £1m fee by heading Nottingham Forest's 1979 Champions Cup winner.

Celtic

Glasgow, Scotland
Founded: 1888
Stadium: Celtic Park (60,506)
Colours: Green and white
hoops/white
League: 42
Cup: 34
League Cup: 14
European Cup: 1967

Celtic and old rivals Rangers are Scottish soccer's greatest clubs, but it was Celtic who first extended that hunger for success into Europe when, in 1967, they became the first British club to win the European Cup.

It was a measure of the way they swept all before them that season that they won every domestic competition as well: the League, the Cup and League Cup. No other team in Europe had, until then, ended the season with a 100 per cent record in four major competitions. In winning the European Cup Celtic also refuted accusations that their Scottish honours owed more to a lack of solid opposition than their own abilities.

Celtic's 1967 team was shrewdly put together by manager Jock Stein, a former Celtic player. As well as new Scottish stars he included veterans such as goalkeeper Ronnie Simpson and scheming inside-left Bertie Auld. In the Lisbon Final they beat former holders Internazionale 2–1 with goals from full-back Tommy Gemmell and centre-forward Steve Chalmers. Sadly, the golden touch did not last. A few months later they were beaten by Kiev Dynamo at the start of their European Cup defence, and were dragged down to fisticuffs in the infamous World Club Cup battle with Racing of Argentina.

In 1970 Celtic returned to the European Cup Final, only to lose to Feyenoord in Milan; and, two years later, they lost only on penalties after two goalless draws in the semi-finals against Inter.

The club had been founded in the east end of Glasgow in 1888 by Irish Roman Catholics, so legend has it, to help raise money to fund soup kitchens.

The venture proved so successful that Celtic were soon considered the richest club in Britain with an annual income running at more than £15,000(!) around the turn of the century. They were among the founding members of the Scottish league.

Celtic's Old Firm rivalry with Rangers was born in that initial decade. The first time they met in the cup final, in 1893, Rangers won but Celtic gained consolation by winning the league for the first time that season. Command was maintained over succeeding years. Between 1905 and 1910 Celtic won five consecutive league titles as well as successive league-and-cup doubles in 1907 and 1908.

It was also in 1906 that Celtic switched from green and white striped shirts to the now-traditional hoops. Celtic were one of the last clubs in Britain to resist the introduction of numbers on players' backs. When they carried off the Champions Cup in 1967 their players, in a concession wore numbers on their shorts rather than shirts.

By the late 1980s Celtic found themselves unable to match Rangers' commercial and playing standards – but only temporarily. In 2001, with Swedish striker Henrik Larsson netting over 50 goals, Celtic took not only the league title, but also both domestic cups. In 2003, they went within a silver goal of regaining European glitter in the UEFA Cup Final.

Celtic captain Neil Lennon takes proud possession of the Scottish Premier League championship trophy in 2007.

Rangers

Glasgow, Scotland
Founded: 1873
Stadium: Ibrox Park (50,471)
Colours: Blue/white
League: 53
Cup: 33
League cup: 26
European Cup-Winners' Cup: 1972

Rangers are the other half of the "Old Firm" – their rivalry with Celtic having dominated Scottish soccer for more than a century. Yet Rangers have never extended that power into Europe, their only prize from virtually non-stop international competition being the 1972 Cup-Winners' Cup win over Moscow Dynamo. Not that their history is short on proud moments.

"Gers" are the fourth-oldest Scottish club, having been created in 1873 by three Protestant families – Campbell, McNeill and Vallance. Initially they played in the east end of Glasgow, then they moved to Paisley Road on the south bank of the Clyde and finally to their now-legendary home of Ibrox Park.

For two years from 1885 Rangers defected from the Scottish game to register with the Football Association. Thus they made a move which has lately, once more, become a subject of speculation since Rangers and their Old Firm rivals Celtic have gained dominant command of the Scottish game, on the pitch and in the bank.

Rangers, like Celtic, were founder members of the Scottish league in 1890 and shared the inaugural league title with Dumbarton. They won the cup for the first time in 1894 and their first outright league championship crown in 1899. Six more titles followed before the outbreak of the first world war and a further 15 – plus six cups – in the inter-war years. These were the great years of the legendary manager Willy Struth and players such as the original "wee blue devil" in winger Alan Morton and domineering captain and halfback David Meiklejohn.

It was under Struth that Rangers secured the first Scottish treble – adding League Cup to the League

Manager Alex McLeish and skipper Lorenzo Amoruso savour the moment after Rangers' Scottish Cup Final victory over Celtic.

and SFA Cup – in 1949. By now another stalwart had emerged in centre half George Young before Rangers sought to extend their all-conquering reach into European club competition. Success proved elusive as Rangers suffered defeats at the hands of Eintracht Frankfurt, Tottenham and Real Madrid.

The start of the 1970s was a time of mixed emotions: 1971 saw the Ibrox disaster, when 66 fans died in a stairway crush at the end of a game against Celtic. A year later, European Cup-Winners' Cup triumph was immediately followed by a European ban after Rangers' celebrating fans ran amok in Barcelona.

The upturn began in November, 1985, when Lawrence Marlboro took control of the club. He brought in Graeme Souness as player-manager. In 1988 David Murray bought Rangers, and Souness revolutionized their image by buying 18 English players and smashing the club's Protestants-only ethic with his £1.5 million capture of Catholic Mo Johnston. Subsequent signings such as Brian Laudrup and Paul Gascoigne enabled Rangers to maintain their league title dominance for a remarkable nine years in a row.

Striker Ally McCoist smashed the club record of 233 goals set 60 years earlier by Bob McPhail and in 1993 and 1999 Rangers secured domestic trebles. McCoist was one of the last outstanding Scots to thrill fans. Under Alex McLeish and Craig Brown the Gers extended their player search far and wide. Even when a new austerity forced them back into domestic "shopping" they still won the league in 2009 and 2010 under Walter Smith.

FRANCE

CORSICA

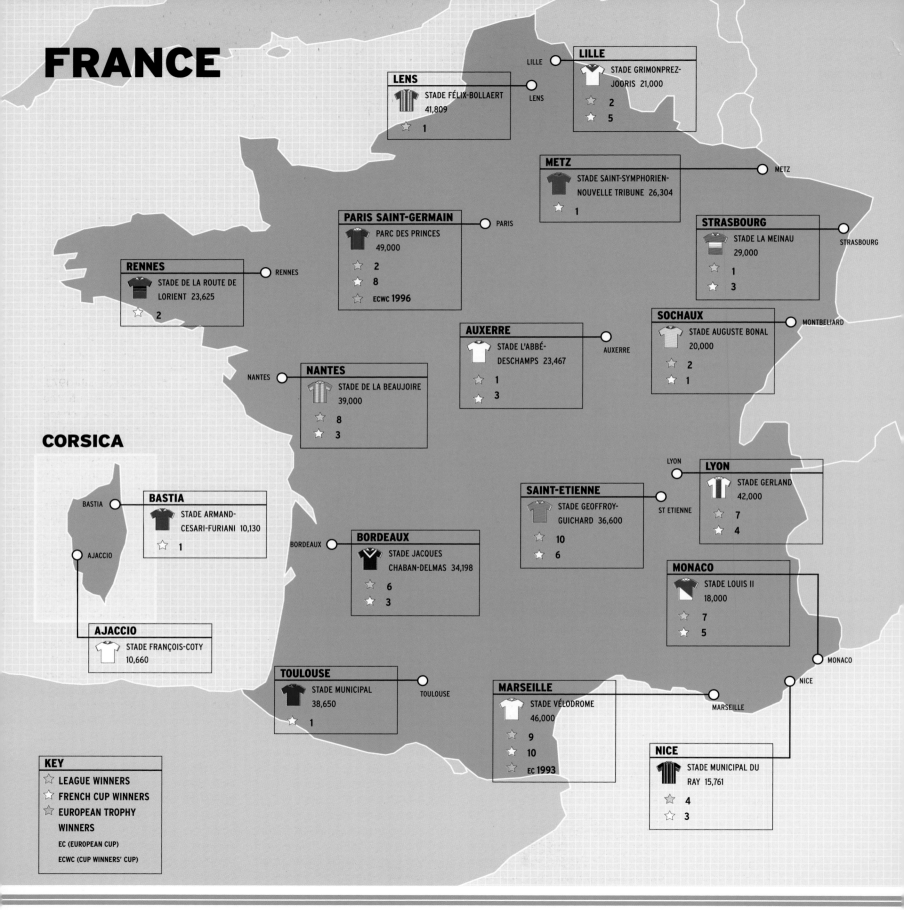

LENS · STADE FÉLIX-BOLLAERT 41,809 · ☆ 1

LILLE · STADE GRIMONPREZ-JOORIS 21,000 · ☆ 2 · ☆ 5

METZ · STADE SAINT-SYMPHORIEN-NOUVELLE TRIBUNE 26,304 · ☆ 1

PARIS SAINT-GERMAIN · PARC DES PRINCES 49,000 · ☆ 2 · ☆ 8 · ☆ ECWC 1996

STRASBOURG · STADE LA MEINAU 29,000 · ☆ 1 · ☆ 3

RENNES · STADE DE LA ROUTE DE LORIENT 23,625 · ☆ 2

AUXERRE · STADE L'ABBÉ-DESCHAMPS 23,467 · ☆ 1 · ☆ 3

SOCHAUX · STADE AUGUSTE BONAL 20,000 · ☆ 2 · ☆ 1

NANTES · STADE DE LA BEAUJOIRE 39,000 · ☆ 8 · ☆ 3

LYON · STADE GERLAND 42,000 · ☆ 7 · ☆ 4

BASTIA · STADE ARMAND-CESARI-FURIANI 10,130 · ☆ 1

SAINT-ETIENNE · STADE GEOFFROY-GUICHARD 36,600 · ☆ 10 · ☆ 6

BORDEAUX · STADE JACQUES CHABAN-DELMAS 34,198 · ☆ 6 · ☆ 3

MONACO · STADE LOUIS II 18,000 · ☆ 7 · ☆ 5

AJACCIO · STADE FRANÇOIS-COTY 10,660

TOULOUSE · STADE MUNICIPAL 38,650 · ☆ 1

MARSEILLE · STADE VÉLODROME 46,000 · ☆ 9 · ☆ 10 · ☆ EC 1993

NICE · STADE MUNICIPAL DU RAY 15,761 · ☆ 4 · ☆ 3

KEY
- ☆ LEAGUE WINNERS
- ☆ FRENCH CUP WINNERS
- ☆ EUROPEAN TROPHY WINNERS
  - EC (EUROPEAN CUP)
  - ECWC (CUP WINNERS' CUP)

Lyon

France
Founded: 1950
Stadium: Gerland (42,000)
Colours: Red and blue
League: seven
Cup: four
League cup: one

Olympique Lyonnais have been the dominant club of the new century in France, setting a record in 2008 with their seventh successive league championship. Off the pitch, ambitious owner Jean-Michel Aulas even forced a change in the law to allow French clubs to pursue finance on the stock exchange.

Lyon were founded in 1950 from a merger between two unsuccessful local rivals, Villeurbanne and FC Lyon. Within one year of becoming a professional club Lyon secured promotion to the top division in 1951 but remained, for years, best-known as a cup-fighting team – though this did reputation did not, initially, extend into Europe. Their debut, in the old Fairs Cup in 1958, saw them crash 1-1, 0-7 to Internazionale. Later they found their feet in the Cup-winners Cup in which they were both quarter and semi-finalists.

The next step upward began in 1993 with the appointment by software millionaire Aulas of ex-France midfielder Jean Tigana as manager-coach. Between 2002 and 2008, Lyon won their record seven consecutive league titles. Even a steady turnover of coaches – Jacques Santini, Paul Le Guen, Gerard Houllier and Alain Perrin were in charge during the title-winning run – did not upset the quality of a team featuring stars such as goalkeeper Greg Coupet, midfielders Juninho Pernambuco and Michael Essien as well as forwards Sidney Govou and Karim Benzema.

Aulas's forward-looking strategy not only earned Lyon membership of the elite 'club' of G-14 clubs and then a founders place in the European Club Association but a Champions League semi-final 'arrival' in 2010.

Marseille

France
Founded: 1898
Stadium: Vélodrome (46,000)
Colours: All white
League: nine
Cup: 10
League Cup: one
European Cup: 1993

No French club had ever won the European Cup before Marseille; and no one will ever forget what happened when they did. Millionaire entrepreneur Bernard Tapie had invested millions in pursuit of European glory. Unfortunately, some of the money had been used to try to fix matches along the road. Barely had Marseille finished celebrating their cup-winning 1-0 victory over Milan in May, 1993, than it emerged that three players from Valenciennes had been paid to "go easy" on Marseille in a league game a week earlier. They were duly banned from their European defence, the French federation revoked their league title and they were further penalised with relegation. Bankruptcy followed.

Marseille's first championship had been celebrated back in 1929. After the war Marseille soon won it again in 1948, but they had slipped into the Second Division by the time ambitious Tapie took over the helm in 1985. Marseille immediately gained promotion, then swept to four league titles in a row.

Monaco

France
Founded: 1919
Stadium: Louis II (18,000)
Colours: Red and white
League: seven
Cup: five
League cup: one

Monaco, thanks to the relaxed tax regime of Monte Carlo, have always been a controversial club. They rely heavily on the Monaco state to underwrite at least half their annual expenditure – not that they have always managed to balance the books.

In 2003 they were threatened with relegation because of their fragile financial status. Ironically, they capitalized on the reprieve to borrow Spanish star Fernando Morientes on loan and embark on a remarkable run to the Champions League final which included a quarter-final victory over Morientes' "proper" club, Real Madrid.

Much of the credit was due to coach Didier Deschamps, a 1998 World Cup winner, and their flying captain Ludovic Giuly.

Founded in 1924 as the Association Sportive de Monaco, they entered the French championship as a professional outfit in 1948 and their subsequent championship wins included 1988 when Arsene Wenger was coach and George Weah their star striker.

Paris Saint-Germain

France
Founded: 1970
Stadium: Parc des Princes (49,000)
Colours: Blue with red
League: two
Cup: eight
League cup: three
European Cup-Winners' Cup 1996

Paris Saint-Germain, remarkably, became the very first club from the French capital to win a European prize when they defeated Rapid Vienna 1-0 in the Cup-Winners' Cup Final in 1996.

Yet PSG had been founded only 26 years earlier – by Parisian fans anxious to fill the gap left by the collapse of professional soccer in the French capital. They did not turn formally full professional until 1973, by which time they had risen to the brink of promotion to the French top division under the enthusiastic presidency of the couturier, Daniel Hechter. The trophy breakthrough arrived with French cup successes in 1982 and 1983 and was extended in 1986 when, under former English teacher Gerard Houllier, Paris won their first league title. Amazingly, it was the first time a Paris club had won the national championship since Racing Club 50 years earlier in 1936.

After Houllier's departure and a shake-up that involved new backing from TV channel Canal Plus, PSG reached European semi-finals in four successive seasons: losing in the UEFA Cup in 1993, the Cup-Winners' Cup in 1994 and the Champions League in 1995, but this hurdle was finally cleared in the 1996 Cup-Winners' Cup. However, their Final victory over Rapid was followed by the departures of coach Luis Fernandez and attacking key Youri Djorkaeff. PSG lost in the Cup Winners' Final to Barcelona the following season – a defeat which sparked years of boardroom turbulence punctuated by six cup and league cup wins

Marseille president Bernard Tapie enjoys his brief taste of European glory.

GERMANY

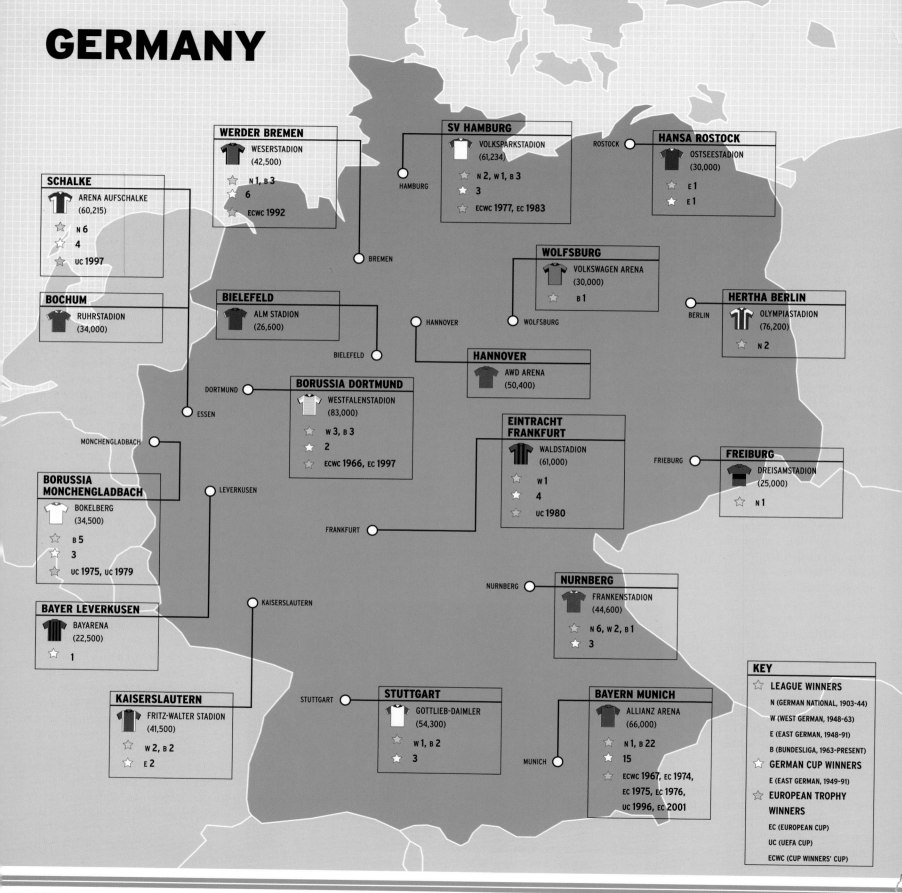

WERDER BREMEN
WESERSTADION
(42,500)
☆ N 1, B 3
☆ 6
☆ ECWC 1992

SV HAMBURG
VOLKSPARKSTADION
(61,234)
☆ N 2, W 1, B 3
☆ 3
☆ ECWC 1977, EC 1983

HANSA ROSTOCK
OSTSEESTADION
(30,000)
☆ E 1
☆ E 1

SCHALKE
ARENA AUFSCHALKE
(60,215)
☆ N 6
☆ 4
☆ UC 1997

BOCHUM
RUHRSTADION
(34,000)

BIELEFELD
ALM STADION
(26,600)

WOLFSBURG
VOLKSWAGEN ARENA
(30,000)
☆ B 1

HERTHA BERLIN
OLYMPIASTADION
(76,200)
☆ N 2

HANNOVER
AWD ARENA
(50,400)

BORUSSIA DORTMUND
WESTFALENSTADION
(83,000)
☆ W 3, B 3
☆ 2
☆ ECWC 1966, EC 1997

EINTRACHT FRANKFURT
WALDSTADION
(61,000)
☆ W 1
☆ 4
☆ UC 1980

FREIBURG
DREISAMSTADION
(25,000)
☆ N 1

BORUSSIA MONCHENGLADBACH
BOKELBERG
(34,500)
☆ B 5
☆ 3
☆ UC 1975, UC 1979

BAYER LEVERKUSEN
BAYARENA
(22,500)
☆ 1

NURNBERG
FRANKENSTADION
(44,600)
☆ N 6, W 2, B 1
☆ 3

KAISERSLAUTERN
FRITZ-WALTER STADION
(41,500)
☆ W 2, B 2
☆ E 2

STUTTGART
GOTTLIEB-DAIMLER
(54,300)
☆ W 1, B 2
☆ 3

BAYERN MUNICH
ALLIANZ ARENA
(66,000)
☆ N 1, B 22
☆ 15
☆ ECWC 1967, EC 1974,
EC 1975, EC 1976,
UC 1996, EC 2001

KEY
☆ **LEAGUE WINNERS**
   N (GERMAN NATIONAL, 1903-44)
   W (WEST GERMAN, 1948-63)
   E (EAST GERMAN, 1948-91)
   B (BUNDESLIGA, 1963-PRESENT)
☆ **GERMAN CUP WINNERS**
   E (EAST GERMAN, 1949-91)
☆ **EUROPEAN TROPHY WINNERS**
   EC (EUROPEAN CUP)
   UC (UEFA CUP)
   ECWC (CUP WINNERS' CUP)

Bayern Munich

Germany
Founded: 1900
Stadium: Allianz Arena (66,000)
Colours: All red
League: 22
Cup: 15
World Club Cup: 1976, 2001
European Cup: 1974, 1975, 1976, 2001
Cup-Winners' Cup: 1967
UEFA Cup: 1996

Bayern Munich are Germany's greatest club and the only one to have climbed every soccer peak: domestic championship and cup, European Champions Cup, European Cup-winners Cup, UEFA Cup and World Club Cup.

The Bavarian club had achieved little before the launch of a unified league in 1963. Until then German soccer had been organized on a regional basis with the "local" winners playing off for the national title. Bayern triumphed only once, in 1932. That record did not earn Bayern a place in the inaugural Bundesliga so they had to go through the play-offs in 1965. After that, they have never looked back.

In 1967 they won their first European trophy, the Cup-winners Cup, with the nucleus of a team that would conquer the world - Sepp Maier in goal, Gerd Müller leading the attack and Franz Beckenbauer as a revolutionary attacking sweeper. This was the role from which he captained his country to victory in the 1972 European Championship and 1974 World Cup.

in 1974 Bayern were at their brilliant best as they defeated Atletico Madrid 4-0 in a replayed Final to win the Champions Cup for the first time. Müller and Uli Hoeness - later the general manager - both scored twice. Victories over Leeds and Saint-Etienne completed a hat-trick of Champions Cups.

Over the years Bayern also proved, financially, to be head and shoulders above the rest of German soccer. In 2001 - with Beckenbauer now as club president - Bayern won a fourth Champions League Cup.

Borussia Dortmund

Germany
Founded: 1909
Stadium: Westfalenstadion (83,000)
Colours: Yellow/black
League: six
Cup: two
World Club Cup: 1997
European Champions Cup: 1997
Cup-Winners' Cup: 1966

Borussia hold a special place in history as Germany's first European winners - in 1966, when they beat Liverpool 2-1 after extra time to win the Cup-winners Cup in Glasgow.

Pride in that achievement extended to superstition when members of that team were flown by Dortmund to the away leg of their 1993 UEFA Cup semi-final against French club Auxerre. The "lucky charms" paid off again though Dortmund subsequently lost to Juventus in the final.

Revenge arrived in style four years later, when Dortmund beat Juventus 3-1 in the Champions Cup Final in Munich. Two goals from Karlheinz Riedle and one from substitute Lars Ricken turned Dortmund into Germany's first European club champions since Hamburg 14 years earlier.

The foundations had been laid at the start of the decade. Dortmund finished Bundesliga runners-up in 1992 then, again, in January 1993 when they paid £3m to bring home attacking sweeper Matthias Sammer from Internazionale of Italy. Sammer, a former East German international, had been sold to Inter only the previous summer by Stuttgart, but he failed to adapt to soccer, life and the language in Italy and Dortmund's enterprise in bringing him home was rewarded with success at home and abroad.

The Westfalenstadion is one of the few modern German stadia which was created primarily for soccer. It was built for the 1974 World Cup finals and expanded to double the capacity 32 years later for the next German World Cup.

Werder Bremen

Germany
Founded: 1899
Stadium: Weserstadion (42,500)
Colours: White/green
League: four
Cup: six
European Cup-Winners' Cup: 1992

Werder Bremen may be one of the least fashionable clubs in Germany. However, over the years, they also have been one of the most consistently successful. Not for Bremen the big splash in the transfer market or the constant changing of coaches. Otto Rehhagel was boss for a decade before being lured away to Bayern Munich in 1995 and his wife was almost as well-known a figure around the Weserstadion. Rehhagel later coached Greece to 2004 European Championship glory.

Bremen won the cup for the first time in 1961, and most recently in 2009. As for the league championship, that was taken home to North Germany in 1965, 1988, 1993 and then again in 2004.

The 1965 team's strength lay in defence, where full-backs Horst-Dieter Hottges and Sepp Piontek were members of the West German squad which finished runners-up at the 1966 World Cup. Piontek went on to greater fame as coach of Denmark's national team, which reached the semi-finals of the 1984 European Championship and the second round of the 1986 World Cup.

In 1992 Bremen won their first European trophy when they defeated Monaco of France in the now-defunct Cup-Winners' Cup final in Lisbon. Star striker Klaus Allofs later became club manager and laid down the financial prudent strategy that resulted league title success in 2004 and a consistent and financially-rewarding presence in the UEFA Champions League.

Midfielder Torsten Frings was a key member of the German side who finished third as hosts at the 2006 World Cup.

SV Hamburg

Germany
Founded: 1887
Stadium: Volksparkstadion (61,234)
Colours: White/red
League: six
Cup: three
European Cup: 1983
European Cup-Winners' Cup: 1977

Hamburg are considered by many to be the oldest league club in Germany and their tradition, from that day to this, has been one of attacking soccer.

The first major trophy could have been theirs in 1922. But when the championship play-off was abandoned because injury-hit Nürnberg had only seven men left on the pitch, Hamburg sportingly declined to accept the title. A year later Hamburg did win the championship, and again in 1928.

They did not win it again until 1960, by which time they were being led by the greatest player in the club's history. Centre-forward Uwe Seeler was four times Hamburg's top scorer in the old regional league system, and after the creation of the Bundesliga was on one occasion the country's leading marksman. He also spearheaded Hamburg's thrilling 1960-61 European Cup campaign, in which they lost to Barcelona only in a play-off in the semi-finals.

Seeler went on to captain West Germany but he had retired by the time Hamburg achieved a European breakthrough and won the Cup-Winners' Cup in 1977. Hamburg beat Anderlecht of Belgium in a final which was the big-occasion debuts of two long-serving internationals, Manni Kaltz and Felix Magath.

Both were stalwarts of the side beaten by Nottingham Forest in the 1980 European Cup Final, when Kevin Keegan tried in vain to stimulate the Hamburg attack. Keegan had returned to England by the time Hamburg beat Juventus in Athens three years later to win the European crown for the first and only time.

HOLLAND & BELGIUM

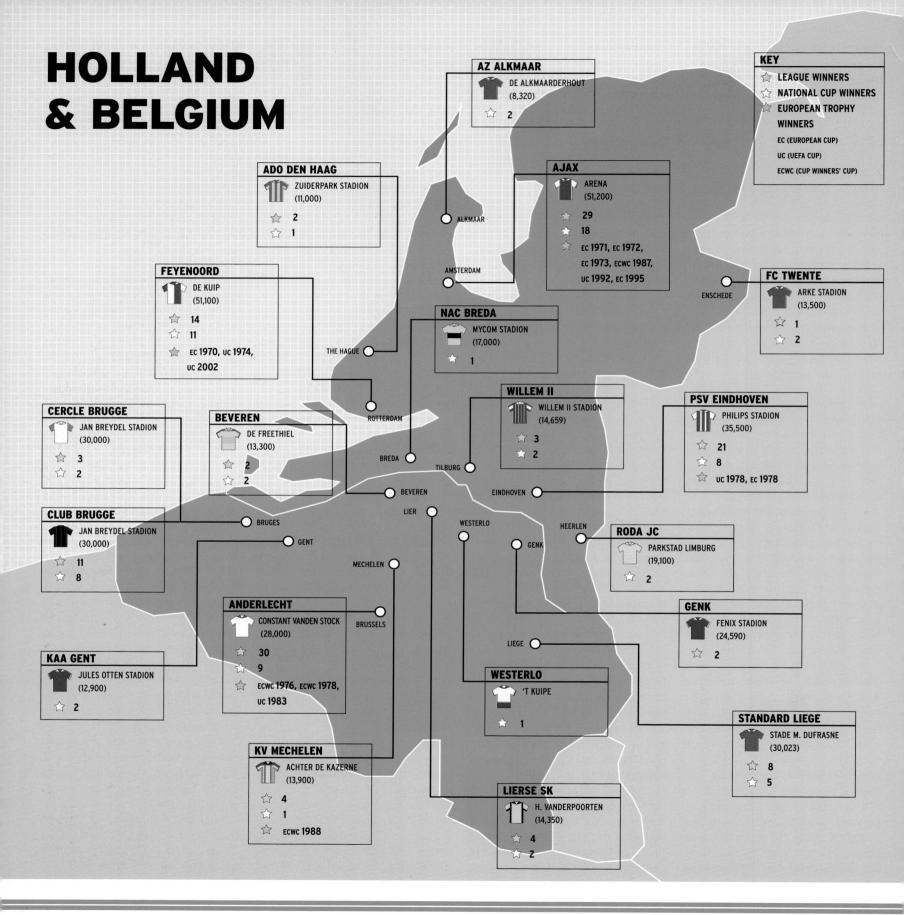

KEY
- ⭐ LEAGUE WINNERS
- ⭐ NATIONAL CUP WINNERS
- ⭐ EUROPEAN TROPHY WINNERS
- EC (EUROPEAN CUP)
- UC (UEFA CUP)
- ECWC (CUP WINNERS' CUP)

AZ ALKMAAR
DE ALKMAARDERHOUT
(8,320)
- ⭐ 2

ADO DEN HAAG
ZUIDERPARK STADION
(11,000)
- ⭐ 2
- ⭐ 1

AJAX
ARENA
(51,200)
- ⭐ 29
- ⭐ 18
- ⭐ EC 1971, EC 1972, EC 1973, ECWC 1987, UC 1992, EC 1995

FC TWENTE
ARKE STADION
(13,500)
- ⭐ 1
- ⭐ 2

FEYENOORD
DE KUIP
(51,100)
- ⭐ 14
- ⭐ 11
- ⭐ EC 1970, UC 1974, UC 2002

NAC BREDA
MYCOM STADION
(17,000)
- ⭐ 1

WILLEM II
WILLEM II STADION
(14,659)
- ⭐ 3
- ⭐ 2

PSV EINDHOVEN
PHILIPS STADION
(35,500)
- ⭐ 21
- ⭐ 8
- ⭐ UC 1978, EC 1978

CERCLE BRUGGE
JAN BREYDEL STADION
(30,000)
- ⭐ 3
- ⭐ 2

BEVEREN
DE FREETHIEL
(13,300)
- ⭐ 2
- ⭐ 2

CLUB BRUGGE
JAN BREYDEL STADION
(30,000)
- ⭐ 11
- ⭐ 8

RODA JC
PARKSTAD LIMBURG
(19,100)
- ⭐ 2

ANDERLECHT
CONSTANT VANDEN STOCK
(28,000)
- ⭐ 30
- ⭐ 9
- ⭐ ECWC 1976, ECWC 1978, UC 1983

GENK
FENIX STADION
(24,590)
- ⭐ 2

KAA GENT
JULES OTTEN STADION
(12,900)
- ⭐ 2

WESTERLO
'T KUIPE
- ⭐ 1

STANDARD LIEGE
STADE M. DUFRASNE
(30,023)
- ⭐ 8
- ⭐ 5

KV MECHELEN
ACHTER DE KAZERNE
(13,900)
- ⭐ 4
- ⭐ 1
- ⭐ ECWC 1988

LIERSE SK
H. VANDERPOORTEN
(14,350)
- ⭐ 4
- ⭐ 2

Map city labels: ALKMAAR, AMSTERDAM, ENSCHEDE, THE HAGUE, ROTTERDAM, BREDA, TILBURG, EINDHOVEN, HEERLEN, BEVEREN, LIER, WESTERLO, GENK, LIEGE, BRUGES, GENT, MECHELEN, BRUSSELS

Ajax

Amsterdam, Holland
Founded: 1900
Stadium: Arena (50,000)
Colours: Red and white broad stripes/white
League: 29
Cup: 18
World Club Cup: 1972, 1995
European Cup: 1971, 1972, 1973, 1995
European Cup-winners' Cup: 1987
UEFA Cup: 1992
Supercup: 1972, 1973, 1995

Ajax, on beating Torino in the 1992 UEFA Cup Final, became only the second team after Italy's Juventus to have won all three European trophies and a full house of all seven titles on offer to clubs. The achievement was a popular one, bearing in mind the entertainment and style the Amsterdam club had consistently provided.

The first hints of glory to come were in evidence in 1966-67 when, under former Dutch international Rinus Michels, Ajax thrashed Liverpool 5-1 in a European Cup tie. Two years later Ajax became the first Dutch side to reach the European Cup Final, though they lost 4-1 to Milan. In 1971 Ajax were back as winners, beating Panathinaikos at Wembley. In the next two Finals, they beat Internazionale, then Juventus. Johan Cruyff was their inspiration and "total football" was their game.

After the sale of Cruyff to Barcelona in 1973, Ajax fell away and it took his return, a decade later, to propel them back to the peaks of the European game. Under Cruyff, the new Ajax generation won the Cup-Winners' Cup in 1987 – his friend and pupil Marco Van Basten scoring the goal which beat Lokomotive Leipzig in the final in Athens. Cruyff's successor Louis Van Gaal then secured the UEFA Cup five years later.

Despite continuing to sell many of their best players, Ajax's 1994-95 squad was statistically their best ever; the team won the League championship without losing a game, and the European Cup for the fourth time.

Anderlecht

Brussels, Belgium
Founded: 1908
Stadium: Constant Vanden Stock/Parc Astrid (28,063)
Colours: White with mauve/white
League: 30
Cup: nine
European Cup-winners' Cup: 1976, 1978
UEFA Cup: 1983
Supercup: 1976, 1978

Anderlecht's international debut was not a happy one: they crashed 12-0 on aggregate to Manchester United. Since then, however, the Royal Sporting Club have earned respect far and wide for an international outlook which has brought success in both the European Cup-Winners' Cup and the UEFA Cup.

Much credit reflects on the coaching work of Englishman Bill Gormlie, a former Blackburn goalkeeper, who helped lay the foundations in the late 1940s and early 1950s.

Equally important was the financial power of the millionaire Constant Vanden Stock. Before his takeover Anderlecht relied mainly on homegrown talent like Paul Van Himst, the greatest Belgian player of all time. As their prestige grew, particularly thanks to the European Cup competitions, they were able to compete in the international transfer market.

A significant coaching influence, in the early 1960s, was Frenchman Pierre Sinibaldi, who perfected a tactical formation which relied on a flat back four, the offside trap and possession soccer in midfield. It worked well against almost all opposition except British clubs, whose more direct style constantly caught defenders on the turn. Thus, the first time Anderlecht reached a European final – in the Fairs Cup in 1970 – they were beaten by Arsenal. European success, in the Cup-Winners' Cup in 1976 and 1978, had to await the more pragmatic coaching approach of Dutchman Wiel Corver and Belgian Raymond Goethals. Later, with Van Himst having returned as coach, they won the UEFA Cup, and in Enzo Scifo produced the finest Belgian player since Van Himst himself.

Feyenoord

Rotterdam, Holland
Founded: 1908
Stadium: De Kuyp (52,000)
Colours: Red and white halves/black
League: 14
Cup: 11
World Club Cup: 1970
European Cup: 1970
UEFA Cup: 1974, 2002

Feyenoord from Rotterdam were founded by mining entrepreneur CRJ Kieboom. Their post-war years were bleak until after the introduction of professionalism in the late 1950s. Then Feyenoord entered their most glorious domestic era, winning the league title six times in 13 years. Their 1965 and 1969 successes brought them league and cup doubles.

They won the European Cup in 1970, with coach Ernst Happel. Feyenoord – and not Ajax – were thus the first Dutch club to break through to European success, and they went on to defeat Estudiantes in the World Club Cup Final.

In 1974, Feyenoord added the UEFA Cup to their trophy room. But later, players had to be sold to balance the books, among them Ruud Gullit. Feyenoord fans have grown increasingly impatient with no league titles to show since 1999.

PSV Eindhoven

Holland
Founded: 1913
Stadium: Philips (30,000)
Colours: Red and white stripes/white
League: 21
Cup: eight
European Cup: 1988
UEFA Cup: 1978

PSV equalled the achievements of Celtic (in 1967) and Ajax Amsterdam (in 1972) when they defeated Benfica on penalties to win the 1988 European Cup.

Surprisingly, considering PSV's position as the sports club of the giant Philips electrics corporation, they were long outshone by Ajax and Feyenoord. For years the Philips company took comparatively little interest in PSV. Only in the past two decades have Philips become seriously involved with club policy and finance.

PSV had won the 1976 UEFA Cup and ten years later the company came up with the funds, and were duly rewarded in 1988 with their sole European Champions Cup victory. An international outlook prompted the signing of top coaches such as Bobby Robson and young Brazilian strikers Romario and Ronaldo. But the inherent financial weakness of the Dutch game means they have never been able to hold their stars long enough for long.

Feyenoord become the first Dutch winners of the Champions Cup.

SAN SIRO, MILAN
Flags of co-hosts AC Milan and Internazionale show off the ground-share ethic which works in Italy but would be beyond discussion in most other European soccer capitals.

ITALY

INTERNAZIONALE
GIUSEPPE MEAZZA (85,700)
- ⭐ 18
- ⭐ 6
- ⭐ EC 1964, EC 1965, UC 1991, UC 1994, UC 1998, EC 2010

PARMA
STADIO ENNIO TARDINI (29,048)
- ⭐ 3

BRESCIA
STADIO MARIO RIGAMONTI (27,500)

UDINESE
STADIO FRIULI (41,662)

CHIEVO VERONA
STADIO MARC ANTONIO BENTEGODI (44,200)
- ⭐ 1

MILAN
GIUSEPPE MEAZZA (85,700)
- ⭐ 17
- ⭐ 5
- ⭐ EC 1963, ECWC 1968, EC 1969, ECWC 1973, EC 1989, EC 1990, EC 1994, EC 2003, EC 2007

BOLOGNA
STADIO RENATO DALL'ARI (39,387)
- ⭐ 7
- ⭐ 2

FIORENTINA
STADIO ARTEMIO FRANCHI (47,350)
- ⭐ 2
- ⭐ 6
- ⭐ ECWC 1961

SIENA
COMMUNALE ARTEMIO FRANCHI (13,500)

JUVENTUS
STADIO DELLE ALPI (70,000)
- ⭐ 27
- ⭐ 9
- ⭐ UC 1977, ECWC 1984, EC 1985, UC 1990, UC 1993, EC 1996

PERUGIA
STADIO RENATO CURI (28,000)

ROMA
STADIO OLIMPICO (75,000)
- ⭐ 3
- ⭐ 9
- ⭐ FC 1961

LECCE
STADIO VIA DEL MARE (41,000)

SAMPDORIA
STADIO LUIGI FERRARIS (40,086)
- ⭐ 1
- ⭐ 4
- ⭐ ECWC 1990

NAPOLI
STADIO SAN PAOLO (45,000)
- ⭐ 2
- ⭐ 3
- ⭐ UC 1989

LAZIO
STADIO OLIMPICO (75,000)
- ⭐ 2
- ⭐ 5
- ⭐ ECWC 1999

REGGINA
STADIO ORESTE GRANILLO (27,690)

Map cities: BRESCIA, UDINE, VERONA, MILAN, TURIN, PARMA, BOLOGNA, GENOA, FLORENCE, SIENA, PERUGIA, ROME, NAPLES, LECCE, REGGIO DI CALABRIA

KEY
- ⭐ LEAGUE WINNERS
- ⭐ ITALIAN CUP WINNERS
- ⭐ EUROPEAN TROPHY WINNERS
  - EC (EUROPEAN CUP)
  - UC (UEFA CUP)
  - FC (FAIRS CUP)
  - ECWC (CUP WINNERS' CUP)

Milan

Italy
Founded: 1899
Stadium: Giuseppe Meazza
(85,700)
Colours: Red and black stripes/white
League: 17
Cup: five
World Club Cup: 1969, 1989, 1990, 2007
European Cup: 1963, 1969, 1989, 1990, 1994, 2003, 2007
European Cup-Winners' Cup: 1968, 1973
Supercup: 1989, 1990, 1995, 2003, 2007

Milan's domination of the European club game for almost two decades from the late 1980s was achieved on a unique stage which would appear to represent the pattern of the future for a sport increasingly controlled by the intertwined commercial interests and demands of big business and television.

In Milan's case, all these strands were in the hands of a puppet-master supreme in media magnate and then prime minister of Italy, Silvio Berlusconi. He had come to the rescue in 1986, investing £20 million to save Milan from bankruptcy and turn the club into a key player in his commercial empire.

Milan had been one of the founders of the Italian Championship back in 1898 but most of the pre-World War Two years were spent in the shadow of neighbours Internazionale – or Ambrosiana as they were then called. After the war Milan achieved spectacular success thanks to their forays into the international transfer market.

Sweden had won the 1948 Olympic title thanks to the inside-forward skills of Gunnar Gren, Gunnar Nordahl and Nils Liedholm, so Milan signed them en bloc and then followed up by paying a then world record £72,000 for Juan Schiaffino – hero of Uruguay's shock World Cup victory in 1950.

Milan were the first major rivals to Real Madrid in the new European Champions Cup – losing to the Spanish club in the 1956 semi-finals, then only after extra-time in the 1958 Final. That was also the year Milan discovered the teenaged Gianni Rivera, whose inside-forward genius inspired Milan to their first Champions Cup victory in 1963.

His partnership with Brazilian centre-forward Jose Altafini destroyed Benfica in the final and skipper and sweeper Cesare Maldini held the cup aloft at Wembley – where he would later enjoy another significant success, this time as manager of Italy, in the 1998 World Cup qualifying event.

Rivera was Milan's figurehead in the 1960s and early 1970s, winning the Champions Cup again in 1969 and the Cup-Winners' Cup in 1973. But even his charisma could not save the club from the scandals inflicted by a string of disastrous presidents.

That was where Berlusconi came in, providing the money which turned Milan into the archetypal "media club" for the 21st century. His power allowed Milan to buy superstars such as Dutchmen Ruud Gullit and Marco Van Basten and later Brazil's Kaka and Cafu but also hold on to Italians such as Franco Baresi and Paolo Maldini, son of Cesare.

The younger Maldini duly went on to emulate his father as a Champions Cup-winning captain with the club and claimed a fifth personal winners' medal after victory over Liverpool in 2007. Milan were fortunate to be in the competition at all after being implicated the previous year in a domestic match-fixing scandal.

Coach Nereo Rocco and captain Cesare Maldini are Wembley winners in 1963.

Milan Presiodent Silvio Berlusconi (holding trophy handle) joins his players after their 2007 UEFA Champions League Final victory over Liverpool at the Olympic Stadium, Athens.

Juventus

Turin, Italy
Founded: 1897
Stadium: Delle Alpi (70,000)
Colours: Black and white
stripes/white
League: 27
Cup: nine
World Club Cup: 1985, 1996
European Cup: 1985, 1996
European Cup-Winners' Cup: 1984
UEFA Cup: 1977, 1990, 1993
Supercup: 1985, 1996

Juventus were founded by a group of Italian students who decided to adopt red as the colour for their shirts. In 1903, however, when the club was six years old, one committee member was so impressed on a trip to England by Notts County's black-and-white stripes that he bought a set to take home to Turin.

In the 1930s Juventus laid the foundations for their legend as the "Old Lady" of Italian soccer – La Vecchia Signora – by winning the league championship five times in a row. Simultaneously they also reached the semi-finals of the Mitropa Cup on four occasions and supplied Italy's World Cup-winning teams with five players in 1934 and three in 1938.

Their own Gianpiero Combi was Italy's victorious captain in 1934, just as another Juventus goalkeeper, Dino Zoff, would be Italy's World Cup-winning skipper in Spain in 1982.

Post-war, the Zebras (after their shirts) scoured the world for talent to match their import-led rivals. First came the Danes, John and Karl Hansen, then Argentine favourite Omar Sivori and the "Gentle Giant" from Wales, John Charles, followed by Spanish inside-forward Luis Del Sol and French inspiration Michel Platini. In 1971 they lost the Fairs Cup Final to Leeds on away goals, but in 1977 beat Bilbao in the UEFA Cup Final under the same rule.

Fabrizio Ravanelli sets off on a trademark glory gallop after scoring for Juventus in the 1996 Champions League Final.

In 1982 no fewer than six Juventus players featured in Italy's World Cup winning line-up, and Antonio Cabrini, Marco Tardelli, Gaetano Scirea, Claudio Gentile and Paolo Rossi helped Juventus to win the 1984 European Cup-Winners' Cup and the 1985 European Cup. The latter success, by 1-0 over Liverpool, is not one that Juventus have ever celebrated, since it was secured amid the Heysel stadium tragedy in Brussels in which 39 Juve fans died in a hooligan-inspired crowd crush before the kick-off.

Seeking new magic in the 1990s, Juventus paid huge fees for Roberto Baggio and Gianluca Vialli. Both shared in the 1995 league and cup double triumph but Baggio then left for Milan on the eve of a season which saw Vialli captain Juventus to victory in the European Champions Cup Final over Ajax in Rome.

Juventus reached the Champions Cup Final again in successive years – 1997 and 1998 – only to lose on each occasion. Both times Juve failed to live up to their favourites' billing against first Borussia Dortmund in Munich in 1997 and then against Real Madrid in Amsterdam in 1998. A further defeat followed – albeit 'only' on penalties to Milan in the first all-Italian final in 2003.

Much worse followed in 2006 when Juve were punished with their first-ever relegation for their part in a major match-fixing scandal. A number of their big-name players unsurprisingly jumped ship rather than play in the second tier, but some – most notably French striker David Trezeguet and Italian duo Alessandro Del Piero and Gianluigi Buffon – stayed in Turin. Their loyalty was rewarded when Juventus bounced back immediately, winning the Serie B title at a canter, then returning to the Champions League in 2009.

Juventus fan's favourite Alessandro del Piero (left).

Bologna

Italy
Founded: 1909
Stadium: Renato Dall'Ara (39,387)
Colours: Red and blue/blue
League: seven
Cup: two

Bologna are one of those clubs who make up the solid backbone of Italian soccer despite all the varying scandals and controversies which assail Calcio. Bologna were among the founder members of the unified top division in 1929-30.

The club not only won the league title six times in the inter-war years but twice carried off the Mitropa Cup, the precursor of today's European club competitions.

They floated around the top half of the league in the two decades after the Second World War and hit a pinnacle of achievement by regaining the league championship shield – the scudetto – in 1964. The manner of victory was astonishing. In the midst of Bologna's duel with Internazionale seven of their players were suspended on doping charges. Bologna had points deducted but these were restored when the players were cleared on appeal due to the confused state of the dope test system. They duly finished level on points at the top with Inter, the reigning world and European champions, whom they then beat 2-0 in a play-off in Rome.

Veteran coach Fulvio Bernardini saw his luck ran out after Bologna then entered the Champions Cup for the only time. Drawn against Belgium's Anderlecht in the first round, they went out on the toss of a coin.

The club have never neared such giddy heights again. In 1982, after a series of power battles and financial disasters, Bologna were relegated for the first time in their history. A year later they slipped straight on through to the Third Division. Later they came back up before dropping all the way back down to the third division and having to fight once more to reclaim a fragile grip on Serie A status.

Fiorentina

Florence, Italy
Founded: 1926
Stadium: Artemio Franchi (47,350)
Colours: All violet
League: two
Cup: six
European Cup-Winners' Cup: 1961

Fiorentina, under new ownership after collapsing into a ruinous bankruptcy which took them down into the Fourth Division, are slowly trying to put back together the pieces of a great reputation for skilful, inventive soccer – founded on the talents of stars such as Giancarlo Antognoni, Daniel Bertoni, Kurt Hamrin and Julinho.

Ironically, however, Fiorentina owed their most notable league success, in 1955-56, to an iron-clad defence. This was the team who conceded a then record of only 20 goals in their 34 league games and remained unbeaten until the last day of the season. The team reached the 1957 Champions' Cup Final, but unluckily had to face Real Madrid in the Spanish capital, and lost 2-0. Fiorentina, however, had the consolation of being the first winners of the Cup-Winners' Cup in 1961.

In the mid-1960s former star Chiappella became coach and built a fine young team which was later guided to the league title by the Swedish manager, Nils Liedholm.

The "Viola" reached a further European final when they lost to Internazionale in the UEFA Cup in 1990. But three years later they suffered the ignominy of relegation for the first time in more than 50 years. An instant revival owed much to the financial power of film-maker Vittorio Cecchi Gori and the acquisition of stars such as Manuel Rui Costa and Gabriel Batistuta.

Catastrophic mismanagement then sent the club careering into bankruptcy in 2002. They were refounded initially as Florentia Viola and had to "buy back" their old name and insignia as they battled up through the lower divisions and, eventually, into the Champions League.

Internazionale

Milan, Italy
Founded: 1908
Stadium: Meazza (85,443)
Colours: Blue and black stripes/black
League: 18
Cup: six
World Club Cup: 1964, 1965
European Champions: 1964, 1965, 2010
UEFA Cup: 1991, 1994, 1998

Internazionale's early years were marked by political issues. They were founded in 1908 out of a members' dispute within AC Milan. Then, in the 1930s, were forced by fascist laws into a name change to rid the club of its foreign associations. As Ambrosiana – the city's patron saint – they were one of the leading lights of the Mitropa Cup.

After the war the rebaptised Internazionale pioneered a tactical revolution. First manager Alfredo Foni, a World Cup-winning full-back before the war, won the league title twice by withdrawing outside-right Gino Armani into midfield; then Helenio Herrera conquered Italy, Europe and the world with an iron-clad catenaccio defence.

Stars such as attacking fullback Giacinto Facchetti, Spanish playmaker Luis Suarez and Italian forward Sandro Mazzola inspired double success in both European Champions Cup and World Club Cup in 1964 and 1965. Not until the late 1980s, however, did Inter then regain their international and domestic status when West German midfielder Lothar Matthäus drove them to the 1989 league title followed by a UEFA Cup hat-trick in the 1990s. Inter regained command after the enforced relegation in 2006 of Juventus for match-fixing and the ageing of neighbours Milan. They won the Serie A crown five years in a row, latterly under coach Jose Mourinho.

Having won titles in a record third country, Mourinho also guided Inter to their first European Champions' crown for 45 years in 2010 before moving on again.

Lazio

Rome, Italy
Founded: 1900
Stadium: Olimpico (75,000)
League: two
Cup: five
European Cup-Winners' Cup: 1999
European Supercup: 1999

Lazio have endured turbulent times since they won the Serie A title on a dramatic final Sunday in 2000. That completed a double after they won the Coppa Italia for the third time. They also reached the Champions League quarter-finals. They had won the last European Cup-Winners' Cup final the previous season. Club president Sergio Cragnotti believed his club were poised to establish themselves amongst Europe's elite.

But things turned sour in 2000-01. Lazio were eliminated from the Champions League and coach Sven-Goran Eriksson left for England. Lazio slipped to sixth in 2002 and went out of the Champions League at the first group stage. The Rome outfit slid deep into debt, Cragnotti quit and the club were then also caught up in the notorious "Moggiopoli" match-fixing scandal.

Lazio had been founder members of the Italian league in 1929-30 but their best pre-war finish was second in 1936-37. They collected their first piece of silverware in 1958 by winning the Italian Cup and collected the league title for the first time in 1974. The title euphoria did not last, however. Lazio were barred from entry to the Champions Cup because of a 12-month ban for crowd trouble and twice subsequently they were relegated.

Cragnotti came to the rescue in 1990 and brought in Eriksson as coach in 1997. In his first season they won the Italian cup and reached the UEFA Cup Final. The next season, 1998-99, they finished league runners-up to Milan and won the last Cup-Winners' Cup Final. Everything at that stage was leading up to the glorious 1999-2000 campaign in which a resurgent Lazio won the league and cup double.

Napoli

Naples, Italy
Founded: 1904
Stadium: San Paolo (45,000)
Colours: Blue/white
League: two
Cup: three
UEFA Cup: 1989

Napoli were, for years, a club with more passion than purpose. The original Naples club were founded in 1904 and became the present Associazione Calcio Napoli in 1926. Relegated in the penultimate pre-war season – 1941-42 – Napoli spent much of the first 20 post-war years hopping between divisions. The "new era" began in 1965 and in the next decade Napoli established themselves as virtual ever-presents in the top four but they had only two Italian Cups to show for it. The step up to European achievement demanded a further coup – signing Maradona from Barcelona for a world record £5 million.

Within a fortnight of the transfer, Napoli had recouped most of the fee in season-ticket sales. Maradona played to sell-out 85,000 crowds and inspired Napoli to win the league title twice, the UEFA Cup and the Italian Cup. The money Napoli made, however, was frittered away. After Maradona's dope-ban exit in 1991, the club collapsed to the brink of bankruptcy and relegation.

Parma

Italy
Founded: 1913
Stadium: Ennio Tardini (29,048)
Colours: All white
Cup: three
Cup-Winners' Cup: 1993
UEFA Cup: 1995, 1999
European Supercup: 1993

Parma were founded on July 27, 1913 – originally under the name of Verdi Foot Ball Club. Five months later the composer disappeared from view as the club committee voted to change titles to Parma Foot Ball Club. In the 1950s Parma appeared to establish themselves in the second division but were relegated in 1965 and slipped right on down into the fourth division.

Finally, in 1986, they gained promotion back to Serie B and, four years later, were in Serie A for the first time in their history. In that first Serie A season they beat Juventus in the Italian cup final, made their way to Europe in the Cup-winners Cup and triumphed thanks to a 3-1 victory over Belgian club Antwerp at Wembley.

Against Arsenal a year later, Parma narrowly failed to become the first club to retain the Cup-winners Cup but their European consolation, a year later, was to beat fellow Italians Juventus for the first of two UEFA Cup triumphs in four years.

Roma

Italy
Founded: 1927
Stadium: Olimpico (75,000)
Colours: All burgundy
League: threeo
Cup: nine
Fairs Cup: 1961

All the fuss afforded the clubs of Milan and Turin over the years has obscured the fact that Roma were one of the first two Italians clubs to win a European trophy. That was in 1961 when Roma beat Birmingham City over two legs to win the Fairs Cup. Roma's team included two popular Argentine forwards in Pedro Manfredonia and Antonio Valentin Angelillo and an Italian goalkeeper in Fabio Cudicini.

Roma came closest to a European prize again in 1984. They were favourites to beat Liverpool in the Champions Cup Final since the venue was their own Stadio Olimpico. But the match ended 1-1 after extra time and Roma proved more nervy in the penalty shoot-out, which they lost 4-2.

Brazilian midfielder Paulo Roberto Falcao, one of the outstanding personalities in Italian soccer in the 1980s, stayed aloof from the shoot-out and his relationship with Roma fans was never quite the same again.

Roma were founded as a result of a merger of four city clubs – Alba, Fortitudo, Roman and Pro Patria. They were members of the inaugural First Division in 1929-30, finishing sixth. Runners-up in 1931 and 1936 they rose to surprise championship winners in 1942 – inspired by the goals of Amadeo Amadei.

The club were nearly bankrupted by relegation in 1951 and then again a decade later after miscalculating the high cost of signing German striker Jurgen Schutz and the Italo-Brazilian centre-forward Angelo Benedetto Sormani for a then world record transfer fee of £250,000.

Fortunately, one of the club's greatest heroes to emerge in the late 1990s, Francesco Totti, was a local boy who cost next to nothing and came up through the youth system.

Sampdoria

Genoa, Italy
Founded: 1946
Stadium: Luigi Ferraris
Colours: Blue/white
League: one
Cup: four
Cup-Winners' Cup: 1990

Sampdoria built a brief reputation, after a take-over by the oil-rich Mantovani family in the early 1980s, as one of Italy's most attractive teams. That was not reflected in as much success as perhaps they deserved with only Cup-Winners' Cup win.

Sampdoria had been founded only in 1946 from the merger of two largely unsuccessful local clubs, Sampierdaranese and Andrea Doria. Hence the club title, Sampdoria. Where neighbours Genoa were the "establishment" club, Sampdoria resorted to the cheque book as a short cut to success and popularity. One of the biggest early signings was Eddie Firmani, from Charlton Athletic. In 1958 Firmani was second in the Italian scoring charts, behind only John Charles of Juventus.

A string of famous coaches failed to prevent Sampdoria's gradual slide towards relegation in 1966. They bounced straight up at first attempt, but went back down in 1975. Tycoon Paolo Mantovani was then a director, and on becoming president in 1979, he launched a one-man revolution.

His drive steered Sampdoria back to Serie A in 1982. Mantovani also provided the finance to purchase English league stars Liam Brady, Trevor Francis and Graeme Souness as well as Roberto Mancini from Bologna. The first tangible sign of success was a cup victory in 1985, which Samp repeated in 1988 and 1989. In due course, England's David Platt and Dutch veteran Ruud Gullit, from Milan, would follow an increasingly well-worn path.

The peak of the Mantovani years was their appearance in the Champions Cup Final in 1992, but they lost in extra time to Barcelona.

UEFA Cup marksman Ciro Ferrara (third from left) gets a celebratory hug from Diego Maradona.

PORTUGAL

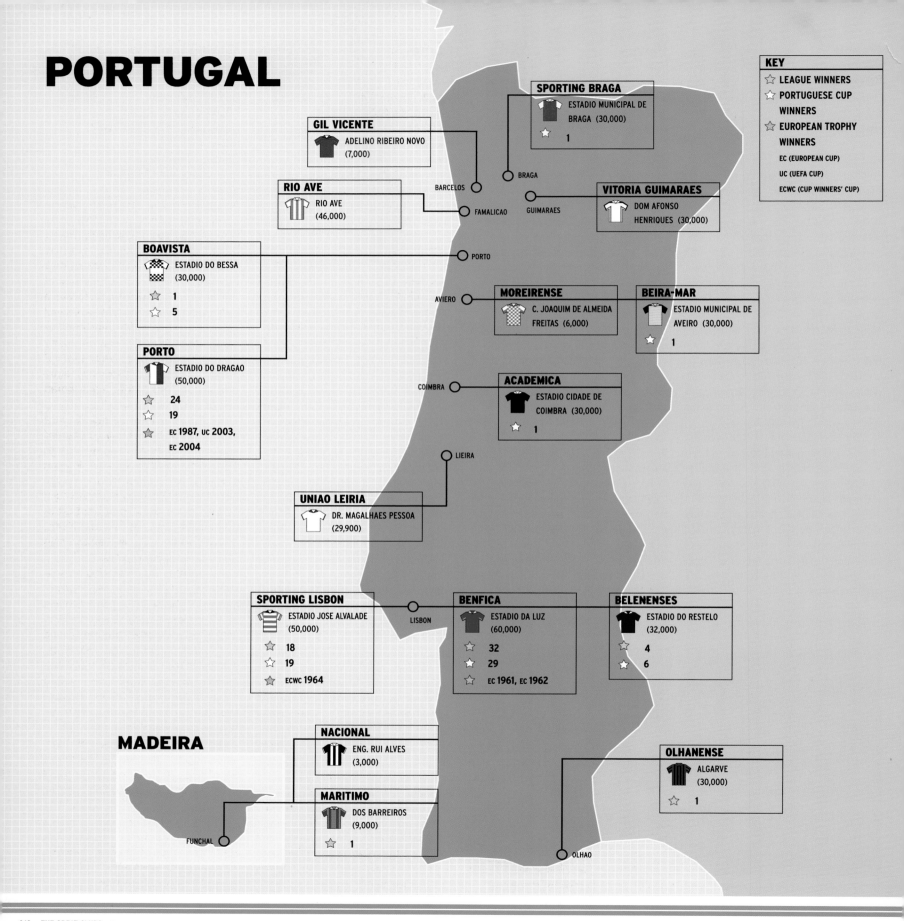

KEY
☆ LEAGUE WINNERS
☆ PORTUGUESE CUP WINNERS
☆ EUROPEAN TROPHY WINNERS

EC (EUROPEAN CUP)
UC (UEFA CUP)
ECWC (CUP WINNERS' CUP)

SPORTING BRAGA
ESTADIO MUNICIPAL DE BRAGA (30,000)
☆ 1

GIL VICENTE
ADELINO RIBEIRO NOVO (7,000)

RIO AVE
RIO AVE (46,000)

VITORIA GUIMARAES
DOM AFONSO HENRIQUES (30,000)

BARCELOS
BRAGA
FAMALICAO
GUIMARAES

BOAVISTA
ESTADIO DO BESSA (30,000)
☆ 1
☆ 5

PORTO

MOREIRENSE
C. JOAQUIM DE ALMEIDA FREITAS (6,000)

BEIRA-MAR
ESTADIO MUNICIPAL DE AVEIRO (30,000)
☆ 1

AVIERO

PORTO
ESTADIO DO DRAGAO (50,000)
☆ 24
☆ 19
☆ EC 1987, UC 2003, EC 2004

ACADEMICA
ESTADIO CIDADE DE COIMBRA (30,000)
☆ 1

COIMBRA

LIEIRA

UNIAO LEIRIA
DR. MAGALHAES PESSOA (29,900)

SPORTING LISBON
ESTADIO JOSE ALVALADE (50,000)
☆ 18
☆ 19
☆ ECWC 1964

LISBON

BENFICA
ESTADIO DA LUZ (60,000)
☆ 32
☆ 29
☆ EC 1961, EC 1962

BELENENSES
ESTADIO DO RESTELO (32,000)
☆ 4
☆ 6

MADEIRA

NACIONAL
ENG. RUI ALVES (3,000)

OLHANENSE
ALGARVE (30,000)
☆ 1

MARITIMO
DOS BARREIROS (9,000)
☆ 1

FUNCHAL

OLHAO

Benfica

Lisbon, Portugal
Founded: 1904
Stadium: Estadio do Benfica/
Da Luz (60,000)
Colours: Red/white
League: 32
Cup: 29
European Cup: 1961, 1962

Benfica are a national institution with their huge stadium – rebuilt for the European finals of 2004 – and 122,000 membership.

Living up to their history is what Benfica believe they owe Cosme Damiao who, on February 28, 1904, organized the first recorded local game of futebol on a patch of Lisbon wasteland. The next day he formed his "team" into a club named Sport Lisboa and, two years later was instrumental in arranging a merger with neighbours Sport Clube de Benfica.

In due course they set their sights on international glory and in 1950 won the Latin Cup and then the European Cup in 1961 and 1962. They introduced one of the most famous Portuguese players of all time in Eusebio, greatest of the many fine players Benfica had discovered in the Portuguese colonies of Angola and Mozambique.

Benfica's boast of only "Portuguese" (including colonial) players was scrapped in the mid-1970s, when the African colonies were cast adrift. The club's command of domestic soccer went with them.

Boavista

Oporto, Portugal
Founded: 1903
Stadium: Bessa (30,000)
Colours: Black and white check
League: one
Cup: five

Boavista have been making a habit of upsetting the odds over the past few years. In 2001 they shocked all Portugal by winning the league for the first time in their history. It was the first time in 53 years that a club from outside the traditional Big Three of neighbours FC Porto, Benfica and Sporting Lisbon had lifted the trophy.

The "draughts board club" were founded by a group of Englishmen on August 1, 1903, some ten years after their richer neighbours, FC Porto. They took their present title of Boavista Futebol Clube in 1909.

By the end of the 1940s and start of the 1950s they had secured a foothold in the top division, albeit marked with a club record victory by 9–0 over Olhanense and club record defeats of 12–1 by Sporting and 11–0 by Benfica.

Not until the 1970s did they establish themselves as a minor force on the national stage. They then won the league in 2001. It was a sensational achievement, given the iron grip held on the title by the Big Three and the fact that not one Boavista player had featured in the Portuguese national team squad who had reached the Euro 2000 semi-finals. The following season they also went on to reach the semi-finals of the UEFA Cup.

FC Porto

Oporto, Portugal
Founded: 1893
Stadium: Dragao (50,000)
Colours: Blue and white stripes/white
League: 24
Cup: 19
World Club Cup: 1987
European Cup: 1987, 2004
UEFA Cup: 2003
Supercup: 1987

Porto were always considered to be number three in the Portuguese soccer hierarchy until their thrilling European Cup victory over Bayern Munich in Vienna in 1987. Events then and since have ensured that, while their trophy count may not yet match that of Benfica, Porto has become an alternative centre of power in the domestic game.

Back in the early 1930s, Porto had been pioneers in the international transfer market. They began by bringing in two Yugoslavs, and that ambition was reflected in Porto's initial championship successes in 1938 and 1939. In those days Porto's home was the old, rundown Campo da Constituciao. They moved on to the 76,000-capacity Estadio das Antas and then built the new Dragao stadium for Euro 2004.

Not only have Porto won the Champions Cup and the UEFA Cup; they also finished runners-up to Juventus in the European Cup-Winners' Cup in 1984.

The creative force behind the club's progress in the 1980s was the late José Maria Pedroto. He led Porto to the cup in 1977 and league title in 1978 and 1979. His work would be carried on by his pupil, former national team centre-forward Artur Jorge, who coached Porto to their 1987 European title. Later, under Brazilian Carlos Alberto da Silva, duly succeeded by Bobby Robson and then Jose Mourinho, Porto enhanced their standing within the European establishment by winning the UEFA Cup in 2003 and then the Champions League, against Monaco, the next year.

Sporting Clube

Lisbon, Portugal
Founded: 1906
Stadium: José Alvalade (50,000)
Colours: Green and white hoops/white
League: 18
Cup: 19
European Cup-Winners' Cup: 1964

Sporting Clube do Portugal last reached a European final back in 1964, when they won the Cup-Winners' Cup. Now Benfica's deadly rivals – the grounds are barely a mile apart – dream of the day when they can bring those old heroes out of retirement obscurity to celebrate a European revival. The late 1980s and early 1990s brought Sporting the worst era in their history, an empty decade following the heady 1981-82 season in which they won the league and cup double under Englishman Malcolm Allison.

In 1992 the new president, José Sousa Cintra, brought in ex-England manager Bobby Robson to try to recapture the Allison magic. Robson was given only 18 months, however, before former Portugal national coach Carlos Queiroz was given the task of reviving the glories of the 1950s, when Sporting took the championship seven times in eight years.

En route to Sporting's sole European trophy, they beat APOEL Nicosia in the second round first leg by a European record 16–1. In the Final against MTK Budapest, an entertaining match saw Sporting go 1–0 down, recover to lead 2–1 then go 3–2 behind before securing a 3–3 draw and a replay. In Antwerp a 20th-minute goal from Morais, direct from a corner, was enough to win the cup.

Their back four of Morais, Batista, José Carlos and Hilario starred in the Portugal team which finished third in the 1966 World Cup finals in England.

The nearest Sporting have since gone to European success was in 2005 when they finished as UEFA Cup runners-up to CSKA Moscow in front of their own fans in Lisbon.

Benfica's Jose Aguas strikes an early goal against Tottenham in the 1962 Champions Cup semi-final.

CAMP NOU, BARCELONA

Calm before the storm... The atmospheric home of Spain's FC Barcelona, hours before a sell-out Champions League tie.

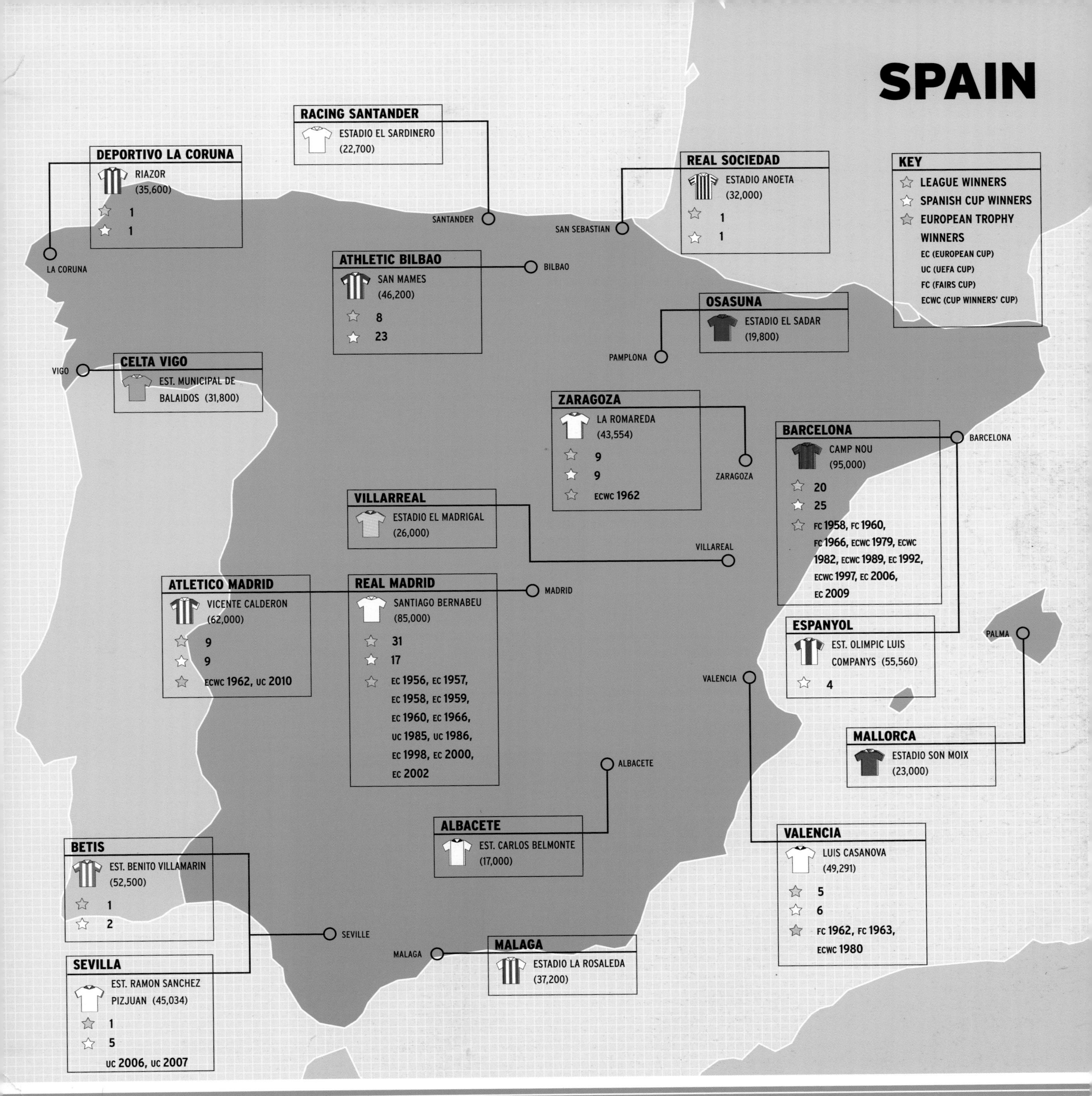
SPAIN
RACING SANTANDER
ESTADIO EL SARDINERO
(22,700)
DEPORTIVO LA CORUNA
RIAZOR
(35,600)
1
1
REAL SOCIEDAD
ESTADIO ANOETA
(32,000)
1
1
KEY
LEAGUE WINNERS
SPANISH CUP WINNERS
EUROPEAN TROPHY WINNERS
EC (EUROPEAN CUP)
UC (UEFA CUP)
FC (FAIRS CUP)
ECWC (CUP WINNERS' CUP)
SANTANDER
SAN SEBASTIAN
LA CORUNA
ATHLETIC BILBAO
SAN MAMES
(46,200)
8
23
BILBAO
OSASUNA
ESTADIO EL SADAR
(19,800)
PAMPLONA
VIGO
CELTA VIGO
EST. MUNICIPAL DE
BALAIDOS (31,800)
ZARAGOZA
LA ROMAREDA
(43,554)
9
9
ECWC 1962
ZARAGOZA
BARCELONA
CAMP NOU
(95,000)
20
25
FC 1958, FC 1960,
FC 1966, ECWC 1979, ECWC
1982, ECWC 1989, EC 1992,
ECWC 1997, EC 2006,
EC 2009
BARCELONA
VILLARREAL
ESTADIO EL MADRIGAL
(26,000)
VILLAREAL
ATLETICO MADRID
VICENTE CALDERON
(62,000)
9
9
ECWC 1962, UC 2010
REAL MADRID
SANTIAGO BERNABEU
(85,000)
31
17
EC 1956, EC 1957,
EC 1958, EC 1959,
EC 1960, EC 1966,
UC 1985, UC 1986,
EC 1998, EC 2000,
EC 2002
MADRID
ESPANYOL
EST. OLIMPIC LUIS
COMPANYS (55,560)
4
PALMA
VALENCIA
MALLORCA
ESTADIO SON MOIX
(23,000)
ALBACETE
ALBACETE
EST. CARLOS BELMONTE
(17,000)
VALENCIA
LUIS CASANOVA
(49,291)
5
6
FC 1962, FC 1963,
ECWC 1980
BETIS
EST. BENITO VILLAMARIN
(52,500)
1
2
SEVILLE
MALAGA
MALAGA
ESTADIO LA ROSALEDA
(37,200)
SEVILLA
EST. RAMON SANCHEZ
PIZJUAN (45,034)
1
5
UC 2006, UC 2007

Barcelona

Spain
Founded: 1899
Stadium: Nou Camp (95,000)
Colours: Blue and red stripes/blue
League: 20
Cup: 25
Club World Cup: 2009
European Cup: 1992, 2006, 2009
European Cup-Winners' Cup: 1979, 1982, 1989, 1997
Fairs Cup: 1958, 1960, 1966
Supercup: 1992, 2009

Barcelona achieved a unique feat when, in 2009, they won all six major prizes open to them: the Spanish league and cup, Champions League, UEFA Supercup, Spanish Supercup then Club World Cup. All the more remarkably, rookie coach Pep Guardiola had been promoted only in the summer of 2008.

Founded in 1899 by a Swiss, Hans Gamper, Barcelona have a string of other successes to their proud name and which go back, in international terms, as far as the Latin Cup of the immediate post-second world war era. They count many glorious triumphs and great players but one of the most impressive of all was that era from the 1950s and into the early 1960s.

In 12 years from 1948 to 1960 Barcelona won the Spanish league six times, the cup five times, the Fairs Cup twice and the Latin Cup twice.

At one time they boasted 20 internationals from seven different nations. That may not appear out of the ordinary in these post-Bosman times but back in the 1950s it was exotic. Two of those imports were Hungarian: Sandor Kocsis and Zoltan Czibor. A third was probably the club's greatest player of all time. Ladislav Kubala was signed after tricking him out of the clutches of Real Madrid. When Kubala lined up for his adoptive Spain in the mid-1950s he became the only player to appear for three countries after winning earlier caps for both Hungary and Czechoslovakia. Later Kubala had a long spell as boss of the Spanish national team.

Back in Kubala's playing days Barcelona were first winners of the Inter-Cities Fairs Cup. Later they carried off the Cup-Winners' Cup three times. But for years their mainstream European efforts in the Champions Cup seemed jinxed. First, in 1961, having apparently achieved the hard part by eliminating the titleholders and their bitter rivals Real Madrid, they lost to Benfica in the final. Barcelona hit the woodwork three times, yet lost 3–2 against the run of play.

In 1973 Barcelona's president, Josep Nunez, believed he had bought the key to Champions Cup glory when he paid a world record £922,000 for superstar Johan Cruyff. He led them from relegation zone to championship and persuaded Barcelona to go back to Ajax and sign Johan Neeskens. But the closest they came to Champions Cup victory was the 1975 semi-final.

The jinx struck again, in even more galling circumstances, in 1986. Barcelona had been frustrated by two unsuccessful years with Diego Maradona as guiding light and only found success once he had left just as Englishman Terry Venables was arriving as team manager. Venables had been recommended by Barcelona's first choice, Bobby Robson, who had refused to break his contract with Ipswich. Under Venables Barcelona won the league then reached the 1986 Champions Cup Final. Controversially, Venables gambled on the fitness of long-time injured striker Steve Archibald to overcome the rank outsiders of Steaua Bucharest. The final was even staged in Seville, yet Barcelona lost in a penalty shoot-out after a goalless draw.

Eventually, it took the return of Cruyff, this time as coach, to steer a new generation of international stars – including Ronald Koeman, Hristo Stoichkov and Michael Laudrup – to long-overdue Champions Cup victory in 1992 over Sampdoria. Domestic success was a stable diet. For instance, Barcelona's 1994 league title was their fourth in a row. But failure to win any sort of trophy in 1995 or 1996 resulted in Cruyff's departure after eight years in charge. He was succeeded by Robson and then by Dutchman Louis Van Gaal, under whom Barcelona won the 1999 League and Cup double.

Fellow Dutchman Frank Rijkaard steered Barcelona back to European primacy, beating Arsenal in Paris, in 2006. He then handed over to Guardiola, midfield anchor under Cruyff, who enjoyed an amazing first season as coach in 2008-09. Barcelona won everything within range, including a Champions League victory over Manchester United secured by a second goal from young superstar Leo Messi. Team-mates included Xavi, Andres Iniesta and Carles Puyol, who achieved even more glory with Spain at the 2010 World Cup Final.

Hristo Stoichkov demands the accolades after scoring against Manchester United.

Argentina's Lionel Messi, Barcelona's own 'Galactico,' shows off his dribbling skills against Real Madrid.

Real Madrid, European champions 1960. Top: Del Sol, Canario, Dominguez, Santamaria, Marquitos, Di Stefano, Gento. Front: Vidal, Zarraga.

Real Madrid

Spain
Founded: 1902
Stadium: Santiago Bernabeu
(85,000)
Colours: All white
League: 31
Cup: 17
World Club Cup: 1966, 1998, 2002
European Cup: 1956, 1957, 1958, 1959, 1960, 1966,
1998, 2000, 2002
UEFA Cup: 1985, 1986
Supercup: 2002

Real Madrid are not only the richest club in the world as well as the most successful, they stand as the greatest club in the world courtesy of a mixture of high-level achievements, high-ego players and a style of soccer which sometimes has proved just too adventurous for their own good.

They are a record nine times champions of Europe, a record 31 times champions of Spain and have also filled their vast trophy salons to bursting point with three World Club Cups, two UEFA Cups and 17 Spanish cups. It all adds up to a soccer honours degree for the club founded by students as Madrid FC (The Real prefix, meaning Royal, was a title bestowed on the club later by King Alfonso XIII).

Madrid were not only among the founders of the Spanish cup and league competitions: it was also the Madrid president, Carlos Padros, who represented Spain in helping launch FIFA in Paris in 1904. In the late 1920s Madrid began a policy of buying big. They paid a then Spanish-record fee of £2,000 for Ricardo Zamora, still revered as the greatest Spanish goalkeeper ever.

The Spanish Civil War left Madrid's Chamartin stadium in ruins. At the time the club had no money, but boasted one of the greatest visionaries in European soccer history. He was Santiago Bernabeu, a lawyer who had been, in turn, player, team manager and secretary, and was now club president.

Bernabeu launched an audacious public appeal which raised the cash to build the wonderful stadium which now bears his name. The huge crowds provided the funds to build the team who dominated the first five years of the European Cup.

But first Bernabeu had to put other building bricks in place. One of the first was an administrator, Raimundo Saporta, who became Bernabeu's right-hand man, club secretary and later executive vice-president. Saporta was also the man who secured the greatest signing in the club's history – Alfredo Di Stefano in 1954.

Di Stefano proved the star of stars even though Bernabeu and Saporta surrounded him with illustrious team-mates such as Hungary's Ferenc Puskas, France's Raymond Kopa, Uruguay's José Santamaria and Brazil's Didi. They won the European Champions Cup for all of its first five years and Di Stefano scored in every final. Their peak was the 7-3 defeat in 1960 of Eintracht Frankfurt.

A 32-year gap followed between Madrid's sixth and seventh wins, in 1966 and 1998. Then, led by home-grown young striker Raul, Real won the revamped Champions League beating Juventus 1-0 in the final. Two years later they repeated the feat, destroying Valencia 3-0. Surprisingly,

weeks later, president Lorenzo Sanz was ousted in elections by the property developer Florentino Perez. He immediately honoured a crucial, alluring election pledge by breaking the world transfer record by paying Barcelona £35m for Portugal's Luis Figo. The first season under Perez was revolutionary. Madrid not only won the league title but Perez negotiated the reclassification of the club's "sports city" training ground so the land could be sold for lucrative development which not only wiped the club's debt but provided further funds for transfer market investment.

In 2001 Perez struck again, signing French star Zinedine Zidane from Italy's Juventus for another world record of £45m. The following May Zidane more than repaid the fee connecting with the magnificent volley which provided Madrid's decisive second goal as they beat Bayer Leverkusen 2-1 in Glasgow to regain the Champions Cup.

However, the subsequent arrivals of David Beckham and Ronaldo confused, rather than improved, the mix. Perez quit as president in 2006 – only to return three years later to launch another spending spree with the world record acquisitions of Kaka from Milan and Cristiano Ronaldo from Manchester United.

Real Madrid, Galacticos Class of '03, with Ronaldo, Figo, Zidane, Roberto Carlos, Raul and Beckham.

Valencia

Spain
Founded: 1919
Stadium: Luis Casanova
(49,291)
Colours: all white
League: seven
Cup: six
European Cup-Winners' Cup: 1980
UEFA Cup: 1962, 1963, 2004
Supercup: 1980, 2004

Valencia, in the early 1960s, underlined Spain's status as the top European nation at club level. Real Madrid had won the European Cup five times; Barcelona had won the Fairs Cup twice and Valencia stepped straight into their footsteps by reaching the Fairs Cup Final in three consecutive years, 1962–64.

Valencia defeated Barcelona and Dinamo Zagreb respectively in the first two. The 1962 victory over Barcelona was an explosive occasion, Valencia winning the first leg 6–2, with a hat-trick from Spanish international Vicente Guillot, then drawing 1–1 in the Catalan capital. A year later Valencia won both legs against Zagreb. But it was not to be third time lucky, as they lost the 1964 Final to Zaragoza.

At domestic level, Valencia won the league for the fourth time in 1971, then the cup for a fifth time in 1979. A year later Valencia regained European allure by winning the Cup-Winners' Cup. The final against Arsenal in the Heysel stadium was a disappointment. Even Argentina's 1978 World Cup hero, Mario Kempes, was unable to engineer a breakthrough, but at least Valencia had the consolation of winning on penalties.

In the late 1990s Valencia sought to regain their earlier pre-eminence with the appointment of Italian Claudio Ranieri as coach and the high-cost purchase of glamour superstars such as Brazil's Romario and Argentina's Ariel Ortega. But it was under the more workmanlike approach of Argentine Hector Cuper that they twice finished Champions League runners-up in successive seasons to Real Madrid and Bayern Munich.

Valencia celebrate a Spanish title success as consolation for double disappointment in Champions League finals.

Athletic Bilbao

Spain
Founded: 1898
Stadium: San Mames (46,200)
Colours: red and white stripes/
white
League: eight
Cup: 23

Athletic – note the English form of the club's title – have not carried off a major trophy since winning the Spanish league and cup double in 1984. But they maintain a unique status courtesy of a Basque soccer pride first inspired by British seamen.

The industrial and maritime links between the Basque province of Vizcaya and Britain were extended in the years years before the Spanish Civil War when the club insisted on employing only British coaches including the legendary Arthur Pentland. In the 1960s Ronnie Allen worked in Bilbao with success and numbered Howard Kendall among his successors. Javier Clemente – a Bilbao product who was later Spain's national coach – visited England frequently to study Liverpool and Ipswich in the days of Paisley and Robson.

Bilbao were founder members of the Spanish top division in 1928 and have never been relegated though they have sometimes survived only by the skin of their teeth. The club proudly claim more supporters in Spain than any other side – benefiting from antipathy in other regions to (Real) Madrid and Barcelona.

Atletico Madrid

Spain
Founded: 1903
Stadium: Vicente Calderon
(62,000)
Colours: Red and white stripes/blue
League: nine
Cup: nine
World Club Cup: 1974
European Cup-winners' Cup: 1962
Europa Cup: 2010

Atletico de Madrid have always existed in the shadow of neighbours Real, but they still rank among the Big Three of Spanish soccer and boast a proud record at international level. Not that life has always been easy. In the late 1930s, after the Spanish Civil War, it took a merger with the Air Force club to keep Atletico in business; in 1959, they just failed to reach the European Cup Final when Real beat them in a semi-final; in the early 1960s they had to share Real's Estadio Bernabeu, because Atletico's Metropolitano had been sold to developers before the new stadium could be completed.

European glory did come to Atletico in the shape of the Cup-winners' Cup in 1962 and in 1974 Atletico secured that elusive place in the European Cup Final but lost. Under controversial owner Jesus Gil there was a league-and-cup double in 1996 before Atletico suffered their first ever relegation in 2000. They bounced back immediately to re-establish their elite status and then win the inaugural Europa League in 2010.

Sevilla FC

Spain
Founded: 1905
Stadium: Sanchez Pizjuan
(45,500)
Colours: all white
League: one
Cup: five
UEFA Cup: 2006, 2007
Supercup: 2006

Sevilla forced their way into European soccer headlines with their decisive victories in the UEFA Cup in both 2006 and 2007. They also carried off the European Supercup in 2006 and cemented their reputation as cup specialists by winning the Spanish cup and Supercup the following year.

On the first occasion Sevilla defeated similar first-time finalists Middlesbrough through goals from Brazilian Luis Fabiano, Italian Enzo Maresca (two) and the Mali spearhead Frederic Kanoute. The following season they edged fellow Spanish rivals Espanyol of Barcelona 3-1 on penalties after a 2-2 extra-time draw. Sevilla's heroes were goalkeeper Andres Palop and coach Juande Ramos – who then left for a short-lived spell in England with Tottenham.

Sevilla won their first domestic title in 1935 when they landed the cup a year ahead of the outbreak of the civil war. They remained a power in the land after the fighting had subsided. They were runners-up in the league in 1940 and 1943 and then champions in 1947 for the first and so far only time.

Their initial foray into the European Champions Cup was a disaster. Qualifying in 1958 as runners-up, since Real Madrid had won both European and Spanish crowns, they came up against the title-holders and crashed to an 8-0 defeat even though Madrid played half the match with 10 men after the expulsion of forward Jose Ramon Marsal. Alfredo Di Stefano scored four goals.

Zaragoza

Spain
Founded: 1932
Stadium: La Romareda
(43,554)
Colours: Blue and white/blue
Cup: six
European Cup-Winners' Cup: 1995
Fairs Cup: 1964

Zaragoza are proof that soccer in Spain is about much, much more than Real Madrid and Barcelona. They have never won the league – second in 1975 remains their best finish. But they have landed the Spanish Cup on six occasions and twice conquered Europe. The first time was in the 1964 Fairs Cup with a superb forward line known as the "Cincos Magnificos" (Magnificent Five); the second time was the Cup-Winners' Cup in 1995.

Zaragoza were founder members of the Spanish Second Division in 1928 and took their present full title after a merger with the Iberia Club de Futbol in 1932. They gained access to the top division in 1936.

In 1962 new president Waldo Marco shocked the fans by selling star Peruvian forward Juan Seminario to Italy's Fiorentina and midfielder or full-back Julio Benitez to Barcelona. But the cash financed the finishing touches to the team of the Magnificent Five forward line.

From 1963 to 1966, Zaragoza played in six finals all against native opposition in Spain, and twice in the Fairs Cup. In 1963 and 1965 Zaragoza were Spanish cup runners-up but in 1964 and 1966 its winners. Their first cup victory became a double when they also won the Fairs Cup, beating Valencia 2-1 in a single match final in Barcelona.

In the middle of all that Marcelino and Lapetra were both members of the Spanish national team which won the 1964 European championship against the Soviet Union.

However defeat by Barcelona in the 1966 Fairs Cup Final sparked a long slide from glory which was not reversed for almost 30 years when Zaragoza won the Cup-Winners' Cup.

Atletico Madrid still wear the stripes bequeathed by original 'parent' club Bilbao.

OTHER EUROPEAN CLUBS

FK Austria

Vienna, Austria
Founded: 1911
Stadium: Horr (10,500) / Prater (62,270)
Colours: Mauve and white
League: 23
Cup: 27

The history of Vienna's Fussball Klub Austria-Memphis began with a game of cricket as the Vienna Cricket and Football Club was founded by the expatriate community in the 1890s. Cricket did not gain universal acceptance, but soccer was another matter, and November 15, 1894 saw the first proper soccer match ever staged in Austria. The Vienna Cricket and Football Club beat 1st Vienna FC – and they have been winning matches and titles ever since.

Changing their name in 1925, FKA notched up many honours in a list which includes runners-up spot in the European Cup-Winners' Cup in 1978, when a team inspired by midfield general Herbert Prohaska became the first Austrian side to reach a modern-day European final. That was long overdue since, in the late 1920s, FK Austria were one of the pioneers of European international club soccer when the Mitropa Cup drew clubs from Austria, Czechoslovakia, Hungary, Yugoslavia, Switzerland and Italy. FK Austria were triumphant in 1933 and 1936. Their delicate style of play, known as the "Vienna School", was modelled on the old Scottish close-passing game and had been taught them by Englishman Jimmy Hogan. His coaching genius contributed mightily to the development of the "Wunderteam" which lost to England in 1932 and then reached the semi-finals of the 1934 World Cup. The backbone of the team was provided by FK Austria. That tradition has been maintained ever since with FKA supplying the largest contingent when the national team reach tournament finals.

IFK Gothenburg

Sweden
Founded: 1904
Stadium: Gamla Ullevi (18,000)
Colours: Blue and white
League: 18
Cup: five
UEFA Cup 1982, 1987

The first members of IFK played not only soccer but also athletics and winter sports, but it did not take long for IFK to became one of Sweden's leading soccer clubs. Apart from eight seasons in the Second Division since the start of the national league, the Blaavit (Blue/white) – as the club are nicknamed – have belonged to the elite. After winning the league in 1969, they were immediately relegated – under-lining their reputation for entertaining, if erratic soccer.

In 1979, Sven-Goran Eriksson was signed from Degerfors as coach. He immediately guided IFK to their first-ever triumph in the cup – defeating Aatvidaberg 6-1 in the final – and in 1982 IFK won the UEFA Cup Final. In 1986 IFK reached the Champions Cup semi-final, losing only on penalties to Barcelona. The following year, they once again won the UEFA Cup.

Kiev Dynamo

Ukraine
Founded: 1927
Stadium: Republic (100,100)
Colours: White/blue
League: 13 Ukraine, 13 Soviet
Cup: nine Ukraine, nine Soviet
European Cup-Winners' Cup: 1975, 1986
European Supercup: 1975

Kiev were founder members of the Soviet top division, yet had to wait until 1961 before they became the first club outside Moscow to land the title. They achieved the league and cup double five years later.

In 1975 Kiev became the first team from the Soviet Union to win a European trophy – the Cup-winners' Cup. They also clinched the league title for the seventh time. In 1986 they won the European Cup-winners' Cup again and key man Igor Belanov was named European Footballer of the Year.

Kiev emerged as the richest club in the independent Ukraine upon the collapse of the Soviet Union, but they failed to translate this into European success and were expelled from the 1995-96 Champions League after officials were accused of trying to bribe a referee.

Moscow Dynamo

Russia
Founded: 1923
Stadium: Dynamo (51,000)
Colours: White/blue
League: 11 Soviet
Cup: one Russia, six Soviet

Dynamo are probably still the most famous of all Russian clubs, having been the first Soviet side to venture out beyond the Iron Curtain in the 1940s and 1950s. Also, they were fortunate enough to possess, in goalkeeper Lev Yashin, one of the greatest personalities in the modern game – a show-stopper wherever he went.

Dynamo's origins go back to the start of soccer in Russia, introduced by the Charnock brothers at their cotton mills towards the turn of the century. The team won successive Moscow championships under the name Morozovsti and, after the Russian Revolution, were taken over first by the electrical trades union and then by the police.

Thus the 1923 date marks the formal setting-up of Moscow Dynamo rather than the original club.

Immediately after the end of the Second World War, Dynamo became a legend as a result of a four-match British tour in the winter of 1945. They drew 3-3 with Chelsea and 2-2 with Rangers, thrashed Cardiff 10-1 and beat a reinforced Arsenal.

Inside-forward Constantin Beskov later became national manager, but it was goalkeeper Alexei "Tiger" Khomich whose reputation lasted long after he had retired to become a sports press photographer. He was succeeded in the team by an even greater goalkeeper in Yashin, who was to become the first Soviet player to be nominated as European Footballer of the Year.

Given Dynamo's leadership, it was appropriate that, in 1972, they became the first Soviet side to reach a European final.

Peter Larsson leads IFK to their 1987 UEFA Cup Final win over Dundee United.

Moscow Spartak

Russia
Founded: 1922
Stadium: Olympic-Lenin/
Luzhniki (102,000)
Colours: Red and white/white
League: nine Russia, 12 Soviet
Cup: three Russia, 10 Soviet

Moscow Spartak, champions of Russia for most of a decaded after the collapse of the Soviet Union, face an enormous challenge. They were a power in the land under the old system, but that was when players were not allowed to move abroad. Now Spartak must regain their domestic command and compete effectively in Europe in an "open" transfer society.

This is all the more challenging because Spartak had, for years, represented the Party line. They play their home matches in what was known as the Lenin stadium in the Luzhniki suburb, and their past heroes included such officially-approved characters as Nikita Simonian and Igor Netto. Spartak's best season in European competitions was 1990–91, when they beat Napoli and Real Madrid to reach the semi-finals of the European Cup, before falling to Marseille. For years the club had been ruled by the most respected members of the managerial old guard in veteran administrator Nikolai Starostin and former national coach Constantin Beskov. Starostin stayed on after the political upheaval, but Beskov handed over the coaching mantle to his former pupil Oleg Romantsev. Despite the loss of sweeper Vasili Kulkov and midfielders Igor Shalimov and Alexander Mostovoi, Romantsev kept Spartak on top of the table. New heroes were left-back and skipper Viktor Onopko, Igor Lediakhov and the forward Mikhail Beschastnikh.

Later luck deserted them as the finished league runners-up three years in a row in 2005, 2006 and 2007.

Rapid

Vienna, Austria
Founded: 1899
Stadium: Hanappi (19,600)
Colours: Green and white/
green
League: 32
Cup: 14

Rapid were founded as the 1st Arbeiter-Fussballklub (First Workers Football Club) but, on changing their name, also set about refining the short-passing style of the "Vienna School" to such good effect that they won the championship eight times between 1912 and 1923. The success story did not end there. In 1930 Rapid became the first Austrian club to win the Mitropa Cup. Several of Rapid's key players were members of the "Wunderteam", the national side who finished fourth in the 1934 World Cup.

Four years later Austria was swallowed up into Greater Germany, and the Austrian league was incorporated into the Greater German championship. To the mischievous delight of their fans, Rapid not only won the German Cup in 1938 (3-2 against FSV Frankfurt in the Final) but also the German championship in 1941. On a day which has entered soccer legend Rapid hit back from 3-0 down to defeat an outstanding Schalke side 4-3 before a 90,000 crowd in the Olympic stadium in Berlin. Their hero was centre-forward Franz "Bimbo" Binder.

Many of Rapid's old heroes returned as coaches, among them Binder, Karl Rappan (who developed the Swiss Bolt system), Edi Fruhwirth and Karl Decker. Great players in the post-war years included wing-half Gerhard Hanappi – an architect by profession, who laid out the designs for the club stadium – tough-tackling defender Ernst Happel and another prolific goal-scoring centre-forward in Hans Krankl. He led Rapid's attack in 1985 in the first of their two defeats in the European Cup-Winners' Cup Final.

Red Star Belgrade

Serbia & Montenegro
Founded: 1945
Stadium: Crvena Zvezda (Red Star) (97,422)
Colours: Red and white stripes/white
League: 25
Cup: 23
World Club Cup: 1991
European Cup: 1991

This may be the most schizophrenic club in the world. In Germany they are known as Roter Stern; in France as Etoile Rouge; in Spain as Estrella Roja; in Serbo-Croat it's Fudbalski Klub Crvena Zvezda; in English, of course, Red Star Belgrade.

Under whichever name, the 1991 European and world club champions stood revered as one of the pillars of the worldwide establishment until civil strife in the former Yugoslavia led to international suspension for both country and clubs. The consequences for the club were dire with transfer monies frozen. A subsequent string of disruptions in national political life plus hooliganism problems and administrative scandals, involving even club legend Dragan Dzajic, all served to add to the problems.

Steaua Bucharest

Romania
Founded: 1947
Stadium: Steaua (30,000)
Colours: Red/blue
League: 23
Cup: 21
European Cup: 1986

Steaua – the word means "Star" – were one of the army clubs created in eastern Europe after the Communist takeovers of political power. Originally known as CCA Bucharest – under which title they won three consecutive championships in the early 1950s – the renamed Steaua won the cup five times in six seasons in the late 1960s and early 1970s.

In 1986 Steaua became the first eastern European team to win the European Cup when they beat Barcelona on penalties in Seville. Their penalty-stopping hero in the climactic minutes was Helmut Ducadam, whose career was ended prematurely by illness soon after. Steaua's power – including the right to sign any player they liked from any other Romanian club – was significantly reduced after the overthrow of the Communist dicatorship of the Ceausescu family.

Red Star's Robert Prosinecki played World Cups for both Yugoslavia and Croatia.

SOUTH AMERICA

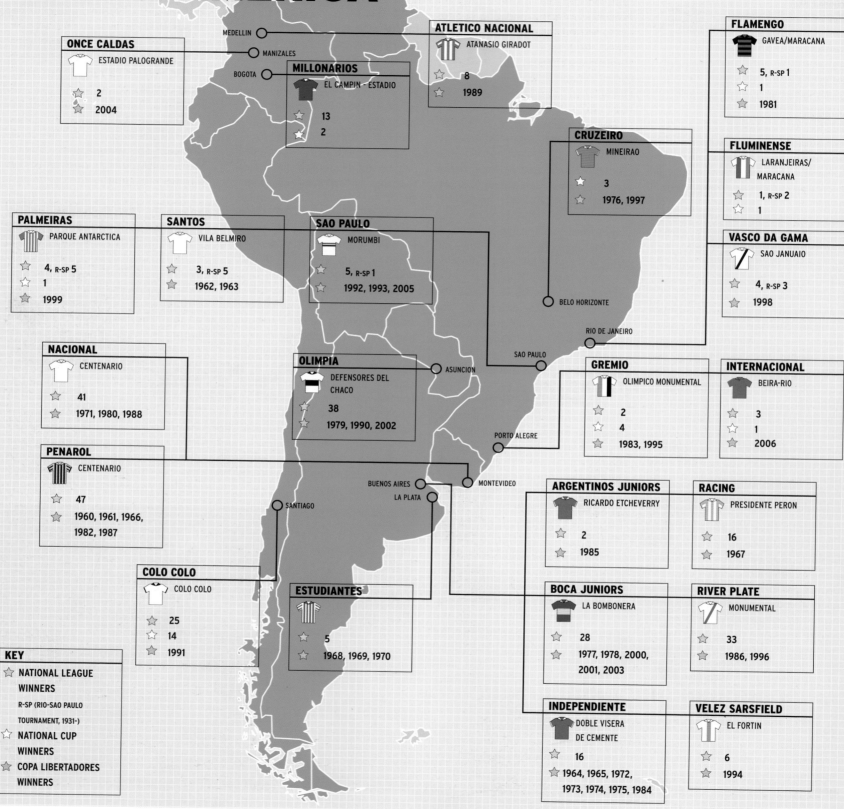

ONCE CALDAS
ESTADIO PALOGRANDE
⭐ 2
⭐ 2004

MILLONARIOS
EL CAMPIN - ESTADIO
⭐ 13
⭐ 2

ATLETICO NACIONAL
ATANASIO GIRADOT
⭐ 8
⭐ 1989

FLAMENGO
GAVEA/MARACANA
⭐ 5, R-SP 1
⭐ 1
⭐ 1981

FLUMINENSE
LARANJEIRAS/MARACANA
⭐ 1, R-SP 2
⭐ 1

CRUZEIRO
MINEIRAO
⭐ 3
⭐ 1976, 1997

VASCO DA GAMA
SAO JANUAIO
⭐ 4, R-SP 3
⭐ 1998

PALMEIRAS
PARQUE ANTARCTICA
⭐ 4, R-SP 5
⭐ 1
⭐ 1999

SANTOS
VILA BELMIRO
⭐ 3, R-SP 5
⭐ 1962, 1963

SAO PAULO
MORUMBI
⭐ 5, R-SP 1
⭐ 1992, 1993, 2005

NACIONAL
CENTENARIO
⭐ 41
⭐ 1971, 1980, 1988

OLIMPIA
DEFENSORES DEL CHACO
⭐ 38
⭐ 1979, 1990, 2002

GREMIO
OLIMPICO MONUMENTAL
⭐ 2
⭐ 4
⭐ 1983, 1995

INTERNACIONAL
BEIRA-RIO
⭐ 3
⭐ 1
⭐ 2006

PENAROL
CENTENARIO
⭐ 47
⭐ 1960, 1961, 1966, 1982, 1987

ARGENTINOS JUNIORS
RICARDO ETCHEVERRY
⭐ 2
⭐ 1985

RACING
PRESIDENTE PERON
⭐ 16
⭐ 1967

COLO COLO
COLO COLO
⭐ 25
⭐ 14
⭐ 1991

ESTUDIANTES
⭐ 5
⭐ 1968, 1969, 1970

BOCA JUNIORS
LA BOMBONERA
⭐ 28
⭐ 1977, 1978, 2000, 2001, 2003

RIVER PLATE
MONUMENTAL
⭐ 33
⭐ 1986, 1996

INDEPENDIENTE
DOBLE VISERA DE CEMENTE
⭐ 16
⭐ 1964, 1965, 1972, 1973, 1974, 1975, 1984

VELEZ SARSFIELD
EL FORTIN
⭐ 6
⭐ 1994

KEY
⭐ NATIONAL LEAGUE WINNERS
R-SP (RIO-SAO PAULO TOURNAMENT, 1931-)
⭐ NATIONAL CUP WINNERS
⭐ COPA LIBERTADORES WINNERS

Map labels: MEDELLIN, MANIZALES, BOGOTA, BELO HORIZONTE, RIO DE JANEIRO, SAO PAULO, ASUNCION, PORTO ALEGRE, BUENOS AIRES, LA PLATA, MONTEVIDEO, SANTIAGO

Boca Juniors

Buenos Aires, Argentina
Founded: 1905
Stadium: Bombonera (58,740)
Colours: Blue with yellow
hoop/blue
League: 31
World Club Cup: 1977, 2000, 2003
South American Club Cup: 1977, 1978, 2000, 2001, 2003, 2007
Copa Sudamericana: 2004, 2005
Recopa Sudamericana: 1990, 2005, 2006, 2008
Supercopa Sudamericana: 1989
Sudamericana Copa de Oro: 1994

Boca are one of the two great clubs in the Argentine capital of Buenos Aires, along with old rivals River Plate. Founded by an Irishman named Patrick MacCarthy and a group of newly-arrived Italian immigrants, they joined the league in 1913 and were immediately caught up in a domestic soccer "war" which saw two championships being organized for most of the 1920s and early 1930s.

Boca bestrode the two eras, winning the last Argentine amateur championship in 1930 and the first unified professional one the following year. Two more titles followed in the next four years, thanks to some fine players including the great Brazilian defender Domingos da Guia.

In the 1940s and 1950s Boca slipped into River Plate's shadow, re-emerging in 1963 when a team fired by the goals of José Sanfilippo reached the final of the South American Club Cup. Winning the title, however, would have to wait until the late 1970s. Then they reached the Final three years in a row – beating Brazil's Cruzeiro in 1977 and Deportivo Cali of Colombia in 1978 before losing to Olimpia of Paraguay in 1979. Boca's rugged style, under Juan Carlos Lorenzo, proved controversial. Not one Boca player figured in the squad which won the 1978 World Cup.

But Boca had already secured their own world crown, beating Borussia Mönchengladbach in the World Club Cup in 1977. Boca rebuilt their team around Diego Maradona in 1981, but it was not until 2000 that they regained world and regional prominence. They won the Libertadores Cup Final three times in four years and share, with Milan, the world record of 18 international titles.

Boca Juniors are a team that knows success.

River Plate

Buenos Aires, Argentina
Founded: 1901
Stadium: Antonio Liberti/
Monumental (76,000)
Colours: White with red sash/black
League: 33
World Club Cup: 1986
South American Club Cup: 1986, 1996
Inter-American Cup: 1986
South American Supercup: 1997

River Plate are one of the two giants of Argentine soccer, Boca Juniors being the other. Traditionally the club from the rich side of Buenos Aires, River were founder members of the first division in 1908, then took a leading role in the "war" which accompanied the introduction of professional soccer in the 1920s. Over the years River have fielded some wonderful teams. In the 1930s they boasted Bernabe Ferreyra, a legendary figure in Argentine soccer; in the late 1940s their high-scoring forward line was so feared and admired they were nicknamed "La Maquina" (The Machine). The names of Muñoz, Moreno, Pedernera, Labruna and Loustau mean little outside Argentina today, but there they inspire awe like Real Madrid in Europe.

Later River produced more great players: Alfredo Di Stefano, who would turn Real Madrid into possibly the greatest team of all time; Omar Sivori, who formed a wonderful partnership with John Charles after joining Juventus; and then 1978 World Cup winners Ubaldo Fillol, Daniel Passarella, Leopoldo Luque and Mario Kempes. In 1986 they were joined in River's Hall of Fame by the likes of goalkeeper Nery Pumpido, centre-back Oscar Ruggeri and schemer Norberto Alonso, after victory in the South American Club Cup provided River with formal confirmation of their lofty status. River really should have succeeded to the crown years earlier, but were runners-up in 1966 to Peñarol and in 1976 to Cruzeiro. In 1986 they made no mistake, beating America of Colombia, then adding the World Club Cup.

Ariel Ortega (top, left) numbers among a host of Argentine heroes who have thrilled fans of River Plate in their aptly-named Estadio Monumental in Buenos Aires.

Santos

São Paulo, Brazil
Founded: 1912
Stadium: Vila Belmiro (20,000)
Colours: All white
São Paulo state league: 18
Brazil championship (incl. Torneo Rio-São Paulo): 8
World Club Cup: 1962, 1963
South American Club Cup: 1962, 1963

The name of Santos will always be synonymous with that of Pele, who played all his mainstream career with the club and returned as a director at the end of 1993 to try to help lift his old club out of the depths of a severe financial and administrative crisis.

Santos had been founded by three members of the Americano club, who stayed home in the port of Santos when their club moved to São Paulo. Santos joined the São Paulo state championship in 1916, became only the second Brazilian club to embrace professionalism in 1933, but did not hit the headlines until the mid-1950s. Then, to organize a host of talented youngsters, they signed the 1950 World Cup veteran, Jair da Rosa Pinto, and discovered the 15-year-old Pele.

To say that Santos were a one-man team, as it often appeared from the publicity, would be unfair. Santos harvested millions of pounds from whistle-stop friendly match tours around the world and reinvested heavily in surrounding Pele with fine players: World Cup winners in goalkeeper Gilmar, centre-back Mauro and wing-half Zito; an outside-left with a ferocious shot in Pepe; and the precocious young talents of right-winger Dorval, schemer Mengalvio and centre-forward Coutinho, Pele's so-called "twin" with whom he established an almost telepathic relationship on the pitch.

Sadly, the constant touring and playing burned out many young players before they had a chance to establish their talent. But not before Santos had scaled the competitive heights as Pele inspired their victories in the South American Club Cup and the World Club Cup in both 1962 and 1963.

One more year and it was all over. Independiente beat Santos in the 1964 South American Club Cup semi-finals, and the spell had been broken. Santos went on touring and raking in cash, capitalizing on Pele's name, for as long as they could.

It was not until 2003 that they returned to the Copa Libertadores final, only to go down to old rivals Boca Juniors.

Santos, from the neighbouring port to Sao Paulo, owed almost everything to the inspiration and then indelible association with the great Pele.

Atletico Nacional

Medellin, Colombia
Founded: 1938
Stadium: Atanasio Giradot
(35,000)
Colours: Green and white stripes/white
League: 10
South American Club Cup: 1989
Inter-American Cup: 1990, 1995
Copa Merconorte: 1998, 2000

Atletico Nacional of Medellin are not the most famous club to come out of Colombia. That honour will always belong to Millonarios. But Nacional earned a place in history by becoming the first club to take the Copa Libertadores, the South American Club Cup, across the Andes to the western side of the continent. Nacional, who provided the base of the Colombian World Cup team in 1990, were in 1954 the first champions of Colombia after the rapprochement with FIFA. Yet it was not until 1971 that they made their debut in the South American Club Cup under Argentine coach Osvaldo Zubeldia. He had earned a fearsome reputation as boss of the rugged Estudiantes de La Plata team which had dominated Argentine and South American club soccer in the late 1960s. He turned Nacional into Colombian champions three times in the mid-1970s and early 1980s. Zubeldia was followed by Luis Cubilla, at whose suggestion, in 1986, Nacional appointed Francisco Maturana as boss. In 1987 and 1988 they were championship runners-up and then, in 1989, won the South American club crown. Sadly, their preparations for the world club showdown with Milan were wrecked when the government halted the league season because of the increasing violence being engendered on the fringes of the game by the drug and betting cartels. Nacional did not emerge with their reputation unscathed. It was not only that Medellin was the centre of the drugs trade; several players were friends of drugs baron Pablo Escobar and when he was killed in 1993 his coffin was draped in a Nacional flag.

Colo Colo

Santiago, Chile
Founded: 1925
Stadium: Colo Colo (50,000)
Colours: White/black
League: 29
South American Club Cup: 1991
Inter-American Cup: 1992
South American Recopa: 1991

Colo Colo, Chilean nickname for a wildcat, were founded by five angry members of the old Magallanes FC. Even though Chilean soccer is generally held to lag far behind that of traditional giants Brazil, Argentina and Uruguay, Colo Colo have an enviable reputation throughout the continent.

The club's vision has always stretched beyond the Andes. Within two years of Colo Colo's foundation, they had sent a team off to tour Spain and Portugal. In 1933 Colo Colo were among the founders of a professional league and in 1941 they set another pioneering trend by introducing a foreign coach in the Hungarian, Ferenc Platko. Record league winners in Chile and the supreme transfer destination for most domestic players, Colo Colo's finest achievement was in winning the 1991 South American Club Cup. They scored a decisive victory over former champions Olimpia of Paraguay. Colo Colo forced a 0-0 draw in Asuncion before winning 3-0 back in Santiago.

Flamengo

Rio de Janeiro, Brazil
Founded: 1895 as sailing club;
1911 as soccer club
Stadium: Gavea (20,000) and
Maracana (130,000)
Colours: Black and red hoops/white
Rio state league: 31
Brazil championship (incl. Torneo Rio-São Paulo): six
World Club Cup: 1981
South American Club Cup: 1981

Flamengo are the most popular club in Brazil, having been formed by dissident members of the Fluminense club under the umbrella of the Flamengo sailing club – which now boasts more than 70,000 members. They first competed in the Rio League in 1912, winning the title two years later. In 1915 they regained the crown without having lost a game. A string of great names have graced the red-and-black hoops over the years, among them defender Domingos Da Guia and the centre-forward Leonidas da Silva. Flamengo ran up a Rio state hat-trick in the mid-1950s, but had to wait until 1981 for their greatest success. Then, riding high on the goals of a new hero, Zico, they won both the South American and World Club Cups.

In the mid-1990s, Flamengo sought to revive the glory days by signing World Cup-winning striker Romario but he later left for rivals Vasco Da Gama.

Fluminense

Rio de Janeiro, Brazil
Founded: 1902
Stadium: Laranjeira (20,000)
and Maracana (130,000)
Colours: Red, green and white stripes/white
Rio state league: 30
Brazil championship (incl. Torneo Rio-São Paulo): 4

Fluminense have yet to win an international trophy, but that does not alter their status as one of South America's great clubs. "Flu" were founded in 1902 by an Englishman named Arthur Cox, and many of their first players were British residents. The club's wealth and upper-class clientele resulted in the nickname "Po de Arroz" ("Face Powder", after the fashion of the time). Today the club's fans wear white powder on their faces as a sign of loyalty. In 1905 Flu were founder members of the Rio de Janeiro league and of the Brazilian confederation; they won the first four Rio (Carioca) championships in 1906–09; and, in 1932, Flu became the first Brazilian club to go professional.

By this time the "Flu-Fla" derby (against Flamengo) had been flourishing for 20 years, the first meeting between the clubs having taken place in 1912. In 1963 their clash drew an official crowd of 177,656 to the Maracana stadium in Rio, which remains a world record for a club game. By 1930 Flu's stadium was the home of the national team and the club had launched a weekly newspaper. A few years later and Flu were ruling the roost with five Rio titles between 1936 and 1941.

In the early 1950s Fluminense's star was the World Cup winning midfield general Didi. In the late 1960s and early 1970s it was another World Cup winner, Brazil's 1970 captain and right-back, Carlos Alberto Torres and in the 1980s the mantle of inspiration-in-chief passed to the Paraguayan Romerito. The closest they came to international glory was in 2008 when they lost the South American Cup final on penalties to LDU Quito.

Adolfo Pedernera (centre) lives up to Millonarios' 'Blue Ballet' nickname against Valencia.

Millonarios

Bogota, Colombia
Founded: 1938
Stadium: El Campin - Estadio Distrital Nemesio Camacho (57,000)
Colours: Blue/white
League: 13

Millonarios remain a legendary name, if only because of the manner in which they led Colombia's fledgling professional clubs into the rebellion which lured star players from all over the world in the late 1940s and the early 1950s. The then club president, Alfonso Senior, later became president of the Colombian federation and a highly-respected FIFA delegate.

Taking massive advantage of an Argentine players' strike, Millonarios led the flight from FIFA and the chase for great players – the legendary Di Stefano, Julio Cozzi, Nestor Rossi and Adolfo Pedernera for example. Nicknamed the "Blue Ballet", they dominated the pirate league. Credit for the club's name goes to a journalist, Camacho Montayo. The club had been founded as an amateur side, Deportivo Municipal, in 1938. But as they pushed for a professional league, so Montayo wrote: "The Municipalistas have become the Millonarios." The name stuck. Millonarios remain a top club but have long lost domestic dominance.

Nacional

Montevideo, Uruguay
Founded: 1899
Stadium: Parque Central (20,000) and Centenario (73,609)
Colours: White/blue
League: 42
World Club Cup: 1971, 1980, 1988
South American Club Cup: 1971, 1980, 1988
South American Recopa: 1988
Inter-American Cup: 1971

Nacional and Peñarol are the two great clubs of Uruguay and bitter rivals on both the domestic and international stages. Nacional were formed from a merger of the Montevideo Football Club and the Uruguay Athletic Club, and in 1903 were chosen to line up as Uruguay's national team against Argentina in Buenos Aires, with Nacional's men winning 3-2.

The club's domestic golden era is considered the years from 1939 to 1943 when they won the league in each of those five years under Scottish manager Williams Reasdale. Nacional's domestic domination was underlined by an 8-0 thrashing of the old enemy, Peñarol.

Later the club extended its status into the international arena. Nacional won the Copa Libertadores for the first time in 1971 when they also went on to secure the first of their three Club World Cup triumphs.

Peñarol

Montevideo, Uruguay
Founded: 1891
Stadium: Las Acacias (15,000) and Centenario (73,609)
Colours: Black and yellow stripes/black
League: 47
World Club Cup: 1961, 1966, 1982
South American Club Cup: 1960, 1961, 1966, 1982, 1987
Inter-American Cup: 1969

Peñarol were the first club to win the World Club Cup three times, but their success is no modern phenomenon. They have been the pre-eminent power in Uruguayan soccer since its earliest days, providing a host of outstanding players for Uruguay's 1930 and 1950 World Cup-winning teams.

Their own international awakening came in 1960, when Peñarol won the inaugural South American Club Cup. They were thrashed by Real Madrid in the World Club Cup, but made amends the next year with victory over Benfica. Peñarol regained the world club crown in 1966, at the expense of Real Madrid, and then again in 1982 when they beat Aston Villa in Tokyo.

By now Peñarol had unearthed another superstar in centre-forward Fernando Morena. He was the latest in a long line of great players, which included the nucleus of the Uruguayan national team who shocked Brazil to win the 1950 World Cup. Goalkeeper Roque Maspoli – later World Club Cup-winning coach in 1966 – captain and centre-half Obdulio Varela, right-winger Alcide Ghiggia, centre-forward Oscar Miguez, right-half Rodriguez Andrade and inside-right Juan Schiaffino all came from Peñarol. Schiaffino was the greatest of all.

Peñarol had been founded as the Central Uruguayan Railway Cricket Club in 1891, and changed their name in 1913 as the British influence waned. The railways sidings and offices were near the Italian Pignarolo district – named after the landowner Pedro Pignarolo – and so the Spanish style of the name was adopted.

São Paulo

Brazil
Founded: 1935
Stadium: Morumbi (150,000)
Colours: White with a red and black hoop/white
São Paulo state league: 21
Brazil championship (incl. Torneo Rio-São Paulo): seven
World Club Cup: 1992, 1993, 2005
South American Club Cup: 1992, 1993

São Paulo's victories over Barcelona and Milan in the 1992 and 1993 World Club Cups in Tokyo left no doubt about which was the finest club side in the world. Those victories also underlined the depth of talent available to São Paulo, since their key midfielder, Rai (younger brother of 1986 World Cup star Socrates), had been sold to French club Paris Saint-Germain in the summer of 1993. Dual success also enhanced the reputation of coach Tele Santana, Brazil's World Cup manager in 1982 and 1986.

São Paulo are, even so, comparative newcomers – having been founded in 1935, at a time when the likes of River Plate, Peñarol and the rest were already well-established powers in their own lands.

Within a decade of being founded, São Paulo developed into the strongest team in the country, winning the state title five times in the 1940s. They imported Argentine inside-forward Antonio Sastre, and the continuing pressure of success led to the construction of the 150,000-capacity Morumbi stadium – the world's largest club-owned sports arena.

In the 1960s São Paulo had to take a back seat to Santos. In 1974 they reached their first South American Club Cup Final (losing to Argentina's Independiente), but it was not until the arrival of Santana, in the late 1980s, that São Paulo emerged from the doldrums. They used the cash to strengthen their squad and were duly rewarded at the highest level. In 2005 they beat Liverpool 1-0 in Japan to become the first winners of the FIFA Club World Championship.

Penarol fans set off flares to match the flair on the pitch.

AFRICA

Al-Ahly

Cairo, Egypt
Founded: 1907
Stadium: Mukhtar El-Tetsh
(50,000)
Colours: Red and white
League: 35
Cup: 35
African Champions Cup: 1982, 1987, 2001, 2005, 2006, 2008
African Cup-Winners' Cup: 1984, 1985, 1986, 1993
African Supercup: 2002, 2006, 2007, 2009
Afro-Asian Cup: 1988
Arab Champions Cup: 1996
Arab Supercup: 1998, 1999
Arab Cup-Winners' Cup: 1995

Al Ahly are an Egyptian institution and their rivalry with Zamalek has dominated the nation's soccer at club level. Generally Al Ahly have had the upper hand. They boast a record number of league titles to go with their record of cup successes. Indeed, Zamalek only broke Al Ahly's iron grip on the championship once between 1948 and 1962, and the club went unbeaten from 1974 through to 1977. Although Zamalek have since had similar success in the African competitions, Al Ahly were the first of the two clubs to win the African Champions Cup in 1982 and they won the Cup-Winners' Cup for three years in succession from 1984 to 1986. Former England manager Don Revie came to manage the club for three unhappy months in 1984, failing to match the success of previous coaching imports such as Nandor Hideguti in 1974, and his successor, fellow Hungarian Aba Kalocsai, up to 1982. In 1999 they were acclaimed the African confederation's Club of the Century.

Asante Kotoko

Ghana
Founded: 1935
Stadium: Kumasi (35,000)
Colours: Red and white
League: 21
Cup: 8
African Champions Cup: 1970, 1983

Soccer started spreading through Ghana at the start of the century, but it was not until the 1920s that the game reached the northern Asante regions, marking the crucial turning-point. In 1930 the Asante Football Association was founded, and it was Asante Kotoko who quickly emerged as not only Ghana's most formidable club, but one of the biggest and most popular in Africa. A taxi driver from Kumasi, Kwesi Kuma, provided the club's unlikely beginnings, forming the Rainbow Football Club after being inspired by Accra teams, Hearts of Oak and Standfast. By 1931, the team had become known as the Titanics, until a local oracle advised a name-change to Kotoko, meaning porcupine. After the Asanthene, the king of the Asante, accepted the club as a gift in 1935, the name Asante Kotoko was confirmed. After establishing themselves as the region's pre-eminent club, Kotoko decided to recruit from areas other than Asante, and won their first league championship in 1959. Although their first attack on the African Champions Cup in 1966 ended with a home defeat, they were finalists in 1967, before clinching the title in 1970, defeating Zairean side Mazembe, who missed a last-minute penalty in the second leg. Defeats in the 1971, 1973 and 1982 African finals followed, despite the presence of stars like Ibrahim Sunday, Robert Mensah and Malik Jabbir in the 1970s, and Joseph Carr, Poku Afriyie and Opouku Nti in the 1980s. Kotoko finally regained the trophy in 1983 with a single Npuko Nti goal against Al Ahly.

Esperance

Tunis, Tunisia
Founded: 1918
Stadium: Olympique (40,000)
Colours: Red and gold
League: 23
Cup: 13
African Champions Cup: 1994
African Cup-Winners' Cup: 1998
CAF Cup: 1996
African Supercup: 1995

Esperance have always been the most respected of Tunisia's club sides, possessing the largest support and a distinctive gold and red strip which marks them out as characteristically Tunisian. But it was not until the late 1980s and early 1990s that they started to make a consistent mark in both Tunisian and African soccer. After their first Tunisian league title in 1941 they had to wait 18 years for the next. Since then, they have taken their overall tally to 14 plus nine cups. Their greatest achievement was in 1994 when they won the African Champions Cup for the first time (they were only the second Tunisian side to lift the trophy) and then scooped the African Supercup and Tunisian league title.

Al-Ahly's Mohamed Emara puts Enugu Rangers under pressure in the CAF Cup.

Razdhi Jaidi of Esperance strikes for goal in Africa's own Champions League.

Gor Mahia

Nairobi, Kenya
Founded: 1968
Stadium: Olympique (40,000)
Colours: Red and gold
League: 12
Cup: eight
African Cup-Winners' Cup: 1987

Gor Mahia, named after a legendary medicine man of the 19th century, have never been the most shy and retiring club: in 1969, they exploded onto the Kenyan soccer scene by finishing runners-up to Nakuru All Stars only a year after their formation, a position they maintained the following year as AFC Leopards won the title. Since then, Leopards and Gor Mahia have waged an almost yearly battle for dominance: from 1979 to 1986, they were the only two clubs to win the title. During the same period, the two teams dominated the East and Central African Club Cup, Gor Mahia running out winners on three occasions, defeating AFC Leopards themselves in 1980 and 1985. Now Gor Mahia claim superiority thanks to their Kenyan Cup triumphs and their African Cup-winners Cup success in 1987, making them the first Kenyan holders.

Hearts of Oak

Accra, Ghana
Founded: 1911
Stadium: International (45,000)
Colours: Red, yellow and blue
League: 21
Cup: nine
African Champions Cup: 2000
African CAF Cup: 2004

Hearts of Oak from the Ghanaian capital were one of the country's first soccer clubs. They achieved minor international celebrity in 1957 when they invited Stanley Matthews to tour the country to help celebrate independence. Matthews was treated as a hero and crowned the Soccerthene, the king of soccer. Hearts of Oak won the first national league in 1965 and were the country's first club to participate in the African Champions Cup, in 1972. They reached the final in 1977 and 1979 before conquering the continent in 1994. Predictably, the Hearts of Oak line-up has always provided the majority of the national side. Sadly it was a Hearts of Oak match against old rivals Asante Kotoko in 2001 which saw one of Africa's worst sports disasters when 126 fans died in a crowd stampede.

Kaizer Chiefs

Naturena, South Africa
Founded: 1970
Stadium: Ellis Park (75,000)
Colours: Gold and black
League: 11
Cup: 12
African Cup-Winners' Cup: 2001

Kaizer Chiefs were born in the imagination of Kaizer Motaung – a former Soweto player. It was a dream he turned into reality when his collection of Orlando Pirates team-mates broke away in 1970 and began their own soccer adventure. Within four years the Chiefs had already won both the South African league and the Top Eight Cup, the league success all the more enjoyable since they took the title from the Pirates. Since then, not only have the club taken their honours list to nine league titles but also added a variety of South African Super Bowl cups, Coca-Cola League Cups and Top Eight Cups. The Chiefs provided three members of host South Africa's squad at the 2010 World Cup finals: goalkeeper Itu Khune, midfielder Reneilwe Letsholonyane and winger Siphiwe Tshabalala – scorer of the dramatic first goal in the tournament.

Zamalek

Cairo, Egypt
Founded: 1925
Stadium: Al Zamalek (35,000)
Colours: All white
League: 11
Cup: 21
African Champions Cup: 1984, 1986, 1993, 1996, 2002
African Cup-winners Cup: 2000
CAF Super Cup: 1994, 1997, 2003
Afro-Asian Cup: 1987, 1997
Arab Cup-winners cup: 2003

Zamalek have spent a long time in the shadow of Cairo rivals Al Ahly but they boast an outstanding record in African club competitions. Their triumph in 1984 was perhaps the sweetest. In the semi-final, Zamalek recovered a 3-1 deficit to beat Algerian side JET to win over two legs, before cruising to a 3-0 aggregate victory over IICC, Nigeria's Shooting Stars, in the final. Two years later, Zamalek became the first Egyptian side to win a second African Cup and have since clinched three further titles. Founded as an Anglo-Egyptian side in 1925, the club's original name was Faruk, after the king of Egypt. In the early 1990s they threatened briefly to overtake rivals Al-Ahly as Egypt's top club.

Patrick Mabedi (right) of Kaizer Chiefs outpaces Lyon's Vikash Dhorasoo.

Zamalek's Hazem Imam holds off Zubeir Zmit of Algeria's Ittihad.

USA

DC United

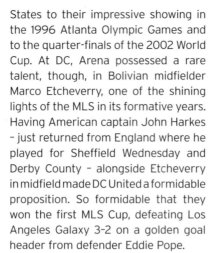

Washington, United States
Founded: 1996
Stadium: RFK (65,000)
Colours: Black and red
MLS League: four
US Open Cup: two
CONCACAF Champions Cup: 1998
Inter-American Cup: 1998

DC United have been one of the success stories of Major League Soccer. United started the inaugural MLS season in 1996 in confident mood, having secured the services of Bruce Arena as coach. In the year leading up to the MLS, he had led the University of Virginia to their seventh Final Four appearance and helped with various national youth sides. He would also coach the United States to their impressive showing in the 1996 Atlanta Olympic Games and to the quarter-finals of the 2002 World Cup. At DC, Arena possessed a rare talent, though, in Bolivian midfielder Marco Etcheverry, one of the shining lights of the MLS in its formative years. Having American captain John Harkes – just returned from England where he played for Sheffield Wednesday and Derby County – alongside Etcheverry in midfield made DC United a formidable proposition. So formidable that they won the first MLS Cup, defeating Los Angeles Galaxy 3-2 on a golden goal header from defender Eddie Pope.

Not only that, but four years later they added the regional CONCACAF title to their honours roll.

Galaxy

Los Angeles, United States
Founded: 1995
Stadium: Home Depot, Carson (35,000)
Colours: Gold and green
MLS League: two
US Open Cup: two
CONCACAF Champions Cup: 2000

Galaxy made international sports headlines in the spring of 2007 when they clinched the signing of former England captain David Beckham from Real Madrid. The Los Angeles based organisation took advantage of new MLS rules that allowed clubs to break the existing traditional wage-cap in order to bring in star-names to boost the profile of the league. Brazil legend Pele said Beckham, the most iconic player of his era, had a promotional potential within the US game which had matched his own in the mid-1970s. But Galaxy were already a power before ex-World Cup defender-turned-director Alexi Lalas landed Beckham and US World Cup skipper Landon Donovan. They were runners-up in the first Major League Soccer play-off and then twice winners of the championship title thanks to an initial strategy of signing players who attracted the local Latin American fan base. Imported stars included the colourful Mexican goalkeeper Jorge Campos.

DC United's Mike Petke shields the ball from Galaxy's Ryan Suarez in the MLS.

JAPAN

Verdy

Tokyo, Japan
Founded: 1991
Stadium: Ajinomoto (50,000)
Colours: Green and white
League: seven
League Cup: six
Emperor's Cup: five

It was no surprise when Kawasaki Verdy ran out comfortable champions of the inaugural J.League season in 1993 and again in 1994. They were overwhelming favourites, having won the previous year's Soccer League Cup – a trophy they duly defended successfully in both 1993 and 1994. In addition to Japanese favourites Kazuyoshi Miura and Nobuhiro Takeda up front, Kawasaki boasted Brazilians Marcio Amoroso and Luis Pereira. Unfortunately, a downturn in fortunes has seen them relegated several times in later years.

Kashima Antlers

Kashima, Japan
Founded: 1991
Stadium: Kashima Soccer (41,000)
Colours: Red and black
League: seven
League Cup: three
Emperor's Cup: three

Kashima take their name from the deer of the Kashima Shrine, and the Antlers rose to runners-up position in the newly-enlarged championship of 1996, before winning their first title in 1997. Zico having retired, it was the responsibility of fellow Brazilians Jurginho, Mazinho and Bismarck to inspire the club's talented Japanese players, adding the Emperor's Cup to their honours. The presence in attack of Mazinho helped inspire Japanese prodigy Atsushi Yanagisawa. The club extended their command of the J.League in 2000 with an unprecedented treble made up of the league, cup and Emperor's Cup.

Two Kashima defenders are needed to overpower Verdy's Takayuki Morimoto, at 15 the J.League's youngest-ever player.

INDEX

Note: italic page numbers refer to illustrations

LIST OF ABBREVIATIONS

The following abbreviations appear throughout this book:

CA   Copa America
CAF   Copa America Final
ECF   European Championship Final

GC   CONCACAF Gold Cup
WCQ   World Cup Qualifier
ECQ   European ChampionshipQualifier
WC   World Cup finals
EC   European Championship finals

ECP   European Championship qualifier play-off
WCP   World Cup qualifier play-off
CC   Confederations Cup
CCF   Confederations Cup Final
WCF   World Cup Final

PICTURE CREDITS